CHINESE CIVILIZATION AND SOCIETY

Chinese Civilization and Society

A Sourcebook

Edited by
Patricia Buckley Ebrey

THE FREE PRESS
A Division of Macmillan Publishing Co., Inc.
NEW YORK

Collier Macmillan Publishers
LONDON

The Free Press
A Division of Macmillan Publishing Co., Inc.
866 Third Avenue, New York, N.Y. 10022

Collier Macmillan Canada, Ltd.

Library of Congress Catalog Card Number: 80–639

Printed in the United States of America

Hard bound printing number

1 2 3 4 5 6 7 8 9 10

Paperback printing number

1 2 3 4 5 6 7 8 9 10

Library of Congress Cataloging in Publication Data
Main entry under title:

Chinese civilization and society.

   Bibliography: p.
   Includes index.
   1. China—Civilization—Sources. 2. China—History—
Sources. I. Ebrey, Patricia Buckley
DS721.C517   951   80-639
ISBN 0-02-908750-3
ISBN 0-02-908760-0 (pbk.)

For Tom and David

Contents

I. THE CLASSICAL PERIOD
Page 1

II. THE HAN DYNASTY
Page 21

III. THE ERA OF DIVISION AND THE T'ANG DYNASTY
Page 45

IV. THE SUNG AND YÜAN DYNASTIES
Page 69

V. THE MING DYNASTY
Page 121

VI. THE CH'ING DYNASTY
Page 177

VII. THE EARLY TWENTIETH CENTURY
Page 243

VIII. THE PEOPLE'S REPUBLIC
Page 333

Preface

This sourcebook came into being because of my belief that listening to what the Chinese themselves have had to say is the best way to learn about China. In teaching Chinese history and culture, however, I found that available translations were of limited use for the kinds of questions students were asking: How different were ordinary Chinese from ordinary Westerners? Did their different religions or philosophies lead to major differences in daily life? Did the Chinese have the same kinds of personal, social, and political problems as we do, or different ones? To help students find answers to these questions, I had to search for sources that could tell us more about the lives, outlooks, and habits of the full range of the Chinese population, not merely philosophers and scholars, but also women, peasants, townsmen, and undistinguished local officials. Since such people seldom wrote essays or autobiographies, I had to look for different kinds of sources—folk songs, plays, moral primers, descriptions, contracts, newspaper articles, and so on.

My efforts to make a sourcebook out of this material could never have succeeded without the generous help of others. Acknowledgment for funding must be made to the National Endowment for the Humanities for an Education Project Grant. This grant allowed me to employ several graduate-student research assistants. Jane Chen, Lucie Clark, Mark Coyle, Nancy Gibbs, Lily Hwa, Jeh-hang Lai, Barbara Matthies, and Clara Yu helped prepare, correct, and polish the translations in this book. Although all the translations we did are attributed to specific translators, they are in fact joint efforts, since in all cases either I as editor or one of the assistants extensively revised the translation to improve accuracy or style. Clara Yu's contribution to this book deserves

particular note; she worked with me from the inception of the project to its completion and is responsible for thirty of the eighty-nine selections.

Over the past five years, I have also regularly profited from the advice and criticisms of colleagues. Robert Crawford and Howard Wechsler helped test the translations in courses at the University of Illinois. Several other faculty members at Illinois have been ready to answer my questions on subjects about which they knew more than I, including Richard Chang, Lloyd Eastman, James Hart, Richard Kraus, Whalen Lai, and William MacDonald. I have also benefited greatly from the reactions and suggestions of professors at other colleges who saw earlier versions of this sourcebook in whole or in part. These include Suzanne Barnett (University of Pudget Sound), David Buck (University of Wisconsin–Milwaukee), Parks Coble (University of Nebraska), Wolfram Eberhard (University of California, Berkeley), Edward Farmer (University of Minnesota), Charlotte Furth (California State University at Long Beach), Peter Golas (University of Denver), John Langlois (Bowdoin College), Susan Mann Jones (University of Chicago), Susan Naquin (University of Pennsylvania), John Meskill (Barnard College), Keith Schoppa (Valparaiso University), Jonathan Spence (Yale University), Philip West (Indiana University), and Arthur Wolf (Stanford University).

Finally, I was fortunate to have excellent clerical assistance from Mary Mann, who typed several versions of this manuscript, and Sandy Price, who helped with the final typing. Christina Pheley conscientiously corrected the page proofs and galleys.

P.B.E.

Suggested Topical Arrangement

RELIGION, COSMOLOGY, AND MORALITY

1. The Metal Bound Box
2. Hexagrams
6. Chuang Tzu
11. The Interaction of Yin and Yang
12. Local Cults*
15. Dedicatory Colophons
21. Book of Rewards and Punishments
22. Precepts of the Perfect Truth Taoist Sect
23. Ancestral Rites*
34. Maxims for Daily Life
35. The Dragon Boat Race*
44. Li Chih's Letters*
45. Parables and Ghost Stories
46. Proverbs About Heaven
47. Almanac
51. Exhortations on Ceremony and Deference
70. Funeral Processions*
72. Birth Customs*
74. Spring Silkworms*
82. The Spring Festival*
83. Lei Feng, Chairman Mao's Good Fighter*
87. The Nature of Diseases

FAMILY AND KINSHIP

⁓ 3. Songs and Poems*
10. Two Women
16. A Woman's Hundred Years
20. Family Division
23. Ancestral Rites*

* Selections that are equally useful for more than one topic are listed under both and marked with an asterisk.

24. The Shrew
25. The Problems of Women
26. Rules for the Fan Lineage's Charitable Estate
42. Family Instructions
43. The Spite of Lotus
58. Marriage Contracts
59. Genealogy Rules
60. Families and Lineages of Yen-yüan County*
61. The Movement Against Footbinding*
70. Funeral Processions*
71. My Wife and Children
72. Birth Customs*
81. The Correct Handling of Love, Marriage, and Family Problems
88. Modern Models for Family Life and Marriage

ECONOMIC RELATIONS

3. Songs and Poems*
7. The Debate on Salt and Iron*
19. Slaves
27. The Attractions of the Capital
29. On Farming
37. Routine Commercial Procedures
38. What the Weaver Said
39. Tenants
41. Merchants in the Ming
49. Permanent Property*
57. The Conditions and Activities of Workers*
64. The Shanghai Builders' Guild
65. On Freeing Slave Girls*
74. Spring Silkworms*
78. The State Budget and the Standard of Living*
80. Developing Agricultural Production*
89. Population Control and the Four Modernizations

GROUP AND COMMUNITY ORGANIZATION

UPPER CLASS AND INTELLECTUALS

THE IMPACT OF THE STATE

REBELLIONS, PROTESTS, AND AGITATION FOR CHANGE

Pronunciation of Chinese Words

Except for a small number of personal and place names well known in variant spellings (Peking, Tientsin, Canton, Chiang Kai-shek, etc.), Chinese words are spelled here according to the Wade-Giles system of romanizing Chinese sounds. Below is a nontechnical explanation of how to pronounce words romanized according to this system.

VOWELS

a as *a* in father
ai as *y* in my
e as *u* in up
ei as *ei* in weigh
i as *ee* in bee
ih as *e* in her
ing as in ring
iu as *iew* in view
o (after h, k, k') as uh
　(after other consonants) as *aw* in law
ou as *oe* in toe
u (after ss, sz, tz, tz') hardly pronounced
　(after y) like *eo* in yeoman

ui (or *uei*) as *way* in sway
ü as *ü* in German *über*

Many other dipthongs are possible, such as *ia*, *iao*, *iai*. Simply add the sounds.

CONSONANTS

ch as *j* in joy (ch' as ch in church)
j is similar to *r* (*jen* is similar to run)
k as *g* in gun (k' as k in kid)
p as *b* in bottle (p' as p in pot)
t as *d* in dot (t' as t in tot)
ts or *tz* as *dz* in adze (*ts'* or *tz'* as *ts* in cats)
hs, the *h* gives aspiration: *hsi* is a breathy she

China today officially uses the Pinyin system of romanization and this system is also being adopted by many authors and publishers. For convenience, a conversion table for Wade-Giles and Pinyin is given below. (Letters not listed are pronounced the same in both systems.)

PINYIN	WADE-GILES	PINYIN	WADE-GILES
b	p	r	j
c	ts', tz'	si	szu
ch	ch'	t	t'
d	t	x	hs
g	k	yi	i
ian	ien	you	yu
j	ch	yu	yü
k	k'	z	ts
ong	ung	zh	ch
p	p'	zi	tzu
q	ch'		

WADE-GILES	PINYIN	WADE-GILES	PINYIN
chi	ji	p'	p
cha, chu, chih	zha, zhu, zhi	szu	si
ch'i, ch'ü	qi, qu	t	d
ch'a, ch'u,	cha, chu,	t'	t
ch'e, ch'ih	che, chi	ts	z
hs	x	ts', tz'	c
j	r	tzu	zi
k	g	yu	you
k'	k	yü	yu
p	b	yüeh	yue

Reference Matter

WEIGHTS AND MEASURES

Chinese weights and measures varied from period to period and indeed from place to place. The equivalents given below are therefore more suggestive than exact.

CHINESE UNIT	APPROXIMATE U.S. EQUIVALENT	APPROXIMATE METRIC EQUIVALENT
ounce (*liang*)	1⅓ ounces	40 grams
catty (*chin* = 16 ounces)	1⅓ pounds	600 grams
picul (*tan* = 100 catties)	133 pounds	60 kilograms
pint (*sheng*)	1 pint	½ liter
peck (*tou* = 10 pints)	½ peck	5 liters
bushel (*hu* = 10 pecks)	1½ bushels	50 liters
inch (*ts'un*)	1 inch	3 centimeters
foot (*ch'ih*, = 10 inches)	1 foot	⅓ meter
li (= 1800 feet)	⅓ mile	½ kilometer
mou	1/6 acre	600 square meters

CURRENCY

The value of money naturally changed as the economy changed. Below are the basic units used.

cash *(ch'ien).* Copper coin issued by the government, "penny."

string of cash *(kuan, tiao, ch'uan).* In theory, one thousand cash strung together through the holes in their centers. Usually "short," i.e. actually missing, 50, 100, 200 coins, etc.

tael *(liang).* An ingot of silver weighing an ounce. Not officially issued by the government, the tael nevertheless became the major unit for larger transactions in the Ming and Ch'ing dynasties.

dollar *(yüan).* Silver dollars were issued from the later nineteenth century to compete with foreign silver dollars gaining popularity. In the twentieth century the dollar became primarily a paper currency and was subject to wild inflation. Inflation was controlled after 1950. In the 1960s and 1970s 100 dollars would be a very good monthly wage for a factory worker or professional.

DATES

Years in the traditional Chinese calendar do not correspond exactly to Western years, since the number of days in them varies. Usually the year starts sometime in late January or February by the Western calendar. The months of the year are closer to lunar months than Western ones are, starting with new moons. The months are referred to by number except when a thirteenth month occasionally has to be added to bring the lunar calendar into line with the solar one. This extra month is called an "intercalary month." Days of the months are numbered or referred to by cyclical characters which provide a series of sixty names. Thus, the 15th day of the third month can also be referred to as the day *keng-shen.* Years can also be labeled with these cyclical characters or numbered within reign periods. Thus, the tenth year of the T'ien-pao reign period was the year *hsin-mao* and largely corresponded to the Western year A.D. 751. Early in the

Republican period the Western calendar was adopted and used for most purposes. In this book traditional Chinese years have been converted to the Western year with which they overlap the most, but months have been left in the Chinese terminology as first, second, third month, etc. For recent decades, when the Western calendar was used, months are translated into their Western equivalents.

THE LOCAL ADMINISTRATIVE HIERARCHY

The hierarchy of local government units was largely the same from the Han through the Ch'ing dynasties, though not all units were in existence at the same time. Their order was as follows:

Central Government
|
Provinces—Headed by Governors
|
Circuits—Headed by Intendants
|
Prefectures—Headed by Prefects
|
Commanderies—Headed by Grand Administors
|
Counties—Headed by Magistrates

THE CIVIL SERVICE EXAMINATION SYSTEM

The hierarchy of the examination system degrees in the Ming and Ch'ing dynasties was as follows:

Sheng-yuan (government students). Those who passed the test given in their prefecture.

Kung-sheng (senior students). Government students specially selected for their merit or seniority.

Chü-jen (recommended men). Those who passed the test given at the provincial seat.

Chin-shih (presented scholars). Those who passed the test given in the capital and the subsequent one given in the palace.

Chronology of Chinese History

5000–2000 B.C.	Neolithic cultures of several distinct types throughout north and central China; use of stone tools and pottery; simple agriculture.
2852–2595 B.C. (specific dates are traditional until 841 B.C.)	Era of the three legendary founding rulers: Fu-hsi, Shen-nung, and the Yellow Emperor.
2357–2198 B.C.	Three Sage Rulers: Yao, Shun, and Yü.
2205–1766 B.C.	Hsia dynasty.
1818–1766 B.C.	Reign of Chieh, model for subsequent "bad last Emperors."

I. THE CLASSICAL PERIOD

ca. 1600–ca. 1100 B.C.	Shang or Yin dynasty, earliest historically and archaeologically documented period; religion stresses divination; human sacrifices at royal tombs.
ca. 1100–256	Chou dynasty.
ca. 1100–770 B.C.	Western Chou dynasty.
1122–1116 B.C.	Reign of founder, King Wu (traditional dates).
1115–1108 B.C.	Regency of Duke of Chou (traditional dates).
ca. 800 B.C.	Poems of the type in the *Book of Poetry* composed.
770–249 B.C.	Eastern Chou dynasty.
722–481 B.C.	Spring and Autumn period. Chou King becomes figurehead with real power devolving to princes of the various states.
604–531 B.C.	Traditional dates of Lao Tzu.
551–479 B.C.	Confucius.
ca. 500 B.C.	Introduction of iron.
403–221 B.C.	Warring States period. "Hundred Schools of Thought."
479–360 B.C.	Mo Tzu.
ca. 400 B.C.	Introduction of copper coins.
372–289 B.C.	Mencius.
369–286 B.C.	Chuang Tzu.
298–238 B.C.	Hsün Tzu.
221–206 B.C.	Ch'in dynasty; unification of China under first imperial state; harsh regime based on ideas of Legalism.
221–210 B.C.	Reign of Ch'in Shih-huang-ti, First Emperor of Ch'in.
215–214 B.C.	Building of the Great Wall.
213 B.C.	Burning of Confucian books.

II. THE HAN DYNASTY (206 B.C.–A.D. 220)

206 B.C.–A.D. 9	Former (Western) Han dynasty with capital at Ch'ang-an.
206–195 B.C.	Reign of founder, Emperor Kao-tsu.
188–180 B.C.	Rule of Empress Lü.
180–157 B.C.	Reign of Emperor Wen; period of general stability and economic growth.
165 B.C.	Examinations required for men recommended for government service, often considered the beginning of the civil service examination system.
141–87 B.C.	Reign of Emperor Wu; establishment of Confucianism as state orthodoxy; geographical expansion.
145–ca. 85 B.C.	Ssu-ma Ch'ien, pioneering historian.
138–126 B.C.	Envoy to Bactria learns of Western countries.
119–110 B.C.	Establishment of monopoly on salt and iron and equable marketing system.
81 B.C.	Debate on Salt and Iron.
A.D. 9–23	Rule of Wang Mang, imperial relative who usurped throne.
A.D. 25–220	Later (Eastern) Han dynasty with capital at Lo-yang.
25–57	Reign of restorer, Emperor Kuang-wu.
64	Founding of White Horse Monastery in Lo-yang, early sign of introduction of Buddhism.
105	First mention of paper.
150	Wang Fu, social and political critic.
184	Rebellion of the Yellow Turbans.
184–215	Five Pecks of Rice Society controls several prefectures.
190–220	Power in the hands of great generals, Ts'ao Ts'ao, Liu Pei, and Sun Ch'üan.

III. THE ERA OF DIVISION (220–589) AND THE T'ANG DYNASTY (618–906)

220–265	Period of the Three Kingdoms: Wei, Han, and Wu.
265–420	Chin dynasty (after 316 in the South only).
283–343	Ko Hung, Taoist philosopher.
ca. 300–500	Foreign monks in China; Buddhist sutras translated into Chinese.
316	North China falls to non-Chinese invaders.
386–589	Northern and Southern Dynasties period; system of equal-land allotments; discovery of tea.
589–618	Sui dynasty; reunification of North and South.
606	*Chin-shih* degree established.
610	Grand Canal built.
618–906	T'ang dynasty.
618–626	Reign of founder, Emperor Kao-tsu.
626–649	Reign of Emperor T'ai-tsung; military expansion; employment of great ministers; intellectual cosmopolitanism.
629	Mosque built in Canton.
684–705	Reign of Empress Wu; growing use of examination system for official recruitment; prominence of Buddism.
700–850	Great age of poetry: Wang Wei (d. 759), Li Po (d. 762), Tu Fu (d. 770), Po Chü-i (d. 846), Han Yü (d. 824).
713–756	Reign of Emperor Hsüan-tsung; flourishing era that ended in disaster.
751	Battle of Talas: Arabs defeat Chinese.
755–763	Rebellion of An Lu-shan, Regional Commander in Northeast China.
843–846	Anti-Buddhist policies adopted.
874–884	Huang Ch'ao Rebellion devastates much of China.

| 907–960 | Period of disunion: Five Dynasties in North, Ten Kingdoms in South. Printing of books; introduction of footbinding. |

IV. SUNG (960–1279) AND YÜAN (1279–1368) DYNASTIES

960–1127	Northern Sung dynasty with capital at K'ai-feng; model era of scholar-official government.
960–976	Reign of founder, Emperor T'ai-tsu.
997–1022	Reign of Emperor Chen-tsung; flourishing of arts and trade.
ca. 1000	Introduction of early-ripening rice.
eleventh century	Revival of Confucianism: Fan Chung-yen (d. 1052), Chou Tun-i (d. 1073), Shao Yung (d. 1077), Chang Tsai (d. 1077), Ch'eng Hao (d. 1085), Ch'eng I (d. 1107).
1065	Beginning of regular triennial civil service examinations.
1069–1076	Wang An-shih (d. 1086) serves as Chief Councillor, attempts to strengthen government financially and militarily by series of reforms known as New Policies.
1076	Conservatives under leadership of Ssu-ma Kuang (d. 1086) and Su Tung-p'o (d. 1101) force Wang An-shih to resign.
twelfth century	Introduction of cotton.
1125–1127	Conquest of North China by the Jurchen tribe, who set up the Chin dynasty.
1127–1279	Southern Sung dynasty with capital at Hang-chou.
1127–1162	Reign of Emperor Kao-tsung. Bitter disputes between the parties who seek to reconquer the North and those wanting peace.
1130–1200	Chu Hsi, philosopher whose interpretations of Confucianism become orthodox during the Ming and Ch'ing dynasties.
1167–1227	Chinggis Khan, unifier of the Mongols and conqueror of most of Asia.
thirteenth century	Development of drama.
1234	Jurchen Chin dynasty falls to the Mongols.
1260	Khubilai becomes Great Khan of the Mongols.
1279	Southern Sung dynasty falls to the Mongols.
1279–1294	Khubilai's reign as emperor of China.
1275–1292	Marco Polo in Khubilai's service.
1351–1368	Red Turban Rebellion.

V. THE MING DYNASTY (1368–1644)

1368–1398	Reign of founder, the Hung-wu Emperor.
1403–1424	Reign of the Yung-lo Emperor; maritime expeditions and expeditions against the Mongols.
1421	Peking becomes capital.
ca. 1400	Appearance of two great novels, *The Romance of the Three Kingdoms* and the *Water Margin*.
1472–1529	Wang Yang-ming, philosopher of the Idealist school of Neo-Confucianism.
1487	Adoption of the "eight-legged" style for civil service examinations.
1527–1602	Li Chih, Confucian individualist.
1535	Portuguese gain right to reside and trade in Macao.
ca. 1550	Appearance of the novels *Journey to the West* and *Chin P'ing Mei*.
1572–1620	Reign of the Wan-li Emperor.
1598–1610	Jesuit missionary Matteo Ricci serves in the imperial court, begins policy of adapting Catholic religion to Chinese society.
1559–1626	Nurhaci establishes a Manchu state.

1604–1626	Tung-lin Academy scholars oppose radicalism in philosophy and moral corruption in government.
1625–1626	Powerful eunuch Wei Chung-hsien purges Tung-lin Academy.
1630–1647	Rebellions in several parts of the country.
1644	Rebel Li Tzu-ch'eng captures Peking and overthrows Ming dynasty; Manchus under Dorgan invade China with aid of Chinese general Wu San-kuei and defeat Li Tzu-ch'eng.

VI. THE CH'ING DYNASTY (1644–1911)

1644–ca. 1680	Ming loyalist resistance to Manchu rule.
1662–1722	Reign of the K'ang-shi Emperor.
1673–1681	Rebellion of the Three Feudatories led by Wu San-kuei.
1680–1733	Lan Ting-yüan, writer and official
1689	Treaty of Nerchinsk between China and Russia, China's first treaty with a foreign power.
1712	Decree freezing the land tax.
1723–1735	Reign of the Yung-cheng Emperor.
1727	Treaty of Kiakhta with Russia.
1736–1795	Reign of the Ch'ien-lung Emperor, consolidation of border areas.
ca. 1750	Completion of the novel *The Scholars*.
1792	Novel *The Dream of the Red Chamber* published.
1793	Macartney Mission from Great Britain.
1796–1804	White Lotus Rebellion and rise of anti-government secret society activity.
1839–1840	Lin Tse-hsü (1785–1850) appointed Special Commissioner of Trade in Canton in an effort to thwart opium smuggling.
1839–1842	Opium War between Britain and China.
1842–1843	Treaty of Nanking and Bogue Supplement fix tariff at 5 percent and establish extraterritoriality and most-favored-nation principle in China. Britain acquires Hong Kong.
1850–1864	T'ai-p'ing Rebellion.
1853–1868	Nien Rebellion.
1855–1878	Moselm Rebellions in Yunnan and Kansu.
1856–1860	Arrow War with Great Britain and allied powers.
1860	Treaty of Peking; Britain acquires Kowloon; Russia gets all lands north of Amur and east of Ussuri Rivers.
1862–1874	Reign of T'ung-chih Emperor, attempts at conservative reform and self-strengthening.
1870	Li Hung-chang (1823–1901) becomes High Commissioner of the Northern Ocean and Governor-General of Chih-li.
1884–1885	China defeated in war with France; establishment of French Indo-China.
1894–1895	China defeated by Japan; treaty of Shimonoseki.
1895–1900	Scramble for concessions.
1898	Hundred Days' Reform attempted by the Kuang-hsü Emperor on advice of K'ang Yu-wei (1823–1901); halted by Empress Dowager Tz'u-hsi.

VII. EARLY TWENTIETH CENTURY

1900–1901	Boxer Rebellion; allied occupation of Peking; indemnity of 450 million taels.
1905	Abolition of the civil service examination system. Sun Yat-sen (1866–1925) founds Revolutionary Alliance in Tokyo.

1911	Wu-ch'ang Uprising; majority of provinces declare independence from Ch'ing government.
1912	China declared a republic; Sun Yat-sen first President, but resigns in favor of Yüan Shih-k'ai (1859–1916); formation of Nationalist Party.
1912–1916	Administration of Yüan Shih-k'ai.
1915–1920	New Culture Movement: Ch'en Tu-hsiu (1879–1942), Hu Shih (1891–1962), Lu Hsün (1881–1936).
1916–1926	Warlord period.
1917	Sun Yat-sen sets up rival government in Canton.
1919	May Fourth Incident.
1921	Founding of Chinese Communist Party in Shanghai.
1921–1923	P'eng P'ai establishes peasant unions.
1923–1924	Sun Yat-sen begins reorganization of Nationalist Party under guidance of Soviet adviser. United front between Communist and Nationalist Parties.
1925	May 30th Incident. Sun Yat-sen dies in Peking.
1925–1935	Vernacular fiction flourishes: Mao Tun (1896–), Lao She (1899–1966), Shen Ts'ung-wen (1902–), Pa Chin (1904–).
1926–1927	Northern Expedition led by General Chiang Kai-shek (1884–1975) reunifies China under Nationalist government.
1927	Chiang attacks Chinese Communists. Nan-ch'ang Uprising. Autumn Harvest Uprising, Canton Uprising.
1927–1937	Nationalist decade at Nanking; industrial and commercial development.
1930–1934	Kiangsi Soviet survives four extermination campaigns.
1931	Mukden Incident; Japanese expansion in Manchuria.
1934	Chiang Kai-shek's New Life Movement.
1934–1935	Long March; Communist headquarters established in Yenan under leadership of Mao Tse-tung (1893–1976).
1936	Sian incident; second United Front.
1937	Marco Polo Bridge Incident leads to full-scale war with Japan; Japanese occupation of East China; Rape of Nanking.
1938	Chiang Kai-shek moves capital to Chungking.
1941	New Fourth Army Incident causes rupture in Communist and Nationalist united front. United States enters war against Japan.
1945	Soviet Union enters war against Japan, invading Manchuria. United States attempts to mediate an accord between Communists and Nationalists.
1946–1949	Civil war between Communists and Nationalists results in Communist victory.

VIII. THE PEOPLE'S REPUBLIC (1949–   )

1949	Mao Tse-tung declares the People's Republic of China in Peking; United States recognizes Nationalist government on Taiwan.
1950	Sino-Soviet friendship pact.
1950–1953	Korean War.
1951	Conquest of Tibet.
1954	Agricultural production cooperatives set up.
1955	Purge of Hu Feng and other intellectuals.
1957	Hundred Flowers Movement in which intellectuals urged to criticize new government, followed by Anti-Rightist Campaign.
1958	The Great Leap Forward and the establishment of People's Communes.
1959	Suppression of uprising in Tibet; Dalai Lama flees to India. Liu Shao-ch'i (1900–1969) replaces Mao as Chairman of the government while Mao retains post

of Chairman of the Party. Defense Minister P'eng Te-huai (1898–1974) purged and replaced by Lin Piao (1907–1971).

1960	Sino-Soviet dispute comes into the open; Soviet advisers withdrawn.
1961–1963	"Three Lean Years" due to natural disasters and Great Leap Forward programs.
1962	Chinese-Indian border war.
1964	Atomic bomb set off in Sinkiang.
1965	Cultural Revolution Group set up to root out revisionism.
1966	Purge of numerous Party officials, high army officers, and intellectuals; huge Red Guard rallies; colleges closed.
1967	Army garrisons at Wuhan mutiny but are reconciled by the mediation of Chou En-lai (1898–1976).
1968	Widespread violence leads to increasing army control in society; Liu Shao-ch'i relieved of all posts.
1969	Sino-Soviet border clashes.
1970	Lin Piao holds great power.
1971	People's Republic replaces Nationalist China in U.N. Lin Piao killed in an air crash after abortive coup against Mao.
1972	U.S. President Nixon visits China.
1973	Anti-Confucius, Anti-Lin Piao Campaign.
1974	Influence of Chiang Ch'ing (1910–) increasing. Legalism praised.
1975	Chiang Kai-shek dies.
1976	Deaths of Chou En-lai and Mao Tse-tung; Hua Kuo-feng becomes Chairman of the Party; Chiang Ch'ing purged.
1977	Teng Hsiao-p'ing (1904–) returns to high office.
1978	New push for economic development; increased contacts sought with the West.
1979	Teng Hsiao-p'ing visits United States. Diplomatic relations between United States and People's Republic of China formally established. China-Vietnam border war.

Introduction

The goal of this book is to explore what anthropologists would call Chinese culture: the system of shared ideas and meanings, explicit and implicit, that the Chinese have used to interpret their world and that have served to pattern their behavior. These are the ideas, concepts, symbols, and mental habits that have pervaded Chinese society and explain why Chinese act in certain ways and why Chinese society has been organized as it has. These include attitudes toward ghosts, child-raising, and master-servant relations, as well as the ideas usually considered philosophical. A full understanding of the culture of the Chinese would let us see them as human beings who are similar to all others yet act and think in distinctive ways. As one scholar put it, "Understanding a people's culture exposes their normalness without reducing their particularity. . . . It renders them accessible: setting them in the frame of their own banalities, it dissolves their opacity."* For a civilization such as China's, encompassing great diversity of class and region, the product of centuries of accumulated experiences, the opacities are not easily dissolved. We can improve our vision, however, by carefully observing what Chinese have said and done. This book provides the kinds of materials—letters, diaries, stories, folk tales, handbooks, contracts, newspaper articles, essays—from which we can observe how Chinese have thought and acted. These sources have been arranged chronologically by major epochs to cover nearly the whole span of Chinese history.

The translations collected here can be read and enjoyed on a number of different levels. Many of the stories, essays, and letters possess an intrinsic interest as works of art, and can be enjoyed for their beauty of

idea and form even without much knowledge of their background. Many selections can also be used as vehicles for gaining a "feeling" for life in the past. What was it like to be a servant girl in the Ming dynasty, or an official in the early Ch'ing? By identifying with an author or character, we can sense the context of his or her life, the fears and ambitions, the limits and possibilities he or she faced. Reading these translations thus can add a more fully human dimension to the study of institutions and events in history by showing how they impinged on the lives of individuals. To make it easier to read them in this way, each translation is prefaced by a brief description of the historical circumstances in which it was written.

For those willing to read more closely, however, these translations have more to offer: they can be "cross-examined" for clues to the content and structure of Chinese civilization. Anything, or nearly anything, Chinese wrote reveals their mental habits, assumptions, or thoughts. But what this indicates about Chinese civilization is not always self-evident. To probe deeper, we must bring to the translations our own questions. Some of the theoretical and conceptual grounds on which we might base our questions are outlined briefly below.

CIVILIZATION, CULTURE, AND SOCIETY

Following a common usage, the culture of China is called a civilization because of its size and complexity. For the past three thousand and more years Chinese culture has been marked by the use of writing, urbanization, social stratification, and a political structure that coordinated a huge population. The dynamics of such a complex culture are

* Clifford Geertz, *The Interpretation of Cultures* (New York, 1973), p. 14.

quite different from those of a simple tribe or small community. Ideas and meanings cannot be fully shared because the paths and methods of communication are varied. People learn how to interpret their world from face-to-face conversation, from visual signs and symbols, from songs, stories, and plays that they hear or see, through the rituals they take part in, and if they can read, through books, letters, posters, and newspapers. Since some people live in villages, some in towns, and others in great metropolises, they do not meet the same range of people or have the same opportunities to see plays or join ceremonies. Since some read and some do not, since some can read anything written in the past thousand years and some can read only the contemporary vernacular, they are not exposed to the same sets of ideas and values. Thus, as the Chinese themselves have been well aware, in a complex civilization such as theirs not everyone living at the same time participates in the same culture. The Chinese recognized distinctions not only of class, sex, and occupation, but also region; they were fond of pointing out the differences between people of the North and South, or even of one county and the next.

Despite such variations in culture, a large body of ideas, attitudes, and assumptions was widely shared among Chinese. For instance, even if practices concerning adoption varied, the notion of filial piety possessed a common core broadly if not universally understood and accepted. And while a gentleman and a peasant did not bow in the same ways to the same people, their expectations of each other's behavior were usually congruent; one expected to condescend, the other to defer.

A first step in analyzing Chinese civilization is discerning the ideational or symbolic elements that make it up. Below is a list of the basic elements of any culture.

This list could easily be expanded by making finer subdivisions, but the range of the components of culture can be seen. These vary in three dimensions: the degree to which they are conscious and articulate, the degree to which they are shaped by existing social structure or political power, and the degree to which they are felt to have moral force.

Values always carry strong moral meaning: certain actions are felt to be better than others and people feel shame or guilt when they do not do them. This evaluative aspect can lead people to strive to meet these values, to strive to appear to meet them, or even to flout them publicly, but they are unlikely to be indifferent to them because their emotions and moral feelings have to some extent been involved.

Laws and rules are different from values because people need not agree with them for them to exist and influence behavior. Perhaps in some ideal, egalitar-

Values	What people say one ought to do or not do; what they consider good and bad. Examples: a person ought to be honest and avoid harming others.
Laws	What the political authorities have decided people should do and are willing to back up with sanctions. Examples: the laws specifying punishments for patricide and highway robbery.
Rules	What a group or its leaders has decided its members should do and backs up by specific group sanctions (expulsion, fines, loss of rights, etc.). Examples: lineage rules specifying loss of rights for marrying into a wife's family.
Social Categories	Ways of thinking about people as types. Examples: thinking of people as monks, grandmothers, kings, criminals, friends. Expecting friends to lend small sums of money, monks not to marry.
Tacit Models	Implicit standards and patterns of behavior that a person knows but does not think about. Examples: knowing the different levels of formality to be used in speaking to women according to whether they are relatives, a friend's relatives, neighbors, or strangers, and married, single, or widowed.
Assumptions	Implicit, not usually articulated ideas and beliefs. Examples: believing that one man's gain is another man's loss, that hard work will be repaid in the end.
Fundamental Categories	Categories and ways of thinking people take for granted and may not recognize even if they are pointed out. Examples: thinking in dualities of good/bad, light/dark, male/female, beastly/godly, square/round, etc.; classifying insects but not plants as living beings.

ian community the laws would represent fully shared agreement on the extent to which ideals should be enforced. But in any complex civilization with great differences in wealth, status, and power, the laws and rules are determined by those with the capacity to do so, not by everyone. Emperors and guild leaders generally take into account the ideals, expectations, and ways of thinking of those they wish to rule, but are not bound by them. China has had alien dynasties, counties have had corrupt magistrates, tenants have had despised landlords, all of whom enforced laws and rules which violated people's own notions of proper social relations. In such situations, sometimes people's notions changed, sometimes people obeyed on the surface while resisting underneath, and sometimes those in power were deposed or expelled. Whatever occurred, the element of coercion played a part.

Social categories and tacit models are not decreed by political rulers but they are closely tied to the existing social structure. That is, a person can "be" a shopkeeper only if he has a conception of what it is to be a shopkeeper and conscious and unconscious models of how to act and how to expect others to act in return. But a culture is not likely to have a category of shopkeepers if there are no shops. Likewise, if economic diversification continues and some shops grow to include hundreds of employees, the culture is likely to develop a further category of "merchant" or "great merchant." Still, in any society there are more theoretically possible categories and models of behavior than the culture actually contains, and those that are present shape the way people act toward each other.

Assumptions, while related to values, categories, and models, operate differently because they are not articulated (except sometimes by the highly educated). Unlike articulated ideals and expectations, they cannot be argued, flouted, masked, or taken into account. People can say, "This man is no ordinary king; he is a king of kings" and invent a new social category. They can also articulate new ideals. But only the most reflective or observant people are likely to say, "Our whole social order is based on an assumption that good is rewarded and evil punished, but since this is not so, we must create a new social order." And if anyone did say this, he would find it difficult to convince others and even more difficult to get them to change their ways.

Fundamental categories are usually unconscious even to the educated. The existence of such categories thus sets even greater constraints on the development of other components of culture. If people are used to thinking of male and female as separate entities, it may be very difficult for them to imagine a social category that male or female could fill equally well; they might be able to think of men filling women's roles, or of male servants and female servants, but they might not be able to think of "farmer" or "painter" without picturing either a male or a female in that role.

To understand Chinese civilization, then, one step is to perceive these various cultural components. Another is to observe how they are interrelated. A culture's laws, values, models, and categories are generally parallel. So, for example, a society that places a high value on filial piety is likely to have laws and rules to enforce it, to have expectations that old parents will be taken care of, to have social categories and tacit models that emphasize kinship and generation, to have basic assumptions about the instinctive nature of parent-child love and the powers of ancestral ghosts, and so on. Even if we cannot decide which comes first—the values, the assumptions, or the patterns of behavior—still we can see that they are related and detect ways in which they reinforce each other. Nevertheless, elements of culture can be contradictory. Expectations often do not match ideals, and even ideals are often in conflict. People may feel strongly that they must be honest, honor commitments, and aid relatives but may encounter situations in which it is impossible to do all three at once. In such cases they must decide which values are more general and take priority; the decisions they make form a part of the process of cultural change.

Chinese civilization has never been uniform and thus cannot be well understood without consideration of the overlapping cultures that constituted it. To take an example, to understand religion in Chinese civilization, we would want to know about values, assumptions, models for ritual behavior, social categories of monk and layman, and so on, not only for some generalized "Chinese" form, but also for any substantial subgroups. Was religion different for the upper and lower classes? For city and village residents? For people in various parts of the country? Despite such differences, were there any key ideas or assumptions that were universally held? If two groups had some but not all elements of religion in common, what is the explanation? Did ideas pass up the social ladder or down? Did educated priests teach people standard religious notions, or did they serve more to rationalize the practices that already existed? Did groups assert their distinctiveness by exaggerating their differences in religious attitudes or practices? Since culture must be transmitted to persist, such questions are important.

One further task involved in understanding Chinese civilization should be mentioned, and it is probably the most difficult of all: discerning how it has changed over time, how much the present is the product of the past, how different the past was from the present. Not only has the content of Chinese culture changed, but its patterns have also. Writing, cities, and state government have existed for over three thousand years; yet literacy, density of settlement, and effective political coordination have greatly increased over the centuries, changing the ways in which cultural values and symbols are shaped and communicated. Nevertheless, every generation inherited a great deal from its predecessors and often proved ingenious in preserving old elements in new environments. Indeed, the durability of China as a civilization is remarkable. Was there anything special in the content or organization of Chinese civilization that made it especially flexible and able to accommodate change without consciousness of continuity being lost?

The purpose of raising these questions about the content, organization, and evolution of Chinese civilization is to suggest some issues with which we might approach the selections in this sourcebook. Understanding Chinese civilization is a daunting task, and many facets may prove beyond our means to comprehend. Still the challenge can be an exciting one, not only because a quarter of mankind is Chinese but also because we ourselves belong to a complex civilization and seeing how another one is put together can teach us much about our own.

WRITTEN MATERIALS AS SOURCES FOR CHINESE CIVILIZATION

When it is impossible to observe a culture firsthand, as it is for all past ones and many present ones, the only recourse we have is to search for other evidence—textual, visual, or physical. For a civilization such as China's, which has left an enormous quantity of written records, the most obvious first step is to read what Chinese have written. Of course,

we could read Western accounts, since for the past several centuries Westerners have described and analyzed what Chinese have said and done; the drawback is that they were writing for Western audiences in Western terms and often could not help distorting or misunderstanding the Chinese. By reading works Chinese wrote for other Chinese, we can achieve direct access to the values, rules, and categories that made up their culture.

Which Chinese books and documents should we read? The study of Chinese civilization, in the sense of the term used here, is a new subject. Scholars have only begun to probe questions such as how the mentality of the upper class changed over time, and how the cultures of the upper class and other groups were interrelated. Therefore, we cannot simply read a few "canonical" texts and deduce the rest. To see both the diversity and the common elements in Chinese civilization, we must read widely from works written by different people, for different purposes, at different times. These fall into three broad categories: (1) personal accounts in which people revealed their thoughts and feelings; (2) what could be called cultural documents, works important because they played a role in communicating components of cultures; and (3) descriptions in which an author characterizes the attitudes and behavior of the other people. (Often a single work such as a novel served more than one purpose and can be used in more than one way.)

The chief danger in using what Chinese have written as a source for their culture is that we might see only the culture of the well-educated, who, needless to say, left many more personal accounts for us to study than the illiterate or semi-literate. Educated men are valuable witnesses and have articulated many attitudes that others could not, but upper class culture was in many ways distinct from that of the rest of the society, and we should not assume that the mental habits of the educated were the same as those of everyone else. The way to avoid this pitfall is to read widely and critically, consulting cultural documents and descriptions as well as personal accounts.

A major difficulty in analyzing culture from personal accounts is the need to sort out shared cultural elements from idiosyncratic ones. No social group is so homogeneous that ideas and attitudes are competely shared; some degree of individual variation always exists. Therefore, if an author expresses resentment for those in authority or shows greater attachment to his brother than to his wife, we have to try to determine whether or not these were common attitudes. If he was giving advice, we must try to detect whether his advice was conventional or highly individual. Sometimes internal evidence is adequate (the author is defensive about holding ridiculed views, for instance), but often our only recourse is to read more widely.

To detect implicit assumptions and unconscious categories from personal accounts we must "read between the lines." We should look especially closely at how an author categorized his subjects and what he took for granted. If his point eludes us or seems illogical, probably he was making an assumption we ordinarily do not make. We should also look at descriptions of behavior to detect the tacit models that lay behind them. If in fiction or anecdotes we find extensive references to tipping, for example, we can try to infer the tacit models for such behavior.

The kinds of people who did not ordinarily write—women, peasants, soldiers, artisans, laborers—still occasionally left personal accounts, usually ones concerned with practical matters such as local events, family affairs, business concerns, or group rules. Even when brief and of limited scope, these can reveal basic categories or assumptions people made. It should be remembered, nevertheless, that the actual choice of words and imagery may well be those of a hired scribe or a cooperative educated gentleman.

Those not able to read learned much of the content of their culture from stories, songs, and plays that they heard or saw. Most of these works did not have authors in the same sense essays or letters do, but they all had audiences who apparently responded to the symbols, concepts, or values they conveyed. Songs and tales carried more than a surface message; that is, tales about orphans did not merely give people images of orphans but used being parentless as a metaphor for aspects of the social structure or human condition. To discover the cultural elements conveyed by popular stories and tales, we must look for recurrent themes and motifs as well as dramatic conflicts and their resolutions.

Components of culture were also transmitted by means of handbooks and guidebooks written for the literate but not highly educated. Again the popularity of such works is evidence that they filled widely felt needs and conformed to standard ways of thinking. Moral primers, sample letters, advice for home

medicine, rules for agriculture all reveal articulated principles and models accepted by broad segments of society.

A further source for the mentality and patterns of acting of those who did not write are fictional and nonfictional descriptions written by upper-class men. While not a substitute for personal accounts, these can still yield valuable information. Some men were knowledgeable and sympathetic witnesses, and their analyses of the habits and attitudes of wives, servants, or tenants may not differ greatly from what such people would have written themselves. But even men who were merely repeating conventional wisdom and showing little real comprehension provide us with useful evidence. If we assume some minimal integration to Chinese civilization, women and peasants had to be able to predict how upper-class men would treat them; thus, even accounts filled with unfair prejudices can be used to infer the prejudices people had to live with.

Selection 10, "Two Women," can serve to illustrate some of the ways written sources can be used to analyze the content and structure of Chinese civilization. This selection consists of two pieces, one a "cultural document," the other a "personal account" and description.

"The Mother of Mencius," from the *Biographies of Admirable Women*, written during the Former Han (202 B.C.–A.D. 9), is a brief didactic tale containing four incidents that show that Mencius' mother knew how to act toward a young son (by removing him from improper influences), an adolescent (by encouraging his study), a newly married son (by promoting harmony between him and his wife), and a full-grown man (by withdrawing into the background and allowing him to pursue his ambitions). While always placing the interests of her son first, the mother of Mencius is not presented as passive. Both astute and assertive, she knows what she should do and proceeds forthwith to do it.

"The Mother of Mencius" cannot be used as a description of the behavior of a particular historical woman, since whatever factual basis it may once have had has been lost behind an accretion of legend. Its importance lies rather in its influence. *The Biographies of Admirable Women*, reissued and enlarged numerous times over the centuries, served to shape general attitudes toward female virtue. Its continued popularity attests to the fact that most people accepted the validity of its premises.

Feng Yen's letter, the second piece, is an entirely different sort of document. His purpose in this letter was to justify to his wife's brother his divorcing her. Since Feng Yen was hardly a detached observer, this source must be used cautiously as a description of household arrangements or the behavior of women. Yet it does contain details of matters Feng Yen could not have distorted without his brother-in-law's knowledge. Thus it seems likely that Feng Yen had five children and no concubines and employed one female servant, and that his wife had an influential relative known as Magistrate Cheng. As a personal account revealing Feng Yen's values, assumptions, and basic ways of thinking, this letter is even more valuable. He explicitly tells us that he considered it a disaster to live in a house dominated by a woman and that he deeply regretted never having taken a concubine. He also clearly reveals what qualities he considered desirable in females. The worst offenses of his wife seem to have been that she was loud, argumentative, jealous, and stubborn. While he probably exaggerated his descriptions of her actual behavior, it does seem that a sweet and agreeable temper were what he would have valued most in a wife. Of next highest importance was neatness and willingness to have more children.

Reading more closely, we can also infer from this letter that Feng Yen considered divorce a major dislocation, to be avoided if at all possible. He delayed divorce because his children were young and there was work to be done in the house, and also perhaps because his wife had influential relatives. In writing to her brother he protests, "I believe that I have just cause, and I am not afraid of criticism." Yet the fact that he feels called upon to make this statement sounds defensive. He also asserts that having arrived at this decision he is abandoning the gentry life, severing relationships with his friends, and giving up his official career. Apparently the humiliation involved in divorce made him reluctant to face his peers.

The biography of the mother of Mencius and the letter by Feng Yen complement each other as sources for cultural attitudes and assumptions about domestic life. People may have widely admired the ideal of the woman of wisdom and courage, and yet many women may have been dominating and quarrelsome like Feng Yen's wife due to their innate personality or the difficult circumstances they found themselves in. Likewise, men may often have preferred the passively

agreeable woman to the quietly assertive one like the mother of Mencius.

Choosing documents such as these two for inclusion in this sourcebook has involved many considerations. Culture may be a "seamless web" of interrelated ideas, attitudes, and ways of thinking, but it can sometimes be more easily grasped when it is analytically divided. In this sourcebook, translations were chosen because they provided insight into the principles underlying seven main topics: (1) cosmology, religion, and morality; (2) family life and kinship organization; (3) economic relations; (4) group structure and community organization; (5) the behavior of the upper class; (6) the impact of state laws and institutions; and (7) movements of protest and rebellion. For earlier periods, especially before the Sung dynasty (960–1279), good sources for these topics were difficult to find. For more recent centuries, however, a vast body of personal accounts, cultural documents, and descriptions survives, and the problem has been selection from among equally good alternatives. In general, personal accounts were chosen because they were vivid, revealing, or interesting to read, or because they provided details on the lives of the kinds of people who seldom wrote. Cultural documents were chosen primarily because they had a wide circulation (as in the case of moral tracts or guidebooks) or because they were typical examples (as in the case of contracts). Descriptions were chosen when they were the only sources available for important topics. For subjects known to be controversial, an effort has been made to include sources from which more than one view can be argued.

A NOTE ON TRANSLATION

Translation is always a balancing act. Fully capturing meaning, style, and mood is seldom possible. If we transpose other peoples' common ways of expression into ways of expression common to us, important elements of the culture are lost to us, for much of culture is communicated in the metaphors and imagery people use. On the other hand, to convey all of the meanings in a text usually results in such bad English that the intelligence, grace, or humor of the original is lost. And even when the style is satisfactory, bringing out too many subtleties from texts, especially popular works, can distort their real meaning. For instance, Buddhist monks certainly read more into technical Buddhist terms than the average layman; to bring out all possible meanings for such terms in a popular moral tract or fictional story would be to misrepresent what it meant to the audience that actually read it. Unfortunately, judging how much an audience understood is nearly impossible. Did most people who invoked the phrase "the tyrant Hsia Chieh" know anything about Hsia Chieh except that he was a famous tyrant? If they did know more, was it very close to the Hsia Chieh of the historical accounts, or was it based on the portrayal of him in popular plays or operas? With our present state of understanding, such problems cannot be adequately solved.

In the translations in this sourcebook, a number of compromises have been made. To make extensive reading more inviting, we have translated into standard, easily intelligible English, often eliminating redundancies but trying to preserve much of the imagery and style of the original. Many selections have been abridged, but omissions are marked with ellipsis points (. . .). Allusions and philosophical terms are translated simply, generally with little explanation. It is hoped that wide reading will give readers a surer sense of what authors and audiences understood by such terms than footnotes ever could.

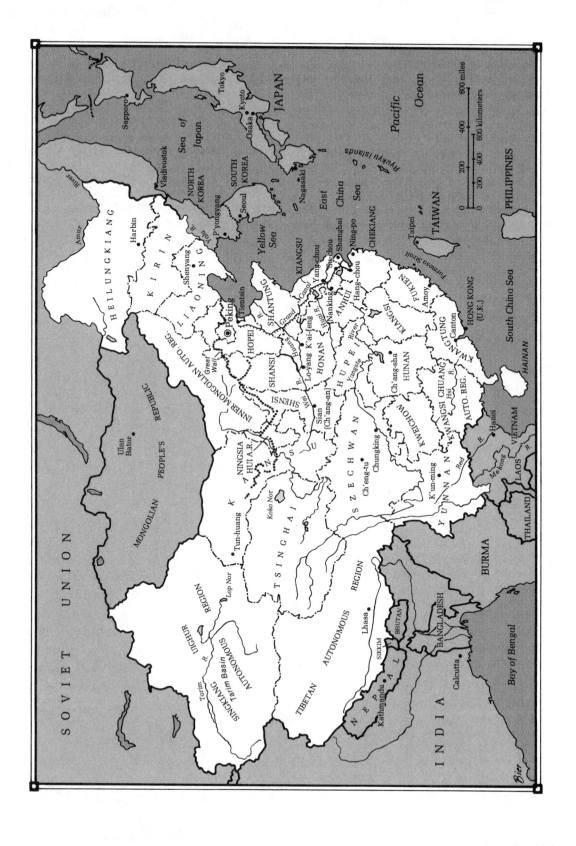

Part One

THE CLASSICAL PERIOD

The archaeological record of human existence in China goes back to the remote past. By the third millennium B.C. neolithic cultures flourished in several parts of the country. It has not yet been possible, however, to link these sites to the earliest heroes described by Chinese historians. With the Shang dynasty (ca. 1600–ca. 1100 B.C.), the historical and archaeological records begin to coincide; the Chinese accounts of the Shang rulers match the diviners' inscriptions on animal bones and tortoise shells found during the past century. Many more sources survive from the Chou dynasty (ca. 1100–256 B.C.), however, for the Chou people, like later Chinese, were meticulous in preserving records.

The Chou house originated in what is now Shensi province in northwestern China, moving eastward to conquer the Shang and establish their rule over much of northern China. The early Chou rulers secured their position by enfeoffing loyal supporters and relatives in different regions, thus establishing a social order somewhat like the feudal system in medieval Europe. The early Chou dynasty was an age when blood kinship was honored and social status distinctions were stressed. Members of the nobility belonged to clans, and their social and political affairs were conducted on a familistic pattern. They were linked both to contemporaries and to their ancestors by bonds of obligation based on kinship. Ancestors were seen as having great influence over the living, with powers similar to but far surpassing those of the living elders of the clan. Even the relationship between lord and peasant was supposed to be a paternalistic one, the peasant serving the lord and the lord concerned about his welfare.

The Chou kingdom remained strong for over two centuries, but its position gradually weakened, until finally in 776 B.C. the capital was sacked by non-Chinese tribes. When the Chou dynasty was revived, a new capital was established in the lower part of the Yellow River valley, marking the beginning of the Eastern Chou. In this period real political power lay with the feudal states. The Chou king continued to reign only because of the prestige of his house and the fact that no one feudal state was strong enough to dominate the others.

The Eastern Chou is divided into two major eras, the Spring and Autumn period (722-481 B.C.) and the Warring States period (403-221 B.C.). During these centuries the numerous states were reduced to a half-dozen powerful ones and the old political and social order gradually broke down. The sixth through third centuries B.C. witnessed a series of fundamental advances, including the introduction of iron, the development of infantry armies, the circulation of money, the beginning of private ownership of land, the growth of cities, and the breakdown of class barriers. During this period also there was a gradual expansion of the culture of the North, southward into the Yangtze River region, and at the same time elements of the indigenous culture of the lusher southern region were incorporated into the culture of the North.

The political disruption and social change of the late Chou drew many men's attention to the problem of how to achieve stability and order. Those who re-

sponded to this challenge included not only military and political leaders but also many philosophers. The foremost philosophers were Confucius (551-479 B.C.) and his followers, who emphasized the preservation of tradition and moral cultivation. They were closely rivaled at the time by the Mohists and Legalists, the former emphasizing frugality and discipline, the latter law and statecraft. Opposed to all of these proposed methods of reform were the Taoists, who preached a return to the Tao or Way, the true condition of man, which had been lost through the process of civilization and could be regained only if people returned to naturalness. The proliferation of philosophy in this period was so great that it came to be known as the period of the "one hundred schools." Without doubt it was one of the most intellectually creative eras in Chinese history.

The major sources for the Classical period are the Book of Documents, the Book of Changes, the Book of Poetry, several historical texts, and the essays and recorded sayings of the philosophers. Selections from each of these kinds of sources are given in Part One.

I.

The Metal Bound Box

Although sources are meager for the religious practices and beliefs of the common people in the Chou period, the classical texts provide abundant evidence of the rituals and beliefs of the nobility and upper class, especially those concerned with ancestor worship and divination. Already widely practiced by the Shang kings, divination gave men a means to communicate with their ancestors and discover their wishes. One common means of divination involved posing a yes-or-no question, then applying heat to a tortoise shell or shin bone to make it crack. The direction of the crack indicated the answer.

Below is an account of an incident in the early Chou in which such religious beliefs played a crucial role. The hero of the story is the Duke of Chou, brother of the founder of the Chou dynasty, King Wu (r. 1122–1116 B.C.). When King Wu died, his son, King Ch'eng (r. 1115–1079 B.C.), was still a child. The Duke of Chou acted as regent for seven years but never attempted to take the throne himself.

This selection is from the Book of Documents, *a collection of purported speeches, pronouncements, and arguments of early kings and their advisers. The oldest of these documents date from the early days of the Chou dynasty, although the one included here is probably of later date. This book became one of the Five Classics, held sacred by the Confucians. Whereas each document deals with a particular political situation, as a group they have been taken to provide an ideal statement of how government should be conducted.*

Two years after he had conquered the Shang dynasty, King Wu became ill and grew despondent. The two Ducal Councillors advised making a reverent divination on behalf of the King. However, the Duke of Chou said, "We must not upset our royal ancestors."

The Duke then took the burden upon himself. He constructed three altars on a single lot of cleared ground. Then he constructed another altar to the south, facing north. Standing there, he arranged the jade disc and grasped the jade baton. Then he addressed his ancestors, King T'ai, King Chi, and King Wen. The scribe recorded his prayer. It read, "Your principal descendant, whose name I dare not utter, has contracted a terrible and cruel illness. Heaven has made you three Kings responsible for your distinguished son. Take me as a substitute for the King. I was kind and obedient to my father. I have many talents and skills, and can serve the ghosts and spirits. Your principal descendant is not as talented or skilled as I, nor can he serve the ghosts and spirits as well. Furthermore, he was given a mandate by the imperial ancestor to lend assistance to the four quarters that he might firmly establish your sons and grandsons here on the earth below. There are no people from the four quarters who do not stand in awe of him. Alas! Do not let the precious mandate which Heaven has conferred on him fail. With him, our royal ancestors will always have a refuge. I now seek a decree from the great tortoise. If you grant my request, I shall take the jade disc and baton and return to await your decree."

He divined with three tortoises, and they all indicated good fortune. He then opened the lock and

3

looked at the writing; it too indicated good fortune. The Duke said, "The configuration shows that the King will not suffer harm, and that I, the small child, have obtained a renewed mandate from the three Kings. It is the long range that must be considered, and so I await my fate. They will take care of our King." The Duke returned and put the scribe's record in a metal bound box. By the next day the King had improved.

After King Wu died, the Duke of Chou's older brother, Kuan Shu, along with his younger brothers, spread rumors around the country that the Duke was not benefiting the young King. The Duke of Chou informed the two Ducal Councillors, "Unless I flee from my brothers, I will not be able to report to our royal ancestors." The Duke then lived in the east for two years, until the criminals were caught. Afterwards, he composed a poem, called "The Owl," which he presented to the young King. King Ch'eng, for his part, did not blame the Duke at all.

In the autumn when the grain was full and ripe but not yet harvested, Heaven sent down a wind accompanied by great thunder and lightning. The grain was completely flattened. Even great trees were up-rooted, and the citizens were very much afraid. King Ch'eng and his officers all put on their ceremonial caps and went to open the great writings in the metal bound box. Then they discovered the burden that the Duke of Chou had taken on himself, how he had wished to substitute himself for King Wu. The two Ducal Councillors and the King then asked the scribe and all of the officers whether this had in fact happened. They replied, "It is true, but, oh, the Duke commanded us not to utter a word about it."

The King took up the writing and cried, saying, "We need not reverently divine. Formerly the Duke worked diligently for the royal family, but I was only a child and did not realize it. Now Heaven has stirred its awesome power to reveal the virtue of the Duke of Chou. I, a small child, must greet him anew, in accordance with the ritual of our state and clan."

King Ch'eng then went out to the suburbs, and Heaven sent down rain and a wind from the opposite direction, so that all the grain stood up straight again. The two Ducal Councillors ordered the citizens to raise up and replant all of the trees which had been flattened. In that year there was a great harvest.

Translated by James Hart

2.

Hexagrams

Another method of divination practiced in the early Chou was the interpretation of hexagrams. To obtain advice a person would randomly draw six milfoil stalks, long or short, to form a hexagram of six broken and unbroken lines. A diviner would then interpret the hexagram arrived at according to traditional meanings associated with each of its lines. These meanings and interpretations became the Book of Changes.

As befits a fortunetellers' handbook, many of the passages in the Book of Changes *are brief, even cryptic, susceptible to varying interpretations. Nevertheless, the* Changes *came to be revered as one of the Five Classics, and over the centuries thousands of scholars have tried to reconstruct its philosophical meanings. The selection below consists of the first hexagram, all whole lines and therefore the strongest, most creative or assertive hexagram, used to represent Heaven; and the second hexagram, all broken lines, therefore the most receptive and yielding hexagram, used to represent Earth. The dualistic principles found in these hexagrams also underlie the theories of Yin (female, receptive, dark) and Yang (male, assertive, bright), which were more fully developed during the late Chou period.*

1. CH'IEN (THE CREATIVE, HEAVEN)

Ch'ien above ═══
Ch'ien below ═══

The Judgment: Ch'ien is the ultimate source. There is great success. There is benefit in perseverance.

Nine at the beginning: There is a hidden dragon. Do not use.

Nine in the second place: See the dragon in the field. It is beneficial to see a great man.

Nine in the third place: The gentleman strives to be creative all day. At night he acts with caution and restraint. There is no fault.

Nine in the fourth place: There is an uncertain leap at the abyss. There is no fault.

Nine in the fifth place: There is a flying dragon in Heaven. It is beneficial to see a great man.

Nine in the sixth place: The overbearing dragon is cause for regret.

Nine in all the lines: There appears a myriad of dragons without heads. This is good fortune.

Commentary: Great indeed is *ch'ien* the ultimate source. The ten thousand things receive their beginnings from it. It governs Heaven. The clouds drift by and the rain falls. All things flow into their forms. The ends and the beginnings are greatly illuminated. The six lines of the hexagram take shape at their own times.

In timely fashion they ride the six dragons and so rule over the heavens. The way of *ch'ien* is change and transformation. Each thing thereby achieves its true nature and destiny and assures that it is in accord with great harmony. There is great benefit and constancy. It stands out from all the things of the world, and the nations of the earth enjoy peace.

The Image: The movements of Heaven have great force. The gentleman invigorates himself and does not become jaded. There is a hidden dragon. Do not use it. The Yang still is buried below. See the dragon in the field. Virtue is everywhere. The gentleman strives to be creative all day. He always follows the correct way. There is an uncertain leap at the abyss. There is no fault in going forward. There is a flying dragon in the heavens. The great man is creative. The overbearing dragon is cause for regret. That which overflows cannot last for long. Nine in all the lines. The virtue of Heaven is not to act as head.

2. K'UN (THE RECEPTIVE, EARTH)

K'un above ☷
K'un below ☷

The Judgment: K'un is the ultimate of receptivity. There is great success. There is benefit in the perseverance of a mare. If the gentleman has a particular goal and attempts to attain it, at first he may lose his way, but ultimately he will achieve it. It is beneficial to make friends in the west and the south, but avoid friends in the east and north. Peaceful perseverance will yield good fortune.

Commentary: Great indeed is that originating in k'un. The ten thousand things all receive life from it when it is in harmonious union with Heaven. K'un contains everything in abundance. Its virtue is in harmony with the infinite. It encompasses all things and illuminates the universe. Each individual thing achieves perfect success. The mare is an animal of the land. It wanders freely over the land. It is gentle and obedient and symbolizes great benefit through perseverance. The gentleman should conduct himself in a like manner. At first he may lose his way, but later by being humbly obedient he will achieve it forever. In the west and south there are friends. One may associate with people of a sympathetic nature. In the east and north there are no friends, but in the end one may gain benefit from this. The good fortune of peaceful perseverance will result from being in harmony with the forces of the Earth.

The Image: The power of the Earth lies in receptivity. The gentleman with great virtue encompasses all things.

Six at the beginning: When one steps on hoarfrost, one knows that solid ice will soon appear.

Comment: When one steps on hoarfrost, one knows that solid ice will appear soon. When the forces of Yin begin to congeal and follow this way, the time of solid ice is about to arrive.

Six in the second place: It is straight, square, and great. Without hustle and bustle there is nothing that does not prosper.

Comment: The movement of six in the second place is straight by means of being square. Without hustle and bustle there is nothing that does not prosper. There is brilliance in the Way of the Earth.

Six in the third place: One's badges are hidden. One can persevere. If in the service of a king, do not try to force affairs but rather bring them to completion.

Comment: One's badges are hidden. One can persevere. At the proper time come forth. If you are in the service of a king, you should have the wisdom to spread greatness.

Six in the fourth place: To be closemouthed like a tied-up sack is neither blameworthy nor praiseworthy.

Comment: To be closemouthed like a tied-up sack is neither blameworthy nor praiseworthy. If one is careful there will be no trouble.

Six in the fifth place: There is great fortune in yellow clothing.

Comment: There is great fortune in yellow clothing. Brilliance lies within.

Six at the top: Dragons do battle in the fields. Their blood is black and yellow.

Comment: Dragons do battle in the fields. Their Way has run its course.

Six in all the lines: There is benefit in steadfast perseverance.

Comment: When all six lines yield six, it shows steadfast perseverance. In this way one can achieve great ends.

Translated by Mark Coyle

3.

Songs and Poems

The best source for the daily lives, hopes, complaints, and beliefs of ordinary people in the early Chou period is the **Book of Poetry.** *Over half of the 305 poems in this classic are said to have originally been popular songs and concern basic human problems such as love, marriage, work, and war. The remainder are court poems, including legendary accounts in praise of the founders of the Chou dynasty, complaints about the decay of royal power and the growing turmoil in the country, and hymns used in sacrificial rites. The four poems given below show something of this range of topics.*

In several ways the **Book of Poetry** *set the pattern for later Chinese poetry: its poems have fairly strict patterns in both rhyme and rhythm, they make great use of imagery, and they tend to be short. As one of the most revered of the Confucian classics, this collection of poems has been studied and memorized by centuries of scholars. The popular songs were regarded as good keys to understanding the troubles of the common people and were often read allegorically, so that complaints against faithless lovers were seen as complaints against faithless rulers.*

I beg of you, Chung Tzu,
Do not climb into our homestead,
Do not break the willows we have planted.
Not that I mind about the willows,
But I am afraid of my father and mother.
Chung Tzu I dearly love;
But of what my father and mother say
Indeed I am afraid.

I beg of you, Chung Tzu,
Do not climb over our wall,
Do not break the mulberry-trees we have
  planted.
Not that I mind about the mulberry-trees,
But I am afraid of my brothers.
Chung Tzu I dearly love;
But of what my brothers say
Indeed I am afraid.

I beg of you, Chung Tzu,
Do not climb into our garden,
Do not break the hard-wood we have planted.

Not that I mind about the hard-wood,
But I am afraid of what people will say.
Chung Tzu I dearly love;
But of all that people will say
Indeed I am afraid.

In the seventh month the Fire ebbs;
In the ninth month I hand out the coats.
In the day of the First, sharp frosts;
In the days of the Second, keen winds.
Without coats, without serge,
How should they finish the year?
In the days of the Third they plough;
In the days of the Fourth out I step
With my wife and children,
Bringing hampers to the southern acre
Where the field-hands come to take good
  cheer.

7

In the seventh month the Fire ebbs;
In the ninth month I hand out the coats.
But when the spring days grow warm
And the oriole sings
The girls take their deep baskets
And follow the path under the wall
To gather the soft mulberry-leaves:
'The spring days are drawing out;
They gather the white aster in crowds.
A girl's heart is sick and sad
Till with her lord she can go home.'

In the seventh month the Fire ebbs;
In the eighth month they pluck the rushes,
In the silk-worm month they gather the
    mulberry-leaves,
Take that chopper and bill
To lop the far boughs and high,
Pull towards them the tender leaves.
In the seventh month the shrike cries;
In the eighth month they twist thread,
The black thread and the yellow:
'With my red dye so bright
I make a robe for my lord.'

In the fourth month the milkwort is in spike,
In the fifth month the cicada cries.
In the eighth month the harvest is gathered,
In the tenth month the boughs fall.
In the days of the First we hunt the raccoon,
And take those foxes and wild-cats
To make furs for our Lord.
In the days of the Second is the great Meet;
Practice for deeds of war.
The one-year-old[1] we keep;
The three-year-old we offer to our Lord.

In the fifth month the locust moves its leg,
In the sixth month the grasshopper shakes its
    wing,
In the seventh month, out in the wilds;
In the eighth month, in the farm,
In the ninth month, at the door.
In the tenth month the cricket goes under my
    bed.
I stop up every hole to smoke out the rats,
Plugging the windows, burying the doors:
'Come, wife and children,
The change of the year is at hand.
Come and live in this house.'

In the sixth month we eat wild plums and
    cherries,
In the seventh month we boil mallows and
    beans.
In the eighth month we dry the dates,

In the tenth month we take the rice
To make with it the spring wine,
So that we may be granted long life.[2]
In the seventh month we eat melons,
In the eighth month we cut the gourds,
In the ninth month we take the seeding hemp,
We gather bitter herbs, we cut the ailanto for
    firewood,
That our husbandmen may eat.

In the ninth month we make ready the stack-
    yards,
In the tenth month we bring in the harvest,
Millet for wine, millet for cooking, the early
    and the late,
Paddy and hemp, beans and wheat.
Come, my husbandmen,
My harvesting is over,
Go up and begin your work in the house,
In the morning gather thatch-reeds,
In the evening twist rope;
Go quickly on to the roofs.
Soon you will be beginning to sow your many
    grains.

In the days of the Second they cut the ice with
    tingling blows;
In the days of the Third they bring it into the
    cold shed.
In the days of the Fourth very early
They offer lambs and garlic.
In the ninth month are shrewd frosts;
In the tenth month they clear the stack-
    grounds.
With twin pitchers they hold the village feast,
Killing for it a young lamb.
Up they go into their lord's hall,
Raise the drinking-cup of buffalo-horn:
'Hurray for our Lord; may he live for ever and
    ever!'

◻◻◻

Lo, we were plucking the white millet
In that new field,
In this fresh-cleared acre,
When Fang-shu arrived
With three thousand chariots
And a host of guards well-trained.
Yes, Fang-shu came
Driving his four dappled greys,
Those dappled greys so obedient,

---

[1] Boar.

[2] Wine increases one's te (inner power) and consequently increases
the probability of one's prayers being answered. That is why we
drink when we wish people good luck.

In his big chariot painted red,
With his awning of lacquered bamboo and his
  fish-skin quiver,
His breast-buffers[1] and metal-headed reins.

Lo, we were plucking the white millet
In that new field,
In this middle patch,
When Fang-shu arrived
With three thousand chariots,
With banners shining bright.
Yes, Fang-shu came
With leather-bound nave and metal-studded
  yoke,
His eight bells jingling,
Wearing his insignia—
The red greaves so splendid,
The tinkling onion-stones at his belt.

Swoop flew that hawk
Straight up into the sky,
Yet it came here to roost.
Fang-shu has come
With three thousand chariots
And a host of guards well-trained.
Yes, Fang-shu has come
With his bandsmen beating the drums,
Marshalling his armies, haranguing his hosts.
Illustrious truly is Fang-shu,
Deep is the roll of the drums,
Shaking the hosts with its din.

Foolish were you, tribes of Ching,[2]
Who made a great nation into your foe.
Fang-shu is old in years,

But in strategy he is at his prime.
Fang-shu has come,
He has bound culprits, captured chieftains.
His war-chariots rumble,
They rumble and crash
Like the clap of thunder, like the roll of
  thunder.
Illustrious truly is Fang-shu,
It was he who smote the Hsien-yün,
Who made the tribes of Ching afraid.

What plant is not faded?
What day do we not march?
What man is not taken
To defend the four bounds?
What plant is not wilting?
What man is not taken from his wife?
Alas for us soldiers,
Treated as though we were not fellow-men!

Are we buffaloes, are we tigers
That our home should be these desolate
  wilds?
Alas for us soldiers,
Neither by day nor night can we rest!

The fox bumps and drags
Through the tall, thick grass.
Inch by inch move our barrows
As we push them along the track.

Translated by Arthur Waley

---

[1] Pear-shaped buffers which hung from the horse's shoulder-girth.
[2] The people later called Ch'u. At this period they were between the Han River and the Yangtze, in northern Hupeh.

4.

The Battle of Chin and Ch'u

One of the aspects of people's lives in the Chou period for which sources are plentiful is warfare. Before the fifth century the conduct of war often seems to have had the character of a great ceremony in which the various actors performed their assigned roles and were judged by how well they fulfilled them. Battles were also seen as great dramas in which human talents and foibles were most fully displayed. Thus, many early attitudes toward human nature and political power can be inferred from the battle stories found in the major narratives.

The following account of a great battle held in 597 B.C. is from the Tso Chronicle, *one of the classical commentaries on the* Spring and Autumn Annals. *The* Annals *is a terse, dry, month-by-month record of items of interest to the court in the state of Lu, the home state of Confucius. While it is one of the Confucian classics, its entries are so brief that they are practically meaningless. The* Tso Chronicle *elaborates on many incidents in the* Annals *and conveys clear moral lessons.*

In the following account, the army of Chin had set out to save the besieged state of Cheng from conquest by Ch'u. When Cheng made peace with Ch'u, the Chin officers debated whether to return home and were ready to do so when two of their soldiers eager to provoke a battle managed to taunt some Ch'u soldiers into fighting.

The soldiers of Chin, afraid that Wei I and Chao Chan would anger the army of Ch'u, had sent out their war chariots to oppose the Ch'u forces. When P'an Tang saw their dust in the distance he sent a horseman to race back with the message, "The Chin army is coming!"

The soldiers of Ch'u, fearful that their king might find himself surrounded by the Chin army, drew up in battle formation. Their Prime Minister, Wei Ao, cried, "Advance! It is better for us to hit them than for them to hit us. The Poem says, 'Ten great chariots went first to open the way.' Let us move first! The Art of War says, 'Move first, and rob your opponent of his will.' Let us attack them!"

Then they advanced rapidly. With the chariot horses galloping and the foot soldiers on the run, they fell upon the Chin army. Chin Commander Hsün Lin-fu did not know what to do, so he beat the signal drum in the midst of the army and shouted, "The first

to cross the river will receive a reward!" The Middle and Lower Armies fought for the boats until the severed fingers could be scooped up in handfuls from the bottoms of the boats. The whole Chin army shifted to the right, except for the Upper Army, which did not move. With the Minister of Works Ch'i in command, the right wing of the Ch'u infantry pursued the Lower Army of Chin. . . .

When asked what to do, Commander Shih Hui replied, "Ch'u's army is now at the peak of its strength. If they gather their forces against us, our army will be annihilated. We had better regroup and leave. Then at least we can share the blame and save our men." Acting as rearguard for their infantry, they retreated and were thus not defeated. . . .

A chariot from Chin became stuck and could not move, whereupon a Ch'u soldier told the charioteer to remove the brace-bar. After that the chariot advanced only a little before the horses wheeled around.

The Ch'u soldier told him to pull out the flagstaff and lay it crosswise, and this time the chariot came free. The charioteer turned back and said, "We are not as experienced at fleeing as are the soldiers of your great state."

Chao Chan of Chin saved his older brother and uncle by giving them his two best horses. Then he turned back with other horses but met the enemy and was not able to escape. He abandoned his chariot and ran into the woods. Just then the Great Officer Feng rode by with his two sons. He told them not to look back, but they did anyway and said, "Venerable Chao is being left behind us." Their father became angry at them and ordered them to dismount. Then he pointed to a tree and said, "Leave your corpses there." He then gave the chariot to Chao Chan, who made his escape. The next day Feng found the corpses of his sons piled beneath the tree to which he had pointed.

Hsiung Fu-chi of Ch'u captured Chih Ying, whose father, Great Officer Hsün Shou, set off in pursuit along with his clansmen. Wei I drove the chariot, and many officers of the Lower Army accompanied them. Every time Hsün Shou wished to shoot, he would select the best arrows but then put them back in Wei I's quiver. Wei I became angry and said, "If you want to save your son, why are you so stingy with these willow sticks? Are you afraid of using up all the willows of Tung Marsh?"

Hsün Shou replied, "Unless I capture other men's sons, how can I get my own son back? I act as I do because I cannot afford to shoot carelessly." He then shot the Officer Hsiang Lao, captured his body, and took it with him in his chariot. Then he shot Kung-tzu Ku-ch'en and took him prisoner. He then turned back with these two prizes in his chariot.

At dusk the army of Ch'u set up a defensive position at Pi. Chin did not have enough troops left to set up a counter position of their own, so they retreated across the Yellow River under cover of darkness. All night long the sounds of their crossing could be heard.

The next day, the Ch'u supply wagons reached Pi, and so the army camped at Heng-yung. P'an Tang said to the King of Ch'u, "My Lord, we should erect a fortress and collect the bodies of the Chin soldiers in it as a war memorial. Your subject has heard that when one conquers an enemy, he should display that fact to his sons and grandsons, so that they will not forget his military achievements."

The King of Ch'u replied, "You do not understand this. In writing, the characters 'stop' and 'spear' fit together to make 'military.' After King Wu conquered Shang, a hymn was written which says, 'Store the shields and spears,/ Encase the arrows and bows./ We seek admirable virtue,/ To extend throughout this great land./ May the king genuinely preserve it.' They also wrote the 'Military' Poem. Its last stanza states, 'You have made your achievement secure.' The third stanza says, 'May we extend this continuously;/ What we seek now is to make it secure.' The sixth stanza says, 'There is peace in ten thousand states,/ And repeated years of plenty.'

" 'Military' means to prevent violence, store weapons, preserve greatness, secure achievements, pacify the people, harmonize groups, and increase wealth. Thus King Wu wanted to make sure that his sons and grandsons did not forget these stanzas. Now I have caused the bones of the soldiers from two states to lie exposed on the battlefield; this is violence. I have made a show of weapons to coerce the feudal lords; this is not storing weapons. Since I have caused violence and have not placed the weapons in storage, how could I have preserved greatness? Furthermore, the enemy state of Chin still exists; so how could my achievement be secure? In many ways I have gone against the people's wishes; so how could they be pacified? I have not been virtuous but have used force against the feudal lords; so how could the groups be harmonized? I have found profit in other men's crises and peace in their disorders. This has given me glory, but how has it increased wealth? There are seven military virtues, but I have not attained a single one of them. What do I have to display to my sons and grandsons? Let us set up an altar to our Ancestral Rulers and announce to them what we have done. Then we should stop there, for what I have done is not a military achievement.

"In ancient times when the enlightened kings chastised the disrespectful, they took the most monstrous offenders and buried them in mounds as a punishment of supreme disgrace. This is the origin of war memorials, and they were used to warn the evil and corrupt. But in the present conflict, there were no criminals. All of the people have been completely loyal, fighting to the death to carry out their rulers' decrees. So what reason is there to build a war memorial?"

So, the King of Ch'u conducted sacrifices to the Spirit of the Yellow River. Then he built an altar for his Ancestral Rulers and announced to them his accomplishment. After this he returned home. . . .

In the autumn, when the army of Chin arrived home, the defeated Commander Hsün Lin-fu requested to be put to death. The Duke of Chin wished to grant his request, but Shih Chen-tzu admonished him, "This must not be allowed. Remember that after the battle of Ch'eng-pu, the army of Chin celebrated with three days of feasting, and yet Duke Wen still had a sad countenance. His advisers said, 'In this time of happiness you are sad. Must there be a time of sadness for you to be happy?' The Duke replied, 'As long as Te Ch'en of Ch'u is still alive, my sadness cannot be alleviated. A caged beast will still fight; how much more so will the Chief Minister of a state!' But after Te Ch'en had been put to death, the Duke's happiness was apparent, and he said, 'Now there is no one left to poison my joy.' This was a double victory for Chin and a double defeat for Ch'u. Because of this, for the next two generations Ch'u was out of con-

tention. At the present time it may be that Heaven is sending a great warning to us; if we would kill our commander Hsün Lin-fu and compound Ch'u's victory, then would we not also be out of contention for a long time? Hsün Lin-fu in serving his ruler has always tried to be completely loyal when in office and to mend his faults when out of office. He is the guardian of the altars to our Gods of Soil and Grain. Why should we kill him? His defeat is like an eclipse of the sun or moon, which does not diminish their brilliance."

The Duke of Chin then restored Hsün Lin-fu to his position.

Translated by James Hart

5.

Confucius

The importance of the Analects *cannot be doubted. As the only reliable record of what Confucius (551–479 B.C.) believed and advocated, it is a highly valuable source for the concerns of a sensitive and intelligent man in the era when the Chou dynasty had begun to fragment. As a sacred book, memorized by beginning students, it influenced the values and habits of thoughts of Chinese for centuries. Many of its passages became proverbial sayings, cited by illiterate peasants who were ignorant of the proverbs' origins.*

The Analects *does not provide carefully organized or argued philosophical discourses. The sayings in it are seemingly haphazardly arranged, and the wisdom they contain is often of a prosaic sort. Yet Confucius' injunctions for men to set high standards for their conduct marks a major development in the history of Chinese thought. Like his predecessors, Confucius accepted the importance of proper performance of ceremonies and respectful obedience to rulers and family elders; yet he invested these practices with new moral meanings.*

Below are some of Confucius' sayings on three of the topics he most frequently addressed. They have been arranged under topical headings for convenience.

THE GENTLEMAN

Confucius said, "The gentleman concerns himself with the Way; he does not worry about his salary. Hunger may be found in plowing; wealth may be found in studying. The gentleman worries about the Way, not about poverty."

Confucius said, "When he eats, the gentleman does not seek to stuff himself. In his home he does not seek luxury. He is diligent in his work and cautious in his speech. He associates with those who possess the Way, and thereby rectifies himself. He may be considered a lover of learning."

Tzu Kung inquired about being a gentleman. Confucius said, "First he behaves properly and then he speaks, so that his words follow his actions."

Ssu-ma Niu asked about the nature of the gentleman. Confucius replied, "The gentleman does not worry and is not fearful." Ssu asked, "Then, can not fearing and not worrying be considered the essence of being a gentleman?" Confucius responded, "If you can look into yourself and find no cause for dissatisfaction, how can you worry and how can you fear?"

Confucius said, "The gentleman reveres three things. He reveres the mandate of Heaven; he reveres great people; and he reveres the words of the sages. Petty people do not know the mandate of Heaven and so do not revere it. They are disrespectful to great people and they ridicule the words of the sages."

Confucius said, "The gentleman must exert caution in three areas. When he is a youth and his blood and spirit have not yet settled down, he must be on his guard lest he fall into lusting. When he reaches the full vigor of his manhood in his thirties and his blood and spirit are strong, he must guard against getting

13

into quarrels. When he reaches old age and his blood and spirit have begun to weaken, he must guard against envy."

Confucius said, "The gentleman understands integrity; the petty person knows about profit."

Confucius said, "For the gentleman integrity is the essence; the rules of decorum are the way he puts it into effect; humility is the way he brings it forth; sincerity is the way he develops it. Such indeed is what it means to be a gentleman."

Confucius said that Tzu Ch'an possessed the way of the gentleman in four areas. In his personal conduct he was respectful; in serving his superiors he was reverent; in nourishing the people he was kind; in governing the people he was righteous.

Confucius said, "The gentleman has nine concerns. In seeing he is concerned with clarity. In hearing he is concerned with acuity. In his expression he wishes to be warm. In his bearing he wishes to be respectful. In his words he is concerned with sincerity. In his service he is concerned with reverence. When he is in doubt, he wants to ask questions. When he is angry, he is wary of the pitfalls. When he sees the chance for profit, he keeps in mind the need for integrity."

Confucius said, "The gentleman is easy to serve but difficult to please. When you try to please him, if your manner of pleasing is not in accord with the Way, then he will not be pleased. On the other hand, he does not expect more from people than their capacities warrant. The petty individual is hard to serve and easy to please. When you try to please him, even if your method of pleasing him is not in accord with the Way, he will be pleased. But in employing people he expects them to be perfectly accomplished in everything."

Confucius said, "The gentleman is in harmony with those around him but not on their level. The small man is on the level of those around him but not in harmony with them."

Confucius said, "The gentleman aspires to things lofty; the petty person aspires to things base."

Confucius said, "The gentleman looks to himself; the petty person looks to other people."

Confucius said, "The gentleman feels bad when his capabilities fall short of some task. He does not feel bad if people fail to recognize him."

Confucius said, "The gentleman fears that after his death his name will not be honored."

Confucius said, "The gentleman does not promote people merely on the basis of their words, nor does he reject words merely because of the person who uttered them."

Confucius said, "The gentleman is exalted and yet not proud. The petty person is proud and yet not exalted."

Tzu Hsia said, "The gentleman has three transformations. Seen from afar he appears majestic. Upon approaching him you see he is amiable. Upon hearing his words you find they are serious."

Confucius said, "If the gentleman is not dignified, he will not command respect and his teachings will not be considered solid. He emphasizes sincerity and honesty. He has no friends who are not his equals. If he finds a fault in himself, he does not shirk from reforming himself."

Tzu Kung said, "When the gentleman falls into error, it is like the eclipse of the sun and moon: everyone sees it. When he corrects it, everyone will look up to him again."

Tzu Kung said, "Does not the gentleman also have his hatreds?" Confucius replied, "Yes, he has his hatreds. He hates those who harp on the weak points of others. He hates those who are base and yet slander those who are exalted. He hates those who are bold but do not observe the proprieties. He hates those who are brash and daring and yet have limited outlook." Confucius then asked, "You too have your hatreds, do you not?" Tzu Kung replied, "I hate those who pry into things and consider it wisdom. I hate those who are imprudent and consider it courage. I hate those who leak out secrets and consider it honesty."

Tseng-tzu said, "The gentleman knows enough not to exceed his position."

Confucius said, "The gentleman is not a tool."

HUMANITY

Tzu-chang asked Confucius about humanity. Confucius said, "If an individual can practice five things anywhere in the world, he is a man of humanity." "May I ask what these things are?" said Tzu-chang. Confucius replied, "Reverence, generosity, truthfulness, diligence, and kindness. If a person acts with reverence, he will not be insulted. If he is generous, he will win over the people. If he is truthful, he will be trusted by people. If he is diligent, he will have great achievements. If he is kind, he will be able to influence others."

Chung-kung asked about humanity. Confucius said, "When you go out, treat everyone as if you were welcoming a great guest. Employ people as if you were conducting a great sacrifice. Do not do unto others what you would not have them do unto you. Then neither in your country nor in your family will there be complaints against you." Chung-kung said, "Although I am not intelligent, please allow me to practice your teachings."

Ssu-ma Niu asked about humanity. Confucius said, "The man of humanity is cautious in his speech." Ssu-ma Niu replied, "If a man is cautious in his speech, may it be said that he has achieved the virtue of humanity?" Confucius said, "When a man realizes that accomplishing things is difficult, can his use of words be anything but cautious?"

Confucius said, "A person with honeyed words and pious gestures is seldom a man of humanity."

Confucius said, "The individual who is forceful, resolute, simple, and cautious of speech is near to humanity."

Confucius said, "The man of wisdom takes pleasure in water; the man of humanity delights in the mountains. The man of wisdom desires action; the man of humanity wishes for quietude. The man of wisdom seeks happiness; the man of humanity looks for long life."

Confucius said, "If a man does not have humanity, how can he have propriety? If a man does not have humanity, how can he be in tune with the rites or music?"

Confucius said, "The humanity of a village makes it beautiful. If you choose a village where humanity does not dwell, how can you gain wisdom?"

Confucius said, "Humanity is more important for people than water or fire. I have seen people walk through water and fire and die. I have never seen someone tread the path of humanity and perish."

Confucius said, "Riches and honors are the things that people desire; but if one obtains them by not following the Way, then one will not be able to hold them. Poverty and low position in society are the things that people hate; but if one can avoid them only by not following the Way, then one should not try to avoid them. If the gentleman abandons humanity, how can he live up to his name? The gentleman must not forget about humanity for even the space of time it takes him to finish a meal. When he is hurried, he must act according to it. Even when he is confronted with a crisis, he must follow its tenets."

Confucius said, "The strong-minded scholar and the man of humanity do not seek to live by violating the virtue of humanity. They will suffer death if necessary to achieve humanity."

Confucius said, "In practicing the virtue of humanity, one should not defer even to one's teacher."

Confucius said, "Is humanity far away? Whenever I want the virtue of humanity, it comes at once."

Tzu-kung asked about the virtue of humanity. Confucius said, "The artisan who wants to do his work well must first of all sharpen his tools. When you reside in a given state, enter the service of the best of the officials and make friends with the most humane of the scholars."

Confucius said, "Only the man of humanity can rightly love some people and rightly despise some people."

Confucius said, "People can be classified according to their faults. By observing an individual's faults, you will know if he is a person of humanity."

Confucius said, "Those who possess virtue will be sure to speak out; but those who speak out do not necessarily have virtue. Those who possess the virtue of humanity certainly have strength; but those who are strong do not necessarily have the virtue of humanity."

Confucius said, "Although there have been gentlemen who did not possess the virtue of humanity, there have never been petty men who did possess it."

FILIAL PIETY

Tzu Yu inquired about filial piety. Confucius said, "Nowadays, filial piety is considered to be the ability to nourish one's parents. But this obligation to nourish even extends down to the dogs and horses. Unless we have reverence for our parents, what makes us any different?"

Confucius said, "When your father is alive, observe his intentions. When he is deceased, model yourself on the memory of his behavior. If in three years after his death you have not deviated from your father's ways, then you may be considered a filial child."

Tseng-tzu said, "I have heard from Confucius that the filial piety of Meng Chuang-tzu is such that it could also be attained by others, but his not changing his father's ministers and his father's government is a virtue difficult indeed to match."

Meng I-tzu inquired about filial piety. Confucius

said, "Do not offend your parents." Fan Chih was giving Confucius a ride in a wagon, and Confucius told him, "Meng Sun questioned me about filial piety and I told him, 'Do not offend your parents.' " Fan Chih said, "What are you driving at?" Confucius replied, "When your parents are alive, serve them according to the rules of ritual and decorum. When they are deceased, give them a funeral and offer sacrifices to them according to the rules of ritual and decorum."

Confucius said, "When your father and mother are alive, do not go rambling around far away. If you must travel, make sure you have a set destination."

Confucius said, "It is unacceptable not to be aware of your parents' ages. Their advancing years are a cause for joy and at the same time a cause for sorrow."

Confucius said, "You can be of service to your father and mother by remonstrating with them tactfully. If you perceive that they do not wish to follow your advice, then continue to be reverent toward them without offending or disobeying them; work hard and do not murmur against them."

The Duke of She said to Confucius, "In my land there is an upright man. His father stole a sheep, and the man turned him in to the authorities." Confucius replied, "The upright men of my land are different. The father will shelter the son and the son will shelter the father. Righteousness lies precisely in this."

Translated by Mark Coyle

6.

Chuang Tzu

The intellectual ferment of the three centuries after Confucius' time led to the writing of many philosophical texts. Those that survive provide rich and varied evidence of people's ideas, assumptions, values, and daily lives. Particularly delightful in this regard is the work entitled Chuang Tzu, *written in part by the early-third century thinker of that name and in part by his followers. As a Taoist, Chuang Tzu took a stand opposed to that of Confucians and most other contemporary philosophical schools; that is, he believed that the efforts of intellectual and political leaders to solve problems through institutional or moral programs would do more harm than good because they necessarily took men away from their natural selves. The* Chuang Tzu *contains parables used to illustrate philosophical points as well as stories lampooning common ideas and rationalizations of his time. The five stories given below illustrate both Chuang Tzu's ideas and his sense of humor.*

Once, when Chuang Tzu was fishing in the P'u River, the king of Ch'u sent two officials to go and announce to him: "I would like to trouble you with the administration of my realm."

Chuang Tzu held on to the fishing pole and, without turning his head, said, "I have heard that there is a sacred tortoise in Ch'u that has been dead for three thousand years. The king keeps it wrapped in cloth and boxed, and stores it in the ancestral temple. Now would this tortoise rather be dead and have its bones left behind and honored? Or would it rather be alive and dragging its tail in the mud?"

"It would rather be alive and dragging its tail in the mud," said the two officials.

Chuang Tzu said, "Go away! I'll drag my tail in the mud!"

🔳🔳🔳

Chuang Tzu and Hui Tzu were strolling along the dam of the Hao River when Chuang Tzu said, "See how the minnows come out and dart around where they please! That's what fish really enjoy!"

Hui Tzu said, "You're not a fish—how do you know what fish enjoy?"

Chuang Tzu said, "You're not I, so how do you know I don't know what fish enjoy?"

Hui Tzu said, "I'm not you, so I certainly don't know what you know. On the other hand, you're certainly not a fish—so that still proves you don't know what fish enjoy!"

Chuang Tzu said, "Let's go back to your original question, please. You asked me how I know what fish enjoy—so you already knew I knew it when you asked the question. I know it by standing here beside the Hao."

🔳🔳🔳

Chuang Tzu's wife died. When Hui Tzu went to convey his condolences, he found Chuang Tzu sitting with his legs sprawled out, pounding on a tub and singing. "You lived with her, she brought up your children and grew old," said Hui Tzu. "It should be enough simply not to weep at her death. But pounding on a tub and singing—this is going too far, isn't it?"

Chuang Tzu said, "You're wrong. When she first died, do you think I didn't grieve like anyone else? But I looked back to her beginning and the time before she was born. Not only the time before she was born, but the time before she had a body. Not only the time before she had a body, but the time before she had a spirit. In the midst of the jumble of wonder and mystery a change took place and she had a spirit. Another change and she had a body. Another change and she was born. Now there's been another change and she's dead. It's just like the progression of the four seasons, spring, summer, fall, winter.

"Now she's going to lie down peacefully in a vast room. If I were to follow after her bawling and sobbing, it would show that I don't understand anything about fate. So I stopped."

🔲🔲🔲

Chuang Tzu went to see Duke Ai of Lu.* Duke Ai said, "We have a great many Confucians here in the state of Lu, but there seem to be very few men who study your methods, sir!"

"There are few confucians in the state of Lu!" said Chuang Tzu.

"But the whole state of Lu is dressed in Confucian garb!" said Duke Ai. "How can you say they are few?"

"I have heard," said Chuang Tzu, "that the Confucians wear round caps on their heads to show that they understand the cycles of heaven, that they walk about in square shoes to show that they understand the shape of the earth, and that they tie ornaments in the shape of a broken disc at their girdles in order to show that, when the time comes for decisive action, they must 'make the break.' But a gentleman may embrace a doctrine without necessarily wearing the garb that goes with it, and he may wear the garb without necessarily comprehending the doctrine. If Your Grace does not believe this is so, then why not try issuing an order to the state proclaiming: 'All those who wear the garb without practicing the doctrine that goes with it will be sentenced to death!'"

Duke Ai did in fact issue such an order, and within

* Lu was the home state of Confucius.

five days there was no one in the state of Lu who dared wear Confucian garb. Only one old man came in Confucian dress and stood in front of the duke's gate. The duke at once summoned him and questioned him on affairs of state and, though the discussion took a thousand turnings and ten thousand shifts, the old man was never at a loss of words. Chuang Tzu said, "In the whole state of Lu, then, there is only one man who is a real Confucian. How can you say there are a great many of them?"

🔲🔲🔲

In ancient times King Wen of Chao was fond of swords. Expert swordsmen flocked to his gate, and over three thousand of them were supported as guests in his household, day and night engaging in bouts in his presence till the dead and wounded numbered more than a hundred men a year. Yet the king's delight never seemed to wane and things went on in this way for three years, while the state sank into decline and the other feudal lords conspired against it.

The crown prince K'uei, distressed at this, summoned his retainers about him and said, "I will bestow a thousand pieces of gold upon any man who can reason with the king and make him give up these sword fights!"

"Chuang Tzu is the one who can do it," said his retainers.

The crown prince thereupon sent an envoy with a thousand pieces of gold to present to Chuang Tzu, but Chuang Tzu refused to accept the gift. Instead he accompanied the envoy on his return and went to call on the crown prince. "What instructions do you have for me, that you present me with a thousand pieces of gold?" he asked.

"I had heard, sir," said the crown prince, "that you are an enlightened sage, and I wished in all due respect to offer this thousand in gold as a gift to your attendants. But if you refuse to accept it, then I dare say no more about the matter."

Chuang Tzu said, "I have heard that the crown prince wishes to employ me because he hopes I can rid the king of this passion of his. Now if, in attempting to persuade His Majesty, I should arouse his anger and fail to satisfy your hopes, then I would be sentenced to execution. In that case, what use could I make of the gold? And if I should be able to persuade His Majesty and satisfy your hopes, then what could I ask for in the whole kingdom of Chao that would not be granted me?"

"The trouble is," said the crown prince, "that my father, the king, refuses to see anyone but swordsmen."

"Fine!" said Chuang Tzu. "I am quite able to handle a sword."

"But the kind of swordsmen my father receives," said the crown prince, "all have tousled heads and bristling beards, wear slouching caps tied with plain, coarse tassels, and robes that are cut short behind; they glare fiercely and have difficulty getting out their words. Men like that he is delighted with! Now, sir, if you should insist upon going to see him in scholarly garb, the whole affair would go completely wrong from the start."

"Then allow me to get together the garb of a swordsman," said Chuang Tzu. After three days, he had his swordsman's costume ready and went to call on the crown prince. The crown prince and he then went to see the king. The king, drawing his sword, waited with bare blade in hand. Chuang Tzu entered the door of the hall with unhurried steps, looked at the king but made no bow.

The king said, "Now that you have gotten the crown prince to prepare the way for you, what kind of instruction is it you intend to give me?"

"I have heard that Your Majesty is fond of swords, and so I have come with my sword to present myself before you."

"And what sort of authority does your sword command?" asked the king.

"My sword cuts down one man every ten paces, and for a thousand li it never ceases its flailing!"

The king, greatly pleased, exclaimed, "You must have no rival in the whole world!"

Chuang Tzu said, "The wielder of the sword makes a display of emptiness, draws one out with hopes of advantage, is behind-time in setting out, but before-hand in arriving.[1] May I be allowed to try what I can do?"

The king said, "You may leave now, sir, and go to your quarters to await my command. When I am ready to hold the bout, I will request your presence again."

The king then spent seven days testing the skill of his swordsmen. Over sixty were wounded or died in the process, leaving five or six survivors, who were ordered to present themselves with their swords outside the king's hall. Then the king sent for Chuang Tzu, saying, "Today let us see what happens when you cross swords with these gentlemen."

Chuang Tzu said, "It is what I have long wished for."

"What weapon will you use, sir," asked the king, "a long sword or a short one?"

"I am prepared to use any type at all. It happens that I have three swords—Your Majesty has only to indicate which you wish me to use. If I may, I will first explain them, and then put them to the test."

"Let me hear about your three swords," said the king.

"There is the sword of the Son of Heaven, the sword of the feudal lord, and the sword of the commoner."

"What is the sword of the Son of Heaven like?" asked the king.

"The sword of the Son of Heaven? The Valley of Yen and the Stone Wall are its point, Ch'i and Tai its blade, Chin and Wey its spine, Chou and Sung its sword guard, Han and Wei its hilt.[2] The four barbarian tribes enwrap it, the four seasons enfold it, the seas of Po surround it, the mountains of Ch'ang girdle it. The five elements govern it, the demands of punishment and favor direct it. It is brought forth in accordance with the Yin and Yang, held in readiness in spring and summer, wielded in autumn and winter. Thrust it forward and there is nothing that will stand before it; raise it on high and there is nothing above it; press it down and there is nothing beneath it; whirl it about and there is nothing surrounding it. Above, it cleaves the drifting clouds; below, it severs the sinews of the earth. When this sword is once put to use, the feudal lords return to their former obedience and the whole world submits. This is the sword of the Son of Heaven."

King Wen, dumfounded, appeared to be at an utter loss. Then he said, "What is the sword of the feudal lord like?"

"The sword of the feudal lord? It has wise and brave men for its point, men of purity and integrity for its blade, men of worth and goodness for its spine, men of loyalty and sageliness for its swordguard, heroes and prodigies for its hilt. This sword too, thrust forward, meets nothing before it; raised, it encounters nothing above; pressed, it encounters

---

[1] The sentence is deliberately cryptic and capable of interpretation on a variety of levels.

[2] These are all feudal states or strategic places of northern China surrounding the State of Chao.

nothing beneath it; whirled about, it meets nothing surrounding it. Above, it takes its model from the roundness of heaven, following along with the three luminous bodies of the sky.[3] Below, it takes its model from the squareness of the earth, following along with the four seasons. In the middle realm, it brings harmony to the wills of the people and peace to the four directions. This sword, once put into use, is like the crash of a thunderbolt: none within the four borders of the state will fail to bow down in submission, none will fail to heed and obey the commands of the ruler. This is the sword of the feudal lord."

The king said, "What is the sword of the commoner like?"

"The sword of the commoner? It is used by men with tousled heads and bristling beards, with slouching caps tied with plain, coarse tassels and robes cut short behind, who glare fiercely and speak with great difficulty, who slash at one another in Your Majesty's presence. Above, it lops off heads and necks; below, it splits open liver and lungs. Those who wield this sword of the commoner are no different from fighting cocks—any morning their lives may be cut off. They are of no use in the administration of the state.

"Now Your Majesty occupies the position of a Son of Heaven, and yet you show this fondness for the sword of the commoner.[4] If I may be so bold, I think it rather unworthy of you!"

The king thereupon led Chuang Tzu up into his hall, where the royal butler came forward with trays of food, but the king merely paced round and round the room.

"Your Majesty should seat yourself at ease and calm your spirits," said Chuang Tzu. "The affair of the sword is over and finished."

After this, King Wen did not emerge from his palace for three months, and his swordsmen all committed suicide in their quarters.

Translated by Burton Watson

---

[3] The stars collectively make up the third luminous body.

[4] The state of Chao, situated in north central China, was never very powerful, and its king, only one among many feudal rulers of the time, in no sense occupied anything that could be called "the position of a Son of Heaven." If the writer has not abandoned all pretense at historicity, he must mean that the king of Chao, if he were to rule wisely, might in time gain sufficient power and prestige to become a contender for the position of Son of Heaven.

Part Two

THE HAN DYNASTY

In 221 B.C., following centuries of warfare between the competing states, China was finally unified by Ch'in, the westernmost of the states. For more than a century this state had been organized along Legalist principles; that is, every effort had been made to strengthen the power of the government through uniformly enforced laws and punishments and through more efficient bureaucratic procedures. Attempts were made to undermine both the old nobility and the patriarchal family and clan and to create in their stead a direct relationship between the ruler (now called the Emperor) and his subjects. With the unification of China these imperial policies were extended throughout the country. Currency and weights and measures were standardized, and attempts were made to eliminate the non-Legalist schools of thought by the famous "burning of the books."

The harshness of Ch'in rule led to an uprising in 209 B.C., and by 207 the second Ch'in Emperor had surrendered. The victor was Liu Pang, a commoner who had proven himself an excellent general. He established the Han dynasty, and his descendants ruled for the next four centuries except for an interregnum (A.D. 9–23) when Wang Mang (a maternal relative of the imperial family) usurped the throne and declared his own dynasty. The period before Wang Mang (206 B.C.–A.D. 9) is generally referred to as the Western or Former Han and the period following him (A.D. 25–220) as the Eastern or Later Han. Western and Eastern refer to the shift in the capital from Ch'ang-an (in modern Shensi) to Lo-yang (in Honan).

The Han government, while publicly repudiating the severity of Ch'in rule, nevertheless built on its heritage of unified control. Despite a brief experiment with giving out large and nearly autonomous fiefs to relatives of the Emperor, the overall trend of the Former Han was toward strengthening the central government. The major difference from the previous Ch'in administration was in the choice of men to staff the government offices. By the first century B.C. it became widely accepted that officials should be men trained in the classics. Thus officials had to reconcile their roles as agents of the Emperor and the court with their Confucian values of integrity and proper behavior. The prestige and influence of government posts steadily rose, and men of wealth and local standing throughout the country began to compete to gain recognition for their learning and character so that they could gain access to office.

Under the stability of Han rule, the population of China increased to over fifty million. The centuries of peace also facilitated the growth of trade and industry and led to improved communication and transportation, all of which helped tie Chinese society more closely together. Cities flourished and the capitals became important cultural centers, attracting men of education and wealth from all over the country. Extensive migrations from areas of hardship to the fertile South also contributed to integrating Chinese society. Thus, while great regional variation in customs and ideas continued to exist, people in different parts of the country were brought into greater contact with each other than ever before.

One of the aims of Legalism under the Ch'in was direct rule by the Emperor of everyone in the society. The Han government retained this policy in its tax and labor service obligations, which were imposed directly on each subject according to age, sex, and imperially-granted rank, instead of on families or communities. This governmental policy ran counter to some strongly entrenched particularistic forces in Chinese society. With the revival of Confucianism in the Han, family values were reasserted, as was emphasis on personal loyalty to friends and neighbors. Forms of social organization based on private relations (kinship, landlord-tenant, teacher-student, patron-client) gained in importance. Thus, whatever the theory, Han China was not a society of independent peasants subject only to the demands of the Emperor and his delegated officials. Rather it was a highly complex society in which individuals were obligated to a wide variety of superiors and subordinates, and a government official might find it impossible to draft peasants who had the protection of powerful landlords.

Because of the loss of most books in the centuries of warfare following the Han, the sources for studying Han society and civilization are not much more abundant than they were for the pre-Han period. Yet there are new kinds of sources. A major intellectual achievement of the Han was the creation of the standard or dynastic history by Ssu-ma Ch'ien (145–ca. 85 B.C.) and Pan Ku (A.D. 32–92). The three standard histories written about the Han give biographies of important men, recount political events, and describe institutional measures. Other sources useful for perceiving the structure and organization of Han society are the essays of writers, classical works and commentaries compiled in this period, collections of popular or inspirational tales and stories, and a few contemporary documents written on wood or carved in stone and fortuitously preserved until today.

7.

The Debate on Salt and Iron

The standard histories of the Han are replete with accounts of the decisions and policies made by the central government. Energetic rulers, such as Emperor Wu (r. 141–87 B.C.), are credited with greatly strengthening the power of the government. Determining how fully these policies were carried out or how they affected the population is often difficult. Sources such as the record of the "Debate on Salt and Iron" nevertheless provide some insight. In 81 B.C., after Emperor Wu's death, Confucian scholars who opposed the fiscal policies he had instituted were invited by his successor to argue their case with the Chief Minister, a man who had been instrumental in establishing them. A record of this debate was made in twenty-four chapters, the first of which is given below.

A major motive for Emperor Wu's fiscal policies had been the need to defend against the non-Chinese nomadic tribes (especially the Hsiung-nu) who lived in the dry regions north of China proper. To protect settlers on the borders from raids by the Hsiung-nu, the government had to mobilize huge armies and build numerous fortifications and encampments. To generate the revenue to pay for these military ventures, Emperor Wu manipulated coinage, confiscated the lands of nobles, sold offices and titles, and increased taxes. He also established government monopolies in the production of iron, salt, and liquor, enterprises that had previously been sources of great profit for private entrepreneurs. Large-scale grain dealing had also been a profitable business, which the government now took over under the name of the system of equable marketing. Grain was to be bought where it was plentiful and its price low and either stored in granaries or transported to areas of scarcity. This procedure was supposed to eliminate speculation in grain, provide more constant prices, and bring profit to the government.

From the start these fiscal ventures were controversial. Those educated in Confucian principles questioned their morality and their effect on the livelihood of the people. They thought that farming was an essential or "root" activity but that trade and crafts produced little of real value and were to be discouraged. Although the government claimed that it was protecting the people from the exploitation of merchants, its critics argued that it was teaching people mercantile tricks by setting itself up in commerce.

In the selection below both sides argued in general terms. They also both used the same rhetorical style, relying heavily on direct and indirect quotations from earlier books. Yet from their debate we can see some of the ways officials and potential officials thought about their responsibilities. From their descriptions of economic conditions we can also gain insight into the state of the economy in this period and the influence of the state on day-to-day economic affairs.

In 81 B.C. an imperial edict directed the Chancellor and Chief Minister to confer with a group of wise and learned men about the people's hardships.

The learned men responded: We have heard that the way to rule lies in preventing frivolity while encouraging morality, in suppressing the pursuit of profit while opening the way for benevolence and duty. When profit is not emphasized, civilization flourishes and the customs of the people improve.

Recently, a system of salt and iron monopolies, a liquor excise tax, and an equable marketing system have been established throughout the country. These represent financial competition with the people which undermines their native honesty and promotes selfishness. As a result, few among the people take up the fundamental pursuits [agriculture] while many flock to the secondary [trade and industry]. When artificiality thrives, simplicity declines; when the secondary flourishes, the basic decays. Stress on the secondary makes the people decadent; emphasis on the basic keeps them unsophisticated. When the people are unsophisticated, wealth abounds; when they are extravagant, cold and hunger ensue.

We desire that the salt, iron, and liquor monopolies and the system of equable marketing be abolished. In that way the basic pursuits will be encouraged, and the people will be deterred from entering secondary occupations. Agriculture will then greatly prosper. This would be expedient.

The Minister: The Hsiung-nu rebel against our authority and frequently raid the frontier settlements. To guard against this requires the effort of the nation's soldiers. If we take no action, these attacks and raids will never cease. The late Emperor had sympathy for the long-suffering of the frontier settlers who live in fear of capture by the barbarians. As defensive measures, he therefore built forts and beacon relay stations and set up garrisons. When the revenue for the defense of the frontier fell short, he established the salt and iron monopolies, the liquor excise tax, and the system of equable marketing. Wealth increased and was used to furnish the frontier expenses.

Now our critics wish to abolish these measures. They would have the treasury depleted and the border deprived of funds for its defense. They would expose our soldiers who defend the frontier passes and walls to hunger and cold, since there is no other way to supply them. Abolition is not expedient.

The learned men: Confucius observed, "The ruler of a kingdom or head of a family does not worry about his people's being poor, only about their being unevenly distributed. He does not worry about their being few, only about their being dissatisfied." Thus, the Emperor should not talk of much and little, nor the feudal lords of advantage and harm, nor the ministers of gain and loss. Instead they all should set

examples of benevolence and duty and virtuously care for people, for then those nearby will flock to them and those far away will joyfully submit to their authority. Indeed, the master conqueror need not fight, the expert warrior needs no soldiers, and the great commander need not array his troops.

If you foster high standards in the temple and courtroom, you need only make a bold show and bring home your troops, for the king who practices benevolent government has no enemies anywhere. What need can he then have for expense funds?

The Minister: The Hsiung-nu are savage and cunning. They brazenly push through the frontier passes and harass the interior, killing provincial officials and military officers at the border. Although they have long deserved punishment for their lawless rebellion, Your Majesty has taken pity on the financial exigencies of the people and has not wished to expose his officers to the wilderness. Still, we cherish the goal of raising a great army and driving the Hsiung-nu back north.

I again assert that to do away with the salt and iron monopolies and equable marketing system would bring havoc to our frontier military policies and would be heartless toward those on the frontier. Therefore this proposal is inexpedient.

The learned men: The ancients honored the use of virtue and discredited the use of arms. Confucius said, "If the people of far-off lands do not submit, then the ruler must attract them by enhancing his refinement and virtue. When they have been attracted, he gives them peace."

At present, morality is discarded and reliance is placed on military force. Troops are raised for campaigns and garrisons are stationed for defense. It is the long-drawn-out campaigns and the ceaseless transportation of provisions that burden our people at home and cause our frontier soldiers to suffer from hunger and cold.

The establishment of the salt and iron monopolies and the appointment of Financial Officers to supply the army were meant to be temporary measures. Therefore, it is expedient that they now be abolished.

The Minister: The ancient founders of our country laid the groundwork for both basic and secondary occupations. They facilitated the circulation of goods and provided markets and courts to harmonize the various demands. People of all classes gathered and goods of all sorts were assembled, so that farmers, merchants, and workers could all obtain what they needed. When the exchange of goods was complete, everyone went home. The *Book of Changes* says, "Facilitate exchange so that the people will not be overworked." This is because without artisans, the farmers are deprived of tools, and without merchants, desired commodities are unavailable. When farmers lack tools, grain is not planted, just as when valued goods are unavailable, wealth is exhausted.

The salt and iron monopolies and the equable marketing system are intended to circulate accumulated wealth and to regulate consumption according to the urgency of need. It is inexpedient to abolish them.

The learned men: If virtue is used to lead the people, they will return to honesty, but if they are enticed with gain, they will become vulgar. Vulgar habits lead them to shun duty and chase profit; soon they throng the roads and markets. Lao Tzu said, "A poor country will appear to have a surplus." It is not that it possesses abundance, but that when wishes multiply the people become restive. Hence, a true king promotes the basic and discourages the secondary. He restrains the people's desires through the principles of ritual and duty and arranges to have grain exchanged for other goods. In his markets merchants do not circulate worthless goods nor artisans make worthless implements.

The purpose of merchants is circulation and the purpose of artisans is making tools. These matters should not become a major concern of the government.

The Minister: Kuan Tzu* said: "If a country possesses fertile land and yet its people are underfed, the reason is that there are not enough tools. If it possesses rich natural resources in its mountains and seas and yet the people are poor, the reason is that there are not enough artisans and merchants."

The scarlet lacquer and pennant feathers from the kingdoms of Lung and Shu; the leather goods, bone, and ivory from Ching and Yang; the cedar, catalpa, bamboo, and reeds from Chiang-nan; the fish, salt, felt, and furs from Yen and Ch'i; the silk yarn, linen, and hemp cloth from Yen and Yu—all are needed to maintain our lives or be used in our funerals. We depend upon merchants for their distribution and on artisans for their production. For such reasons the ancient sages built boats and bridges to cross rivers; they domesticated cattle and horses to travel over mountains and plains. By penetrating to remote areas, they

were able to exchange all kinds of goods for the benefit of the people.

Thus, the Former Emperor set up iron officials to meet the farmers' needs and started the equable marketing system to assure the people adequate goods. The bulk of the people look to the salt and iron monopolies and the equable marketing system as their source of supply. To abolish them would not be expedient.

The learned men: If a country possesses a wealth of fertile land and yet its people are underfed, the reason is that merchants and workers have prospered while agriculture has been neglected. Likewise, if a country possesses rich natural resources in its mountains and seas and yet its people are poor, the reason is that the people's necessities have not been attended to while luxuries have multiplied. A spring cannot fill a leaking cup; the mountains and seas cannot satisfy unlimited desires. This is why [the ancient emperor] P'an Keng practiced communal living, [the ancient emperor] Shun concealed the gold, and [the Han dynasty founder] Kao-tsu prohibited merchants and shopkeepers from becoming officials. Their purpose was to discourage habits of greed and to strengthen the spirit of sincerity. Now, even with all of the discriminations against commerce, people still do evil. How much worse it would be if the ruler himself were to pursue profit!

The *Tso Chronicle* says: "When the feudal lords take delight in profit, the officers become petty; when the officers are petty, the gentlemen become greedy; when the gentlemen are greedy, the common people steal." Thus to open the way for profit is to provide a ladder for the people to become criminals!

The Minister: Formerly the feudal lords in the commanderies and kingdoms sent in the products of their respective regions as tribute. Transportation was troublesome and disorganized and the goods often of such bad quality as not to be worth the transport cost. Therefore, Transport Officers were appointed in every commandery and kingdom to assist in speeding the delivery of tribute and taxes from distant regions. This was called the equable marketing system. A Receiving Bureau was established at the capital for all the commodities. Because goods were bought when prices were low and sold when prices were high, the government suffered no loss and the merchants could not speculate for profit. This was called the balancing standard.

The balancing standard safeguards the people from unemployment; the equable marketing system

---

* I.e., Kuan Chung, a famous minister of the seventh century B.C. noted for his economic policies.

distributes their work fairly. Both of these measures are intended to even out goods and be a convenience for the people. They do not provide a ladder for the people to become criminals by opening the way to profit!

The learned men: The ancients in placing levies and taxes on the people would look for what they could provide. Thus farmers contributed their harvest and the weaving women the products of their skill. At present the government ignores what people have and exacts what they lack. The common people then must sell their products cheaply to satisfy the demands of the government. Recently, some commanderies and kingdoms ordered the people to weave cloth. The officials caused the producers various difficulties and then traded with them. They requisitioned not only the silk from Ch'i and T'ao and the broadcloth from Shu and Han, but also the ordinary cloth people make. These were then nefariously sold at "equable"

prices. Thus the farmers suffered twice over and the weavers were doubly taxed. Where is the equability in this marketing?

The government officers busy themselves with gaining control of the market and cornering commodities. With the commodities cornered, prices soar and merchants make private deals and speculate. The officers connive with the cunning merchants who are hoarding commodities against future need. Quick traders and unscrupulous officials buy when goods are cheap in order to make high profits. Where is the balance in this standard?

The equable marketing system of antiquity aimed at bringing about fair division of labor and facilitating transportation of tribute. It was surely not for profit or commodity trade.

Translated by Patricia Ebrey

8.

Rules for Visiting

Manners and everyday rituals serve to mold interpersonal relations and orient people in everyday affairs. Although people may not consider such gestures as bowing, shaking hands, or motioning for others to go first as anything more than politeness, the habits of deference and respect they ingrain cannot help but extend into other realms of social life.

Highly precise descriptions of rituals and good manners supposedly dating from the Chou period were edited during the Han to form three classic texts. The Record of Ritual *and the* Ritual of the Chou Dynasty *concern the ceremonies of the rulers and officials at court. The* Ceremonies and Rituals, *the text from which the following selection was taken, describes the etiquette and ceremonial observances of the* shih, *a term which means upper-class, educated men, and here is translated as "gentlemen." While the specific rules given in this selection, such as the kinds of gifts to be used, were not necessarily always followed, this text continued to provide a basic outline for social intercourse for many centuries.*

THE CEREMONIES FOR VISITS BETWEEN GENTLEMEN

In winter one presents a freshly killed pheasant and in summer a dried one. The bird is held up in both hands, the head to the left.

The visitor: "I have desired an interview for some time, but have had no justification for asking for one. Now his honor So-and-so has commanded me to visit."

The host: "The gentleman who introduced us has ordered me to grant you an interview. But you, sir, are demeaning yourself by coming. Please return home, and I shall hasten to present myself before you."

The guest: "I cannot disgrace you by obeying this command. Be good enough to end by granting me this interview."

The host: "I do not dare to set an example of how a reception of this kind should be conducted, and so I persist in asking you to return home, and I shall call on you without delay."

The guest: "It is I who do not dare to show that example, and so I persist in asking you for an interview."

The host: "Since I have failed to receive permission to decline this honor, I shall not press it further. But I hear that you are offering me a gift, and this I must decline."

The guest: "Without a gift I cannot dare to come into your presence."

The host: "I am not worthy of these ceremonies, and so I must persist in declining."

The guest: "If I cannot have the support of my gift, I dare not pay you this visit; so I persist in my request."

The host: "I also am decided in declining; but as I cannot secure your consent, how dare I refuse?"

Then the host goes to meet the guest outside the gate, and there bows twice, answered by two bows from the guest. Then the host, with a salute, invites him to enter. The host goes in by the right side of the door, the guest holding up the present and entering by the left. When they enter the courtyard the host bows twice and accepts the present, the guest bows twice as he hands it to him, and then starts going out. Then the host invites him to carry out the visit, and the guest returns and complies. When the guest leaves, the host escorts him outside the gate and bows twice.

When the former host pays his return visit, he takes the other's present with him. He says: "Recently when your honor demeaned himself by visiting me, you commanded me to an interview. I now ask permission to return your gift to the attendant."

The host: "Since I have already secured an interview, how could I now refuse to grant one?"

The guest: "I do not dare to ask for an interview; I only presume to request permission to return the gift by your attendant."

The host: "Since I have already obtained an interview by the help of this gift, I must persist in declining to receive it back."

The guest: "I dare not listen to such a speech, so I will press my request through your attendant."

The host: "Since I cannot secure your consent to my declining, I dare not but obey."

Then the guest enters, carrying the present. The host bows twice and receives it, the guest bowing twice as he gives it. On departure, the host escorts him outside the gate and bows twice.

When a gentleman visits an official, the latter declines altogether to receive his present. At his entrance the host bows once, acknowledging their difference in rank. When the guest withdraws, he escorts him and bows twice.

When a gentleman calls on his former superior, the host formally declines the visitor's gift: "As I have not been able to receive your consent to my declining, I dare not persist in it."

Then the guest enters, lays down his gift, and bows twice. The host replies with a single bow. When the guest leaves, the host sends the attendant to return the gift outside the gate.

The attendant: "So-and-so sends me to hand back your gift."

The guest: "Since I have already obtained an interview, I venture to decline to receive the gift."

The attendant: "So-and-so has issued his commands to me, and I cannot myself take the initiative in this matter. I must press his request on you."

The guest: "I am the humble servant of His Excellency, and am not capable of observing the ceremonies of a visitor with his host; so I venture to persist in declining."

The attendant: "Since So-and-so has ordered me, I dare not take it upon myself to make decisions in this matter, but persist in this request."

The guest: "I have repeatedly declined, without receiving his honor's permission to do so. How then dare I not obey?" He thus bows twice and receives the present back.

The lower officials, in visiting one another, use a live wild goose as a present. It is wrapped in a cloth, its feet bound with a cord, and is carried like the pheasant. In visits among the higher officials, a live lamb is presented. It is wrapped in a cloth, with the four legs bound in front. The head is held to the left as a fawn is held. The ceremonial is the same as that observed in visits exchanged between gentlemen.

At their first interview with the ruler, visitors carry a gift, holding it on a level with the girdle. Their deportment shows a respectful uneasiness. When commoners have an interview with their ruler, they do not assume dignified carriage, but hurry along both in advancing and retreating. Gentlemen and officials lay down their present and kowtow twice. To this the ruler responds with a single bow.

If the visitor is from another state, the usher is sent to hand him back his gift, saying: "My unworthy ruler has sent me to return your present."

The visitor replies: "A ruler has no ministers beyond his own borders, and therefore I dare not refuse to do as he commands." Then kowtowing twice, he receives it back.

Anyone who sees his ruler on business stands

directly in front of him when he faces south. If that is impossible, then the minister faces squarely east or west, and not in whatever direction the ruler happens to face. If the ruler is in the hall, the minister goes up the steps nearest the ruler, without making any distinction between directions.

Except to answer questions, in addressing the ruler a person composes himself before speaking. In speaking with the ruler, one talks of official business; with an official, of service to the ruler; with older men, of the control of children; with young people, of their filial and brotherly duties; with the common man, of loyalty and geniality; with those in minor offices, of loyalty.

In speaking to an official, one begins by looking him in the face; toward the middle of the interview one looks at his breast, and at the end of the interview one's eyes are again directed to his face. The order is never changed, and is used in all cases. In talking to one's father, the eyes are allowed to wander, but not higher than the face, nor lower than the girdle. If one is not speaking when the other is standing, one looks at his feet, and, if he sits, at his knees.

When one is sitting in attendance on a great man, should he yawn, stretch himself, ask the time of day, order his dinner, or change his position, then one must ask permission to retire. When one is sitting in attendance at night, if the great man should ask the time of night or start eating pungent things to prevent sleepiness, one may ask permission to retire.

If the ruler invites a guest to dinner, after the ruler makes an offering, the guest begins the meal by first tasting all the foods. He then drinks and awaits the ruler's command before beginning to eat. If there is anyone in charge of tasting the food, then the guest waits until the ruler has eaten before he eats. If the ruler gives him a cup of wine, he gets off his mat, kowtows twice, and then receives the cup. He then returns to his mat, sits down, and pours a libation. When he has emptied the cup, he waits until the ruler has emptied his, and then hands back his empty cup.

When he is leaving, the guest takes his shoes, goes quietly to one side, and puts them on. If the ruler rises on his account, the gentleman says: "There is no reason why you, Ruler, should get up, but your servant does not dare presume to decline the honor." If by any chance the ruler should escort him to the gate, he does not dare to look at him, but goes away immediately after taking his leave. In the case of an official, he declines the honor of being escorted. When he goes down the steps, and the ruler follows, he declines again. When he is escorted to the door, he declines for the third time.

Should a retired official call on a gentleman and ask to see him, the gentleman requests permission to decline. Not receiving it, he says: "I am not in a position to be visited by his honor, but not being able to secure permission to decline, I hurry to wait on him." Then he anticipates the visitor by going out and bowing to him first.

Unless a man is sent on a mission by his ruler, he does not call himself an official of his ruler. A gentleman calls himself the "old one" of his ruler.

When bearing a present of silk, one does not walk with great strides but deports himself with an anxious uneasiness. A person carrying jade steps carefully, lifting his toes and dragging his heels.

In speaking of himself to his ruler, a gentleman or official calls himself "Your servant." A speaker residing at home within the capital calls himself "Your servant of the market-place well"; and if in the country, "Your servant of the grass and fields." A commoner calls himself "Your servant the grass-cutter." A man from another state calls himself "Your servant from outside."

Translated by Patricia Ebrey

9.

Social Relations

Since holding office came to confer great prestige, in the Han, competition among the educated for the available offices became increasingly intense. Posts generally had to be obtained through recommendations, either from the official in charge of the commandery where one lived or from a high official. Men were supposed to be selected above all for their moral character, and it was believed that character could best be judged by those personally acquainted with the candidate. From the beginning, critics of this system pointed out that officials often recommended friends, relatives, and men of wealth and influence.

The following essay by Wang Fu (ca. 100–150) is an attack on the whole system of recommendations and its assumption that worthy but poor and powerless scholars would be recognized. It is also a personal account in which Wang Fu reveals his own view of his social world. Although known in literary circles and the author of a large book of essays, Wang Fu never gained an official post; his failure to do so probably contributed to the bitterness of his criticisms.

In a style typical of essays written in this period, Wang Fu alludes to a large number of historical figures whose names would have been familiar to his contemporaries. In this translation the historical contexts have been filled in to make Wang Fu's points clear.

It is said, "With people, the old friends are best; with things, the new ones are best." In other words, brothers may drift apart as time goes by, but it is normal for friends to become closer with the passage of time.

Nowadays this is not so. People often seem to miss those they hardly know but forget close friends; they turn away from old friends as they seek new ones. Sometimes after several years friendships become weaker and weaker, and friendships of long standing break down. People not only discard the ancient sages' instruction to treasure old friends but also break oaths of enduring fidelity.

What are the reasons for these changes in attitude toward friendship? Careful analysis makes them clear. There are common tendencies and normal ways of operating in the world. People compete to flatter and get close to those who are wealthy and prominent; this is a common tendency. People are also quick to snub those who are poor and humble; this is a normal way of operating. If a person makes friends with the rich and prominent, he will gain the benefits of influential recommendations for advancement in office and the advantages of generous presents and other emoluments. But if he makes friends with the poor and humble, he will lose money either from giving them handouts or from unrepaid loans.

A powerful official may be as evil as the tyrant Chieh and the bandit Tao Chih, but if he rides in a magnificent carriage to summon scholars to him, they will take it as a great honor and flock to his service. How can a person avoid being drawn to those who can render him tangible benefits? A scholar may have the combined talents of Yen Hui and Pao Shang-yen, yet if he wears poor clothing when he pays visits, others will feel insulted and will look with dread upon the prospect of further calls. How can a person not avoid those who will bring him disadvantage? Therefore, those who are rich and prosperous find it easy to get along in society, while those who are poor and humble find it difficult to secure a place in the world.

The poor, if they wear fine clothes, are regarded as extravagant and ostentatious, but if they wear coarse clothing, they are taken to be in dire straits and difficulties. If they walk slowly, people say they are weak from hunger, but if they walk fast, they are accused of trying to flee from debts. If the poor do not visit others, they are regarded as arrogant, but if they come around too often, they are suspected of trying to sponge free meals. If they come empty-handed, they are taken for insincere friends, but if they bring a gift, they are regarded as degenerate. If they are confident and self-assured, they are regarded as unvirtuous. All these are the woes of being an unemployed scholar, poor and without rank.

The poor scholar, being in a humble position, has much to bear. At home he has to put up with his wife's complaints. Outside he must endure the cutting remarks of the scholar-officials. At banquets his gifts are small and considered inadequate. His own parties are simple and not up to others' standards. He is not rich enough to come to the aid of friends in need, and his power is too meager to save them. A friendship may have been long and cordial, but since the poor scholar is unable to save his friend in need, the relationship weakens. Once this occurs, the humble scholar becomes more and more aware of his own low status, while the other individual busies himself with cultivating relationships with more useful persons and forgets his old friend.

Since friendship is founded on mutual advantage, when disadvantage arises the friendship breaks down. An oath of friendship is meaningless and eventually will be discarded. Those who communicate often become close friends because they see advantage to themselves in the relationship. A commoner will act as follows. If a person can be useful, he will draw near to him. Being close to him, he will gradually develop a feeling of love for him. Because he thinks the friend is right, he will regard him as capable, and so he will turn his heart toward him and praise him happily. A commoner will keep his distance from those whom he regards as unable to render him benefits. Because they are distant, after a time he begins to

feel hatred for them. Because he hates them, he always considers them in the wrong, and so feels disgust for them. Once he feels disgust for them, his heart naturally turns away from them and he slanders them. Therefore, even if one's friendship with a wealthy and prominent man is a new one, it will become closer and closer every day; and although one's friendship with a poor and humble man is of long standing, it will tend to become weaker and more distant. These are the reasons why a poor scholar cannot compete with officials for friends.

Rulers do not understand what causes people to form friendships, and so they readily believe the words of their high officials. This is why honest scholars are always excluded from court while crafty persons always get their way. In the past when Wei Ch'i lost his power, his retainers abandoned him to serve in another place. When the general Wei Ch'ing lost imperial favor and was no longer able to shower his subordinates with rewards from the court, they left him to serve the newly powerful general Huo Ch'ü-ping. The retainers of the Chao general Lien P'o and of the Han general T'i Kung came and went, depending on whether their benefactors were in power or not. These four gentlemen were all capable and all had illustrious pasts, yet the loyalty of their subordinates wavered with the amount of power they had. How much more would this happen to those who became really poor and humble!

Only those who have the heroic virtue of the ancients will not desert their superiors and friends in such a fashion. When these people make commitments to friends, they do not abandon them their whole life long. If they love someone, their concern for him can only become greater as his situation worsens. The *Book of Poetry* says, "The virtuous man, the princely one, is uniformly correct in his deportment. His heart is as if it were tied to what is correct." Only during the cold of winter, when all other trees have lost their leaves, do people realize that the pine trees resist the cold and do not shed their needles. Likewise, it is only when difficulties are encountered that a person's virtue can be noticed. Yu Ying and Yu Jang gave their lives to retain their master's good grace. Chuan Chu and Ching K'o sacrificed their lives to render service to their masters. It is easy to die, but to die for one's master willingly when he has encountered hard times is difficult indeed. . . .

Most scholars are very shortsighted, concerned only about the present moment. If they think that a powerful man will be of use to them, they rush to his service; but if they think that someone will be of no use, they are quick to avoid him. Those who burn for rapid promotion and advancement compete with one another to get close to persons of prominence but can find no time to associate with the humble. They scrape and claw to make their way to the front but have little time to concern themselves with those who have been left behind. When the Minister Han An-kuo lost his official post, he sent some five hundred golden artifacts to the newly powerful Grand Commandant Tien Fen to seek a position. Yet not once did he give any assistance to a poor but capable scholar. Likewise the Minister Ti Fang-chin was eager to recommend Shun Yu-ch'ang, a relative of the empress, for promotion, but was unable to recommend even one humble scholar. Now, both Han An-kuo and Ti Fang-chin were good and loyal officials of the Han dynasty, and yet they still acted in such a snobbish way. How can one expect virtue from officials who are inferior to them? This is the reason that crafty, calculating individuals can worm their way up the official ladder while ordinary scholars slip ever more into obscurity. Unless the realm has a brilliant ruler, there may be no one to discern this.

Not everyone desires riches and honors; not everyone scorns poverty and humbleness. People can differ drastically in their preferences and goals. Hsü Yu refused to accept the dragon-throne, which the sage-king Yao offered to him, yet small men fight bitterly to gain a mere Magistrate's post. Mencius declined a stipend of 10,000 bushels, but there are small men who grasp after a salary of one peck. . . . Po I did not regret the need to gather wild vegetables to support himself, and Tsao Fu was content to dwell in a tree. From these cases one can see that gentlemen's intentions are varied. Therefore I say to the gentlemen of today: Although you may be rich and powerful, you must not look down upon those who are poor and humble, nor demand their submission to you.

The *Book of Poetry* says, "Virtue is light as a hair, but few are able to lift it." In this world there are four basic virtues which people are rarely able to acquire fully: reciprocity, fairness, respect, and perseverence. Reciprocity is the basis of knowledge. Fairness is the basis of righteousness. Respect is the basis of propriety. Perseverence is the basis of fidelity. When these four types of virtues are established, they form the basis for the achievement of the four kinds of good behavior, and the one who possesses them can be re-

garded as a true worthy. Those who do not possess these four virtues or types of good behavior—perhaps not having even one of them—are considered small men. . . .

In this world there are three things which are loathsome indeed. These may be summed up as follows: first, to express in words extremely warm affections toward others while one's heart holds nothing but cold feelings; second, to express in writing dear thoughts toward others while in fact one's thoughts are rarely with them; third, to make appointments with others while having already decided not to show up at all. If people are always suspicious of others' words, they may fear that they will dismiss the genuine sentiments of a true worthy. But if people are quick to believe what they are told, they will be often fooled. This is why those disingenuous, mediocre people are so disgusting. . . .

Alas! The gentlemen of today speak nobly but act basely. Their words are upright, but their hearts are false. Their actions do not reflect their words, and their words are out of harmony with their thoughts. In talking of antiquity they always praise the conduct of Po I, Shu Ch'i, Ch'ü Yüan, and Yen Hui; but when it comes to the present, their only concern is the scramble for official ranks and positions. In their lofty speeches they refer to virtuous and righteous persons as being worthy. But when they actually recommend people for office, they consider only such requirements as influence and prominence. If a man is just an obscure scholar, even if he possesses the virtue of Yen Hui and Ming Tzu-chien, even if he is modest and diligent, even if he has the ability of I Yin and Lu Shang, even if he is filled with the most devoted compassion for the people, he is clearly not going to be employed in this world.

Translated by Lily Hwa

10.

Two Women

The family has always been considered by the Chinese as the fundamental unit of their society. During the Han, family virtues, especially filial piety and female constancy, were widely celebrated. The Classic of Filial Piety gained popularity, and Liu Hsiang (79–8 B.C.), an eminent scholar and bibliographer, wrote Biographies of Admirable Women, a collection of accounts of the gallant deeds and unselfish behavior of women of antiquity. Many of these women epitomized a single virtue—for instance, loyalty to the ruler, self-sacrifice to help husband or father, or preservation of chastity under duress. As seen in the account below, however, the mother of the great Confucian philosopher Mencius (372–289 B.C.) had several virtues.

Reading this account does not reveal what women were like in the Han, but it does show us what people admired in women. No fiction has survived from the Han which could give us portrayals of women in ordinary life. We do have, however, one description of a real but far-from-ideal woman written by her husband, Feng Yen. It is found in a letter he addressed to his wife's younger brother to explain his reasons for divorcing her. Hardly a detached observer, Feng Yen nevertheless cannot help but reveal his own attitudes toward female character and the institution of marriage.

THE MOTHER OF MENCIUS

The mother of Mencius lived in Tsou in a house near a cemetery. When Mencius was a little boy he liked to play burial rituals in the cemetery, happily building tombs and grave mounds. His mother said to herself, "This is no place to bring up my son."

She moved near the marketplace in town. Mencius then played merchant games of buying and selling. His mother again said, "This is no place to bring up my son."

So once again she moved, this time next to a school house. Mencius then played games of ancestor sacrifices and practiced the common courtesies between students and teachers. His mother said, "At last, this is the right place for my son!" There they remained.

When Mencius grew up he studied the six arts of propriety, music, archery, charioteering, writing, and mathematics. Later he became a famous Confucian scholar. Superior men commented that Mencius' mother knew the right influences for her sons. The *Book of Poetry* says, "That admirable lady, what will she do for them!"

When Mencius was young, he came home from school one day and found his mother was weaving at the loom. She asked him, "Is school out already?"

He replied, "I left because I felt like it."

His mother took her knife and cut the finished cloth on her loom. Mencius was startled and asked why. She replied, "Your neglecting your studies is very much like my cutting the cloth. The superior person studies to establish a reputation and gain wide knowledge. He is calm and poised and tries to do no wrong. If you do not study now, you will surely end up as a menial servant and will never be free from troubles. It would be just like a woman who supports herself by weaving to give it up. How long could such a person depend on her husband and son to stave off hunger? If a woman neglects her work or a man gives up the cultivation of his character, they may end up as common thieves if not slaves!"

Shaken, from then on Mencius studied hard from morning to night. He studied the philosophy of the Master and eventually became a famous Confucian scholar. Superior men observed that Mencius' mother understood the way of motherhood. The *Book of Poetry* says, "That admirable lady, what will she tell them!"

After Mencius was married, one day as he was going into his private quarters, he encountered his wife not fully dressed. Displeased, Mencius stopped going into his wife's room. She then went to his mother, begged to be sent home, and said, "I have heard that the etiquette between a man and a woman does not apply in their private room. But lately I have been too casual, and when my husband saw me improperly dressed, he was displeased. He is treating me like a stranger. It is not right for a woman to live as a guest; therefore, please send me back to my parents."

Mencius' mother called him to her and said, "It is polite to inquire before you enter a room. You should make some loud noise to warn anyone inside, and as you enter, you should keep your eyes low so that you will not embarrass anyone. Now, you have not behaved properly, yet you are quick to blame others for their impropriety. Isn't that going a little too far?"

Mencius apologized and took back his wife. Superior men said that his mother understood the way to be a mother-in-law.

When Mencius was living in Ch'i, he was feeling very depressed. His mother saw this and asked him, "Why are you looking so low?"

"It's nothing," he replied.

On another occasion when Mencius was not working, he leaned against the door and sighed. His mother saw him and said, "The other day I saw that you were troubled, but you answered that it was nothing. But why are you leaning against the door sighing?"

Mencius answered, "I have heard that the superior man judges his capabilities and then accepts a position. He neither seeks illicit gains nor covets glory or high salary. If the Dukes and Princes do not listen to his advice, then he does not talk to them. If they listen

to him but do not use his ideas, then he no longer frequents their courts. Today my ideas are not being used in Ch'i, so I wish to go somewhere else. But I am worried because you are getting too old to travel about the country."

His mother answered, "A woman's duties are to cook the five grains, heat the wine, look after her parents-in-law, make clothes, and that is all! Therefore, she cultivates the skills required in the women's quarters and has no ambition to manage affairs outside of the house. The *Book of Changes* says, 'In her central place, she attends to the preparation of the food.' The *Book of Poetry* says, 'It will be theirs neither to do wrong nor to do good,/ Only about the spirits and the food will they have to think.' This means that a woman's duty is not to control or to take charge. Instead she must follow the 'three submissions.' When she is young, she must submit to her parents. After her marriage, she must submit to her husband. When she is widowed, she must submit to her son. These are the rules of propriety. Now you are an adult and I am old; therefore, whether you go depends on what you consider right, whether I follow depends on the rules of propriety."

Superior men observed that Mencius' mother knew the proper course for women. The *Book of Poetry* says, "Serenely she looks and smiles,/ Without any impatience she delivers her instructions."

Translated by Nancy Gibbs

LETTER FROM FENG YEN TO HIS BROTHER-IN-LAW

Man is a creature of emotion. Yet it is according to reason that husband and wife are joined together or put asunder. According to the rules of propriety which have been set down by the Sage, a gentleman should have both a primary wife and concubines as well. Even men from poor and humble families long to possess concubines. I am old and approaching the end of my life, but I have never had a concubine. I will carry regret for this into my grave.

My wife is jealous and has destroyed the Way of a good family. Yet this mother of five children is still in my house. For the past five years her conduct has become worse and worse day after day. She sees white as black and wrong as right. I never err in the slightest, yet she lies about me and nags me without end. It is like falling among bandits on the road, for I constantly encounter unpredictable disasters through this woman. Those who slander us good officials seem to have no regard for the deleterious effects this has on the welfare of the country. Likewise, those who indulge their jealousy seem to have no concern for the unjust strain this puts on other people's lives.

Since antiquity it has always been considered a great disaster to have one's household be dominated by a woman. Now this disaster has befallen me. If I eat too much or too little or if I drink too much or too little, she jumps all over me like the tyrant Hsia Chieh. If I play some affectionate joke on her, she will gossip about it to everyone. She glowers with her eyes and clenches her fists tightly in anger over things which are purely the product of her imagination. I feel a severe pang in my heart, as though something is poisoning my five viscera. Anxiety cuts so deeply that I can hardly bear to go on living. My rage is so great that I often forget the calamities I might cause.

When she is at home, she is always lounging in bed. After she gave birth to my principal heir, she refused to have any more children. We have no female servants at our home who can do the work of weaving clothes and rugs. Our family is of modest means and we cannot afford a man-servant, so I have to work myself like a humble commoner. My old friends see my situation and feel very sorry for me, but this woman has not the slightest twinge of sympathy or pity.

Wu Ta, you have seen our one and only female servant. She has no hairpins or hair ornaments. She has no make-up for her face, looks haggard, and is in bad shape. My wife does not extend the slightest pity to her, nor does she try to understand her. The woman flies into a rage, jumps around, and yells at her. Her screaming is so shrill that even a sugar-peddler's concubine would be ashamed to behave in such a manner.

I should have sent this woman back long ago, but I was concerned by the fact that the children were still young and that there was no one else to do the work in our house. I feared that my children, Chiang and Pao, would end up doing servants' work. Therefore I retained her. But worry and anxiety plunge like a dagger into my heart and cause me great pain. The woman is always screaming fiercely. One can hardly bear to listen to it.

Since the servant was so mistreated, within half a year her body was covered with scabs and scars. Ever since the servant became ill, my daughter Chiang has had to hull the grain and do the cooking, and my son Pao has had to do all sorts of dirty work. Watching my children struggle under such labor gives me distress.

Food and clothing are scattered all over the house. Winter clothes which have become frayed are not patched. Even though the rest of us are very careful to be neat, she turns the house into a mess. She does not have the manner of a good wife, nor does she possess the virtue of a good mother. I despise her overbearing aggressiveness, and I hate to see our home turned into a sty.

She relies on the power of Magistrate Cheng to get what she wants. She is always threatening people, and her barbs are numerous. It seems as if she carries a sword and lance to the door. Never will she make a concession, and it feels as if there were a hundred bows around our house. How can we ever return to a happy family life?

When the respectable members of our family try to reason with her, she flings insults at them and makes sharp retorts. She never regrets her scandalous behavior and never allows her heart to be moved. I realize that I have placed myself in a difficult position, and so I have started to plan ahead. I write you this letter lest I be remiss in keeping you informed of what is happening. I believe that I have just cause, and I am not afraid of criticism. Unless I send this wife back, my family will have no peace. Unless I send this wife back, my house will never be clean. Unless I send this wife back, good fortune will not come to my family. Unless I send this wife back, I will never again get anything accomplished. I hate myself for not having made this decision while I was still young. The decision is now made, but I am old, humiliated, and poor. I hate myself for having allowed this ulcer to grow and spread its poison. I brought a great deal of trouble on myself.

Having suffered total ruin as a result of this family catastrophe, I am abandoning the gentry life to live as a recluse. I will sever relationships with my friends and give up my career as an official. I will stay at home all the time and concentrate on working my land to supply myself with food and clothing. How can I think of success and fame?

Translated by Lily Hwa

II.

The Interaction of Yin and Yang

The concepts of Yin and Yang, first elaborated in the late Chou period, provided the basis for Chinese cosmology and proto-scientific thinking. Underlying the theory of Yin and Yang is the assumption that all things are interrelated and interdependent; no part has a life of its own but is shaped by and helps to shape other constituent parts in a continuum of interactions. Out of the primordial Tao (Way) occur the cosmic forces of Yin (female, dark, passive) and Yang (male, bright, assertive). These two forces are not in contention but complement each other. All things contain some Yin and some Yang, although in most cases one predominates. For instance, during the day Yang is predominant but at night Yin is more powerful; yet each moment is a particular blend of Yin and Yang. The framework of Yin and Yang was used to discover correspondences between different realms. Fire, for instance, was seen as corresponding to joy, the heart, the planet Mars, summer, south, and so on, because they also were overwhelmingly Yang in nature. Through such theoretical elaboration, Yin and Yang also came to provide a way of thinking about the working of nature and, in particular, the human body and its diseases

Below is a selection from the Yellow Emperor's Classic of Medicine, *the basic medical text of traditional China. It was supposed to have been written during the third millennium* B.C. *by the mythical Yellow Emperor, but it most likely was put in final form during the Han dynasty. It reveals the essential role the concepts of Yin and Yang played in Chinese scientific thought.*

The Yellow Emperor said: "The principle of Yin and Yang is the foundation of the entire universe. It underlies everything in creation. It brings about the development of parenthood; it is the root and source of life and death; it is found within the temples of the gods. In order to treat and cure diseases one must search for their origins.

"Heaven was created by the concentration of Yang, the force of light; Earth was created by the concentration of Yin, the force of darkness. Yang stands for peace and serenity; Yin stands for confusion and turmoil. Yang stands for destruction; Yin stands for conservation. Yang brings about disintegration; Yin gives shape to things. . . .

"The pure and lucid element of light is manifested in the upper orifices, and the turbid element of darkness is manifested in the lower orifices. Yang, the element of light, originates in the pores. Yin, the element of darkness, moves within the five viscera. Yang, the lucid force of light, truly is represented by the four extremities; and Yin, the turbid force of darkness, stores the power of the six treasures of nature. Water is an embodiment of Yin, as fire is an embodiment of Yang. Yang creates the air, while Yin creates the senses, which belong to the physical body. When the physical body dies, the spirit is restored to the air, its natural environment. The spirit receives its nourishment through the air, and the body receives its nourishment through the senses. . . .

"If Yang is overly powerful, then Yin may be too weak. If Yin is particularly strong, then Yang is apt to be defective. If the male force is overwhelming, then there will be excessive heat. If the female force is overwhelming, then there will be excessive cold. Exposure to repeated and severe cold will lead to fever. Exposure to repeated and severe heat will induce chills. Cold injures the body while heat injures the spirit. When the spirit is hurt, severe pain will ensue. When the body is hurt, there will be swelling. Thus, when severe pain occurs first and swelling comes on later, one may infer that a disharmony in the spirit has done harm to the body. Likewise, when swelling appears first and severe pain is felt later on, one can say that a dysfunction in the body has injured the spirit. . . .

"Nature has four seasons and five elements. To grant long life, these seasons and elements must store up the power of creation in cold, heat, dryness, moisture, and wind. Man has five viscera in which these five climates are transformed into joy, anger, sympathy, grief, and fear. The emotions of joy and anger are injurious to the spirit just as cold and heat are injurious to the body. Violent anger depletes Yin; violent joy depletes Yang. When rebellious emotions rise to Heaven, the pulse expires and leaves the body. When joy and anger are without moderation, then cold and heat exceed all measure, and life is no longer secure. Yin and Yang should be respected to an equal extent." . . .

The Yellow Emperor asked, "Is there any alternative to the law of Yin and Yang?"

Ch'i Po answered: "When Yang is the stronger, the body is hot, the pores are closed, and people begin to pant; they become boisterous and coarse and do not perspire. They become feverish, their mouths are dry and sore, their stomachs feel tight, and they die of constipation. When Yang is the stronger, people can endure winter but not summer. When Yin is the stronger, the body is cold and covered with perspiration. People realize they are ill; they tremble and feel chilly. When they feel chilled, their spirits become rebellious. Their stomachs can no longer digest food and they die. When Yin is the stronger, people can endure summer but not winter. Thus Yin and Yang alternate. Their ebbs and surges vary, and so does the character of their diseases."

The Yellow Emperor asked, "Can anything be done to harmonize and adjust these two principles of nature?"

Ch'i Po answered: "If one has the ability to know the seven injuries and the eight advantages, one can bring the two principles into harmony. If one does not know how to use this knowledge, his life will be doomed to early decay. By the age of forty the Yin force in the body has been reduced to one-half of its natural vigor, and an individual's youthful prowess has deteriorated. By the age of fifty the body has grown heavy. The ears no longer hear well. The eyes no longer see clearly. By the age of sixty the life-producing power of Yin has declined to a very low level. Impotence sets in. The nine orifices no longer benefit each other. . . .

"Those who seek wisdom beyond the natural limits will retain good hearing and clear vision. Their bodies will remain light and strong. Although they grow old in years, they will stay able-bodied and vigorous and be capable of governing to great advantage. For this reason the ancient sages did not rush into the affairs of the world. In their pleasures and joys they were dignified and tranquil. They did what they thought best and did not bend their will or ambition to the achievement of empty ends. Thus their allotted span of life was without limit, like that of Heaven and Earth. This is the way the ancient sages controlled and conducted themselves. . . .

"By observing myself I learn about others, and their diseases become apparent to me. By observing the external symptoms, I gather knowledge about the internal diseases. One should watch for things out of the ordinary. One should observe minute and trifling things and treat them as if they were big and important. When they are treated, the danger they pose will be dissipated. Experts in examining patients judge their general appearance; they feel their pulse and determine whether it is Yin or Yang that causes the disease. . . . To determine whether Yin or Yang predominates, one must be able to distinguish a light pulse of low tension from a hard, pounding one. With a disease of Yang, Yin predominates. With a disease of Yin, Yang predominates. When one is filled with vigor and strength, Yin and Yang are in proper harmony."

Translated by Mark Coyle

12.

Local Cults

During the Han, and certainly earlier, local cults played an important part in the religious lives of Chinese in all social strata. Shrines were dedicated to various kinds of spirits and deities, including the ghosts of local residents, the spirits of mountains or rivers, and mythical culture heroes and ancient rulers. Shrines were places where individuals could make offerings when asking the gods for help and also served as focal points for communal festivals. Occasionally when a shrine was constructed or repaired a stone would be carved to record the deed. Such stones have seldom survived, but in over a dozen cases the texts were recorded by history-conscious scholars sometime after A.D. 1000. These inscriptions testify to the nature and origins of specific local cults during the Han.

Below are the texts of three such inscriptions dating from the mid-second century A.D. From them we can infer the powers people imputed to gods and spirits and the significance they gave to maintaining shrines and making offerings. We can also see aspects of the social process by which construction of a shrine was initiated and financed.

INSCRIPTION FOR PRINCE CH'IAO

Prince Ch'iao is an immortal from a past age whose divinity has been known for a long time. Not knowing in what period it arose, I inquired widely of Taoist experts. Some said Ying-ch'uan, some said Yen-meng. When this city was first built, this mound was here. The tradition passed down from former people was that it was the grave of a Prince, but as his line of descent had not continued, no one had maintained it. How many years went by, no one could remember.

Then in the twelfth month of A.D. 136, on the night of the winter festival, there was a sound of crying at the top of the grave. Wang Po, who lived nearby, heard it and marvelled at it. At dawn he made an offering at the grave and looked around. Then Heaven sent a heavy snow, and although there were no human tracks to be seen, he saw the traces of a large bird near the place of the sacrifice. Everyone thought it was the spirit.

Some time later, a person appeared in front of the grave. He was wearing a large hat and a single red gown and carried a bamboo pole. He shouted to a young woodcutter, Yin Yung-ch'ang, "I am Prince Ch'iao. Never again take the trees from the front of my grave!" In a moment he had disappeared.

The Magistrate, Wan Hsi of T'ai-shan, looked into the sayings of the elders and learned that this was an auspicious response to some influence. He examined the evidence and believed that there was proof. Then he built a temple in order to give peace to the spirit. From that time on, ardent Taoists have come here from afar. Some would play lutes and sing of the "great unity." Some would meditate long in order to pass through Cinnabar Hill.* The sick and emaciated would cleanse their bodies, pray for cures, and be blessed immediately. However, if they were not reverent, they would have a relapse. Therefore, it

* Cinnabar Hill is a home of immortals.

became known that this grave mound with its great power was really that of an immortal.

In the eighth month of A.D. 165 the Emperor sent an emissary to offer sacrifices in order to honor this spirit. The solicitous dignity was just right. The Administrator of the Kingdom, Wang Chang (styled Po-i) of Tung-lai, thought that since the spirit had been honored by the Emperor, there should be an inscription to show to later generations. The common people were proud of the similarity to the recognition of Lao Tzu by Yin Hsi at the barrier.* Then with the help of Chief Aide Pien Ch'ien-fang and the gentlemen and clerks, the stone tablet was set up. On the black stone the spirit is praised and his merit recorded. People who search for the Way now have something to read.

INSCRIPTION FOR SAN-KUNG MOUNTAIN

The people believed that a period of famine and hardship had occurred because the gods of the San-kung, Yü-yü, and San-t'iao Mountains were on the west sides of the peaks, on the far side from them. Then when the officials and common people made offerings, clouds gathered and rains fell throughout the area. Later when the Tibetans raided and there were locusts, drought, and unseasonal weather, the people wandered away. Thus, sacrificial offerings became rare and libations were not performed. Since then, the weather has been intemperate.

Then there came a learned Taoist who traced the origins of these problems. He concluded that the divine power of the San-kung has been difficult to preserve because it is in a place difficult to reach. Therefore, a lucky piece of land to the east of the kingdom seat was selected by divination, and a shrine and altar raised near Heng Mountain. A pair of columns stand on either side of the gate. Sacrifices have been offered and wine presented in order to please the god. The god enjoys his position and sweet rain has repeatedly fallen, the response as quick as a shadow or an echo. There is great abundance within the borders of the kingdom and grain sells for three cash a bushel. The common people have neither illness nor suffering and live into old age.

The Chief Aide, Yen Fu (of Lu kingdom); the Officer of the Five Bureaus, Yen Chi; the Clerk of the

Department of Population, Chi Shou; the Officer of Construction, Wang Ch'eng; the Magistrate of Yüan-shih, Mao K'ung; the Assistant, Wu Yin; the Court Officer, Kuo Hung; the Clerk of the Department of Population, Ti Fu; and the Workman, Sung Kao, engraved this stone as a record of it.

INSCRIPTION FOR THE SPIRIT TOWER AT CH'ENG-YANG

This concerns the mother of Lord Yao.

In ancient times Ch'ing-tu lived in Ch'iung-ching. Of the Yi lineage, she was endowed with the best virtue and behaved according to the most appropriate rites. She modeled herself on the interaction of Yin and Yang, and attained to the brilliance of the sun, moon, and stars. On an excursion by the bank of the Yellow River, she was influenced by the red dragon and thus gave birth to [the mythical sage king] Yao. Later when Yao asked about his ancestry, Ch'ing-tu informed him of the river dragon. Yao went to three rivers and a dragon came and gave him the diagrams.* With these, he personally carried out sage government and took care of his people. His glory was like a fiery sun: at first dark but later brighter and brighter. Subsequently he went from being a noble to being ruler.

When Ch'ing-tu died, she was buried here. It was desired that no one know of the place, so it was named Spirit Tower. On top is a yellow room where Yao offered sacrifices. At the bottom he ran some water to please the dragon. Turtles played and fish jumped in the water there; flat fish with sleek scales appeared among the pebbles at the dark bottom; rushes grew along the edges of the tower. For a long time it was a center of worship, but dynasties changed, and it was abandoned and not repaired.

The five interacting forces went through their cycles and the Han dynasty received a long span. The people of Han revived what had been destroyed and continued what had been discarded. So, like Yao had done, they continued the sacrifices. In a year the flat fish again appeared. Therefore the Spirit Tower's Attendant and Guard sent a messenger to offer the fish to the throne because they could prolong life. Later, the Way was in decline and blocked. Subsequently,

---

* That is, in both cases it was a commoner who had recognized the greatness of someone others had ignored.

* The "River Diagrams" were revered by Confucians for their cosmological significance.

under Wang Mang's rule,* the offerings were stopped.

The former Minister of Punishments, Chung Ting, began to ponder: "The great Han has flourished and its virtue has reached the four directions. Why has great peace not yet arrived, the portents not yet appeared? Why, instead, have barbarians frequently encroached on us and our armies frequently been disturbed? Since the Emperors are not inattentive, why does the sun decline and not reappear?" The Minister examined the classics and checked the records and the secret diagrams of the Yellow and Lo rivers. He concluded that since the Han founder had been conceived through a red dragon, he was a descendant of Yao. Thus Yao's shrine ought to be repaired to its original design, and in repairing the Yellow Hall the sage's intentions should be sought. At that time disasters occurred and the Minister thought Heaven was making known its will. Several times he petitioned the throne, explaining these basic principles, proposing that one should draw forth the lucky omens and block unlucky ones for the future blessings of the Han dynasty. The court closely examined his proposal and the Emperor accepted his plan that every year in the spring and fall a great animal sacrifice should be made.

At this time the Minister of Punishments was due for a new appointment. Repeatedly he asked to retire, and finally his wish was granted. He was given the title Great Palace Grandee and returned home to re-pair the Yellow Hall. In a good month, on a lucky day, he drew up the plan and set up the boundaries. He assembled the workers and the area was leveled. Everything was in accord with both Heaven and Earth, beautifully painted in five colors.

A column was set up which seemed to penetrate to Heaven. The gate faced the east, and in front there was a large hall for worship of the gods. The floor was made of stone slabs to keep it cool. It could be used for dances. . . .

At the time, the Grand Administrator of Ch'i-yin, Shen Huang of Wei commandery, and the Magistrate of Ch'eng-yang, Kuan Tsun of Po-ling, each sent a Great Officer to assist. Minister Chung managed and directed it. Before long the project was completed. The essence of the gods relies on human beings; it will disappear if abandoned and flourish if preserved.

The Minister led a group of his clan's poor and rich to buy a stone tablet, all contributing fairly. On it deeds and teachings were recorded, and it was set up outside the central gate.

By divination the Minister selected a day and everyone came to worship sincerely. They first made reverent offerings, then prayed for blessings. They asked the spirits to enjoy the offerings, to send sweet rain, to let the grains ripen, to bring the foreign wastelands to submission, to bring prosperity to the ten thousand states and the multitudes of people.

Translated by Patricia Ebrey

---

* Wang Mang, a relative of the mother of a child Emperor, usurped the throne from A.D. 9 to 23.

13.

Uprisings

The collapse of the Han was hastened by the outbreak in 184 of a large-scale rebellion staged by followers of the "Way of Great Peace." Although this uprising was suppressed within a year, other rebels, preaching similar doctrines and using similar principles of organization, appeared throughout the country and proved difficult for the government to defeat or control. Little is known about these rebels or the societies they formed except what was reported to the court by unsympathetic observers. Therefore, we cannot even state for certain whether the leaders were religious prophets or anti-dynastic rebels.

Below are three slightly divergent accounts contained in three histories of the period. The first deals exclusively with Chang Chüeh, the leader of the "Way of Great Peace." The second discusses the doctrines and practices of four rebel religious leaders, with particular emphasis on Chang Hsiu, who gained control of Han-chung in west-central China. The third piece describes Chang Lu, who was associated with Chang Hsiu, although these last two selections differ on who was leader and who was follower.

CHANG CHÜEH

Chang Chüeh of Chü-lu called himself the "Great Worthy Leader" and devoted himself to the Way of the Yellow Emperor and Lao Tzu. He accepted many disciples who would kneel, bow, and confess their faults to him. He cured illnesses with holy water and prayers, and when the sick recovered, the common people came to believe in him.

Chang Chüeh sent eight disciples to different parts of the country to convert everyone to his faith, thereby propagating this delusion. After some ten years, he had several hundred thousand followers scattered through the commanderies and kingdoms. Everyone in the eight provinces of Ching, Hsü, Yu, Chi, Ch'ing, Yang, Yen, and Yü [that is, eastern and central China] followed him. Then he set up thirty-six Directors, who were like generals. A Great Director had over ten thousand people under him, a Lesser

Director six or seven thousand. Each had Chiefs below him. Chüeh's followers falsely proclaimed, "Green Heaven is already dead. Yellow Heaven must be established. The year *chia-tzu* [184] will be a propitious one for the whole world." They wrote the characters *chia-tzu* in mud on the gates of government offices in the capital and the provinces.

In 184, the Great Director Ma Yüan-i and others gathered twenty or thirty thousand men in Ch'ing and Yang provinces and planned an uprising to be staged in the city of Yeh. Ma Yüan-i went back and forth from the capital several times, secretly plotting with several eunuch Palace Secretaries, including Feng Hsü and Hsü Feng. It was agreed that the uprising would begin on the 5th day of the third month in all parts of the country. But before the rebellion began, one of Chang Chüeh's disciples, T'ang Chou of Chi-nan, reported it to the authorities. Ma Yüan-i was consequently executed by being drawn and quartered in the capital, Lo-yang. Emperor Ling for-warded Chou's report to the three Ducal Ministers and the Capital Area Inspector, who ordered the Imperial Commissioner to direct the Ducal Ministers' subordinates in investigating who in the palace, government, guards, and among the common people were followers of Chang Chüeh. In the end, over a thousand people were executed, and an emissary was sent to Chi province to arrest Chüeh and his men. When Chüeh learned that his plan had been exposed, he sent messengers galloping day and night to inform his followers in each region, who then all rebelled.

To distinguish themselves, the rebels wore yellow turbans, so people at the time referred to them as the "Yellow Turbans." They also called them the "Ant-like Bandits." These rebels killed people to sacrifice to Heaven. Chang Chüeh called himself General, Duke of Heaven. His younger brother Pao was called General, Duke of Earth, and his next younger brother Liang was called General, Duke of Man. Wherever they went they burned government buildings and pillaged villages and towns. The local and regional governments collapsed, and most of the officials fled. Within ten days the whole country had risen up and the capital was trembling.

HETERODOX BANDITS

In the Hsi-p'ing period [172–177] there were great uprisings of religious bandits, including Lo Yao in the San-fu area [that is, around Ch'ang-an]. In the Kuang-ho period [178–183] there was Chang Chüeh in the east and Chang Hsiu in Han-chung. Lo Yao taught people the method of redemption; Chüeh had his Way of Great Peace; and Hsiu had the Way of Five Pecks of Rice. In the Way of Great Peace a leader would hold a staff with nine joints while reciting spells and prayers and would instruct people to bow their heads and think of their faults, after which he would give them holy water to drink. Sick people who got better within a few days were said to have faith; those who did not were said to lack it.

Chang Hsiu's teaching was largely the same as Chang Chüeh's, but he also set up quiet rooms where sick people would stay and think about their faults. He also had people serve as "Debauchers" and "Wine Offerers." The "Wine Offerers" were in charge of the five thousand characters of the *Lao Tzu*, and the people who made everyone recite it were called "Debauchers." The "Demon Clerks" were in charge of the

prayers for the sick. These prayers were offered by writing the name of the sick person and explaining the crimes he had confessed to. Three copies would be made, one sent up to Heaven by being placed on top of a hill, one buried in the earth, and one immersed in water. These were called the "Letters to the Three Officials." The families of sick people had to contribute five pecks of rice as a standard rule, and therefore the leaders were called "Teachers of the Five Pecks of Rice." In reality all this was merely wanton perversion, of no use in curing illness. Still, simple people were deceived by it and competed with each other to join.

Later Chang Chüeh was executed and Chang Hsiu died. When Chang Lu came to Han-chung, he elaborated on the local populace's faith in Chang Hsiu's teaching. He instructed believers to set up "Charity Houses," which were stocked with grain and meat for the use of travelers. He taught personal redemption; those with minor faults would repair roads for a hundred paces to wipe out their offenses. He followed [the classical text] the *Ordinances of the Months*, prohibiting killing in the spring and summer. He also prohibited alcohol. All those who strayed into his area had no choice but to accept his doctrines.

CHANG LU

At the end of the Han period, Chang Ling of P'ei kingdom was studying the Way at Crane-Cry Mountain in Shu. He wrote the *Book of the Way* and called himself "Originator of the Great Purity," thus deluding the common people. After he died, his son Heng continued to propagate this religion, and in turn was succeeded by his son Lu. The Governor of I province, Liu Yen, became a believer in this demoniacal religion; Lu's mother was somewhat attractive and became a frequent visitor to Liu Yen's house.

In the Ch'u-p'ing period [190–193], the Governor appointed Lu a major and sent him to Han-chung, which had been cut off from the rest of the country. When Lu arrived, he acted benevolently, teaching his religion and establishing charity houses stocked with meat and grain. Travelers were to take only enough to fill their bellies but no more. Those who took more could expect to be made sick by the demons. In the markets Lu had all prices standardized. Those who committed offenses would be forgiven three times and then punished. Those who learned of the religion but did not become believers were called "the demon's soldiers" and were later made "Offerers of Wine." In Pa commandery the common people, both Chinese and non-Chinese, largely found this a useful religion. Since contributions were specified as five pecks of rice, it was generally known as the "Rice Religion."

When Su Ku was made Grand Administrator of Han-chung, Lu sent his associate Chang Hsiu to attack the city where Su Ku was stationed. . . .Lu then gained control of Han-chung. One after another, he killed all the representatives sent by the central government. Governor Liu Yen had to inform the government that the "Rice Rebels" had cut the roads. When Liu Yen's son Chang became Governor, Lu became even more overbearing. This angered Chang, who in the year 200 killed Lu's brother. Lu then led the non-Chinese Tu Huo, P'u Hu, Yüan Yueh, and others to rebel against the Governor. Lu's representatives at court also became more arrogant. Once the court realized that Lu could not be controlled, it gave him the titles of Chief of the Secretaries and Grand Administrator of Hai-ning. No Magistrates were appointed to serve under him. Instead, he governed his people through the "Offerers of Wine". . . .

In 215 [the de facto ruler of the North] Ts'ao Ts'ao went west to attack Lu, who fled to Pa-chung where he was welcomed by [the de facto ruler of the Southwest] Liu P'ei. . . . [In the end], Lu submitted to Ts'ao Ts'ao and sent a hostage. Ts'ao Ts'ao made him a general and enfeoffed him as the Marquis of Hsiang-p'ing; he also enfeoffed his five sons as feudal lords.

Translated by Patricia Ebrey

Part Three

THE ERA OF DIVISION AND THE T'ANG DYNASTY

By the late-second century, the Han government was unable to maintain order. Its overthrow, initiated in 184 by peasant rebels, was completed by the generals assigned to suppress them. By the early-third century a stalemate had been reached with three warlords— one in the North, one in the Southeast, and one in the Southwest—each controlling distinct territories. With the abdication of the last Han Emperor in 220, each of these warlords proclaimed himself ruler, beginning what is known as the Three Kingdoms Period (220–265). The northern state, Wei, was the strongest, but before it had succeeded in unifying the realm, it was overthrown by an internal coup. Its successor, the Chin (265–420), unified China in 280. This display of strength was only temporary, however, for the northern non-Chinese tribes—such as the Hsiung-nu, Chieh, and Hsien-pei—now posed a threat. In 311 the Chin dynasty lost its capital, and the court had to flee to the relatively undeveloped area south of the Yangtze River near modern Nanking. Thus began a period of nearly three centuries (316–589) when the North and South were ruled independently. Both experienced a succession of dynasties, but in the North the rulers were ethnically non-Chinese.

The four centuries of division from the fall of the Han until the reunification of the Sui in 589 are historically important for a number of reasons. They marked a serious setback to central government control and allowed the flourishing of all sorts of private social and political relations, with the concomitant growth of regionalism and greater class distinctions. Aristocracy developed at the top and types of personal bondage at the bottom. The division into North and South allowed autonomous development of the rich southeast area, while at the same time leading to the incorporation of many non-Chinese customs and institutions in the North. The new religion of Buddhism found a receptive audience among many social groups and came to pro-

vide an entirely new world outlook, first to the upper class, but also by the end of the period to ordinary commoners, who could hear monks deliver sermons and could visit holy places and temples.

The division of China into North and South, while largely following natural geographic divisions, was never stable. Attempts at conquest were regularly undertaken, and in 589 the Sui dynasty in the North finally succeeded in defeating the southern state of Ch'en. The Sui itself, however, lasted only two reigns, and was succeeded by the T'ang dynasty (618–906), founded by a member of one of the Sui noble houses.

Elements of centralized, bureaucratic control had been gradually introduced in the North from the midfifth century on but under the T'ang were more fully developed. The T'ang proved generally successful in curbing private power and status, ruling and taxing peasants directly, and even in limiting the authority of the Buddhist church. Reunification and peace led to a cultural flowering, especially in literature. By the eighth and ninth centuries the opening up of wider trade and communication had stimulated the economy, which in many ways had stagnated since the Han. The capital cities of Ch'ang-an and Lo-yang became great metropolises, Ch'ang-an and its suburbs growing to house over two million inhabitants.

Although stronger and more glorious than its predecessors, the T'ang bore many structural similarities to them. When compared to the Sung and later dy-nasties, the T'ang was still "early imperial," not "late imperial." The martial aggressiveness and expansiveness of the Han and Northern dynasties were still retained through at least the first half of the T'ang. The ruling class was still strongly shaped by aristocratic tendencies; men admired old families, and members of old families found the avenues to status and influence easily accessible. The nascent examination system had not yet come to determine the composition of more than a fraction of the upper class. And although the commercial economy grew in the T'ang, it had not yet produced the great commercial cities of the Sung.

The sources available for analyzing the content and organization of Chinese culture during the Era of Division and the T'ang are much like those for the Han, except for one fortuitous difference—the discovery by Aurel Stein in 1907 of a large cache of late Northern dynasty and T'ang documents in a sealed cave temple in Tun-huang (a city on the northwest edge of China proper, sufficiently arid for paper to survive over a thousand years). These documents and ones discovered by subsequent expeditions are important for social and cultural history because they contain types of sources not normally published and preserved, such as bills of sale, contracts, guides to the composition of letters, elementary textbooks, moral and ritual primers, and popular ballads and tales. Several documents from Tun-huang are among the sources translated in Part Three.

14.

Ko Hung's Autobiography

The third and fourth centuries A.D. *were periods of social and political turmoil. The warfare between the separate kingdoms, internal coups, struggles among the aristocratic families, and finally invasion by a series of non-Chinese tribes made life insecure and political activity highly risky. In this period many men turned away from Confucian scholarship and political concerns, searching for spiritual and intellectual insight elsewhere. Poetry, Taoist philosophy, mysticism, and searches for immortality through drugs and alchemy all flourished.*

Ko Hung (283–343), whose autobiographical account follows, was in many ways a typical figure of his period. He was trained in the military arts, and despite his scholarly proclivities, was called on to perform military service. He came from a well-established family and, from his own testimony, was frequently asked to evaluate his friends and acquaintances as potential candidates for office. (The system of recruitment to office in this period was supposed to be based on local opinion of candidates' character and ability, but in practice family status was what counted.) Ko Hung never rejected traditional Confucian virtues, but wanting more, became interested in Taoist philosophy and the use of drugs to achieve the spiritual freedom of an immortal. A man of perception, Ko Hung's account is revealing both of his world and of himself.

I was my father's third son. Because I was born late, my parents spoiled me and did not make me study. When I was thirteen my father passed away, so I was left without his guidance and had to endure the hardships of hunger and cold. I took on the farming chores myself. Having no inheritance whatsoever, I had only stars to look upon and the grass to tread on.

Since our family library had been completely lost in the repeated wars, there was nothing I could read in my leisure after farming. I was therefore forced to shoulder my satchel and walk long distances to borrow books. Because I could rarely get an entire book from one household, this task was rather time-consuming. Moreover, I had to cut firewood and sell it in order to buy paper and writing brushes and do my copying by the light of fires amidst the fields and gardens. For these reasons, I was not introduced to literature at an early age. And because I constantly lacked paper, I would write on both sides of each sheet; as a result, no one could decipher my writing.

Not until I was sixteen did I start reading the *Classic of Filial Piety*, the *Analects*, the *Classic of Poetry*, and the *Classic of Changes*. As I was too poor to travel far in search of teachers and learned friends, I was shallow in my knowledge and understanding. Although I could not understand the profundity of books, I was avid to read them; I would silently recite the texts and carefully memorize the key points. The books that I went through ranged from the classics, histories, and the various philosophical treatises to short, miscellaneous essays—altogether nearly ten thousand chapters. Because I was slow and forgetful by nature, because I did not have many ideas or a set goal, my knowledge was meager and I had doubts about many points. Nevertheless, in my writings I have found occasion to cite these sources.

I never became a pure scholar of Confucianism or fit to be a teacher. In fact, I only glanced at the River Chart, the Lo Text, and the apochryphal books. I was not fond of astrology, arithmetic, the nine divisions of the sky, the three treasures of man, the "great union," the "flying talismans," and such things. I wanted no part of these arts because they cause people much trouble but have little to offer. In my later years I studied the methods of divination based on observation of the wind and the air, the auspicious and inauspicious elements, and the cycle of the agents. I learned only the main ideas, however, and not the fine points of practice. I figured that people who specialize in these arts are all employed by others, and therefore practicing them was no different from taking public office. Since I was not pressed by circumstances to struggle with such matters, I saw more to gain in studying philosophy. Thus I gave them up.

According to the *Imperial Library Catalog* and the *Treatise on Bibliography*, there were 13,299 volumes of books in all [in the Han], and since the Wei dynasty [220–265], all genres of literature have doubled in quantity. Realizing this made me aware of how many books I had never seen. Since so many books were not available in the area south of the Yangtze River, I decided to go to the capital to search for rare works. However, it so happened that there was a rebellion, and I had to turn back midway, much to my regret.

Now that I am approaching my fortieth year, my life-long ambitions are waning; I think only of further reducing my ambitions and converting my actions into nonaction. All that I do is till my fields to eke out a living, and my efforts to achieve broad learning diminish day by day. I am an unrefined person; my nature is dull, my speech slow, and my appearance ugly. I never try to hide my shortcomings. I wear a soiled hat, dirty shoes, and worn-out clothes but am not embarrassed by them. Clothing styles change quickly and frequently. Sometimes people all of a sudden wear broad collars and wide belts; at other times they dress up in tightly fitted clothes with long, slender sleeves. Sometimes robes are so long that they sweep the ground, while at other times they are too short to cover the feet. I, however, stick with one style and do not follow the whims of the world.

When I speak I am straightforward and matter-of-fact, never sarcastic or playful. If I am not in the company of the right kind of people, I keep silent all day. This is why people call me "the scholar who embraces simplicity," a sobriquet which I have adopted for my writings.

I was born with a weak constitution and further was subjected to many illnesses. Thus, on top of being too poor to afford carriages or horses, I am too feeble to travel on foot. Anyway, travel is something that does not appeal to my nature; the corrupt custom of discarding the fundamental and pursuing the trivial, of placing too much emphasis on making friends and paying visits, makes me apprehensive. For these reasons, I have lived in quiet seclusion in my humble residence and have not rushed to visit others. I am not even acquainted with the rich and influential people who reside nearby.

My clothes do not protect me from the cold, my roof does not keep me from the rain, my food does not save me from being weak, and I am not known outside of my own house—yet none of this causes me worry. I am too poor to keep a servant, my bamboo fences have crumbled, thorny thistles grow thick in my yards, and weeds block the steps. To go out of my gate I have to push away the bushes; to get into my room I have to brush aside the tall grass. People unsympathetically criticize me for aiming at the faraway and ignoring the close-at-hand, when the truth of the matter is that I do not have anyone to do the housework.

Being ignorant of the etiquette for visiting superiors, I never pay visits to high officials. I do, however, make an effort to go and express my condolences to families who have lost an elderly member and to visit the seriously ill. Yet, though I intend to present myself on every such occasion, I often fail to do so because of my own frequent illnesses. I am often criticized on this account, and I admit my own faults, but they do not worry me; I am fully sympathetic toward the bereaved and the ill, but my own illnesses prevent me from carrying out my intentions. As long as I do not have a bad conscience, why should I argue with those who do not understand me? Those who are discerning, nevertheless, do forgive me, for they know that I am not trying to cultivate an image of loftiness for myself.

Most people in this world enjoy having intimate friends and are given to probing into others' secrets. Yet I find it quite a task to know someone well. (The sages also found it difficult.) Casual acquaintances who are congenial in conversation but poles apart in spirit do more harm than good. Although I cannot cut off all contacts as Chu Kung-shu did, I pay no special attention to a person until I have cleared away all my doubts about him and have come to know him thoroughly. Although this is one more reason why I am disliked by so many, I will not change my ways.

Those who hasten to chase after distinguished personages and wait deferentially at the gates of influential families all hate me for being different from them. They slander me, saying that I am haughty and that I disregard established custom. I, however, base my behavior on my conscience and do not listen to others' praise or slander.

It troubles me how nowadays people often pride themselves on their own strong points and despise others on account of their shortcomings. I admit that my abilities as a scholar are slight, yet whenever I talk with someone, I estimate his knowledge and keep the conversation within that limit; I do not deliberately direct it to what he does not know. Whenever I argue a point with a scholar, I bring forth my main points. If he should be too prejudiced by his own opinions to comprehend my ideas, I merely explain the direction of my ideas in general terms, in order to inspire him, not pressing so hard that he is trapped by his own arguments. If he thinks the matter over thoroughly on his own, often he realizes his mistakes and comes to the correct understanding. If I judge that it is useless to talk to someone, even though he comes to me with questions, I often say that I do not know the answer in order to avoid wasting words.

By nature I have a deep aversion to bothering officials and superiors. In the course of my life I have saved several good friends who were in distress, and in these cases I forced myself to speak with the officials in power. Yet I never let these friends know what I did for them, for it was because I could not bear to see them wronged that I secretly assisted them. Otherwise, even when my closest relatives, who would gladly do me favors, are in power, I never trouble them with written or oral requests. It is true that when I run out of food or desperately need medicine, I appeal to my friends and accept their help if they offer it. Whenever I have received favors from others, I have repaid them in subtle ways over a long period of time, so that they were not aware of it. Yet I do not lightly accept gifts from those who are not the right kind of people. When I have food for ten days, I share it with people who are in need; however, if I do not have enough for myself, I do not give away my own food—for I do not ostentatiously display little acts of virtue. Sometimes the good-natured common people of the village offer me wine and food. Even though they are not my equals, I do not decline their invitations, and later I repay them at my leisure. I once explained my motives by remarking that Shih-yün's refusal to accept food from his own brothers and Master Hua's keeping himself aloof from his over-

friendly company were but hypocritical acts performed to win a reputation and were not in accordance with the broad-mindedness required of people in high positions.

Those I abhor are the unprincipled men who do not work diligently at the principal occupations of farming and silk production but instead use unethical means to obtain undue profits. Such men control public opinion and sell their recommendations for gain. They use the power of their positions to extort money. Sometimes they accept bribes from the guilty and consequently wrong those who are in the right; at other times they harbor criminals fleeing for their lives. They appropriate corvée labor for their own purposes, thereby interfering with the public good; or they hoard currency or commodities to force the value up; or they dominate the markets to rob the commoners of their profit; or they encroach on others' land, destroying the livelihood of the orphaned and the weak; or they wander from one government office to another to look for profits to be made. In this way they impress their wives and concubines, angle for fame, and seek offices. I will have nothing to do with such people. For these reasons, the vulgar sort hate me since I dislike them, and it is only natural that we should become alienated. In my alley there are no traces of carriages and horses; in my livingroom there are no incompatible guests; my courtyard is so quiet one can set up bird nets; on my furniture dust accumulates.

Since the time I was old enough to understand things, I have never uttered a word concerning others' faults or private affairs. This comes naturally to me, for I do not even make fun of the defects of servants or little children. I never discuss my opinions of people's characters, nor do I like to criticize people on their selection of friends. When I am forced by my elders to give my evaluations, then I mention only a person's excellent qualities, or in evaluating his writing ability, raise only his good points. Because I never criticize others' shortcomings, I have never offended anyone through criticism. Occasionally I am asked by the higher-ups to give my opinion of officials, clerks, or common citizens. If the person is superior in morality and ability, I report on his achievements; if he is greedy, violent, stupid, or narrow-minded, I reply that I do not know him. As a result, I have been rather severely criticized for being overcautious and for failing to distinguish good from bad and black from white. However, I have never cared to change my ways. I have often observed that those who are fond of discussing others' personalities are not always fair in their comparisons and critiques. Those who are praised by them take it for granted and are not particularly grateful to them; whereas those who are offended regard them with a hatred more ferocious than that caused by a blood feud. I am therefore even more cautious and no longer talk about other people. I even leave the evaluation of the younger members of my own family and lineage to others. When people criticize me for this, I answer as follows: "It should be the easiest for me to evaluate myself. But if someone asks me to compare myself with other men, ancient and modern, I do not know who to consider my equal. How can I then take another person and give an evaluation of him?"

During the T'ai-an period [302–303], Shih Ping led a revolt in six provinces which brought about the decline of the dynasty. The rightful rulers of the state were disobeyed and the loyalist army was opposed. The Commander-in-Chief asked me to take the position of Commandant and lead troops. After repeated urgings, I agreed, taking into account that the country was endangered by the rebels, that the ancients saw it as one's obligation to act in emergencies, and also that martial law was not to be challenged freely. Thus, I drafted several hundred men and joined other regiments in an attack on a rebel general. On the day we broke into the rebel's city, money and silk were piled in heaps and valuables and curios covered the ground. All the other regiments set their soldiers loose upon the riches, and they loaded cart after cart, basket after basket. I alone gave orders that my soldiers were not to leave their positions. By beheading those who collected loot, I made sure no one else dared to set down their staffs. As expected, several hundred rebels burst forth to ambush us. As all the other brigades were out looting, there were no troops to speak of, and those there were were all so heavily laden with booty, they had no will to fight. Frightened and confused, many were killed or wounded, and defeat was imminent. Only my men maintained enough discipline to avoid casualties. I was thus instrumental in saving the other regiments from a disastrous defeat. Later, in another battle, we killed a minor commander of the rebels, seized large quantities of armor, and took many heads. When I reported our victory to headquarters, the Commander-in-Chief conferred on me the title of Wave-Conquering General. All the generals were awarded, according to custom, a hundred bolts of cloth, which they sealed up or sent home. I was the only one to distribute it among my officers, soldiers,

and needy friends. I exchanged the last ten bolts for meat and wine and feasted my men, earning me much praise and attention.

When the rebellion was suppressed, I discarded my weapons and armor and set out for Lo-yang in the hope of obtaining rare books. I did not at all intend to be rewarded for my military deeds, having long admired Lu Lien for not accepting gold from Liao-ch'eng, and Pao-hsü for refusing a reward for saving Ch'u. Yet it so happened that while I was on my way, the capital was plagued by a major rebellion, blocking the route to the north. Furthermore, Ch'en Min staged an uprising in Chiang-tung, cutting off my return route. Moreover, at that time an old friend of mine, Chi Chün-tao of Ch'iao-kuo, was appointed as the governor of Kuang-chou, and he petitioned the throne to appoint me as his military councillor. Although this position was not what I wanted, it provided a way to escape south, so I forced myself to accept it. I was ordered to leave early in order to draft soldiers. After I left, Chi Chün-tao was killed, so I stayed at Kuang-chou, where I was frequently offered positions by the authorities. I declined them all, thinking that riches and high positions may be attained gradually but should not be amassed quickly. Besides, the trivialities one has to attend to in such posts are quite bothersome.

Honor, high posts, power, and profit are like sojourning guests: there is no way of keeping them when they are due to depart. Prosperity and glory will all come to an end, just like the spring flowers that quickly wither away. When I chance to have them, I do not rejoice; nor do I grieve when I lose them. They are not worth all the regret and blame, worry and anxiety they cause. Furthermore, I figure that I am by nature lazy and untalented. With these two characteristics, even if I could cringe, kneel, and rush about in the mundane world, I would certainly fail to obtain fame or high position—which is beside the fact since I could never bring myself to do so! It is better for me to cultivate the Way of the Taoists, Ch'ih Sung-tzu and Prince Ch'iao, and depend solely on myself.

I am hoping to ascend a famous mountain where I will regulate my diet and cultivate my nature. It is not that I wish to abandon worldly affairs, but unless I do so, how can I practice the abstruse and tranquil Way? Besides, to comprehend these matters is truly difficult, requiring considerable discussion and questioning. For these reasons, I neither visit nor send letters to powerful officials. However, even those scholars who refrain from visiting others cannot refuse to receive callers, who invariably become an obstacle to concentration. It is not that the Way is found in the mountains and forests; the reason the ancient practitioners of the Way always had to enter the mountains and forests was that they wished to be away from the noise of the world and keep their minds tranquil. Now I am about to fulfill an old wish; I will leave my hometown and go to Mount Sung in order to walk in the paths of Fang-p'ing and Master Liang.

Fortunately, I have put my mind to it and completed my philosophical works, including the *Inner Chapters* and the *Outer Chapters*. Now I only need to finish the selection and rearrangement to make it ready for later readers. When I was fifteen or sixteen I thought that my poetry, prose-poems, and miscellaneous writings were good enough to be circulated. At the age of twenty I carefully looked through those writings and found them very unsatisfactory. It was not that I had become more talented, but that I was a little better read and was able to differentiate between the beautiful and the ugly. Thereupon I threw out most of my writings, retaining less than one-tenth. Today, besides my philosophical works, I have another one hundred-odd volumes. I am not quite finished editing them yet, and it grieves me that I do not have the time to work on them.

When other people finish writing something, they are immediately satisfied. Being untalented and slow-witted, I have never been able to satisfy myself. Whenever I compose something, I feel that with every change of wording I can further improve it. Yet, because of my laziness, and because of the volume of my works, I have not been able to go over them enough times. When I passed twenty, I figured that it would be better to establish the tenets of my own philosophy than to waste my energy and time writing short, trivial compositions. Thus I now have a draft of my philosophical writings. It was written during a time of warfare and rebellion. As I wandered from place to place, homeless, some of my works were lost. Still, I never abandoned my writing brush. This continued for more than a decade, until 304, when my works were finally completed. They consisted of twenty chapters of the *Inner Chapters*, fifty chapters of the *Outer Chapters*, one hundred chapters of stone inscriptions, eulogies, poetry, and free verse, and thirty chapters of military strategies and proclamations, memorials, and commentaries. I also wrote ten chapters of *Biographies of Immortals*,

ten dealing with those who are normally not recorded, and ten chapters of *Biographies of Recluses*, dealing with those who are lofty-minded and seek no place in officialdom. In addition, I made selections from the Five Classics, seven histories, the philosophers, military treatises, esoteric skills, and miscellaneous strange events. These totaled 310 chapters. I also made a separate index of my anthology. My *Inner Chapters* belong to the Taoist school, as they discuss immortals, longevity medicines, ghosts and devils, transformations, the nurture and extension of human life, and the aversion of evil and misfortune. My *Outer Chapters*, which discuss the success and failure of men and the good and evil in the world, belong to the Confucian school.

At the end of the autobiographical notes to his *Records*, Emperor Wen of Wei [r. 220–227] mentioned such arts as playing chess and fencing. This gave me the idea to do something similar. But rather than boast of my own modest skills, I will give an account of what I do not know. I am physically clumsy and slow by nature and have few amusements or hobbies. As a child, I could not compete with other children in throwing tiles or wrestling. Throughout my life, I have never tried cock-fighting, drake-fighting, dog-racing, or horse-racing. Whenever I see people engaged in gambling, I try not to even glance at them; but if I have to watch, I do not pay close attention. Thus, to this day, I do not know how many rows there are on a chessboard, or the names of the chessmen. Another reason for my aversion is that I object to the way chess disturbs people's thoughts and wastes their time: this trivial art makes officials reduce their political undertakings, scholars ignore their studies, commoners forget their crops, and merchants lose their business. When engaged in a game at the marketplace, the players are fired up inside and worried in appearance. They lose their sense of righteousness and shame and become rivals; they take each other's money and develop hatreds and feuds. Long ago, the gaming of Duke Min of Sung and the Crown Prince of Wu led to their violent deaths and rebellion; the seven feudal states were overthrown as a result and the dynasty nearly toppled. This example provides an obvious lesson for all later generations.

I have often observed the players in a chess game. Overwhelmed by shame and anger, they hit and kick each other and abuse each other with foul language, much to the detriment of their friendship. Since grudges can start from small matters, it is not worth doing things which can cause so many regrets. Confucius warned against sleeping during the day, a sentiment that I do not fully share. Sleeping during the day produces no benefit, but neither does it cause resentments or give rise to quarrels and lawsuits. Even the Sage had to wear out the binding string of his books three times before he had completely familiarized himself with the classics. How then can an ordinary person of our time learn everything? I believe that playing all the games there are is less worthwhile than reading a short essay. Thus, finding no pleasure in games, I do not play them. Only the vulgar sort are attracted to them.

When I was young, I learned archery, but my strength was not up to drawing a bow as heavy as Yen Kao's. I studied it because archery is one of the six arts of a gentleman, and enables a person to defend himself against bandits and robbers and to hunt for birds and animals. When I was in the army, I myself shot at pursuing horsemen, who fell at the flicker of my bowstring. By killing two rebels and one horse, I escaped death myself. I also received instruction on sword-and-shield, single sword, and double lances. For all of these there are verbal formulae and essential skills needed to defeat the opponents. There are also secret methods that are as clever as magic and, used against the unknowing, guarantee victory every time. Later, I also learned the art of the seven-foot staff, which can be used to defeat people with daggers and lances. However, this is also a trivial art of no urgency; it does not have to be used any more than the unicorn's horn or the phoenix's spur. Besides the above-mentioned, I hardly know anything else. . . .

Because I am untalented and unlearned, whether I restrain myself or indulge freely, my practices are always ill-suited to the times, my actions against the ways of the world, my utterances out of tune with the customary, my steps out of line with the majority. At home, I do not have the advantage of being rich, like Chin and Chang; out in the world, I do not have friends in high office. Although the road I have traveled is broad, I do not have the feet of a unicorn; although the universe is wide, I do not have the wings of the great roc. Thus, I have not been able to soar high like a hawk, helping to govern our country, nor have I been able to bring glory to my parents or to be remembered by posterity. My qualities are not entrusted to official historians to record; my words are not inscribed on bells and tripods. For these reasons, on finishing my writings, I composed this autobiographical chapter—although it will not make up for any failure on my part, at least it will be preserved for the future.

Translated by Clara Yu

15.

Dedicatory Colophons

[*Buddhism differed markedly from earlier Chinese religions and philosophies. It was a universal religion appealing to individuals of all countries and all social stations. It had a founding figure, the Gautama Buddha (ca. 563–483 B.C.) and a body of scriptures called sutras said to be records of the sermons of the Buddha. Its most devoted followers became monks and nuns and formed a part of a large, complex, organized church. Buddhist philosophy accepted the Indian conviction that sentient beings pass through endless reincarnations as people, animals, or gods, moving up or down according to the karma, or good and bad deeds, that they have accumulated. The major insight of the Buddha was that life is inevitably sorrowful because of men's desires. Yet he offered hope, teaching that men could escape the cycle of rebirths by moral conduct that leads to enlightenment.*

Buddhism in China flourished during the Age of Division and the T'ang dynasty developing a great many sects and schools of thought. Most ordinary believers, however, probably were little concerned with the subtle differences in metaphysics or theology between these sects. Treatises and commentaries to sutras, therefore, are not adequate sources for the motivations and thoughts of the ordinary believer. Better sources are ballads, tales, sermons, and the explanatory colophons added to sutras. Making copies of sutras was a way to gain religious merit. At the end of the sutra text the person doing the copying or paying for it often added a note (or colophon) explaining his or her motivations. Five such colophons from pre-T'ang and T'ang sutras found at Tun-huang are given below.

1

Recorded on the 15th day of the fourth month of 531.

The Buddhist lay disciple Yüan Jung—having lived in this degenerate era for many years, fearful for his life, and yearning for home—now makes a donation of a thousand silver coins to the Three Jewels [the Buddha, the Law, and the Monastic Order]. This donation is made in the name of the Celestial King Vaisravana. In addition, as ransom money,* he makes a donation of a thousand to ransom himself and his wife and children, a thousand more to ransom his servants, and a thousand more to ransom his

---

* Ransom from their present existences.

domestic animals. This money is to be used for copying sutras. It is accompanied by the prayer that the Celestial King may attain Buddhahood; that the disciple's family, servants, and animals may be blessed with long life, may attain enlightenment, and may all be permitted to return to the capital.

2

Happiness is not fortuitous: pray for it and it will respond. Results are not born of thin air: pay heed to causes and results will follow. This explains how the Buddhist disciple and nun Tao-jung—because her conduct in her previous life was not correct—came to be born in her present form, a woman, vile and unclean.

Now if she does not honor the awesome decree of Buddha, how can future consequences be favorable for her? Therefore, having cut down her expenditures on food and clothing, she reverently has had the *Nirvana Sutra* copied once. She prays that those who read it carefully will be exalted in mind to the highest realms and that those who communicate its meaning will cause others to be so enlightened.

She also prays that in her present existence she will have no further sickness or suffering, that her parents in seven other incarnations (who have already died or will die in the future) and her present family and close relatives may experience joy in the four realms [earth, water, fire, and air], and that whatever they seek may indeed come to pass. Finally, she prays that all those endowed with knowledge may be included within this prayer.

Dated the 29th day of the fourth month of 550.

3

Recorded on the 28th day of the fifth month of 583.

The Army Superintendent, Sung Shao, having suffered the heavy sorrow of losing both his father and mother, made a vow on their behalf to read one section each of the following sutras: *The Sutra of the Great Assembly of Buddhas, The Nirvana Sutra, The Lotus Sutra, The Benevolent King Sutra, The Golden Light Sutra, The Sutra of the Daughter of Prasenajit,* and *The Master of Medicine Sutra.* He prays that the spirits of his parents will someday reach the Pure Land* and will thus be forever freed from the three unhappy states of existence and the eight calamities and that they may eternally listen to the Buddha's teachings.

He also prays that the members of his family, both great and small, may find happiness at will, that blessings may daily rain down upon them while hardships disperse like clouds. He prays that the imperial highways may be open and free of bandits, that the state may be preserved from pestilence, that wind and rain may obey their proper seasons, and that all suffering creatures may quickly find release. May all these prayers be granted!

* The Pure Land is the paradise promised by the Amita Buddha.

4

The preceding incantation has been translated and circulated.

If this incantation is recited seven, fourteen, or twenty-one times daily (after having cleansed the mouth in the morning with a willow twig, having scattered flowers and incense before the image of Buddha, having knelt and joined the palms of the hands), the four grave sins, the five wicked acts, and all other transgressions will be wiped away. The present body will not be afflicted by untimely calamities; one will at last be born into the realm of immeasurably long life; and reincarnation in the female form will be escaped forever.

Now, the Sanskrit text has been re-examined and the Indian Vinaya monk Buddhasangha and other monks have been consulted; thus we know that the awesome power of this incantation is beyond comprehension. If it is recited 100 times in the evening and again at noon, it will destroy the four grave sins and the five wicked acts. It will pluck out the very roots of sin and will ensure rebirth in the Western Regions. If, with sincerity of spirit, one is able to complete 200,000 recitations, perfect intelligence will be born and there will be no relapses. If 300,000 recitations are completed, one will see Amita Buddha face to face and will certainly be reborn into the Pure Land of tranquillity and bliss.

Copied by the disciple of pure faith Sun Szu-chung on the 8th day of the fourth month of 720.

5

The lay disciple Madame Tuan (nee Chang) has ever lamented that the fragrant orchid, like a bubble, blooms for but one day, and that separation from loved ones causes so much sorrow. She wonders how it can be that Heaven feels nothing for the calamities it inflicts, and causes the worthiest to be the first to be cut down, just as the young tree is the first to wither and the tallest blossoms are the first to fall.

Thus, on behalf of her deceased third son, Commissioner Tuan, an officer of the local commandery, she has reverently had this section of the *Golden Light Sutra* copied. Now that the transcription is completed, she prays that her son's spirit may visit the blue heavens, that he may mingle with the immortals, that he may travel in person to the Pure Regions and listen to sutras being recited under the tree. She also prays that he may never pass through the three unhappy states of existence or the eight calamities, but will gather karma sufficient to enable him to proceed joyfully to the Lotus Palace and the Flowering Throne, that he will never again suffer a short life but enjoy longevity in the Pure Land and may be perpetually reborn only there.

His loving mother, thinking of him, prays that the karma for both of them may be good and that they may both enjoy the fruits of salvation.

Recorded on the 9th day of the sixth month of 900 in the Great T'ang Dynasty.

Translated by Lucie Clark and Lily Hwa

16.

A Woman's Hundred Years

Among the documents at Tun-huang were the texts of ballads and popular songs containing Buddhist themes or messages. Some of these were didactic pieces composed by monks to use in preaching, but others appear to have been works of popular origin inspired by the basic ideas of Buddhism. The following song, concerning the life cycle of a woman, falls into the latter category. Stressing how life inevitably leads to change and sorrow, it plays upon a familiar Buddhist theme of the transience of life but does not make explicit reference to Buddhist principles. Its message was probably one widely understood by ordinary people in the T'ang.

At ten, like a flowering branch in the rain,
She is slender, delicate, and full of grace.
Her parents are themselves as young as the rising moon
And do not allow her past the red curtain without a
  reason.

At twenty, receiving the hairpin, she is a spring bud.
Her parents arrange her betrothal; the matter's well done.
A fragrant carriage comes at evening to carry her to her
  lord.
Like Hsiao-shih and his wife, at dawn they depart with
  the clouds.

At thirty, perfect as a pearl, full of the beauty of youth,
At her window, by the gauze curtain, she makes up in
  front of the mirror.
With her singing companions, in the waterlily season,
She rows a boat and plucks the blue flowers.

At forty, she is mistress of a prosperous house and makes
  plans.
Three sons and five daughters giver her some trouble.
With her ch'in* not far away, she toils always at her
  loom,
Her only fear that the sun will set too soon.

At fifty, afraid of her husband's dislike,
She strains to please him with every charm,
Trying to remember the many tricks she had learned since
  the age of sixteen.
No longer is she afraid of mothers- and sisters-in-law.

At sixty, face wrinkled and hair like silk thread,
She walks unsteadily and speaks little.
Distressed that her sons can find no brides,
Grieved that her daughters have departed for their
  husbands' homes.

At seventy, frail and thin, but not knowing what to do
  about it,
She is no longer able to learn the Buddhist Law even if
  she tries.
In the morning a light breeze
Makes her joints crack like clanging gongs.

At eighty, eyes blinded and ears half-deaf,
When she goes out she cannot tell north from east.
Dreaming always of departed loves,
Who persuade her to chase the dying breeze.

At ninety, the glow fades like spent lightning.
Human affairs are no longer her concern.
Lying on a pillow, solitary on her high bed,
She resembles the dying leaves that fall in autumn.

* A stringed instrument.

56

At a hundred, like a cliff crumbling in the wind,
For her body it is the moment to become dust.
Children and grandchildren will perform sacrifices to her
 spirit,
And clear moonlight will forever illumine her patch of
earth.

Translated by Patricia Ebrey and Lily Hwa

17.

The Examination System

The T'ang was the first dynasty in which examinations came to play an important role in selecting men for office. With this change in the system of recruitment also came a change in the life of those who aspired to office. Although most such men still were from established families and well connected, they now had to devote more effort and energy to preparing for the examinations by studying the classics and practicing literary composition. If they passed they became chin-shih (presented scholars) and were eligible for prestigious posts in the government.

Whatever the seriousness of the examinations, men could also laugh at their distortions and excesses. The following anecdotes are supposed to be based on true incidents and were included in an anthology of gossip and vignettes compiled in the late T'ang. Some of these anecdotes were intended to poke fun at the way men acted, others to record noble aspirations and deeds.

Hsiao Ying-shih passed the imperial examination in 735. Proud of his talent, he was unequaled in conceit and arrogance. He often took a pot of wine and went out to visit rural scenic areas. Once during such an outing, he stayed at an inn, drinking and chanting poetry by himself. Suddenly a storm arose, and an old man dressed in a purple robe came in with a page boy to take shelter. Because of their informality, Hsiao Ying-shih treated them rather insolently. In a short while, the storm was over, the rain stopped, carriages and retinues came, and the old man was escorted away. Flustered, Hsiao Ying-shih inquired about the old man's identity, and the people around him said, "That was the Minister of the Board of Civil Office."

Now, Hsiao Ying-shih had gone to see the Minister many times, yet had not been received. When he heard that the old man was none other than the Minister himself, he was flabbergasted.

The next day, Hsiao brought a long letter with him and went to the Minister's residence to apologize. The Minister had him brought into the hallway and scolded him severely. "I regret that I am not related to you in any way, otherwise I would like to give you some good 'family discipline,'" said the Minister. "You are reputed to be a literary talent, yet your arrogance and poor manners are such that it is perhaps better for you to remain a mere *chin-shih* (presented scholar)."

Hsiao Ying-shih never got anywhere in officialdom, dying as a Chief Clerk in Yang prefecture.

◧◧◧

Lu Chao was from I-ch'un of Yüan-chou. He and Huang P'o, also from the same prefecture, were equally famous. When they were young, Huang P'o was wealthy, but Lu Chao was very poor. When they were ready for the imperial examination, the two of them decided to set out on the trip together. The Prefect gave a farewell dinner at the Pavilion of Departure, but Huang P'o alone was invited. When the party was at its peak, with lots of wine and music, Lu Chao passed by the Pavilion, riding on an old, weak horse. He traveled some ten *li* out of the city limits, then stopped to wait for Huang P'o to join him.

The next year, Lu Chao came back to his hometown, having been awarded the title of *chuang-yüan* [number one]. All the officials from the Regional Commander on down came out to welcome him, and the Prefect of Yüan-chou was greatly embarrassed.

Once when the Prefect invited him to watch the Dragon Boat Race, Lu Chao composed a poem during the banquet which read:

> "It is a dragon," I told you.
> But you had refused to believe.
> Now it returns with the trophy,
> Much in the way I predicted.

Lu Hui's mother's brother was Cheng Yü. As his parents died when he was small, Lu Hui was brought up in his mother's family, and Cheng Yü often encouraged him to take the imperial examination and become a *chin-shih*. Lu Hui was recommended for the examinations for the "widely brilliant" in the early part of 870, but in 880, bandits encroached on the capital, forcing him to flee to the south. At that same time Cheng Yü's son Hsü was stationed in Nanhai as a Regional Commander. Lu Hui and Cheng Hsü had gone to school together, but when Hsü was already a county official, Hui was still a commoner. The two of them, however, equally enjoyed the favor of Cheng Yü.

During the ten years in which Cheng Hsü rose to become a Governor-General, Lu Hui remained a destitute scholar. Once again he managed to escape an uprising and came to Cheng Hsü, carrying but one sack of personal belongings. Cheng Hsü still treated him kindly. At this time, the Emperor was on the expedition to Shu, and the whole country was in turmoil. Cheng Hsü encouraged Lu Hui to seize the opportunity to advance himself. "How long can a man live?" he said to Lu Hui. "If there is a shortcut to riches and fame, why insist on going through the examination?"

But Lu Hui was adamant. Cheng Hsü asked his friends and assistants to try to persuade Lu Hui to give up the exams; he even left the seat on his right-hand side vacant for Lu Hui to occupy. Lu Hui therefore said to him, "Our great nation has established the examination system for the outstanding and the talented. I do not have the ability and dare not dream

of such honors. However, when he was alive, my uncle again and again encouraged me to take the examinations. Now his study is empty and quiet, but I cannot bring myself to break our agreement. If I have to die as a mere student, it is my fate. But I will not change my mind for the sake of wealth. I would sooner die."

When Cheng Hsü saw Lu Hui's determination, he respected him even more than before. Another ten years passed before Lu Hui finally passed the examination under the Lord of Hung-nung, and he died as one of the highest officials in the whole empire.

Liu Hsü-po and Lord P'ei of T'ai-ping had once sat close to each other during the imperial examination. When Lord P'ei became the administrator of the imperial examinations, Liu was still only a candidate for the examination. On the day when the examinees were tested on their "miscellaneous essays," Liu presented a poem to the chief examiner, his old classmate:

> I remember evenings like this twenty years ago:
> The candles were the same, so was the breeze.
> How many more years will I have, I wonder,
> To wear this gunny robe,
> And to wait to reach you.

The Chief Minister Wang Ch'i was appointed chief examiner in the imperial examinations during the Ch'ang-ch'ing period (821–824). He had Po Min-chung in mind as the candidate for the *chuang-yüan* [number one] but was displeased with Min-chung's close association with Ho Pa-chi, a talented but eccentric man. Therefore, Wang Ch'i had a confidant reveal his displeasure to Min-chung, hinting to him to break off his friendship.

This messenger went to see Po Min-chung and told him the Chief Minister's intentions. "I will do as you say," Min-chung readily agreed.

In a little while Ho Pa-chi came to visit, as usual, and the servants lied to him, saying that Min-chung was not home. He waited a little, then left without saying a word. A moment later, Po Min-chung rushed out and ordered the servants to send for Ho. When he arrived, Min-chung told him everything, and then said, "I can be a *chin-shih* under any examiner. I can't, however, wrong my best friend for this reason." The two of them then merrily drank wine and took a nap.

This whole sequence took place right before the eyes of the messenger from the Chief Minister, and he left in a fury. When he returned to the Chief Minister, he told him the story and thought this was the end of Po Min-chung. But Wang Ch'i said instead, "I only thought of taking Po Min-chung; now I should also consider Ho Pa-chi."

⬛⬛⬛

Hsü T'ang was from Ching county of Hsüan-chou and had been taking the examinations since he was young. In the same village there was a man named Wang Tsun, who had served as a minor government clerk when young. After Hsü T'ang had taken the examination, Hsü T'ang treated him with contempt. still but a low functionary in the government. Yet Wang Tsun wrote good poetry, although no one knew about it because he kept it a secret.

One day, Wang Tsun resigned from his post and set out for the capital to take the imperial examination. As he was approaching the capital, he met Hsü T'ang, who was seeing some friends off at the outskirts of the city.

"Eh," Hsü T'ang asked him, "what are you doing here in the capital?"

"I have come to take the imperial examination," answered the former functionary.

Upon hearing this, Hsü T'ang angrily declared, "How insolent you are, you lowly clerk!" Although they were now fellow candidates for the imperial examination, Hsü T'ang treated him with contempt. But in the end, Wang Tsun passed the examination and became very famous. Hsü T'ang did not pass until five years later.

⬛⬛⬛

P'eng K'an and Chan Pi were both from I-ch'un of Yüan-chou, and their wives were sisters. P'eng K'an passed the imperial examination and became a *chin-shih*, whereas Chan Pi remained a mere functionary in the county.

At the celebration banquet given by P'eng K'an's in-laws, all the guests were either high officials or renowned scholars. P'eng K'an was seated at the head of the table, and the whole company was enchanted by his exuberant character. When Chan Pi arrived at the banquet, he was told to eat his food in the back room.

Seeing that Chan Pi was not even disturbed by this, his wife scolded him severely: "You are a man, yet you cannot push yourself ahead. Now that you are so humiliated where is your sense of shame?" These words stimulated Chan Pi, and he began to study very hard. Within a few years, he also passed the imperial examination.

Previously, P'eng K'an used to insult Chan Pi. On the day when the results of the imperial examination were announced, P'eng K'an was out in the countryside, donkey riding for pleasure. Suddenly a servant boy came running and reported to him the good news about Chan Pi. P'eng K'an was so shocked that he fell off his saddle.

This is the origin of the lampoon that spread throughout Yüan-chou:

> When Chan Pi the exams did pass,
> P'eng K'an fell off his ass.

⬛⬛⬛

Hua Ching was from Chien-chou, and was very famous for his prose-poem compositions. When he visited Ta-liang, he attended public feasts and became acquainted with a eunuch Army Inspector. Later, Hua Ching went to the capital and passed the imperial examination. One day, when he was riding side by side with his fellow *chin-shih*, he saw this person on a busy street and saluted him. This shocked the public and gave rise to many libelous tales. Hua Ching ended up without promotion and died as a mere scholar in the Imperial Academy.

⬛⬛⬛

Chang Shu and Ts'ui Chao-wei were both sent up from Hsi-ch'uan to take the examination in the early years of Chung-ho [881–884]. While there the two of them went together to have their fortunes told.

At the time, Chang Shu was reputed for his literary talent, and was generally known as the "number-one-to-be." Even Ts'ui Chao-wei was regarded as inferior to him. However, the fortune-teller hardly paid any attention to Chang Shu but looked Ts'ui Chao-wei over and told him, "You will definitely pass the imperial examination and come out on top." Then, seeing that Chang Shu was annoyed, the fortune-teller said to him, "As to you, sir, you will also pass, but not until Mr. Ts'ui here becomes the Minister and you pay homage to him."

When they were taking the examination that year, Chang Shu had a death in the family and had to withdraw while Ts'ui Chao-wei turned out to be the "number one." Frustrated, Chang Shu vented his indignation in writing lines such as "I had followed you a thousand miles but only lost your tail during the morning's storm." Naturally, Ts'ui Chao-wei was very disturbed. At a drinking party, Ts'ui Chao-wei toasted Chang Shu, asking him to drink a huge horn-shaped goblet of wine. When Chang declined, Ts'ui said to him, "Just drink it, and when I become the Chief Minister, I will let you be the number-one." Chang walked out in a fury, and the two of them became foes.

Seven years later, Ts'ui was appointed Chief Minister by the Emperor, and Chang Shu later passed the examination under the chief-examiner Lord P'ei. As predicted, Chang had to pay homage to Ts'ui.

Translated by Clara Yu

18.

Household Registration

One of the most important ways the early T'ang government affected the lives of ordinary people was through its policies of allotting land and assessing taxes according to age, sex, and marital status. That is, every male from eighteen to sixty years of age was supposed to receive twenty mou of "inheritable land" and eighty mou of "personal share land." Men over sixty were to receive forty mou of "personal share land" and widows thirty mou, unless they lived in households without adult males, in which case their allotment would be raised to fifty mou. The major taxes were assessed in uniform amounts on all males aged twenty-one to fifty-nine.

To make this system work, the government had to keep detailed records on every household in the country. From documents preserved at Tun-huang, it is clear that in the first century and a half of T'ang rule, a genuine effort was made to keep up such records. Although there was not enough land for everyone to receive a full allotment, the government kept track of what each person had, and of the ages, departures, and honors (which conferred tax exemptions) of its males. Records on women seem to have been kept more casually, probably since whether a woman died or left a household had no effect on its taxes and seldom any on its allotment.

Below are two household registration records for families in Lung-lo district of Tun-huang county recorded in 747.

Household head: Ts'ao Szu-li, 56, Deputy Guard (Rank conferred on the 16th day of the ninth month of 723 under Ho Chih-t'ai. His great-grandfather was Kao, his grandfather K'uo, his father Chien. A rank 8 household, at present not taxed.)

Step-mother: Sun, 60, widow (Died this year.)

Wife: Chang, 58, housewife

Younger brother: Ling-hsiu, 28, able-bodied man (Died this year.)

Son: Ling-chang, 18, youth (Died in 745.)

Deceased younger brother's wife: Wang, 25, widow (Omitted from record last year.)

Daughter: Niang-niang, 31, woman

Daughter: Miao-yin, 21, woman

Daughter: Miao-hsien, 17, girl

Daughter: Chin-chin, 15, girl

Daughter: Shang-chen, 13, girl

Younger brother: En-ch'in, 42, able-bodied male (Left in 727.)

Deceased elder brother's son Hsiung-chang, 23, Pillar of State (Rank conferred in 710 by Yüan-shuang, due to privilege inherited from his father Te-chien. In 745 omitted from record. Great-grandfather Kao, grandfather K'uo, father Chien.)

Deceased elder brother's son: Hsiung-yü, 17, boy (Omitted from record in 745.)

Younger sister: Fa, 43, woman

Altogether they should receive 364 *mou* of fields. (They now have 62 *mou* and are owed 202 *mou*. 61 *mou* is inheritable land, one *mou* is personal share, and one *mou* is for house and garden.)

Plot 1: 15 *mou* of inheritable land
15 *li* west of the county seat. Elevated. Borders: east, a ditch; west, Ts'ao Ch'ih's property; south, Tien Hsiang-fu's property; north, the house.

Plot 2: 6 *mou* of inheritable land

10 *li* west of the county seat. Clay. Borders: east, their own fields; west, ditch; south, ditch; north, ditch.

Plot 3: 9 *mou* of inheritable land

7 *li* west of the county seat. Elevated. Borders: east, ditch; west, Ts'ao Ch'ih's property; south, ditch; north, Chao I's property.

Plot 4: 11 *mou* of inheritable land

7 *li* west of the county seat. Elevated. Borders: east, Chang Ts'ung-chiao's property; west, ditch; south, ditch; north, gully.

Plot 5: 4 *mou* of inheritable land

10 li west of the county seat. Elevated. Borders: east, government lands; west, ditch; south, road; north, ditch.

Plot 6: 4 *mou* of inheritable land

10 *li* west of the county seat. Elevated. Borders: east, ditch; west, Kao Shen-t'ung's property; south, same; north, ditch.

Plot 7: 12 *mou,* 11 of which is inheritable land and 1 personal share land 11 *li* west of the county seat. Elevated. Borders: east, own land; west, Kung T'u-ch'üeh's property; south, ditch; north, ditch.

Plot 8: 1 *mou* of house and garden land.

□□□

Household head: Liu Chih-hsin, 29, able-bodied male (Rank 9 household, presently taxed.)
Grandmother: Wang, 69, elderly widow
Mother: So, 49, elderly widow

Wife: Wang, 21, able-bodied wife (In 744 omitted from the record.)
Younger brother: Chih-ku, 17, boy
Younger sister: Hsien-yün, 29, woman
Younger sister: Wang-wang, 7, girl
Altogether they should receive 163 *mou.*

(They have already received 68 *mou,* 20 of inheritable land and 47 of personal share, and one of house and garden land. 95 *mou* not yet received.)

Plot 1: 20 *mou* of inheritable land

7 *li* west of the county seat. Flat. Borders: east, Chia A-pen's property; west, ditch; south, ditch; north, own fields.

Plot 2: 10 *mou* of personal share land

7 *li* west of the county seat. Flat. Borders: east, house; west, ditch; south, ditch; north, Liu Shan-cheng's property.

Plot 3: 30 *mou* of personal share land

7 *li* west of the county seat. Flat. Borders: east, ditch; west, graveyard; south, Shih Sheng-ming's property; north, road.

Plot 4: 6 *mou* of personal share land

10 *li* west of the county seat. Flat. Borders: east, ditch; west, Buddhist establishment; south, ditch; north, Li Huai-chung's property.

Plot 5: 1 *mou* of personal share land

10 *li* west of the county seat. Flat. Borders: east, Pei Szu-liang's property; west, ditch; south, ditch; north, Cheng Szu-hung's property.

Plot 6: 1 *mou* of house and garden land

Translated by Patricia Ebrey

19.

Slaves

Although the exact legal forms varied from period to period, in all dynasties a small but significant segment of the population had unfree or demeaned status. Such people included slaves, hereditary serfs, and members of households that had hereditary obligations to the government as laborers, soldiers, or craftsmen. Slaves, who could be bought and sold and treated very much as their masters wished, always had the lowest status. Some slaves were the descendants of convicts or prisoners of war; others had become slaves because their parents had sold them in times of duress. T'ang law recognized slavery but also included many provisions intended to prevent the impressment or sale into slavery of free men.

The following three documents from Tun-huang show ways in which people dealt with slavery. The first is a bill of sale or contract. Its format is similar to that used for the sale of a house, land, or draft animals and includes certain traditional features, such as the requirement that the two parties should have met face to face and that the contract be witnessed. The second document is an official record of the sale of a slave. Although notifying the government was not required to make a sale legal, some buyers and sellers apparently felt more secure with government certification. The third document, a sample statement of manumission from a model letter writer, shows something of the value placed on being a free man and the merit to be achieved from the act of freeing slaves.

1

A contract executed on the 12th day of the eleventh month of 991.

On this day the Functionary, Han Yüan-ting, having expenses to meet and lacking sufficient stores of silk, sells his household slave Chien-sheng, aged about twenty-eight. The slave is being sold to the monastery dependent, Chu Yüan-sung, then to Chu's wife and sons, etc. The price of the slave has been fixed at a total of five bolts of silk, consisting of both finished and unfinished goods.* This day the buyer has remitted three bolts of unfinished silk. The fifth month of next year has been established as the deadline for

the delivery of the remaining two bolts of finished silk.

After the woman and the goods have been exchanged and the sale completed, it is agreed that the sons and daughters of the Chu family shall be masters of this slave forever and ever, from generation to generation. If in future a relative of the seller should reclaim this slave, it is ordered that Han Yüan-ting and his wife, Seventh Daughter, seek out an adequate slave as replacement. If an imperial amnesty should be declared subsequent to the sale, it may not be used to reopen discussions among the negotiants.

The two parties to the contract have met face to face and have reached their agreement after joint discussions. If one of the parties should default, he shall be fined one bolt of decorated silk and two large rams—all to be turned over to the non-defaulting

---

*Bolts of plain silk of standard size and quality were used as a unit of currency for larger transactions in the T'ang and even formed a part of the standard tax payment.

party. In light of the chance of this contract's not being made in good faith, the following persons have witnessed it and will serve as its guarantors:
(Note: In case this woman should prove to have a sickness, a waiting period of ten days has been agreed upon. Beyond this time withdrawal from the agreement will be impossible.)

The woman whose person is being sold, Chien-sheng
The seller of the woman, her mistress, Seventh Daughter
The seller of the woman, her master, Han Yüan-ting
A relative by marriage, who has participated in the discussions, Fu-chen
A witness, Monk Ch'ou-ta, of the Pao-en Monastery
A witness, Monk Lo Hsi-an, Master in the Law and the Discipline, Lung-hsing Monastery

(Additional note: In place of one of the bolts of finished silk it has been decided to furnish six lengths of Chu serge and six lengths of white serge, making a total of twelve lengths, each measuring between ten and twenty feet. These goods are to be delivered by the fifth month of next year.)

2

The entry of the guild merchant Wang Hsiu-chih states, "I have sold the Tatar slave, To Pao, thirteen years of age, to Hui-wen for twenty-one bolts of unfinished silk. Please issue an official certificate to the buyer." According to An Shen-ch'ing and other guarantors, this slave is indeed of humble origin. Moreover, the Tatar slave, To Pao, is willing to be sold by [Wang] Hsiu-chih and Wang already has had full payment. . . .

The guild merchant Wang Hsiu-chih sold the Tatar slave To Pao to [Hui-wen] for twenty-one bolts of unfinished silk. We have examined the matter and have verified it. Based on the pledge of the guarantors we issue an official certificate to [Hui-wen]. We are now asking for a prefectural seal to validate this contract.

If there has been any fraud, [we are willing to accept the appropriate punishment].

[Prefectural seal]

Owner of the silk
Master of the slave, the guild merchant, Wang Hsiu-chih,
age sixty-one
Tatar slave, To Pao, age thirteen
Guarantor[——] commoner, An Shen-ch'ing, age fifty-nine*
Guarantor, the guild merchant Chang Szu-lu, age forty-eight
Guarantor, a commoner of Tun-huang prefecture, Tso Huai-chieh, age fifty-seven
Guarantor, frontier guard Wang Feng-hsiang, age thirty-six
Guarantor, frontier guard Kao Ch'ien-chang, age thirty-three
Chief market official, Hsiu-ang, issues the certificate
clerk [——] *

3

SAMPLE STATEMENT OF MANUMISSION

Oh, you multitude of male and female slaves: I have heard that whoever frees his slaves will receive blessings as high as the highest mountain peaks, but whoever enslaves good people will incite hatred as deep as deepest hell.

You slaves are humble persons who labor hard and long. You rise early and conduct yourselves with submission and deference all day long. Even at night you find no rest. Thinking of your hardships has caused me deep remorse, so I have pledged to my ancestors to set you free.

I hope that, like captured fish returning to the sea, you will frolic again joyfully in the waves, or like fallen willow wands you will rise up again with the coming of spring. You may go wherever you wish. There will be no interference with your actions, nor shall my posterity set any bondage on you.

Although state laws exist, I prefer to settle this matter person to person. If ever I violate this settlement, you may freely present this statement to the officials.

Master of the slaves being freed
Brothers
Posterity
Guarantor in person
Witness in person
Village and District representative
(Village) elder
Official
Official

Translated by Lucie Clark

*Original text is damaged and certain words cannot be deciphered.

20.

Family Division

The financial basis of family life in China was based on the principle of joint ownership of property by all male members of the family under the control of the family head. Since at least the Han, equal inheritance had been the standard practice and each son was considered to have a right to a full share of the property. Family harmony was thought best served when property was left intact until the parents or at least the father died. If the father enjoyed a long life, married sons and their wives and children might pool their resources and use a common purse for decades. Should frictions become too great, however, an early division of the property would be possible. Even after the parents died, if there were young brothers or sisters not yet married or orphaned nieces or nephews, division of the family property would often be delayed until they had grown up and were better able to take care of themselves. When the time came for the property finally to be divided, it was often a traumatic occasion, when latent hostilities could easily rise to the surface.

Since division of property was a financial arrangement, it was important to list the provisions made and record the agreement of the various parties. Below are two blank agreements people could use for this purpose; they come from manuals of sample documents found at Tun-huang.

1

Brothers come from the same womb, share the same vital essences, and have strong affections toward each other. They complement each other like luxuriant leaves and stately boughs, and think that they will stay together forever. Little do they realize that one day they will part like birds that fly in different directions—each to a corner of the four seas. Just as winters and summers alternate, the bramble shrubs become withered and branches detach from each other, their time for parting eventually comes.

Elder brother, A, and younger brother, B, now have, in the presence of neighbors and relatives of various branches, meticulously divided into two parts their estate and fields outside of the city as well as their house, other property, miscellaneous objects,

and livestock in the city. The details are clearly itemized below.

Afterwards, each brother is in charge of his own share of the family property, and there are to be no complaints or quarrels over it. Should either of them violate this agreement, he will be fined a bolt of fine silk for government use and fifteen bushels of wheat as ration for the military.

This document is drawn up as evidence of the agreement. From now on, each of the brothers has his own household. When the tree has grown too big, its branches will part. When the leaves become scattered, the attachment will be lost. Even the four black birds of the Heng Mountain have to fly their separate ways when their feathers turn dark. This agreement on the division of family property is based on the same principle.

2

It has been said that the bonds between men are measured against the life of mountains and that the love between brothers outlasts rocks. Now, when we, uncle and nephews, chose to share our property instead of each guarding his own, we were like brothers, for ours is a blood relation, and we had no wish to separate. We have gotten along well with each other, and everything has been smooth and harmonious. Our wives have been humble and respectful, always behaving according to propriety. We have appeased the city god by preserving the neighborly ways of K'ung Huai. The bramble shrubs in our courtyard have been blessed with luxuriant growth. For three generations we have been a family of Confucian scholars. In this age when customs are corrupt and the human mind is shallow, our family teaching has kept alive a vigorous spirit, and our Confucian tradition has withstood the prevalent ways of the world. The brothers of the family have always agreed on the same principles. However, we are afraid that later generations of our family may have a different frame of mind, and that they may raise objections and spread rumors. Therefore, at the present time, while our family is prosperous and has seen generations of filial sons, we have decided to divide the family property, before later misunderstandings arise.

The three nephews, A, B, and C, lost their parents in their childhood, and their uncle has acted as their parent—bringing them up and educating them. The nephews, having not repaid the uncle for his kindness, now decide to divide their property with him. Their affection for their uncle being the same as before, they wish to see him have what he needs for his pleasure and livelihood. Thus they have taken inventory of their estate, fields, carriages, cattle and horses, other properties and miscellaneous possessions and divided them into two equal parts, one part to be held by the uncle and the other to be shared by the nephews.

[list]

All the above listed properties, daily utensils, and miscellaneous things have been examined by close relatives in the presence of the uncle and the nephews. Three times have they checked everything, and they agree that the division is fair, equal, and impartial. Our posterity should now be free of suspicions and quarrels. However, the relation between the two households is to remain the same. The elders are to guide the youngsters, teaching them righteousness and diligence, and preventing them from becoming prodigal or unfilial sons who are laughed at by others or soil our family name.

We have thus drawn up this document for the division of our family property. If any member of either household in later generations should make criticisms or spread rumors, he will be committing the five unfilial sins, and there will be an everlasting curse on his house. If there should be anyone who, in disregard of propriety, acts rebelliously, he will be fined silk if he is an adult, and cast out from the family if he is a youngster. If anyone should start arguing about the shares of the family property, he will be fined one bolt of fine silk for government use.

This document is drawn up as evidence of the division of our family property, lest later generations should fail to understand the agreement.

Translated by Clara Yu

Part Four

THE SUNG AND YÜAN DYNASTIES

From the mid-ninth century the T'ang government progressively lost control of the country and, like the Han before it, was finally destroyed by ambitious generals who seized control of the armies in the wake of peasant rebellions. After the official demise of the T'ang in 906, the North witnessed five successive dynasties, the last overthrown by the Sung, destined to rule for three centuries (960–1279).

A number of the intervening dynasties had been ethnically non-Chinese, reflecting the growing strength of Turkic, Tibetan, Mongol, and Tungusic peoples in the dry regions north of China. Considerable territory which the T'ang had controlled in its heyday was never recovered by the Sung. Then in 1127 most of North China was lost to the Jurchen, a semi-nomadic tribal confederation, which established the Chin dynasty. The Jurchen in turn succumbed in 1234 to the Mongols, then rapidly building up a pan-Asian empire. When the Sung lost North China to the Jurchen, a "temporary" capital was established at modern Hang-chou, and a vigorous social, intellectual, and economic life was maintained in South China until it also fell to the Mongols in 1279. The Mongol dynasty in China, called the Yüan (1234–1368), always remained an alien dynasty. Non-Chinese, including Marco Polo and many Central Asians, were assigned to governmental posts, and the Mongols themselves maintained their identification as warriors. When the dynasty collapsed through internal weakness and rebellion, the Mongol nobility and armies largely withdrew to modern Mongolia.

Chinese civilization underwent a number of fundamental changes during the Sung dynasty. These involved especially the means by which cultural values, ideas, and assumptions were communicated. Unprecedented wealth was created by a commercial revolution (begun in the mid-T'ang), by technological improvements in industry, and by the great extensions of wet-field rice cultivation. In the new commercial cities, dif-

ferent social groups and classes were brought into greater contact with one another, and contact of a new sort, based more on commercial relations and less on the paternalistic social relations of master and retainer or tenant (although such relations also persisted into modern times). Even town and countryside became more closely integrated as extensive marketing networks developed.

Accompanying these changes were new forms of communication. In the cities, storytellers could attract large audiences. Like Buddhist monks in earlier periods, they transmitted cultural ideals and principles to the illiterate. Their importance went even further, however, since they dealt with secular themes in addition to religious ones and, by responding to popular demand, probably served as much to acquaint the educated with the attitudes and ways of thinking of commoners as the other way around.

An even more important development was the invention of printing. With books now more widely available and much less expensive, literacy and a familiarity with the works of the ancient and modern masters became less a preserve of the most privileged. Increased access to education also served to undermine aristocratic ideals and reduce emphasis on birth. Moreover, printing led to publishing, in considerable numbers, works addressed to those with a general, rather than a classical or literary education. These include popular moral tracts, guides for farming, handbooks for rituals, and books of moral, social, or economic advice. Such works are all highly useful as "cultural

documents," texts that played a role in shaping people's conceptions of their world. Several are included in Part Four.

During the Yüan dynasty most of the economic advances of the Sung slowed or were even temporarily reversed. Mongol oppression and mismanagement led to a setback in industrial innovation and commercial growth. Nevertheless, urban life remained vibrant, publishing continued, and popular drama in particular matured.

During the Sung dynasty the culture and way of life of the scholarly gentleman acquired a characteristic style that lasted for centuries. The decline of aristocratic habits and ideals, the increase in wealth, the intellectual excitement caused by the early Neo-Confucian teachers and philosophers, and the great growth in importance of the examination system for recruitment to office probably all influenced this development. From the Sung to the end of imperial China, the way of life of educated men who aspired to hold office or move in cultivated circles involved years if not decades of intensive study, the formation of close student-teacher relationships, which could last well into adulthood, and often the cultivation of artistic, literary, or antiquarian interests. During the Yüan dynasty, although many upper-class men found political careers impossible or uninviting, their intellectual, literary, and artistic pursuits were not hampered and indeed seem to have thrived.

21.

Book of Rewards and Punishments

With the spread of printing came the frequent publication of moral and religious tracts, our surest sources for popular values and attitudes. From the Sung through the Ch'ing dynasties, the brief Book of Rewards and Punishments *was perhaps the most popular and widely circulated of these tracts. It is usually classified as a work of popular Taoism, probably because its text is anachronistically attributed to Lao Tzu, the sixth century* B.C. *Taoist sage. In fact, like most other tracts, it is a highly eclectic product. The Buddhist concepts of karma and salvation run throughout the piece. The importance of retribution, immortality, nature, and cosmology stem largely from Taoist notions. Nevertheless, many of the virtues extolled are traditional Confucian ones.*

The Grand Elder [i.e., Lao Tzu] has said that calamity and misfortune cannot gain entrance of their own into a person's life; it is the individual alone who calls them in. Good and evil are requited as automatically as shadow follows form. In keeping with this principle, Heaven and Earth have spirits who judge transgressions. These spirits take into account the lightness or gravity of the evil deeds that human beings have committed and then deduct from those individuals' life spans correspondingly. After diminishing the culprits' life expectancy, they reduce them to poverty and visit upon them innumerable calamities. Everyone comes to hate them. Punishment and misfortune pursue them wherever they go; happiness and pleasure flee from them. An unlucky star torments them. When their allotted time is up, death claims them. There are also spirit rulers of the constellations of Three Towers and Northern Scoop, who reside far above the heads of people and who keep track of their foul deeds and wickedness. They may shorten an individual's life a hundred days or twelve years. There are also three spirits of the body, which reside within the human organism. On each *keng-shen* day [once every

sixty days] they ascend to the Heavenly Ruler and inform him of the transgressions and harmful deeds of the people over whom they watch. On the last day of the month the Kitchen God does likewise. When individuals have been found guilty of a serious transgression, they are punished by a loss of twelve years from their allotted life span. For minor transgressions, they suffer the loss of one hundred days of life.

There are hundreds and hundreds of occasions for transgressions, large and small. People who want to achieve immortality must first of all avoid these occasions. They must recognize the path of righteousness and enter upon it; they must recognize the way of evil and stay clear of it. They do not tread the byways of depravity, nor do they poke into the private affairs of others. They accumulate virtue and gain merit and have compassion for all living things. They exhibit loyalty to their ruler, filial obedience to their parents, true friendship to their older brothers. By conducting themselves with propriety, they influence others. They take pity on orphans and are kindly toward widows; they venerate the elderly and are warmhearted toward the young. They will not permit

71

themselves to do any harm even to an insect, a plant, or a tree. They consider it proper to feel sorry when others suffer misfortune and to rejoice when others enjoy good fortune, to aid those in need and to assist those in danger. They look upon the achievements of others as if they were their own achievements, and they regard the failures of others as if they were their own failures. They do not dwell on the shortcomings of others, nor do they brag about their own strong points. They put a stop to what is evil and praise what is good. They give much and seek little. They accept honors only with misgivings. They show favor to people without seeking anything in return. When they share things with others, they do not regret it later. They are called good people and everyone reveres them. The Way of Heaven protects them from harm. Happiness and good fortune follow them everywhere; the depravities of the world keep their distance from them. The spirits watch over them; whatever they undertake results in success. Thus, they can hope to become immortal. Individuals who desire to achieve heavenly immortality should establish in themselves the 1,300 good qualities, and those who aim for earthly immortality should establish within themselves the 300 good qualities.

Evil persons, on the other hand, are devoid of righteousness, as their actions reflect. They turn their backs on the correct principle and equate wickedness with capability. They act heartlessly and do injury and harm. In stealth they rob the law-abiding. They insult their ruler and their parents behind their backs. They are rude to their teachers and rebellious toward those they are supposed to serve. They deceive the ignorant and slander their fellow students. They are treacherous and lying and bring charges against their ancestors. They are perverse, without human-heartedness, vicious, and selfish. Their priorities of right and wrong are out of place, and they turn their backs on their duties.

In office they are tyrannical toward their subordinates and take credit for their work, while at the same time being obsequious toward their superiors and currying their favor. If they receive some kindness, they show no gratitude. They brood over grievances incessantly. They are contemptuous of the common people and bring disorder and confusion into the state. They extend rewards to the unrighteous and dole out punishments to the innocent. They will have some people executed to get their hands on their wealth and will have other people fired from their jobs to grab their positions. In war they kill those they

have captured and slaughter those who have surrendered. They dismiss the upright, dispose of the virtuous, mistreat orphans, and harass widows. They ignore the law and take bribes. They take straight for crooked and crooked for straight, treating light crimes as grave ones and watching the resultant executions with glee. They know that they are doing wrong but refuse to change; they know what is right but refuse to act upon it. They blame others for their own wickedness. They obstruct the arts and sciences. They slander wisdom and morality, insult the Way and virtue.

Evil persons shoot creatures that fly and hunt those that run, stirring up hibernating animals and rousing roosting fowl. They block up animals' dens and overturn birds' nests, injuring hens and breaking their eggs. They hope for others' ill-fortune and ruin in order to secure advantage for themselves. They let others bear risks to preserve their own safety and fleece people to enrich themselves. They present things of poor quality as good. They disregard the public good for their own private advantage. They take credit for others' achievements. Concealing others' good points, they exaggerate their bad points. They expose people's private affairs. They squander the wealth of the nation. They break up friends and families. They insult the things people love. They lure others into doing evil. They get their way by intimidating people to seek triumphs by ruining others. They destroy crops while they are just sprouting up and flowering. They break up marriages. If they have ill-gotten wealth, they bristle with pride over it. They shamelessly shirk the responsibility for their acts. Quick to claim credit, they are equally quick to deny fault. They are like marriage brokers who wed people to misfortune and like peddlers who sell people evil.

Evil people buy themselves false reputations. Their hearts are nests of wicked intentions. They deprecate the strong points of others while covering up their own shortcomings. They use power tyrannically to intimidate others, not hesitating to inflict cruel and even fatal injury on people. They cut up cloth without cause and cook animals they have slaughtered senselessly, waste the five grains, mistreat animals and other living creatures, wreck people's homes, confiscate their wealth, and destroy their homes by letting loose floods and starting fires. They throw the plans of others into confusion and thereby thwart their achievements. They break tools and make them worthless to workers. When they see others prosper, they desire to have them censured and exiled. If they encounter a rich and prosperous man, they hope he will be brought to ruin. At the sight of a beautiful woman, their hearts brim over with lust. Having borrowed, they wish their creditors would die to avoid repaying them. If their wishes are not met, they curse and burn with hatred. When they notice others having a bit of bad luck, they say it must be recompense for their transgressions. When they see persons who are deformed and crippled, they laugh at them. They play down any praiseworthy talents they observe in others. They resort to magic to get rid of their enemies and use poison to kill trees. They fly into a rage at their teachers and are obstinate toward their elders. They go to violent extremes to satisfy their lusts and desires. They are more than happy to employ tricks and mischief to achieve their ends and gain wealth by plundering. Promotion they seek by cunning and deceit. They are unfair in rewarding and punishing. In indulging their pleasures they go beyond all moderation. They are cruel and severe to those below them, loving to instill fear in people.

Evil persons murmur against Heaven, blame others, curse the wind, and decry the rain. They engage in quarrels and lawsuits. Foolheartedly they become involved in cliques and factions. They use women to advise them and do not follow the teachings of their parents. As soon as they find something new, they abondon the old. They say "yes" with their mouths when their hearts say "no." They covet riches and take advantage of their superiors by deceiving them. They invent wicked stories to defame and ruin innocent people; and while defaming others, they praise their own straightforwardness. They slander the spirits and boast of their own rectitude. They reject virtue and adopt rebelliousness. They turn their backs on those who are close to them and embrace distant acquaintances. They call on Heaven and Earth to witness their misdeeds. If they give something away, they soon regret it. They will borrow money with no intentions of repaying it. They crave those things they have no right to attain. They bend every effort to make an extravagant display.

Evil people's lustful desires go beyond all restraint. Although their hearts are poisonous, they put on a compassionate demeanor. They sell people contaminated food to eat; they deceive people by teaching falsehoods. They give a short foot, a narrow measure, a light pound, a small pint; they take the bad and mix it in with the good, trying to pass the whole lot off as top quality. In such ways they accumulate dishonest profits. They lure good people

into disgraceful acts, deceiving and tricking the ignorant. Their avarice is insatiable. They curse those who seek rectitude. Their drunkenness leads them to sedition. They fight with their families.

A man with these evil traits is without loyalty and virtue, a woman without kindness and obedience. Men like this do not live in harmony with their wives. Women of this sort do not respect their husbands. On every occasion such men love to brag, such women are moved by jealousy. Such men act badly toward their wives and children; such women show no sense of propriety before their fathers-in-law and mothers-in-law. These evil people treat the spirits of their ancestors with contempt. They disobey the orders of their superiors. Their activities benefit no one. They revel in duplicity. They curse themselves and others. Both their loves and their hatreds are based on prejudice.

These evil people skip over wells and hearths and jump over food and people [all of which exhibits a great disrespect for the spirits]. They commit infanticide and perform abortions. Many are their dark and depraved activities! On the sacred days at the end of the month and at the end of the year, they sing and dance with great frivolity. On the first of the month and in the mornings they shout and curse. They snivel, spit, and even urinate toward the north [which is the position of the Emperor and the gods]. They hum, sing, and even cry in front of the hearth [which is the dwelling place of the Kitchen God]. Moreover, they use the fire of the hearth to burn incense. They light filthy firewood to cook their food. They lounge around at night shamelessly naked. They inflict punishments during the eight prohibited periods of the year. They spit at shooting stars and point at the rainbow [by which they manifest their disdain for cosmological phenomena]. They point at the stars unceremoniously and regard the sun and the moon with disrespect. They go hunting and burn wood during the prohibited spring months, curse foully in the direction of the north, and without any reason kill tortoises and hack up snakes [which act as representatives of the gods].

For this sort of wickedness the Judge of Destiny shortens the culprit's life span twelve years or one hundred days, depending on the gravity of the offenses. Should sentence be passed and death occur without the complete expiation of the crimes, then retribution is extended to the sons and grandsons. In cases in which a man has swindled another person out of his money, the burden of restitution is reckoned and passed on to his wife, his children, and all his household to be made good until sooner or later death devours them all. If death itself does not take them, then they are visited by such calamities as floods, fires, robberies, disinheritance, loss of property, disease, and slander in order to make restitution for the crime. In cases in which people kill others unjustly, it is as if they were to hand over their swords so that they themselves in turn could be slain. In cases in which people have acquired ill-gotten wealth, it is just as if they had gulped down rotting meat to satisfy their hunger or had drunk poisoned wine to quench their thirst: they derive a short-lived satisfaction, but death soon ensues. But if within their hearts people rise toward goodness, even if they have not yet achieved it, the spirits of good fortune will watch over them. On the other hand, if within their hearts people sink toward evil, even if they have not yet been totally debased, the spirits of misfortune will pursue them.

A person who has been guilty of doing evil but later changes, repents, ceases to indulge in wickedness, and follows the good completely can attain happiness and success little by little. This can be called changing disaster into blessing.

Therefore, good people are of virtuous speech, virtuous demeanor, and virtuous behavior. If they maintain these three modes of virtue every day, in three years' time Heaven will definitely shower them with its blessings. Wicked people are of evil speech, evil demeanor, and evil behavior. If they maintain these modes of evil every day, in three years' time Heaven will definitely rain down disaster upon them. How then can we not but endeavor to act properly!

Translated by Mark Coyle

22.

Precepts of the Perfect Truth Taoist Sect

Buddhist and Taoist monks were familiar figures in villages and towns throughout China. Even areas that had no monasteries nearby undoubtedly had a few temples or shrines taken care of by monks or priests, who could also perform religious ceremonies for the local residents. Monks, like doctors, geomancers, and merchants, were usually literate and educated in their specialty but generally did not aspire to the intellectual or cultural level of the literati. While learned monks associated with leading scholars, the typical monk would have been more likely to mix with townsmen and prosperous farmers.

The outlook and behavior of monks was shaped by their study of classical religious texts as well as the traditions and practices of the sect to which they belonged. The selection below sets forth the founding principles of the Perfect Truth (Ch'üan-chen) Taoist sect. The twelfth and thirteenth centuries witnessed a Taoist reformation, which culminated in the formation of three reform Taoist sects. These sects preached a rejection of the alchemical and magical practices characteristic of the preceding centuries. Perfect Truth, the largest of the three, was founded by an eccentric ascetic, Wang Che (b. 1180), and represented a fusion of the "Three Teachings" (Taoism, Buddhism, and Confucianism). Although the Perfect Truth sect eventually reincorporated much of the popular beliefs and magic it had originally rejected, it outlived the other two sects and has remained the most prominent Taoist sect into the twentieth century. The founding principles given below were directed primarily at Taoist monks and concern matters of both doctrine and monastic practice.

On the Cloistered Life

All those who choose to leave their families and homes should join a Taoist monastery, for it is a place where the body may find rest. Where the body rests, the mind also will gradually find peace; the spirit and the vital energy will be harmonized, and entry into the Way *(Tao)* will be attained.

In all action there should be no overexertion, for when there is overexertion, the vital energy is damaged. On the other hand, when there is total inaction, the blood and vital energy become sluggish. Thus a mean should be sought between activity and passivity, for only in this way can one cherish what is permanent and be at ease with one's lot. This is the way to the correct cloistered life.

On Cloud-like Wandering

There are two kinds of wandering. One involves observing the wonders of mountains and waters; lingering over the colors of flowers and trees; admiring the splendor of cities and the architecture of temples; or simply enjoying a visit with relatives and friends. However, in this type of wandering the mind is constantly possessed by things, so this is merely an empty, outward wandering. In fact, one can travel the world over and see the myriad sights, walk millions of miles and exhaust one's body, only in the end to confuse one's mind and weaken one's vital energy without having gained a thing.

In contrast, the other type of wandering, cloud-like wandering, is like a pilgrimage into one's own nature and destiny in search of their darkest, innermost mysteries. To do this one may have to climb fearsome mountain heights to seek instruction from some knowledgeable teacher or cross tumultuous rivers to inquire tirelessly after the Way. Yet if one can find that solitary word which can trigger enlightenment, one will have awakened in oneself perfect illumination; then the great matters of life and death will become magnificent, and one will become a master of the Perfect Truth. This is true cloud-like wandering.

On Book-Learning

In learning from books, one who merely grasps onto the literal sense of words will only confuse his eyes. If one can intuit the true meaning behind the words and bring one's heart into harmony with it, then the books themselves can be discarded. One must therefore first attain an understanding of meanings and locate the principles behind them; then one should discard the principle and internalize the meaning into one's heart. When the meaning is understood, then the mind will withdraw from externals, and in time will naturally become responsive to reality. The light of the mind will overflow, the spirit of wisdom will become active, and no problem will be insolvable.

Thus one should diligently cultivate the inner self, never letting one's mind run wild, lest one lose his Nature and Destiny. If one cannot fully comprehend the true meanings of books, and only tries to read more and more, one will end up merely jabbering away before others, seeking to show off one's meager talent. This will not only be detrimental to one's self-cultivation but it may do harm to one's spirit and vital energy. In short, no matter how many books one reads, they will be of no avail in attaining the Way. To understand fully the deep meaning of books, one must incorporate them into one's mind.

On the Art of Medicine

Herbs are the treasures of the hills and the waters, the essence of the grass and the trees. Among the various herbs there are those which are warm and those which are cold; properly used, they can help in supplying elements to or eliminating them from the body. There are active and less active medicines, those that work externally and internally. Therefore people who know thoroughly the power of herbs can save lives, while those who do not will only do further harm to the body. Therefore the man of the Way must be expert in this art. But if he cannot be, he should not pursue it further because it will be of no use in the attainment of the Way and will even be detrimental to his accumulation of merits. This is because those who pride themselves in such knowledge crave after worldly goods, and do not cultivate the Truth. They will pay for such transgression either in this life or the next. The Perfect Truth Taoist must pay heed to this.

On Residence and Covering

Sleeping in the open air would violate the sun and the moon, therefore some simple thatched covering is necessary. However, it is not the habit of the superior man to live in great halls and lavish palaces, because to cut down the trees that would be necessary for the building of such grand residences would be like cutting the arteries of the earth or cutting the veins of a man. Such deeds would only add to one's superficial external merits while actually damaging one's inner credits. It would be like drawing a picture of a cake to ward off hunger or piling up snow for a meal—much ado and nothing gained. Thus the Perfect Truth Taoist will daily seek out the palace hall within his own body and avoid the mundane mind which seeks to build lavish external residences. The man of wisdom will scrutinize and comprehend this principle.

On Companionship

A Taoist should find true friends who can help each other in times of illness and take care of each other's burials at death. However he must observe the character of a person before making friends with him. Do not commit oneself to friendship and then investigate the person's character. Love makes the heart cling to things and should therefore be avoided. On the other hand, if there is no love, human feelings will be strained. To love and yet not to become attached to love—this is the middle path one should follow.

There are three dimensions of compatibility and three of incompatibility. The three dimensions of compatibility are an understanding mind, the possession of wisdom, and an intensity of aspiration. Inability to understand the external world, lack of wisdom accompanied by foolish acts, and lack of high aspiration accompanied by a quarrelsome nature are the three dimensions of incompatibility. The principle of establishing oneself lies in the grand monastic community. The choice of a companion should be motivated by an appreciation of the loftiness of a person's mind and not by mere feelings or external appearance.

On Sitting in Meditation

Sitting in meditation which consists only of the act of closing the eyes and seating oneself in an upright position is only a pretense. The true way of sitting in meditation is to have the mind as immovable as Mount T'ai all the hours of the day, whether walking, resting, sitting, or reclining. The four doors of the eyes, ears, mouth, and nose should be so pacified that no external sight can be let in to intrude upon the inner self. If ever an impure or wandering thought arises, it will no longer be true quiet sitting. For the person who is an accomplished meditator, even though his body may still reside within this dusty world, his name will already be registered in the ranks of the immortals or free spirits *(hsien)* and there will be no need for him to travel to far-off places to seek them out; within his body the nature of the sage and the virtuous man will already be present. Through years of practice, a person by his own efforts can liberate his spirit from the shell of his body and send it soaring to the heights. A single session of meditation, when completed, will allow a person to rove through all the corners of the universe.

On Pacification of the Mind

There are two minds. One is quiet and unmoving, dark and silent, not reflecting on any of the myriad things. It is deep and subtle, makes no distinction between inner and outer, and contains not a single wandering thought. The other mind is that mind which, because it is in contact with external forms, will be dragged into all kinds of thoughts, pushed into seeking out beginnings and ends—a totally restless and confused mind. This confused mind must be eliminated. If one allows it to rule, then the Way and its power will be damaged, and one's Nature and Destiny will come to harm. Hearing, seeing, and conscious thoughts should be eliminated from all activities, from walking, resting, sitting, or reclining.

On Nurturing One's Nature

The art of cultivating one's Nature is like that of playing on the strings of a musical instrument: too great a force can break the string, while too weak a pull will not produce any sound; one must find the perfect mean to produce the perfect note. The art of nurturing one's Nature is also like forging a sword: too much steel will make the sword too brittle while too much tin will make it too malleable. In training one's Nature, this principle must be recognized. When it is properly implemented, one can master one's Nature at will.

On Aligning the Five Primal Energies

The Five Primal Energies are found in the Middle Hall.* The Three Primal Energies are located at the top of the head. If the two are harmonized, then, beginning with the Green Dragon and the White Tiger [the supreme Yin-Yang pair], the ten thousand gods in the body will be arranged in perfect harmony. When this is accomplished, then the energy in the hundred veins will flow smoothly. Cinnabar [symbol for Nature] and mercury [symbol for Destiny] will coalesce into a unity. The body of the adept may still be within the realm of men, but the spirit is already roving in the universe.

On the Union of Nature and Destiny

Nature is spirit. Destiny is material energy. When Nature is supported by Destiny it is like a bird buoyed up and carried along by the wind—flying freely with little effort. Whatever one wills to be, one can be. This is the meaning in the line from the *Classic of the Shadowy Talismans:* "The bird is controlled by the air." The Perfect Truth Taoist must treasure this line and not reveal its message casually to the uninitiated. The gods themselves will chide the person who disobeys this instruction. The search for the hidden meaning of Nature and mind is the basic motif of the art of self-cultivation. This must be remembered at all times.

On the Path of the Sage

In order to enter the path of the sage, one must accumulate patiently, over the course of many years, merit-actions and true practices. Men of high under-

---

* The "Five Primal Energies, the Middle Hall," etc., represent terminology from the so-called "Five-Element School."

standing, men of virtue, and men who have attained insight may all become sages. In attaining sagehood, the body of the person may still be in one room, but his nature will already be encompassing the world. The various sages in the various Heavens will protect him, and the free spirits and immortals in the highest realm of the Non-Ultimate will be around him. His name will be registered in the Hall of the Immortals, and he will be ranked among the free spirits. Although his bodily form is in the world of dust, his mind will have transcended all corporal things.

On Transcending the Three Realms

The Three Realms refer to the realms of desire, form, and formlessness. The mind that has freed itself from all impure or random thoughts will have transcended the first realm of desire. The mind that is no longer tied to the perception of objects in the object-realm will have transcended the realm of form. The mind that no longer is fixed upon emptiness will further transcend the realm of formlessness. The spirit of the man who transcends all three of these realms will be in the realm of the immortals. His Nature will abide forever in the realm of Jade-like Purity.

On Cultivating the Body of the Law

The Body of the Law is formless form. It is neither empty nor full. It has neither front nor back and is neither high nor low, long nor short. When it is functioning, there is nothing it does not penetrate. When it is withdrawn into itself, it is obscure and leaves no trace; it must be cultivated in order to attain the true Way. If the cultivation is great, the merit will be great; if the cultivation is small, the merit will be small. One should not wish to return to it, nor should one be attached to this world of things. One must allow Nature to follow its own course.

On Leaving the Mundane World

Leaving the mundane world is not leaving the body; it is leaving behind the mundane mind. Consider the analogy of the lotus; although rooted in the mud, it blossoms pure and white into the clear air. The man who attains the Way, although corporally abiding in the world, may flourish through his mind in the realm of sages. Those people who presently seek after non-death or escape from the world do not know this true principle and commit the greatest folly.

The words of these fifteen precepts are for our disciples of aspiration. Examine them carefully!

Translated by Whalen Lai and Lily Hwa

23.

Ancestral Rites

The classical ritual texts, such as the Record of Ritual *and the* Ceremonies and Rituals, *were based on the practices of an age with a social system very different from imperial China's. Hence, although always revered, these classics became less and less useful as practical guides to family rituals. From at least the T'ang dynasty, more up-to-date handbooks were regularly written and circulated. One guide was written by the historian and conservative statesman Ssu-ma Kuang (1019–1086). His book contains instructions on cappings, weddings, funerals, ancestor worship, forms of address to be used in letters, and other questions of etiquette. Although his rules and advice were aimed most directly at the upper class, they also seem to have provided models for members of other social groups when they wished to carry out an event in the most proper way.*

Below are the instructions Ssu-ma Kuang gave for the rites honoring ancestors. As early as the Shang dynasty ancestor worship had been practiced by nobles. By the Han, it had become an important part of the religious life of the common people, involving offerings to recent ancestors in homes, at gravesites, or in specially constructed shrines. By the Sung dynasty this system had been more fully elaborated. Domestic ancestral rites, of the sort described below, played an important part in fostering the solidarity of close relatives, while worship at graves or in temples was becoming important to the formation and coherence of lineages.

All ancestor worship should be conducted in the second month of a season [the first month being reserved for imperial ceremonies].

First, the master of the household, his younger brothers, sons, and grandsons, dressed in their formal attire, attend to the divination of an auspicious day for the ceremony. This is done outside of the Image Hall. The master of the household stands facing west, and all the others file behind him in one line, ordered according to their ranks in the family, from north to south. A table is set in front of the master on which are placed incense burners, incense boxes, and milfoil stalks. The master inserts his official tablet in his girdle, lights the incense, and addresses the diviner as follows:

"I would like to present a yearly offering to my ancestors on such-and-such a day. Please determine whether it is an auspicious day."

Then he steps back and hands the milfoil stalks to the diviner, who then performs the divination, facing west. If the proposed date turns out to be inauspicious, then the master of the household names another. When finally an auspicious day is found, all present enter the Image Hall. The master now stands facing north, with his sons and grandsons in file behind him as before, except that now they are ordered according to their ranks from west to east.

The master inserts the official tablet in his girdle, advances to light the incense, then returns to his former position. The deliverer of prayers now comes out from the left of the master, turns to face east, inserts his official tablet in his girdle, takes out the written prayer from his breast pocket, and kneels down to read: "Your filial grandson, officially entitled such-and-such, will on such-and-such a day offer the yearly sacrifice to his departed grandparents. This is to report to you that the date has been found auspicious and that the offering will be made." He then puts the prayer sheet away in his pocket, takes out his official tablet, and rises. After he has returned to his former position, the master of the household bows to the memorial tablets of the ancestors, and everyone exits.

Three days before the date set for the ceremony, the master of the household leads all the male members of the family (above ten years of age) to the outer quarters of the house to observe abstinence, while the women do so in the inner quarters. Thus, although there is wine-drinking, there is no disorder. Meat-eating is allowed, but strong-smelling foods such as onion, leek, and garlic are prohibited. During this period the family members do not attend funerals, nor do they listen to music. All inauspicious and unclean matters are avoided, so that everyone can concentrate on the memory of the departed ancestors.

On the day before the ceremony, the master organizes all the male members of the family and the assistants to dust and sweep the place where the sacrifice will be held, to wash and clean the utensils and containers, and to arrange the furniture. The places for the departed ancestors are so arranged that each husband and wife are side by side, arranged according to proper ranking from west to east, and all facing south. The mistress of the house supervises the women of the household in cleaning the cooking utensils and preparing the food, which should include five kinds of vegetables and five kinds of fruits and not more than fifteen dishes of the following sorts: red stew, roast meat, fried meat, ribs, boiled white meat, dried meat, ground meat, special meats other than pork or lamb, foods made of flour. (If the family is poor, or if certain items cannot be obtained at a particular location or time, then merely include several items from each category, that is, vegetable, fruit, meat, flour-foods, and rice-foods.)

The assistants prepare a basin with a stand for washing hands and set it on the southeastern side of the eastern steps. To the north of the stand is set a rack of towels for drying hands. (These are for the relatives.) Then, on the east side of the eastern steps another basin and some towels are set; these,

however, are without a stand or a rack. (These are for the assistants.)

On the day of the ceremony, all members of the family rise early and put on formal attire. The master and the mistress lead the assistants to the hall for the ceremony. In front of every seat, on the south side of the table, the assistants place vegetables and fruits, and on the north side, wine cups, spoons, chopsticks, teacups and saucers, and sauce bowls. Next they put a bottle of water and a bottle of wine on a table above the eastern steps. To its east is placed a table with a decanter, wine cups, knives, and towels on it. An incense table is placed in the center of the hall, with an incense burner and an incense box on it. An ash bowl is set on the east side, and a burner, a water bottle, an incense ash ladle, and a pair of tongs are set on the west side. Water is poured into the washing basins.

In the morning, when the cook reports that all the foods have been prepared, the master and mistress go to the Image Hall together. Two assistants carry the memorial tablets in a bamboo basket, and, with the master taking the lead and the mistress following him, all the members of the family form two rows, the men on the left-hand side and the women on the right-hand side. In this order they proceed to the hall of the ceremony. The basket is then placed at the top of the western steps, to the west of the burner.

The master and mistress now wash their hands and carry the memorial tablets to the seats: those of the male ancestors first, those of the female ones next. Afterwards, the master leads all the men in the family to form one line, from west to east according to their ranks, below the eastern steps, all facing north. The mistress, likewise, leads all the women in the same order, from east to west, below the western steps, also facing north. The assistants to the ceremony form another line, from west to east, behind the men. When all have taken their proper positions, they bow together to greet the spirits of the ancestors.

The master than ascends the eastern steps and goes to the south of the incense table. He puts his official tablet in his girdle and lights the incense. Then he bows and returns to his former position. The deliverer of prayers and the assistants to the ceremony now wash and dry their hands. One assistant ascends the steps, opens the wine bottle, wipes the mouth of the bottle, and pours the wine into the decanter. Then he takes the wine cup, fills it with wine from the decanter, and makes a libation toward the west.

The cook and servants have by now put the foods

for offering on a table placed on the east side of the washing basin and towel rack. The men now wash their hands. Then, following the example of the master, they put down their official tablets and hold up bowls of meat—the master ascends from the eastern steps, all the others from the western steps—and place them in front of the memorial tablets of the ancestors, to the north of the vegetables and fruits. Afterwards, they take up their official tablets and return to their former positions. Now the women wash and dry their hands. Led by the mistress, they first carry the foods made of flour, ascend the western steps, and set them down to the north of the meats. Then they carry the foods made of rice, ascend the western steps, and set them down to the north of the foods made of flour. Afterwards they descend and return to their former positions.

The master now ascends the eastern steps, goes to the wine table, and turns to face west. An assistant takes the wine cup of the great-grandfather in his left hand and that of the great-grandmother in his right hand; another assistant, in the same manner, holds the cups of the grandparents and a third holds the cups of the parents. The three assistants now go to the master, who, after putting his official tablet away in his girdle, pours wine into the cups. With these cups in their hands, the assistants walk slowly back to the tables to set them down in their former positions. The master takes out his official tablet again, approaches the seats of his great-grandparents, facing north. One assistant now takes the wine cup of the great-grandfather and stands on the left side of the master; another holds the cup of the great-grandmother and stands on the right side of the master. The master, putting away his official tablet, kneels and receives the cup of the great-grandfather, offers a libation, and returns the cup to the assistant, who puts it back where it was. The master then takes out his official tablet, prostrates himself on the floor, then rises and steps back a little.

The deliverer of prayers steps out from the left of the master, turns to face east, puts away his official tablet, takes out the written prayer, kneels down and reads:

On such-and-such a day, of such-and-such a month, of such-and-such a year, your filial great-grandson, officially titled as such-and-such, presents the soft-haired sacrifice (for lamb; if a pig is offered, then he should say "hard-haired" sacrifice) and good wine in the yearly offering to his great-grandfather, officially titled such-and-such, and great-grandmother (give honorary title here). O that you enjoy the food!

He then rolls up the prayer sheet and puts it back into his pocket. Then he takes out his official tablet and rises. The master bows to the memorial tablets.

Next they proceed with the same ceremony at the seats of the grandparents and those of the parents, except that the prayer is slightly modified, so that for the grandparents it reads: "Your filial grandson presents the yearly offerings . . . ," and for the parents, "Your filial son . . .", etc.

When this first round of offerings is completed, the deliverer of prayers and the master descend and return to their former positions. Now the second round of offering begins. (This is usually performed by the mistress herself or some close relative.) The offerer washes her hands if she has not done so already, ascends through the western steps, pours the wine and offers libations, just as the master has done. The only difference is that there is no reading of prayers.

When this second round of offerings is completed, the master ascends the eastern steps, takes off his official tablet, holds the decanter, and fills all the wine cups. Then he takes up his official tablet again and steps back to stand on the southeast side of the incense table, facing north. The mistress ascends the western steps, places spoons in the bowls of millet, and straightens the chopsticks. The handles of the spoons should point to the west. She now goes to stand on the southwest side of the incense table and faces north. The master bows twice at the memorial tablets and the mistress bows four times.

One assistant now removes the tea leaves and another ladles soup for the ancestors, both starting from the western end. When this is done they leave, and the deliverer of prayers closes the door for the ancestors to dine in private. The master now should stand on the east side of the closed door, facing west, with all male members of the family in a file behind him; the mistress stands on the west side of the closed door and faces east, with all female members of the family in a file behind her. In this manner all persons wait for the duration of a meal. Then the deliverer of prayers ascends and approaches the door, facing north. He coughs three times to warn the ancestors before opening the door.

The assistants now go to the north of the table

with the water, and the master comes in to take his position, facing west. The deliverer of prayers ascends the western steps and approaches the seat of the great-grandfather. He puts his official tablet in his girdle and raises the wine cup, slowly walks to the right of the master, turns to face south, and offers the cup to the master, who, after putting his official tablet away in the girdle, kneels down to receive the cup and to sip the wine.

An assistant then hands a container over to the deliverer of prayers, who uses a spoon to take a few grains of millet from the bowl of each ancestor and puts them in the container. He then carries the container and walks up to the left of the master, turns to face north, and offers the master this blessing: "Your grandfather commands me to confer many blessings on you, the filial grandson, enabling you to receive prosperity from Heaven, your fields to produce abundantly, and you to live a long life."

The master places the wine cup in front of him, takes up his official tablet, prostrates himself on the floor, rises, and bows. Then he puts his official tablet away in his girdle and kneels to receive the millet. He tastes a little of it, then puts the rest in his left sleeve. An assistant is standing on his right side, and the master gives the container of the millet to him. The master then folds the edge of his left sleeve over his fingers, takes up the wine cup, and drinks from it. Another assistant is standing on his right side, to whom the master gives the cup. On the left side of the master another assistant is holding a plate. He now puts the plate on the floor, and the master lets the millet fall from his sleeve into the plate, which is then carried out. The master takes up his official tablet, prostrates himself, rises, and goes to stand at the top of the eastern steps, facing west. After the master receives the blessed millet, the deliverer of prayers holds up his official tablet and steps back to the top of the western steps, facing east. When the master has taken his position at the top of the eastern steps, the deliverer of prayers announces the completion of the ceremony. Then he descends and takes his former position. All present bow to the memorial tablets, except for the master, for he has received the blessing. Afterwards, the master descends and bows with everyone else to bid the ancestors farewell.

The ceremony having been completed, the master and mistress ascend to take down the memorial tablets and put them back into the bamboo basket, the tablets of the female ancestors being taken down first, then those of the male ancestors. Two assistants carry the basket to the Image Hall, followed by everyone in the family in the same manner as when the tablets were brought out.

At this point the mistress returns to supervise the removal of the offerings. The wine that remains in the cups, together with that in the decanter, is poured into a pot and sealed. This is the "blessed wine."

The assistants bring the offered foods back to the kitchen, where they are removed from the special containers into ordinary bowls and plates, and the special containers are carefully washed and put away under the supervision of the mistress. A small portion is taken from each item of the offered foods, and put into food boxes, which are sealed together with some "blessed wine," and dispatched, with a letter, to relatives and friends who are ardent observers of rites and rituals. This activity the master supervises. (The food sample is precious because it is left by the ancestors' spirits; it does not have to be rich in itself.)

The assistants now help set up the feast. The men and women are seated separately: the master and all the other male members of the family in the main hall, the mistress and the other female members of the family in the inner quarters. Tables and chairs are set; fruits, vegetables, sauces, wine cups, spoons, chopsticks, and knives are all placed in their proper places. Then wine is poured into decanters, and the hot foods that were offered to the spirits are warmed up.

First, the master of the household takes his seat, and all the other male members of the family offer their good wishes to him. They should stand according to their ranks in the family, just as during the preceding ceremony, and for both men and women the right side ranks higher than the left side. The eldest among them (either a younger brother of the master or his eldest son) stands a trifle ahead of everyone else. An assistant holds the wine decanter and stands on his right. Another assistant holds the wine cup and stands on his left. This eldest of the males then sticks his official tablet in his girdle, kneels, and takes the decanter in his right hand and the wine cup in his left. He then pours the wine and offers good wishes: "Now that the memorial ceremonies have been completed, our ancestors have been offered good food. We wish that you will receive all the five blessings, protect our lineage, and benefit our family."

The assistant who was holding the decanter then steps back, and the one who was holding the cup presents the wine to the master of the household. The eldest male prostrates himself, rises, and returns to his former position. Then he bows to the master together with all the other males. The master then orders the assistant to bring the decanter and the cup of the eldest male member. He pours wine into the cup himself, declaring, "Now that the offerings to our ancestors are successfully accomplished, we celebrate the good fortune of the five blessings bestowed on us; I hereby share them with all of you."

The assistant then hands the cup to the eldest male who, after putting away his official tablet in his girdle, kneels down to receive the wine. After he drinks the wine, he gives the cup back to the assistant, prostrates himself, then rises. The master then orders the assistant to pour wine for everyone. When this is done, all the males again prostrate themselves, and they are then ordered to be seated by the master.

Meanwhile, in the inner quarters, all the female members of the family salute the mistress and are in turn offered wine by her; the procedure is the same as that for the male members, except that it is all performed from a standing position with no kneeling or prostrating. When the round of drinking is over, the assistants bring in the meats. Afterwards, the women come to the main hall to offer their congratulations to the master, who then offers wine to the eldest female member (either a younger sister of his or the eldest daughter), who receives it without kneeling down.

But all other procedures are the same as performed by the males. Then the men come to the inner quarters to offer their good wishes to the mistress, where the procedure is exactly as the one in the main hall.

Next the assistants bring in the foods made of flour, and all the assistants offer their good wishes to the master and mistress, in the same way that the female members saluted the mistress, but they are not offered wine.

Then the foods made of rice are brought in. After this, wine is liberally drunk, and wine games are played, and the offered food consumed. The number of rounds of wine-drinking is decided by the master. When the offered food and wine are used up, other food and wine is brought in. When the feast is over, the leftovers are given to the servants. The master distributes them to the servants of the outer quarters, and the mistress to the servants of the inner quarters, reaching down even to the lowliest in rank, so that the foods are entirely consumed on that day.

Whenever ancestor worship is performed, sincerity in one's love and respect for one's ancestors are what is most significant. Thus, those who are ill should only do as much as they can, but the young and strong should naturally follow the ceremonies closely.

Translated by Clara Yu

24.

The Shrew

Marriage in China, as in most societies, was a matter of considerable concern to the two families involved. At all social levels weddings were expensive, involving an exchange of presents, a procession in which the bride was brought to her new home, feasting, and rituals symbolizing the new status of the bride and groom. To the bride, marriage marked a major turning point; it brought her new duties and incorporated her into a new and probably unknown family. For the groom and his family, a new bride meant help with household chores and a mother to bear children, but they knew that as an outsider she might prove a disruptive force in a previously stable household.

No source provides as good evidence of the dynamics of marriage as fiction written in the vernacular language. Before the Sung almost all texts were written in a literary language, of great beauty to those well read in the classics and histories but unintelligible if read aloud. But in the Sung dynasty professional storytellers entertained audiences at fairgrounds, temples, and markets with tales of supernatural beings, historical heroes, or contemporary domestic comedies. These stories were sometimes recorded in the vernacular in which they were told, to form "prompt books." "The Shrew," given below, is such a story. It is set in the Northern Sung but seems to have been put into near present form in the Southern Sung or Yüan dynasty.

She declaims whole chapters extempore—
  let no one despise her gift!
Each speech brings her fresh enemies;
  her fate moves men to pity.
Though she lacks the persuasion of the wise Tzu-lu
May her tale yet win a laugh from you.

These lines refer to former days in the Eastern Capital, where dwelt a gentleman by the name of Chang Eminent, who had in his house much gold and silver. Of his two grown-up sons, the older was called Tiger, the younger, Wolf. The older son had already taken a wife, the younger was not yet married. In the same city was another gentleman, Li Lucky, who had a daughter named Ts'ui-lien, aged sixteen and uncommonly pretty, accomplished in the art of the needle, and conversant even with the Classics, Histories, and Hundred Philosophers. She was, how-

ever, somewhat too ready with her tongue. In speaking to others, she composed whole essays, and the flow of her speech became a flood. Questioned about one matter, she answered about ten, and when questioned about ten, she answered about a hundred. There is a poem to prove it:

Asked about one thing, she tells about ten—indeed a feat!
Ask her ten things, she'll tell you a hundred—rare talent!
Her speech is ready, her words come swift—truly a marvel!
Regard her not as common; she is no ordinary maid.

The story went that in the same city was a Madam Wang who went to and fro between the two families to arrange about a marriage. The family stations corresponding, a match was agreed upon, and a propitious day and hour chosen for the wedding. Three days before the event, Li Lucky said to his wife, "Our

84

daughter is faultless in most respects; only her tongue is quick and you and I cannot be easy about it. Should her father-in-law prove hard to please, it were no trifling matter. Besides, the mother-in-law is certain to be fussy, and they are a large family with older brother, sister-in-law, and numerous others. What shall we do?" And his wife said, "You and I will need to caution her against it." With this, they saw Ts'ui-lien come before them, and when she found that the faces of both her parents were clouded with grief, and their eyebrows closely knit, she said:

Dad as bounteous as Heaven, Ma as bounteous as Earth,
To arrange this match for me today!
The man finds a wife, the maid a mate,
It's time for rejoicing: be gay for luck!
A fine husband, people all say,
Possessed of riches and many precious things, and well
  connected,
Clever and nimble,
Good at the Double-Six, chess, and all the gentle arts.
He composes verse and antithetical couplets on demand;
He even knows trade and commerce, selling and buying.
How do you like him for a son-in-law
That bitter tears should fall in drops?

When Li Lucky and his wife had heard her to the end, they were exceedingly angry. They said, "We were grieving even because your tongue is as sharp as a blade. We feared that when you entered your husband's house you might talk too much and offend against the proprieties, and thus incur the displeasure of your parents-in-law and everyone else, and become a laughing stock. So we called you, to caution you to talk as little as possible. But higgledy-piggledy, you come out again with a long discourse! What a bitter lot is ours!" Ts'ui-lien, however, said in reply:

Dad, ease your mind; Ma, be consoled;
Brother, rest assured; sister-in-law, stop worrying;
It is not that your daughter would boast of her cleverness
But from childhood she has been on her mettle:
She can spin, she can weave,
She makes dresses, does patching and embroidery;
Light chars and heavy duties she takes in her stride,
Has ready the teas and meals in a trice;
She can work and hand-mill and pound with the pestle;
She endures hardship gladly, she is not easily tired,
Thinks nothing of making dumplings and cookies,
Prepares any soup or broth, does to a turn some cutlet or
  chop.
At night she is vigilant,
Fastens the backdoor and bolts the gate,

Scrubs the frying pan, shuts the cupboard,
Tidies up the rooms both in front and behind,
Makes ready the beds, unrolls the quilts,
Lights the lamp, asks the mother-in-law to retire,
Then calls out "Rest well" and returns to her room:
Thus shall I serve my parents-in-law,
And would they be dissatisfied?
Dear Dad and Ma, let your minds be at rest—
Besides these set tasks, nought matters more than a fart.

When Ts'ui-lien had finished, her father rose from his chair to beat her. But the mother pleaded with him, and loudly reproved her saying, "Child, your father and I were worried just because of your sharp tongue. From now on, talk less. The ancients say, 'Loquacity earns the hatred of many.' When you enter your husband's house, be wary of speaking. A thousand times remember this!" Ts'ui-lien thereupon said, "I know now. From this time onwards I will keep my mouth shut."

On the eve of the wedding, Mrs. Li said to Ts'ui-lien, "Old grandfather Chang next door is a neighbour of long standing, and you grew up, as it were, under his very eyes. You should go over and bid him farewell." And Mr. Li also said, "That would be right." Ts'ui-lien then went over to the neighbours', crossed their threshold, and spoke in a loud voice:

Grandpa Chang, hearken; grandma Chang, hearken;
Hearken to my speech, you two old ones.
Tomorrow at dawn I mount my bridal sedan;
Today I am come to make the announcement.
My parents are frail, they have no support;
Pray keep an eye on them morning and night.
If my brother and his wife offend you in any way,
Forgive them for my parents' sake.
When I return a month after the event,
I shall myself come to ask you pardon.

Grandfather Chang replied: "Little lady, set your mind at rest. Your father and I are dear old friends. I shall certainly look after him morning and evening. And I shall ask my aged spouse to keep your mother company. On no account let it trouble you."

When Ts'ui-lien returned from bidding grandfather Chang farewell, Li Lucky and his wife said to her: "Child, you should now tidy up and go to bed early. Tomorrow you have to rise before daybreak to attend to things." Ts'ui-lien then said:

Dad, retire first; Ma, retire first;
You are not like us young ones.

Sister-in-law and brother can keep me company
While each part of the house I tidy up.
The young can watch all through the night;
Older folk, when they try it, fall a-dozing.

When Ts'ui-lien had spoken, the father and mother were greatly vexed. They cried, "Have done! Have done! As we were saying, you would never change. We will now retire. You can tidy up with your brother and sister-in-law, and then 'Early to bed and early to rise.' "

When Ts'ui-lien saw that her parents had gone to rest, she hurriedly went to the door of her brother's room and shouted aloud:

Do not pretend to be drunk, sister-in-law and brother,—
How distressing even to think of you two!
I am your own dear little sister
And shall be home just one more night.
However could you two act in this way,
Leaving all the chores to me,
Shutting your door, ready to fall asleep?
Sister-in-law, how ungracious of you!
I am at home but this short while—
Would it matter so much if you lent a hand?
You cannot wait to send me away
That the two of you may be free and easy.

Ts'ui-lien finished speaking, and the brother remonstrated with her, saying, "How could you still behave like this? With Dad and Ma there, I am not in a position to scold you. Go and rest now, and get up early tomorrow. Your sister-in-law and I will attend to whatever has to be done." So Ts'ui-lien went back to her room to sleep. In a little while the brother and sister-in-law had tidied up each part of the house, and the entire family retired for the night.

Li Lucky and his wife woke up after a good sleep. They called out to Ts'ui-lien, saying, "Child, what time is it now? Is it fine or rainy?" Then Ts'ui-lien broke into speech:

Dad, do not rise yet; Ma, do not rise yet;
I do not know if it be rainy or fine;
I do not hear the watch being sounded—nor the cock crow.
The streets are quiet, none are conversing;
I only hear Mrs. Pai next door
  making ready to grind her bean-curd,
And old father Huang opposite pounding his sticky rice.
If not still the fourth watch,
Certainly it would be the fifth.
Let me rise first,
Start the fire, chop the wood and fetch the water.
Next let me scrub the pot,

Boil water with which to wash my face,
And comb my hair till it is smooth and shining.
Let everyone else rise early, too,
Lest the bridal procession find us all in a flurry.

Then father, mother, brother, and sister-in-law all rose from their beds. And the father and mother said in an outburst of rage, "All too soon it will be bright in the east. Yet instead of attending to your toilet, you are busy wagging your tongue." But Ts'ui-lien said in reply:

Dad, do not scold; Ma, do not scold;
See how cleverly I adorn myself in my room.
My raven black hair I flatten around each temple,
Mix powder and rouge and rub them on my cheeks,
Then paint my red lips and pencil my eyebrows.
A golden ear-ring I wear in each lobe;
Silver and gold, jade and pearl, I pin all over my head;
Pendants of gems and tinkling bells I attach to my
  sides.
You are marrying me off today,
But, oh! my Dad and Ma, how could I leave you?
I bethink me of the favours of giving suck and rearing
And teardrops wet through my scented silk handker-
  chief.
Hark, I hear voices outside the house—
Despite myself I grow alarmed.
But today is my lucky day:
Why go on tattling and prattling like this?

Ts'ui-lien stopped. However, when her toilet was done, she went straight into her parents' presence and said:

Dad, hear my report; Ma, hear my report;
The dumplings are steamed, the noodles are cut,
The viands and box of delicacies are laid out.
I have them all ready, and now wait patiently
Even while the drum-beats give out the fifth watch.
Mark how our own rooster crows right on the hour!
We must send for the relatives who planned to see me off.
It would matter little if Ma's sister and Uncle's wife stayed
  away,
But how wicked of Dad's own sister!
She sets no store by her words.
She promised to be here by the fifth watch only yesterday;
The cock has crowed, yet there is no trace of her.
When, later, she enters our gate, I must just—
Instead of a final invitation—
Offer her a resounding slap with all five fingers outstretched.

Angry though they were at her words, Li Lucky and his wife forbore to speak out. Mrs. Li said, "Child, go

and ask your brother and sister-in-law to rise now and
attend to things. The bridal procession will soon be
here." When Ts'ui-lien heard her mother say this, she
hurriedly went to the door of the brother and sister-
in-law, and shouted aloud:

Dear sister-in-law, dear brother, you are no longer children.
From now on I shall seldom be home;
You could at least have risen early today—
Will you sleep until broad daylight?
It's time to unbolt the gate and open the windows;
Next, you might light the candles and aromatic incense;
Then give the ground, within and without, a sweeping:
The bridal sedan is expected any moment,
And if the hour be missed and my parents-in-law annoyed,
The pair of you shall hear from me!

The brother and sister-in-law swallowed the affront
and kept silent, and they attended to various tasks in
the house. Then Li Lucky said to Ts'ui-lien, "Child,
you should go before the family shrine, make obeisance to your ancestors and bid them farewell. I have
already lit the candles and incense; so do it while we
wait for the bridal procession. May the ancestors protect you and you be at peace in your husband's
home." Thus instructed, Ts'ui-lien took a bunch of
lighted incense sticks and went before the shrine, and
even as she made obeisance, she prayed aloud:

Shrine that guides the household,
You sages that were our ancestors,
This day I take a husband,
Yet shall not dare keep my own counsel:
At the solstices and equinoxes, and the beginning of each
  season,
I still will offer up the smoke of incense.
I pray to your divine wisdom
Ten thousand times that you pity and hearken!
The man takes a wife, the maid a mate—
This is in the nature of things—
May there be good fortune and rejoicing!
May husband and wife both remain sound and whole,
Without hardship, without calamity,
Even for a hundred years!
May they be merry as fish in water
And their union prove sweeter than honey,
Blessed with five sons and two daughters—
A complete family of seven children—
Matched with two worthy sons-in-law,
Wise and versed in etiquette,
And five daughters-in-law, too,
Paragons of filial piety.
May there be grandsons and granddaughters numerous
To flourish generation after generation.

May there be gold and pearls in heaps
And rice and wheat to fill in a granary,
Abundance of silkworms and mulberry trees,
And cattle and horses drawn up neck to neck,
Chickens, geese, duck and other fowl,
And a pond teeming with fish.
May my husband obey me,
Yet his parents love and pity me;
May the sister-in-law and I live in harmony
And the older and the younger brother be both easy to
  please;
May the servants show full respect,
And the younger sister take a fancy to me.
And, within a space of three years,
Let them die, the whole lot,
And all the property be left in my hands:
Then Ts'ui-lien would be happy for some years!

When Ts'ui-lien had finished her prayer, there was a
din outside the gate. It was a confused noise of many
musical instruments, above which rose the shrill notes
of pipes and singing. The procession from the bridegroom's family, carriage, horsemen and all, was at
the gate. And the astrologer accompanying the procession chanted in verse:

Roll up your bead curtain and fasten it with jade hooks;
A perfumed carriage, followed by noble horses, has reached
  your gate.
Be liberal in your happy-omened tips on this auspicious
  occasion
And in wealth, honour, and splendour pass a hundred
  autumns.

Li Lucky then asked his wife to fetch money to
reward the astrologer, the match-maker, the grooms,
and other attendants. But when Mrs. Li came out with
the banknotes, Ts'ui-lien snatched them from her,
saying,

Let me distribute these notes—
Dad, you are not used to this; Ma, you are not used to this;
Brother and sister-in-law, you too are not used to this
  dealing.
Hey, all of you there, come and stand before me!
Be it less or more, it is as I shall apportion.
To the sedan-bearers, five thousand copper cash;
Mr. Astrologer and the match-maker each get two and a half.
Keep your money well, do not start a row;
If any of you lose it, you have but yourself to blame.
Look, there's another thousand cash note remaining—
Take it, match-maker, and buy a cake
To comfort your dotard of a husband at home.

The astrologer, the sedan-bearers, and the others were all aghast when they heard this. They said, "We have seen thousands of brides but never one so quick in speech." They gaped and put their tongues out and, swallowing their anger, crowded around Ts'ui-lien and helped her on to the bridal sedan.

While they were on their way, the match-maker kept on admonishing Ts'ui-lien, "Little lady, when you reach the gate of the house of your parents-in-law, on no account open your mouth." Before long, the procession reached the gate of the Chang home and the sedan chair was let down. The astrologer chanted:

The sound of nuptial music is heard all over the capital;
The Weaving Maid this day weds the Divine Cowherd.
The relatives of this house come forth to receive the treasure;
The bride in her finery accepts her mouthful of rice—
     a custom from time immemorial.

To go on with the story, the match-maker held up a bowl of rice and shouted aloud: "Little lady, open your mouth to receive the rice." Upon this, Ts'ui-lien in her bridal sedan burst out in rage:

Shameless old bitch! Shameless old bitch!
One moment you tell me to shut my mouth, and the next
     you ask me to *open* it!
Oh! the unfathomable glibness of match-makers!
However could you change your "don'ts" at once into "dos"?
Are you drunk already so early in the day
That foolishly you open *your* mouth, lying and wagging
     your tongue?
Just then while you walked by my sedan,
You warned me on no account to open my mouth.
I have only now been set down before the gate—
Why then do you ask me to open my mouth?
Blame me not for calling you names—
Really you are but a painted old bitch.

The astrologer then said, "Bride, cease your anger. She is the match-maker. You go too far in your words. There is no precedent for such behaviour in a bride." But Ts'ui-lien replied:

Mr. Astrologer, you are a man of learning;
How then could you be so dull of apprehension?
Not to speak when one ought to is, by definition, slow-
     witted.
This bawd of a match-maker will be the death of me!
She says the bridegroom's family is wealthy and high-
     ranking,
Possessed of riches and precious things, much silver and
     gold;

A calf or horse they would kill for their table;
Their gate is made of sandal and sapanwood;
They have silks, gauzes, brocades in numberless rolls,
And pigs, goats, cattle, and horses all in droves.
Yet even before I enter the house, they dish up this cold rice:
Better be poor than wealthy and high-ranking in *this*
     fashion.
Hard indeed to endure a family so uncouth
As would serve up cold rice and expect me to swallow it!
Had I no regard for the faces of both parents-in-law,
I could beat you till you saw stars!

Ts'ui-lien having had her say, the match-maker was so incensed that she tasted not a drop of wine but, like a whiff of smoke, vanished into the house, neither minding Ts'ui-lien's descent from the bridal sedan, nor the ensuing ceremony at the altar.

But the relatives of the bridegroom's family crowded around Ts'ui-lien and escorted her into the ceremonial hall, where they made her stand with her face to the west. The astrologer, however, announced: "The bride will turn and face the east. The stars of good luck are all in the east today." At this, Ts'ui-lien again burst out:

Just then it was west, and now I must face east.
Will you drag the bride about as you would lead a beast?
Having turned round and round, tending in no fixed direc-
     tion,
I am so vexed, my heart is afire:
I cannot tell who my mother-in-law
Nor who my father-in-law is
Amidst this noisy crowd of relatives even to the ninth degree,
With the younger brother and sister adding to the confusion.
The red paper tablet is placed in the centre
And red silken lanterns, several pairs of them, are lit.
But, wait, my father-in-law and mother-in-law
     are not yet deceased.
Why then should there be a lamp for the dead?

Old Chang Eminent and his wife were furious when they heard this. They exclaimed: "It was earlier agreed that our son would marry the daughter of a respectable family. Who would have known it would turn out to be this ill-mannered, ill-bred, long-tongued, wayward peasant girl?" And all the relatives of the nine degrees gaped, utterly confounded.

Finally the astrologer said, "This child has been spoilt at home. She has only just arrived today. You will need to train her gradually. Let us proceed with the ceremony of bowing before the altar, to be followed by the bowing to the relatives." And when the ceremony was over and all the relatives, old and young, had been introduced, the astrologer, chanting in verse, requested the bride and groom to enter the nuptial chamber for the stewing of the bed curtains:

The newly wed move their steps across the lofty hall;
Nymph and god together enter the nuptial chamber.
Be liberal in your happy-omened tips on this auspicious
    occasion—
Scatter the grain in all directions, that *Yin* and *Yang* min-
gling may increase.

Wolf went in front, with Ts'ui-lien behind him. The astrologer, holding before him a peck containing a mixture of the five grains, followed them into the nuptial chamber.

   The newly wedded couple sat on the bed while the astrologer chanted with the grain in his hand:

Scatter the grain east of the bed curtains—
Red candles cast their shadows where thick screens enfold.
Long may youthful charms bloom, not fade;
Eternal spring prevail in the painted hall!

Scatter the grain west of the bed curtains—
Pennants and ribbons stream down the corners of the bed.
Lift the veil and you will see the goddess's face;
The godlike bridegroom attains his laurel branch.

Scatter the grains south of the bed curtains—
Nuptial bliss long to linger over!
A gentle breeze in moonlight cools hall and bower,
Flapping two belts adorned with the "heir bearing" plant.

Scatter the grain north of the bed curtains—
That overflowing beauty between her eye-brows!
In the warmth of the embroidered curtains on a night in
  spring
The moon goddess detains her favoured guest.

Scatter the grain above the bed curtains—
A pair of intertwining mandarin ducks!
May you dream tonight of the bear
And the pearl-oyster falling on to your palm!

Scatter the grain within the bed curtains—
A pair of jade hibiscus under the moon!
It's as if one encountered a fair immortal,
Wrapped in crimson clouds, alighting from Mount Wu.

Scatter the grain under the bed curtains—
Some say a golden light will shine in the room.
Share now the lucky dreams of this night:
Bring forth next year a man child and win enhanced
  standing.

Scatter the grain in front of the bed curtains—
Hovering in the air is neither mist nor smoke,

It is the coiled-dragon-incense fume:
The student at last meets his fairy bride.

Scatter the grain behind the bed curtains—
Man and wife agreeing, long cherish each other.
From of old "Wife chimes in when husband sings";
Do not then roar like the proverbial lioness.

To go on with the story, the astrologer had not yet completed the ceremony of strewing the bed curtains, when Ts'ui-lien sprang up and, groping about, found a rolling-pin, with which she dealt him two smart blows in the sides, and roundly abused him: "You skunk of a windbag. It's your own wife who would be the lioness." And without further ado she drove him out of the bridal chamber, shouting after him:

Scatter the grain indeed! I ask you, to what purpose?
Having littered that way, again to litter this way,—
Beans, rice, wheat, barley all over the bed.
Just pause to think: Ain't it a pretty sight?
The parents-in-law are rude and rash,
The bride's untidy and careless, they'll say.
And if the husband should pretend to be vexed
He would say the wife was slatternly.
Off with you at once—out of the gate.
And spare yourself more blows from my rolling-pin.

The astrologer took his beating and went out through the gate. The bridegroom, Wolf, was now roused and exclaimed: "Of the thousands of misfortunes, to have married this peasant woman! Strewing the bed curtains is an ancient ceremony." To this, Ts'ui-lien said in reply:

Husband, husband, be not angry,
Hear me and judge the right and wrong for yourself.
The mere thought of that man tries my patience,
Littering beans and barley all over the place.
Yet you ask no one to sweep them away;
Instead you say, I lack womanly obedience.
If you vex me any further,
You too I will drive out with him,
Shut my door, sleep by myself.
"Early to bed and early to rise" as I please.
And "Amitabha" chant my prayers
With my ears undisturbed in careless solitude.

And Wolf, at a loss what to do with her, went out to join in the feasting and toast his guests.

   By nightfall the feast broke up and the relatives all went home. Sitting alone in the nuptial chamber, Ts'ui-lien thought to herself: "Soon my husband will come into the room and his hands are certain to rove in some wild ecstatic dance. I have to be prepared." So she stood up, removed her jewelery, undressed and, getting into bed, rolled herself tightly in a quilt and slept. Now, to go on with the story, Wolf came in and undressed, and was about to go to bed, when Ts'ui-lien stunned him with a thundering cry:

Wretch, how ridiculously mistaken in your designs!
Of a truth, what an uncouth rustic!
You are a man, I a woman;
You go your way, I go mine.
You say I am your own bride—
Well, do not call me your old woman yet.
Who was the match-maker? Who the chief witness?
What were the betrothal presents? How was the gift of tea?
How many pigs, sheep, fowl and geese? How many vats of wine?
What floral decorations embellished the gifts?
How many gems? How many golden head ornaments?
How many rolls of silk gauze thick and thin?
How many pairs of bracelets, hat pins, hair pins?
With what should I adorn myself?
At the third watch late at night,
What mean you to come before my bed?
At once depart, and hurry away,
Lest you annoy my folk at home.
But if you provoke my fiery temper,
I will seize you by the ears and pull your hair,
Tear your clothes and scratch your face;
My heavy hand with outstretched fingers shall fall pat on your cheek.
If I rip your hair-net, don't say I did not warn you,
Nor complain if your neatly coiled hair get dishevelled.
This is no bawd's lane.
Nor the dwelling of some servile courtesan.
What do I care about silly rules like "Two and two make four"?
With a sudden laying about of my fist
I'll send you sprawling all over the room.

When Wolf heard his bride declaim this chapter, he dared not approach her, nor utter even a groan, but sat in a far-off corner of the room.

To go on with the story, soon it was indeed almost the third watch, and Ts'ui-lien thought to herself: "I have now married into his family. Alive, I shall remain one of their household; dead, I shall dwell among their ghosts. If we do not sleep in the same bed tonight, when tomorrow my parents-in-law learn about it, they will certainly blame me. Let it be, then! I will ask him to come to bed." So she said to Wolf:

Dumb wretch, do not say you are drunk!
Come over, I will share the bed with you.
Draw near me and hear my command:
Fold your hands respectfully before you; tread on your toes; do not chatter.
Remove your hair-net and off with your cap;
Gather up your garments, socks, and boots;
Shut the door, lower the curtain,
And add some oil to the lamp grown dim.
Come to bed, and ever so softly
We'll pretend to be mandarin ducks or intertwining trees.
Make no noise, be careful of what you say;
When our conjugal rites are completed, you'll curl up next my feet,
Crooking your knee-joints, drawing in your heels.
If by chance you give even one kick,
Then know it's *death* for you!

And the story went that the whole night through Wolf indeed dared not make the least noise. They slept until dawn, when the mother-in-law called out: "Wolf, you should ask your bride to rise early, finish her toilet, and come out to tidy up." So Ts'ui-lien spoke out:

Do not hurry, do not rush;
Wait till I have donned my everyday clothes.
Now—vegetables with vegetables, ginger with ginger,
Each variety of nuts into a separate pack.
Pork on one side, mutton on the other;
We'll sort out the fresh fish from boiled tripe.
Wine by itself, away from the broth;
Salt chicken and smoked venison should not be mixed.
In the cool of this time of year
They will keep yet a good five days.
Let me set apart some neat slices
To serve on the third morn with tea for the aunts.
And if the relatives do not eat them all,
The parents-in-law can have the left-overs as a treat.

When the mother-in-law had heard this, she was a long while speechless. She wanted to scold Ts'ui-lien but was afraid she would only make herself a laughing stock. So she swallowed her anger and endured in silence until the third morn, when the bride's mother called in to present her gifts. And when the two mothers-in-law had met, Mrs. Chang could no longer contain herself: she recounted from beginning to end how Ts'ui-lien had inflicted blows on the astrologer and how she had abused the match-maker, how she had insulted her husband and how she had slighted her parents-in-law. Upon hearing this account, Mrs. Li grew exceedingly ashamed. She went straight to her daughter's room and said to Ts'ui-lien, "What did

I warn you against when you were still at home? I told you not to jabber and chatter when you entered your husband's house, but you never listened to me. It is only the third day, yet your mother-in-law made many complaints about you just then, causing me to be in fear and trepidation, and unable to utter a word in reply." Ts'ui-lien, however, said:

Mother, don't start a row yet;
Listen while I relate it in each particular.
Your daughter is no untaught peasant woman;
There are some matters you little know about.
On the third morn the new daughter-in-law enters the
  kitchen
(Ha ha, to relate this would but earn me ridicule)
Two bowls of thin rice porridge with salt was all they
  provided
And, to serve with the meal, not even tea but plain boiling
  water!
Now, you, their new relation, make your first call,
At once they start their tittle-tattle:
Regardless of white or black, true or false,
Harassing me is all they are bent on.
My mother-in-law is by nature too impetuous,
The things she says are none too proper.
Let her beware—lest driven to my last resource,
With a bit of cord and a swing from the noose
I leave her to answer for my corpse.

When the mother found Ts'ui-lien talking in this way, she could not very well scold her. And without drinking her tea or tasting the wine, Mrs. Li instantly took leave of her new relations, mounted her sedan-chair, and returned home.

To go on with the story, Wolf's older brother, Tiger, now began to shout in the house: "What kind of a family are we now? It was said at first that brother would be marrying a well-behaved young woman. Who would have expected it to be this tavern waitress who chatters the whole day, wagging her tongue and declaiming sentences and maxims? It is quite outrageous!" Ts'ui-lien heard him and said in reply:

  Brother-in-law, you err against ritual;
  I did not in the least provoke you.
  A full-grown, manly pillar of society
  To call his sister-in-law a glib tavern waitress!

Tiger then called to Wolf and said, "Haven't you heard the old saying: 'Teach a wife when she first comes to you'? Though you need not go so far as to beat her, you might at least lecture her now and then;

or else go and tell her old bawd of a mother." At this, Ts'ui-lien exclaimed:

Busy-body of a brother-in-law!
I did not dip my fingers in your bowl of rice.
Though I may be a bit loquacious,
There's husband and mother-in-law, to keep me in order.
Your new relations did not provoke you—
Why then do you call my mother a bawd?
Wait till I go back when the month is over;
I will tell my own dear brother at home.
My brother is a hotheaded firebrand;
You will perhaps know me better
When his fist and hand shall both at once hit out,
And like a tortoise in a drought you'll crawl in vain for
  shelter.

Tiger was enraged by her speech and, laying hands upon Wolf, thought to give the brother a thrashing. But his wife, Mistress Ssu, ran out from her room and said, "To each his own; how should brother's wife concern you? It was said of old: 'Don't wear your clean shoes to tread on a dunghill.'" At once Ts'ui-lien burst out again:

Sister-in-law, don't start trouble;
This kind of conduct would never do.
Was it not enough for brother-in-law to shout at me
But you must step forward to scold some more?
It ever has been: when the wife is dutiful, the man shuns all
  ills
And succeeds in the highest enterprise.
Go off then quickly, back to your room,
And sit in hiding in some secure corner.
Sister-in-law, I did not provoke you—
Why then do you liken me to dung?
Since we must die even if we lived to a hundred,
Shall you and I now fight it out?
And if any mishap befell me,
Before Yama, King of the Underworld, I would not let you
  off.

The daughter of the house, Wolf's younger sister, heard this. She went into her mother's room and said, "You are her mother-in-law. Why don't you keep her under control? How very unseemly it would be if she carried on like this unchecked! People would only laugh at us." But when Ts'ui-lien saw the younger sister thus engaged, she called out after her:

Younger sister, how wicked of you
To sneak within to incite your mother!
If my mother-in-law should beat me to death,

I would carry you off with me to the king of hell.
My father is by nature pugnacious—
He's not one to endure wrongs meekly—
He would insist on a hundred priests, Taoist and Buddhist,
To conduct services seven nights and seven days,
And a pine-wood coffin with a solid block for base,
And mother-in-law and father-in-law to burn paper-money
    for me.
You, younger sister, and sister-in-law, would wear mourn-
    ing headscarves,
And brother-in-law could prostrate himself as my heir,
And the relatives of the nine degrees would carry the bier.
The funeral ended, your troubles would start afresh:
Accusations would have sped to the local and high courts,
Whose judges with all your silver you would bribe in vain.
Even had you millions upon millions of strings of cash,
You would spend them all and still forfeit your lives.

The mother-in-law now came out and said to Ts'ui-
lien, "Luckily you have been my daughter-in-law
only these three days; had you been these three years,
would any of us in this family, old ones and young
ones, ever get to speak at all?" Ts'ui-lien replied:

You are too easily swayed, my mother-in-law;
When older folk grow slack, they lose the respect of the
    young.
Dear younger sister, do not tempt fortune too far;
Must you splutter all before your mama,
Exaggerating heavily the lightest rumours?
To which the old fool listening and readily believing,
Stings me to the quick with this remark or that
In words unfit for the ear.
If any mishap befell me,
Rest assured the old one would pay with her life.

When the mother-in-law heard this, she went straight
back to her room. And she said to the old gentleman.
"Just look at that new daughter-in-law of ours. Her
tongue is as sharp as a blade, and she has insulted
each member of the family in turn. You are her
father-in-law. Don't be afraid to summon and reprimand her." The old gentleman said, "I am the father-
in-law, and so hardly in a position to reprimand her.
However, let me ask her for some tea to drink, and we
can then see what happens." His wife then said,
"When she sees you, she will not dare wag her
tongue."

Thereupon Mr. Chang gave the order: "Ask Wolf's
wife to brew some mid-day tea." When Ts'ui-lien
heard the father-in-law calling for tea, she hurriedly
went into the kitchen, scrubbed the pot and boiled the
water. She then went to her own room and took out a

variety of nuts, and returning to the kitchen, made
bowls of tea, which she placed on a tray. Holding the
tray before her, she went into the ceremonial hall,
where she arranged the chairs. She then went before
her parents-in-law, saying "Pa and Ma will please
have their tea in the hall." And she also went to the
sister-in-law's room and said: "Brother and sister-in-
law will please have tea in the hall." Mr. Chang then
remarked: "You were all saying the new daughter-in-
law had a sharp tongue. Now when I order her to do
something, she dare not raise her voice." His wife rejoined: "Since this is so, you shall give her all the
orders."

In a little while the entire family were gathered in
the ceremonial hall, and sat down in order of seniority. And they saw Ts'ui-lien come forward with
her tray to address them:

Pa, have tea; Ma, have tea;
Brother and sister-in-law, come and have your tea.
If younger sister and younger brother would like tea,
They can help themselves to the two bowls on the oven.
But hold your bowls well, the pair of you, and tread with
    care
Lest the hot tea scald your hands and you cry "Oh! oh!"
This tea we call Granny's Tea;
The name is homely, the taste delicious.
Here are two chestnuts freshly roasted brown,
Half a pinch of fried white sesame seeds,
Olives from south of the Yangtze, and mixed nut kernels,
And walnuts from beyond the Great Wall, and shelled
    haws.
You two venerable ones will eat them slowly
Lest all unawares you lose a tooth or two.

When the father-in-law found her speaking in this
manner, he said in a rage: "A female person should be
gentle and staid, and sober in speech: only then is she
fit to be a daughter-in-law. Was there ever a long-
tongued woman like this one!" But Ts'ui-lien again
spoke out:

Venerable Pa, venerable Ma,
And brother and sister-in-law too, sit you down,
You two old ones, do not scold me
But listen to your daughter-in-law's account:
She is not stupid nor is she sly;
From childhood on, she was straight and blunt,
And unkind words, once uttered, slip clean out of her mind.
Pa and Ma, do not detest her overmuch;
But if you really disapprove, then—repudiate her:
She will not grieve nor be afraid;
She will mount her sedan and return home.

No new husband shall she think of—neither one who would
  dwell with her parents
Nor one who would take her to his own house.
She will not put on powder and rouge, nor adorn herself,
But, as in mourning, wear white from top to toe,
And so wait on her parents and end her days.
I remember many ancient men of wisdom:
Chang Liang and K'uai Ch'e were skilled in argumentation,
Lu Chia and Hsiao Ho ever ready with some learned al-
  lusion;
Ts'ao Chih and Yang Hsiu were no less ready in wit;
The eloquence of Chang I and Su Ch'in swayed the Warring
  States,
And Yen-tzu and Kuan Chung overcame mighty princes
  through persuasion;
And there were Ch'en P'ing with his six stratagems, and
  Li Tso-chü,
And the twelve-year-old official Kan Lo, and the disciple
  Tzu-hsia himself:
These ancients all excelled in making speeches;
They regulated their households, governed their kingdoms,
  and pacified the Empire.
If Pa would stop me from speaking,
Then you must stitch up my mouth.

Mr. Chang cried, "Have done! Have done! Such a
daughter-in-law would one day bring down the family name and be a reproach to the ancestors." And he
called Wolf before him and said, "Son, put your wife
away. I will find you another, a better wife." Though
Wolf assented to this, he could not find it in his heart
to cast her off. And Tiger and his wife both pleaded
with the father, saying, "Let her be taught
gradually." But Ts'ui-lien, having heard them, once
more spoke up:

Pa, do not complain; Ma, do not complain;
Brother and sister-in-law, do you not complain.
Husband, you need not persist in clinging to me;
From now on, each will do as he pleases.
At once bring paper, ink, slab, and brush,
Write out the certificate of repudiation and set me free.
But note: I did not strike my parents-in-law nor abuse the
  relatives;
I did not deceive my husband nor beat the humble and
  meek;
I did not go visiting neighbours, west or east;
I did not steal nor was I cozened;
I did not gossip about this person nor start trouble with that
  one;
I was not thievish nor jealous nor lewd;
I suffer from no foul disease; I can write and reckon;
I fetched the water from the well, hulled the rice and
  minded the cooking;

I spun and wove and sewed.
Today, then, draw up the certificate as you please,
And when I carry away my dowry, do you not resent it.
In between our thumb-prints add these words:
"Never to meet again, never to see each other."
Conjugal affection is ended,
All feelings dead;
Set down on paper many binding oaths:
If we chance upon each other at the gate of hell,
We shall turn our heads away and not meet.

Wolf, because his parents had decided for him, wrote
out the document with tears in his eyes, and the two
of them affixed their thumb-prints. The family called
for a sedan-chair, loaded the trousseau on it, and sent
Ts'ui-lien home with the certificate of repudiation.

In the Li family, Ts'ui-lien's father, mother,
brother, and sister-in-law all blamed her for her sharp
tongue. But she said to them:

Dad, do not shout; Ma, do not shout;
Brother and sister-in-law, do you not shout.
It is not that your lassie would sing her own praises,
But from childhood she has been of high mettle.
This day I left their household,
And the rights and wrongs of the affair I will leave off.
It is not that my teeth are itching to speak,
But tracing patterns and embroidering, spinning and
  weaving,
Cutting and trimming garments, in all these I am skilled.
True it is, moreover, I can wash and starch, stitch and sew,
Chop wood, carry water, and prepare choice dishes;
And if there are silkworms, I can keep them too.
Now I am young and in my prime,
My eyes are quick, my hand steady, my spirits bold;
Should idlers come to peep at me,
I would give them a hearty, resounding slap.

Mr. Li and his wife cried: "Have done! Have done!
The two of us are now old; we can no longer keep you
under our control. What we are afraid of is that some
indiscretion or other would make you simply an object of ridicule. Poor, pitiful one!" But Ts'ui-lien went
on:

Your daughter was destined at birth to a lonely, wretched
  life—
She married an ignorant, foolish husband!
Though I might have endured the severity of his father and
  mother,
How could I have borne those sisters-in-law?
If I but moved my lips,
Off they went and stirred up the old ones.
Besides, such venom lay behind their scolding,

It soon led to blows and kicks,
From which began an incessant to-do;
Then all at once they wrote the certificate of dissolution.
My one hope was to find contentment and peace at home—
How should I expect even Dad and Ma would blame me?
Abandoned by the husband's family and my own,
I will cut off my hair and become a nun,
Wear a straight-seamed gown and dangle a gourd from a
 pole,
And carry in my hands a huge "wooden fish."
In the daytime from door to door I shall beg for alms;
By night within the temple I shall praise the Buddha,
Chant my "Namah,"
Observe my fasts and attend to my exercises.
My head will be shaven and quite, quite bald;
Who then will not hail the little priestess?

And having spoken, she removed her ornaments and
changed out of her gay garments into a suit of cotton
clothes. She then went before her parents, joined the
palms of her hands to perform a Buddhist salute, and
bade them farewell. And she turned and bade her
brother and sister-in-law farewell. And the brother
and sister-in-law said to her: "Since you have chosen
to take the vows, let us accompany you to the Clear
Voice Temple in the street in front." Ts'ui-lien
however, replied:

Brother and sister-in-law, do not accompany me, I will go
 by myself;
And when I am gone, you can be easy and free.
As the ancients put it well:
"Though here not welcome, elsewhere I shall be."
Since I am renouncing the world
And shall have my head shaven,
All places may be my home—
Why only the Clear Voice Temple?
Unencumbered and without a care,
I too shall be free and easy.

She would not cling to wealth and rank;
Wholeheartedly she embraced her vows.
She donned her nun's brocade robes
And constantly fingered her beads.
Each month she kept her fasts;
Daily she offered up fresh flowers,
A Bodhisattva she might not become:
To be Buddha's least handmaid would still content her!

Translated by H. C. Chang

25.

The Problems of Women

Although China produced a number of distinguished women poets, women seldom wrote fiction, diaries, or essays, and of what they did write, little has survived. Therefore, it is impossible to describe with certainty how women reacted to common experiences such as marriage, the birth of children, and the death of spouses or children. The best sources we have are fictional accounts that appealed to women as well as men, and the essays and letters of men who seem to have been relatively astute and sympathetic observers of women.

Below are a number of brief essays on some of the problems women faced and what their fathers, sons, and husbands could do to help them. They were written by Yüan Tsai (flourished 12th c.) and form part of a book of practical advice he wrote, which also discussed how to raise children, how to live harmoniously in a large family with several grown brothers, how to arrange marriages that will fare well, how to manage a family business, and how to divide the family property when division becomes necessary. Although focusing especially on the problems of complex families with many members, Yüan Tsai explicitly addressed his advice as much to merchants and townsmen as to scholars and officials.

Women Should Not Take Part in Affairs Outside the Home

Women do not take part in extra-familial affairs. The reason is that worthy husbands and sons take care of everything for them, while unworthy ones can always find ways to hide their deeds from the women.

Many men today indulge in pleasure and gambling; some end up mortgaging their lands, and even go so far as to mortgage their houses without their wives' knowledge. Therefore, when husbands are bad, even if wives try to handle outside matters, it is of no use. Sons must have their mothers' signatures to mortgage their family properties, but there are sons who falsify papers and forge signatures, sometimes borrowing money at high interest from people who would not hesitate to bring their claim to court. Other sons sell illicit tea and salt to get money, which, if discovered by the authorities, results in fines.

Mothers have no control in such matters. Therefore, when sons are bad, it is useless for mothers to try to handle matters relating to the outside world.

For women, these are grave misfortunes, but what can they do? If husbands and sons could only remember that their wives and mothers are helpless and suddenly repent, would that not be best?

Women's Sympathies Should Be Indulged

Without going overboard, people should marry their daughters with dowries appropriate to their family's wealth. Rich families should not consider their daughters outsiders but should give them a share of the property. Sometimes people have incapable sons and so have to entrust their affairs to their daughters' families; even after their deaths, their burials and sacrifices are performed by their daughters. So how can people say that daughters are not as good as sons?

Generally speaking, a woman's heart is very sympathetic. If her parents' family is wealthy and her husband's family is poor, she wants to take her parents' wealth to help her husband's family prosper. If her husband's family is wealthy but her parents' family is poor, then she wants to take from her husband's family to enable her parents to prosper. Her parents and husband should be sympathetic toward her feelings and indulge some of her wishes. When her own sons and daughters are grown and married, if either her son's family or her daughter's family is wealthy while the other is poor, she wishes to take from the wealthy one to give to the poor one. Her sons and daughters should understand her feelings and be somewhat indulgent. But taking from the poor to make the rich richer is unacceptable, and no one should ever go along with it.

Orphaned Girls Should Have Their Marriages Arranged Early

When a widow remarries she sometimes has an orphaned daughter not yet engaged. In such cases she should try to get a respectable relative to arrange a marriage for her daughter. She should also seek to have her daughter reared in the house of her future in-laws, with the marriage to take place after the girl has grown up. If the girl were to go along with the mother to her step-father's house, she would not be able to clear herself if she were subjected to any humiliations.

For Women Old Age Is Particularly Hard to Bear

People say that, though there may be a hundred years allotted to a person's life, only a few reach seventy, for time quickly runs out. But for those destined to be poor, old age is hard to endure. For them, until about the age of fifty, the passage of twenty years seems like only ten; but after that age, ten years can feel as long as twenty. For women who live a long life, old age is especially hard to bear, because most women must rely on others for their existence. Before a woman's marriage, a good father is even more important than a good grandfather; a good brother is even more important than a good father; a good nephew is even more important than a good brother. After her marriage, a good husband is even more important than a good father-in-law; a good son is even more important than a good husband; and a good grandson is even more important than a good son. For this reason

women often enjoy comfort in their youth but find their old age difficult to endure. It would be well for their relatives to keep this in mind.

It Is Difficult for Widows to Entrust Their Financial Affairs to Others

Some wives with stupid husbands are able to manage the family's finances, calculating the outlays and receipts of money and grain, without being cheated by anyone. Of those with degenerate husbands, there are also some who are able to manage the finances with the help of their sons without ending in bankruptcy. Even among those whose husbands have died and whose sons are young, there are occasionally women able to raise and educate their sons, keep the affection of all their relatives, manage the family business, and even prosper. All of these are wise and worthy women. But the most remarkable are the women who manage a household after their husbands have died leaving them with young children. Such women could entrust their finances to their husbands' kinsmen or their own kinsmen, but not all relatives are honorable, and the honorable ones are not necessarily willing to look after other people's business.

When wives themselves can read and do arithmetic, and those they entrust with their affairs have some sense of fairness and duty with regard to food, clothing, and support, then things will usually work out all right. But in most of the rest of the cases, bankruptcy is what happens.

Beware of Future Difficulties in Taking in Female Relatives

You should take into your own house old aunts, sisters, or other female relatives whose children and grandchildren are unfilial and do not support them. However, take precautions. After a woman dies, her unfilial sons or grandsons might make outrageous accusations to the authorities, claiming that the woman died from hunger or cold or left valuables in trunks. When the authorities receive such complaints, they have to investigate and trouble is unavoidable. Thus, while the woman is alive, make it clear to the public and to the government that the woman is bringing nothing with her but herself. Generally, in performing charitable acts, it is best to make certain that they will entail no subsequent difficulties.

Before Buying a Servant Girl or Concubine, Make Sure of the Legality

When buying a female servant or concubine, inquire whether it is legal for her to be indentured or sold before closing the deal.* If the girl is impoverished and has no one to rely on, then she should be brought before the authorities to give an account of her past. After guarantors have been secured and an investigation conducted, the transaction can be completed. But if she is not able to give an account of her past, then the agent who offered her for sale should be questioned. Temporarily she may be hired on a salaried basis. If she is ever recognized by her relatives, she should be returned to them.

Hired Women Should Be Sent Back When Their Period of Service Is Over

If you hire a man's wife or daughter as a servant, you should return her to her husband or father on comple-tion of her period of service. If she comes from another district, you should send her back to it after her term is over. These practices are the most humane and are widely carried out by the gentry in the Southeast. Yet there are people who do not return their hired women to their husbands but wed them to others instead; others do not return them to their parents but marry them off themselves. Such actions are the source of many lawsuits.

How can one not have sympathy for those separated from their relatives, removed from their hometowns, who stay in service for their entire lives with neither husbands nor sons? Even in death these women's spirits are left to wander all alone. How pitiful they are!

Translated by Patricia Ebrey

---

* In other words, do not buy a girl who was kidnapped, only one whose parents consented to her sale.

26.

Rules for the Fan Lineage's Charitable Estate

From the Sung dynasty until modern times many Chinese have belonged to organized patrilineal kinship groups called lineages. An important aspect of the strength and durability of these lineages has been the provision for common property handed down in perpetuity in the form of "charitable estates." The income from such property was used to cover lineage expenses and provide material benefits for lineage members. Usually the estates were started by successful men who donated land or money to the lineage.

Fan Chung-yen (989–1052), a famous statesman, was the first to establish such an estate. The rules he laid down for its use and management are given below. In later generations his descendants made many amendments to these rules to accommodate new situations as the lineage and its property grew, amendments that reflected the difficulty of preventing fraud, keeping competent managers, and maintaining a sense of common goals. Nevertheless, the basic provision set up by Fan Chung-yen survived several centuries.

1. One pint of rice per day may be granted for each person whom a branch has certified to be one of its members. (These quantities refer to polished rice. If hulled rice is used, the amount should be increased proportionately.)

2. Children of both sexes over five years of age are counted in the total.

3. Female servants may receive rice if they have borne children by men in the lineage and the children are over fifteen or they themselves are over fifty.

4. One bolt of silk for winter clothing may be granted for each individual, except children between five and ten years of age who may receive half a bolt.

5. Each branch may receive a rice ration for a single slave, but not any silk.

6. Every birth, marriage, death, or other change in the number of lineage members must immediately be recorded.

7. Each branch should make a list of those entitled to grain rations. At the end of the month the manager should examine these requests. He must not make any prior arrangements or exceed the stipulated monthly rations. The manager should also keep his own register in which he records the quantity due each branch based on the number of its members. If the manager spends money wastefully or makes advance payments to anyone, the branches have the authority to require him to pay an indemnity.

8. For the expenses of marrying a daughter, thirty strings of cash may be granted, unless the marriage is a second one, in which case twenty strings may be granted.

9. For the expenses of taking a first wife, twenty strings may be granted (but nothing for a second wife).

10. Lineage members who become officials may receive the regular rice and silk grants and the special

grants for weddings and funerals if they are living at home awaiting a post, awaiting selection, or mourning their parents. They may also receive the grants if they leave their families at home while they serve in Szechwan, Kwangtung, or Fukien, or for any other good reason.

11. For the expenses of mourning and funerals in the various branches, if the deceased is a senior member, when mourning begins, a grant of ten strings of cash may be made, and a further fifteen at the time of the burial. For more junior members, the figures are five and ten strings respectively. In the case of low-ranking members or youths under nineteen, seven strings for both expenses; for those under fifteen, three strings; for those under ten, two strings. No grant should be made for deceased children under seven, or slaves or servants.

12. If any relatives through marriage living in the district face dire need or unexpected difficulties, the branches should jointly determine the facts and discuss ways to provide assistance from the income of the Charitable Estate.

13. A stock of rice should be stored by the Charitable Estate from year to year. The monthly rations and the grants of silk for winter clothing should start with the tenth month of 1050. Thereafter, during each year with a good harvest, two years' worth of grain rations should be hulled and stored. If a year of dearth oc-

curs, no grants should be made except for the rice rations. Any surplus over and above the two years' reserve should be used first for funeral and mourning expenses, then marriage expenses. If there is still a remainder, winter clothes may be issued. However, if the surplus is not very large, the priorities should be discussed, and the amount available divided up and granted in equitable proportions. If grants cannot be made to all entitled to them, they should be made first to those who have suffered bereavement, next to those with weddings. In cases where more than one death has occurred at the same time, senior members take precedence over junior ones. Where the relative seniority of those concerned is the same, the grant should be made on the basis of which death or burial took place first. If, after paying out the rations and the allowances for marriages and burials, a surplus still remains, it must not be sold off, but hulled and put into storage for use as rations for three or more years. If there is a danger that the stored grain might go bad, it may be sold off and replaced with fresh rice after the autumn harvest. All members of the branches of the lineage will carefully comply with the above rules.

Tenth month, 1050.
Academician of the Tzu-cheng Hall, Vice-President of the Board of Rites, and Prefect of Hang-chou, Fan. Sealed.

Translated by Patricia Ebrey

27.

The Attractions of the Capital

The two Sung capitals, K'ai-feng and Hang-chou, were not merely administrative centers; they were also flourishing commercial cities. Both were located at centers of communication—K'ai-feng at the juncture of the Yellow River and the Pien Canal, Hang-chou midway between the Yangtze and the seacoast, at the other end of the canal. In these two cities, with their concentration of people and wealth, a distinctly urban style of life evolved. Numerous amenities, including a great variety in food, entertainment, and luxury goods, were available to city residents. The division of labor reached a very high level, with many workers engaged in highly specialized enterprises. Below is a description of the city of Hang-chou written in 1235. At that time the city encompassed seven to eight square miles.

MARKETS

During the morning hours, markets extend from Tranquility Gate of the palace all the way to the north and south sides of the New Boulevard. Here we find pearl, jade, talismans, exotic plants and fruits, seasonal catches from the sea, wild game—all the rarities of the world seem to be gathered here. The food and commodity markets at the Heavenly-View Gate, River Market Place, Central Square, Pa Creek, the end of Superior Lane, Tent Place, and Universal Peace Bridge are all crowded and full of traffic.

In the evening, with the exception of the square in front of the palace, the markets are as busy as during the day. The most attractive one is at Central Square, where all sorts of exquisite artifacts, instruments, containers, and hundreds of varieties of goods are for sale. In other marketplaces, sales, auctions, and exchanges go on constantly. In the wine shops and inns business also thrives. Only after the fourth drum does the city gradually quiet down, but by the fifth drum, court officials already start preparing for audiences and merchants are getting ready for the morning market again. This cycle goes on all year round without respite.

By far the most exciting time of the year is the Lantern Festival. Rows upon rows of businesses and private residences are all richly decorated, and numerous tents are set up for various spectacles and activities. (It is impossible for me to give an exhaustive description here.) During the Lung-hsing reign [A.D. 1163–1164], the Imperial Temple and the Noble Ladies' Quarters were located at Central Square, opposite the present imperial dye and bleach works. Once, after performing the state sacrifice, Emperor Hsiao-tsung [r. 1162–1189] stopped to see the lantern displays. We saw the rows of imperial attendants in front of the curtain of the Emperor's carriage, and the piles of cash that they spent to buy food. They also gave out cash and gifts liberally to the onlookers, some of whom were fortunate enough to get real gold or silver pieces.

Whenever there is an imperial procession or a religious parade, the carriages form a spectacular, long wall, the tip of one touching that of another.

On the lot in front of the wall of the city building, there are always various acting troupes performing, and this usually attracts a large crowd. The same kind of activity is seen in almost any vacant lot, including those at the meat market of the Great Common, the herb market at Charcoal Bridge, the book market at the Orange Grove, the vegetable market on the east side of the city, and the rice market on the north side. There are many more interesting markets, such as the candy center at the Five Buildings, but I cannot name them all.

COMMERCIAL ESTABLISHMENTS

Various businesses are designated by the word "company" (*hang*), which is a taxation category imposed by the government and is used for all businesses dealing in commodities, regardless of their size. Even physicians and fortunetellers are included. Other trades sometimes also borrow the word "company" for their own use, such as liquor company and food company. Some businesses are called "gatherings" (*ho*), such as a flower gathering, fruit gathering, dried-fish gathering. . . . Artisans sometimes call their businesses "workshops" (*tso*), such as comb workshop, belt workshop, gold-and-silver plating workshop. There are some businesses that use unusual names; for example, shops dealing in the "seven treasures" (gold, silver, pearl, amber, etc.) may call themselves curio companies, whereas a bathhouse may be designated a fragrant-water company.

In general, the capital attracts the greatest variety of goods and has the best craftsmen. For instance, the flower company at Superior Lane does a truly excellent job of flower arrangement, and its caps, hairpins, and collars are unsurpassed in craftsmanship. Some of the most famous specialties of the capital are the sweet-bean soup at the Miscellaneous Market, the pickled dates of the Ko family, the thick soup of the Kuang family at Superior Lane, the fruit at the Great Commons marketplace, the cooked meats in front of Eternal Mercy Temple, Sister Sung's fish broth at Penny Pond Gate, the juicy lungs at Flowing Gold Gate, the "lamb rice" of the Chih family at Central Square, the boots of the P'eng family, the fine clothing of the Hsüan family at Southern Commons, the sticky rice pastry of the Chang family, the flutes made by Ku the Fourth, and the Ch'iu family's Tatar whistles at the Great Commons.

WINE SHOPS

Among the various kinds of wine shops, the tea-and-food shops sell not only wine, but also various foods to go with it. However, to get seasonal delicacies not available in these shops, one should go to the inns, for they also have a menu from which one can make selections. The pastry-and-wine shops sell pastries with duckling and goose fillings, various fixings of pig tripe, intestines and blood, fish fat and spawn; but they are rather expensive. The mansion-style inns are either decorated in the same way as officials' mansions or are actually remodeled from such mansions. The garden-style inns are often located in the suburbs, though some are also situated in town. Their decoration is usually an imitation of a studio-garden combination. Among other kinds of wine shops are the straight ones which do not sell food. There are also the small retail wine shops which sell house wine as well as wine from other stores. Instead of the common emblem—a painted branching twig—used by all other winehouses, they have bamboo fences and canvas awnings. To go drinking in such a place is called "hitting the cup," meaning that a person drinks only one cup; it is therefore not the most respectable place and is unfit for polite company.

The "luxuriant inns" have prostitutes residing in them, and the wine chambers are equipped with beds. At the gate of such an inn, on top of the red gardenia lantern, there is always a cover made of bamboo leaves. Rain or shine, this cover is always present, serving as a trademark. In other inns, the girls only keep the guests company. If a guest has other wishes, he has to go to the girl's place. . . .

The emblems of wine shops are a branching twig painted red, crimson curtains with laces of red and gold tones, and a gardenia lantern. It is said that this convention started with the visit of Emperor Kuo (of the Five Dynasties) to the P'an-lou winehouse in Pienching.

The wine chambers are usually named. If the building has several stories, they may be distinguished by the term "mountain." Thus there may be a first mountain, a second mountain, a third mountain, etc. These "mountains" are figurative heights indicating the capacity for wine. For this reason, when you go to a wine shop, refrain from going upstairs if you only intend to order a few drinks and to stay for a short time. If you do not order too many drinks, you can sit downstairs, in the area designated as "tables facing the door and the streets."

After you are seated, the waiter will bring you a few sample delicacies. He will then ask you what you would like to have and in what quantity. Only afterwards will he bring you your order. People who are unfamiliar with this custom often start eating these samples and make themselves the laughingstock of the day.

The expenses incurred on visiting an inn can vary widely. If you order food, but no drinks, it is called "having the lowly soup-and-stuff," and is quite inexpensive. If your order of wine and food falls within the range of 100–5000 cash, it is called a small order. However, if you ask for female company, then it is most likely that the girls will order the most expensive delicacies. You are well advised to appear shrewd and experienced, so as not to be robbed. One trick, for instance, in ordering wines is to give a large order, of say, ten bottles, but open them one by one. In the end, you will probably have used only five or six bottles of the best. You can then return the rest. . . .

RESTAURANTS

Most restaurants here are operated by people from the old capital, like the lamb rice shops which also serve wine. There is an art to ordering dishes: if you wish to fill yourself quickly, then you should first order the heavy items (such as bean soup, rib-and-rice, sticky-rice, etc.) and then the light ones (such as fried gizzards, tripe, and kidneys); if you prefer to enjoy the good taste of the foods before you fill yourself, then order the light dishes first and the heavy ones last.

The so-called Southern style is a misnomer. These restaurants were originally established in the old capital to serve Southerners who were not used to the Northern diet. Now that they *are* in the South, the term Southern style becomes misleading. At any rate, noodles and seafood are the specialty of these restaurants, and each has its own house menu.

There are special food shops such as meat-pie shops and vegetable-noodle shops, but these are not very formal, and therefore you should not invite your guests to eat there. The vegetarian restaurants cater to religious banquets and vegetarian dinners. The Ch'ü-chou rice shops are reputed for steamed rice and home-style food; they are good places to go to eat your fill but not suitable for elegant company.

There are also shops specializing in snacks. Depending on the season, they sell a variety of delicacies from fried meats, pastries, stewed ginger, and soy beans to pickled pig's feet. In the evening, food venders of all sorts parade the streets and alleys, supporting trays on their heads or carrying baskets on a pole, and chanting their trade songs. The residents in the capital are used to them, but visitors from other parts of the country find them a curious breed. . . .

TEAHOUSES

In large teahouses there are usually paintings and calligraphies by famous artists on display. In the old capital, only restaurants had them, to enable their patrons to while away the time as the food was being prepared, but now it is customary for teahouses as well to display paintings and the like.

The teahouses also sell salted soybean soup in the winter and plum-flower wine in the summer. During the Shao-hsing reign [1131–1162], teahouses used to play the plum-flower wine tune and serve tea with a ladle just as in wine shops.

Often many young men gather in teahouses to practice singing or playing musical instruments. To give such amateur performances is called "getting posted."

A "social teahouse" is more of a community gathering place than a mere place that sells tea. Often tea-drinking is but an excuse, and people are rather generous when it comes to the tips.

There is a special kind of teahouse where pimps and gigolos hang out. Another kind is occupied by people from various trades and crafts who use them as places to hire help, buy apprentices, and conduct business. These teahouses are called "trade heads."

"Water teahouses" are in fact pleasure houses, the tea being a cover. Some youths are quite willing to spend their money there, which is called "dry tea money."

Other jargon calls for explanation: A "teakettle carrier" does more than just bring wine and tea to private households; he also carries messages and functions as a social go-between. "Dirty tea" designates the kind of street vagabonds who, in the name of selling tea, actually beg for cash or gifts.

THE FOUR DEPARTMENTS AND SIX OFFICES

For the households of the noble and the wealthy, there are the Four Departments and Six Offices in charge of entertainment. They manage dinner parties and keep related matters in good order. In the commercial areas of the capital, one can also find people who specialize in these matters. Thus, whenever there is occasion for an elaborate party, a middle-class household simply hires these professionals to manage everything.

The Setup Department is responsible for preparing the place for the occasion: setting up tents and awnings, banquet tables and seats; providing screens, embroidered hangings, paintings, calligraphy, and so on. The Kitchen Department is in charge of the design, purchase, and preparation of food. The Tea and Wine Department takes care of the drinking needs of the guests, offering tea and drinks, warming up wines, and opening wine bottles. It is also responsible for ushering guests to their seats and for escorting them out at the end of the feast. The Serving Department specializes in serving food and drinks and in waiting on the guests.

The Fruit Office is in charge of making decorative arrangements of various kinds of fruits, as well as supplying seasonal fruits that go well with wines. The Sweetmeats Office supplies preserved fruits and sweetmeats as appetizers. The Vegetable Office provides pickled and fresh vegetables that please the eye as well as the palate. The Oil and Candle Office is in charge of illumination, performing such duties as setting up candle holders and lanterns, snuffing candles, and lighting incense. The Perfume and Medicine Office is equipped with medicine chests and supplies sachets, exotic perfumes, and herb medicines that help sober up the guests who have had too much to drink. The Decor Office is responsible for hanging up paintings and decorations, designing and displaying flower arrangements, as well as for keeping the banquet hall clean and orderly.

If the professionals of the Four Departments and Six Offices are competent, then both the host and the guests will be much more at ease. On the other hand, if these people should make mistakes, the guests will also understand that it is not the host's fault. After the banquet, compensations and tips should be meted out in the following order: the chef first, the persons in charge of tea and wine next, the entertainers last.

ENTERTAINMENT CENTERS

The entertainment centers commonly called "tiles" are places where people gather and are just as easily dispersed. It is not clear when the term first came into use, but in the old capital the entertainment centers were places where many dissipated people—scholars as well as commoners—gathered, and where many young men were ruined.

In these centers there are schools for musicians offering thirteen different courses, among which the most significant is opera. The old music schools had such divisions as flute department, big-drum department, stick-drum department, clapper department, balloon-guitar department, zither department, dance department, singing department, opera department, and military acts department. Each of these had a department head, above whom were school administrators, disciplinary officers, and masters of ceremonies. All were filled by appointment. The players wore loose robes of purple, scarlet, or green, with yellow aprons. The actors wore headdresses; the other musicians wore ordinary caps. There were also boys' and girls' troupes, as well as a military band; the latter gave rise to the present-day custom of the band of musicians on horseback parading behind the Emperor's carriage. . . .

In each scene of an operatic performance there are four or five performers who first act out a short, well-known piece, which is called the gorgeous piece; then they give a performance of the opera itself, which is called the second piece. . . . The opera is usually based on history and teaches a moral lesson, which may also be political criticism in disguise. . . . A miscellaneous act is a comic scene taken from an operatic performance. In the old capital, the stock characters of a miscellaneous act were the rustic villagers from Shantung or Hopei, who were the funniest country bumpkins in the eyes of the citizens of the capital. . . .

The hundred games used to be the official entertainment of the old capital. Wrestling and fighting are categorized as butting games; there are also displays of different styles of boxing techniques. The experts in kicking games feature in the ritual plucking of the golden rooster at the general pardon after an Emperor's coronation. They can climb high poles, do somersaults, walk on stilts, juggle spears, do the death dance, play with swords, display horsemanship, and so on.

The various skills of the entertainers have their respective high-sounding names. Their acts include: kicking bottles, juggling plates, kicking musical stones, twirling drumsticks, kicking writing brushes, playing ball. There are also performances with trained insects, fish or bears, fireworks, fire shows, water shows, puppet shows, and marksmanship of all kinds.

Puppet shows include string-puppets, cane-top puppets, water-puppets, and flesh-puppets. The stories are usually fictitious and fantastic. Shadow plays originated in the old capital. At first the figures were made with white paper; later they were made of leather and painted various colors. The stories of the shadow plays are pretty much the same as those used by the storytellers; generally speaking, they are a mixture of truth and fiction. The loyal and righteous are given a handsome appearance, whereas the wicked and treacherous are depicted as monstrously ugly—a kind of implicit criticism that is easily understood by the people in the streets. The storytellers can be divided into four groups: those who specialize in social tales, mysteries, and miracle tales; those who deal with military adventures; those who explicate sutras by telling religious tales; and those who relate historical events. . . .

CLUBS

For men of letters, there is a unique West Lake Poetry Society. Its members include both scholars residing in the capital and visiting poets from other parts of the country; over the years, many famous poets have been associated with this society. People interested in verse riddles may join such clubs as South Studio, North Studio, or West Studio, all of which are situated on the right bank of the Che River. People who like sports form various football and archery clubs.

The Upper Indian Temple has a Luminous Society, the members of which are wealthy Buddhists from the city and its suburbs. They donate incense, candles, and cash to help the temple with its expenses. The Tea Society provides free tea for the believers whenever any of the Buddhist temples holds a service. The Dharma Propagation Temple in the city has a Purifying Society, which gathers men on the 17th day and women on the 18th day of each month for preaching and explicating sutras. At the end of each year it also holds a seven-day-and-seven-night service. In the West Lake region, a let-live campaign is launched in the fourth month of each year to return fishermen's catches to the lake. There are also numerous Sutra Societies associated with various temples, which hold rituals on the birthdays of various saints and deities.

Other groups include the Physical Fitness Club, Anglers' Club, Occult Club, Young Girls' Chorus, Exotic Foods Club, Plants and Fruits Club, Antique Collectors' Club, Horse-Lovers' Club, and Refined Music Society.

GARDENS

The gardens within the city limits include Ten-Thousand-Pines Ridge, Garden of Good Views, Eastern Mountains, Plum Pavillion, etc. . . . Outside of the eastern New Gate there are the Eastern Imperial Garden and Five-Willows Imperial Garden. To the west of the city is the Vista Imperial Garden. . . . To the west of the South Mountain Long Bridge there is Revels Imperial Garden; in front of the Pure Mercy Temple there is a Screen-Mountain Imperial Garden; facing the Cloud Summit Tower there is a Pearl Garden. . . . I do not know all the names of the private gardens owned by the noble and the wealthy families. The garden next to Pao Mountain is most famous for its peach blossoms. Other gardens specialize in rare plants. . . .

BOATS

The capital is encircled by a river on the left side and by West Lake on the right; thus the most convenient way to travel is by boat. The boats for hire on West Lake vary greatly in size. Some are fifty feet long and have a capacity of more than one hundred passengers; others are twenty to thirty feet long and can take thirty to fifty passengers. All of them are exquisitely constructed, with carvings on the railings and paintings on the beams. They sail so smoothly that the passengers may forget that they are on water. These boats are for hire in all seasons and never lack patrons. They are also well equipped with everything; a tourist can get on board in the morning, drink wine, and enjoy himself; at dusk he may walk home by following a trail. It is not tiring but is rather expensive. Some wealthy families have their own pleasure boats, and these are even more exquisitely built and more luxuriously fitted out.

Dragon boat competitions are held in spring at the West Lake and in autumn at the Che River. The dragon boats are light and swift and make a grand spectacle. . . . In early and mid-autumn there are swimmers in the Che River, who, brandishing pennants and poles, display the most breath-taking skills. I believe this is a unique attraction of the capital.

SPECIALTY STORES

The commercial area of the capital extends from the old Ch'ing River Market to the Southern Commons on the south and to the border on the north. It includes the Central Square, which is also called the Center of Five Flowers. From the north side of the Five Buildings to South Imperial Boulevard, there are more than one hundred gold, silver, and money exchanges. On the short walls in front of these stores, there are piles of gold, silver, and copper cash: these are called "the money that watches over the store." Around these exchanges there are also numerous gold and silversmiths. The pearl marts are situated between the north side of Cordial Marketplace and Southtown Marketplace. Most deals made here involve over 10,000 cash. A score of pawnshops are scattered in between, all owned by very wealthy people and dealing only in the most valuable objects.

Some famous fabric stores sell exquisite brocade and fine silk which are unsurpassed elsewhere in the country. Along the river, close to the Peaceful Ford Bridge, there are numerous fabric stores, fan shops, and lacquerware and porcelain shops. Most other cities can only boast of one special product; what makes the capital unique is that it gathers goods from all places. Furthermore, because of the large population and busy commercial traffic, there is a demand for everything. There are even shops that deal exclusively in used paper or in feathers, for instance.

WAREHOUSES

In Liu Yung's [ca. 1045] poem on Ch'ien-t'ang, we read that there were about ten thousand families residing here; but that was before the Yüan-feng reign [1078–1085]. Today, having been the "temporary capital" for more than a hundred years, the city has over a million households. The suburbs extend to the south, west, and north; all are densely populated and prosperous in commerce as well as in agriculture. The size of the suburbs is comparable to a small county or prefecture, and it takes several days to travel through them. This again reflects the prosperity of the capital.

In the middle of the city, enclosed by the Northern Pass Dam, is White Ocean Lake. Its water spreads over several tens of *li*. Wealthy families have built scores of warehouse complexes along this waterfront. Each of these consists of several hundred to over a thousand rooms for the storage needs of the various businesses in the capital and of traveling merchants. Because these warehouses are surrounded by water, they are not endangered by fires or thieves, and therefore they offer a special convenience. In other commercial centers such as Sha-shih and Huang-ch'ih of T'ai-p'ing prefecture there are no such facilities.

HUSTLERS

These are the same breed of people as the retainers of Prince Meng-ch'ang.* They have no regular profession, but live off of other people by providing trivial services.

Some of these hustlers are students who failed to achieve any literary distinction. Though able to read and write, and play musical instruments and chess, they are not highly skilled in any art. They end up being a kind of guide for young men from wealthy families, accompanying them in their pleasure-seeking activities. Some also serve as guides or assistants to officials on business from other parts of the country. The lowliest of these people actually engage themselves in writing and delivering invitation cards and the like for brothels.

There are others who make their living entertaining at private parties. In the past some of these people were quite well versed in activities such as play-acting, jesting, playing musical instruments, juggling, singing, reciting poems, playing wine games, swimming, and boxing. Some who specialize in training birds are called leisure practitioners. They train hawks, eagles, pigeons, doves, quail, and cocks for fighting and gambling.

There are also professional go-betweens, nick-named "water-treaders," whose principal targets are pleasure houses, where they flatter the wealthy young patrons, run errands for them, and help make business deals. Some gather at brothels or scenic attractions and accost the visitors. They beg for donations for "religious purposes," but in fact use the money to make a living for themselves and their families. If you pay attention to them, they will become greedy; if you ignore them, they will force themselves on you and will not stop until you give in. It requires art to deal with these people appropriately.

THE THREE TEACHINGS

There are civil and military schools inside as well as outside the capital. Besides lineage schools, capital schools, and county schools, there are at least one or two village schools, family schools, private studios, or learning centers in every neighborhood. Often the

* A prince of the state of Ch'i in the third century B.C. famous for attracting retainers.

students' recitation of texts from one school is echoed by that of another. In the years when the imperial examinations are held, the students from the capital sometimes do quite well.

Buddhist temples are numerous. There are around one hundred Zen monasteries (such as the Yin Spirit and Great Filial Piety monasteries) and a similar number of the Vinaya Sect temples (such as the Bright Blessings and Spirit of Longevity temples) and seminaries (such as the Great Dharma Propagation, Grove of Wisdom, and Source of Wisdom seminaries). There are also convents, religious societies, and various places of worship. Whenever a big monastery holds a service, these small groups also attend. Some of the masters are highly accomplished.

Taoist worship is held in the Imperial Great Unity Temple, the Eternal Happiness Temple, and various other temples, studios, and halls. The Taoist temples house monks who have abandoned the mundane world, as well as masters from all parts of the country. There have been frequent reports of miracles and epiphanies of divine beings, which other people have recorded.

Translated by Clara Yu

28.

The Mutual Responsibility System

Periodically through Chinese history, the government tried to organize people down to the village level to make them easier to rule. One recurrent method was to group people into units of five or ten households, then group five or ten of these units into a superior unit, and so on, in successive levels up to the county (hsien). In 1070 the statesman Wang An-shih (1021–1086), as one of his many reforms, introduced the Mutual Responsibility System (pao-chia). Modeled on earlier systems, ten households formed a pao, with a head chosen from among the household heads of the pao. Five pao formed a large pao, also with a head, and ten large pao formed a general pao. The duties of these various pao were supposed to be restricted to detecting and reporting criminals, but other duties, involving tax collection and military service, tended to be added from time to time.

Below is a notice about the functioning of the Mutual Responsibility System posted by Chen Te-hsiu (1178–1235) while he was Magistrate of a county in Fukien province. From it we can infer some of the people's uneasiness about the system as well as some of the practical difficulties the government faced in trying to enforce it. This notice is also evidence of the kind of knowledge ordinary people would have had about government policies, since certainly few of them ever read the formal regulations or proclamations.

NOTICE ABOUT THE MUTUAL RESPONSIBILITY SYSTEM IN P'U–CH'ENG

In ancient times people regarded an obligation toward a neighbor as a significant matter. They considered themselves friends whether they were in the village or elsewhere. They assisted each other in the duties of guarding their villages and they supported each other in times of illness. Our local units of today are actually derived from such ancient practices, but now very few people realize the meaning of such organizations, and neighbors often treat each other like strangers.

Recently the Mutual Responsibility System (*pao-chia*) has been reactivated by the government. This is something which pleases me very much, for not only can the Mutual Responsibility System provide us with protection against the unexpected, but it will promote the ancient practice of neighborly relationships among people who live in close proximity. Because of uncertainties as to how to make the division into geographical units, this system has not yet been put into effect. Nevertheless, people in the various communities have already expressed suspicion about the system out of fear that it will mean obligatory labor. I have listened attentively to the arguments of the elders and would like to point out that the practice of the Mutual Responsibility System will be limited primarily to dealing with thefts and negligence. For instance, if one family is robbed, it usually cannot catch the thief; whereas when the whole community is engaged in the search, the thief will have no place to hide. If a house is on fire and the family cannot extinguish it, the neighbors will offer their assistance, and the fire will certainly be put out. Military activities such as fighting against rebels from other parts of the nation will be the responsibility of the militia forces, the recruited soldiers, and the national guard; our people will not be required to perform such duties.

Generally, only one man per family will be required to enlist. Poor scholars with no servants and single men who are old or physically unfit are exempt from duty. Every five days there will be a roll call, just to keep a rough count of the number of people involved. Sometimes there will be a call to patrol the region, but usually it will not be necessary. These are my plans, but up to now most of our citizens have not understood them and thus have been skeptical of the program. They fail to see that the Mutual Responsibility System is designed to protect them, not disturb them, and that they have nothing to be apprehensive about. I have lived here six years, and all the people in this city are my neighbors. I have always wanted to meet each one of you, yet there never seemed to be an opportune occasion. I would like to hold a general assembly now, but my resources do not allow it. I will, however, make a joint sacrifice with one hundred neighboring families at our local temple in the middle of this month. I will provide all the offerings which will, after the ceremony, be shared by everyone present—scholars, farmers, artisans, or merchants—without discrimination. This will be in accord with the ancient principle of community harmony. As to the seating, however, there will be assigned areas for each group.

On that day I will explain to you the meaning of a friendly neighborhood as well as the purpose of the Mutual Responsibility System to dispel your doubts. I will have the gathering announced in all areas under my administration and have this notice posted on doors so that everyone will be informed of it.

Translated by Clara Yu

29.

On Farming

A major factor in allowing the population of Sung China to reach 100 million was the continued expansion of settlement in the South and the development of forms of intensive wet-field rice cultivation. This increase in wet-field cultivation changed the nature of agricultural work for a large share of China's peasants. Growing two or sometimes even three successive crops on the same field came to be common, part of a general tendency toward applying more time, labor, and fertilizer to smaller pieces of land. Because these techniques were so productive, the government often took steps to encourage their adoption, even distributing illustrated guides.

Below are selections from a treatise on farming written by Ch'en P'u in 1149. It discusses both wet-field cultivation and methods used for vegetables and other crops. This treatise was aimed at those actively engaged in agriculture and enjoyed wide circulation for several centuries. This and other popular texts on agriculture are the best sources we have for what peasants thought of their daily work.

FINANCE AND LABOR

All those who engage in business should do so in accordance with their own capacity. They should refrain from careless investment and excessive greed, lest in the end they achieve nothing. The *Tso Chronicle* says, "Profit comes from a little; confusion comes from a lot." In the farming business, which is the most difficult business to manage, how can you afford not to calculate your financial and labor capacities carefully? Only when you are certain that you have sufficient funds and labor to assure success should you launch an enterprise. Anyone who covets more than he can manage is likely to fall into carelessness and irresponsibility; under such conditions, he cannot reap even one or two out of every ten portions, and success will certainly elude him. Thus, to procure more land is to increase trouble, not profit.

On the other hand, anyone who plans carefully, begins with good methods, and continues in the same way can reasonably expect success and does not have to rely on luck. The proverb says, "Owning a great deal of emptiness is less desirable than reaping from a narrow patch of land." Too true! I have the following example to prove my point. In ancient times there was a great archer, P'u Ch'ieh, who was able to draw a delicate bow and string two orioles on one arrow, high in the clouds. The reason he could achieve such dexterity in aiming was that he had more strength than needed to draw the bow. If the bow had been heavier than he could handle, he would have trembled and staggered under its weight; then how could he have gotten his game? By extension, for the farmer who is engaged in the management of fields, the secret lies not in expanding the farmland, but in balancing finance and labor. If the farmer can achieve that, he can expect prosperity and abundance.

TOPOGRAPHY

Concerning mountains, rivers, plateaus, lakes, and swamps, their altitudes differ and so their temperatures and degrees of fertility do also. Generally speaking, high lands are cold, their springs chilly, their soil cool. When the *Tso Chronicle* says, "In the high mountains there is more winter," it refers to the constant windy cold. Also, these areas are more prone to droughts. On the other hand, low lands are usually fertile but prone to flooding. Thus, different methods of land management are required for different terrain.

In the case of high land, choose a spot where water can converge and dig a reservoir of appropriate size. (For every ten *mou* of land, two to three *mou* should be set aside for the reservoir.) In late spring and early summer when rainfall is frequent, strengthen the embankments and deepen and widen the reservoir so that it will have enough space to contain the water. On the embankments plant mulberry and pomegranate trees on which cows can be tethered. The cows will be comfortable under the shade of the trees; the embankments will be strengthened because the cows constantly tread on them; and the mulberry trees will grow beautifully because of the nourishing water. Whenever there is a drought, the water in the reservoir can be released for irrigation, and whenever there is heavy rainfall, the crops will not be harmed by floods.

As to low lands, because they are easily flooded, you must study their topography and build high, wide embankments surrounding the area most likely to be inundated. On the slopes of the embankments vegetables, hemp, wheat, millet, and beans can be planted. On either side you can also plant mulberry trees and raise cows. Because of convenient water and grass, the cows can be successfully raised with little effort.

For lakes and marshy swamps, use the "rape-turnip soil" system. First, bind logs together to form a base for the field. Let the base float on water but remain tied to land. Then lay the "rape-turnip soil" on the wooden platform and plant there. As the platform floats on water, it rises and falls with the water level, so the crops are never lost to floods.

PLOWING

Early and late plowing both have their advantages. For the early rice crop, as soon as the reaping is completed, immediately plow the fields and expose the stalks to glaring sunlight. Then add manure and bury the stalks to nourish the soil. Next, plant beans, wheat, and vegetables to ripen and fertilize the soil so

as to minimize the next year's labor. In addition, when the harvest is good, these extra crops can add to the yearly income. For late crops, however, do not plow until spring. Because the rice stalks are soft but tough, it is necessary to wait until they have fully decayed to plow satisfactorily.

In the mountains, plateaus, and wet areas, it is usually cold. The fields here should be deeply plowed and soaked with water released from reservoirs. Throughout the winter, the water will be absorbed, and the snow and frost will freeze the soil so that it will become brittle and crumbly. At the beginning of spring, spread the fields with decayed weeds and leaves and then burn them, so that the soil will become warm enough for the seeds to sprout. In this way, cold as the freezing springs may be, they cannot harm the crop. If you fail to treat the soil this way, then the arteries of the fields, being soaked constantly by freezing springs, will be cold, and the crop will be poor.

When it is time to sow the seeds, sprinkle lime in the wet soil to root out harmful insect larvae.

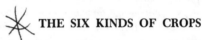 ## THE SIX KINDS OF CROPS

There is an order to the planting of different crops. Anyone who knows the right timing and follows the order can cultivate one thing after another, and use one to assist the others. Then there will not be a day without planting, nor a month without harvest, and money will be coming in throughout the year. How can there then be any worry about cold, hunger, or lack of funds?

Plant the nettle-hemp in the first month. Apply manure in intervals of ten days and by the fifth or sixth month it will be time for reaping. The women should take charge of knotting and spinning cloth out of the hemp.

Plant millet in the second month. It is necessary to sow the seeds sparsely and then roll cart wheels over the soil to firm it up; this will make the millet grow luxuriantly, its stalks long and its grains full. In the seventh month the millet will be harvested, easing any temporary financial difficulties.

There are two crops of oil hemp. The early crop is planted in the third month. Rake the field to spread out the seedlings. Repeat the raking process three times a month and the hemp will grow well. It can be harvested in the seventh or the eighth month.

In the fourth month plant beans. Rake as with hemp. They will be ripe by the seventh month.

In mid-fifth month plant the late oil-hemp. Proceed as with the early crop. The ninth month will be reaping time.

After the 7th day of the seventh month, plant radishes and cabbage.

In the eighth month, before the autumn sacrifice to the god of the earth, wheat can be planted. It is advisable to apply manure and remove weeds frequently. When wheat grows from the autumn through the spring sacrifices to the god of the earth, the harvest will double and the grains will be full and solid.

The *Book of Poetry* says, "The tenth month is the time to harvest crops." You will have a large variety of crops, including millet, rice, beans, hemp, and wheat and will lack nothing needed through the year. Will you ever be concerned for want of resources?

HOUSING

The ancient kings who reigned over subjects in all four directions and took advantage of the earth in the right seasons must have had good principles. They decreed that five *mou* of land should be set aside for housing, out of which two and a half *mou* were for a cottage erected in the center of the fields.

In the period of plowing and sowing, move into this cottage to facilitate management and provide supplies for the farm workers. At the same time start a garden and plant vegetables. Along the walls, mulberry trees can be planted for the breeding of silkworms. In this manner you will live up to the system exemplified by the ancients.

When the ninth month has come, transform the vegetable garden into a harvest processing area. In the tenth month, when the harvest is done and the year's work finished, you can rest as compensation for your labor of plowing and sowing in the spring. Now move the whole family, both old and young, back to the house. For if you stay too long in the cottage in the fields, your house will become dilapidated as a result of neglect.

FERTILIZER

At the side of the farm house, erect a compost hut. Make the eaves low to prevent the wind and rain from entering it, for when the compost is exposed to the moon and the stars, it will lose its fertility. In this hut, dig a deep pit and line it with bricks to prevent leakage. Collect waste, ashes, chaff, broken stalks, and fallen leaves and burn them in the pit; then pour manure over them to make them fertile. In this way considerable quantities of compost are acquired over time. Then, whenever sowing is to be done, sieve and discard stones and tiles, mix the fine compost with the seeds, and plant them sparsely in pinches. When the seedlings have grown tall, again spinkle the compost and bank it up against the roots. These methods will ensure a double yield.

Some people say that when the soil is exhausted, grass and trees will not grow; that when the *ch'i* [material force] is weak, all living things will be stunted; and that after three to five years of continuous planting, the soil of any field will be exhausted. This theory is erroneous because it fails to recognize one factor: by adding new, fertile soil, enriched with compost, the land can be reinforced in strength. If this is so, where can the alleged exhaustion come from?

WEEDING

The *Book of Poetry* says, "Root out the weeds. Where the weeds decay, there the grains will grow luxuriantly." The author of the *Record of Ritual* also remarks, "The months of mid-summer are advantageous for weeding. Weeds can fertilize the fields and improve the land." Modern farmers, ignorant of these principles, throw the weeds away. They do not know that, if mixed with soil and buried deep under the roots of rice seedlings, the weeds will eventually decay and the soil will be enriched; the harvest, as a result, will be abundant and of superior quality.

There is method to weeding. In the Chou dynasty, Minister T'i, who was in charge of weeding, ruled that, "In the spring the weeds begin to sprout and grow, and in the summer one has to go and cut them down daily." This is to say, in the summer the weeds grow easily, therefore one should labor every day to curb their growth. "In the autumn one should hoe them with measure." This means chopping off the seeds so that they will not reach the soil. "In winter one should go and plow the fields daily." That is because the crops have now been reaped, and plowing through the roots of the weeds will expose them to snow and frost, so that they decay and not revive the next year. Also, they can serve as fertilizer for the soil.

CONCENTRATION

If something is thought out carefully, it will succeed; if not, it will fail; this is a universal truth. It is very rare that a person works and yet gains nothing. On the other hand, there is never any harm in trying too hard.

In farming it is especially appropriate to be concerned about what you are doing. Mencius said, "Will a farmer discard his plow when he leaves his land?" Ordinary people will become idle if they have leisure and prosperity. Only those who love farming, who behave in harmony with it, who take pleasure in talking about it and think about it all the time will manage it without a moment's negligence. For these people a day's work results in a day's gain, a year's work in a year's gain. How can they escape affluence?

As to those with many interests who cannot concentrate on any one and who are incapable of being meticulous, even if they should come by some profit, they will soon lose it. For they will never understand that the transformation of the small into the big is the result of persistent effort.

To indulge in pleasure and discard work whenever the chance arises and to meet matters only when they become urgent is never the right way of doing things. Generally speaking, ordinary people take pride in having the prosperity to indulge in temporary leisure. If there should be a man who remains diligent in prosperity, everyone else will mark him as a misfit, so great is their lack of understanding!

Translated by Clara Yu

30.

A Schedule for Learning

The behavior and outlook of members of the upper class cannot be adequately understood without some apprecia-tion of the experiences they went through while students. Elementary instruction in reading and writing might re-quire only three or four years, but gaining mastery of the classical texts and sufficient literary skills to be able to take the civil service examinations was a long process, continuing from early childhood through the late teens or early twenties. The hours spent at school or with tutors were intended to develop not only young men's intellectual skills, but also their manners and above all their character.

Beginning in the late Sung period, education was strongly influenced by the Neo-Confucian teachings of Chu Hsi (1130–1200) and his followers. A Schedule for Learning by Ch'eng Tuan-li (d. 1345) is an example of a Neo-Confucian treatise on education. This book, much of which consists of judicious quotation from earlier writers, was composed for the use of Ch'eng's own students. It proved highly popular, and the Ministry of Education during the Yüan dynasty had copies of it sent to teachers in all prefectures. Below are three pieces from the first chapter: Ch'eng's preface, the rules for a local school established by two disciples of Chu Hsi during the Southern Sung, and a memorial to the throne on the principles of education written by Chu Hsi himself.

PREFACE

Nowadays, fathers and older brothers who wish to benefit their youngsters give them an education and yet hardly two or three out of every ten of our youths actually achieve anything academically. This is not solely the fault of the youngsters and their teachers; the elders, for their lack of foresight, should also share the blame. Before the youngsters have studied and understood the nature of things, they are forced by their elders to compose essays. The teachers, though aware of the danger of such a practice, nevertheless wish to display their own talents; they are therefore willing to comply with such requests. In this way, the sequence of the learning process is confused. Instead of attaining their goals by a shortcut, the youngsters end up not getting anywhere at all. Not only are their writings worthless, but they usually do not even know

one book thoroughly. Months and years go by; when they finally realize their mistakes and begin to regret them, they have become too old. Furthermore, when incorrect methods are used in the beginning, various wrong ideas are likely to stick because of the impor-tance of first impressions. This in turn causes the students to wander on the periphery of true learning all their lives, ignorant of their own mistakes.

The sequence of teaching practiced by Confucius was as follows: first he made the students concentrate their minds on the Way; then he taught them virtues; then he made them act in accordance with the princi-ple of humanity. Only after these principles had been incorporated in their daily lives did the students begin to study. In the *Ritual of Chou* the Grand Educator listed the six arts after the six virtues and six model behaviors, which clearly indicates the order of significance. Our present system of selecting govern-

113

ment officials still regards personal virtue as the first criterion; next comes knowledge of the classics and the ability to govern, with writing ability as the last consideration. This is a very reasonable system. The examinations on the classics, furthermore, are based on the teachings of Master Chu Hsi, combining study of philosophy with advancement in officialdom, much to the benefit of those who devote themselves to the Way. This is what the civil service examinations of the Han, T'ang, and Sung dynasties lacked, and therefore scholars are now offered a rare opportunity. Unfortunately, our students fail to take advantage of this system.

Our students try to follow the teachings of Master Chu in their study of the classics, yet they are ignorant of his method of study. Because they have no method, they tend to use flowery language to promote themselves. During the period when the teachings of Master Ch'eng flourished, Hu Wen-ting lamented the wordiness of most people's writing. I fear that the same trend is returning in our time. To correct the situation, I have compiled a "Schedule for Learning," which I would like to share with my friends. This work is based on the selection of Master Chu's method of study compiled by Fu Han-ch'ing. I have also included other helpful theories by scholars in earlier eras.

In my humble opinion, if we wish to study the classics, to understand the nature of things, to be familiar with all political theories, to investigate our institutions, to be well versed in everthing ancient and modern, to wield language at will, and finally, to popularize our discoveries and contributions throughout the entire nation, we should follow this schedule for learning. For it is the purpose of this work to differentiate between the essential and the trivial and to retain a proper order of progress. In this manner we will not forget what we have learned thoroughly, and we will review and reflect daily on what has not yet been fully digested until it becomes a part of ourselves. Eventually, mind and reason will become one, and a profound tranquility will be achieved amidst constant changes and movements. There will be a convergence of the self and the Way, and virtues will be reflected naturally in our discourse and writings, which will become models for our contemporaries as well as for posterity. Our method is thus not to be compared with the ordinary methods of studying one narrow subject.

Written by Ch'eng Tuan-li, in the eighth month,

1315, at the Academy for Establishing Virtue in Ch'ih-chou.

SCHOOL REGULATIONS ESTABLISHED BY MASTERS CH'ENG AND TUNG

All students of this school must observe closely the following regulations.

1. *Ceremonies held on the 1st and 15th of every month.* At daybreak, the student on duty for that day will sound his clappers. At the first round of the clappers, you should rise, wash your face, comb your hair, and put on proper clothing. By the second round of the clappers, you should be dressed either in ceremonial robes or in summer robes and gather in the main hall. The teachers will then lead you to the image of Confucius, to which you will bow twice. After the incense has been lit, you will make two more bows.

Afterwards, the teachers walk over to the southwestern corner, and you line up in order of your ages in the northeast. Then you pay respect to the teachers by making two bows to them, while the teachers accept the salutation, standing erect. An older student then comes forward and delivers a short speech; this is followed by two more bows to the teachers. Afterwards, the teachers retire into a room, and you form a circle and bow to each other twice. When this is done, you go to your seats.

2. *Daily salutations held in the morning and in the evening.* On ordinary days, the student on duty sounds the clappers as described above. At the second round of the clappers you will enter the hall and line up to wait for the teachers to come out. Then the teachers and you bow to each other with hands folded in front. Next, you divide into two groups and bow to each other, after which you begin your daily studies.

At night, before bedtime, the clappers are sounded again. You must all gather to repeat the same ceremony as in the morning.

Whenever there is an assembly of students, such as at a group lecture, a dinner, or a tea, the salutations are the same as just described. For a lecture, you should wear ceremonial robes or summer robes. For all other occasions you may dress less formally.

3. *Daily behavior.* You should have a defined living area. When in a group you will be seated according to your ages. When sitting, you must straighten your

backs and sit squarely in the chair. You should not squat, lean to one side, cross your legs, or dangle your feet. At night, you should always wait for the elders to go to bed first. After they are in bed, you should keep quiet. Also, you should not sleep during the day.

4. *Gait and posture.* You should walk slowly. When standing, keep your hands folded in front. Never walk or stand in front of an elder. Never turn your back on those who are your superiors in age or status. Do not step on doorsills. Do not limp. Do not lean on anything.

5. *Looking and listening.* Do not gape. Do not eavesdrop.

6. *Discourse.* Statements should always be verifiable. Keep your promises. Your manners should be serious. Do not be boisterous or playful. Do not gossip about your neighbors. Do not engage in conversations about vulgar matters.

7. *Appearance.* Be dignified and serious. Do not be disobedient. Do not be rough or rude. Do not be vicious or proud. Do not reveal your joy or anger.

8. *Attire.* Do not wear unusual or extravagant clothing. Yet do not go to the other extreme and appear in clothes that are ragged, dirty, or in bad taste. Even in your private quarters you should never expose your body or take off your cap. Even in the hottest days of summer you should not take off your socks or shoes at will.

9. *Eating.* Do not fill yourself. Do not seek fancy foods. Eat at regular hours. Do not be discontent with coarse fare. Never drink unless on a holiday or unless you are ordered to do so by your elders. Never drink more than three cups or get drunk.

10. *Travel.* Unless you are called upon by your elders, ordered to run errands by your teachers, or faced by a personal emergency, you are not allowed to leave the campus at will. Before your departure and after your return you should report to your teacher. You must not change your reported destination, and you must return by the set time.

11. *Reading.* You should concentrate on your book and keep a dignified appearance. You should count the number of times you read an assigned piece. If, upon completion of the assigned number, you still have not memorized the piece, you should continue until you are able to recite it. On the other hand, if you have memorized the piece quickly, you should still go on to complete the assigned number of readings.

Only after a book has been thoroughly learned should you go on to another. Do not read too many things on a superficial level. Do not attempt to memorize a piece without understanding it. Read only those books which expound virtues. Do not look into useless writings.

12. *Writing.* Do not scribble. Do not write slanted or sloppy characters.

13. *Keep your desk tidy.* The assigned seats should be kept in order. Your study area should be simple but tidy. All book chests and clothing trunks should be locked up carefully.

14. *Keep the lecture halls and private rooms clean.* Each day one student is on duty. After sounding the second round of the clappers, he should sprinkle water on the floor of the lecture hall. Then, after an appropriate wait, he should sweep the floor and wipe the desks. The other cleaning jobs should be assigned to the pages. Whenever there is cleaning to be done, they should be ordered to do it, regardless of the time of the day.

15. *Terms of address.* You should address those who are twice your age as "elder," those who are ten years older than you as "older brothers," and those who are about your age by their polite names. Never address one another as "you." The same rules should be followed in letter writing.

16. *Visits.* The following rules should be observed when a guest requests to visit the school. After the teacher is seated and the student on duty has sounded the clappers, all students, properly dressed, enter the lecture hall. After the morning salutation, the students remain standing; only when the teacher orders them to retire may they leave. If the guest should wish to speak to a student privately, he should, after seeing the teacher, approach the student at his seat. If the student finds the visitor incompatible, he is not obliged to be congenial.

17. *Recreation.* There are rules for the playing of musical instruments, for archery, as well as for other games. You should seek recreation only at the right time. Gambling and chess games are lowly pastimes and should be avoided by our students.

18. *Servants.* Select those who are prudent, honest, and hardworking. Treat them with dignity and forbearance. When they make mistakes, scold them or report to the teacher. If they do not improve after being punished, report to the teacher to have them discharged. A student should not expel his page at will.

If you can follow the above regulations closely, you are approaching the true realm of virtue.

MEMORIAL BY MASTER CHU

Of all the methods of learning, the first is to explore the basic principle of things. To get at the basic principle of things, one must study. The best way to study is to proceed slowly and in sequence, so as to learn everything well. In order to learn everything well, one must be serious-minded and able to concentrate. These are the unchanging principles of study.

There is a principle for everything under the sun: there is a principle behind the relationship between an Emperor and his subjects, between a father and his son, between brothers, between friends, and between man and wife. Even in such trivial matters as entering and leaving a house, rising in the morning and going to bed at night, dealing with people and conducting daily affairs, there are set principles. Once we have explored the basic principles of things, we will understand all phenomena as well as the reasons behind them. There no longer will be doubts in our minds. We will naturally follow good and reject evil. Such are the reasons why learning should begin with the exploration of the true principles of things.

There are many theories about the principles of things in our world, some simple, others subtle, some clear, others obscure. Yet only the ancient sages were able to formulate a constant, eternal theory of the world, and their words and deeds have become the model for the ages. If we follow the teachings of these ancient sages, we can become superior men; if not, we will become ignorant fellows. We are inspired by the superior men who govern the realm within the four seas; we are frightened by the ignorant ones who lose their lives. All these deeds and results are recorded in the classics, historical writings, and memorials to the throne. A student who wishes to comprehend the basic truth of things yet fails to study these materials might as well place himself in front of a wall—he will not get anywhere. This is why I say that study is the only key to the comprehension of the principles of the world.

People who dislike studying are often indolent, careless, and without perseverance. On the other hand, those who like studying often tend to be too ambitious with regard to volume and range. The latter, barely having begun a subject, are already eager to probe into its ultimate meaning; before they have thoroughly understood one work, they already are anxious to start another. For this reason, they are busy studying all the time yet always feel hurried and unsettled, as if they were chasing or being chased by something. They can never achieve the serenity of leisure and confidence, nor can they feel contented. Furthermore, they are never able to retain a prolonged interest in learning. Consequently, they are essentially no different from those who are indolent, careless, or without perseverance. This is what Confucius meant when he said, "Speeding will not get you to your destination," and what Mencius meant when he said, "One who advances too fast will retreat just as quickly."

If we take care to avoid these pitfalls, correct our study habits, and concentrate on one subject at a time, eventually all the works we have studied will begin to make sense in a larger context, in the same way that all the blood vessels are connected in a complicated system. Gradually, we will become naturally involved in our studies, and our minds will become one with the principle of things. Then to follow good and avoid evil will become the most natural course. Such a gradual process of acquiring essential knowledge is the ideal method for learning.

The comprehension of essential knowledge depends on the mind. The mind is the most abstract, most mysterious, most delicate, and most unpredictable of all things. It is always the master of a person, for everything depends on it, and it cannot be absent for even a second. Once a person's mind wanders beyond his body, he will no longer have control over himself. Even in movements and perception he will not be the master of himself, let alone in the comprehension of the teachings of ancient sages or in the investigation of the true nature of the myriad things. Therefore Confucius said, "If a gentleman is not serious-minded, he will not inspire awe and his learnings will not be solid." And Mencius said, "There is no principle in learning other than the freeing of the mind." If a person can really concentrate his mind on learning and observation and not be distracted by various desires and temptations, there will be no obstacles to his comprehension of the nature of things, nor any impropriety in his contacts with people. This is why concentration is the basis of learning. I, your humble subject, have tried these principles in the course of my own studies and found them most effective. I believe that even if the ancient sages should return to life, they would have no better methods for educating people. I believe these principles are fit even for the education of Kings and Emperors.

Translated by Clara Yu

31.

Kuo Pi's Diary

The life of upper-class men involved not only study and official service but also refined pursuits such as collecting antiques or old books and cultivation of the arts—especially poetry-writing, calligraphy, or painting. For many individuals these interests totally overshadowed any philosophical, political, or economic concerns; others usually sober-minded found in them occasional outlets for creative activity and aesthetic pleasure. A large share of the informal social life of upper-class men was oriented around these refined pastimes, as they gathered to compose or criticize poetry, to view one another's treasures, or to patronize young talents.

The diary of Kuo Pi, from which sixteen days are given below, illustrates the kind of relationships that existed between poetry, painting, calligraphy, and connoisseurship, and shows something of their place in the social and cultural life of a group of upper-class men. Kuo Pi was a scholar and artist of the early-fourteenth century who painted landscapes and bamboo and was noted for his calligraphy. (About a half dozen of his paintings have been preserved until today.) Diary writing does not seem to have been practiced to any appreciable extent before the Sung, and for the next several centuries most diaries, like Kuo Pi's, were records of trips.

THE SIXTH MONTH, 1309

12th day

Staying at Hsing-hua. Mr. Chan Te-jun invited me for dinner. The guests were the same as yesterday except for Kung Tzu-fang. Tzu-fang is the nephew of Tzu-chung, and lives in Kao-yu. After dinner, I accompanied the others to Ultimate Truth Taoist Monastery, where we sat under four catalpa trees to catch some breeze. I wrote twenty wine poems for Chao Po-ch'ien.

13th day

I painted a picture of a carved stone for Mr. Chan. The stone was less than one foot long and six or seven inches high. Its shape was very unusual and yet no trace of a chisel could be detected. It was as though it had been carved by fairies. When I finished painting

the stone, I asked Mr. Wang, the painter, to come see it. Then with my coconut cup I started drinking, and by noon I was already drunk. Yesterday I went with Kung Tzu-fang, Tsang Tzu-hsüan, and Hsü Kuei-yen to visit Ching-kung at the county school. There we ran into Mr. Chao and Mr. Huang. All of us sat on the ground and enjoyed a chicken and a jug of wine. When finished with the wine, we went our separate ways.

14th day

Staying at Hsing-hua. Liu Chü-ch'uan's newly made wine had just matured; its taste was pure and its flavor unique. In the morning he brought over a pot, and we enjoyed several cups with Mr. Chan. At noon Liu barbecued two birds, and we drank some wine together. The guests included me, Huang Chung-wen, Li Ching-kung and others. After the wine, Hu

Tzu-chen's brother-in-law, Tsang Tzu-hsüan, hired a small boat and invited me, Kung Tzu-fang, and Hsü Sheng-chih to visit the Lotus Flower Swamp. Chao Po-ch'ien also came along. After a little while Mr. Chan, his son, and Liu Chü-ch'uan also joined us in another small boat. After lingering for some time, we went to Righteous Road Monastery. The master in the monastery prepared wine for us, but I cannot say very much for its taste. Next we went back to the boats and picked lotus seeds. By this time the sun was setting and a breeze began to blow. We made cups out of lotus leaves and drank wine from them. Those who could not hold their liquor all got drunk. Not until the moon had risen on the horizon did we return. It was a very merry day, except for the mosquitoes—they somehow spoiled the fun.

15th day

Staying at the Chan household at Hsing-hua. County Assistant An Tou and Warden Hsing came over. Mr. Chan prepared wine for them and served melons. At night I sat with Mr. Chan on the bridge. With a cool breeze blowing and the moon shining, we drank some wine and enjoyed the melons.

16th day

I made a calligraphy scroll for Mr. Chan. At noon I drank wine.

17th day

Staying at Hsing-hua. It has been extremely hot every night. I perspired so much, I felt I had been rained on. The mosquitoes in Hsing-hua are big and ferocious. When you sit unsheltered, they swarm over to attack, and there are so many of them that you feel as if sand had been thrown at you. In the evening, Chü-ch'uan invited me to enjoy the cool breeze at the county school. Later I had a few cups of wine with Li, Tsang, and Huang.

18th day

Staying at Hsing-hua. Hu Tzu-chen, Li Ching-kung, Wang Shih-chung, and I went to the county school and visited Huang Chung-wen in his office. The evening was unbearably hot. Mr. Chan took a row-boat out onto the lake to get some cool air; yet he too was bothered by the mosquitoes and came back disappointed. That day, Mr. Chan showed us an ancient bronze vessel with a horse on top and two lines of text

under it: "Excellent for the elders, suitable for the young," and "Worthy elders—good sons and grandsons." When one strikes the bronze, it makes a sound.

19th day

Had breakfast at Hu Tzu-chen's. It rained in the evening, then became cooler.

20th day

Painted a picture of orchids for Wang Shih-chung. I went to Original Goodness Monastery with Kung Tzu-fang and Tsang Tzu-hsüan to get some cool air. Next we stopped at Four Sages Taoist Monastery. Kung and Tsang invited Hsü Tung-hsi, Hsü Sheng-chih, and me, then all five of us went to visit Liu Tung-an. We pooled our money to buy some wine and enjoyed the fragrance of the lotus flowers, not returning until dark. Later I went to the county seat and in the Great Hall I found a plaque which read: "Hall of Admiration for Fan." They say the plaque was made because Fan Wen-cheng had once been Magistrate here.* In the evening I talked Te-jun into settling some business.

21st day

Staying at the Chan residence at Hsing-hua. Liu Chü-ch'uan came and had lunch with me. Kung Tzu-fang and Hsü Sheng-chih bought some paper and asked me to do calligraphy and bamboo drawings for them.

22nd day

I gave my writings to Chan Te-jun. For my farewell dinner he had a goose cooked. The guests included Hu Tso-fang and me. Warden Hsing came over. Using a poem by Wei Su-chou, I made a calligraphy scroll for Te-jun.

23rd day

The Customs Commissioner A-pan paid me what was due. Li Ching-kung and Chao Po-ch'ien, hearing that I was leaving, presented me with ten catties of yellow fish and brought a roll of paper to ask for samples of my drawing and calligraphy. Warden Hsing requested a screen with my calligraphy and bamboo

---

* Fan Chung-yen, author of the rules for the Charitable Estate, selection 26 above.

drawings. He offered me presents of two geese, some noodles, and wine cups. I took the wine cups, which were in the Li-chao style.

24th day

Everything was set for the trip and I was about to board the boat, when suddenly a heavy downpour started. It continued all day and I had to stay for another day. Hsü Tung-hsi, who is very good at portraits, brought with him two rolls of paper to ask for one of my bamboo drawings. Hu Tzu-chen made me a present of his calligraphy. He also asked me for a title for Master Wen's painting of grapes and my bamboo drawings. I also painted two old trees for Mr. Chan. Afterwards I packed.

25th day

In the morning I took leave of Mr. Chan and his son. They gave me a coconut-scoop and a square ink-block for presents. They asked Wang Shih-chung to accompany me to the pier in the rain. Unfortunately, the local officials had appropriated all the boats for catching locusts. I had to ask Wang Shih-chung to negotiate with the county government before I was able to leave. That day, Hsü Sheng-chih and Kung Tzu-fang paid eight thousand cash for the boat fare. By dinner time the three of us had arrived at Kao-yu county. We went to visit Eastern Peak Temple and left our belongings at Kung Tzu-fang's house. In the evening I took a bath and felt refreshed. Compared to Hsing-hua, Kao-yu had practically no mosquitoes. I slept soundly until midnight. When I woke up my bed was filled with silvery moonlight.

26th day

In the morning, Kung Tzu-fang and I went to Heavenly King Monastery. There we visited Master Hai and took a look at the newly constructed pavilions. Tzu-fang served me breakfast. Afterwards, on our way to the county seat, we passed Cho-ying Bridge; then we went to the county school to pay our respects to Confucius. At the back of the school there was a pavilion called Love-Lotus, with a plaque written by Ch'ien Ch'un-fu. Further back there was Literary Journey Pavilion, which was built by Ch'en Mao-shu and inscribed by Yen Wu-feng. At the side of the pavilion was a shrine in which were statues of Sun Hsin-lao and Ch'in T'ai-hsü. Later I went with Tzu-fang to the market to drink some tea. Returning,

I passed by the gate of the painter Chang Hsin-chien. When he learned that we were from the same village, he asked me to stay for a cup of tea and showed me his paintings. Next I went to Hsü Sheng-chih's house, but he happened to be out. At his door, I came across Master Kung Tzu-hsiang, and we talked about an encounter we had had thirteen years earlier. The two of us then went up to Westerner Buddhist Monastery, the magnificent architecture of which impressed me. Tzu-hsiang dragged me to his place for lunch. He showed me a purple bull painted by Hsü Hsi and a few other specimens of paintings and calligraphy. Then he brought paper and asked me to do some ten scrolls of calligraphy for him. His three sons were waiting on us; the oldest is called Li-fu, the youngest Po-ya, but the name of the second I cannot recall. After lunch, Tzu-hsiang accompanied me back to Tzu-fang's house. Tzu-hsiang's residence is called Heavenly Lodge. According to him, there is a "Fair Lady Well" in front of it. Hsü Sheng-chih came by to see me and left me a pig's head and some pastry as presents. In the evening Tzu-fang cooked a goose and drank wine with me. Li-fu brought paper, asking me for some calligraphy. Tzu-fang's brother was also present. Tzu-fang is the son of Yüeh-hsi. Even in the summer heat, he treats me like a guest, with extreme hospitality.

27th day

In the morning Tzu-fang accompanied me to the outskirts of Kao-yu City to board my boat. I took breakfast in the boat. At noon I got to Chao-po and changed boats. At that time it started raining very hard, making it impossible to get to shore. Thus, through the pouring rain I rode in a boat which was very damp and narrow. All the riders were common people so that there was no one to talk to. Fortunately, the wind was perfect, and I reached Yang-chou by dinner time. I stopped to see Sheng Mao-shih. The two of us then went to a bathhouse. Afterwards, we returned to his place for some wine. Mr. P'ei Chün-te also drank with us. At night I stayed at an inn.

Translated by Clara Yu

Part Five

THE MING DYNASTY

Peasant rebellions and internal weakness brought to an end the Yüan dynasty and allowed the establishment of a Chinese dynasty, the Ming (1368-1644). The early Ming was a period of recovery from some of the set-backs of Mongol rule, but many Yüan institutions were retained, since the forms and institutions of the Sung could not be directly or fully restored. The Mongol capital at Peking was made the Ming capital in 1421 and except for brief periods has remained the capital of China until today. Economic revival led to a high level of commercial activity and handicraft production, but not to the innovative and burgeoning spirit of the early Sung. Nevertheless, the Ming seems to have been one of the most prosperous periods of Chinese history. It was during these centuries that the great potential of South China came to be fully exploited. Many new crops such as cotton, maize, and sweet potato were widely cultivated, and industries such as porcelain and textiles flourished.

The Ming is generally considered the first truly despotic or autocratic Chinese dynasty (if the Yüan is considered an alien dynasty). The problems of central control of a huge, complex empire appeared pressing to the early Emperors, who were intent on assuring personal control of the machinery of the bureaucracy and finding ways to keep the officials in line. The Jurchen and Mongol innovation of provincial governments, consisting of branches of the central government, was developed further as a way to cope with the difficulty of direct central control of the whole empire. The Censorate, Imperial Guard, and eunuchs were all used to keep the Emperor informed of possible wrongdoing throughout the country. The arbitrary actions of the Emperors undoubtedly demeaned the status of high officials and often jeopardized their welfare, but it seems unlikely that the reach of the government was actually any more autocratic at the level of villages, whose affairs were still left pretty much to elders and local notables.

Sources for the Ming are even more varied than for the Sung. Particularly valuable are sources such as genealogies, charters, and other records of group activities. These provide us with considerable evidence of the proclivity of peasants and townsmen to form corporate groups of various sorts, such as lineages, guilds, village associations, and secret societies. Such groups were probably common before the Ming, but they cannot be as well documented. The major reason for forming corporate groups seems to have been to gain protection from the casual mistreatment or exploitation of powerful people, such as officials, large landowners, or rich merchants. Once one group of people had organized to protect their own interests, others would imitate them so as not to be left isolated. Indeed, by the Ming there is evidence that isolated individuals, without groups to support them, often lived precarious lives or had to put themselves under the protection of a landlord or employer who could take advantage of their weak position.

Vernacular fiction is another valuable source for the structure and content of social life and culture which becomes plentiful only in the Ming. The development of fiction in the vernacular language had begun in the Sung with storytellers, and had progressed further in the Yüan, when drama flourished. During the Ming the stories that had evolved through oral and dramatic performances were written down as short stories and four long novels, **Journey to the West, Romance of the Three Kingdoms, Water Margin,** *and* **Chin P'ing Mei.** *This colloquial fiction is a valuable source for understanding Chinese civilization for two reasons. First, many stories contain realistic portrayals of social life; while often exaggerated to provide a humorous effect, the conversations and behavior of tradesmen, servants, bullies, concubines, government clerks, teachers, and so on are colorfully portrayed and must often have corresponded to a social type recognized by the audience. The second value of fiction is as a repository of themes, images, and symbols that proved popular even if those reading or hearing of them never had encountered any such person or situation. Much like myths and folk tales, stories of bandits, treacherous women, and docile servants could dramatize the conflicts of everyday life and resolve them in ways emotionally satisfying, even if unrealistic. The great love, from at least the Yüan period on, of stories of the outlaws in the* **Water Margin** *saga must be seen in this way—not as evidence that Chinese peasants and townsmen admired bandits (whom they probably considered a scourge if they were ever unfortunate enough to live within their reach), but as evidence that the flouting of authority provided symbols that helped make sense of life as people actually found it. Selections from both* **Water Margin** *and* **Chin P'ing Mei** *are included in Part Five.*

32.

Proclamations of the Hung-Wu Emperor

In 1368 Chu Yüan-chang (1328–1398) founded the Ming dynasty, the first commoner to become Emperor in 1500 years. He was an orphan, his parents having died in an epidemic when he was sixteen. For four years he was a monk and even for a while begged for his living. During the chaotic years of the fall of the Yüan dynasty, he became a rebel leader. In 1356 his group seized Nanking and in 1368 Peking. Known by his reign title as the Hung-wu Emperor, he is famous as both a conscientious and a despotic ruler. In the two proclamations below, the Emperor discusses two topics which were to worry social and political observers for the rest of imperial China: the corruption of high officials who were placed in positions that made extortion or acceptance of bribes all too easy; and the disruptive and dishonest activities of the assorted underlings, runners, guards, and servants who did the bidding of officials and controlled ordinary people's access to them.

These proclamations can be read as a personal testament of the values and thoughts of a man who rose meteorically within the Chinese social system. From these proclamations we can also draw inferences about the working of the bureaucracy and its probable effects on people's lives.

AN IMPERIAL EDICT RESTRAINING OFFICIALS FROM EVIL

To all civil and military officials:

I have told you to refrain from evil. Doing so would enable you to bring glory to your ancestors, your wives and children, and yourselves. With your virtue, you then could assist me in my endeavors to bring good fortune and prosperity to the people. You would establish names for yourselves in Heaven and on Earth, and for thousands and thousands of years, you would be praised as worthy men.

However, after assuming your posts, how many of you really followed my instructions? Those of you in charge of money and grain have stolen them yourselves; those of you in charge of criminal laws and punishments have neglected the regulations. In this way grievances are not redressed and false charges are ignored. Those with genuine grievances

have nowhere to turn; even when they merely wish to state their complaints, their words never reach the higher officials. Occasionally these unjust matters come to my attention. After I discover the truth, I capture and imprison the corrupt, villainous, and oppressive officials involved. I punish them with the death penalty or forced labor or have them flogged with bamboo sticks in order to make manifest the consequences of good or evil actions.

Those who have died from their punishments are mute. However, those who survive confuse the truth by speaking falsely. Lying to their friends and neighbors, they all say they are innocent. They complain, "The Court's punishments are savage and cruel." This kind of slander is all too common. Yet I had clearly warned my officials from the beginning not to do anything wrong. Too often they have not followed my words, thereby bringing disaster upon themselves.

123

When a criminal commits a crime or when a good person mistakenly violates the law, he is going to be punished. Among these guilty ones there will always be some who are so afraid of being flogged or of dying that they will try to bribe the law-enforcement officials with gold and silk. The law-enforcement officials, for their part, place no value on bringing glory to their ancestors, their wives and children, or themselves; nor do they seek to preserve their own lives. The guilty persons, afraid of death, use money to buy their lives. The officials, not afraid of death, accept the money, thereby putting their lives in danger of the law. Yet later, when they are about to be punished or are on their way to the execution ground, they begin to tremble in fear. They look up to Heaven and they gaze down at the Earth. They open their eyes wide, seeking for help in every direction. Alas, by then it is too late for them to repent their actions! It is more than too late, for they now are no longer able to preserve their lives.

For example, the former Vice-President of the Board of War, Wang Chih, accepted a bribe of 220,000 cash for making up false reports on run-away soldiers and other matters. I questioned him face to face, "Why are you so greedy?"

He replied, "Money and profit confused my mind. They made me forget my parents and my ruler."

I then asked, "At this moment what do you think about what you did?"

"Facing punishment," he replied, "I begin to feel remorse, but it is too late."

Alas, how easily money and profit can bewitch a person! With the exception of the righteous person, the true gentleman, and the sage, no one is able to avoid the temptation of money. But is it really so difficult to reject the temptation of profit? The truth is people have not really tried.

Previously, during the final years of the Yüan dynasty, there were many ambitious men competing for power who did not treasure their sons and daughters but prized jade and silk, coveted fine horses and beautiful clothes, relished drunken singing and unrestrained pleasure, and enjoyed separating people from their parents, wives, and children. I also lived in that chaotic period. How did I avoid such snares? I was able to do so because I valued my reputation and wanted to preserve my life. Therefore I did not dare to do these evil things.

For fourteen years, while the empire was still unpacified, I fought in the cities and fields, competing with numerous heroes, yet never did I take a woman or girl improperly for my own pleasure. The only exception occurred after I conquered the city of Wu-ch'ang. I was enraged at Ch'en Yu-liang's invasion, so after I took over the city, I also took over his former concubine. Now I am suddenly suspicious of my own intentions in that case. Was it for the beauty of the woman? Or was it the manifestation of a hero's triumph? Only the wise will be able to judge.

In order to protect my reputation and to preserve my life, I have done away with music, beautiful girls, and valuable objects. Those who love such things are usually "a success in the morning, a failure in the evening." Being aware of the fallacy of such behavior, I will not indulge such foolish fancies. It is not really that hard to do away with these tempting things.

DISMISSAL OF EXCESSIVE LOCAL STAFF BECAUSE OF THEIR CRIMES

Among those with no redeeming features, the worst are the riffraff found in the prefectures of Su and Sung. It is indeed a great misfortune that these ne'er-do-wells can cause such great disturbances among the cities' inhabitants. For the average town dweller there are four types of occupation. These idle riffraff engage in none of them, but just hang around, concerned only with establishing connections with the local officials. In the city and suburbs of Sung-chiang alone there are 1350 persons who do not engage in any actual production but busy themselves only with currying favor with local officials. In the city and suburbs of Su-chou, 1521 individuals fall into this category. Alas, those who engage in productive work are few, while those who shirk work are many!

These idlers understand neither the hardships of the farmer nor the hard labor of other occupations. They work for the local government, calling themselves the "little warden," the "straight staff," the "record staff," the "minor official," and the "tiger assistant"—six types in all, each with a different name.

Even during the farmers' busiest season these idle persons will go to the fields to make trouble and interrupt agricultural activities. When it is time to transplant rice, and the farmers, with rice sprouts in their hands, are busy with their chores, these idlers will come into the fields, clutching an official dispatch. They will drag people away from the irrigation water wheel and arrest them on the spot. They have even been known to take the rice sprouts out of a farmer's hands and arrest him right in his field. Yet when formal official matters are not really pressing, government officials are not supposed to interrupt agricultural work. Therefore, how could one interrupt the farmer as he farms with something that is really nothing?

At this time, if I were to thoroughly eradicate this riffraff, in addition to those already imprisoned, I would have to deal with no less than 2000 people from each of these two prefectures. These men take part in none of the four useful occupations. They utilize the prestige of the government to oppress the masses below. If people outside the government do not know how wicked these men are, they are going to say that I am harsh in my punishments, since they see only the severity of the law. They do not know that certain persons have used the name of the court and the government to engage in evil practices.

In the morning I punish a few; by evening others commit the same crime. I punish these in the evening and by the next morning again there are violations. Although the corpses of the first have not been removed, already others follow in their path. The harsher the punishment, the more the violations. Day and night I cannot rest. This is a situation which cannot be helped. If I enact lenient punishments, these persons will engage in still more evil practices. Then how could the people outside the government lead peaceful lives?

What a difficult situation this is! If I punish these persons, I am regarded as a tyrant. If I am lenient toward them, the law becomes ineffective, order deteriorates, and people deem me an incapable ruler. All these opinions can be discerned in the various records and memorials. To be a ruler is indeed difficult.

I have exterminated the vicious riffraff in the prefectures of Su-chou and Sung-chiang. Evil persons in other areas, seeing this edict, take heed. Discontinue your evil practices and you will perpetuate your good fortune and prosperity. But if you violate this edict, you will be exterminated and your family will be broken. Be cautious! Be cautious!

Translated by Lily Hwa

33.

Laws Against Theft and Robbery

A basic element in the operation of the government of traditional China was a tension between Confucian and Legalist political theories, or, perhaps more accurately, gentle and tough versions of Confucianism. From the Han dynasty on, the theory of government through moral example and the rules of ritual was officially propounded; nevertheless, the need for carefully specified and often harsh laws was widely recognized. Each of the successive dynasties issued a highly detailed legal code that was an attempt to cover all possible sorts of offenses. The specification of punishments was determined in part by the hierarchical and familial principles of Confucian ritual, such as the view that an offense by a junior against a senior was much more serious than one in which the offender was the social or familial superior. The written code itself tended to provide harsh penalties, but a degree of compassion for mitigating circumstances was built into the automatic review process. Thus, after a case had been decided, higher judges would often reduce the penalty one or two grades below what was specified in the law, commuting execution to exile, exile to a beating, and so on.

What was the impact of the laws and legal procedures on the lives of ordinary people? People were encouraged to settle disputes out of court, and, indeed, did often avoid formal litigation, seeking justice instead through personal retaliation or group sanctions. Still, the importance of the written code should not be overlooked. Chinese laws, like any laws by which people are governed, reflected social relations and commonly accepted social values, and in turn served to reinforce them. Moreover, the existence of severe penalties, especially for crimes of violence and ritual impropriety, served as a restraint on many social activities. These aspects of the law can easily be seen in the statutes given below. They are nine of the twenty-eight statutes classifed under theft and robbery in the Ming code of 1373.

STEALING GOVERNMENT EDICTS AND ORDERS

All principals or accessories to the crime of stealing an edict which has received the great imperial seal shall be beheaded. The crime of stealing the documents of any Magistrate or government office shall be punished with 100 blows, and the criminal shall be branded on the arm. If any corrupt motive is proved, the theft shall be punished according to the most severe among the different laws applicable to the case. If the edict stolen was concerned with the collection of supplies for the army, or was connected with a military operation, both principals and accessories shall be strangled.

STEALING THE KEYS TO THE GATE OF A FORT OR CITY

All principals or accessories to the crime of stealing the key to the gate of the imperial capital shall be sentenced to 100 blows and exile to the distance of 3000 *li*. The crime of stealing the key to the gate of any other city, town, fortress, or barrier station shall be punished with 100 blows and exile for three years.

The crime of stealing the key to a granary, treasury, or other government building or public office shall be punished with 100 blows and the thief shall be branded on the arm.

STEALING MILITARY WEAPONS AND EQUIPMENT

All those found guilty of stealing ordinary military weapons or equipment shall be punished in proportion to the amount and value of the articles stolen according to the law applicable to theft in ordinary cases. However, those who steal any weapons or equipment which it is unlawful for the people in general to possess shall, at the minimum, be punished as severely as is provided by the law prohibiting the possession of such articles. When soldiers in actual service steal from each other, they shall be punished according to the law against theft in ordinary cases, except that if the articles stolen are voluntarily surrendered to the government, the punishment shall be less in each case by two degrees.

STEALING TIMBER FROM TOMBS

All principals and accessories to the offense of stealing trees growing within the boundaries of the imperial tombs shall be punished at the minimum with 100 blows and three years' exile. Anyone found guilty of stealing trees growing in a private burial ground shall be punished with at least 80 blows. If the value of the timber cut down and carried away is considerable, it shall be estimated, and the punishment increased in every case, by one degree above what would have been legally inflicted for an ordinary theft of the same amount.

EMBEZZLEMENT OF PUBLIC PROPERTY

When any of the persons entrusted with public property kept in government treasuries and storehouses are found guilty of being principals or accessories to the offense of embezzling any part of such property, they shall be punished according to the scale given below, without any regard to the number or extent of the shares into which the embezzled property may have been divided. The offender shall also be branded or marked on the arm between the wrist and the elbow with the following words: "stealer of government

grain/stores/silver." Each character will be distinctly marked and shall measure one and a half inches square.

Value less than	1	tael of silver		80 blows
Value exceeding	1	tael of silver		90 blows
"	"	5	taels of silver	100 blows
"	"	$7\frac{1}{2}$	" " "	60 blows and exile for 1 year
"	"	10	" " "	70 blows and exile for $1\frac{1}{2}$ years
"	"	$12\frac{1}{2}$	" " "	80 blows and exile for 2 years
"	"	15	" " "	90 blows and exile for $2\frac{1}{2}$ years
"	"	$17\frac{1}{2}$	" " "	100 blows and exile for $2\frac{1}{2}$ years
"	"	20	" " "	100 blows and permanent exile at 2000 *li.*
"	"	25	" " "	100 blows and permanent exile at 2500 *li.*
"	"	30	" " "	100 blows and permanent exile at 3000 *li.*
"	"	40	" " "	Death by being beheaded

ROBBERY

All principals or accessories in an attempt to seize the property of another by force shall be punished with 100 blows and perpetual exile to the distance of 3000 *li.* If the attempt succeeds, both principals and accessories shall be beheaded. Whenever stupefying drugs or other means are used to deprive a person of the use of his senses in order to take his property, the crime shall be punished as a robbery. If thieves caught in the act of stealing refuse to surrender and continue their resistance to the point of wounding someone, they shall be beheaded. When a female is raped in the course of a theft, the punishment is also beheading. Accessories to the theft who were not involved in the killing, wounding, or raping do not receive this increased punishment. A thief who discards stolen goods when pursued, but then defends himself by force and refuses to surrender, shall be punished according to the law for ordinary cases of criminals who refuse to surrender.

STEALING FROM RELATIVES

Anyone who steals from a relative with whom he lives shall suffer a punishment five degrees less severe than that which is legally inflicted in ordinary cases of theft of the same value. Similarly, all persons guilty of stealing from relatives of the third degree of mourning shall suffer a punishment four degrees less severe; in the case of stealing from relatives of the fourth degree, the punishment shall be three degrees less severe; and in cases of relatives of the fifth degree, the punishment will be lessened two degrees.* Finally, the punishment for stealing from any relative outside the mourning grades shall be one degree less than in ordinary cases. Persons who steal from their relatives shall not be subject to being branded for their offense.

In cases of robbery among relatives, when an elder relative has robbed a junior one, a reduction in the punishment shall be allowed similar to that already described in cases of theft. If a junior relative has robbed a senior one, the punishment shall be the same as that inflicted in ordinary cases. But if the robbery is accompanied by the additional crime of killing or wounding the junior or senior relative, the offender shall be punished according to whichever of the penalities is more severe.

If the junior of two relatives who live together induces a stranger to steal family property, he shall suffer a punishment two degrees more severe than in ordinary cases of using and consuming without permission a part of the joint family property, but the punishment shall not exceed 100 blows. The stranger induced to steal shall be punished one degree less severely than in ordinary cases of stealing, and shall not be branded. Should the robbery result in killing or wounding the senior, the junior relative will be punished according to the appropriate statute on killing or wounding. The stranger, if he was unaware of

what was being done, shall be punished according to the statute on robbery. If the stranger killed someone without the knowledge of the junior relative, the junior relative will receive the heavier punishment provided by the statute on juniors killing or injuring their senior relatives.

If a slave or hired worker who lives with his master steals from the master or from another slave or servant, the punishment shall be one degree less severe than in ordinary cases of theft, and the thief shall not be branded.

OBTAINING PROPERTY UNDER FALSE PRETENSES

All persons who obtain public or private property by fraudulent means or under false pretenses shall be punished with the same degree of severity as if they were guilty of stealing an equal amount, except that they shall not be branded. In all cases of relatives defrauding one another, the punishment shall be reduced as in cases of theft between relatives. When any person entrusted with the custody of property fraudulently takes any part of it for his own use, he shall be punished in the same manner as if he had embezzled it. When the offense amounts to attempt only, the punishment in each of the several cases shall be less than is provided above by two degrees. In general, whenever any type of property is fraudulently obtained, whether by asserting a false claim or by deceiving the owner with a fabricated story, or by prevailing on the owner to allow the property out of his possession, it shall be treated as theft except that the offender shall not be branded.

THE UNLAWFUL SEIZURE AND SALE OF FREE PERSONS

All persons guilty of entrapping or enticing a free person by the use of tricks or false pretenses, and who then offer that person for sale as a slave, shall be punished with 100 blows and perpetual exile to the distance of 3000 *li*. If the purpose was to sell the victims as wives or concubines, or for adoption as children or grandchildren, the punishment shall be 100 blows and three years' exile. If this offense results in a person being wounded, the offender shall suffer death by strangulation. When such victims are killed, the offender shall be beheaded. The kidnapping victim shall not in any of the above cases be liable to any punishment but shall be restored to his family. Any-

---

* Mutual mourning obligations between relatives were divided into five grades. The first grade was for the closest relationships (such as father and son) and the fifth grade for relatively distant ones such as between third patrilineal cousins.

one who receives the children of free parents with the promise to adopt them but instead sells them afterwards to others shall be punished according to this law.

When people consent to being taken away, those who sell them as slaves shall be punished with 100 blows and three years' exile. Those who, under the same circumstances, sell such persons as wives or concubines or for adoption as children or grandchildren shall be punished with 90 blows and exiled for two and a half years. The persons who voluntarily allow themselves to be sold shall be punished also, their punishment one degree less severe than those who sell them. When the sale of a person willing to be sold is proposed but not completed, the punishment shall be less severe by one degree. When the persons kidnapped or enticed away are under ten years of age, they shall not be held responsible for giving their consent, and the kidnappers shall be punished according to the law for unlawful seizure.

The offense of entrapping or enticing away for sale a person's slave shall be punished one degree less severely than that of kidnapping a free person. Any person who sells his children or grandchildren as slaves shall be punished with 80 blows. Any person who sells his younger brother or sister, his nephew or niece, his maternal grandchild, grandniece, grand nephew, his own concubine, or the wife of his son or grandson shall be punished with 80 blows and two years' exile. The punishment inflicted for the sale of the concubine of a son or grandson shall be two degrees less severe. Whoever sells his younger first or second cousin or their children or grandchildren shall be punished with 90 blows and exiled for two and a half years. In any of the preceding cases, when a sale is made with the consent of the party sold, the punishment shall be less severe by one degree. In general, also, when the sale has not been completed, the punishment shall always be one degree less severe. Junior relatives who consent to be sold shall not in any case be liable to punishment and shall simply be restored to their families. Any person who sells his wife as a slave or who sells any relative beyond the third mourning grade as a slave shall suffer the ordinary punishment for seizing and selling free persons.

If the purchasers were in collusion with the kidnappers, they shall suffer equal punishment with the kidnappers. Any person who is a broker in such a sale shall be punished one degree less severely than the principal offender and the money shall be turned over to the government. If the purchaser or broker was unaware of the illegality of the sale, he shall not be punished and the money shall be returned to him.

Translated by Patricia Ebrey

34.

Maxims for Daily Life

As seen in selection 11, "The Interaction of Yin and Yang," an ancient element in the Chinese world view was a habit of looking at the universe as an organic whole made up of interdependent parts related to one another in terms of Yin and Yang. Although metaphysical and scientific texts employing Yin-Yang analysis are abundant, we need other sources to understand to what extent these concepts permeated ordinary people's ways of thinking. The following selection, from a farmer's encyclopedia, is useful in this regard. Other parts of this book discuss such subjects as plowing and sowing techniques, silk production, remedies for animals' illnesses, and information on weather. The section here consists of miscellaneous advice and precautions to be taken in daily life, and shows how Yin-Yang thinking was intermingled with empirical, practical advice.

USEFUL SAYINGS

1. Intemperate daily living and unwise expenditure of strength will lead to injury of the veins and arteries. Injury to the Yang results in nosebleeds; injury to the Yin results in kidney disease.

2. Looking too long harms the spirit; standing too long harms the bones; walking too long harms the tendons; sitting too long harms the circulation; reclining too long harms the *ch'i* [vital energy].

3. In the spring you should go to sleep late and rise early so that your mind will be devoid of anxiety and your *ch'i* will be vented. Failure to do so will injure the heart and in the autumn malaria and dysentery will follow.

4. In the autumn you should go to sleep early and rise early so that your mind will be calm and your spirit and *ch'i* will be collected. Failure to do so will damage the lungs, and in the winter indigestion and diarrhea will result.

5. In the winter you should go to sleep early and rise late so that cold will be expelled and warmth pre-

served and nothing will be lost through the skin. Failure to do so will harm the kidneys, and in the spring you will become listless and exhausted.

6. Excessive joy causes the Yang to fall; excessive anger causes the Yin to snap; excessive shock leads to madness; excessive fear leads to injury of the kidneys.

7. If you have forgotten something and exert yourself to search for it but fail, then you will experience the "wailing of the lungs." When this happens, the lungs become feverish, their leaves become scorched, and weakness and illness result.

8. Too much sorrow leads to the exhaustion of membranes and capillaries; it also leads to the collapse of the heart, which then, in turn, leads to frequent urination specked with blood. Eventually, apoplexy follows.

9. Too many unfulfilled thoughts, too many erotic thoughts, or too much sexual activity will result in the weakening of the tendons and involuntary ejaculation.

10. You should not harbor hatred or love too deeply

or your nature will be harmed and your spirit injured. . . .

11. While conversing or laughing, you should also strive to cherish your energy and *ch'i*. If you laugh too much, then the kidneys will turn and the waist will hurt.

12. The eyes are the mirrors of the body. If you see too much, then the mirror becomes blurred. The ears are the windows of the body. If you listen too much, then the windows will close themselves. The face is the dwelling place of the spirit. If the heart is sorrowful, then the face will become withered. The hair is the flower of the brain. When the brain declines, the hair turns white.

13. If the *ch'i* is clear, the spirit flows smoothly. If the *ch'i* is muddy, the spirit becomes faint. If the *ch'i* is confused, the spirit becomes cumbersome. If the *ch'i* is weak, the spirit departs.

14. If you rise late, your spirit will not be clear.

ADVISABLE PRACTICES

1. At the fifth drum (daybreak), rub your palms until they become very warm, then use them to "iron" your face and chin. This will diminish wrinkles. Use them to "iron" your eyes and your eyesight will sharpen.

2. When getting up in the morning, use your two hands to massage the area of your kidneys, then do the same on the soles of your feet. In this way you can avoid diseases such as beriberi.

3. At the cock's crow, knock your teeth thirty-six times, lick your lips, and rinse your mouth. Roll your tongue over the palatal area three times. This will kill worms and cure other weaknesses.

4. The teeth should be knocked in the morning as well as at night, in order to collect energy.

5. If sudden misfortune or inauspicious happenings occur, you should knock your left teeth thirty-six times. This is called "chiming the heavenly bell." To become immune to wicked *ch'i*, knock your right teeth, which is called "striking the heavenly music-stone." Knocking on the center teeth is called "hitting the heavenly drum." Ill-luck will turn into good fortune as a result of this practice.

6. Traveling in early morning, you should keep some cooked ginger in your mouth, which will prevent you from being harmed by fog and dew. If your stomach is full and you have drunk some liquor, you will be able to dissolve the damp and poisonous *ch'i*.

7. When you are tired from traveling and your bones ache, you should sleep in a warm place.

8. If you have traveled too much, then you should, while sleeping, face the corner of a wall and curl your legs up. The next day you will find that your legs are no longer tired.

9. Traveling through the mountains, you may often be harassed by mountain spirits and ghosts. Some of them can even transform themselves and appear as humans. Therefore, you should hang a clear, nine-inch-long mirror on your back, so as to avoid all evil spirits. For, although these spirits can change their forms, they cannot do so in the mirror; therefore, when they see their real form in the mirror, they will disappear, not daring to harm you.

10. When you have to cross rivers, in red ink write the character Yü and wear it on you.* In this way you can avoid the dangers of wind and waves.

11. Whenever you finish a meal, rinse your mouth with warm water. By doing this you will prevent dental problems.

12. After each meal, roll a small piece of paper in your nostrils to induce sneezing several times. In this way the *ch'i* will have a clear passage without obstacles, and your spleen and stomach will be healthy, the phlegm dissolving itself.

13. Eating little at supper and sleeping without covering your face can lead to longevity.

14. After supper, a slow walk in the yard will ensure good health.

15. Before going to bed, take some phlegm-dissolving herbs.

16. Knock your teeth before going to bed. This will make them sturdy.

17. While sleeping, you should curl your legs up; while awake, you should extend your limbs.

18. Put some musk in your pillow, and it will repel the evil and disturbing elements. The "pupil-brightening" chrysanthemums can sharpen your eyesight.

19. Sleeping at night, you should extend one leg and flex the other. Whether you sleep on your side or on your back, you should keep the two legs together. In this way you can be free of worries about involuntary ejaculation.

* Yü was the legendary founder of the Hsia dynasty, famous for having calmed extremely severe floods.

20. Before going to bed, you should set one shoe facing upward and the other facing downward. You will have no nightmares if you do so.
21. If a person has a nightmare, you should take some of the dust from the beam of the house and blow it into his nostrils. He will then wake up instantly.
22. When you rise during the night, use the rug as shoes or walk on it, so as to keep your feet warm. Then you will not be harmed by the wicked cold.
23. When you rise during the night, sit up and try to touch the soles of your feet. In this way you will not suffer twisted tendons.
24. Spit out some saliva (at this time you should not speak) to apply to boils and sores, and the swelling will go down. Lick the back of your thumbs and rub them against your eyes, then you can keep your eyesight sharp until old age.
25. Before a child can speak, give him some "replenishing" herbs. They will enter the blood vessels of his kidneys.

Translated by Clara Yu

35.

The Dragon Boat Race

Festivals play a major role in people's lives: like rituals, they give impressive and dramatic representations that shape people's ways of thinking; they break up the monotony of life and often serve to strengthen group identification or solidarity; they give vent to emotions that cannot acceptably be expressed in more direct fashions.

One of the most popular seasonal festivals in China took place on the 5th of the fifth month, which occurred sometime in June according to the Western calendar. The nature of the festival varied from area to area, but where there were rivers, boat races were traditional. The following selection is a description of the boat race as it was performed in Hunan in the late Ming. The account was written by Yang Szu-ch'ang (1588–1641), a native of the area. He makes it clear that the races were not simple diversions but occasions for the expression of intense competition.

The dragon boat race originated in the old Yüan and Hsiang regions as a ceremony to call back Ch'ü Yüan.* Being north of the Tung-t'ing Lake, our Wu-ling is part of Yüan (Ch'ang-sha, south of the Lake, is in the old Hsiang) and therefore the boat race flourishes here. Since we inherited it directly from the state of Ch'u of the Chou dynasty it is only natural that our boat race cannot be matched by that of any other province.

The boat race is held at the center of the prefectural seat. The most distant places from which boats still come are Yü-chia-kang, fifteen *li* downstream, and Pai-sha-tu, thirty-five *li* upstream. On the day of the festival, flagmen and drummers on boats going to and fro make a deafening noise heard for about fifty *li*. The race course runs for about ten *li* along the southern shore from Tuan-chia-tsui to Ch'ing-ts'ao-tsui and along the northern shore from Shang-shih-

kuei. The river is wide there and well suited for a race course. The southern shore is covered with grass, forests, and snowy white sands. On the northern shore are high buildings with beautifully painted balconies and old city walls. The spectators gather there. . . .

The current popular belief is that the boat race is held to avert misfortunes. At the end of the race, the boats carry sacrificial animals, wine, and paper coins and row straight downstream, where the animals and wine are cast into the water, the paper coins are burned, and spells are recited. The purpose of these acts is to make pestilence and premature death flow away with the water. This is called "sending away the mark." Then the boats row back without flags and drumbeating. They will be pulled onto land and housed in huts on the shore till the next year, as this year's races are over. About this time the people have rites performed to ward off fires. Also, those who are ill make paper boats in the same color as the dragon boat of their region and burn them at the shore. . . .

Shamans are employed during the boat races in

---

* Ch'ü Yüan (332–295 B.C.) was the archetype of the loyal minister who lost the favor of his King through slander. In despair, he threw himself into the river to drown.

order to suppress evil influences.* Sometimes people go to the mountains to invite famous shamans, called "mountain teachers," who are especially skillful. The night before the race, the headman provides sacrificial animals and wine and asks the shaman to perform. The shaman jumps head over heels from the bow to the stern. Buckwheat is scattered and a fire is lighted. This is called "brightening the boat." Drums are beaten throughout the night to ward off the influences of opposing shamans, who, if caught, might be beaten to death.

On the day of the races the shaman makes an oil fire to launch the boat. He can foresee unfailingly the victory or defeat of the boat from the color and height of the flame. The god he serves is called the Immortal of Hsi-ho-sa. The shaman's spells include "the furious fire of the violent thunder burning Heaven." His finger-charms include "arresting the front dragons," "stopping the devil-soldiers," and "moving the mountains and overturning the seas." With his trouser legs rolled up and his feet bare, he jumps seven steps and then throws water into the fire. When the fire rises again, the boat starts. Some sentences of his spell are: "The Heaven fire burns the sun. The Earth fire burns the five directions. The thunder fire, executing the law, burns to death the various inauspicious things. The dragon boat taking to the water will float at will in the five lakes and four seas." The outer side of the bottom of the boat is swept with a bundle of reeds from stem to stern in order to prevent anything from being hung on the boat by an enemy. The other ceremonies, being secret, cannot be described.

The man chosen as the headman of a racing boat must be brave and have a family. Several days before, he distributes steamed cakes and pieces of paper to those who belong to his region and is repaid in money. On the top of the pieces of paper pictures of dragon boats are printed and on the bottom some sentences are written.

Supplying food and wine during the race is assigned to rich men, who are honored if they contribute generously. Others supply food because they have made a vow to do so. On the day of the races there are small boats in the river bringing food. They are decorated with two trees of paper money and colored silks, and musicians play in them. The boatmen must force in the food and wine beyond the point of

satiation until nothing is left. Otherwise anything left has to be thrown into the water together with the dishes and chopsticks.

In the evening when the boats return, the people take the water in the boats, mix it with various grasses, and use it to wash their bodies. This is said to prevent bad luck and is a kind of purification.

The boatmen are all familiar with the water and are expert swimmers, but the headman, flagman, drummer, and clapper need not be able to swim, as the oarsmen are responsible for their lives. On the day of the races all wear on their heads the charms furnished by the shaman and stick small reddish-yellow flags with egret feathers in the hair at their temples to ward off evil. The spectators display red or green pieces of silk, some with sentences written on them, and give them to the passing dragon boats as presents. As a boat passes by its home base, the people set off fireworks, wave their fans, and applaud. If the boat belongs to some other place, they shout ridicule at it, some of them getting angry and even throwing tiles at it. The boatmen respond by grabbing their oars or gesturing to show their willingness to fight. . . .

Each boat belongs to a distinct region, and the people of its home base quarrel with those of the others about who won and who lost. Even the children and women do not admit defeat. Most men who have moved away from where their ancestors lived are still loyal to the boat of their ancestral region. But others who have moved do not root for any boat, which makes them despised by their neighbors as cowardly. At this time, while playing chess, guessing fingers, and even when drinking, people say nothing but "victory." Sometimes they shout "tung, tung" to imitate the sound of the drums; sometimes they wave their sleeves to accompany the rowing and cry "victory! victory!" It is the custom to have this kind of enthusiasm for the races. Officials, stationed within the territories of the different boats should not join the contending groups, but, in fact, they are also divided according to the popular way of thinking. . . .

The people watch the boat races from the shore. Along the northern shore from Ch'ing-p'ing-men to Shih-kuei, about five or six li, are buildings of three or four stories in which space can be reserved by paying an advance fee of up to several hundred cash. On the day of the races, the people, carrying wine bottles and food boxes, ride on carts and horses or walk along the roads to get there by mid-morning. Tables are covered with fruit and food for sale. The best fruits

---

* Shamans are holy men able to communicate with the spirits, usually by going into trances. They had played a part in popular religion since the classical period.

are the "plums from the Han family" and the "wheat-yellow peaches"; the food includes shad and vegetables. When the start of the race is announced, everyone stops talking, laughing, or leaning against the balustrades. Attentively they watch, wondering which is their boat and whether it will meet victory or defeat. All too quickly victory is decided. Then some are so proud it seems as if their spirits could break the ceiling, and some have faces pale as death and seem not to know how to go down the stairs. . . .

The people can only rent space in buildings within their respective regions. Those who belong to the flower or the white boat do not enter the region of the black boat; those of the black or the red boat do not enter that of the flower boat. No one would do so consciously unless he wanted a fight, because sometimes terrible consequences result.

Because there are too few buildings for all the spectators, there are numerous food shelters on the southern shore and house boats in the river. People on the southern shore can see quite clearly as the boats cross the river from the northern to the southern bank. When a boat nears a bank, if it does not belong to their region, people fling stones at it, and the men on the boat wave their oars menacingly. The spectators' boats in the river often obstruct the route of the racing boats. If a boat happens to be just in front of a racing boat and cannot get out of the way, it can be broken to pieces in seconds. . . .

The victorious boat rows with its stern forward. The men hold their oars vertically, dance, and beat gongs on the boat. When they pass a losing boat, they threaten it. Those losing try to do the same but with less spirit, or if a little further behind, they silently acknowledge defeat. At sunset the boats disperse. At the home of the headmen, feasts are prepared and the boatmen all gather to dine. At the victor's home, food and wine are especially abundant and his neighbors, relatives, and friends come to offer congratulations. The next day, the door of his house will be beautifully decorated with colored silk, and a feast and a dramatic performance will be held. Some people write sentences or short poems on the city gates to ridicule the losers, or tie up a dog or a tortoise with some grass and fruit and place them there for the same purpose. When the men of the defeated boats happen to pass by, they lower their heads and go on their way. Their relatives or friends sometimes send such things to them to make fun of them.

From the fourth month the people begin to talk enthusiastically about the boats. In the fifth month the race is held and victory and defeat are decided. Yet even by the eighth or ninth month the people are still not tired of the subject.

Translated by Patricia Ebrey

36.

Village Ordinances

In every dynasty villages were allowed considerable self-government, and by the Ming many villages had assemblies that set and enforced their own rules or ordinances. Although these ordinances did not have the force of law in the official courts established by the central government, they are a valuable historical source because they indicate the principles by which villages, or at least village leaders, thought their affairs should be run. They also show the kinds of restraints people could be placed under by decisions of their neighbors.

The following three sample village ordinances come from encyclopedias for daily reference published in the late Ming with titles such as The Complete Compilation of Everything the Gentry and Commoners Need to Know *and* The Complete Book of Practical Information Convenient for the Use of Commoners.

PROHIBITION ORDINANCE

In the imperial court there are laws; in the village there are ordinances. Laws rule the entire nation; ordinances control only one area. Although laws and ordinances differ in scope, the matters they deal with are equally significant.

Each year we set up ordinances for our village, and yet, to our deep regret, they are denigrated by the greedy and overturned by the influential. As a result, they are rendered ineffective, customs deteriorate, and incalcuable damage is done by our people and their animals.

The problem is not that ordinances cannot be enforced; rather, it is that those in charge of the ordinances are unequal to their posts, and those who design them are incompetent. Recently we have followed the suggestion of the villages and grouped all households into separate districts, each with a fixed number of members. On the first and the fifteenth of each month, each district will prepare wine and hold a meeting to awaken the conscience of its residents. In this manner, contact between the high and low will be established, and a cycle will be formed. Anyone who violates our village ordinances

will be sentenced by the public; if he thinks the sentence is unfair, he can appeal to the village assembly. However, let it be known that no cover-up, bribery, blackmail, or frame-up will be tolerated; such evil doings will be exposed by Heaven and punished by thunder. We know that even in a small group there are good members as well as bad ones; how can there be a lack of honest people among our villagers?

From now on, our ordinances will be properly enforced and the morality of our people will be restored. The village as a whole as well as each individual will profit from such a situation, and there will be peace between the high and the low, their morality and custom having been unified. Thus, what is called an "ordinance" is nothing but the means to better ourselves.

ORDINANCE PROHIBITING GAMBLING

This concerns the prohibition of gambling. Those who are farmers devote their time to their work and certainly do not gamble. It is the unemployed vagrants who have the gambling disease—a disease which is detrimental to social customs and ruins family fortunes. Unfortunately in our village the population increases daily, and the proper behavior does not prevail. As a result vagrancy becomes the fashion. Among us there are homeless rovers who, lacking occupations, form gangs and occupy themselves solely with gambling. They either bet on card games or play with dice; vying to be the winner, they continue day and night, without food or sleep. They have nothing with which to support their parents or their wives and children. Thus, unlawful intents are born, and wicked schemes are hatched. In small offenses they dig holes or scale walls, using all the cunning they have to steal from others; in more serious cases they set fires and brandish weapons, stopping at nothing. If we fail to prohibit gambling, the situation will become impossible. This is why we are gathered here to enact an ordinance for the prohibition of gambling. From now on those in question should repent for their past sins and reform their souls; they should espouse duty and kindness; they should tend to their principal occupations. Should there be anyone who persists in this evil practice and fails to honor this ordinance, he will definitely be punished. The light offenders will be confined, upon the decision of our village assembly, and the serious ones will be brought to the officials for sentence.

Our purpose is clearly stated in the above, and this notice is not posted without good reason.

PROHIBITION ON TRAVEL AT NIGHT

This ordinance is drawn up by so-and-so to prohibit travel at night, for the purpose of safeguarding our village.

In ancient times, night travel was strictly prohibited, and violaters were punished without exception. Robbers and thieves were prevented from climbing walls and boring holes in houses, to the benefit of all the inhabitants of the area.

Recently, however, night-wanderers, instead of resting at night, have dared to saunter around at will. Because of this we have prepared wine and called for this meeting to draw up a strict ordinance. As soon as the sun sets, no one will be allowed to walk about; not until the fifth drum will traffic be allowed to start again. We will take turns patrolling the streets, carrying a bell, and clapping the nightwatchman's rattle. He who sights a violator will sound his gong, and people in every household will come out with weapons to kill the violator on the spot. Should anyone fail to show up for roll call at the sound of the gong, he will be severely punished upon the decision of the village assembly.

We have made copies of this ordinance to be posted at various places so that night-wanderers will be warned and thieves and rogues will not prevail.

Duly enacted.

Translated by Clara Yu

37.

Routine Commercial Procedures

Wherever a money economy prevails, commercial transactions such as buying and selling, borrowing money, and renting houses are important parts of people's daily lives. Because most economic relations potentially involve conflicts of interest, they need to be regulated by well-understood traditions, written agreements, or both. By the T'ang dynasty, contracts seem to have been in wide use in China, and thereafter even illiterate peasants realized the importance of having a piece of paper to prove the original terms of an agreement. Private financial agreements could be drawn up by any two individuals, usually with the aid of a mediator or a witness. Experts in legal matters were not normally consulted, but to ensure that most foreseeable problems had been dealt with, people could consult sample contracts.

Below are a number of blank contracts taken from a late Ming reference book similar to the ones that contained the village ordinances above. Most of these contracts and bills of sale state that the transaction was legal and had not been coerced. They also carefully specify who is responsible if anything goes wrong. Very often the weaker party (the man seeking to borrow money, be hired, sell his child, and so on) clearly accepts the brunt of the responsibility should anything unexpected happen. Such economic relations surely must have also shaped social relations.

SAMPLE CONTRACT FOR THE SALE OF A HOUSE

The undersigned sellers, _____, unable to sustain themselves, agree to sell their part of the house with _____ rooms, together with the main structure of _____ rooms, encompassing _____ to the east, _____ to the west, _____ to the south, _____ to the north, its boundary clearly stated in the above, including the tiles on the roof and the land on which the house is constructed (for those who do not sell the land, just state: "the foundation of the house"), complete with doors and windows, all in sound condition, to the buyer, _____. This transaction is mediated by _____.

On this date, all three parties negotiated the price, which comes to _____ only. The deed and the full payment were exchanged, leaving no outstanding debts.

Before this transaction, all the sellers' relatives involved were consulted. The house has not been previously sold or mortgaged. Should any questions arise, the sellers assume full responsibility.

This transaction is completed out of the free will of the seller and the buyer; there has been no pressure from any creditor to sell the house as payment for debts. After the sale, the buyer will have full control of the property and there should be no other disputes. (In cases where only the house is for sale, then state: "The sellers will vacate the premises on the date selected by the buyer, their non-compliance or resistance being prohibited.") Should either party violate any terms of this contract, he will have to

138

compensate the other party with an amount equivalent to half of the total sale price.

This contract is drawn up as evidence of the sale.

SAMPLE CONTRACT FOR
THE MORTGAGE OF A HOUSE*

The undersigned mortgagor, _____, because of inadequate funds, agrees to mortgage his house of _____ rooms, encompassing _____ to the east, _____ to the south, _____ to the west, _____ to the north, its boundary clearly stated in the above, through a mediator to the mortgagee, _____, for _____ amount of silver, which has been received in full. The house is now available for immediate occupancy by the mortgagee.

It is agreed that the sum received will not accrue any interest and the house will not yield any rent. The mortgage will remain effective until _____ year, at which time the mortgagor will, by reimbursing the mortgagee for the sum specified above and presenting this contract as evidence, reclaim his property.

If the mortgagor is unable to pay back the mortgagee at the specified time, the latter will be entitled to continue occupancy of the house; the mortgagor will also be fined _____ amount.

It is further stated that there are no prior mortgages on the house, nor are there any questions as to its ownership. Should any such question arise, it will be the sole responsibility of the mortgagor.

This contract is drawn up as evidence of the present mortgage transaction.

SAMPLE CONTRACT FOR
THE SELLING OF CATTLE

The undersigned seller, _____, agrees to sell a water buffalo (bull/cow), its age as indicated by its teeth, its body intact, having four limbs, head and tail, to the buyer, _____, for use in ploughing. The seller, the buyer, and the mediator have agreed on the price, _____, which is to be paid in full on the same day this contract is signed. The condition of the merchandise has been examined by the buyer; the seller assumes full responsibility for its origin.

This contract is drawn up as evidence of the sale.

---

* Note the difference between this kind of mortgage and our own: in this case the owner of the house is essentially "pawning" his house for a sum of money; he cannot live in the house until he repays the loan.

SAMPLE CONTRACT FOR
THE PURCHASE OF A CONCUBINE

The undersigned, _____, from _____ village, has agreed to give in marriage his own daughter _____, aged _____ years, to the second party, _____, as a concubine, through the mediator, _____.

On this date the undersigned has received _____ amount as betrothal payment. He agrees to give his daughter away on the date selected by the second party. He will not dare to cause any difficulties or to extort more money from the second party. He also guarantees that the girl has not been previously betrothed, and that there is no question as to her origin. Should such questions arise, or should the girl run away, he will be held responsible. Should the girl die of unexpected circumstances, it is her fate, and not the responsibility of the second party.

This contract is drawn up as evidence of the agreement.

SAMPLE CONTRACT FOR
THE SELLING OF A SON FOR ADOPTION

The undersigned, _____, from _____ county, _____ village, is unable to raise his own son _____, aged _____ years, because of poverty. After consulting his wife and relatives (uncle/ brother _____ and _____, etc.), he has decided to sell the child, through a mediator, to _____ as an adopted son.

On this date the undersigned received _____ amount of money from the second party, and the transaction was completed. The second party agrees to raise the child, who will be at his disposal for marriage, will be as obedient to him as a servant, and will not avoid labor or run away. This contract is signed out of the free will of both parties, there being no prior sales, and no questions as to the origin of the child; nor is the seller forced by a creditor to sell the child as payment for debts. From now on the child belongs to his new owner; alive, he shall never return to his original family; dead, he shall not be buried in the graveyard of his original family. Should he run away or be kidnapped, only the seller and the mediator are responsible; should the child die of unexpected circumstances, it is his fate, and not the responsibility of his owner.

This contract, stamped with the palm prints of the

child, is to be held by the owner as evidence of the transaction.

SAMPLE CONTRACT FOR
HIRING A WORKER

The undersigned, _____, in order to support his family, agrees to work for _____ for one year as a laborer. The wages of _____ have been agreed on by both parties and are to be drawn by the employee at set intervals.

After the contract becomes effective, the hired worker will not avoid labor, but will devote himself to it. Should any unpredictable misfortune befall him, it is his fate, and not the responsibility of his master. If he should fail to work, deductions will accordingly be made from his daily wages.

This contract is drawn up as evidence of the agreement.

SAMPLE CONTRACT FOR FORMING
A BUSINESS PARTNERSHIP

The undersigned, _____ and _____, having observed that partnerships bring profit and enterprise brings success, have agreed to pool their capital for profit. As witnessed by a mediator, _____, they have each contributed _____ as capital, and will cooperate sincerely in their business venture. The profit yielded will be divided between them each year to provide for their families. The capital will remain untouched to serve as the fountainhead of the business. Each individual will take care of his own personal expenses and not draw from the capital, nor should business and private expenditures be in any way mixed in bookkeeping. The two parties have taken an oath by drinking blood-wine to work together in harmony and share both profits and losses. They will not disagree, feud, or seek separate profits. The party that breaks this contract will be persecuted by gods and men alike.

This contract is drawn up in two copies as evidence of the agreement.

Translated by Clara Yu

38.

What the Weaver Said

By the Ming dynasty, textile production had become a major industry involving considerable specialization and establishment of large and small workshops, networks of brokers, and markets. Cotton cloth was woven mainly by peasants working in their homes as a means of gaining extra income. Fancy silks, however, were generally produced in workshops by weavers paid wages. Below is an account of a weaver in such a workshop written by the scholar and teacher Hsü I-k'uei (d. ca. 1400). His purpose in recording his conversation with the weaver was to provide a moral lesson, but there is no reason to doubt his description of what he saw and heard.

When I lived in Hsiang-an Ward in Ch'ien-t'ang. I had a wealthy neighbor who employed live-in weavers. Late every evening one of them would start to sing and the rest would join in. From the sound of their voices, they seemed to be cheerful. "How happy they are!" I sighed.

One morning I walked over there and found it to be just a rickety old house. There were four or five looms in a room, arranged in a row from the north to south, and about ten workers, all of whom were laboring with both hands and feet. They looked pale and spiritless. I called one worker over and said, "From what I have seen, your work is very hard. Why are you still so happy?"

The worker replied, "Happiness is determined by the thoughts in a person's mind. If he isn't greedy, he can be happy with very little. But those who are greedy may earn a thousand strings of cash a day and still always feel unhappy. Though my job is a humble one, I can earn two hundred strings of cash a day. The master provides me with food and clothes, so I can use my wages to support my parents, wife, and children. We are far from having delicious food, yet neither are we suffering from hunger or cold. I consider my life a normal one; I am not discontent, and

the material I weave is very beautiful and highly valued by people. Thus, the master can easily sell the products and we are able to earn our wages easily. Since this is all we really want, our inner contentment naturally comes out in our voices as we sing together. We do not think of the hardship of the work.

"Not long ago, there was a weaver employed in another workshop. He earned approximately the same amount of money as we do. Yet, after working for a while, he started to complain: 'I am a more skillful weaver than anyone else, but I still get the same wages. I am going to work for someone who will pay me twice as much.' Later on, one workshop owner did offer him double. The master examined his work and noticed that it was indeed superior, and the other weavers, after seeing his skill, also respected him highly. The master was very happy, thinking, 'This one weaver's work is better than that of ten others put together. It is well worth doubling his pay.' After working for a while, the weaver again became dissatisfied. He thought, 'I am such a superior weaver that if I leave this occupation and engage in another, I will undoubtedly be superior in that one, too. If I take employment under a high official, by playing up to him and serving him whole-heartedly, I will be able to gain great wealth and glory for myself. Why should I work in a weaving factory forever?'

"Eventually, he did take a position serving a high official. He worked among the slaves taking care of carriages and horses, and for five years did not find anything he could consider an opportunity for wealth and glory. Then one day, after another five years had passed, he provoked the official, who became infuriated and dismissed him and refused to see him ever again. By that time, the weaver had already forgotten his former trade. Moreover, people were disgusted with his arrogance and inability to be content, and no one wanted to hire him to weave. In the end he died of hunger and cold.

"I took this person as a warning. How could I fail to feel content and happy?"

This worker is indeed content, and exemplifies what Lao Tzu meant when he said, "One who knows how to be satisfied will always be satisfied." This is why I recorded his story. At the time of our conversation, there were about ten workers present. The one who talked to me was named Yao.

Translated by Lily Hwa

39.

Tenants

Ever since the late Chou dynasty, when free buying and selling of land became common, tenancy was a recurrent problem. Some farmers would flourish and buy more land while others, for whatever reason, would be reduced to selling property. They would then have to work the land of others as hired hands or as tenants paying their landlords either a fixed share of the harvest or a fixed yearly sum. Tenancy was always considered a social and political evil because large landowners stood to gain too much local power. Often they would protect their tenants from tax and labor service obligations to the government, thereby attracting more tenants but also reducing the government's revenues. From the Han through the T'ang, the government repeatedly tried to limit landholdings and tenancy, but after mid-T'ang great variation in the size of landholdings was legally tolerated.

How did tenants look upon their position? Contracts are one of the few sources that can give us a clue to this question. Although contracts would usually have been composed by the master or a scribe, their content was so important to the tenant that it must often have been deeply impressed on his mind. Below are two contracts from an estate in Hui-chou, in Anhui province, which date from the late Ming. In certain parts of China, including the Hui-chou area, tenants were often obligated to perform nonagricultural duties for their masters, such as helping at festivals, weddings, and funerals. Such tenant-servants were acquired through contracts, and their status was often hereditary. The two contracts here show two common ways a person could become a tenant-servant: in exchange for gravesites; or to gain the right to marry the widow of another tenant-servant. After these two contracts is the brief description from a local history of an abortive revolt of tenant-servants in this area during the upheavals that accompanied the fall of the Ming.

1

The servants Hu Sheng-pao, Hu Chu-pao, Hu Ch'ih-pao, and the sons and grandsons of the four Hu branch families, draw up this contract. Previously our ancestors, Hu Ang and Hu Sheng, besought from Master Hung Shou one piece of open land, the Lower Pond Hill, located in our county, for the purpose of burying our ancestors, Hu Fu and his wife. Since then, fifteen more coffins have been buried there. Each coffin occupies the space of nine paces. Kept in this cemetery was also one small coffin of the master's family and one stone tablet. Our ancestors had drawn

up statements specifying that we could bury no one outside these given spaces. It stated that we could only have further burials in the master's cemetery with his permission. It is agreed that the descendants of our Hu family will observe this regulation in perpetuity; no arbitrary burial is allowed. If there are any violations of this rule, the master can present the case to the court and have us punished as violators.

Recently because of our failure to perform adequately our duty of escorting his children to school, the master expressed his intent to present the case to court. All the four branch families, realizing our weak position, pleaded for forgiveness and were willing to accept punishment. It is agreed that from now on, whenever there are marriages, funerals, or sacrifices in the master's house, we will offer our services.

The master, in consideration of the fact that we live far away from his estate and that the servants on the estate are sufficient, only requests us to send over two people to help with the sacrifice and cleaning during the Clear and Bright Festival [for honoring the dead]. In addition, on occasions when members of the master's family are going to school, going to the examinations, or responding to the call to serve in public office, the descendants of the four families will each dispatch one person to serve for one day. We dare not refuse the call for service. We also agree to keep watch carefully over the master's family graveyard.

After the drawing up of this contract, the descendants of the four Hu families will observe the regulations in perpetuity. Should there be any violations, the master can present the case to the court and have us punished as violators.

In order to guarantee the agreements, we draw up this contract as evidence.

Dated on the 17th day of the twelfth month of 1605.
The servants who draw up the contract, Hu Sheng-pao,
Hu Hsi-pao, and their sons and grandsons, Hu Ch'i, Hu
Ch'eng-ming and Hu Yen-kuei,
Hu Chu-pao, Hu Ch'u and their sons and grandsons, Hu
Hsi-sun, Hu Hsia-lung, Hu Ch'ih-pao and Hu She-ch'i
Hu Chi, Hu Ch'i-pao and their sons and grandsons, Hu
She-fu and Hu She-lung
The person who wrote the contract, Hu Ch'eng-ming

2

Tenant Wang Meng-hsi draws up this contract. The resident-tenant Lü San of the Old Father Temple Estate, Hu Family Mountain, passed away, leaving behind him his widow, Chü-hsiang, nee Lin, and two sons. The elder son is Yu-shou; the younger one is Pao-shou. They are both young and weak and unable to perform the duty of cultivating the field for the estate.

The master, considering that I have not been married, permitted me to marry the widow, Lin, to enter her family, to raise her two children, and to pay the rent to the master.

Previously Lü San had separated his property from that of Lü Hsing. I will take possession of the house and lands which belonged to Lü San. Upon entering the widow's house, I will carefully serve the master, diligently cultivate the land, and earnestly raise the two children. I do not dare to come or go at will or to make trouble. Later on if I have children of my own, I will divide my earnings and the field and the house equally among all of them. If I am lazy or indolent, the master can proceed against me.

In order to guarantee this agreement, I have drawn up this contract as evidence.

Dated on the 27th day of the eleventh month of 1634.
The person who drew up the contract, Wang Meng-hsi
(sign)
Younger cousin, Lü Hsing (sign)
Roommate Lin Fa-hu (sign)

3

Yi county and Hsiu-ning county were both under the jurisdiction of Hui-chou. In the fourth month of 1645, before the Ch'ing troops had arrived, the tenant-servants in these counties formed twelve stockades and demanded the return of their contracts from their masters. If their masters acted in any way against their will, they were killed and their houses burned. The tenant-servants all said: "The Emperor has been replaced; our masters should now be our servants." Masters and servants began to address each as "brothers." In weddings, the bride and groom had to walk, for there were no servants to carry them. This situation bore a resemblance to the rebellion of Chiang-yin, except it seemed even worse in Yi county.

When this revolt reached Hsiu-ning, the people of good birth there were all in a quandary. They subsequently formed seventy-two societies, with the wealthy contributing food and silver to ensure local security. The county Magistrate, Ou-yang Hsüan, was from Chiang-hsi. He invited the gentry of the county to a banquet, during which he made a tearful declaration that he would now raise troops. Chin Sheng and Huang Keng also mobilized their own troops. For this reason, the tenant-servants did not dare make any more moves.

Translated by Lily Hwa and Clara Yu

40.

Shih Chin, the Nine-Dragoned

From at least the late Sung, Chinese storytellers and dramatists delighted audiences with tales of the 108 heroes and outlaws of Liang-shan. Based on an actual gang active in the last decades of the Northern Sung, this legend grew over the years and these bandits came to be credited with numerous feats of strength, daring, and cruelty. An episodic novel about the members of this bandit gang, called Water Margin, *developed from this long oral tradition and probably was put in its present form in the fifteenth century.*

The section of this novel given below recounts how one young man came to embark on a career that would eventually lead him to join the bandits of Liang-shan. This episode provides descriptions of social customs, such as ways of treating teachers and guests. Moreover, by contrasting the docility and weakness of villagers and servants with the behavior of the hero, it suggests some reasons why Chinese peasants, townsmen, and even members of the upper class were so attracted to stories of the reckless pursuit of honor and profit.

Let us now tell about Instructor Wang Chin and his mother. After leaving the Eastern Capital, they traveled for over a month, taking their meals on the road, stopping at night and setting out early in the morning. Finally one evening, Wang Chin, walking behind his mother's horse with the luggage on his shoulders, said to her, "Heaven has taken pity on us. We have escaped. Soon we'll be in Yen-an prefecture, where Minister Kao cannot arrest us even if he wants to."

Mother and son were so overjoyed that they went past the inn where they should have stopped. "It's so late now, and there's not a single village in sight. Where can we spend the night?" Just as they were worrying themselves with these thoughts, they caught the glimmer of a light through a patch of woods some distance away. Wang said to his mother, "We'll be all right now. We'll just go there and beg to stay for the night and be on our way again early tomorrow."

When they turned into the woods, they found a large farmhouse surrounded by a mudwall, lined by some two to three hundred willow trees. Instructor

Wang went to the gate of the village and knocked. Finally, a servant came out. Setting down his load, Wang saluted the servant, who asked their purpose.

"Let me explain," Wang said. "My mother and I were so eager to go a little farther that we went beyond the last inn and found ourselves in the middle of nowhere. So, we would like to stay overnight in your village. We will pay for the lodging and leave promptly in the morning. We hope you can help us."

"Wait here a moment," said the servant, "while I ask my master. If he says so, you may stay." The servant went in, and eventually came out again to say, "Our master says to show you in."

Wang helped his mother dismount, then picked up his luggage again and entered with the servant. He led the horse to the threshing ground, set down his luggage, and tied the horse to a willow tree. Mother and son now went to the main hall to meet the master of the house.

The master was an old man of over sixty, his hair and beard completely white. He wore a warm wadded cap, a straight-cut loose robe belted by a black silk sash, and leather boots. When Wang Chin saw him, he hurried to salute. The old man stopped him, saying, "Don't stand on ceremony. You are travelers and must be exhausted. Please be seated." Wang and his mother sat after the usual preliminaries. The old man asked them, "Where are you from? Why have you arrived here late at night?"

Wang replied, "My name is Chang. I am originally from the Capital, but I lost all my money in business. Now that I have no way to make a living, I'm on my way to Yen-an prefecture to stay with relatives. Today, because we were eager to cover as much distance as possible, we missed the last inn. We hope to stay at your village overnight and will be on our way again early tomorrow morning. We will be happy to pay the standard rate for the lodgings."

"No problem," said the old man. "Who in this world can carry his own house over his head when he travels? I suppose you haven't eaten yet, have you?" Then he ordered a servant to bring food.

In no time a table was set right in the hall, and the servants brought out a tray with four kinds of vegetables and a plate of beef. They set the plates on the table, warmed some wine, and poured it into cups. The master of the house said, "In this backwater area, we do not have much to offer our guests. Please don't take offense."

Wang rose from his chair to thank him. "My mother and I have intruded on you and troubled you. We don't know how to repay you for your kindness."

"Please—no such nonsense!" the old man said. "Come, have some wine."

At his urging, mother and son drank some five or seven cups of wine. Afterwards rice was served, and they took their meal. When the dishes were cleared away, the old man showed the pair to the guest room where they would spend the night. Wang then made another request, "The horse that my mother rode—could you please take care of it, too? I will also pay for its stall and feed."

"No problem at all. I myself also have a few horses and mules. I'll just tell the servants to put your horse in the stable and feed it with the others."

Thanking him, Wang brought his luggage to the room. A servant lit the lamp and brought them hot water for washing their feet. The old man went back to his inner quarters to rest. Thanking the servant, Wang and his mother closed the door and went to bed.

The next morning, Wang and his mother did not get up. When the old man passed by the guest room, he heard the mother groaning. So he called out, "Sir, it's dawn, time to get up."

When Wang heard him, he hurried out of the room and saluted him. "I have been up for a long time," he said. "Sorry for all the trouble we caused you last night."

The old man then asked about the groaning. Wang explained, "Sir, I won't hide it from you. My mother is exhausted from riding and last night she suffered pains in her heart."

"Don't worry," said the old man, "let your mother stay a few days in my house. I have a good prescription for heart pain, and I'll send a servant to the town to fill it for her. Tell her to relax and take her time resting." Wang Chin again expressed his thanks.

But let's not go into every detail. In short, Wang and his mother stayed at the farm while she took her medication. In about a week's time, Wang felt that his mother had recovered and prepared to leave. On his way out to the stable in the back of the house to see his horse, he passed an open yard where he saw a young man practicing with a cudgel. He was naked from the waist up and tattooed all over with blue dragons. About eighteen or nineteen, his face was as bright and shiny as a silver plate.

After watching him for a while, Wang Chin inadvertently remarked, "That's very good! But you're still making mistakes and couldn't beat a real master."

This remark infuriated the young man, who shouted at Wang, "Who are you? How dare you put me down? I've studied with seven or eight famous teachers. There's no way you can beat me! I dare you to fight with me."

Hardly had he finished speaking when the old man appeared and scolded him, "Don't be rude."

"But this jerk laughed at my fencing techniques."

The old man then asked Wang if he knew martial arts. "Rather well," he replied. Then he asked who the young man was, and the old man told him he was his son. Wang said, "Since he is the young master of the house, I wouldn't mind giving him a few hints to improve his skills—that is, if he wishes to learn."

"That would be great," said the old man, who then told the youth to pay Wang Chin the obeisance due a teacher.

This the young man would have nothing to do

with. Now even more angry than before, he said to his father, "Dad, don't listen to this jerk. I'll be his student only if he can win over this cudgel of mine."

"If the young master doesn't think I'm his equal," Wang Chin said, "we can spar just for fun."

Hearing this, the young man, who already occupied the center of the yard, whirled his cudgel so swiftly that it looked like a windmill. He called out to Wang Chin, "Come on, come on! I'm not a man if I'm afraid of the likes of you."

Wang Chin laughed, but did not make a move.

The old man then said to him, "Sir, since you are willing to teach my son, why don't you go ahead and try the cudgel with him?"

"I'm afraid that I may hurt him, which would be embarrassing."

"It doesn't matter," the old man said. "Even if you break his arm or leg, it is all his own fault."

"In that case, forgive me for my audacity." Saying that, Wang Chin picked a cudgel from the weapon rack. Then he went to the center of the yard and struck a pose.

The young man looked at him, then, whirling his cudgel, rushed at him. Wang turned and ran, trailing his cudgel on the ground. The young man, flourishing his cudgel, ran after him. Now, Wang suddenly turned around, raised his cudgel, and crashed down on the young man, who lifted his cudgel to meet the blow, only to find that Wang Chin had changed direction. Wang swiftly drew back the cudgel, and thrusted it toward the young man's chest. With one twirl, he knocked the cudgel out of the young man's hands and threw him to the ground.

Wang dropped his own cudgel and hastened to help him get up, apologizing. The young man scrambled to his feet, then immediately pulled over a stool and forced Wang to sit on it. He knocked his head on the ground in front of Wang Chin and said, "I've wasted my time with those worthless teachers. You are now my teacher; please instruct me."

"I haven't been able to think of a way to repay all the trouble my mother and I have caused these many days. I would be glad to teach you."

Delighted, the old man told his son to get dressed, and together they took Wang Chin to the inner guest hall. There they ordered the servants to kill a sheep and prepare various wines, foods, fruits, and sweets. Wang Chin's mother was invited to join them. After the four of them were seated and the wine was served, the old man rose to make a toast. Then he said to Wang, "Sir, you are such a master of martial arts, surely you must be a head instructor in the army. My son may have eyes, but he failed to recognize a hero."

Wang Chin laughed and said, "To tell you the truth, my name is not Chang. I am Wang Chin, Head Instructor of the 80,000-man imperial army in the Eastern Capital, and I spent my life playing with weapons. You see, the new Commander of the Imperial Army, Kao, was once given a beating by my father. When he became the Commander, he sought to vent his old hatred on me. Unfortunately I was under his command and in no position to argue with him. That's why I fled with my mother in the hopes of getting a job with the Commander-in-Chief of Yen-an prefecture. It wasn't my plan to come here. You and your son have been very kind to us, curing my mother and looking after us for so many days. I feel very indebted to you. If your son is willing to learn, I'll do all I can to teach him. But what he has learned so far is only show, of no value in combat. I must teach him again from the beginning."

"Do you understand how wrong you were, my son? Come over and pay respect to your teacher again!"

The young man once more knocked his head on the ground before Wang Chin, while the old man told him, "Sir, for generations our family has lived here in Hua-yin county with Little Flower Mountain right in front of us. This village is called Shih Family Village and contains three to four hundred families, all named Shih. Since his childhood, my son has been entranced by the martial arts and unwilling to learn farm work. His mother scolded him to no avail and eventually died of anger and frustration. Unable to control him, I've had to let him do what he wants. I don't know how much money I've spent for his teachers. I even had a famous artist tattoo his arms, shoulders, and chest with nine dragons, which resulted in his being called 'Shih Chin the Nine-Dragoned' by people here in the county. Sir, now that you are here, it will be great if you can help him complete his training. I will reward you handsomely for it."

Wang Chin, now highly pleased, replied, "Rest assured, sir, I will not leave until I've taught him everything."

From the day of that banquet, Instructor Wang and his mother stayed in the village. Everyday Shih

Chin would come and beg Wang to teach him the techniques of the eighteen weapons of war, and Wang taught him everything from scratch. Shih Chin's father was in the Hua-yin county seat serving as a village headman.

Time slipped quickly by. Within a little more than half a year Shih Chin had mastered the skills of all eighteen weapons: the lance, battle-hammer, bow, crossbow, jingal, whip, truncheon, double-edged sword, chain, hooks, axe, battle-axe, as well as the three-pronged spear, halberd, shield, cudgel, spear, and rake. With Wang putting his heart into teaching the young man, Shih Chin learned the secret techniques of each weapon. When Wang saw that he had mastered them all, he thought to himself, "Nice as it is to be here, I can't stay forever." So, one day, he said it was time to go to Yen-an. Shih Chin, however, wouldn't let him go, saying, "Don't leave. I'll take care of you and your mother till the end of your days. How about it?"

"My good brother," Wang replied, "you have been very kind, and everything is very nice here. But I'm afraid that Commander Kao will send someone to arrest me. You'd be implicated, not a very good prospect. For these reasons, I've decided to go to the Commander-in-Chief in Yen-an. It's on the border where people are needed. I'll be able to get a job there and settle down."

When Shih Chin and his father found that they couldn't change Wang Chin's mind, they prepared a farewell feast for him. To show their gratitude, they presented him with a platter on which lay two rolls of satin and 100 taels of silver.

The next day Wang Chin packed his luggage and got his horse ready, and he and his mother bade their host farewell. Wang helped his mother onto the horse, and they started their journey to Yen-an. Assigning a servant to carry Wang's luggage, Shih Chin escorted him for a distance of 10 *li*, so reluctant was he to let his teacher go. Then he bowed to the ground to him, and they parted in tears. Shih Chin returned home with his servant, while Instructor Wang again shouldered his bundles and walked behind his mother's horse on their way to Kuan-hsi.

We will now leave Wang Chin, who went to seek a career in the military, but continue our story of Shih Chin, who returned to his village.

Everyday Shih did nothing but train to increase his strength. As he was in his prime and unmarried, he would get up before dawn to practice his skills and during the day would spend all his time in the back of

the village riding on horseback and shooting arrows. Less than half a year had passed in this way when one day his father fell ill. He did not improve for many days, and Shih Chin sent all over for doctors to care for him, but the old man could not be cured and passed away.

For the sake of his father, Shih Chin selected the best coffin and outer casket. He engaged monks to pray for him, to hold memorial services through the forty-nine day mourning period, and to establish merits for the old man in the next world. He also engaged Taoist priests to set up an altar and perform a dozen redemption services to ensure his passage to Heaven. Then Shih Chin selected an auspicious day and a propitious hour for the burial. All the three to four hundred families of the village joined in the funeral procession in mourning dress. They buried his father in the ancestral graveyard on the mountain west of the village. From then on, Shih Chin's family estate lacked a manager, for he would not concern himself with farm work; the only thing he enjoyed was challenging others to spar with him using various weapons.

Three or four months after the old man's death, on a very hot day in the middle of the sixth month, Shih Chin was idling away his time and pulled up a bench to sit in the shadow of the willow trees near the threshing ground. A breeze wafted through the pine grove on the other side, and Shih Chin exclaimed, "Ah, what a good, cool breeze!" Just then he saw someone peeping out from behind the trees. "What are you up to—you who are spying on my village?" shouted Shih Chin. He jumped up and went around on the other side of the trees, where he found the hunter Li Chi, nicknamed "Rabbit-lancer."

"Li Chi, what are you searching for in my village? Are you planning to rob us?"

Stepping forward, Li Chi said, "Sir, I was just going to have a drink with 'Shorty' Ch'iu I-lang. When I saw you there resting, I didn't dare to intrude."

"I have a question for you," Shih interposed. "You used to bring by game to sell in our village, and I paid you for it. Why have you stopped doing it? Is it because you think I don't have the money to pay you any more?"

"Sir, how dare I even dream of such a thing! The truth is that I haven't had any game to sell."

"Nonsense," said Shih Chin. "Little Flower Mountain is so big; I can't believe that there isn't a deer or rabbit on it."

"Haven't you heard?" said the hunter. "There's a

band of robbers in the mountains now. They've built themselves a hideout and gathered some five to seven hundred men and over a hundred good horses. The chief is called Chu Wu, nicknamed 'Clever Strategist,' the second in command is Ch'en Ta, nicknamed 'Gorge-leaping Tiger,' and the third in command is Yang Ch'un, 'White-speckled Snake.' These chiefs lead their men to raid people's houses. Even the Hua-yin county government can't handle them and is now offering a reward of 3000 strings of cash to anyone who captures them. But who dares? Since we hunters don't even dare climb the mountain to hunt for game, how can I have any for sale?"

"I've heard about these bandits," said Shih Chin, "But I didn't know they'd gotten so powerful. Sooner or later they'll bring trouble. Well, Li Chi, if you ever have any game, bring some by." Li Chi bowed and left.

As Shih Chin went back into the house, he thought, "These bandits are growing so strong. Inevitably, they'll come to our village to make trouble. In that case—." He then ordered the servants to butcher two fat buffalos and bring out some good home-brewed wine. After burning a stack of paper coins for the gods, he sent servants out to invite over all the three or four hundred farmers of the Shih Family Village. When they arrived, Shih Chin seated them in the main hall according to seniority. As the servants poured wine for the guests, Shih Chin told them, "I have learned that there are three great bandits on Little Flower Mountain, who have gathered five to seven hundred men and taken them looting. Having become so strong, sooner or later they will come to our village to bother us. I've especially invited you here to discuss this matter. In case they should come, we ought to be prepared. If the bamboo clappers at my house are sounded, all of you should come with arms to help me. If something happens to any of you, we'll do the same. In this way we will help each other and together we'll protect our village. If the chiefs themselves should come here, I'll take care of them."

All the people said, "Sir, we farmers all depend on you to make the decisions. When the clappers are sounded, we'll all come to help." They thanked Shih Chin for the wine, and each went back home to get his weapons ready. Shih Chin also began precautionary measures; he repaired his doors and walls, set up watch stations, and got his armor, weapons, and horses ready.

Now let's turn to the three chiefs, who were

holding a conference in their hideout at Little Flower Mountain. The leader, "Clever Strategist" Chu Wu, was from Ting-yuan and could fight with a sword in each hand. Although not particularly skilled in fighting, he knew military maneuvers well and was clever at strategy. The second in command was Ch'en Ta, from Yeh-ch'eng, whose weapon was a steel lance with a white tip. The third one, Yang Ch'un, was from the Chieh-liang county of P'u-chou, and he used a big, long-handled sword. At the conference, Chu said to Ch'en and Yang, "I heard that the Hua-yin county government has offered 3000 strings of cash to anyone who captures us. I'm afraid that we'll have to put up a fight. Since we're low on both money and food, we'd better go get some. Not only are we short now, but we need to stock up provisions for a long war."

Ch'en Ta the "Gorge-leaping Tiger" added, "You're right. We'll go to Hua-yin county and ask to 'borrow some rations' from them and see what they say."

"Don't go to Hua-yin county," injected the "White-speckled Snake" Yang Ch'un. "Let's go to P'u-ch'eng county and run no risks."

Ch'en said, "P'u-ch'eng has very few people and not a lot of cash or food. We'll do better in Hua-yin. The people there have lots of money and grain."

"Elder brother, you don't understand," explained Yang. "To raid Hua-yin, we must pass Shih Family Village. That 'Shih Chin the Nine-Dragoned' is a tiger of a man, not to be provoked. He'll never let us pass."

"Brother, what a coward you are! If you can't even get through a mere village, how can we fight the government soldiers?"

"Elder brother, don't underestimate Shih Chin. He's really something," Yang Ch'un warned.

Chu Wu concurred. "I've also heard that the man is extremely brave and capable. Let's not go that way, brother."

At this Ch'en Ta yelled, "Shut your traps, you two! Don't tell me how great he is and how worthless we are. He's just a man and doesn't have three heads or six arms." Then he called out to his followers, "Get my horse ready! We'll attack the Shih Family Village right now. And afterwards we'll take Hua-yin county."

Chu Wu and Yang Ch'un tried to dissuade him, but Ch'en Ta wouldn't listen. He put on his armor and mounted his horse, selected some one hundred and fifty men, then, to the accompaniment of drums and gongs, descended the mountain heading straight for Shih Family Village.

Shih Chin was just getting his weapons and horses ready when a servant reported the bandits were coming. He ordered the bamboo clappers sounded. When the farmers all around Shih Family Village heard the clappers, they gathered together, three or four hundred of them. Bearing lances and staves, they rushed over to Shih Chin's place. There they saw the young man. On his head was a flat-topped turban; on his body a vermilion mail over a blue padded silk robe; on his feet a pair of green boots; and around his waist a wide leather belt. In front and behind, he wore metal plates as shields; on his back hung a bow and a quiver of arrows; in his hand he held a three-pointed, double-edged sword with four holes on which eight large metal rings were attached. A servant led forth a fiery red horse, which Shih Chin mounted, his sword in hand. In front of him were some forty strong retainers and behind some ninety farm laborers. The farmers of the Shih clan made up the rear of this procession. Shouting and yelling, they all made straight for the crossroad north of the village.

Ch'en Ta had led his men dashing down Little Flower Mountain and ordered them to take position. Shih Chin saw that Ch'en Ta wore a red concave cap, a gilded iron breast plate over a red padded robe, high boots, and a woven belt seven feet long. He rode on a tall white horse and held in horizontal position a steel spear eighteen feet long. His men, who had split into two groups and stood on either side, were shouting and yelling. The two leaders then approached each other to talk.

Ch'en Ta looked at Shih Chin and bowed from his horse. Shih addressed him in a loud voice, "You and your men kill, set fires, and rob people of their possessions. These are all capital offenses. You all have ears and ought to have heard of me! How dare you come here looking for trouble?"

Ch'en Ta answered, "We are short of food up in our mountain hideout and are on our way to Hua-yin county to borrow some. We only wish to pass your village; we wouldn't dare touch even a blade of grass here. If you let us pass now, we will thank you on our return."

"Nonsense! I am the village headman and was just about to go and capture you. How dare you ask to pass through my village! If I let you go, I myself will be implicated when the county Magistrate hears of it."

"Within the four seas all men are brothers," said Ch'en Ta. "Please let us pass."

"Cut the idle talk! Even if I let you go, there is someone else who wouldn't. Ask him; if he's willing to let you pass, you may."

"My good man," asked Ch'en Ta, "whom am I to ask?"

"Ask this sword in my hand," replied Shih Chin. "If he lets you go, so will I."

Ch'en Ta grew very angry and said, "You've driven me beyond endurance. Don't you be presumptuous with me!"

Shih Chin, now also incensed, flourished his sword and spurred on his horse in the direction of Ch'en Ta, who raised his spear and charged at Shih Chin. Their horses drew near, and a long fight ensued. Finally, Shih Chin faked a mistake and allowed Ch'en Ta to thrust the spear toward his chest. At that instant Shih suddenly turned sideways, and Ch'en, his spear in hand, lunged right in front of him. With great ease Shih stretched out his long arm and, with a twist of his strong waist, lifted Ch'en from his saddle. Then, seizing him by the woven belt he wore, Shih tossed him to the ground. Ch'en Ta's horse galloped away like a gust of wind.

Shih ordered his servants to tie Ch'en up. After chasing the bandits away, Shih returned home, where he tied Ch'en to a pillar in the center of the courtyard. He announced that he would capture the other two leaders and then go for the reward. Then he gave everyone a round of drinks and told them to return to their homes for the time being. They all applauded him. "You're a real hero, sir!"

Let's leave this joyous drinking crowd and return to Chu Wu and Yang Ch'un, who had stayed in their mountain hideout, holding their breath. They sent out some men to find out what had happened, and these men returned with the defeated bandits leading Ch'en Ta's riderless horse. "Bitter, bitter news!" they cried. "Brother Ch'en wouldn't listen to the chiefs and now has lost his life." Upon Chu Wu's inquiry, the men reported the details of the battle and concluded, "He couldn't measure up to the invincible Shih Chin."

Chu Wu said, "This is all because he wouldn't listen to me."

"Let's all go out there and fight to the death!" said Yang Ch'un.

"That won't help any," Chu said. "If even Ch'en is not Shih Chin's equal, you won't have a chance. I do have a plan, but if it doesn't work, it'll be the end of both of us." Then he whispered his plan to Yang Ch'un, adding, "There's no other way."

"An excellent plan!" exclaimed Yang. "Let's go at once; there's no time to lose."

Back in the village, before Shih Chin's anger had

abated, a servant ran in so fast that it seemed he had wings. "The bandit leaders Chu Wu and Yang Ch'un have come here themselves," he reported.

"Those guys are doomed. I'll send them both to the Magistrate. Bring my horse!" Shih Chin ordered. Meanwhile, the bamboo clappers were sounded everywhere, and all the farmers gathered. Shih Chin mounted his horse, but before he could depart from the village gate, he saw that Chu Wu and Yang Ch'un had already walked up to it. The pair of bandit chiefs dropped to their knees, four streams of tears flowing down their cheeks.

"What's going on?" Shih Chin got off his horse and shouted at them. "Why are you kneeling?"

Chu Wu replied in tears, "The three of us were forced to become bandits because we were persecuted by the law. When we became blood-brothers, we made a vow: 'Though we were not born on the same day, we will die on the same day.' We dare not compare our bond with that between the heroes of the Three Kingdoms, Kuan Yu, Chang Fei, and Liu Pei, but that is what we aspire to. Ch'en Ta, my younger brother, wouldn't listen to my advice and offended you. You captured him and we have no way of convincing you to release him, so we have come here to die with him. We beg you to send all three of us to the Magistrate and collect the reward. We swear that we will not even bat an eye, for we want to die at the hands of such a hero as you."

When Shih Chin heard this, these thoughts ran through his mind: "What brotherly love! If I turn these people in for a reward, all the heroes in the world will hold me in contempt for such an unworthy act. Since ancient times it has been said, 'A tiger does not eat a piece of offered meat.'" Aloud he said, "You two, come inside with me."

Chu Wu and Yang Ch'un were unafraid. They followed Shih into the inner hall and there again fell on their knees and asked to be tied up. Shih asked them to rise many times but they refused. As a hero naturally admires heroic qualities, Shih Chin finally said to them, "Since there is such a bond between you, I would be less than a real man if I were to send you to the Magistrate. Why don't I release Ch'en Ta and return him to you."

"No," said Chu Wu. "That would implicate you, which won't do. It's better for you to send us in and collect the reward."

"That I will not do," Shih Chin said. "Will you eat and drink with me?"

"We are not even afraid to die," Chu Wu replied. "Why should we be afraid of your wine and meat?"

Very pleased with this reply, Shih released Ch'en and prepared wine and food for the three right in the inner hall. Chu Wu, Yang Ch'un, and Ch'en Ta thanked him for his clemency. After a few rounds of drinks, they grew warmer toward each other. When the dinner ended, the three thanked their host again and together set out for the mountain. Shih saw them off at the village gate and then returned home.

When Chu Wu and the others arrived at their mountain hideout, they took their seats, and Chu said, "If we hadn't used this scheme to win his sympathy, we wouldn't have emerged alive. Although we achieved our goal, we must admire Shih Chin for his sparing us on the grounds of our brotherly love. Let's send him some presents one of these days to thank him."

In short, on a moonless night about a fortnight later, the three bandit leaders gathered thirty taels of slim gold ingots and commanded two of their men to take the gift to Shih Family Village. When the servants reported that two men were knocking at the gate, Shih Chin quickly threw on his clothes and hurried out. "What is it?" he asked the men.

"Our three chiefs send their repeated regards. They have sent us here with a small token of their gratitude for your sparing their lives. Please do not refuse it, sir."

At first Shih Chin would not accept the gift, but when he thought of the givers' good intention, he relented. He ordered the servants to serve the messengers plenty of wine, and, before leaving, gave them some odd silver as a tip. Half a month later, Chu Wu and his men succeeded in obtaining some large pearls in the course of their exploits, and they again sent some men on a midnight mission to present the pearls to Shih Chin, who once more accepted the gift.

Another half month passed, and Shih Chin thought to himself, "Those three men have been very respectful to me. Let me send them something in return." So, the next day he ordered a servant to send for a tailor and he himself went into town to buy three pieces of red embroidered silk, which he asked the tailor to use to make three robes. Then he selected three fat sheep to be cooked and placed in large boxes. He instructed two servants to deliver the presents. Shih Chin's head servant, named Wang Ssu, was quite capable in dealing with officials and had a way with words. For these reasons, the villagers all called him "Peerless Diplomat." On this occasion, Shih Chin picked him and another trusted servant for the mission. They took the boxed presents to the foot of the mountain, and, after being interrogated by Chu Wu's men, were shown to the leaders. Chu and the other leaders were very pleased; they accepted the silk robes, the fat sheep, and the wine. They also tipped the two messengers with ten taels of silver. After having a dozen drinks, the two returned to the village and conveyed to Shih Chin the bandit leaders' best wishes. From then on, Shih Chin and the three chiefs maintained constant contact. Wang Ssu was repeatedly sent to the mountain with presents, and the chiefs reciprocated with messengers bearing gold and silver for Shih Chin.

Time went by and soon it was the eighth month. Shih Chin wished to talk with the chiefs and so sent Wang Ssu to Little Flower Mountain with an invitation for Chu, Ch'en, and Yang. He would hold a banquet on the evening of the Mid-Autumn Festival and wanted them to join him for wine and viewing the full moon.

Wang Ssu ran up the mountain and delivered the invitation. After reading it, Chu Wu was delighted and the three chiefs immediately wrote a reply, promising their attendance. They rewarded Wang Ssu with some four or five taels of silver and let him drink a dozen cups of wine before he departed. At the foot of the mountain, however, he chanced to see one of the bandits who often brought presents to the village. The latter would not let him leave, but dragged him to a roadside wine house, where Wang Ssu drank another dozen cups of wine. After the two parted, Wang Ssu headed for his village. The wind blew down from the mountain, and, as he was walking, the wine began working on him. He staggered along, swaying with every step. Hardly had he walked ten *li* when he saw a grove of trees in front of him. Once in it, he passed out on the lush green ground.

It so happened that the "Rabbit-lancer" Li Chi was looking for rabbits at the foot of this slope. He recognized Wang Ssu of Shih Family Village and hurried to the grove to help him get up. That proved impossible but he caught sight of some silver showing from Wan Ssu's shoulder bag. Li Chi thought to himself, "He is drunk. But where did he get all this silver? Well, why shouldn't I take some?" Just as it was destined that the stars of the Dipper were to end up in one place, so Heaven provided this opportunity. Li Chi untied the shoulder bag and, with a toss of the hand, threw its contents on the ground—the letter and all! He picked up the letter and, since he could read a little, opened it. He saw the words "Chu Wu, Ch'en Ta, Yang Ch'un of Little Flower Mountain." The letter itself contained words that he did not know, but he sure knew those three names. He

thought, "When will a hunter like me ever get rich? Yet the fortune-teller said that this year I would come into a large fortune. This must be it! Didn't the Hua-yin county government offer three thousand strings of cash to get those bandits? I can't believe this Shih Chin! The other day when I went to his village to see 'Shorty' Ch'iu, he said I was there on the prowl for things to steal. Who'd think he's the one who runs around with bandits!" The hunter took the silver and the letter, then went straight to Hua-yin county to report to the officials.

Let's now talk about Wang Ssu. He woke up in the middle of the night, bathed in moonlight. When he jumped up in alarm, he found himself surrounded by pine trees. He fumbled around, but the bag and the letter were both gone! A search turned up nothing but the empty bag in the grass, which made him very worried. "The silver doesn't matter," he thought, "but the letter—what am I going to do? I don't know who took it." Then a plan occurred to him and he said to himself, "If I return to the village and say I've lost the letter, Master Shih will surely become enraged and kick me out of the village. It would be better to tell him there wasn't a written reply. How is he ever to find out the truth?"

His plan formed, Wang Ssu sped back to the village as if he had sprouted wings on his back. By the time he arrived, it was close to daybreak. When Shih Chin saw him, he asked, "Why so late?"

The servant replied, "Thanks to you, my lord, the three chieftains would not let me go, entertaining me with drinks half the night. That's why I'm so late."

"Have you brought back a letter or reply?"

"The three chieftains wanted to write a reply, but I told them, 'My lords, since you have decided to accept the invitation, there is really no need to put it in writing. I have had quite a few cups of wine; if I should lose the letter, it would be no laughing matter.'"

Shih Chin was very pleased with this answer. "You are really capable," he said. "No wonder people call you 'Peerless Diplomat.'"

Wang Ssu continued, "And I did not dare to delay even a moment. I ran straight back here, without taking one minute's rest on the road."

Then Shih Chin said, "Since they are coming, let's send some people to town to get fruit and wine for the feast."

Time passed quickly, and soon it was the Mid-Autumn Festival. The weather was beautiful and Shih Chin ordered his servants to kill a fat sheep and some hundred chickens and geese for the banquet. As evening drew near, the three chiefs on Little Flower Mountain ordered most of their men to stay behind to keep watch at the hideout, picking only a few to accompany them. Each of the three carried a big sword in his hands and another hanging from his waist. They did not mount their horses but instead walked down the mountain. On arrival at Shih Family Village, Shih Chin received them, and after the usual ceremonies, brought them to the back courtyard, where a feast had been prepared. The three chiefs were shown to the seats of honor, whereas Shih Chin himself sat across from them. As soon as the front and the back gates were barred, the drinking commenced. Servants took turns pouring the wine, while others carved and served the mutton. After they had had a couple of drinks, a bright full moon pushed itself above the eastern horizon.

Shih Chin and the three chiefs were chatting when suddenly they heard loud shouts from outside the wall and saw the glare of torches. Greatly startled, Shih Chin jumped up from his seat and said, "My three good friends, please remain seated. I'll go find out what is happening." Then he ordered the servants not to open the gates.

Pulling a ladder against the wall, he climbed up and looked out. He saw the Sheriff of Hua-yin on horseback; behind him were two leading officers and three or four hundred soldiers. The entire village was surrounded. Shih Chin and the three chiefs thought to themselves, "We're done for!" In the light of the torches, they could see gleaming steel-pronged spears, swords, five-pointed spears, and hooks, all as thick as hemp stalks in a field. The two leading officers yelled out, "Don't let the bandits escape!" . . .

"Now, what are we to do?" asked Shih Chin.

The three chiefs knelt down to the ground and said, "Older brother, you are innocent. We don't want to involve you. You must tie us up and give us up for the reward. It wouldn't look good to get you implicated in this."

"I will do nothing of the kind," said Shih Chin. "Otherwise people will think that I have tricked you into coming here in order to turn you in for the reward, and I'll become a universal laughing-stock. No, I'll live or die with you. Please get up and stop worrying; we'll think of something. But first let me get to the bottom of things." At that he climbed the ladder again and called out, "Why do you two officers come here in the middle of the night to bother me?"

They replied, "Sir, you still won't confess? Here, this is your accuser, Li Chi."

"Li Chi," shouted Shih Chin, "why do you falsely accuse me?"

"At first I did not know what it was. I picked up a letter from Wang Ssu, and read it in front of the county Magistrate; then the whole matter came out."

Shih turned to Wang Ssu, "Didn't you say that there was no written reply? What was this letter, then?"

"I was drunk and forgot about the letter."

At this Shih Chin gave out a loud cry, "You moron! Now what are we to do?"

The officers and their men, all afraid of Shih Chin, did not dare to come in to get him. The three chiefs pointed toward the outside and said, "Just give them a reply." Shih got the message and called out, "Officers, you don't have to bother. Please step back, and I'll have them tied up and send them out to you for the reward."

The two officers, afraid as they were of Shih Chin, consented, "We don't want to make any trouble. We'll just wait for you to bring them out and then go together with you to the Magistrate for the reward."

Getting off the ladder, Shih Chin came to the main hall. He first had Wang Ssu brought to the backyard, and, with one thrust of the sword, killed him. Then he ordered some servants to pack up all the valuables and others to light some thirty or forty torches. Meanwhile, Shih and the three chiefs put on their armor and picked their weapons from the rack. Each had a short sword hanging from his waist and a big sword in his hand. By the time they set fire to the thatched huts in the rear of the village, the servants had also packed their own belongings.

When the crowd outside saw the fire, they all ran toward the back of the village, and Shih Chin took this opportunity to set fire to the main section. Then he flung open the gates and, with a loud cry, rushed out, killing whoever was in his way. Right behind Shih were Chu and Yang; then came Ch'en with the bandits and Shih's servants. They fought their way out and deceived their enemies by pretending to go one direction while actually heading in another.

Shih Chin was a true tiger no one could stop. Against the background of the fire and confusion, he hewed open a passage through his enemies and came face to face with the two leading officers and Li Chi. When Shih saw them his anger rose, just as the saying goes, "When enemies meet they recognize each other clearly." The two officers, seeing that the outlook was bad for them, turned and ran. Li Chi wanted to do likewise, but before he could, Shih Chin caught up with him. He raised his sword and, with a downward blow, cut him in two. The two officers were trapped in their flight by Ch'en Ta and Yang Ch'un. Each gave a blow with his big sword, and the two lives were ended. The Sheriff was so scared that he retreated at full gallop. Terrified, each of the soldiers ran for his life. Soon all had disappeared.

Shih Chin led the men, running and fighting, straight to Little Flower Mountain. Entering the hideout, they sat down, and after they had rested a moment or two, Chu Wu and the other chiefs ordered their men to kill cows and horses for a feast to celebrate the victory. We need not go into the details.

A few days later, Shih thought to himself, "I was in such a hurry to save these three people, I set fire to my village. Although I salvaged the valuables, all the furniture and heavy things are lost." As he worried about his future, he decided that it was not a good idea to stay. So he spoke his mind to the three chiefs, "My teacher, Instructor Wang, is now working for the Commander-in-Chief of Kuan-hsi. I had wanted to go and look for him when my father passed away. Now that I have lost everything, including my house and my fortune, I will go look for him."

Chu Wu and the others said, "Older brother, don't leave. Stay a little longer. We can talk it over later. If you don't want to become a bandit, you can wait till the whole thing has cooled down, then we will rebuild your village for you, and you can still be a good citizen."

"I appreciate your kindness," Shih Chin said. "But my mind is made up. If I can find my teacher, I will be able to become an officer and will have a good life ahead of me."

Chu Wu said, "Older brother, if you don't mind the small size of this hideout, you can stay and be a chief. You'll be happy here."

"I am a man with no criminal record," said Shih Chin, "and must not bring shame to my deceased parents. Don't ever again mention the subject of my joining you as a bandit."

After a few more days' stay, Shih insisted that he had to go, despite the best efforts of Chu and the others to make him stay. Shih Chin left all his men with the bandits. Taking only a little silver and a bundle of clothes, he entrusted the rest of his belongings to the chiefs. He put on a white brimmed fur hat with a red tassel, and under it a soft black scarf, tied under his chin with a yellow ribbon. On his body he wore a uniform of white silk belted with a sash of plum-red color. On his legs he wore black-and-white garters tied in a zig-zag pattern and on his feet hemp sandals suited for travel in the hills. At his side hung a "wild goose feather" sword.

Swinging his bundle over his shoulders, Shih Chin picked up his big sword and bade farewell to Chu and the other chiefs. All Chu Wu's men accompanied him down the mountain, where they parted in tears. Then Chu Wu and the men returned to their hideout.

Translated by Clara Yu

41.

Merchants in the Ming

As seen in selection 7, "The Debate on Salt and Iron," early Confucian views were distrustful of the profit motive and consequently of commercial activity in general. With the extensive commercialization that occurred in later dynasties, such extreme views came to be tempered but did not disappear altogether.

How did merchants and others involved in commercial activities react to such negative conceptions? How did they view their own place in the world? Unfortunately, few active merchants wrote memoirs, though many scholars and officials from Ming times onward came from commercial families. Therefore, we have to approach this question indirectly by looking at what was written about merchants and at the models of behavior held up for them to emulate.

Below is an essay on merchants written by Chang Han (1511–1593), a Ming official whose family had established its fortune through the textile industry. It shows ambivalent feelings toward merchants and commerce not atypical of the period. Following it are two biographies of admirable merchants, respected for their skills in business but also for their virtue and generosity. They were included in a collection of biographies compiled by Wang Tao-k'un (1525–1593), a high official and writer who was the son and grandson of salt merchants.

ESSAY ON MERCHANTS

Money and profit are of great importance to men. They seek profit, then suffer by it, yet they cannot forget it. They exhaust their bodies and spirits, run day and night, yet they still regard what they have gained as insufficient. . . .

Those who become merchants eat fine food and wear elegant clothes. They ride on beautifully caparisoned, double-harnessed horses—dust flying as they race through the streets and the horses' precious sweat falling like rain. Opportunistic persons attracted by their wealth offer to serve them. Pretty girls in beautiful long-sleeved dresses and delicate slippers play string and wind instruments for them and compete to please them.

Merchants boast that their wisdom and ability are such as to give them a free hand in affairs. They believe that they know all the possible transformations in the universe and therefore can calculate all the changes in the human world, and that the rise and fall of prices are under their command. They are confident that they will not make one mistake in a hundred in their calculations. These merchants do not know how insignificant their wisdom and ability really are. As the *Chuang Tzu* says: "Great understanding is broad and unhurried; little understanding is cramped and busy."

Because I have traveled to many places during my career as an official, I am familiar with commercial activities and business conditions in various places. The capital is located in an area with mountains at its back and a great plain stretching in front. The region is rich in millet, grain, donkeys, horses, fruit, and vegetables, and has become a center where goods from distant places are brought. Those who engage in commerce, including the foot peddler, the cart peddler, and the shopkeeper, display not only clothing and fresh foods from the fields but also numerous luxury items such as priceless jade from K'un-lun, pearls from the island of Hai-nan, gold from Yunnan, and coral from Vietnam. These precious items, coming from the mountains or the sea, are not found in central China. But people in remote areas and in other countries, unafraid of the dangers and difficulties of travel, transport these items step by step to the capital, making it the most prosperous place in the empire. . . .

South of the capital is the province of Honan, which is the center of the empire. Going from K'ai-feng, its capital, northwards to Wei-chung, one can reach the Yangtze and Han rivers. Thus, K'ai-feng is a great transportation center; one can travel by either boat or carriage from this spot to all other places, which makes it a favorite gathering place for merchants. The area is rich in lacquer, hemp, sackcloth, fine linen, fine gloss silk, wax, and leather. In antiquity, the Chou dynasty had its capital here. The land is broad and flat, the people are rich and prosperous, and the customs are refined and frugal. . . .

In general, in the Southeast area the greatest profits are to be had from fine gauze, thin silk, cheap silk, and sackcloth. San-wu in particular is famous for them. My ancestors' fortunes were based solely on such textile businesses. At the present time, a great many people in San-wu have become wealthy from the textile industry.

In the nation's Northwest, profits are greatest in wool, coarse woolen serge, felt, and fur garments. Kuan-chung is especially famous for these items. There is a family named Chang in that area which has engaged in the animal-breeding business generation after generation. They claim to have 10,000 sheep. Their animal-breeding enterprise is the largest in the Northwest and has made them the richest family in the area. In the surrounding areas of Yen, Chou, Ch'i, and Chin, many other people have also become rich from animal breeding. From there, merchants seeking great profits go west to Szechwan and south to Kwangtung. Because of the nature of the special products from the latter area—fine and second-grade pearls, gold, jade, and precious woods—profits can be five- or ten-fold or more.

The profits from the tea and salt trades are especially great but only large-scale merchants can undertake these businesses. Furthermore, there are government regulations on their distribution, which

prohibit the sale of tea in the Northwest and salt in the Southeast. Since tea is produced primarily in the Southeast, prohibiting its sale to the non-Chinese on the northern border is wise and can be enforced. Selling privately produced salt where it is manufactured is also prohibited. This law is rigidly applied to all areas where salt was produced during the Ming dynasty. Yet there are so many private salt producers there now that the regulation seems too rigid and is hard to enforce.

Profits from selling tea and the officials' income from the tea tax are usually ten to twenty percent of the original investment. By contrast, merchants' profits from selling salt and the officials' income from the salt tax can reach seventy to eighty percent of the original invested capital. In either case, the more the invested capital, the greater the profit; the less the invested capital, the less the profit. The profits from selling tea and salt enrich the nation as well as the merchants. Skillful merchants can make great profits for themselves while the inept ones suffer losses. This is the present state of the tea and salt business.

In our Chekiang province it appears that most of the rich gain their wealth from engaging in salt trade. But the Chia family in Wu-ling became rich from selling tea and have sustained their prosperity for generations. The "Book of Chou" says: "If farmers do not work, there will be an insufficiency of food; if craftsmen do not work, there will be an insufficiency of tools; if merchants do not work, circulation of the three necessities will be cut off, which will cause food and materials to be insufficient."*

As to the foreign trade on the northwestern frontier and the foreign sea trade in the Southeast, if we compare their advantages and disadvantages with respect to our nation's wealth and the people's well-being, we will discover that they are as different as black and white. But those who are in charge of state economic matters know only the benefits of the Northwest trade, ignoring the benefits of the sea trade. How can they be so blind?

In the early years of the frontier trade, China traded sackcloth and copper cash to the foreigners. Now we use silk and gold but the foreigners repay us only with thin horses. When we exchanged sackcloth and copper cash for their thin horses, the advantage of the trade was still with China and our national wealth was not endangered. But now we give away

---

* The "Book of Chou" is a section of the *Book of Documents*, one of the oldest of the classics.

gold and silk, and the gold, at least, will never come back to us once it flows into foreign lands. Moreover, to use the silk that China needs for people's clothing to exchange for useless, inferior horses is clearly unwise.

Foreigners are recalcitrant and their greed knows no bounds. At the present time our nation spends over one million cash yearly from our treasury on these foreigners, still we cannot rid ourselves of their demands. What is more, the greedy heart is unpredictable. If one day they break the treaties and invade our frontiers, who will be able to defend us against them? I do not think our present trade with them will ensure us a century of peace.

As to the foreigners in the Southeast, their goods are useful to us just as ours are to them. To use what one has to exchange for what one does not have is what trade is all about. Moreover, these foreigners trade with China under the name of tributary contributions. That means China's authority is established and the foreigners are submissive. Even if the gifts we grant them are great and the tribute they send us is small, our expense is still less than one ten-thousandth of the benefit we gain from trading with them. Moreover, the Southeast sea foreigners are more concerned with trading with China than with gaining gifts from China. Even if they send a large tribute offering only to receive small gifts in return, they will still be content. In addition, trading with them can enrich our people. So why do we refrain from the trade?

Some people may say that the Southeast sea foreigners have invaded us several times so they are not the kind of people with whom we should trade. But they should realize that the Southeast sea foreigners need Chinese goods and the Chinese need their goods. If we prohibit the natural flow of this merchandise, how can we prevent them from invading us? I believe that if the sea trade were opened, the trouble with foreign pirates would cease. These Southeast sea foreigners are simple people, not to be compared to the unpredictable Northeast sea foreigners. Moreover, China's exports in the Northwest trade come from the national treasury. Whereas the Northwest foreign trade ensures only harm, the sea trade provides us with only gain. How could those in charge of the government fail to realize this?

Turning to the taxes levied on Chinese merchants, though these taxes are needed to fill the national treasury, excessive exploitation should be prohibited. Merchants from all areas are ordered to stop their carts and boats and have their bags and cases ex- amined whenever they pass through a road or river checkpoint. Often the cargoes are overestimated and thus a falsely high duty is demanded. Usually merchants are taxed when they enter the checkpoint and are taxed again at the marketplace. When a piece of goods is taxed once, the merchant can still make some profit while complying with the state's regulations. But today's merchants often are stopped on the road for additional payments and also suffer extortions from the clerks. Such exploitation is hard and bitter enough but, in addition, the merchants are taxed twice. How can they avoid becoming more and more impoverished?

When I was Vice-President of the Board of Public Works in Nanking, I was also in charge of the customs duties on the upper and lower streams of the Black Dragon River. At that time I was working with Imperial Censor Fang K'o-yung. I told him: "In antiquity, taxes on merchants were in the form of voluntary contributions based on official hints, not through levies. Levying taxes on merchants is a bad policy. We should tax people according to their degree of wealth or poverty. Who says we cannot have good government!" Fang agreed with me, so we lowered the taxes on the merchants some twenty percent. After the taxes were lowered, merchants became willing to stop at the checkpoints. All boats stop when they should and the total tax income received from merchants increased fifty percent. From this example one can see that the people can be moved by benevolent policies.

THE BIOGRAPHY OF CHU CHIEH-FU

Chu Chieh-fu, whose formal name was Chieh, started as a Confucian scholar. He was from T'un-hsi of Hsiu-ning and his father, Hsing, was a salt merchant who lived away from home at Wu-lin. Hsing had taken Shao-chi of Wu-lin as his concubine but she was barren. Later, when he returned home for his father-in-law's birthday, his primary wife became pregnant and gave birth to Chieh-fu. In his early childhood, Chieh-fu lived in Wu-lin with his father and went to school there. Shao-chi, relying on the father's favor, did not treat him as her son. Chieh-fu, however, served her respectfully and worked diligently in school. At the age of fourteen, he officially registered Wu-lin as his native place and was designated an official student of that place. Shortly thereafter, his father died at Wu-lin. His concubine took the money and hid it with some of her mother's relatives and would not return to her husband's hometown. Chieh-fu wept day and night, saying, "However unworthy I may be, my late father was blameless." Finally the concubine arranged for the funeral and burial of her husband in his hometown. Thus, everything was done properly.

After the funeral, Chieh-fu was short of funds. Since for generations his family had been in commerce, he decided not to suffer just to preserve his scholar's cap. Therefore he handed in his resignation to the academic officials and devoted himself to the salt business. He thoroughly studied the laws on salt merchandising and was always able to talk about the strengths and weaknesses of the law. When the envoy from the Salt Manufacturing Division asked for his suggestions, Chieh-fu would respond promptly. Therefore, all the other salt merchants respected him as their leader.

During the Chia-ching period [1522–1567], salt affairs were handled by the Central Law Officer, who increased the taxes suddenly, causing great inconvenience for the merchants. They gathered in Chieh-fu's house and asked him to serve as their negotiator. Chieh-fu entered the office and stated the advantages and disadvantages of the new law eloquently in thousands of words. Leaning against his couch, the Central Law Officer listened to Chieh-fu's argument and finally adopted his suggestion.

At that time, the merchants suffered greatly from two scoundrels who often took them to court in the hopes of getting bribes from them. During tense moments at trials, the merchants usually turned to Chieh-fu as their spokesman. Being lofty and righteous, he always disclosed the scoundrels' crimes and condemned them. The merchants thus esteemed Chieh-fu for his virtue and wanted to give him a hundred taels of gold as a birthday present. But he protested: "Even if my acts have not been at the lofty level of a knight-errant, I did not do them for the sake of money." Thus, the merchants respected him even more and no longer talked about giving him money.

When there was a dispute among the merchants which the officials could not resolve, Chieh-fu could always mediate it immediately. Even when one group would go to his house and demand his compliance with their views, he would still be able to settle the dispute by indirect and gentle persuasion. Hence, people both far and near followed each other, coming to ask him to be their arbitrator. Yet, after settling a

dispute, Chieh-fu would always step aside and never take credit himself.

The populace in T'un-hsi city where Chieh-fu lived was militant and litigious. When he returned home for his father's funeral, slanderous rumors were spread about him, but Chieh-fu humbled himself and never tried to get back at the instigators. Later, when he grew rich rapidly, people became even more critical. Chieh-fu merely behaved with even greater deference. When the ancestral shrine fell into disrepair, Chieh-fu on his own sent workmen to repair it. When members of his lineage started talking about it, he had the workmen work during the day and consulted with his relatives in the evening. Finally the whole lineage got together and shared the task with him.

Once Chieh-fu bought a concubine in Wu-lin who bore a child after only a few months. His family was about to discard the child but Chieh-fu upbraided them, saying, "I love my children dearly. How could I cause someone else's child to die in the gutter?" He brought the child up and educated him until he was able to support himself.

In the past many wealthy merchants in the eastern provinces had striven to associate themselves with the gentry. But for several years the merchants had been barely scraping by, limiting their access to such friendship. Yet when Chieh-fu was in East Yüeh for business he became acquainted with some members of the gentry there. He gained a reputation for his hospitality, and even when common people visited him they always received the best treatment. Some people came to rely upon Chieh-fu as much as if he were a relative. If he did not offer them enough, they would complain, "You stupid little rich merchant, why are you so stingy with me?"

Chieh-fu finally discontinued his salt business and ordered his son to pursue a different career. By that time he was already planning to retire to his hometown. Then in 1568 a Central Law Officer who was appointed to inspect the salt business started to encourage secret informants. Soon Chieh-fu was arrested, an enemy having laid a trap for him. However, the official could not find any evidence against him. But then Ho, whose son Chieh-fu had once scolded, came forward to testify. Consequently, Chieh-fu was found guilty. When the litigation against him was completed, he was sentenced to be a frontier guard at Ting-hai. The merchants said, in describing Chieh-fu's case: "Beating the drum, the official seized a lamb and claimed it to be a tiger; pretending to net a big fish, he actually aimed at the big bird."

When Chieh-fu received his sentence to enter the army, he controlled his feelings and immediately complied. His son, fearing his father would acquire a bad name, suggested that he send a petition to the Emperor. Chieh-fu merely sighed and said, "Your father must have offended Heaven. The truth is that the Central Law Officer is a representative of his Heavenly Majesty, not that your father is falsely charged."

Frontier General Liu had heard of Chieh-fu and therefore summoned him to work in his own encampment. At that time, a friend of the General's moved to Hsin-tu upon his retirement. The General sent Chieh-fu to Hsin-tu as his personal messenger but within a short time Chieh-fu became seriously ill. He advised his son, Cheng-min: "Your father's name has been recorded in the official labor records. Now he is about to die as a prisoner. Never let your father's example stop you from behaving righteously. Remember this." Then, at the age of sixty-five, he died.

THE BIOGRAPHY OF GENTLEMAN WANG

In 1556, Mr. Wang, who was ninety years old at the time, was given the highest prefectural title by imperial decree and from that time on has been treated with the courtesies due an elder. As the histories testify, in ancient times emperors often honored venerable old men so as to receive the benefit of their constant advice. Even at his great age Mr. Wang is a man of the highest integrity; therefore I now extol his deeds in order to show my respect for virtuous old men.

Mr. Wang's formal name is T'ung-pao and polite name Ch'u-ch'üan. He is from Yen township of She county. His ancestors were originally from T'an-mo but a number of them split away from the family and moved to Yen township. (It is said that Mr. Wang and I are descended from a common ancestor.) Even as a teenager, he was famous for his skill in making money.

Mr. Wang lives in Shang-hai. Being open and confident he has attracted the respect of many capable and prosperous people who compete to attach themselves to him. At first, Mr. Wang's capital was no greater than the average person's. Later, as he grew more prosperous every day, the number of his associates also steadily increased. To accommodate his apprentices, Mr. Wang built buildings with doors on four sides. Whenever customers came, they could be taken care of from all four directions; thus, no one ever had to wait very long.

Mr. Wang set up the following guidelines for his associates: do not let anyone who lives in another county control the banking; when lending money, never harass law-abiding people unnecessarily or give them less than they need; charge low interest on loans; do not aim at high profit and do not ask for daily interest. These principles led customers to throng to him, even ones from neighboring towns and provinces. Within a short time, Mr. Wang accumulated great wealth; in fact, of all the rich people in that area he became the richest.

Mr. Wang liked to help people and to give assistance to the poor. If anyone among his kinsmen could not afford a funeral for his parents, Mr. Wang would always buy some land and build a tomb for him. As soon as he heard someone could not make ends meet, he would buy land to rent to him. Whenever he was out traveling and met some unburied spirit, he would bid his servants bury it and present some offerings.

During the Chia-ching period [1521–1567], there was a serious drought, and the Prefect proposed opening the granary. Considering the hardship this would cause the people, Mr. Wang sent a written report to the Prefect, as follows:

> This proposal will cause starving people to travel here from hundreds of *li* away to wait for the distribution. Even if there are no delays en route, they may die before they get here. Yet if we make them stay home and wait for a pint of food, it will be like abandoning them to die in the gutters. I suggest that we exchange the grain for money and distribute it around the area. All the wealthy people ought to donate some money to help the poor. I myself will start with a donation of a hundred taels of gold.

The Prefect accepted his suggestion and everyone said that this was much more convenient. Then Mr. Wang also prepared some food to feed people in his own county and caused similar actions to be taken throughout the whole of Shang-hai. Thus most people in this area survived.

Once Tung-ching Bridge in Wu-hui was damaged and Mr. Wang donated a hundred strings of cash for repairs. From then on, whenever a dike or bridge was built, he would donate a similar sum to promote such community activities.

Mr. Wang once had a dream in which three Taoist priests approached his house. And, indeed, the next day he received a picture which matched his dream. He regarded the priests as gods and worshipped them sincerely. Later he was almost poisoned but escaped the disaster by tipping over the poison. Another time when he was traveling from Tan-yang, the driver, with evil intentions, was leading him down the wrong road. Fortunately, he met an old man who cautioned him and he escaped. Mr. Wang himself said that it must have been because of the gods' help that he survived each time. Hence, he spent several thousand taels of gold to construct a Three Taoist Temple near Mt. Lion. This was reported to Emperor Shih-tsung, who conferred a tablet upon the temple with these words on it: "A divine manifestation." The local people have recourse to this temple in cases of flood, drought, disease, and suffering.

When some bullies encroached upon the ancestral temple on Mount Ling and occupied his ancestral cemetery in Yeh village, Mr. Wang repaired all the damage, sparing no expense; thereafter, everyone praised him as a righteous man.

When the "island barbarians"* raided Shang-hai, some of Mr. Wang's associates fled with his money. Nevertheless, he remained unmoved and made no inquiries. Neighbors came to see him, saying, "Mr. Wang, please cheer up. Really this loss is as insignificant as plucking a hair out of a horse's skin."

Mr. Wang smiled and replied, "Where can the hair grow when there's no skin left? When these people first came to join me, it was unexpected; now that they have gone, I myself remain unchanged and bear no resentment." Within a short time, his business revived; yet Mr. Wang still remained unmoved. Hence, people said that he was a man of wisdom because neither success nor frustration could affect him.

Whenever there was a dispute, Mr. Wang could always resolve it immediately, even if it was quite serious. When Magistrate Hsü was in charge of Shang-hai, he imprisoned someone named Chu, who died in jail. The victim's father then presented a petition to the Emperor which worried the Magistrate. The officials, elders, and local leaders were willing to offer the father a thousand taels of gold on the Magistrate's behalf, but on discussing it, they decided only Mr. Wang could settle the matter, and indeed he persuaded the father to accept the terms. Then the Magistrate was transferred to another position. Upon learning this fact, the officials, elders, and local leaders all quickly dispersed. Mr. Wang sighed and said, "It isn't easy to collect a thousand taels of gold but I will not break the promise made to the Magistrate in trouble." He then paid the thousand taels of gold and the Magistrate was out of his difficulties. Even when Magistrate Hsü was dismissed soon thereafter, Mr. Wang did not voice any concern, and after two years Hsü returned the thousand taels of gold to him.

Later when Mr. Chu set up dikes, a dispute occurred which involved thousands of people. The official tried to straighten out the merits of the case, but still it could not be resolved. Therefore the official asked Mr. Wang to take a hand in the matter. He successfully mediated the dispute merely by sending out a long letter. Later he was singled out to promote good community relations in Lin-ho and resolved all the quarrels there. Thus everybody praised him, saying, "Mr. Wang is capable of mediating disputes. He has the manner of a gentleman of national stature, and even the gentlemen of antiquity were not his equals."

When Mr. Wang is at home he is always in high spirits. He likes to make friends with the chivalrous youths. In his later years he has become particularly fond of chess, often staying up all night until he either wins or loses a game. The youths say that Mr. Wang is no ordinary person, that he must have received instruction from Heaven.

Now Mr. Wang is almost one hundred years old. He has at least thirty sons and grandsons living at home with him. It is said, "One who seeks perfection will attain it." This describes Mr. Wang perfectly.

Translated by Lily Hwa

---

* I.e., pirates from Japan, the Ryukyus, and so on.

42.

Family Instructions

Lineages were not only concerned with common property and joint ancestor worship; they also played important roles as higher authorities on family matters. Family disputes concerning matters such as inheritance would often be referred to the leaders of the lineage for a decision. Lineage councils would also help parents discipline unruly or disobedient children, especially grown ones. To facilitate making judgments in such cases, lineages often compiled and published rules for proper family behavior and advice on achieving family harmony. On the whole, traditional precepts and Neo-Confucian moral values were upheld and reiterated, although some adjustments were often made because of the difficulties poor members of the lineage might have in observing some standards.

The following instructions for family activities and behavior are from the preface to a late-Ming genealogy of the Miu lineage in Kwangtung province.

WORK HARD AT ONE OF THE PRINCIPAL OCCUPATIONS

1. To be filial to one's parents, to be loving to one's brothers, to be diligent and frugal—these are the first tenets of a person of good character. They must be thoroughly understood and faithfully carried out.

One's conscience should be followed like a strict teacher and insight should be sought through introspection. One should study the words and deeds of the ancients to find out their ultimate meanings. One should always remember the principles followed by the ancients, and should not become overwhelmed by current customs. For if one gives in to cruelty, pride, or extravagance, all virtues will be undermined, and nothing will be achieved.

Parents have special responsibilities. *The Book of Changes* says: "The members of a family have strict sovereigns." These "sovereigns" are the parents. Their position in a family is one of unique authority, and they should utilize their authority to dictate matters, to maintain order, and to inspire respect, so that the members of the family will all be obedient. If the parents are lenient and indulgent, there will be many troubles which in turn will give rise to even more troubles. Who is to blame for all this? The elders in a family must demand discipline of themselves, following all rules and regulations to the letter, so that the younger members emulate their good behavior and exhort each other to abide by the teachings of the ancient sages. Only in this way can the family hope to last for generations. If, however, the elders of a family should find it difficult to abide by these regulations, the virtuous youngsters of the family should help them along. Because the purpose of my work is to make such work easier, I am not afraid of giving many small details. . . .

2. Those youngsters who have taken Confucian scholarship as their hereditary occupation should be sincere and hard-working, and try to achieve learning naturally while studying under a teacher. Confucianism is the only thing to follow if they wish to bring glory to their family. Those who know how to

keep what they have but do not study are as useless as puppets made of clay or wood. Those who study, even if they do not succeed in the examinations, can hope to become teachers or to gain personal benefit. However, there are people who study not for learning's sake, but as a vulgar means of gaining profit. These people are better off doing nothing.

Youngsters who are incapable of concentrating on studying should devote themselves to farming; they should personally grasp the ploughs and eat the fruit of their own labor. In this way they will be able to support their families. If they fold their hands and do nothing, they will soon have to worry about hunger and cold. If, however, they realize that their forefathers also worked hard and that farming is a difficult way of life, they will not be inferior to anyone. In earlier dynasties, officials were all selected because they were filial sons, loving brothers, and diligent farmers. This was to set an example for all people to devote themselves to their professions, and to ensure that the officials were familiar with the hardships of the common people, thereby preventing them from exploiting the commoners for their own profit.

3. Farmers should personally attend to the inspection, measurement, and management of the fields, noting the soil as well as the terrain. The early harvest as well as the grain taxes and the corvée should be carefully calculated. Anyone who indulges in indolence and entrusts these matters to others will not be able to distinguish one kind of crop from another and will certainly be cheated by others. I do not believe such a person could escape bankruptcy.

4. The usual occupations of the people are farming and commerce. If one tries by every possible means to make a great profit from these occupations, it usually leads to loss of capital. Therefore it is more profitable to put one's energy into farming the land; only when the fields are too far away to be tilled by oneself should they be leased to others. One should solicit advice from old farmers as to one's own capacity in farming.

Those who do not follow the usual occupations of farming or business should be taught a skill. Being an artisan is a good way of life and will also shelter a person from hunger and cold. All in all, it is important to remember that one should work hard when young, for when youth expires one can no longer achieve anything. Many people learn this lesson only after it is too late. We should guard against this mistake.

5. Fish can be raised in ponds by supplying them with grass and manure. Vegetables need water. In empty plots one can plant fruit trees such as the pear, persimmon, peach, prune, and plum, and also beans, wheat, hemp, peas, potatoes, and melons. When harvested, these vegetables and fruits can sustain life. During their growth, one should give them constant care, nourishing them and weeding them. In this way, no labor is wasted and no fertile land is left uncultivated. On the contrary, to purchase everything needed for the morning and evening meals means the members of the family will merely sit and eat. Is this the way things should be?

6. Housewives should take full charge of the kitchen. They should make sure that the store of firewood is sufficient, so that even if it rains several days in succession, they will not be forced to use silver or rice to pay for firewood, thereby impoverishing the family. Housewives should also closely calculate the daily grocery expenses, and make sure there is no undue extravagance. Those who simply sit and wait to be fed not only are treating themselves like pigs and dogs, but also are leading their whole households to ruin. . . .

OBSERVE THE RITUALS AND PROPRIETIES

1. Capping and wedding ceremonies should be carried out according to one's means. Funerals and burials, being important matters, should be more elaborate, but one should still be mindful of financial considerations. Any other petty formalities not found in the *Book of Rites* should be abolished.

2. Marriage arrangements should not be made final by the presenting of betrothal gifts until the boy and girl have both reached thirteen; otherwise, time might bring about changes which cause regrets.

3. For the seasonal sacrifices, the ancestral temple should be prepared in advance and the ceremonies performed at dawn in accordance with [Chu Hsi's] *Family Rituals* and our own ancestral temple regulations.

4. For burials one should make an effort to acquire solid and long-lasting objects to be placed in the coffin; but one need not worry as much about the tomb itself, which can be constructed according to one's means. The ancients entrusted their bodies to the hills and mountains, indifferent to whether their names

would be remembered by posterity; their thinking was indeed profound.

5. Sacrifices at the graves should be made on Tomb-Sweeping Day and at the Autumn Festival. Because the distances to different mountains vary, it is difficult to reach every grave on those days. Therefore, all branch families should be notified in advance of the order of priority: first, the founding father of our lineage; then ancestors earlier than great-great-grandfather; next, ancestors down to each person's grandfather. Established customs should be followed in deciding how much wine and meat should be used, how many different kinds of sacrificial offerings should be presented, and how much of the yearly budget should be spent on the sacrifices. All of these should be recorded in a special "sacrifice book" in order to set standards.

6. Not celebrating one's birthday has since ancient times been regarded as an exemplary virtue. An exception is the birthdays of those who are beyond their sixty-first year, which should be celebrated by their sons and grandsons drinking to their health. But under no circumstances should birthdays become pretexts for heavy drinking. If either of one's parents has died, it is an especially unfilial act to forget him or her and indulge in drinking and feasting. Furthermore, to drink until dead-drunk not only affects one's mind but also harms one's health. The numbers of people who have been ruined by drinking should serve as a warning.

7. On reaching five, a boy should be taught to recite the primers and not be allowed to show arrogance or laziness. On reaching six, a girl should be taught *Admonitions for Women* and not be allowed to venture out of her chamber. If children are frequently given snacks and playfully entertained, their nature will be spoiled and they will grow up to be unruly and bad. This can be prevented if caught at an early age.

8. When inviting guests to dinner, one should serve not more than five dishes or more than two soups. Wine and rice should also be served in the right proportion.

9. When attending a funeral service, one should bring only incense and paper money, never hand-towels, fruit, or wine, and should stay for only one cup of tea.

10. Gifts presented to us on the occasion of ancestor worship are to be properly compensated for by cash.

If the gift box contains a pig's head, the corresponding return would be one-tenth of a tael of silver; for two geese and wine it would be three-tenths of a tael; for a lamb and wine, half a tael; a pig and wine, one tael. In addition, two-hundredths of a tael should be placed in an envelope and presented as a token compensation for fruit and wine. Whether or not these are accepted, and whether or not another present is given in return, depends on the other party. For ceremonies held in our own village, each person should contribute two-hundredths of a tael of silver, and four people should share one table. Those who have contributed yet fail to attend the banquet will get their money back in the original envelope. This is to be stated in the village agreements and to be practiced by all.

PROHIBIT EXTRAVAGANCE

1. All our young people should wear cotton clothes and eat vegetables. Only on special occasions such as ancestor worship or dinner parties are they to be allowed to drink wine, eat meat, and temporarily put on new clothes. They are fortunate enough to be sheltered from hunger and cold; how dare they feel ashamed of their coarse clothing and coarse food! Also, they should do physical labor. As long as they are capable of carrying loads with their hands and on their backs, they have no need to hire servants. They are fortunate enough not to be ordered around by others; how dare they order other people around! They should learn to cherish every inch of cloth and every half-penny, thereby escaping poverty.

2. Among relatives, presents should not be exchanged more than twice a year, and the gifts should not cost more than one-tenth of a tael of silver. Relatives should agree to abide by the principle of frugality and refuse any gift exceeding this limit. This rule, however, does not include celebrations and funerals, for which custom should be followed.

3. Ordinarily, custom dictates the foods to be offered guests. However, relatives and friends who visit each other often can be served just a dish of fish and another of vegetables. Ssu-ma Wen Kung once wrote:

> My father was a Prefect. Whenever a guest came to visit, he would always serve wine. Sometimes there were three rounds of drinking, and sometimes five; but never were there more than seven rounds. The wine was bought from the common market. The only sweets were

pears, nuts, dates, and persimmons; the only dishes were dried or hashed meats, vegetables, and thick soup; the plates were either porcelain or lacquer. That was the way officials of that time entertained their guests. They met often and were courteous to each other. Though the food was cheap, their friendships were deep.

From now on, whenever a guest comes to visit, we should not have many dishes and should not force the guest to drink too much. Our aim should be to have the congenial mood last a long time, and the host and the guest enjoy it together.

Since our branch of the family has many members, when a visitor comes, it is difficult to have everyone present for dinner. Instead, only some members of the family will be asked to share the company of the guest. This is designed to save expense. The members will all have their turns at being invited and should not compete among themselves, lest jealousy or suspicion arise.

EXERCISE RESTRAINT

1. Our young people should know their place and observe correct manners. They are not permitted to gamble, to fight, to engage in lawsuits, or to deal in salt privately. Such unlawful acts will only lead to their own downfall.

2. If land or property is not obtained by righteous means, descendants will not be able to enjoy it. When the ancients invented characters, they put gold next to two spears to mean "money," indicating that the danger of plunder or robbery is associated with it. If money is not accumulated by good means, it will disperse like overflowing water; how could it be put to any good? The result is misfortune for oneself as well as for one's posterity. This is the meaning of the saying: "The way of Heaven detests fullness, and only the humble gain." Therefore, accumulation of great wealth inevitably leads to great loss. How true are the words of Lao Tzu!

A person's fortune and rank are predestined. One can only do one's best according to propriety and one's own ability; the rest is up to Heaven. If one is easily contented, then a diet of vegetables and soups provides a lifetime of joy. If one does not know one's limitations and tries to accumulate wealth by immoral and dishonest means, how can one avoid disaster? To be able to support oneself through life and not leave one's sons and grandsons in hunger and cold is enough; why should one toil so much?

3. Pride is a dangerous trait. Those who pride themselves on wealth, rank, or learning are inviting evil consequences. Even if one's accomplishments are indeed unique, there is no need to press them on anyone else. "The way of Heaven detests fullness, and only the humble gain." I have seen the truth of this saying many times.

4. Taking concubines in order to beget heirs should be a last resort, for the sons of the legal wife and the sons of the concubine are never of one mind, causing innumerable conflicts between half brothers. If the parents are in the least partial, problems will multiply, creating misfortune in later generations. Since families have been ruined because of this, it should not be taken lightly.

5. Just as diseases are caused by what goes into one's mouth, misfortunes are caused by what comes out of one's mouth. Those who are immoderate in eating and unrestrained in speaking have no one else to blame for their own ruin.

6. Most men lack resolve and listen to what their women say. As a result, blood relatives become estranged and competitiveness, suspicion, and distance arise between them. Therefore, when a wife first comes into a family, it should be made clear to her that such things are prohibited. "Start teaching one's son when he is a baby; start teaching one's daughter-in-law when she first arrives." That is to say, preventive measures should be taken early.

7. "A family's fortune can be foretold from whether its members are early risers" is a maxim of our ancient sages. Everyone, male and female, should rise before dawn and should not go to bed until after the first drum. Never should they indulge themselves in a false sense of security and leisure, for such behavior will eventually lead them to poverty.

8. Young family members who deliberately violate family regulations should be taken to the family temple, have their offenses reported to the ancestors, and be severely punished. They should then be taught to improve themselves. Those who do not accept punishment or persist in their wrongdoings will bring harm to themselves.

9. As a preventive measure against the unpredictable, the gates should be closed at dusk, and no one should be allowed to go out. Even when there are visitors, dinner parties should end early, so that there

will be no need for lighting lamps and candles. On very hot or very cold days, one should be especially considerate of the kitchen servants.

10. For generations this family has dwelt in the country, and everyone has had a set profession; therefore, our descendants should not be allowed to change their place of residence. After living in the city for three years, a person forgets everything about farming; after ten years, he does not even know his lineage. Extravagance and leisure transform people, and it is hard for anyone to remain unaffected. I once remarked that country living has all the advantages, and that the only legitimate excuse to live in a city temporarily is to flee from bandits.

11. The inner and outer rooms, halls, doorways, and furniture should be swept and dusted every morning at dawn. Dirty doorways and courtyards and haphazardly placed furniture are sure signs of a declining family. Therefore, a schedule should be followed for cleaning them, with no excuses allowed.

12. Those in charge of cooking and kitchen work should make sure that breakfast is served before nine o'clock in the morning and dinner before five o'clock in the afternoon. Every evening the iron wok and other utensils should be washed and put away, so that the next morning, after rising at dawn, one can expect tea and breakfast to be prepared immediately and served on time. In the kitchen no lamps are allowed in the morning or at night. This is not only to save the expense, but also to avoid harmful contamination of food. Although this is a small matter, it has a great effect on health. Furthermore, since all members of the family have their regular work to do, letting them toil all day without giving them meals at regular hours is no way to provide comfort and relief for them. If these rules are deliberately violated, the person in charge will be punished as an example to the rest.

13. On the tenth and twenty-fifth days of every month, all the members of this branch, from the honored aged members to the youngsters, should gather at dusk for a meeting. Each will give an account of what he has learned, by either calling attention to examples of good and evil, or encouraging diligence, or expounding his obligations, or pointing out tasks to be completed. Each member will take turns presenting his own opinions and listening attentively to others. He should examine himself in the matters being discussed and make efforts to improve himself. The purpose of these meetings is to encourage one another in virtue and to correct each other's mistakes.

The members of the family will take turns being the chairman of these meetings, according to schedule. If someone is unable to chair a meeting on a certain day, he should ask the next person in line to take his place. The chairman should provide tea, but never wine. The meetings may be canceled on days of ancestor worship, parties, or other such occasions, or if the weather is severe. Those who are absent from these meetings for no reason are only doing themselves harm.

There are no set rules for where the meeting should be held, but the place should be convenient for group discussions. The time of the meeting should always be early evening, for this is when people have free time. As a general precaution the meeting should never last until late at night.

14. Women from lower-class families who stop at our houses tend to gossip, create conflicts, peek into the kitchens, or induce our women to believe in prayer and fortune-telling, thereby cheating them out of their money and possessions. Consequently, one should question these women often and punish those who come for no reason, so as to put a stop to the traffic.

15. Blood relatives are as close as the branches of a tree, yet their relationships can still be differentiated according to importance and priority: parents should be considered before brothers, and brothers should be considered before wives and children. Each person should fulfill his own duties and share with others profit and loss, joy and sorrow, life and death. In this way, the family will get along well and be blessed by Heaven. Should family members fight over property or end up treating each other like enemies, then when death or misfortune strikes they will be of even less use than strangers. If our ancestors have consciousness, they will not tolerate these unprincipled descendants who are but animals in man's clothing. Heaven responds to human vices with punishments as surely as an echo follows a sound. I hope my sons and grandsons take my words seriously.

16. To get along with patrilineal relatives, fellow villagers, and relatives through marriage, one should be gentle in speech and mild in manners. When one is opposed by others, one may remonstrate with them; but when others fall short because of their limitations, one should be tolerant. If one's youngsters or servants

get into fights with others, one should look into oneself to find the blame. It is better to be wronged than to wrong others. Those who take affront and become enraged, who conceal their own shortcomings and seek to defeat others, are courting immediate misfortune. Even if the other party is unbearably unreasonable, one should contemplate the fact that the ancient sages had to endure much more. If one remains tolerant and forgiving, one will be able to curb the other party's violence.

PRESERVE THE FAMILY PROPERTY

1. The houses, fields, and ponds that have been accumulated by the family should not be divided or sold. Violators of this rule will be severely admonished and barred from the ancestral temple.

2. Maps of the family graves should be printed. The graves are to be well taken care of and frequently repaired. The custodians of the graves should be treated well.

3. Books constitute the lifeline of a family. A record should be kept of their titles. They should be aired out at regular intervals, stored in a high chamber, and kept from being dispersed. In this way we can keep intact our ancestors' writings.

4. Paintings, maps, books, scrolls, and utensils should be stored in separate wooden cabinets. There should be a notebook in which all these are registered. Whenever an item is loaned to someone, a slip of paper with the description of the item should be temporarily pasted on the shelf. When the item is returned, it should be replaced in its original position.

5. There are many thieves in the country; therefore, one should be careful not to leave clothing and other objects about. Doors should be locked and carefully guarded. Be prepared! On noticing anything suspicious, look into it immediately and take preventive action, in order to achieve maximum security.

6. In order to cultivate the moral character of the young, one must severely punish those who are so unruly that they have no sense of righteousness or who so indulge their desires that they destroy their own health. One should also correct those who have improper hobbies, such as making too many friends and avoiding work, indulging in playing musical instruments and the game of Go, collecting art and valuables, composing music, singing, or dancing. All these hobbies destroy a person's ambition. Those who indulge in them may consider themselves free spirits; yet little do they know that these hobbies are their most harmful enemies.

7. If among patrilineal and affinal relatives and fellow villagers there are people who give importance to propriety and are respected for their learning and ability, one should frequently visit them to request advice and offer one's respects. Then, in case of emergencies in the family, one will be able to obtain help from them. Besides, receiving frequent advice is good in itself. By contrast, to make friends with the wrong sort of people and join them in evil deeds is to set a trap for oneself. If one is jealous of upright gentlemen and avoids upright discourse, misfortune will strike, the family will be ruined, lives may even be lost. Then it will be too late for regrets.

8. Scholars, farmers, artisans, and merchants all hold respectable occupations. Scholarship ranks the highest; farming is next; and then craft and business. However, it should be up to the individual to measure his ability against his aspirations as well as to find the most suitable occupation for himself. In these family instructions, I have given first place to the profession of scholarship, but have also devoted a great deal of attention to the work of farmers, artisans, and merchants. These family instructions attempt to show the correct procedures to be followed in everyday life. If one truly understands them and fulfills the duties appropriate to his way of life; if one upholds public and private obligations; if one can in good conscience invite Heaven's favor, then misfortune will stay away and bliss will enter without conscious effort on one's part. In this way, a person can face his ancestors without shame and instruct his posterity; there are no other secrets to having good and capable descendants.

Translated by Clara Yu

43.

The Spite of Lotus

Polygamy is probably the aspect of the Chinese kinship system most foreign to Western experience. Although it is undoubtedly true that the vast majority of Chinese men could never afford more than one wife, still the existence of polygamy colored Chinese life in a variety of ways. Poor families were affected as the suppliers of daughters. They were always aware that if they could not afford to marry their daughters off, they could sell them to rich men. This step meant turning an economic liability into an asset, but most people tried to avoid it, not only because they worried about the happiness of their daughters but also because their own prestige was involved. For families of modest means, polygamy meant that if the first wife failed to produce a surviving son after perhaps ten years of marriage, a second wife or concubine might well be acquired.

In families of prosperous merchants, landlords, scholars, and officials, polygamy naturally was of even greater importance. Most members of such families would have spent at least a part of their lives in complex households in which one man had two or more mates; besides a wife from a family of similar social status, he would have concubines or secondary wives of lower social origins. Men in such families could also establish liaisons with maids which might or might not result in the maid's being raised to the status of concubine.

Fiction is the only source that gives any details about the interpersonal dynamics of such polygamous households. Below is an episode from the novel Chin Ping Mei, *of uncertain authorship, first published in 1610. This book recounts the varied adventures of Hsi-men Ch'ing, a congenial but unambitious and undisciplined heir of a prosperous commercial family whose household had grown to include a wife and five concubines. In the episode below, Lotus, the newest concubine, who could be tender and solicitous of Hsi-men, demonstrates the malice she could vent on her competitors. Naturally, the events described here cannot be taken as typical of polygamous households; people undoubtedly fantasized as much about having a harem as about becoming a bandit. Nevertheless, even their fantasies are of interest if we are to understand the dynamics of polygamous families.*

Now that she was the favorite, Lotus became more and more intent on having her own way. She was never at peace. Suspicious of the others, she was constantly peeping from behind doors and spying through cracks. One day, in a bad mood over nothing, she upbraided her maid Plum. Plum was not the docile type who could accept criticism quietly, so to vent her anger she ran off to the kitchen, where she pounded her fists on the tables and pans. Snow, the fourth wife, watched all this and teased her, "You silly little thing. If you want a man so much, can't you look elsewhere? Why must you have your fits here?"

Angry already, Plum now lost her temper. "How dare anyone insult me!" she declared. When Snow saw fit to ignore her, Plum ran back to her mistress. She embellished the incident and told Lotus, "That one says you personally handed me over to the master so that we could keep him all to ourselves."

Plum's story did nothing to improve Lotus's bad

mood. That morning she had risen earlier than usual to help Moon, the principal wife, get ready for a funeral. She had been so tired she took a nap, and was just going back to her own suite. On her way there she ran into Jade, the third wife.

"Why are you looking so worn out?" Jade asked.

"Don't ask me! I had to get up early," Lotus replied, then added, "Sister, where are you coming from?"

"I stopped at the kitchen."

"Did the one there tell you anything?"

"No, not that I can think of."

Lotus did not let on what was bothering her, but she was forming a hatred for Snow. She and Jade sat down and passed some time doing needlework. After finishing the tea and cakes Plum and Chrysanthemum set out, they decided to play a game of chess. But no sooner had their game become exciting than Hsi-men was announced and entered the room.

Hsi-men gazed in satisfaction at the two well decked-out ladies. Silk hair nets revealing curls at their temples, earrings of blue sapphire, white silken dresses with red bodices and embroidered skirts, tiny arched and pointed slippers—how exquisite their taste was! "Just like a couple of courtesans, worth at least a hundred taels of silver!" he teased.

"Courtesans, my word! You have one in your household, but she's in back, not here," Lotus bantered back.

Jade rose to withdraw, but Hsi-men caught her and drew her back into the room. "Where would you be going? As soon as I arrive you try to escape! Tell the truth—what have you two been doing in my absence?"

"Nothing wrong," Lotus answered. "We were both feeling low, so we started a game of chess." Lotus helped him put the chessmen back and commented that he had returned from the funeral rather early.

"Yes, there were a lot of officials there and it was terribly hot, so I made a quick exit."

When Jade asked about Moon, Hsi-men said she would be coming later in the sedan chair and that he had sent two servant boys to meet her. He sat down next to them and asked, "What were your stakes in this game?"

"Oh, we were just playing for the fun of it," Lotus answered.

"Then let me challenge you each to a game.

Whoever loses forfeits a tael of silver to pay for a party."

"But we don't have any money with us." Lotus objected.

"Never mind. You can give me a hairpin as security."

First he played with Lotus and she lost. He began to reset the pieces for a game with Jade, but Lotus suddenly tipped over the board, causing the chessmen to fall in a jumble. Then she ran out of the room and into the garden.

Hsi-men chased her and found her picking flowers. "What a spoilsport! You run away because you lost, my lovable little oily-mouth," he called to her, panting.

Coyly, Lotus looked up at him. "What a villain, to pursue me just because I lost! You wouldn't dare do that to Jade!" She playfully pelted him with blossoms. Hsi-men went up to her and took her in his arms, then stuck out his tongue to give her a piece of candy from his mouth.

Their diversions were soon interrupted by Jade who called, "Moon has just returned. We'd better go."

Lotus broke loose from Hsi-men and said she would talk to him more later. Then she hurried after Jade to pay her respects to Moon.

Moon asked them, "What makes you two so merry?"

"Lotus lost a tael of silver playing chess with the master, so she will have to host a party tomorrow," Jade answered. "You must come."

Moon smiled and Lotus soon took her leave. She rejoined Hsi-men in the front suite and had Plum light some incense and draw a hot bath so that later they could amuse themselves like a couple of fish.

Although Moon was Hsi-men's principal wife, her ill-health usually kept her from fulfilling all the duties of the mistress of the house. Grace, the second wife, performed most of the social duties such as paying visits and receiving guests, and handled the household budget. Snow, the fourth wife, took charge of the servants and was the chief cook. Wherever Hsi-men was in the house, if he wanted something to eat or drink, he would send his request to Snow via one of the maids of the lady he was visiting.

That night Hsi-men stayed with Lotus. They drank some wine, took a bath, and went to bed. The next morning things started to happen. It began when

Hsi-men cajoled Lotus by promising that right after breakfast he would go to the temple market to buy her some pearls. But when he told Plum to fetch him breakfast (ordering lotus-seed cakes and carp soup), the girl would not budge.

Lotus intervened, "There's a person in the kitchen who says I induced Plum to yield to you so that she and I could keep you for ourselves. She called us all sorts of names. So don't make Plum go there."

"Who are you referring to?"

"I don't want to name names. Even the pots and pans have ears around here. Just send Chrysanthemum instead."

Hsi-men did as he was told. More than enough time passed to have cooked two breakfasts and Lotus had the table all set, but Chrysanthemum still did not return. Hsi-men was near to losing his patience, so Lotus sent Plum after all, telling her, "Go see where that slave is dallying. She must've taken root someplace!"

Reluctantly Plum complied and found Chrysanthemum standing in the kitchen. "You depraved slave," she scolded. "Mistress will cut you to pieces! What's keeping you? Master is out of patience! He wants to go to the market and I must bring you back with me at once."

She would have continued, but Snow interrupted, "Silly wench, you behave like some Mohammedan on a feast day! Isn't the pot made of iron? Will the soup get hot just by sitting in it? I have some gruel ready, but instead he wants cakes and soup. What kind of a worm is at work in his stomach?"

This was more than Plum could take. "Impudence! Do you think I came here for the fun of it? Are you going to get the stuff ready or not? Just wait! Master will be furious when I tell him about this!" Dragging Chrysanthemum by the ear, she turned to go.

As they left, Snow shouted, "That slave and her mistress are both too cocksure! But my time will come!"

"Maybe it will! What do I care?" Plum retorted.

Still in a huff, Plum produced Chrysanthemum before her mistress, who noticed how pale her face was. "What's the matter?" Lotus asked.

"Ask her! I found her standing in the kitchen. That person was taking forever to prepare a little breakfast! All I said was that the master was in a rush and you wanted to know what was keeping her. That kitchen woman called me a slave wench and other ugly things. She even reviled the master calling him some extravagant Mohammedan! Does she think he needs her permission before asking for something? She complained that he wouldn't eat her gruel! She seems to think the purpose of a kitchen is not cooking but cursing!"

"What did I tell you!" Lotus exclaimed. "We shouldn't have sent Plum. I knew that that one would pick a quarrel and insinuate that Plum and I had made you into our exclusive property! Oh, why do I have to endure such insults!"

Her outburst produced immediate effect: Hsi-men dashed into the kitchen and began kicking Snow. "You evil bag of bones! What gives you the right to curse the girl I sent to fetch some breakfast? You call her a slave? If you want to see a slave, look at the reflection in your own puddle!"

Snow knew better than to talk back to Hsi-men, but as soon as he left she turned to Lai Pao's wife. "What evil luck I'm having! You are my witness. You saw her prance in here like some demon! Did I say the least thing to her? But off she goes with that little maid and tells lies to the master so that he abuses me for no fault of mine! Just wait! I'll be on the lookout! Sooner or later that impudent slave wench and her mistress will make a false move!"

Unknown to Snow, Hsi-men had paused to listen outside the door. Convulsed with rage, he barged back in and pummeled her. "You depraved slave, you slut! Tell me now you didn't insult her! I heard you with my own two ears!" He kept hitting her until she could not take the pain any longer, then stormed off, leaving her shrieking.

Hearing the commotion, Moon, who had just risen and was having her hair dressed, sent her maid Jewel to investigate. Jewel came back and related the whole story. "He's never wanted cakes before," Moon remarked. "But Snow should have done his bidding as quickly as possible, and certainly she shouldn't have scolded the maid over nothing."

She sent Jewel back to the kitchen to tell Snow to finish the breakfast. So, in the end, Hsi-men got his meal and was off to the market with one of the servant boys.

Snow could not get over how she had been mistreated. As soon as Hsi-men was out of the house she went to Moon's room to give her version of the incident. Little did she know Lotus had followed her and was eavesdropping outside the window to every-thing she told Moon and Grace. "You have no idea what this woman is capable of!" Snow ranted. "She is absolutely man-crazy and can't stand to spend even a single night alone! Even a dozen husbands wouldn't be enough for her! She got rid of her first husband by poisoning him! Just imagine what she's planning for us! She's turned our husband into some kind of beady-eyed chicken who never notices the rest of us!"

"Now, now," Moon tried to calm her, "weren't you at fault? He did send the maid for the cakes, and if you had sent her right back with them, none of this would have happened. There wasn't any call for you to provoke her."

"I was the one who got provoked! That maid was impertinent even when she used to work for you, but you never objected when I corrected her, even the time I hit her with the back of a knife. What makes her so privileged now that she works for Lotus?"

"The fifth mistress is outside," Jewel warned as she came in.

The next moment Lotus entered. Looking straight into Snow's face, she stated, "If you know for a fact that I had poisoned my first husband, then why didn't you stop the master from bringing me here? That way you wouldn't have had to worry about me getting him all for myself. As for Plum, she doesn't belong to me. If you object to the current arrangements, let her wait on Moon again. Then I wouldn't care if you picked quarrels with her. But don't worry—there's a simple solution to everything. When the master comes back I'll ask him to write out a letter of divorce!"

"I really don't understand why you two have to squabble," Moon interjected. "If only you both talked a little less . . ."

"But Lady," Snow objected, "her mouth pours forth words like a river! No one is a match for her! If she lost her tongue she could still make the master believe anything by merely rolling her eyes! If she had her way, all of us, except perhaps you, would be driven out of here!"

For a while Moon let them hurl insults back and forth at each other. Then when Snow said, "You call me a slave, but you're the real slave," and seemed on the point of striking Lotus, Moon ordered Jewel to remove Snow from the room.

Back in her own suite, Lotus took off her clothes, removed her makeup, and mussed up her dark hair. In this disheveled condition, she threw herself on her bed and sobbed.

When Hsi-men returned that evening with four ounces of pearls, he found Lotus in this state, demanding a divorce. "I never cared anything about your money," she protested through her tears. "It was just that I loved you. But what do I get in return but insults? Now I'm called a husband murderer! It would be better if I didn't have a maid, since anyone who works for me has to put up with such treatment!"

Lotus's tale turned Hsi-men into a demon. He whirled through the house until he set down on Snow. Grabbing her hair in one hand, he thrashed her with his short stick, not stopping until Moon came to restrain him.

"Let's everyone behave," Moon said, then addressing Snow, added, "Don't upset the master."

"You culprit! You evil bag of bones!" Hsi-men railed at Snow. "I heard what you called them in the kitchen! Just let me catch you one more time!"

All this Snow suffered because of Lotus's spiteful scheming. There's a verse to prove it:

> Lotus depended on her husband's favor
> To make Snow suffer deep humiliation.
> Using gratitude to accumulate hatred—
> The consequences will take centuries to unfold.

Hsi-men returned to Lotus's room and took from his sleeve the pearls he had bought her. Lotus was no longer petulant; Hsi-men had taken her side and fought her battles for her. She repaid his affection tenfold and his delight in her only increased.

Translated by Patricia Ebrey

44.

Li Chih's Letters

Among Chinese intellectuals there were always some individualists and iconoclasts who were at odds with the social or intellectual world around them. While such men never represented more than a tiny proportion of the population, their experiences and ideas are often particularly instructive because they reveal points of tension or conflict within the society. Below are five letters by one such iconoclast, Li Chih (1527–1602).

Li Chih was one of the extraordinary scholars who appeared during the intellectually tumultuous final decades of the Ming dynasty. He came from a commercial family in the area of Ch'üan-chou, a major southeastern seaport and trading center. He passed the provincial examinations at the age of twenty-six but did not go on for the highest degree, the chin-shih. From 1555 to 1581 he held several lower and mid-level governmental posts but did nothing to distinguish himself in the civil service. In 1585 he retired to a Buddhist temple and devoted himself to study and writing.

Li Chih's philosophy was eclectic, incorporating elements of Buddhism and Taoism into Confucianism. He laid stress on the original goodness of the human mind, which in its pristine state, the "infant mind," would make sound moral judgments. He criticized the prevailing ethical system of the Chu Hsi school of Neo-Confucianism as an arbitrary, rationalistic, and artificial dogma. From these ideas Li developed theories of individualism and personal freedom. He asserted that each individual should seek his own Way, his own position in the natural scheme, following his own enlightened self-interest. He thought that people should not be required to follow a given pattern of behavior and that true ethical action should include expression of the emotions and bodily appetites. Li Chih's personal eccentricities and abusive manner, as well as his unorthodox ideas, made him many enemies during the course of his life. He was eventually arrested for his heterodoxy and committed suicide in jail.

LETTER TO CHUANG CH'UN-FU

Jih-tsai has arrived and I have learned that her funeral is over [i.e., Li Chih's wife's funeral]—this is something to be glad of. I lived with her for more than forty years and we knew each other well. As I have sojourned at Pien-chou a long time and the place has become like a home town to me, I naturally feel sad when I have to leave. I feel the same about leaving her, except that the affection between husband and wife is stronger. Besides the intimacy between pillows and sheets, I also had her diligence, her

wise financial management, and her assistance at home. She and I respected each other and treated each other with sincerity. We also lived up to filial duty, friendship, loyalty, and obligation, and we helped others, sometimes at great cost to ourselves. We were much more truthful than the scholarly sort of today who seek only a virtuous name but not virtuous deeds. It is all the more difficult for me to be separated from her now because, besides her love and affection, I will also greatly miss her deeds, merits, good advice, and virtues.

My wife, Huang I-jen, was your mother-in-law.

Her only fault was that she never listened to anyone as far as learning was concerned, which was regrettable. Were my bosom made of iron and stone, I could not but feel sorrowful. What is more, when two married people approach old age and are called back to Heaven separately, without even being able to bid farewell to each other—isn't it a most grievous thing? Ah, let it be, let it be!

After I received the sad news of her departure, I dreamed of her every night, but she was always alive and well in my dreams. Did she really come here to be with me? Or did her spirit come to me because I thought of her? I recall that she was always very prudent; seldom would she cross the threshold to enter my meditation abode. Yet, what is wrong with coming to the meditation abode once in a while? She never reached the graceful carefreeness which goes beyond the boundaries of worldly virtues.

The point is, once we recognize the fact that the soul is the only true existence, then where is the demarcation between man and woman? If, after her departure from this world, I-jen is still bound by those old behavior codes, she will never be able to reach a carefree state. The existence of the soul proves that the being itself is deathless and by nature boundless. Therefore, how can one better oneself with boundaries and limits? The very carefreeness of the soul is itself the Pure Land and the Paradise: there is no other Heavenly world.

Ch'un-fu, you should burn this letter for the soul of your mother-in-law so that she may know my wishes. Tell her not to covet the joy of reincarnation, for, once she is placed in a woman's womb to be reborn, she will be deprived of her awareness of the other world. Tell her not to yearn to be worshipped as a Heavenly being, for once reborn in Heaven, she will instantly forget her wish of her previous life to be carefree. Once the retributions end, the karma is in turn manifested, and one is reborn into the six paths of existence with no end to it.

Judging from your mother-in-law's behavior on earth, doubtless she is now in Heaven. Let her mark my words well: although she is already in Heaven, she should remember to wait for me and meet me when my days come to an end. In this way we will be able to rely on each other through many lives, without being separated by mistake. If she temporarily entrusts her thoughts to Buddhism, it will be excellent; but even if she cannot, should she meet some old friend of mine whom I have always respected, she

could also follow him while she waits for me. But do tell her that she should by no means covet rebirth.

Ch'un-fu, be sure to burn incense and paper money for your mother-in-law. Read my letter to her three or five times. Enjoin her repeatedly in front of her image. Recite my letter to her clearly and loudly. My I-jen will receive the message.

TO TSENG CHI-CH'ÜAN

I hear that you intend to shave your hair and become a monk. You really should not do so.

You have a wife and concubines, as well as a house and land. What is more, you do not yet have a son. Now, without a son, to whom are you going to entrust your family and possessions? To desert them without a reason is not only unkind but irresponsible. If you have really transcended life and death and seen through human existence, then it is preferable to cultivate yourself at home.

I should like to ask you some hypothetical questions: Can you really hold a monk's bowl to beg for food from door to door? Or can you really fast for several days without begging for a meal from people? If you can do neither, but still have to rely on farming for a livelihood, then isn't it more practical to cultivate yourself at home?

In the beginning, when I had just started studying the Way, not only did I have a wife and family, I also was an official who had to travel tens of thousands of *li*. But I felt that my learning increased day by day. Later on, I stayed in Ch'u to be close to my good friends and teachers, but my wife would not stay with me; I had to let my son-in-law and my daughter accompany her home. There she had her daughter, nephew, and others waiting on her constantly. I handed over to her whatever savings I had from my offices. As I alone was away from home, I did not need to worry about her and was able to stay down here and enjoy the company of my friends. The reason why I shaved my hair was that various people at home always expected me to return and often actually traveled a thousand *li* to pressure me to return and to bother me with trivial, worldly affairs. So I shaved my hair to show them that I had no intention of returning. Also, the ignorant people down here eyed me as a heretic, so I let myself behave as such to satisfy them. And yet was my sudden decision to shave my hair based primarily on these reasons? In addition, I knew I was getting old and would not stay in this world of men for long; that was the true reason. Now you, sir, are in your prime years, the fittest time to beget children, to live, to aspire for greatness. Furthermore, you do not own too much land and your estate is not very large. This is the ideal condition in which to live—unlike those rich men who are tied down with so many financial worries that they do not have even one minute of leisure.

Now, tell me, why do you have to discard your hair in order to learn the Way? I, for one, did not get rid of mine and leave home when I started studying it. Do mark my words and bear them in mind.

ON READING THE LETTER TO JO–WU FROM HIS MOTHER

Jo-wu's mother wrote to him, "I am getting older year after year. I have been a widow since you were eight and have brought you up. You left me to become a monk and that was all right. But now you want to leave in another sense to go to Chin-kang. Even your teacher waited until his parents passed away before becoming a monk. If you want to go away, you can wait until I have died. It will not be too late then.

"You say that even when you live close to me, you have never been able to help me in any way. Yet, when I am ill or indisposed, it is convenient to have you around. That way I do not worry about you. You also are carefree, not having to worry about me. Thus we both live with peace of mind, and where there is peace of mind there is tranquility. Why are you set on leaving home to seek for quiet? Besides, Ch'in Su-ko, who has always been generous to you, has bought you the temple. You always think in terms of the Way; I, however, think in terms of the ways of the world. I believe that what harmonizes with the ways of the world also conforms to the Way.

"Now, even if you forget about my old age, you have an obligation to care for your two small children. Even after your teacher became a monk, he took care of his sons during the famine years. This was because he could not put them out of his mind. For should he have failed to take care of them, they would have become roving good-for-nothings and the butt of insults and ridicule.

"Now you want to cultivate sereneness of the mind, but are you going to be concerned about your children? I do not believe you can be unconcerned about them. The fact is that you are concerned, but out of fear of being ridiculed by others, you hide your feelings. Let me ask you this: which is more honest, which is better, 'concerned but refusing to be involved,' or 'concerned and involved'? The way I see it, if you take care of your children, although it may seem that you are concerned, yet because you can thus achieve peace of mind, you are actually not concerned. On the other hand, if you do not take care of them, you are seemingly unconcerned, yet because your mind feels secret pangs, you are in fact concerned. You ought to examine your own mind. If you can achieve a peaceful mind, then that is the eternal dwelling place, that is the Chin-kang you are looking for.

"Why do you only listen to others? To listen to others and not to examine your own mind is to be manipulated by circumstances. Once you submit to that, there will be no peace of mind for you. . . . I fear for you: You now find Lung-t'an not quiet enough and wish to go to live in Chin-kang. Should you someday find Chin-kang not quiet enough, where else are you going to go? You always talk only of the 'Way'; I wish now to talk to you about 'mind.' If you do not believe me, ask your teacher. If what matters is the surroundings, then you should indeed go and dwell in Chin-kang. If what matters is the mind, however, then you have no need to go away. If your mind is not serene, then even if you should travel to the other side of the sea, you would still not find quiet, let alone in Chin-kang."

On reading the letter, I sighed. I congratulate you on having a mother who is a real Buddha. From morning till night you have with you a teacher of the mind. She speaks with the voice of the ocean tide and teaches the ultimate truth which can never be contradicted. In comparison, the rhetoric of our peers is neither to the point nor effective. We are like those who talk about food, acting as though we could feed people with our mere words. All we achieve is making people laugh at each other, yet we do not even feel ashamed of ourselves. In retrospect, I realize that the several pages I wrote to you were mere exaggerations which would impress the foolish but had no bearing whatsoever on the truth. I now beg you to destroy my letters so that your godly mother may not read them, lest she say that I have spent all my life expounding harmful ideas. I also wish you would circulate your mother's letter and make students of Buddhism read it from time to time, so that they will learn to study true

Buddhism. As long as one studies true Buddhism, one is a real Buddha. Even if a person has never recited "Amita" once, Amita will lead him to the correct path. Why is this? Because, to study Buddhism one has to cultivate virtuous behavior and filial piety. If one can get to see Amita by studying false Buddhism, then what kind of Buddhism did Amita himself study to become what he is? I am sure he was but an ordinary man who exhibited filial virtues and benevolence.

When one gives voice to one's deepest emotions, one can penetrate a reader's heart like a spear and move him to tears. I am sure you feel the same as I. No one who ever reads your mother's letter will be able to hold back his tears.

LETTER TO LIU HSIAO-CH'UAN

I look forward earnestly to seeing your father and also to seeing you. Do I have to invoke Heaven to testify to my sincerity?

And yet the season is still the "great cold" period of the year. How does an old man like me dare to travel? Also, since the tenth month I have been studying the *Book of Changes* with Jo-hou at night. We study one hexagram per night because during the night it is quiet with no visitors or affairs interfering, only the five or six of us who take this seriously and argue and analyze until the second nightwatchman's drum. It will take us four and a half months to finish the book. A couple of the most serious-minded are guests from a thousand *li* away who came here with their families and rented nearby houses to be close to my Eternal Rewards Meditation Abode. It would not be right to desert them abruptly.

In my opinion you should come here. Take a light boat and let the river carry you conveniently down here. You will soon be listening to explications of the *Book of Changes* and be purged of your despondency. Jo-hou is an unworldly man whose only concern is study. Although he seldom travels, he is no less a scholar for it. You should come here to meet him. Why are you guarding your home so stupidly, like a child or a woman? By all means, do come down here. I will be standing on tiptoe watching for you. You cannot, should not, and will not disappoint me! What is so precious about your office that you have to shut yourself up in there, watching over everything? Believe me, you will fall ill because of it. You are a man, yet you do not have the all-transcending spirit

to seek for teachers and friends in the wide world. Instead you ask an old man to travel to you. How absurd! Do come down here quickly, immediately!

If you come, come by yourself. Do not bring anybody with you, for I do not like other people. Such people as Chen-ting and K'ang-kun who accompanied your uncle two years ago on the lake made me so sick that I still flinch at the thought of them. Such people are the most pitiful creatures on earth. Those who study the *Book of Changes*, on the contrary, are very refined, very diligent, and very interesting; they are where the real joy of the Way lies.

If you come, bring a lot of rice and firewood in your boat, since these things are expensive here. In the Chiao household there are more than six hundred people to be fed, and yet there is not even one *mou* of land to bring in income. Hardly able to support me, how can they feed my guests? Now, remember to bring rice. The firewood you can forget.

Writing in a hurry, I have not been careful about details. Please excuse me.

THE WILL OF MR. LI CHO-WU

Since spring I have been ill most of the time and I am eager to depart this world. I am glad that this will is to fall into the hands of my good friends. This is quite rare and I am very fortunate; do believe how important it is to me.

When I die, you should hurry to select a high mound outside the city. Dig a rectangular grave facing south, ten feet long, five feet wide, and only six feet deep. When the rectangle is completed according to scale, then dig another two feet five inches into the earth to make a smaller rectangle six and a half feet long and two feet five inches wide within the first rectangle. In this smaller rectangle rest my body. Spread five reed mats at the bottom of the grave and lay me on top. Who can say that this is not clean? As long as my mind is restful in there, it is paradise. Do not fall for the customary sounds and sights and thereby act against my wish. Although Ma Ch'eng-lao can afford a pompous burial for me, it is better to let me rest peacefully. This is my most important wish! Now my spirit is dispersing and in no time I will be enjoying my body's resting place.

Before setting me down in the rectangle, put my body on a board. Let me be dressed in the clothes I die in. Do not provide new clothes for me, lest my body feel ill at ease. Yet do cover my face with a piece of cloth. Put my head on a pillow as usual. Cover my whole body with a white sheet and use a footbinding strip to tie the sheet around my body, lacing it from my feet up. At the fifth drum when the temple gate is opened, have four strong men carry me out evenly to the grave.

At the grave you can then lay me down on the reed mats and take the board back to its owner. After my body is down, put twenty to thirty wooden boards across the rectangle, then another five sheets of reed mat over them. Then you can put the soil back in the grave, pounding it solid and even. Pile more soil on top of the grave so that my body's dwelling place is recognizable. Plant trees around the grave and place a tombstone in front of it with the words, "Tomb of Mr. Li Cho-wu." Each word should be four feet square. You can ask Chiao I-yüan to write it; I believe he will not decline the request.

Those of you who wish to remain at my tomb site must do so out of sincerity. If you are indeed sincere, Master Ma will certainly see to it that you are taken care of; you will not have to worry. Those who are not concerned with me may go wherever they wish. While I was alive I never wanted any relatives to follow me; naturally after I die I will not need to be attended by them. This should be clear.

Please do not change a word of what I have written.

The 5th day of the second month,
The Will of Li Cho-wu.

Please listen to me and do what I ask of you.

Translated by Clara Yu

Part Six

THE CH'ING DYNASTY

Although the Ming was overthrown by peasant rebellions of the usual sort, the next dynasty was founded not by a warlord or rebel leader but by the chieftains of the Manchus, a non-Chinese tribe living in the hilly forests and plains to the northeast of China proper, the large area generally called Manchuria. The Manchus had long been in contact with the Mongols and Chinese and for decades had been building up political and military institutions capable of governing sedentary farming populations.

Like the Mongols, the Manchus were alien conquerors; yet their dynasty, the Ch'ing (1644–1911), did not represent nearly as fundamental a break with Chinese traditions. The Manchus tried to maintain their own identity and traditions, but left Chinese political institutions and customs largely intact. In fact, in many respects the eighteenth century was the apogee of Chinese civilization. Some two to three hundred million people lived peaceably in an empire even bigger than China today, stretching from Manchuria, through Mongolia, and into Central Asia and Tibet. Traditional scholarship and arts flourished under the patronage of the Ch'ing Emperors, and even in rural areas schools were common and basic literacy relatively high.

Yet during the Ch'ing dynasty the stability of traditional Chinese civilization was being undermined by the steady increase in the size of the population. By 1850 the population reached about 400 million. This demographic change affected many other aspects of life. By the beginning of the nineteenth century, the pressure of population on available land resources was becoming acute. All of the land which could profitably be exploited using traditional methods was already under cultivation, so any increase in food supply had to come from less and less rewarding additions of labor or marginal land. As a consequence, the prospect of widespread suffering became very real, especially in times of drought or flood. The government structure did not keep pace with the population's growth; in fact, it remained static in size during the Ch'ing period, so that government services and control became weaker, stretched thin to cover two or three times as large a population as before. At the local level, more authority was taken over by the gentry, especially by men who had passed the lower-level civil service examinations.

The growing importance of the "examination gentry" was a major social development of late imperial China. Since at least the Ming period, competition in the examinations had been fierce; by the nineteenth century it was brutal. Of the two million students who sat for the first, or prefectural, examination in any given year, only 30,000 passed to become sheng-yüan (government students). Even these men had only about a one to two percent chance of rising high enough to become officials, for only 1,500 passed the provincial examination as chü-jen (recommended men) and only 500 the metropolitan examination as chin-shih (presented scholars). Only the chin-shih could count on becoming officials. The sheng-yüan and many of the chü-jen remained local gentry with only unofficial responsibilities and sources of income. Those with extensive landholdings could maintain the way of life of cultivated literati, but others were often forced into marginal positions.

At the same time that these demographic and social changes were beginning to weaken the Ch'ing government, China was threatened by a new kind of foreigner who arrived by sea. China's defeat by the British in the Opium War of 1840–1842 set in action a chain of events both humiliating and threatening. Westerners came to occupy privileged positions in a number of "treaty ports" along China's coast and acquired territorial rights to small parts of China such as Hong Kong. They sold manufactured goods that competed with Chinese industries. Their missionaries gained the right to try to convert Chinese to Christianity. Most troubling of all, their armies and navies repeatedly proved themselves superior to China's, raising fundamental questions about how China could strengthen herself and what, if anything, she should copy from these foreigners.

Although the vast majority of the Chinese never saw a Westerner during this period and changed few of their habits or attitudes, by the end of the dynasty the foreign threat had come to have far-reaching effects. Intellectual leaders and high officials were divided into reformers and conservatives. The gentry as a whole was demoralized, convinced that the dynasty was on an inevitable downward slide. Peasants and townsmen in port cities, or areas where missionaries were active or modern enterprises such as railroads were being introduced, protested these intrusions and the changes they were causing. From the time of the great and devasting T'ai-p'ing Rebellion (1850–1864) until the overthrow of the Ch'ing dynasty in 1911, instability and restiveness seem to have pervaded almost all segments of Chinese society.

Sources for the Ch'ing period are much like those for the Ming, although even more plentiful. Genealogies, gazetteers, fiction, and personal memoirs all survive in greater quantity. One new kind of source seldom available before the Ch'ing is original documents, such as contracts, agreements, account books, and so on, which accidentally survived into the twentieth century and then were preserved by scholars who recognized their value to legal, institutional, and economic history. A few such documents are translated in Part Six.

45.

Parables and Ghost Stories

Stories of divine retribution and of ghosts and spirits were popular in China from at least the Han dynasty. Such tales not only were entertaining and morally uplifting, but also provided explanations of some of the unusual experiences and strange twists of fate that people encountered. The conceptual foundations of these tales were varied. Some were based on beliefs derived from Buddhism, such as karma and reincarnation. Others made use of popular notions that the world of nature contained a wide variety of spirits, including some that could move back and forth between the human and spirit worlds. Yet others depended on the belief that human beings had two kinds of "souls," a hun and a p'o. The hun normally dissipated on death, but the p'o became a ghost which, if properly fed and cared for by its descendants, caused no trouble and could even help them. If the p'o was neglected or had been the victim of a violent crime, it could cause considerable mischief or harm to living people.

The following nine stories of the supernatural are probably of popular origin, even though they were recorded by educated men who may have been skeptical of some of their elements. The first three are from a collection compiled by P'u Sung-ling (1640–1715), and the last six from a similar compilation made by Yüan Mei (1715–1797).

PLANTING A PEAR TREE

A peasant was selling his pears at the marketplace. They were unusually sweet and fragrant and the price was extremely high. When a Taoist priest dressed in rags and tatters came begging in front of his cart, the peasant shooed him away but the priest refused to leave. The peasant became angry and began to revile him with loud curses. The priest said, "You have a few hundred pears on your cart. I am only asking for one of them which will not be a great loss to you. Why do you get so angry?"

Spectators gathered around them, and some tried to persuade the peasant to give the priest a pear of inferior quality and thus be rid of him, but he stubbornly refused. A clerk from a nearby shop found the clamor unbearable, bought a pear, and handed it to the priest, who humbly thanked him and said to the crowd, "People like me who have renounced their

properties and homes fail to understand the selfish conduct of others. I myself have some high quality pears which I would like to share with you."

Someone in the crowd asked, "If you already had pears, why didn't you eat them instead?"

The priest answered, "Because I needed a seed to grow them from." He then raised the pear to his mouth and munched at it. Keeping the seeds in one hand, he unshouldered his hoe and dug a hole a few inches deep. He dropped the seeds into it and covered it up again with the dirt. He then asked the bystanders to bring him some hot water. A busybody ran to a neighboring shop and procured a bowl of hot water, which the priest poured over the dirt.

All eyes in the marketplace were fixed on the dirt, and soon a sprout emerged and grew bigger and bigger until it became a large tree with luxuriant leaves. The tree burst into blossom and soon large, fragrant clusters of pears were hanging from every branch.

The priest climbed to the top of the tree, picked the pears, and passed them to the crowd. In a moment they were gone. Then, with his hoe, the priest chopped down the tree, hoisted it, complete with leaves and branches, onto his shoulder, and strolled quietly away.

Now, from the moment the priest began his trick, the peasant had joined the crowd watching intensely and had quite forgotten his own business. After the priest departed, he turned to tend his cart and found that his pears had disappeared and the cart was completely empty. Then he realized that the pears which the priest had given away were actually his own. After a closer look at his cart, he saw that its handle had been broken off. Greatly enraged, he hurried off after the priest. When he turned a corner, he found his broken handle on the ground. Then he realized that this was what the priest had chopped down. The priest, however, was nowhere in sight. The people in the marketplace all had a good laugh at the peasant's expense.

Translated by Nancy Gibbs

FORTY STRINGS OF CASH

In Hsin City in the household of Minister Wang there served a head steward who had considerable personal fortune. One night the steward dreamt that a man rushed into his house and said to him, "Today you will return the forty strings of cash you owe me."

The steward asked who he was but the man gave him no answer and instead walked into the women's quarters. When the steward woke up he learned that his wife had just given birth to a baby boy. Recognizing this as a retribution for an old unpaid debt, he set aside forty strings of cash in a closet and spent that money only on food, clothing, and medicine for the baby.

When the child was between three and four, the steward noticed that only 700 cash of the original sum was left in the closet. When the boy was carried to him by a wet nurse for some playful teasing, the steward said to him, "The forty strings of cash are almost all repaid; therefore you can leave now." Almost immediately the child's face changed color, his head fell back, and his eyes stared vacantly. When they examined him they found that he had stopped breathing. So, taking the rest of the money left in the closet, the steward paid for the child's funeral expenses.

In the past, an old man with no children consulted many exalted Buddhist priests about his childless condition. One priest said to him, "If you do not owe anything to anybody and if no one owes you anything, how can you hope to have children?" Indeed, a good son is repayment of a debt owed you. A bad son is a creditor whose birth should bring no happiness and whose death should cause no sorrow.

Translated by Nancy Gibbs

THE THREE STATES OF EXISTENCE

Liu Hsiao-lein, who received his *chü-jen* degree at the same time as Mr. Wen Pi, can remember his previous states of existence. Once he told the complete story, as follows.

"I came from a respectable family but, after leading a life of dissipation, I died at the age of sixty-two and was led to the King of the Underworld. His Highness treated me courteously, invited me to sit down, and offered me a cup of tea. But I noticed that the tea in his cup looked clear, while my tea looked murky with thick sediment. I suspected that mine was the potion that makes one forget all about his past existence. When the King looked away, I poured my tea under the table and pretended to have drunk it.

"A record showing the good and evil deeds of my life was brought before the King for examination. After reading it, he became very angry and ordered his attendants to drag me away and punish me by sending me back to earth as a horse. Immediately I was taken away by these devils to a house with a door sill so high that I was unable to step over. While I was struggling to cross the threshold, a devil whipped me so hard that I jumped with the pain, and the next thing I knew, I was a horse in a stable.

"'The mare just had a nice colt,' I heard people say. Although I was aware of all the goings on, I was not able to speak. Feeling very hungry, I had no choice but to be nursed by the mare.

"After four or five years I had grown to be a straight and sturdy horse; but I was so afraid of the whip that I would run away at its very sight. When the master rode me, he used a saddle-cloth and rode at a leisurely pace so I was able to endure it. But when the servants rode me, they never used a saddle-cloth and they dug their heels into my sides so violently that the pain penetrated into my inner organs. Unable to endure this, I refused food for three days and died.

"When I returned before the King of the Underworld, he discovered that I had not completed my term of punishment and accused me of dodging my sentence. The horse hide was torn off me and I was further punished by having to return to earth as a dog. Feeling very depressed, I did not wish to move; but the devils came at me and whipped me until I scrambled away to an open field thinking that death would be preferable. I hurled myself over a cliff and fell on the ground, unable to move.

"When I looked around, I found myself among a litter of puppies whose mother was suckling and licking me. I realized that once more I had come back to the world of mortals. Later, although garbage and wastes looked disgusting to me, they smelt appetizing. Still I did not wish to eat. During those years I often wished to die but I was afraid that I would again be accused of escaping my term of punishment.

"One day I bit my master's leg and tore it badly. He was very angry and had me destroyed. The King of the Underworld was so enraged by my behavior that he had me beaten and condemned to return as a snake. First I was shut in a dark, stifling room; but gradually I climbed up the wall and escaped through a crevice. When I next saw myself, I was a snake lying low in the grass. Then I made myself a vow never to harm any living thing. I fed on berries and leaves for some years always remembering not to kill myself or incite others to kill me by injuring them.

"One day as I was lying in the grass I heard a carriage coming. Intending to get out of its way, I crossed the road, but the wheels ran over me and I was cut in two. The King was quite surprised to see me back so soon. With humility I told him my story. He accepted my innocence and pardoned me so I was permitted to be born once again as a human being."

This was Mr. Liu's story. At birth, he was able to speak fluently. After one reading he was able to commit anything to memory. In 1621 he received his *chü-jen* degree. All this life he told people to put saddle-clothes on their horses and that the pain a horse feels from being kicked in the ribs is much worse than from being whipped.

Translated by Nancy Gibbs

MATCH-MAKING FOR GHOSTS

In the southern region of Chiang-p'u, there once lived a woman whose maiden name was Chang married to a man named Ch'en. After seven years Ch'en died, and as she was not able to manage her daily needs, she remarried a man also named Chang. By coincidence, Chang's wife had also been dead for seven years; therefore their match-maker thought it was Heaven's will that the two should get together.

Hardly had they been married for a fortnight when Mrs. Chang became possessed by the spirit of her dead husband and scolded herself: "You have no conscience! To think that you would betray me and marry a common bum!" She then slapped her own cheeks with her hands. The Chang family burned paper money to offer to the ghost and tried many ways to pacify him, yet he continued to harass his former wife.

Next, Mr. Chang also became possessed by his dead wife and reproached himself: "You are heartless! Now you only know the new wife and no longer remember the old one!" He also started hitting himself with his hands, and the whole family panicked.

It so happened that, just at that time, the same match-maker, whose name was Ch'in, was at the scene and said jokingly, "Before, I have always made matches for living beings, but what should stop me from making a match for dead ones? Since Mr. Ch'en is here asking for his wife, and you are here asking for your husband, why don't you two get together and leave those two alone? That way you will not be lonely in the underworld, and the living couple can also live in peace. What's the point of making a scene here?"

Now a coy expression came to Mr. Chang's face and in his former wife's voice he said, "The same idea also occurred to me. Yet I am very ugly. I don't know if Mr. Ch'en will take me, and it's not proper for me to propose. Now that you, madam, have expressed such kind thoughts, could I ask you to speak to him about it?"

Ch'in the match-maker then asked both families, and everybody consented. Suddenly the possessed Mr. Chang smiled and said again, "It is a good idea—yet, although we are ghosts, we should not have an illicit affair; otherwise all the other ghosts would look down upon us. The match-maker must cut paper-men to bear my sedan-chair; provide wedding music of gongs and drums; set up a banquet; and give us the 'conjugal drink' to conclude the wedding ceremony. Only then can we leave you in peace."

The Chang family obeyed everything that she said, and the couple was never troubled again. Meanwhile, it became a legend among the folk of neighboring regions that in a certain village, a match-maker named Ch'in had made a match for two ghosts.

Translated by Clara Yu

SAINT PIG

In the late Ming dynasty, a pig was raised in the Hua-shan Buddhist Monastery. It had lived a great many years, until all its hair had fallen out. It was a vegetarian and would not eat anything unclean. Whenever it heard the monks recite the scriptures, it would kowtow and piously touch the feet of the statue of Buddha with its head. All the monks in the monastery therefore called it "Saint Pig."

One day when the pig was very old and ill and about to die, the abbot of the monastery, Chan-i, was about to leave for some distant place to preach. He summoned his disciples and said to them, "If Saint Pig should die, you must butcher it into pieces, and distribute its meat to treat the neighbors of this monastery." All the monks verbally agreed, but in their hearts thought it wrong to do so.

A little later Saint Pig died, and the monks secretly buried it instead of carrying out Chan-i's order. When he returned, he asked how his disciples had disposed of the pig, and the monks then told him the truth: "The Law of Buddha forbids killing; therefore we have buried it."

Hearing this, Chan-i was greatly alarmed and went straight to where the pig had been buried. He thumped the ground with his staff and cried, "I have let you down! I have let you down!" When the monks asked the reason for his grief, Chan-i said, "Thirty years from now, in a certain village, there will be a righteous official who, though innocent, will be tortured by extreme punishment, and that official will be none other than Saint Pig. You see, Saint Pig was a government official in his previous life. Because he had acted against his conscience, he knew that he would not be able to escape an ill fate. He had therefore requested to be reincarnated as a base animal and come here to have his soul alleviated from suffering. I had therefore determined to relieve him of his guilt by slaughtering him, and now you ignorant disciples, you have mismanaged the whole thing. And yet, this must also be his unalterable fate."

Under the reign of the Ch'ung-chen Emperor [1628–1644], in a certain village there was a member of the National Academy and the Tung-lin Party by the name of Cheng Man. His character was beyond reproach, yet his uncle falsely accused him of beating his mother with a staff, and he suffered the punishment of slow death by dismemberment. The whole empire grieved over the injustice. Only then did ordinary people recognize that Chan-i (who had already passed away) had a thorough understanding of the law of causality.

Translated by Clara Yu

MALARIA SPIRIT

When Ch'en Ch'i-tung, the Shang-yüan Magistrate, was young, he stayed at the temple of Kuan-ti in T'ai-p'ing. Sharing a room with him was a certain Mr. Chang, who had contracted malaria. One day Ch'en became tired at noon and lay down on the bed facing Chang. Outside the door he saw a pale boy whose clothes, hat, shoes, and socks were all black. Although the boy looked in and stared at Chang, Ch'en did not question him, taking him to be someone from the temple. A few moments later Chang had a spasmodic fit, which subsided as soon as the boy departed.

Another day, when Ch'en was sleeping, he suddenly heard Chang crying out deliriously and wildly vomiting phlegm. Ch'en, startled from his sleep, saw the boy standing in front of Chang's bed, merrily dancing and looking around as if very satisfied with himself. Ch'en now realized that this was a malaria spirit. He rushed forward to attack the boy, but whatever part Ch'en touched was unbearably cold. The boy ran out like a gushing wind. Ch'en chased him up to the central courtyard, where the boy vanished. Chang's sickness was cured, but Ch'en's hands turned a blackish color, as if smoked, that did not go away for several days.

Translated by Clara Yu

CH'EN BLOWS AWAY A GHOST

Ch'en Kung-p'eng lived on terms of friendship with his fellow villager Li Fu. One autumn evening he strolled in the moonlight over to Li's house to have a chat with him. "I just tried to talk my wife into getting me some wine," Li told him, "but she wouldn't. Please sit down for a moment. I'll go buy some, and we can then enjoy the moonlight together."

Ch'en sat down and opened an anthology of poetry to read while waiting. Then outside the gate a woman appeared, wearing a dark gown, her hair disheveled. She opened the gate and entered, but left again when she saw Ch'en. Ch'en supposed she was one of Li's family, who would not enter in the presence of a stranger, so he turned sideways to avoid being seen by her. She returned with something in her sleeves, which she hid under the sill of the gate, before entering the house. Ch'en, curious to know what she had hidden there, went over to the sill and saw a foul-smelling cord stained with blood. It now occurred to him that the woman was the ghost of a hanged person. He took the cord, hid it in his boot, and sat down as if nothing had happened.

After a short while, the woman with the disheveled hair came out of the house and groped around in the spot where she had hidden the cord. Unable to find it, she flew into a rage and dashed straight toward Ch'en, crying, "Give it back to me."

"Give *what* back to you?" Ch'en asked. The woman did not reply. Drawing herself up to her full height, she opened her mouth and blew a puff of ice cold wind over him, which made his hair stand up on end and his teeth chatter. Meanwhile, the lamplight sputtered and turned greenish, as if about to go out.

"The ghost has breath," Ch'en thought. "Do I have none?" So he too blew at the woman, and where his breath hit her she grew hollow. First her belly was bored right through, then followed her chest and her head. In a little while she vanished altogether, just as a light vapor dissolves in the air.

After some time Li entered, the wine he had purchased still in hand, crying loudly that his wife had hanged herself over their bed. Ch'en smiled and said, "She's all right. The ghost's rope is still in my boot." He told Li what had happened, and they went inside to untie the woman. They gave her ginger water to drink and she came around. When asked why she desired death, the wife said, "We're very poor, and yet my husband does not stop entertaining guests. He took my only hairpin to buy wine. I was very upset, yet I couldn't cry because a guest was sitting out there. Suddenly by my side I found a woman with disheveled hair. Claiming to be a neighbor, she told me that my husband hadn't taken my hairpin in order to entertain his guest, but to go to the gambling house. These words increased my grief and indignation. I was also worried because, if my husband failed to come home tonight, the guest wouldn't

leave, and it would be very embarrassing to explain the situation to him. The woman with disheveled hair then made a noose and said, 'Through this you will pass into the boundless delights of Buddha's realm.' I put my head through the noose, but her hands could not draw it tight, and the noose slackened time and again. The woman then said, 'I will go fetch my Buddha-cord, and it will make a Buddha of you.' She went out to get the cord but didn't return, and I was left in a trance or dream until you came to save me."

They made inquiries and, sure enough, some months before a village woman in the neighborhood had hanged herself.

Translated by Clara Yu

A GHOST'S LEG CAUGHT IN THE DOOR

One day, Yin Yüeh-heng, who lived outside the northeast gate of Hang-chou, was returning home from the Sand River Rapids with half a pound of water chestnuts in his bosom. He passed by Alms Bowl Lake, a deserted area where scarcely anyone lived. In the vast open field there stood a few untended graves. Suddenly he felt the contents of his bosom lose their weight; he reached for the water chestnuts he had bought, but they were gone. He returned to look for them, and found them in the graveyard, peeled and broken into pieces, piled on top of a grave. Yin picked them up, put them back in his bosom, and hurried home.

Hardly had Yin finished eating the water chestnuts when he fell ill and loudly exclaimed, "I had not tasted water chestnuts for a long time, and all I wanted was to satisfy my long-unfulfilled desire for them. And you had to take them all away again. How very stingy! Now that I'm here in your house, I won't leave until I've eaten my fill."

The family was greatly frightened, and immediately set out food to redeem the guilt of their master. In cases such as these, it is the custom of the people in Hang-chou to close the gate as soon as the ghosts have left. Now Yin's family also followed this custom, but they closed the gate too hastily, and Yin again cried loudly: "When you have guests, you should treat them with respect. Now you shut the door before I've gotten outside! My leg is injured and hurts a lot. Unless you prepare another feast for me, I'll never leave this house."

The family had to appease the ghost again with prayers and sacrifices, upon which Yin got a little better, but often the disease would return. He never recovered and finally died of the consequences.

Translated by Clara Yu

THE DEVIL IN A WOODEN COLLAR

In Huai-an there lived a man named Li, who had a very loving relationship with his wife. When Li died of illness in his thirties, even after his body was lying in the coffin, his wife could not bear to have the lid nailed down. She wept daily from morning till night and often would lift up the lid to gaze on him.

In former times, the custom was that when someone died, his ghost was expected to return on the seventh day. On this day, all Li's relatives, including the nearest ones, had withdrawn from the room, and yet the wife would not leave. She set her children in the next room and sat down within the curtains of her dead husband's bed to await him.

At the second watch-drum, a blast of cold wind rose and the lamplights turned green. She then saw a devil with red hair and round eyes, its height more than a hundred feet. In its hand it held an iron fork. With a rope this devil pulled the husband into the room through the window. But as soon as the devil saw the sacrificial wine and food placed in front of the coffin, it dropped its fork and rope, sat down, and started to gulp down the food, belching with each gulp. Meanwhile, the husband walked around and touched the furniture that had belonged to him when he was alive, sighing with sorrow. When finally he came to the bed and raised the curtains, his wife burst into tears and clasped him in her arms. But he was cold and intangible like a wisp of an icy cloud. She then wrapped him up in a quilt. At this, the red-haired devil rushed forth and tried to take the dead man away from her. The wife cried out so loudly that all her children ran to her rescue, and the red-haired devil fled.

The wife and her children put the wrapped-up *hun* into the coffin, and it gradually showed signs of life. They then put him on the bed and fed him with rice-gruel. The man finally came around at daybreak. The iron fork which the devil left behind was now discovered to be made of paper, like those people burn for spirits. Once more the husband and wife lived together for over twenty years. The wife, who was then sixty, was praying one day in the temple of the God of Walls and Moats when in a trance she saw two bowmen carrying a criminal with a wooden collar round his neck. On looking closer she recognized that the collar-wearer was none other than the red-haired devil. He cursed her with these words: "It was my gluttony that allowed you to trick me into this collar for twenty years. Now that I have seen you again, do you think I will let you escape?"

As soon as the wife reached home, she died.

Translated by Clara Yu

46.

Proverbs About Heaven

Proverbs are a valuable source for understanding common assumptions and ways of thinking that people take as so obvious and well-accepted that they do not have to be argued; merely by invoking the proverb or saying, one is certain that others will understand. It is true that the repertoire of proverbs contains many that are mutually contradictory (such as two given below: "Heaven helps the good man," and "Heaven is high and the Emperor far away"). In such cases, most people probably would acknowledge believing both, not as statements of universal applicability, but still as "truths."

Below are some proverbs collected in China in the nineteenth and early twentieth centuries. They occurred in everyday speech but in a variety of contexts. All of these proverbs concern Heaven, which literally means "sky." Heaven is not Paradise, a place where souls go after death (such as the Pure Land of the Buddhists); rather it is closer to the Western concept of Providence or the Supreme Being.

1. The net of Heaven is large and wide but it lets nothing through.
2. All things have their root in Heaven.
3. Heaven produces and Heaven destroys.
4. The heart of the people is the heart of Heaven.
5. It is easy to oppress the people beneath you but difficult to deceive Heaven above.
6. Men can be imposed upon but not Heaven; men can be deceived but not Heaven.
7. Men's whispers sound like thunder in Heaven's ears; their secret thoughts flash like lightning before Heaven's eyes.
8. The slightest virtue, although unseen by men, is surely seen by Heaven.
9. Men see only the present; Heaven sees the future.
10. When men's desires are good, Heaven will certainly further them.
11. Heaven helps the good man.
12. To depend upon men is not as good as to depend upon Heaven.
13. A fire started by men is called a fire; a fire started by Heaven is called a calamity.
14. Men should beware of coveting riches; when riches come through covetousness, Heaven's calamities follow.
15. Those who accord with Heaven are preserved; those who rebel against Heaven perish.
16. Heaven sets the price of fuel and rice.
17. Great blessings come from Heaven; small blessings come from man.
18. Because men do not like the cold, Heaven does not cause winter to cease.
19. Man would order things thus and so but Heaven's way is never such.
20. Heaven responds to man as promptly as shadow to form or echo to voice.
21. Heaven never produces a man without providing him clothes and food.
22. For each man produced by Heaven, Earth provides a grave.

23. Man depends on Heaven as a ship on her pilot.
24. It is Heaven's role to declare a man's destiny; it is man's role to shorten or lengthen his days.
25. When you have done your duty, listen to the will of Heaven.
26. Heaven and Earth are the greatest; father and mother are the most honored.
27. Death and life are predetermined; riches and honors depend upon Heaven.
28. Heaven complies with the wishes of good men; happiness springs naturally in harmonious homes.
29. Heaven is high and the Emperor far away.
30. Heaven does not spare truth; Earth does not spare its treasures.
31. Heaven is man on a large scale; man is Heaven on a small scale.
32. Heaven never stops a man from making a living.
33. In our actions we should accord with the will of Heaven; in our words we should accord with the hearts of men.
34. If Heaven above lets fall a plum, open your mouth.

47.

Almanac

The most widely circulated books in traditional China were probably the annually published almanacs. These books gave a variety of information considered to have a bearing on activities undertaken on each day of the year. The theory behind them was the Han and pre-Han notions of the correspondence between the human and the cosmic realms and the interconnections between all phenomena based on the forces of Yin and Yang and the five elements. Long after political thinkers had ceased to pay much attention to interpreting portents from Heaven, such beliefs remained strong in people's personal lives. For major events, such as marriages, funerals, departures for distant places, or the undertaking of new enterprises, almost no one would fail to choose a lucky day or at least avoid an unlucky one. He could consult an almanac himself or ask a diviner or other expert to do it for him. Many people, however, used almanacs much more frequently, often as a routine aid in making decisions.

To give a sense of what these almanacs were like and how they could be used, the section of an 1894 almanac covering the first five days of the year is given below.

FIRST DAY OF THE FIRST MONTH

Name in the sixty-day cycle: chi-mao. *Element:* earth. *Constellation:* wei. *Quality:* relievedness. *Anniversaries:* Birth of Maitreya Buddha. *Auspicious stars:* Sui-ho, etc. *Genie:* forest. *Location of womb spirit:* front gate.* *Western date:* February 6, 1894.

Forecast: Avoid breaking bills of exchange, digging wells or ponds, visiting the sick, draining water, moving into a new residence. On this day, the God of Joy is to be found in the northeast direction; the God of Wealth in the north; the God of Rank in the south; the God of Misfortune in the west. The hour between midnight and 1 A.M. is the most auspicious for offering incense, starting journeys, and welcoming the God of Rank to his shrine (face the south when doing

this), for the auspicious stars T'ien-te, Yüeh-te, and T'ein-tao gather their force in this hour. Between the hours of 3 and 5 A.M. it is good to welcome the God of Prosperity or personages who may bring good luck for the year. The hours 11 A.M. to 1 P.M. are also propitious. The hours 5 to 7 P.M., however, are characterized by "brokenness" and those between 3 and 5 P.M. are characterized by "interception." As the path is either empty or lost in these hours, avoid them, or use them with discretion.

SECOND DAY

Cyclical name: keng-ch'en. *Element:* metal. *Constellation:* chi. *Quality:* fullness. *Anniversary:* Birth of General Ch'e. *Auspicious stars:* T'ien-en, etc. *Inauspicious stars:* Fu-tuan, etc. *Genie:* earth. *Location of womb spirit:* pestle, mill, and chicken coop. *Western date:* February 7, 1894.

---

* Womb spirits are the souls of fetuses which reside in various parts of the house before birth. Pregnant women and members of their families must be sure not to harm the spirits if they want to avoid miscarriages, birth defects, and so on.

Forecast: Avoid doing business. Mourners should refrain from weeping on this day. A propitious day for bathing, praying for good fortune, repairing walls, sewing clothing, knitting fishing nets, and hunting.

THIRD DAY

Cyclical name: hsin-szu. *Element:* metal. *Constellation:* tou. *Quality:* evenness. *Anniversary:* Death of Emperor Kao-tsung; birth of Sung the Immortal. *Auspicious stars:* T'ien-en, etc. Inauspicious stars: Ch'ung-jih, etc. *Genie:* spirit. *Location of womb spirit:* kitchen, stove, bed. *Western date:* February 8, 1894.

Forecast: Avoid making soy sauce or starting journeys. Propitious for repairing roads.

FOURTH DAY

Cyclical name: jen-wu. *Element:* wood. *Constellation:* niu. *Quality:* steadiness. *Auspicious star:* T'ien-en, etc. *Inauspicious stars:* Szu-ch'i, etc. *Genie:* fire. *Location of womb spirit:* storage, pestle. *Western date:* February 9, 1894.

Forecast: Avoid draining water, divination for construction, entering school, fishing, felling trees. Propitious for sacrifices, praying for good fortune and sons, presenting memorials, meeting friends, starting journeys, marriages, adding family members, moving, exorcising, sewing clothes, repairs and construction, breaking earth for construction, erecting pillars and placing ridgepoles, doing business, starting new businesses, receiving profits, planting, and interring. The auspicious hours are 1–3 A.M., 7–11 A.M.

FIFTH DAY

Cyclical name: kuei-wei. *Element:* wood. *Constellation:* nü. *Quality:* firmness. *Auspicious stars:* T'ien-en, etc. *Inauspicious stars:* Fan-chih, etc. *Genie:* mountain. *Location of womb spirit:* bedroom, bed, toilet. *Western date:* February 10, 1894.

Forecast: Avoid lawsuits or taking medicine. Propitious for meeting friends, catching animals, taking up new offices, entering school, capping and pinning, marriages, adding new family members, starting journeys.

Translated by Clara Yu

48.

Taxes and Labor Service

One way any government affects the people under it is by imposition of taxes and obligatory service. In traditional China, taxes were recognized as inevitable, though periodic reforms were made to rationalize their collection or make their burdens more equitable. Labor service obligations, by contrast, were considered undesirable, and ever since the T'ang dynasty efforts had been made to do away with them or commute them to cash payments. However, for local officials to hire workers whenever something needed to be done would have cost too much, and time and again they would draft people to serve without pay.

Assessing the impact of government policies such as taxation is always difficult, since most discussions of policies and institutions are written from the point of view of the rulers, not the ruled. Thus we have full descriptions of what laws were issued and how institutions were supposed to work, but few accounts of how they were perceived by those most affected by them. In the case of taxes and service obligations, one group that often felt particularly burdened was well-to-do but not high-ranking households, including the households of lower-degree holders. From the government's point of view, poor people could not bear all the burdens of paying and collecting taxes, since they simply did not have the resources. At the same time it was too difficult to exploit fully the upper gentry and high officials because of their political power and many privileges. Thus more and more obligations were placed on lesser landlords.

The following essay reveals some of the complaints of this group. It is an account of the tax and labor service systems as they actually operated in Sung prefecture (in the modern Shanghai area) in the seventeenth century. The author, Yeh Meng-chu, composed this account as part of a comprehensive description of his native area entitled **Perceptions of the Era.** *He relied on the recollections of old people for some of his evidence but also had personal experience with aspects of the system. His particular grievance about the treatment he received for tax arrears in 1661 should not be taken as a typical experience; the early Ch'ing government, intent on consolidating its authority, dealt especially severely with the gentry of this area as a warning to others elsewhere. In other places severe penalties were rarely imposed.*

TAXES

Our prefecture's taxes are the highest in the country. Su-chou yields more tax income than does the whole province of Chekiang. The land encompassed by Sung prefecture, although only one-third the size of Su-chou, yields half as much tax income as Su-chou. From this one can see that Su and Sung prefectures are the most heavily taxed in the whole southeast delta area, and that Sung prefecture's taxes are by far the highest.

I have talked with old people about how things were during the Lung-ch'ing [1567–1572] and Wan-li periods [1573–1620], and they all say that at that time local produce was abundant and the people were happy. Officials were not punished for their performance in tax collection, and the common people were not disturbed by tax-prodders. Today our taxes are not much higher than before, but the officials make strenuous efforts to collect them, piling one penalty on top of another for failure to pay, and, since the people are drained of all their riches, their overdue taxes never get paid. . . .

Throughout the Ming dynasty, officials considered their tax collection accomplished when they had collected eighty percent of the required amount, and the people who paid eighty percent of their taxes were considered law-abiding subjects, even those who only paid sixty to seventy percent were considered "cooperative." Moreover, because peace had existed for a long time, the regulations had become routine. As there were extensive stores of grain, the tax grain to be shipped out could be reduced in quantity. There were priority expenses that had to be met, such as the salaries of government officials, the wages for workers, the expenses for schools, and the allowance for the salaried students; but other expenses could be delayed. The yearly repair of government buildings, city walls, and storage structures did not have to be done on time. The alms granaries had to be filled, but not necessarily with the first round of collected tax grain. The yearly rewards for scholars who passed the civil service examination and the traveling expenses for the new candidates could not be ignored but they did not have to be given regularly, and the traveling expenses for those on the waiting list could be deferred. The soldiers who defended our cities had to be paid; yet the seasonal display of their training and equipment could be omitted. Other such cases where the expenses might be delayed were innumerable. So, when sixty or seventy percent of the tax was collected, it was ready to be shipped. When eighty percent was collected, some revenue could even be set aside as savings. In this way, taxes were collected in installments and the revenue was spent as actual needs arose. Officials were not punished for neglecting their tax-collection duties, and the people were not squeezed dry.

Beginning with this dynasty, things changed. In the fifth month of 1645, an imperial decree was issued to reduce the taxes of the southeast delta area by fifty percent. As a result, local governments had to reduce all taxes that could be delayed and to cut out all but urgent expenses. It was true that, owing to the good intention of the Emperor, the yearly taxes, though not quite as low in the reigns of Lung-ch'ing and Wan-li, were much lighter than before. And yet,

when non-urgent expenses were cut, everything else was absolutely necessary, and officials could no longer balance out by appropriating funds set aside for non-urgent matters to supply immediate needs. Furthermore, much of the tax revenue was used to pay the soldiers. Since they had to be paid in full, taxes also had to be paid in full. Consequently, a local official now had to collect one hundred percent of the taxes before his duties were fulfilled, and he had to punish those who did not pay the full amount. For this reason, all local officials concentrated on their tax-collection duties and paid little attention to the welfare of the people.

As to the taxpayers, some were law-abiding, others were defiant. Their fields also varied in quality, as did their yearly harvests. . . . All these factors made it impossible to obtain a one hundred percent tax collection. Moreover, although the tax was lowered, people were accustomed to the old ways and failed to anticipate the consequent strict execution of the law, so many continued to owe taxes. As a result, many Magistrates lost their posts because of their failure to collect all the taxes due. The county Revenue Officer usually counted the newly collected tax against the old deficit. The transferral of county officials also caused problems because the new and old Magistrates evaded their responsibilities to each other. Often Magistrates had to rent houses and stay near their former post because of unfinished tax business. This situation continued until the last years of Shun-chih [1644–1661], when the Prefect of Chiang-ning was unable to solve the problem and blamed the gentry, the literati, and the government functionaries. He proposed to the throne that they be punished. The order was first applied to Wu-hsi county in Chang and the Chia-ting county in Su, and then, in the fifth month of 1661 the new tax law was adopted in the four prefectures Su, Sung, Chang, Chen, and the county of Li-yang. It required an explanation for delayed tax payments and stipulated that the owed amount be paid up by the end of the year.

Now, while it was true that the gentry, literati, and government functionaries did owe taxes, the sum was barely ten percent of the amount owed by the common people. Besides, there were mistakes in the records when the law was first implemented. The bookkeepers, who did not comprehend the seriousness of the matter, only recorded rough figures for the taxes paid by individuals from one day to another. Sometimes a completed payment was erroneously recorded as still outstanding; other times, a small unpaid amount was mistakenly recorded as a large one. Sometimes, the name of the person who had paid up his taxes failed to show up on the record; other times, such a person's name failed to be deleted from the list of delinquents.

In its severity, the new law made no distinction of how high one's office was or how much or how little tax one owed. All the government officials on the list of delinquents were to be dismissed from their offices and all the gentry in retirement were to be demoted in rank. Consequently, 2,171 local gentry and literati and 11,346 lower degree holders were listed as offenders and were scheduled to be dismissed or demoted. At first, it was reported that these offenders were to be extradited to the capital to be severely punished, and all hearts pounded. Then it was decided that those who could pay up before the imperial decree arrived could avoid extradition, bringing some relief. But still, hundreds were unable to pay up by that date and were released only if they managed to clear their debts before the scheduled extradition. Those people certainly would not have remained prisoners if they had had some way out.

Then officials began to collect unpaid taxes for the previous ten years, and the citizens, frightened of the devasting consequences, rushed in to pay, selling their estates at any price. Sometimes, a person would face several deadlines on one day, or would be called upon to appear before several officials. When he tried to comply with one, he would have to ignore the others. The officers were as fierce as wolves and tigers, and the literati were treated as if they were common criminals. At such moments, the only course for many was to borrow. And yet, the monthly interest was twenty to thirty percent and one day's delay in payment would result in compounded interest. . . . Consequently, when a person borrowed ten taels of silver, he would only get nine to begin with, and this would be equivalent to little more than eight taels of pure silver. When he brought in the latter amount to the revenue office, it would be regarded as little more than seven taels. If he should fail to meet the deadline for the tax payment, then he might spend more than half of his loan just to appease the tax collectors. One month later, the officers would be out for his blood again, in packs. A person who owned one hundred *mou* could have his land, his house, his pots and pans, even his children confiscated and still be in debt for the taxes. Fettered by the law and driven by the whip, he would be too desperate to make a wise decision. That is why so many people abandoned their property and fled to other areas and still congratulated themselves on having preserved their lives. That was the saddest episode in the history of the tax system.

On the 15th day of the eleventh month of 1662 there was a rumor that all unpaid taxes had to be paid up by the end of that day and those who failed to do so would be exiled to the most desolate areas of the country. People turned panicky and fought to pay their taxes, so much so that the tax collectors were not able to handle the rush. Later it was discovered to be only a rumor, yet everyone's heart had sunk in fear. . . . At this time the Emperor was young and the state was ruled by four regents who were strict and allowed no exceptions. . . . The officials Chang Jen-an and Yeh Fang-ai were demoted because they both owed one-thousandth of a tael of silver. The county student Ch'eng P'i-chieh was dismissed from office because he owed 0.7 of one-thousandth of a tael. From these cases one can see the severity of the law. . . .

In 1675 warfare broke out and military funds were short, so selling offices was widely resorted to. A regulation was put into effect that those who had been impeached in 1660, as long as they had no other offenses, could regain their former status if they were able to contribute 500 to 600 taels of silver, depending on their former ranks. Those who could ship rice, beans, and straw to the dangerous regions of Ch'in, Ch'u, Min, and Yüeh would be eligible for a fifty-percent reduction of their contribution.

However, fifteen years had elasped since 1660. The young and strong had become weak and old and had little enthusiasm for self-promotion; they found it difficult enough just to maintain a livelihood. Furthermore, because of the widely practiced system of buying offices, there no longer were any standards for high officials. One did not have to pass the civil service examination; one did not have to have seniority; all one needed to become a high official was riches. For these reasons, of the formerly impeached literati and gentry, few submitted money to regain their status.

I was one of the impeached officials, implicated by some relatives and friends. At the time, my demotion came as such a shock to everyone that those friends and relatives felt very guilty; had there been some way to compensate me for the wrongs I had suffered, they could easily have been persuaded to assist me financially. Yet now, so many years later, the guilty feelings have worn down; even if I were to call on them for help, they probably would not respond. Besides, I have grown old and have lost my ambition. Why should I exchange ten times the wealth of my household to gain a blue scholar's robe?

Yet, as I watch the world go by, I cannot help reflecting on this matter. I have kept various documents which I have appended to show that there was room for leniency in my case. Yet we were unable to make ourselves heard at the time, and when our Emperor finally changed his mind, there was no longer a set correlation between human feelings and justice. This must have been my predestined course in life, but it is a curious course for fate to take.

LABOR SERVICE

Our prefecture ranks first not only in land taxes but also in labor service. This phenomenon is not found in any other province or prefecture.

The heaviest duties used to be the "transportation of cloth" and the "northern transportation of rice." At first our county had to supply one person per year to attend to the transportation of cloth; later, the number increased to three. Their task was to buy cloth of various colors and quality with state revenue, then ship it to the capital by boat. Each year our county supplied twenty-three persons to undertake the northern transportation of rice. Their task was to select more than 13,000 piculs of fine white rice and glutinous rice and ship it to the capital for the Court of Imperial Entertainments to use in supplying the granaries for the officials' salaries. Only the richest people were assigned such duties. In addition to the northern transportation of rice, there was also a shipment of rice to the south, to Nanking. For this shipment two persons were assigned each year from our county. Besides these duties there was tax collection. Each year forty-eight persons were drafted for collection of the county revenue—a total of more than 200,000 taels of silver. Another thirty-eight persons were assigned to exchange the 110,000 piculs of tax rice for silver and hand it over to the transporters.

All the above duties were categorized as "heavy" ones and were reassigned and reviewed every five years. "Light" duties included "Expediting Tax Prodder" and "Hastening Tax Prodder." These were reassigned and reviewed every ten years. Only landowners were assigned to them. There was also a "Public Works Superintendent" responsible for the repair and maintenance of city walls, public halls, ponds, and waterways, as well as other miscellaneous duties.

When the labor service rules were first implemented, there were subsidies for transportation expenses, for loss of rice in refining, and for the cost of labor. Because these were important duties, the system was worked out in detail. But it gradually deteriorated so that, for instance, the people responsible for transportation and delivery were told to collect the taxes themselves. But this was not the worst. These people, because of their service obligations, became subject to continual extortion: at home they faced unreasonable demands from the local government headquarters; en route they were at the mercy of various local runners and lower government officials; arriving in the capital, they became victims of insatiable officials from all government departments and often were detained for a whole year without being able to obtain a discharge. Thus, those assigned to transportation and delivery suffered extremely.

As to those who served as tax collectors, many had to hire bookkeepers and accountants of their own. Others had to deal with powerful gentry and officials who protected their relatives. These relatives would underpay or pay in low quality silver, and the tax collectors did not dare to protest. They also had to entertain and present gifts to the continually arriving local functionaries. All these expenses, plus having to make up taxes not paid, brought great suffering to the tax collectors.

Those who were assigned the task of grain exchange, on the other hand, were sometimes even able to make a profit, provided they were shrewd and encountered good times. The reason was that, for each picul of rice, the tax payer actually had to pay another three pecks of rice to cover wastage. This practice was so well established that even the influential and the powerful dared not ignore it. Generally, there is a large amount of bran in the tribute rice and cunning exchange workers would mix even more bran in it. . . . After 1646 or 1647, however, the government tightened the rules and stipulated that tribute rice would have to be sifted and tossed against the wind before it could be submitted. Consequently, people began to select good quality rice for taxes. Before it was deposited in the granaries, there were inspectors who carefully examined its quality. If they found unhusked grains, they would punish the exchange workers. As a result, some corrupt practices were eliminated, but exchange workers could be blackmailed by the transporters. . . . This financial burden, to which were added presents for the officials and other miscellaneous expenses, amounted to a total expenditure which was often twice as much as the value of the rice. Thus, in the end no one performing grain exchange duties could escape bankruptcy and people began to fear this duty as a trap.

It was not until 1646 that Imperial Inspector T'u Kuo-pao, sensitive to the people's distress, ordered prefectures and county governments to make detailed studies of the possible simplification of the three major labor service duties, namely, the transportation of cloth, the northern transportation of rice, and the collection of taxes. He also ordered that the prefecture and county governments take over collection and transportation. As a result, an unnecessary source of waste was eliminated as the heavy labor service duties were terminated.

The only remaining complaint was that the government clerks tended to make excessive deductions when they weighed the silver that people handed in as taxes. Later it was ruled that the taxes be handed in in sealed envelopes and that there be no weighing at the clerk's counter. This made it impossible for the clerks to touch the silver; even a small child could go and pay taxes, for he would be treated in the same manner as a powerful personage. As a result, the people were instantly relieved of another hardship.

The abolition of the grain exchange began in 1658. Chu Hao-an, a member of the gentry, was in charge of local exchanges; he submitted memorials to the Imperial Court explaining the disadvantages of the system, and requested that the government take over this duty just as it had taken over the northern transportation of rice, cloth transportation, and tax collection. . . .

The only labor service left was that of tax prodding in the local units. One might argue that, all the heavy duties having been abolished, the light ones would not have been too burdensome. But one immediately is forced to recognize that corruption had sunk so deep that the chore of prodding taxes on the local level had become even more onerous than the supposedly heavy duties.

In the first place, during the inspection and assignment of duties held every seven years, the clerks and the heads of villages tried to distort facts to suit their private ends. Consequently, people who had large pieces of land sought the support of important of-

ficials or local influential people, or paid bribes to get away with light duties. Under such circumstances labor service duties fell upon middle-income families and ones even less well-off. Those who owned several hundred *mou*, several tens of *mou*, or sometimes even only several *mou* had to serve in place of the wealthy.

Each time tax collection began, if the government clerks had not received enough payoff, they would keep all the law-abiding households for themselves so as to extort profits from them and assign the tax collectors only the most uncooperative ones. Often they would order a person of low income to collect the tax from someone well-to-do, or have someone ignorant collect from someone cunning, or make a commoner collect tax from the gentry. As a result, not only could these collectors fail to collect anything, but often they would not even get to see the tax payer in question. They might linger at the doors of the influential for days on end, allowed to see them only when the deadline was past. They would have to bribe the officials and make up the deficit themselves. After they had used up all their own resources, they would be whipped every day and driven to the loan sharks who charged 100 cash for each cash borrowed. Still they could not possibly clear their debts. Eventually they would lose not only all their belongings but their lives as well.

The system of the "Expediting Tax Prodder" was later changed into the "Rice Bin Superintendent System" *(wu-t'un)* which was equally corrupt; the "Rice Bin Superintendent System" was then replaced by the "Tax Chief System" *(li-t'ou)* which was even more disastrous. Consequently, as soon as people heard that duties were being assigned, the whole countryside would be in an uproar. Only the government clerks and runners would rejoice since they were the ones who would profit from the system. They would extort money from the individuals to whom they assigned the duties. Each tax prodder was responsible for a separate area and had to guarantee its tax. Each had to pay the expenses of the initial meetings, the banquets, the transportation, the clerks' fees, and the presents at festivals, harvest, and New Year. With these and other expenses, a tax prodder would have to spend at least several hundred taels of silver each year. But this was limited to cases where tax collection was completed before the deadline. Should the prodders fail to meet the deadline, then runners bearing arrest warrants would rush out one after another. As fierce as wolves and tigers, they would demand that the expenses for their transportation, lodging and meals be paid by the prodders, and they would stay night and day until the collection was completed. Consequently, the village tax prodders greatly feared the city government functionaries. . . .

Originally the duty of the "Public Works Superintendent" was confined to public construction. . . . Later on, however, local officials and influential gentry began to treat the "Public Works Superintendent" as a private servant. If a river were located close to a gentry family's graveyard, then the family would order the "Public Works Superintendent" to dredge it; if a public pond were near their residence, they would demand that the "Public Works Superintendent" repair it. They would make up various excuses to persuade the local government to grant their requests, and the officials would knowingly comply, thereby establishing a system of corruption. Thus, an official might dispatch one hundred workers for a job which required only ten so that the gentry would receive payoffs from people who wished to be exempted from their assigned duty. Should there be no construction work, the official would extort twenty to thirty taels of silver from each, on the pretext that they had neglected their duties.

The miscellaneous duties also increased day by day. During the Ming dynasty there were many types of labor service but never any miscellaneous duties, which came into being only after the heavy duties were abolished. Thus, in the early years of the Shunchih reign [1644–1661], when the government was trying to eliminate the Mao pirates, people were drafted as sailors; when troops were mobilized from other areas, people had to take care of the provisions for the horses; when warships were being built, people had to work as drillers and wood-purchasers. Later, when the pirates penetrated inland, people were assigned to build bridges and to place castiron chains and stockades along the beaches. They also had to repair forts, bonfire platforms, and patrol stations along the coast.

[When a military action was developing] all the common people who were assigned duties were filled with fear and resorted to bribing their way out of the assignments. For each district, it would take from a few dozen to one or two hundred taels to get out of an assignment; yet once a person escaped one, he would immediately be assigned to some other. As a result, those who succeeded in getting out of all assignments became bankrupt. And those individuals who did report for their duties were subject to so many ploys

that they eventually would end up paying more than those who bribed the officials. Only then would those who had bribed their way out feel that they had gotten their money's worth, and only then would the people who actually served regret that they had not offered bribes in the first place. . . .

The tiger-like runners imposed themselves on the tax collectors to such an extent that the latter had to stock up on wine and food and keep their chimneys smoking, not to mention other expenses they had to bear. I had a rather wealthy neighbor, Mr. Ku, who used to send his children to study under my instruction. Later he was ruined by labor service duties. He told me that in order to accommodate the runners, he once had to make twenty-four meals in one day. Between 1664 and 1665, he abandoned his estate and fled. It is not hard to discern why the people all lived in fear!

When Han Shih-ch'i, an Imperial Inspector, heard of these evils, he made tours incognito to find out the truth before giving formal inspection. Often having found out about corrupt officials and their accomplices, he would order them severely punished. The miscellaneous labor service duties were then suspended, and, in fact, the entire system was about to be revised.

When an "Equal Land and Equal Labor System" was first promulgated in Chia and Hu prefectures of western Chekiang, the people of Su and Sung prefectures unsuccessfully requested to have it adopted for them too. When Li Ying-tou was reappointed as the Magistrate of Lou, he saw the harm caused by the "Tax Chief System" and worried about the people's exodus to other districts. Therefore he drew up a petition explaining the advantages of the "Equal Land and Equal Labor" method. . . . When instituted, this method disregarded the land boundaries previously established. Rather, all the land in a county was measured again and divided into set numbers of mutual responsibility units, each having a set size. Then the landowners were told to measure their land with *chia* as a unit. Regardless of the number of *chia* he owned, each landowner would have his own account with the taxing agency, and he would pay his taxes according to the size of his land. Those whose land was less than a *chia* were to combine their land with that of their relatives and friends so as to make up a *chia*. The landowners would then submit their records to the county government, which would group them into new mutual responsibility units according to the order of their submitted records. In this way each landowner paid his own taxes, and the various duties such as "Expediting Tax-Prodder" and "Hastening Tax-Prodder" were eliminated.

As itinerant high officials seldom came to inspect, the local government needed only to keep the courier station clean; Magistrates could now settle local cases based on evidence produced by the plaintiff and the defendant [and did not need the report of the "Head of a Mutual Responsibility Unit"]. When a waterway was blocked, the people of the respective mutual responsibility unit themselves would clean it; thus it was no longer necessary for the government to send laborers great distances to do the job. In this way there was no longer any need for the "Superintendent of Public Works." . . . Village heads and local officials were no longer able to use their power to extort money from the people, and landowners were able to retain their dignity and pay their taxes upon demand. The practices of tax evasion, over-taxing, and other wicked devices were now completely eliminated; and people no longer regarded landed property as a source of misfortune. Many who had run away in previous years now returned to their homes, and the hardship of the common people was also greatly reduced.

Although it is possible that after a long time this new law will also become corrupt, if one compares the labor service laws of 1662, 1663, and 1664 with the present law, one may say that, for the present, the people have been rescued from boiling water and placed on dry land. However, some gentry dislike the new law because it creates equality between the classes. . . . They do not realize that the spirit of the new law is not to demote the gentry class, but to promote the commoners. The law only seems to obliterate the principle that gentlemen work with their minds while ordinary people do physical work. The gentry fails to realize that the number of gentlemen is far smaller than that of the commoners and that the descendants of the gentry of today will most likely become commoners tomorrow, with only a few retaining their high status. Should the government return to the old law, it would benefit the gentry class very little. Moreover, when these same gentlemen are studying and discussing the Way or busy holding office, what they are most concerned with is the life of the commoners; but when they retire from office, they are actually assisting in depriving the people of their well-being and pushing them into boiling water. This I cannot understand at all. . . .

Should the new law someday become corrupt, it is the responsibility of its administrators to make minor revisions according to the circumstances. However, in essence, the method incorporated in this law can be kept without change for a hundred generations.

Translated by Clara Yu

49.

Permanent Property

A steady source of income was generally a prerequisite for upper-class life, making possible lengthy education and preparation for official careers. The traditional way to assure such income was landholding, though from the Sung dynasty on, many fortunes were undoubtedly amassed through commerce or industry, and in all periods family fortunes could be greatly augmented by successful government careers.

The essay below presents one man's perception of the importance of landholding to members of the upper class and discusses some of the practical difficulties involved in their lives, which combined scholarship, officeholding, and estate management. The author, Chang Ying (1638–1708), was a prominent official who lived in an agriculturally productive area of Anhui province. He addressed this essay to his sons. It should be readily apparent that Chang Ying's views on landholding and the life of the landlord differed considerably from those of his older contemporary, Yeh Meng-chu, seen in the previous selection.

All worldly things that once were new will eventually age. A house that has stood for a long time will decay; clothes worn for a long time will become shabby. Cattle, slaves, and horses are costly when purchased, yet ten years later they are no longer the same, and after another ten years they do not even exist. Only land remains new through hundreds and thousands of years. Even if, due to negligence, the soil becomes barren, once fertilizer is applied, it becomes rich again. With cultivation desolate land becomes productive; with irrigation dry land becomes arable; with weeding neglected soil becomes fertile. Since time immemorial man has not had to worry about the land becoming worn out or ruined, nor about its running away or becoming scarce. Indeed, land is truly precious.

Nowadays the young heirs of large estates wear fancy clothes, ride strong horses, and seek pleasure to their hearts' content in song and dance. A fur garment easily costs scores of gold taels; a feast, several taels. The price of grain in our area has been low for

the past decade so that now ten piculs of grain will barely pay for a feast and a hundred piculs will scarcely buy a fur garment; but the young heirs act ignorant of this. They do not wish to know that the peasants, bodies soaked and feet muddy, toil all year round to produce a hundred piculs of grain. Furthermore, with the unpredictability of floods and droughts, one year's harvest does not guarantee the next. I have heard that in Shensi province there is an annual famine and with each famine the price of a picul of grain goes up six or seven taels. Yet young heirs of today will sell precious grain cheaply merely to satisfy a desire for another fur garment or another feast. How can one not be deeply disturbed by these matters?

The ancients have a saying: "Use the products of the earth sparingly and you will be content." The youthful heirs should be made to observe the toil of the peasants and should be made to keep accounts when the granaries are opened for grain-sale. They should observe how it takes a strong man to carry one picul of grain, and how what four or five men can carry sells for only one gold tael, a tael which can be carelessly spent, disappearing who knows where. Such experiences should make the youthful heirs less wasteful. But what hope is there? The young heirs of today live sheltered lives; well fed and warmly clothed, they do not realize that precious resources should be conserved, and casually cast them away like dirt.

Those who accumulate wealth will always worry about fire, flood, or robbery, since valuables can suffer instant misfortune. Indeed, the commoner who accumulates ten taels of gold stops sleeping soundly at night. Land alone is not subject to fire, flood, or robbery, for even the most violent cannot snatch away one single inch of it. Thousands of *mou* of land may be worth ten thousand taels of gold, yet not one man is needed to stand guard. Should war or riot drive a person from his home, he may return to find his house gone, his livestock lost, his belongings vanished—but his land will always be there. The land that belonged to the Changs will still belong to the Changs; that which belonged to the Lis will still belong to the Lis. As soon as one has rooted out the weeds and tilled the soil, one will have a prosperous farm again. Indeed, nothing else under the sun is as secure as land. How can one fail to try to preserve it?

It is better to seek wealth from Heaven and Earth than from other men. I have seen people lend out money for interest secured by mortgages on tillable land. In three to five years they have a return as great as the original sum lent, but the borrower, despite appearing grateful, may become contentious and resentful and may refuse to pay back the principal. I have heard of poor scholars who, having saved several dozen gold taels, lend it out in this manner, but when they become more prosperous it becomes less advantageous for them to do so (because of the enmity incurred).

The profit from land is different. Those who sow half-heartedly reap lightly; those who sow diligently reap abundantly. Some can harvest three times in four seasons, others twice in a year. The main fields can be used for rice and wheat; the side plots and border mounds for hemp, beans, peas, cotton and so on. Every little piece of land will produce a few pennies of income. Therefore, it is worth pondering the proberb, "The land does not begrudge its treasures." In the beginning the land nourishes our grandfathers, then our fathers; soon it will nourish our sons and grandsons. It is a humble benefactor and a tireless servant. It never complains of its labor as it produces in great variety. Those who enjoy its benefits need not have scruples. Although they gain a great deal, they do not feel the discomfort brought by unjustified profit; thus they can face Heaven, Earth, and the spirits of their ancestors. They have no need to scheme and they are spared the jealousy of others. Is there anything that can compare with land?

I have said that one should not sell one's land, yet everywhere in the world we see people doing just that. Even the wise frequently do so. Why? The reason is debt, and debt comes from mismanagement. Those who do not know how to budget expenses according to income will eventually become so deeply in debt that they have to resort to selling land that has been in their families for generations. Therefore we may say that unwise management leads to debt and debt leads to selling of land—which leads to poverty. To stop the process before it starts, one should begin by budgeting expenses.

A simple, long-lasting way to do this is the "regulating expenses according to income" method devised by Lu So-shan. His procedure is to figure out the total income for the year, deduct taxes from it, then divide the rest into three parts. Set one part aside to provide for a year of poor harvests. Divide the remaining two parts into twelve portions and spend one portion each month. In this manner, if the crops are good every year, one is in conformity with the ancients' principle of "saving one-third of what one reaps." Should there be a poor harvest one year, then one may make up shortfalls with the previous year's savings; should there be bad harvests several years in a row, one can use the savings accumulated over many years. Only in this way can the need for contracting debts be avoided. In contrast, if each year's income is spent each year, then whenever there is a flood or drought, one will have to resort to selling land. To think that people should fail to recognize such obvious logic! . . .

Mismanagement of household economy is not the only cause of debt and land sale; other causes include indulgence in gambling, women, and extravagances—the dangers of which go without saying. The most ridiculous people of all are those who sell their land to pay for marriage expenses. For as long as there are sons and daughters there will be marriages, but they can be arranged according to one's means, with the savings from past harvests. How can one sell a generations-old resource to provide luxury and splendor for a moment? Do these people think that after the marriage they could be full without food or warm without clothing? Alas, what stupidity!

Anyone who does not want to sell his estate should carefully consider how to preserve it by making the best possible use of it. This can be done two ways, through wise selection of farm tenants and through the establishment of adequate irrigation.

An apt proverb says, "A good tenant is better than a fertile field." If tenants are idle and incompetent, the fields will deteriorate despite the owner's labor and planning. The owners of fields are like loving parents who entrust their baby to cruel servant girls, ignorant of the baby's suffering. There are three advantages to good tenants: first, they sow on time; second, they nourish the land with diligence; third, they control irrigation wisely.

The ancients said, "Timing is of utmost importance in farming." He who tills the fields a month early gets an extra month's benefit; therefore, winter is the best season for ploughing and spring only second best. He who sows a day early gets a day's benefit; therefore, the late crops should be sown before the first day of autumn. As for nourishing the land, the ancients referred to manure as "that which makes a hundred *mou* a field." They also observed, "It is not enough to fertilize only in bad years." The *Book of Poetry* says, "Where weeds decay grains grow abundantly." If one is diligent, one *mou* can produce as much as two. The field does not expand, yet the tenant can have more than enough and the owner can also reap profits. To apply water wisely depends a great deal on timing. It should be collected, held, and released only at the right times. Only good, experienced farmers have such knowledge.

Inferior tenants have three shortcomings: they miss the opportune time for tilling; they are not diligent in nourishing the land; and they do not know the best methods of irrigation. If there happens to be a good year and rain falls at the right time, then even bad tenants will have a good harvest and their defects will be hidden. Yet, when there is a drought, the difference between good and bad tenants will be instantly clear. In a bad year, the landowner can get double the usual price for his grain, unless he is prevented by incompetent tenants. . . .

The estate managers often prefer bad tenants to good ones. Good tenants have prosperous households, have the self-respect not to flatter, have a simple and straightforward manner, are thrifty and will not take unreasonable orders from the managers. Bad tenants, on the other hand, are idle and insolent, will cajole the managers, and will do anything to satiate the managers' greed. Because of these differences, managers prefer bad tenants to good ones, not in the least concerned about the condition of the owner's fields. Moreover, managers welcome floods and droughts, for in such times land rent cannot be paid in full and they can tamper with the revenue. Beware of such age-old corruption and evil practices.

Wherever good tenants live, the farm houses are tidy and neat, the gardens and yards are lush, the trees are abundant. All these are beyond the control of the land owner and his managers. Yet a good tenant can keep up everything himself. A bad one is just the opposite, making the selection of tenants a highly important task. . . .

The young heir of an estate should carefully inspect his farm twice a year, each spring and autumn. In addition, he should occasionally drop by unexpectedly. He should not merely visit. First, he should learn any boundaries of his fields which are not easy to remember. He should ask experienced tenants to point them out to him, if necessary, repeating his request a second or even a third time; usually after five or six times he will know them. Whenever he has a doubt, he should feel free to question; he should not be afraid of looking silly, otherwise he will remain ignorant all his life. Second, he should observe the tenants to determine whether they save, whether they are strong, whether they are frugal, and whether they are improving the land. With these facts, he should be able to judge which are the good tenants and which the inferior. Third, he should closely inspect the irrigation system to determine the depth of the reservoirs and the strength of the embankments, so as to decide what kinds of repairs are needed. Fourth, he should investigate the state of the woods and hill land. Fifth, he should apprise himself of the fluctuations in the price of grain. These steps will give him firsthand knowledge of his estate.

If, however, a young man merely listens to his managers while sitting under the eaves of the farm house, he will gain nothing but a little rest, a meal, and a night's lodging. His eyes will not encounter the fields, nor his feet the farm paths. Meanwhile, the managers will gather the tenants around him to make a great uproar with their complaints. Some will want to borrow seed grain, others to borrow food against their rent; some will say their ponds are leaking, others that their houses are collapsing. In this way they will intimidate their master, who will be so embarrassed that he will escape at the first opportunity.

He will learn nothing in response to his questions about the borders of his fields, the diligence of his tenants, the produce of the forests, or the value of the crop. When he returns to the city and meets his friends, this one will greet him and say, "I have just come back from my farm," and that one will say, "I have just inspected my fields." And the master himself will respond, "I have just arrived from my farm. How tiresome it was!" Alas! What is the use! This is what I did myself when I was young, and I still regret it. The heir of an estate should never take its management as something vulgar or petty to be avoided, nor should he inherit title to it without taking up the responsibility. Think carefully about the business of farming and compare it with receiving handouts from others: which is nobler and which baser?

A family's wealth and esteem provide but temporary glory. What one depends on ultimately for supporting one's descendants is farming and studying. An estate should be worth two or three thousand taels of gold before its heir goes to live in the city. Why is this so? Such an estate yields a yearly income of some one hundred taels, which must cover firewood, vegetables, poultry, pork, fish, shrimp, pickled and minced food, as well as expenses incurred by invitations among relatives, social occasions, and entertainment. When the harvest is good, grain brings only a low price, and even when the harvest is poor the price is not much better. Therefore the income from his estate will barely allow the young heir to keep up with his expenses. In short, those with estates worth less than one thousand taels should definitely not live in the city. By living in the country, the heir can cultivate a few acres of land himself, doubling his

yield, and making it possible to support a household of eight people. He can raise chickens and hogs in his own pens, grow vegetables in his own garden, keep fish and shrimps in his own pond, and from the adjacent mountains take firewood. In this manner he can live weeks and months without having to spend more than a few cash. Besides, living in the country, there will be fewer social occasions. Even when visitors come, it will only be necessary to treat them to chicken and rice. The women, if diligent, can weave cloth. The heir can wear cotton clothes and ride a feeble donkey, there being no need for glamour. All these things a city-dweller cannot do. Living in the country, the heir can till the land and enjoy his studies. He can also employ a teacher for his sons. Such a life is serene and simple. Not a coin in his pocket, he will not be bothered by robbers and thieves.

My father knew the art of country living very well. What he left for us did not amount to much, yet he lived better than city-dwellers who had several thousand taels' worth of property. Furthermore, life among mountains and waters is leisurely and free from money worries. What a shame it is that people should fail to see this point! If, after success in studies, one becomes a renowned official and is able to afford living in the city, then moving there is fine. If, after one or two generations, country living is again advisable, then move back. In this manner, one alternates city living and country living, farming and studying, and the family lineage will be long and prosperous, a highly desirable state of affairs.

Translated by Clara Yu

50.

Lan Tíng-yüan's Casebook

Magistrates, the officials in charge of counties (hsien), were the only representatives of the central government most people ever encountered. Their manner of enforcing laws, conducting trials, and collecting taxes affected the lives of all residents of the county. Local political life therefore cannot be understood without considering the behavior of Magistrates.

Below are two cases which Lan Tíng-yüan (1680–1733) included in a record of his official experiences. Lan was from a scholarly family of Fukien province and was the author of several books. He never passed even the chü-jen examinations, yet because of his participation in a military campaign and his reputation for knowledge of the coastal area, he was introduced to the Emperor. Thereafter he was appointed Magistrate of P'u-ning and Ch'ao-yang counties in Kwangtung. His description of his activities is best read as a personal account; although he did not hesitate to brag, he also could not help but reveal the values, assumptions, and prejudices that he brought with him to his post as Magistrate.

THE SPIRIT OF THE KING OF THE THREE MOUNTAINS TELLS EVERYTHING

One day Ch'en A-kung rushed in to see me and begged me to try to discover the fate of his daughter.

He said, "My daughter, Ch'in-niang, is married to Lin A-chung. They live in the neighboring village. She has been married for three years but has had no children. A-chung's mother is very cruel and despises my daughter for coming from a poor family. On the 13th day of the ninth month when I went to see her, I could find no trace of her. I don't know whether she has been beaten to death, sold off as a servant, or remarried into another household."

"Does your daughter often come back to visit you?" I asked.

He replied, "She came to see me in the eighth month and went back to her husband on the 6th day of the ninth month. You can ask Wang A-sheng about this."

When I made inquiries into the case, A-chung's mother, Mrs. Hsü, complained that the charges were unfair. She said, "I have been a widow for seventeen years and have one daughter-in-law. But from the time of her marriage she has visited her parents every month. In the seventh month she went home twice. On the 6th day of the eighth month she went home again. On the 17th and the 24th day of the eighth month and on the 3rd day of the ninth month we unsuccessfully asked her to come back. I have no idea why she did not come back. Then on the 13th day of the ninth month Ch'en A-kung came bursting into my home demanding to know the fate of his daughter. I am sure A-kung has evil designs and has merely hidden his daughter away, hoping to marry her to someone else."

I questioned Ch'en A-kung. "When exactly did your daughter leave your house? Did she walk or go by sedan chair? Who accompanied her?"

He replied, "My daughter told me she wanted to

return to her husband on the 6th of the ninth month. I am a poor man and could not afford to hire a sedan chair to take her home, so I sent her brother, A-chü, to accompany her half way. They set out walking from my house."

I asked, "What is the distance between your two residences?"

"It is over ten *li*," he answered.

A-chung and his mother cried out, "She did not come back. You can ask the neighbors."

I asked Wang A-sheng, "When and where did you see Ch'en A-kung's daughter return to her husband's place?"

A-sheng said, "I only heard about it from A-chü. I did not actually see them go. A short distance from my home lies King of the Three Mountains Temple. On the 6th day of the ninth month, while I was hoeing my garden on the left side of the road, I saw A-chü coming back from the temple. He told me he had been asked by his father to accompany his sister who was returning to her husband. I asked him, 'Where is your sister now?' 'Already gone,' he replied. That is what I heard, and I know nothing else of the matter."

"Is the Ch'en family rich or poor?" I asked.

A-sheng said, "They are very poor."

"How far is it from A-kung's house to the temple?"

"About three *li*."

I pressed him further, "How many *li* are there between the Lin family residence and the temple?"

"That distance is around six or seven *li*."

With anger in my voice I demanded an explanation from A-kung. "Your daughter is married and your family is not rich, yet you let her come home all the time in spite of the extra expense it brings you. How is this? When her husband's family tried to get her back, you would not let her go. On the 3rd day of the ninth month her husband requested that she return home, but you refused to let her. Why then would you all of a sudden send her home of your own free will on the 6th? Now let us consider the rest of your story. You did not instruct your boy to accompany her all the way to her husband's place but had him turn back in mid-journey. What were your intentions in bringing in A-sheng, who had no connection with the case? Your son said that he had just casually mentioned a word of the affair to A-sheng, and yet you have cited this as your main piece of evidence. I suspect you have plotted to remarry your daughter and have caused all this commotion."

A-kung cried bitterly and loudly, "Father and child are most dear to each other. Although my family is poor, we have enough vegetables and water to make a tasty meal. When my daughter's husband urged her to come home, I didn't want her to leave, but later I realized that I was doing wrong to keep her and that I should let her go back. Isn't it reasonable that I should try to do the right thing in order to make up for my previous selfishness? As for my son's returning after going only half way, the boy is still only a youngster, and so I didn't dare let him wander too far from home. I asked him to accompany her only half way because I figured my son-in-law's home would then be close enough for her to get there without danger. My son returned home quite soon after they departed so I scolded him because I thought perhaps he had not accompanied her even half way. He defended himself, saying, 'I passed the temple and Uncle A-sheng saw me!' Now my daughter is missing and I am under suspicion. I am certainly one who appreciates the principle that a woman must be faithful to her husband all through her life. How then could I possibly let my daughter remarry when her husband is still alive?"

I questioned A-chü, a boy of ten years. He said, "I escorted my sister to the front of the temple and then returned."

I asked, "Why didn't you take her all the way to her husband's place?"

"My father ordered me to take the livestock out to pasture, so I let my sister continue on alone after going half way."

I threatened him, saying, "Your sister was kept home to be remarried. How dare you lie to me? If you do not tell me the truth, I will cut off your fingers."

A-chü was terrified. He cried but said nothing more. I tried several ways to trick him, but he always replied, "No, not so."

I then asked him, "Is there a monk at the temple?"

"No," he replied.

"Are there any beggars?"

"No."

"Is there any family around the temple?"

"No."

"Is there a tree, creek, river, or pond there?"

"No."

"Are there any neighbors around your home?"

"No, there aren't any neighbors."

I really suspected that Ch'en A-kung had sold his daughter, but he was cunning and stubborn, and A-chü was still quite young. Therefore I could not use threats of torture to break the case. Then it came to me that southerners are afraid of ghosts and spirits. I would try to bring this to bear on the case.

Calling in the plaintiff and the defendant, I said, "Since neither of you has any substantial evidence to back up your allegations, it is rather difficult for me to make a judgment in this case. But since the boy and girl passed by the temple, the spirit of the King of the Three Mountains must know the true story. You all go home for the time being, and I will send an official dispatch to ask the spirit about the matter. I will resume court tomorrow."

The next day I called Ch'en A-kung straight into the courtroom and, pounding on the table, reviled him: "What kind of human being are you? You have hidden away your daughter and remarried her. Then you adopted the tactics of a shyster lawyer and came running with the first accusation so as to throw your opponent off balance. Who do you think you're fooling? Even though you lie to men, you cannot deceive Heaven. You know that Heaven is but three feet above our heads and that there are gods watching us all the time! The King of the Three Mountains has told me all. Are you still obstinate enough to stick to your story? I know who it was your daughter remarried, where she got married, and how much you received for her. If you do not buy her back, I will order that you be punished under the press."

A-kung was so frightened that he could not answer back. He groveled on the floor, kowtowed, and begged for forgiveness.

I said, "If you get your daughter back, I will pardon you."

He blurted out, "Yes, certainly I will. It was the extreme poverty of my family that forced me to let my daughter remarry. She is now married into the Li family of Hui-lai, who paid three taels for her. I will sell my cow to buy her back."

I ordered A-kung to be whipped thirty strokes and then to be clapped into the wooden collar for public humiliation in town. I gave him a stern warning: "If you redeem your daughter and bring her back, I will release you. If you don't, I will leave you in the collar until you die."

A-kung thereupon sent his wife, Wang, to Hui-lai to buy back the daughter. The Li family demanded that she pay double the original price they had given for the girl, so Wang was forced to sell her youngest daughter as well as the cow to raise the money. Hearing of these events, the greedy first husband saw an opportunity to make six taels. He told Wang that he could not accept Ch'in-liang back because she had

lost her chastity and secretly came to terms with her, releasing Ch'in-liang from all obligations to him for six taels. After he got the money from Wang, he married another girl. Ch'in-liang remained with the Li family and did not have to be redeemed.

While all this was going on, A-kung was forced to remain in the collar for nearly two months and almost died. He moaned to his wife, "I regret that I did not sell the cow and our youngest daughter in the first place so that I could have avoided such a punishment. If I had only known that the King of the Three Mountains would tell everything! Now that the affair is finished, you must petition the Magistrate to let me go."

When Wang told me what her husband said, I laughed and released him.

DEPRAVED RELIGIOUS SECTS DECEIVE PEOPLE

The people of Ch'ao-yang believed in spirits and often talked about gods and Buddhas. The gentry regarded Ta Tien [of the T'ang Dynasty] as their great Buddhist master, and ladies of the gentry families joined together to go to the temples to worship the Buddha. In this way, heretical and depraved teachings developed and the so-called Latter Heaven sect became popular.

The origin of the Latter Heaven sect is unknown. Chan Yü-ts'an and Chou A-wu first preached it in our area, claiming to have received the teaching from a white-bearded Immortal. When the former Magistrate apprehended them, they ran away with their families but later returned to Ch'ao-yang. The sect also called itself the "White Lotus" or the "White Willow." (It probably belonged to the "White Lotus Society" but found it expedient to use other names.)

Chan Yü-ts'an's wife, Lin, was thought to be the "Miraculous Divine Lady." She claimed to possess the ability to summon wind and rain and to give orders to gods and spirits. She was the leader of the Latter Heaven sect and was assisted by her paramour, Hu A-ch'iu, who called himself the "Pen Peak Divine Gentleman." These two cast spells and used magic charms and waters to cure illness and to help pray for heirs. They even claimed to be able to help widows meet their deceased husbands at night.

The people of Ch'ao-yang adored them madly; hundreds of men and women worshipped them as their masters. People from Ch'eng-hai, Chieh-yang, Hai-yang, Hui-lai, and Hai-feng made pilgrimages here carrying gifts of money, animals, wine, and flowers to offer in worship. On the 10th day of the second month of winter on my return from the prefectural city I was informed of these events. By this time members of the sect had already constructed a large building in the northern part of the county where they established a preaching hall and gathered several hundred followers. They hired actors for a period of two days to celebrate the opening of their church. I dispatched runners to apprehend the sect leaders, but the runners were afraid to offend the gods lest the soldiers of hell punish them. Besides, the local officials and many of the influential families favored the sect. So they all escaped.

I, therefore, went to the place myself, pushed my way into the front room, and arrested the Divine Lady. Then I went further into the house to search for her accomplices. The place was like a maze, filled with concealed rooms. Even by day one had to light a torch to get around, or one would bump into people in the dark and easily get lost. It was indeed an ideal place to hide criminals. As I proceeded on my search, above the Divine Lady's bedroom, in a dark, concealed chamber, I seized Yao A-san, Yang Kuang-ch'in, P'eng Shih-chang, and about a dozen other men. Similarly, above the Divine Gentleman's bedroom I found a wooden seal of the Empress Lady of the Moon, a heretical sutra, incense, a wig, and clothes, but at this time I had no idea of how they were used. I looked all around for the Divine Gentleman. Finally, the local rowdies as well as certain influential families, knowing they could no longer hide him, handed over Hu A-ch'iu. Through questioning him, I learned of all his occult tricks.

In fact, these charlatans had no special powers whatsoever but used incense and costumes to bewilder people. The foolish people who trembled on just hearing the names of gods and spirits were impressed when they saw that the Divine Lady had no fear of gods and goddesses. Hu A-ch'iu. who accompanied her, wore rouge, female clothing, and a wig. People believed Hu was the genuine Empress Lady of the Moon and never suspected he was a man.

When these pious women entered his bedroom and ascended to the upper chamber, they would be led to worship the Maitreya Buddha and to recite the charms of the Precious Flower Sutra. Then stupefying incense was burned and the women would faint and fall asleep so the leaders of the sect could do whatever they pleased. (This incense was also called soul-bewildering incense; people who inhaled it would feel tired and want to sleep.) Later the sect members would cast spells and give the women cold water to drink to revive them. The so-called "praying for heirs" and the "meeting with a deceased husband" occurred while the women were dreaming and asleep.

The members of the Latter Heaven sect were extremely evil; even hanging their heads out on the streets would have been insufficient punishment for their crimes. However, this had been a year of bad harvest, so the villagers already had lots of worries. Moreover, the case involved many people, including members of local gentry families. Therefore, sympathetic to the people's troubles and wanting to end the matter, I destroyed the list of those involved which the culprits had divulged during the trial.

I had Lin, the "Divine Lady," and Hu A-ch'iu beaten and put in the collar, placing them outside the court so that the people could scorn them, beat them, and finally kill them. As to Ch'an Yü-ts'an, the man who had allowed his wife to commit such a heinous crime, and his accomplices, Yao A-shan and some ten other people, they were all beaten and put in the collar as punishment. I inquired no further into the matter so that the other accomplices could repent and start a new life. I confiscated the sect's building, destroyed the concealed rooms, and converted it into a literary academy dedicated to the worship of the five great [Neo-Confucian] teachers. Thus the filthy was swept away and the clean restored.

In my leisure time, on the days of the new and the full moon, I went to the academy to lecture or discuss literature with the people of the county. Chang P'i gave 100 bushels of grain for the salary of a teacher, allowances for the students, and the expenses of the spring and autumn school sacrifices. As formal study developed, heretical beliefs ceased to exist. The morality and customs of the people also changed for the better. Commander Shang and Governor Yang heard about the elimination of the depraved sect and sighed in admiration: "Without the elimination of this sect, great damage would have occurred. It is a marvelous accomplishment to have gotten rid of it. The Magistrate expelled the evil but refrained from seeking fame for himself. Had he not done so, many people in the area would have been put into jail and many women would have committed suicide by night. It is indeed an act of great mercy to preserve others' reputations."

Translated by Jeh-hang Lai and Lily Hwa

51.

Exhortations on Ceremony and Deference

In the Ch'ing dynasty, on the first and fifteenth of every month local officials or scholars were required to give lectures to the populace, explaining the Sacred Edict of the K'ang-hsi Emperor (Sheng-tsu, r. 1662–1722) and the amplifications of the Yung-cheng Emperor (Shih-tsung, r. 1723–1735). The lecturers were to use the local vernacular and draw examples from everyday life so that the moral messages would reach the uneducated. A number of officials published their lectures as guides for other officials. The one translated here, on the ninth maxim, was by an eighteenth-century Salt Commissioner named Wang Yu-p'u.

This text is useful for three purposes. It provides another source for judging how people's lives were affected by the government, since exhortations and instructions were one of the major ways the government tried to influence people. At the same time, the lecture was based on the moral attitudes most people recognized as correct and so can also be used as a source for how it was generally thought people should behave. Probing further, one can also see evidence of common social frictions and situations in which disapproved conduct was more the rule than the exception.

DEMONSTRATE CEREMONY AND DEFERENCE IN ORDER TO IMPROVE POPULAR CUSTOMS

His Majesty's meaning is as follows:

In the empire there are what are called popular customs (*feng-su*). What are *feng* and *su?* A Han dynasty scholar said that the hearts of all the common people in the world contain feelings of benevolence, justice, propriety, wisdom, and sincerity. But people in the North are generally hardy, those in the South generally delicate. Where people's temperaments are fast-paced, business is executed promptly; where they are slow, work is performed more leisurely. People of one place do not understand the dialect of those in the other. All this proceeds from the fact that the climate (*feng-ch'i*) is different in every place and men feel a certain influence from it. This is the reason for the word *feng*.

Further, what people here like, people there hate.

On occasions when one is active the other is at rest. There is no fixed mode; everybody acts according to the common practices (*su*) of his locality. This is the reasons for the word *su*.

Popular customs vary greatly: in some places people are kindly, in others, reserved; in some places they are extravagant and pompous, in others frugal and simple. Because the customs of every place differed, the ancient sages created ceremonial practices in order to standardize conduct. The sage [Confucius] said that to secure the ease of superiors and bring order to the people, nothing is better than ceremony (*li*). This sentence teaches us that ceremony is extremely important. Were Heaven and Earth to depart from the forms of ceremony, they would no longer be Heaven and Earth. Were the myriad creatures to depart from ceremonial forms, they would no longer exist. The forms of ceremony are vast and its uses are manifold. Were reason and virtue, benevolence and justice to depart from ceremony, they could no longer be true reason and virtue, benevolence and justice. Were the honorable and the mean, the noble and base, to depart from ceremony, one could no longer distinguish between them. Were the rituals for manhood, marriage, mourning, and ancestor worship to depart from ceremony, one could not conduct those rituals. In fact, if Emperor Shih-tsung, in offering sacrifices to Heaven or to the temple of his ancestors, or in giving private feasts, were to depart from ceremony, those things could not be performed. In a word, ceremony is the root of all customs.

But when you practice ceremonial behavior, there should be no awkward stiffness; all should be natural and easy. The essence of ceremony is contained in the word "deference." The Sage said that as long as ceremony and deference were used, there would be no difficulty in ruling the empire. If these two words, ceremony and deference, are sufficient to regulate the vast concerns of an empire, shouldn't it be even easier to regulate an individual or a family through them? The Sage also said a ruler who wants the common people not to fight must first set an example for them of ceremonial behavior and deference. Thus it may be seen that this word, deference, is also the root of the practice of ceremony.

Were I now to speak of the details of rituals and ceremonies, you soldiers and common people probably would have difficulty learning them because they are so numerous. But you all possess the basic elements of ceremonial behavior. For example, you know that there should be filial piety towards parents, honor and respect for superiors, harmony between husband and wife, affection among brothers, honesty among friends, and mutual responsibility among those of the same lineage. This proves that internally you already possess the basic elements of ceremony and deference. Why then make a fuss about the externals? If you could really, in dealing with others, be extremely cooperative, in conducting yourselves be extremely obliging, in the family express the affection appropriate between parents and children, elder and younger brothers, in your villages maintain accord between the old and the young, the great and the small, then those habits of struggling over minor differences and getting into noisy disputes would be reformed and the tendency toward indulgent and degenerate conduct would be restrained.

If I had no desire which might induce you to compete or me to steal; if I never allowed momentary anger to get me into a fight; if I never held you in contempt because you are poor and I am rich; if you didn't try to hurt me because you are strong and I am weak; if everybody became kind, without any sign of pettiness; then this would be true ceremony and deference, and in the fullest sense there would be honor and justice.

Though everyone knows how to talk of ceremony and deference, they do not all practice it. Why don't they practice it? Because at present they only know how to use the rules of ceremony to reprove others, not how to use them to correct themselves. For example, if we are quarreling, you'll say I'm impolite and I'll say you are. One will say, "Why don't you yield to me?" And the other will reply, "You haven't yet yielded to me. Why should I yield to you?" At length the animosities become so complex that they cannot be disentangled. What gain is there in that? You should think a little and say, "Although he is without proper manners, where are my manners? Although he hasn't yielded to me, in the beginning why didn't I yield to him?" If both parties would admit part of the blame, wouldn't numerous disputes be avoided?

It is just that people love to quarrel and will not give in to others. For instance, a scholar who has a rough idea of how to compose a few verses of various kinds of poetry regards himself as the literary prodigy of the day and disdains to cast an eye on others. But if he realized that the subjects of study are inexhaustible and that the empire possesses an abundance of learned men, he would say, "The books I have read are only a fraction of what men have written and my compositions don't amount to even a spot of brightness among the whole lot." Automatically he would be modest and defer to others. He who really acts with modesty and deference is a virtuous and worthy scholar.

Farmers are also in the habit of quarreling about their fields. I say that you have encroached on the dike a little; you say that I have ploughed a furrow too many. Perhaps some animal, an ox or a sheep, has trodden down the grain, and this gives rise to a quarrel. Or perhaps one person dams up the water till it overflows his own fields, not letting it pass by and irrigate those of his neighbor, and this leads to a struggle. Craftsmen are also quick to get into violent quarrels. You want to keep me down and I want to keep you down; I try to turn your employer against you and you try to turn mine away from me. We each care for our own prosperity only, with no regard to whether the other lives or dies.

Merchants and shop owners are even worse. When

you see me earning money, you become jealous; when I see you making a profit, my eyes turn red with envy. When a particular kind of trade is profitable, you want to engage in it, and so do I. When trading conditions are good in a certain place, you will conceal it from everyone else and secretly hurry there yourself. Knowing that a certain kind of goods is losing value, a merchant will trick people into taking them off his hands and afterwards go and insist on getting the payment. There are others who, beginning trade with empty hands, borrow money at high rates but are a long time in repaying their bills. This is what is called "You seek high [interest] while I seek delay [in repayment]." Others get into disputes about the scales used or the quality of coins. There are so many sources of disputes that it would be an endless task to mention all of them. To sum it up, people will not yield to each other on anything; if only they would yield, they would all become honest and generous men.

As to you soldiers living in camp, you can't avoid having rough and crude personalities. At work and at rest you use your swords and staffs and engage in combat. Everybody says that soldiers, because of their very nature, do not understand ceremony. Therefore, from now on you must try to understand the principle of yielding and ceremony. In your village try your best to show deference to others and to temper the roughness of your personalities.

Let all of you—scholars, farmers, artisans, merchants, and soldiers—take care in practicing ceremonial deference. If one place becomes good, then many places will become so, and finally the entire realm will be in excellent harmony. Won't we then have a world in perfect concord?

In an ancient book it says, "The humble gain; the self-satisfied lose." These two phrases are exceptionally apt. How do the humble gain? Humility consists of modesty and mildness. Men of the present day can't perceive their own faults at all. Therefore they perpetually quarrel, not realizing that strife is the road to the destruction of their families and their personal ruin. In every affair, great or small, retreat a step and you will certainly gain the advantage. For example, suppose a man curses me, and I let pass a couple of phrases. If he is a good man he will naturally feel sorry. If he is a bad man, on seeing that his curses have no effect, he will give up. Wouldn't this prevent a lot of trouble? Do you think that by his cursing me he will rise to greater glory, or that I by bearing with him will fall into disgrace? If I defer to

him in this way, people will just praise how good I am and will all want to join me, perhaps confiding to me the secrets of their hearts or entrusting to me their money. If he is so overbearing, people will all hate and avoid him. If he runs into trouble, who will pay attention to him? Haven't I then gained the advantage?

Among the ancients there was a man named Lou Shih-te. He once asked his brother, "Suppose that someone spit in your face. How would you react to him?" When his brother said he would just wipe it off, Lou Shih-te said, "If you wipe it off, the man will hold you in even greater contempt. Just accept it with a smile and wait until it dries of its own accord." Just think, meek Lou Shih-te afterwards rose to become Prime Minister. Isn't this evidence that "the humble gain"?

How do the self-satisfied lose? Self-satisfaction occurs when a person is impressed with his own importance. It does not refer only to property owners and officials who rely on their money and influence to deceive and humiliate others and thus invite disaster. It also refers to young men who call their elders "old fogies" and even if they are poor or feeble do not address them in a respectful manner; it also refers to young men who tell local officials and gentry, "We will not cringe before you" and arrogantly try to gain the upper hand. This emotion of self-satisfaction will inevitably lead a man to exceed what is appropriate to his station. He will undertake daring acts, bringing on calamity. This shows how "the self-satisfied lose."

The principles taught by these two sentences may be compared to an earthen vessel. When the vessel is empty (= modest) it can still gain. If it is full (= self-satisfied), you cannot put more things into it, and if you force them you may overturn the vessel or break it into pieces. From this can be seen how the humble gain and the self-satisfied lose. These principles may also be compared to a man who has some chronic disorders. Knowing that his body is weak, he will be careful in all matters, not daring to eat much food or indulge in wine or women. Consequently he may enjoy a long life. The man who doesn't have the slightest health problem, by contrast, will depend on his strength and vigor. He will eat and then go right to sleep, take off his clothes in drafty places, and show not even the least moderation in regard to wine and women. Then one day he gets an incurable illness. Aren't these accurate examples of how the humble (= cautious) gain and the self-satisfied lose?

Formerly there was a Mr. Wang Yen-fang who

was exceptionally ready to defer to others. Once a cattle thief, when captured, said, "I will willingly receive my punishment, but please don't inform Wang Yen-fang." When Wang heard of this, he sent someone to give the thief a piece of cloth and persuade him to become good. From this incident the thief became so reformed that when he saw someone drop his sword in the road he stood guarding it till the owner came back to get it. In antiquity there also was a Mr. Kuan Yu-an who was equally deferential. When an ox belonging to another family came and ate the young shoots of his field, he was not at all angry, but took the ox, tied him to a tree, and brought him grass to eat. Because he was so accommodating and humble, all the people of his village reformed. In a time of rebellion, the bandits didn't bother him, and those who had fled from danger came to him for protection. Just think of it: when one man knows how to yield, a whole district can be reformed, and even bandits can be influenced. Aren't ceremonial behavior and deference then real treasures?

Furthermore, if you compete over things, you don't get any more for it; if you yield, neither do you have any less. The ancients said it very well: "A person who always makes way for others on the road won't waste one hundred steps in his whole life. He who always gives in on questions of boundaries won't lose even a single section over the course of his life." Hence it can be seen that yielding and ceremony bring gain and never humiliation. Then why not yield? Emperor Shih-tsung hopes that you all will listen to the instructions of the former Emperor Sheng-tsu and examine yourselves by them.

If you are able to get along with others, those who are rude will imitate you and learn to get along. If you are able to manage business fairly, those who are dishonest will learn to be fair by following you. When one person takes the lead, all the rest will follow. When one family follows, then the whole village will do the same. From near to far, everywhere people will be good. At first it will take effort, but constant practice will make it easy. Men will become honest and popular customs pure and considerate. Only this would constitute full adoption of the meaning of Emperor Shih-tsung's repeated instructions to you.

Translated by Patricia Ebrey

52.

Village Organization

Many matters of social and political importance were left to local residents to initiate themselves. Often local gentry or village elders would call residents together to make decisions or to undertake village projects. They might also approach neighboring villages to gain their cooperation for projects of mutual benefit. Should any controversy arise, however, they could always appeal to the Magistrate.

The two documents below show some of the forms and mechanisms of such village and intervillage organization. The first is a water-use agreement originally recorded in 1828 and still in use in the early twentieth century. When first drawn up, the rights to water were divided among different people on a twenty-one-day cycle. Over the years, however, many people had sold their rights, and these changes were recorded by pasting new sections into the original agreement. The second document, dating from 1875, is a stone inscription recording how residents of several villages in what is now Inner Mongolia had gone about establishing a temple and attached market.

RECORD OF THE OLD SOUTH DITCH

The Old South Ditch is the lower stream of Dog-Head Spring. During the early Ming period, the water in the spring was so abundant that it often overflowed on its course north of Wu Family Estate, through Small Great-Water Village and East Great-Water Village, to the Seven-Mile River. The elders of our village (East Great-Water Village) traced the source of the spring because they wanted to dredge the area and cut an irrigation ditch to channel water first eastward, then northward, and finally back eastward so that the spring would irrigate all the fields of the villagers. However, the spring gushed forth so strongly that the irrigation ditch was unable to contain it. Therefore, the village elders built a small canal south of Small Great-Water Village to channel some of the water to the Seven-Mile River and thus reduce the volume flowing into the irrigation ditch at East Great-Water Village. This small canal also made it easier to close the sluice gate while the ditch

was being dredged in the spring and summer. It was at this time that the irrigation ditch was given the name Dog-Head River, and the name South Ditch fell out of use.

During the Lung-ch'ing period [1567–1573], White-Berth, Big-Worthy, and other villages observed the unused water running down the canal to the Seven-Mile River and decided to tap it with irrigation ditches of their own. Our village, however, was reluctant to let them do this, so they appealed the matter to the Magistrate, Ti Ming-shih. He went to inspect the river system himself, and, seeing all the unused water running down the canal to the Seven-Mile River, he issued an order to the elders of our village which read: "It is better to share water with neighboring villagers than to let it go to waste. And if two more ditches are built, East Great-Water Village will also enjoy the benefits of further irrigation."

The village elders did not dare to oppose the Magistrate's order. So White-Berth, Big-Worthy, and the other villages constructed a stone sluice gate on the small drainage ditch south of Small Great-Water Village. They also built a circulation ditch and another ditch to the north.

Since the people of East Great-Water Village had dredged the Dog-Head River, it would have been unfair to put them on a par with the people of the other villages when it came to sharing labor and benefits. It would also have been unfair for the other villages to drain off too much water and leave East Great-Water Village without enough for irrigation. Therefore, Magistrate Ti ordered the other villages to share the expenses of repairing the upper stream sluice gates and of dredging the upper reaches of Dog-Head River. He required us only to dredge the part of the river below the north ditch. Thus, we would start the work, and the other villages would finish the job.

Magistrate Ti ordered that the eight villages along the circulation ditch use only 40 percent of the irrigation water but permitted East Great-Water Village to use 60 percent. This made a distinction between those with the right to the surplus. So that the two other ditches would not widen after years of use and thus drain off more than 40 percent of the water, Magistrate Ti ordered a stone sluice gate two feet narrower than the width of the Dog-Head River to be built on the circulation ditch. The north ditch had a rather deep bottom, thus allowing more water to flow through it, so the Magistrate ordered that stones be put on its bottom and sides, thus decreasing the flow of water to the allotted 40 percentage. With these precautions, he hoped that the 40–60 ratio could be maintained and that water usage would cause no problems for later generations.

With the construction of the circulation ditch and the north ditch, the lower stream of the Dog-Head River became the southernmost irrigation ditch. For this reason it became known again as Old South Ditch. Thus the water came to be divided between East Great-Water Village and the other villages of the area.

Those villagers who were in charge of water distribution on the Old South Ditch were dubbed Old Man and Little Tithing. Those persons who had the most land had to furnish personnel for these positions—they could not decline the job. It cost five cash to use water for one day and one night. Furthermore, each person was limited to the water he could take in a given cycle of twenty days. This water usage procedure could not be altered, and it became the standard water distribution system for the Old South Ditch. Unfortunately, with the construction of the

stone sluice and the placing of stones on the river bed, not as many people could take full advantage of the irrigation ditch.

Because water was distributed on a cash basis, the strong could not snatch it away from the weak. Relying on the wisdom and fairness of Magistrate Ti, the villagers complied with all these regulations and the elders of the village handed down the benefits of these rules to us. Therefore, we have recorded these events on the first page of our village record so that later generations may be aware of them.

Translated by Lily Hwa

INSCRIPTION FOR THE NEWLY ERECTED TEMPLE-MARKET "OUR LADY"

We have heard that one who does a job well does it thoroughly, and one who starts something should also finish it. This is the wise teaching of the ancient sages and the rule for us to follow.

On the northeast side of the city of T'o-ke-t'o, there are densely populated villages and extensive farmland. Whenever the field work gets heavy, hiring farmhands from distant regions becomes a problem. Those who discussed the problem in the past noted that the village of Shih-li-teng is situated in the center of all these communities; if a temple-market could be built there, they reasoned, all people in the area would benefit. However, although this was proposed several times, nothing came of it.

In 1874, the village of Shih-li-teng again brought up the proposal. All the people liked the idea, yet they also realized how difficult it would be to put into practice. The chairman of the meeting, Shih Ju-ch'i, and others, volunteered to undertake the task. "Whether we succeed or not," they said, "we will do our best and not shirk our responsibilities."

The decision having been made, it was announced to all the villagers, who began collecting funds among themselves and soliciting donations from the neighboring communities, which willingly contributed to this cause. On an auspicious day in the fourth month, the land was measured and the ground broken. From then on, workers and materials gathered at the site, designers, builders, sculptors, and painters cooperated with each other, and the new temple-market was completed in a matter of months.

On the opening day of the market, hundreds of different kinds of goods were brought in from all over, and people came from all directions. The quiet village now acquired a new look. The donors were all pleased with the speedy construction, and the employers were also happy because now it was easy to hire farmhands.

Yet a construction project without a written record is like an enterprise half-finished, and an enterprise half-finished defeats all the effort already spent. We would like later generations to understand our reasons for building the temple-market, and we would like to solicit their continuous effort to maintain the place properly. They should repair the building and the walls of the temple; they should try

hard to bring business to the market; they should also do their best to ensure orderly transaction of business here. It is important to appease the gods and to satisfy the people, for this will bring our village as well as the surrounding communities a good reputation.

Composition by the Confucian scholar Ts'ui P'ei-yü of Tai-chou.
Calligraphy by the Licentiate Ts'ui Fu-shih of Tai-chou. Tablet erected by Committee Chairman She Wei-han and twelve others, on an auspicious day of the fourth month of 1875.

Translated by Clara Yu

53.

The Village Headman and the New Teacher

Although documents such as tenancy contracts, village agreements, and legal cases provide insight into various elements in rural social, economic, and political relations, no source conveys so well the atmosphere of village life as fiction. Even though none of the major novels centers around villagers, a number of them have vignettes in which rural life is portrayed.

The following selection is from the long, episodic novel The Scholars, *written by Wu Ching-tzu (1701–1754). This book was the first and perhaps the most successful novel of social satire, and contains delightful parodies of hypocrites and pompous fools of various stations in life. The chapter that follows presents a realistic though undoubtedly exaggerated description of how affairs were decided in one village.*

PROVINCIAL GRADUATE WANG MEETS A FELLOW CANDIDATE IN A VILLAGE SCHOOL; CHOU CHIN PASSES THE EXAMINATION IN HIS OLD AGE

In Hsueh Market, a village of Wen-shang county, Shantung, there lived over a hundred families, all of whom worked on the land. At the entrance to the village was a Kuan-yin Temple with three halls and a dozen empty rooms. Its back door overlooked the river. Peasants from all around contributed to the upkeep of this temple, and only one monk lived there. Here the villagers would come to discuss public business.

It was the last year of the Cheng-hua period[1] of the Ming Dynasty, when the country was prosperous. One year, on the eighth of the first month, just after New Year, some of the villagers met in the temple to discuss the dragon lantern dance which is held on the fifteenth. At breakfast time the man who usually took the lead, Shen Hsiang-fu, walked in, followed by

[1] 1487.

seven or eight others. In the main hall they bowed to Buddha, and the monk came to wish them a happy New Year. As soon as they had returned his greeting, Shen reproved him.

"Monk! At New Year you should burn more incense before Buddha! Gracious Heaven! You've been pocketing money from all sides, and you ought to spend a little of it. Come here, all of you, and take a look at this lamp: it's only half filled with oil." Then, pointing to an old man who was better dressed than most: "Not to mention others, Mr. Hsün alone sent you fifty catties of oil on New Year's Eve. But you are using it all for your cooking, instead of for the glory of Buddha."

The monk apologized profusely when Shen had finished. Then he fetched a pewter kettle, put in a handful of tea leaves, filled the kettle with water, boiled it over the fire and poured out tea for them. Old Mr. Hsün was the first to speak.

"How much do we each have to pay for the lantern dance in the temple this year?" he asked.

"Wait till my relative comes," said Shen. "We'll discuss it together."

As they were speaking, a man walked in. He had red-rimmed eyes, a swarthy face, and sparse, dingy whiskers. His cap was cocked to one side, his blue cloth gown was greasy as an oil vat, and he carried a donkey switch in one hand. Making a casual gesture of greeting to the company, he plumped himself down in the seat of honour. This was Hsia, the new village head for Hsueh Market.

Sitting there in the seat of honour, he shouted: "Monk! Take my donkey to the manger in the back yard, unsaddle it, and give it plenty of hay. After my business here I have to go to a feast with Bailiff Huang of the county yamen." Having given these orders, he hoisted one foot on to the bench, and started massaging the small of his back with his fists, saying, "I envy you farmers these days. This New Year I've got invitations from everybody in the magistrate's yamen, literally everybody! And I have to go to wish them all the season's greetings. I trot about on this donkey to the county seat and back until my head reels. And this damned beast stumbled on the road and threw me, so that my backside is still sore."

"On the third I prepared a small dinner for you," said Shen. "I suppose it was because you were so busy that you didn't come."

"You don't have to remind me," said Village Head Hsia. "Since New Year, for the last seven or eight days, what free time have I had? Even if I had two mouths, I couldn't get through all the eating. Take Bailiff Huang, who's invited me today. He's a man who can talk face to face with the magistrate. And since he honours me like this, wouldn't he be offended if I didn't go?"

"I heard that Bailiff Huang had been sent out on some business for the magistrate since the beginning of the year," said Shen. "He has no brothers or sons, so who will act as host?"

"You don't understand," said Hsia. "Today's feast is given by Constable Li. His own rooms are small, so he is using Bailiff Huang's house."

Eventually they started discussing the dragon lanterns. "I'm tired of managing it for you," said Village Head Hsia. "I took the lead every year in the past, and everyone wrote down what contribution he would make, and then failed to pay up. Heaven knows how much I had to pay to make good the deficit. Besides, all the officials in the yamen are preparing lanterns this year, and I shall have too much to watch. What time do I have to look at the lanterns in the village? Still, since you've mentioned it, I shall make a contribution. Choose someone to be responsible. A man like Mr. Hsün, who has broad lands and plenty of grain, should be asked to give more. Let each family pay its share, and you'll get the thing going." Nobody dared disagree. They immediately came down on Mr. Hsün for half the money, and made up the rest between them. In this way they raised two or three taels of silver, a record of the contributors being made.

The monk then brought out tea, sugar wafers, dates, melon seeds, dried beancurd, chestnuts, and assorted sweets. He spread two tables, and invited Village Head Hsia to sit at the head. Then he poured out tea for them.

"The children are growing up," said Shen, "and this year we must find them a teacher. This temple can be used as a school."

The others agreed.

"There are a lot of families who have sons who should be in school," said one of them. "For instance, Mr. Shen's son is Village Head Hsia's son-in-law. Hsia is always getting notices from the magistrate, so he needs someone who can read. But the best thing would be to find a teacher from the county seat."

"A teacher?" said the village head. "I can think of one. You know who? He's in our yamen, and he used to teach in chief accountant Ku's house. His name is Chou Chin. He's over sixty. The former magistrate placed him first on the list of county candidates, but he's never yet been able to pass the prefectural examination. Mr. Ku employed him as tutor for his son for three years; and his son passed the examination last year, at the same time as Mei Chiu from our village. The day that young Ku was welcomed back from the school he wore a scholar's cap and a broad red silk sash, and rode a horse from the magistrate's stable, while all the gongs and trumpets sounded. When he reached the door of his house, I and the other yamen officials offered him wine in the street. Then Mr. Chou was asked over. Mr. Ku toasted his son's teacher three times and invited him to sit in the seat of honour. Mr. Chou chose as entertainment the opera about Liang Hao, who won the first place in the palace examination when he was eighty; and Mr. Ku was not at all pleased. But then the opera showed how Liang Hao's pupil won the same distinction at seventeen or eighteen, and Mr. Ku knew that it was a compliment to his son. That made him feel better. If you want a teacher, I'll invite Mr. Chou for you." All the villagers approved. When they had finished their tea the monk brought in some beef noodles, and after eating these they went home.

The next day, sure enough, Village Head Hsia spoke to Chou Chin. His salary would be twelve taels of silver a year, and it was arranged that he should eat with the monk, whom he would pay two cents a day. It was settled that he should come after the Lantern Festival, and begin teaching on the twentieth.

On the sixteenth the villagers sent in contributions to Shen Hsiang-fu, who prepared a feast for the new teacher to which he also invited Mei Chiu, the new scholar of the village. Mei Chiu arrived early, wearing his new square cap, but Chou Chin did not turn up till nearly noon. When dogs started barking outside, Shen Hsiang-fu went out to welcome the guest; and the villagers stared as Chou Chin came in. He was wearing an old felt cap, a tattered grey silk gown, the right sleeve and seat of which were in shreds, and a pair of shabby red silk slippers. He had a thin, dark face, and a white beard. Shen escorted him in, and only then did Mei Chiu rise slowly to greet him.

"Who is this gentleman?" asked Chou.

They told him, "He is Mr. Mei, our village scholar."

When Chou Chin heard this, he declared it would be presumptuous on his part to allow Mei to bow to him. And although Mei Chiu said, "Today is different," he still refused.

"You are older than he is," said the villagers. "You had better not insist."

But Mei Chiu rounded on them, "You people don't understand the rule of our school. Those who have passed the prefectural examination are considered senior to those who have not, regardless of age. But today happens to be exceptional, and Mr. Chou must still be honoured."

(Ming Dynasty scholars called all those who passed the prefectural examination "classmates," and those who only qualified for this examination "juniors." A young man in his teens who passed was considered senior to an unsuccessful candidate, even if the latter were eighty years old. It was like the case of a concubine. A woman is called "new wife" when she marries, and later "mistress"; but a concubine remains "new wife" even when her hair is white.)

Since Mei Chiu spoke like this, Chou Chin did not insist on being polite, but let Mei Chiu bow to him. When all the others had greeted him too, they sat down. Mei and Chou were the only two to have dates in their tea cups—all the others had plain green tea. After they had drunk their tea two tables were laid, and Chou Chin was invited to take the seat of honour, Mei Chiu the second place. Then the others sat down in order of seniority, and wine was poured. Chou Chin, cup in hand, thanked the villagers and drained his cup. On each table were eight or nine dishes—pig's head, chicken, carp, tripe, liver, and other dishes. At the signal to begin, they fell to with their chopsticks, like a whirlwind scattering wisps of cloud. And half the food had gone before they noticed that Chou Chin had not eaten a bite.

"Why aren't you eating anything?" asked Shen. "Surely we haven't offended you the very first day?" He selected some choice morsels and put them on the teacher's plate.

But Chou Chin stopped him and said, "I must explain—I am having a long fast."

"How thoughtless we have been!" exclaimed his hosts. "May we ask why you are fasting?"

"On account of a vow I made before the shrine of Buddha when my mother was ill," said Chou Chin. "I have been abstaining from meat now for more than ten years."

"Your fasting reminds me of a joke I heard the other day from Mr. Ku in the county town," said Mei Chiu. "It is a one character to seven character verse about a teacher." The villagers put down their chopsticks to listen, while he recited:

> A
> Foolish scholar
> Fasted so long,
> Whiskers covered his cheeks;
> Neglecting to study the classics,
> He left pen and paper aside.
> He'll come without being invited next year.

After this recitation he said, "A learned man like Mr. Chou here is certainly not foolish." Then, putting his hand over his mouth to hide a smile, he added, "But he should become a scholar soon, and the description of the fasting and the whiskers is true to life." He gave a loud guffaw, and everybody laughed with him, while Chou Chin did not know which way to look.

Shen Hsiang-fu hastily filled a cup with wine and said, "Mr. Mei should drink a cup of wine. Mr. Chou was the teacher in Mr. Ku's house."

"I didn't know that," said Mei Chiu. "I should certainly drink a cup to apologize. But this joke was not against Mr. Chou. It was about a scholar. However, this fasting is a good thing. I have an uncle who never ate meat either. But after he passed the prefectural examination his patron sent him some sacrificial meat, and my grandmother said, 'If you don't eat this, Confucius will be angry, and some terrible calamity may happen. At the very least, he will make you fall sick.' So my uncle stopped fasting. Now, Mr. Chou, you are bound to pass the examination this autumn. Then you will be offered sacrificial meat, and I'm sure you will stop fasting."

They all said this was a lucky omen, and drank a toast to congratulate Chou Chin in advance, until the poor man's face turned a mottled red and white, and he could barely stammer out his thanks as he took the wine cup. Soup was carried in from the kitchen with a big dish of dumplings and a plate of fried cakes. They assured Chou Chin that there was no animal fat in the cakes, and pressed him to eat some. But he was afraid the soup was unclean, and asked for tea instead.

While they were eating the dessert, someone asked Shen, "Where is the village head today? Why hasn't he come to welcome Mr. Chou?"

"He has gone to a feast with Constable Li," said Shen.

"These last few years, under the new magistrate, Mr. Li has done very well," said someone else. "In one year he must make about a thousand taels of silver. But he is too fond of gambling. It's a pity he's not like Bailiff Huang. Bailiff Huang used to play too, but later he turned over a new leaf and was able to build a house just like a palace—it is very grand."

"Since your relative became the village head," said Mr. Hsün to Shen Hsiang-fu, "he's been in luck. Another year or two, and I suppose he will be like Bailiff Huang."

"He's not doing badly," said Shen. "But it'll be several years before his dream of catching up with Bailiff Huang comes true."

With his mouth full of cake, Mr. Mei put in: "There *is* something in dreams." And turning to Chou Chin he asked: "Mr. Chou, these past years, during the examinations, what dreams have you had?"

"None at all," replied Chou Chin.

"I was fortunate," said Mei Chiu. "Last year on New Year's Day, I dreamed that I was on a very high mountain. The sun in the sky was directly above me, but suddenly it fell down on my head! Sweating with fright, I woke up and rubbed my head, and it still seemed hot. I didn't understand then what the dream meant, but later it came true!"

By this time all the cakes were finished, and they had another round of drinks. By then it was time to light the lamps, and Mei Chiu and all the others went home, while Shen Hsiang-fu produced blue bedding and escorted Mr. Chou to the temple to sleep, where he settled with the monk that the two empty rooms at the back should be used for the school.

When the day came to start school, Shen Hsiang-fu and the other villagers took their sons, large and small, to pay their respects to the teacher; and Chou Chin taught them. That evening, when he opened the envelopes containing their school fees, he found there was one-tenth of a tael of silver from the Hsün family with an extra eight cents for tea, while the others had given only three or four cents or a dozen coppers apiece; so altogether he had not enough for one month's food. He gave what he had to the monk, however, promising to settle his account later.

The children were a wild lot. The moment Chou Chin took his eyes off them, they would slip outside to play hopscotch or kick balls. They were up to mischief every day, yet he had to sit there patiently and teach them.

Soon more than two months had passed and it began to grow warm. One day after lunch, Chou Chin opened the back gate and went out to stroll on the river bank. It was a small country place, with some peach trees and willows beside the stream, their pink and green beautifully intermingled. Chou Chin enjoyed the scenery until it began to drizzle. Then he went back to his doorway to watch the rain falling on the river and mist shrouding the distant trees, making them look even lovelier. The rain was beginning to fall more heavily when a boat came downstream—a small craft with a matting roof which could not keep out the wet. As it approached the bank, he saw a man sitting in the middle of the boat and two servants in the stern, while in the bow were two hampers. They reached the bank and the man ordered the boatman to moor the boat, then stepped ashore followed by his servants. He was wearing a scholar's cap, a sapphire-blue gown and black slippers with white soles. His beard was combed into three tufts, and he looked a little over thirty. Coming to the temple gate he nodded to Chou Chin, then entered saying to himself, "This seems to be a school."

"Yes," said Chou Chin, accompanying him in and greeting him.

"And you, I suppose, are the teacher?"

"That is correct."

"How is it we don't see the monk?" the stranger asked his servants.

But just then the monk hurried in, saying, "Please take a seat, Mr. Wang, and I'll make tea for you." Then he told Chou Chin, "This is Mr. Wang Hui, a new provincial scholar. Please sit down and keep him company while I go to make tea."

The newcomer showed no false modesty. When the servants drew up a bench he promptly sat himself down in the place of honour of it, leaving the teacher to take a lower seat.

"What is your name?" he demanded.

Knowing that this man was a provincial scholar, Chou Chin replied, "Your pupil is called Chou."

"Where did you teach before?"

"In the family of Mr. Ku of the county yamen."

"Aren't you the man who came first in that test which my patron, Mr. Pai, supervised? He said that you were teaching in Mr. Ku's family. That's right. That's right."

"Do you know my former employer, Mr. Ku, sir?"

"Mr. Ku is one of the secretaries in our office. He is one of my sworn brothers too."

Presently the monk brought in tea, and when they had drunk it Chou Chin said, "I read your examination essay over and over again, sir. The last two paragraphs were particularly fine."

"Those two paragraphs were not by me."

"You are too modest, sir. Who else could have written them?"

"Although not by me, they were not by anybody else either," said the scholar. "It was the first day of the examination, on the ninth, getting on for dusk; but I had still not finished the first essay, and I said to myself, 'Usually I write very quickly. What makes me so slow today?' As I was racking my brains, I dozed off on the desk. Then I saw five green-faced men leaping into the cell. One of them made a mark on my head with a big brush which he had in his hand, then darted away. Then a man in a gauze cap, red robe, and golden belt came in, who shook me and said, 'Mr. Wang, please get up!' I woke up, trembling, bathed in icy sweat, and taking the pen into my hand began to write without knowing what I was doing. From this one can see that there *are* spirits in the examination school. When I made this statement to the chief examiner, he said that I ought to pass the very highest examination."

He was speaking with great gusto, when a small boy came in with a written exercise. Chou Chin told him to put it down, but Wang Hui said, "You go ahead and correct it. I have other things to see to." Then the teacher went to his desk while Wang Hui said to his servants, "Since it is dark and the rain has not stopped, bring the hampers here and tell the monk to cook a peck of rice. Order the boatman to wait. I shall leave tomorrow morning." He told Chou Chin, "I have just come back from visiting the graves of my ancestors, and did not expect to run into rain. I shall spend the night here."

While he was speaking, he caught sight of the name Hsün Mei on the little boy's exercise, and gave an involuntary start. he pursed his lips and his face was a study, but Chou Chin could not very well question him. When Chou Chin had finished correcting the exercise and sat down again as before, Wang Hui asked, "How old is that boy?"

"Seven."

"Did he start school this year? Did you choose that name for him?"

"I didn't choose the name. At the beginning of the term his father asked the new village scholar, Mei Chiu, to choose a name for him. And Mr. Mei said, 'My own name seems to be an auspicious one, so I will give it to him and hope that he will turn out like me.' "

"This is certainly a joke," said Wang Hui with a short laugh. "On the first day of this year I dreamed that I was looking at the list of metropolitan examination results. My name was on it—that goes without saying. But the third name was that of another man from Wen-shang county called Hsün Mei, and I wondered at this, since there was no provincial scholar from my county called Hsün. Fancy it's turning out to be this little student's name! As if I could be on the same list as he!" He burst out laughing, then went on, "It's obvious that dreams are unreliable. Fame and achievement depend upon study, not upon any supernatural forces."

"Some dreams do come true, though," said Chou Chin. "The day that I arrived here, Mr. Mei told me that one New Year's Day he dreamed that a great red sun fell on his head, and that year, sure enough, he passed the prefectural examination."

"That doesn't prove anything," retorted Wang Hui. "Suppose he does pass the prefectural examination and have a sun falling on his head—what about me? I have passed the provincial examination. Shouldn't the whole sky fall on my head?"

As they were chatting, lights were brought in, and the servants spread the desk with wine, rice, chicken, fish, duck, and pork. Wang Hui fell to, without inviting Chou Chin to join him; and when Wang Hui had finished, the monk sent up the teacher's rice with one dish of cabbage and a jug of hot water. When Chou Chin had eaten, they both went to bed. The next day the weather cleared. Wang Hui got up, washed and dressed, bade Chou Chin a casual good-bye, and went away in his boat, leaving the school-room floor so littered with chicken, duck, and fish bones, and melon seed shells, that it took Chou Chin a whole morning to clear them all away, and the sweeping made him dizzy.

When the villagers heard about Wang Hui's dream that Mr. Hsün's son would pass the metropolitan examination in the same year as himself, most of them thought it a great joke, and Hsün Mei's classmates took to calling him Dr. Hsün. But their fathers and elder brothers were annoyed. Out of spite, they went to congratulate Mr. Hsün on being the father of a metropolitan graduate, until he was so angry he could hardly speak.

Shen Hsiang-fu told the villagers secretly, "Mr. Wang could never have said such a thing. It's all made up by that fellow Chou. He saw that the Hsün family was the only one in the village with money, so he spun this yarn to flatter them, in the hope that they would send him more food during festivals. Only the other day I heard that the Hsüns sent some dried bean curd to the temple; and they have often sent him dumplings and cakes too. Depend on it, this is the reason."

Everyone was indignant, and Chou Chin's position became precarious. But since he had been introduced by the village head, they could not dismiss him; and he went on teaching as best he could for a year. At the end of that time, however, Village Head Hsia also became convinced that the teacher was a fool, because Chou Chin did not come often enough to flatter him. So Hsia allowed the villagers to dismiss him.

Having lost his job, Chou Chin went home. He was extremely hard up. One day his brother-in-law, Chin Yin-yu, came to see him and said, "Don't take offence at what I say, brother. But all this study doesn't seem to be getting you anywhere, and a bad job is better than none. How long can you go on like this—neither fish, flesh, nor fowl? I am going to the provincial capital with some other merchants to buy goods, and we need someone to keep accounts. Why don't you come with us? You are all on your own, and in our group you won't want for food or clothes."

"Even if a paralytic falls into a well, he can be no worse off than before," thought Chou Chin. "It can't hurt me to go." So he consented.

Chin chose an auspicious day, and they set off with a party of merchants to the provincial capital, where they stayed in a merchants' guild. Since Chou Chin had nothing to do, he strolled through the streets until he saw a group of workmen who said that they were going to repair the examination school. He followed them to the gate of the school and wanted to go in, but the gateman cracked his whip and drove him away.

That evening he told his brother-in-law how much he wanted to look over the examination school, and Chin had to tip the gateman to get him in. Some of the other merchants decided to go too, and asked the guild head to act as their guide. This time they simply sailed through the gate of the school, because the gateman, whose palm had been greased, made no attempt to stop them. When they reached the Dragon Gate, the guild head pointed to it, and said, "This is the gate for Scholars." They went into a corridor with examination cells on both sides, and the guild head told them, "This is Number One. You can go in and have a look." Chou Chin went in, and when he saw the desk set there so neatly, tears started to his eyes. He gave a long sigh, knocked his head against the desk, and slipped to the ground unconscious.

Translated by Yang Hsien-yi and Gladys Yang

54.

Boat People

The Boat People are a minority group in Kwangtung with a distinct dialect and distinct customs. Considered socially inferior by other Chinese of the area, they found it difficult to acquire educations or rise to positions of influence within the larger Chinese society. Consequently Boat People did not write books we can use to probe their values and culture; we must instead make the best use we can of accounts written by outsiders. Since any minority's world view and social situation will be strongly influenced by how they are treated by others, such sources can be very revealing. The following description of the history and customs of the Boat People is from the gazetteer of Kao-yao county published in 1826. Like most gazetteer entries, this one was composed by quoting from three earlier local histories.

The origin of the Boat People (*tan-hu*) cannot be traced. Boats are their homes and fishing is their occupation. During the Chin dynasty [265–420], there were five thousand households of them outside of the control of the government. Since the T'ang dynasty [618–906], they have paid taxes to the government. In the early years of the Hung-wu period [1368–1398] of the Ming dynasty, they were registered by households and headmen were appointed for each district. They were under the jurisdiction of the Bureau of Rivers and Lakes and paid annual taxes in fish. During the Ch'ung-chen period [1628–1643], the Bureau of Rivers and Lakes of Kao-yao county was abolished and the Boat People were placed under Sung-t'ai station. Under our dynasty, they pay taxes to the local county.

The Boat People can endure cold and can dive deeply into the water. Whenever passengers in boats drop articles into the water, they always have Boat People retrieve them. The local inhabitants classify them as "Boat People" and refuse to marry them. They will not even allow them to settle on the land.

Therefore day and night they have to crowd together on their boats. The fish they catch are barely enough to feed them and none of them, male or female, have enough clothes to cover their bodies.

Every year they must pay taxes at the end of the spring and the beginning of summer. Those who live in the upstream area of Antelope Strait pay 87, while those who live in the downstream area pay 94. The taxpayers are further classified as "Boat People units" or "worker units." The latter are those who are hired to fish for others while the Boat People units are independent fishing households who are responsible for sending their own taxes to the government. The worker units act not only as tenants for commoners but also as servants. As they are in extreme poverty those who monopolize the business are able to hire them for low wages. They give the tenants several years' advance salary, but such wages are insufficient to keep them from suffering cold and hunger. Thus, year after year the tenant fishermen are unable to pay the government tax.

The Boat People by nature are stupid and illiterate. They are afraid of seeing officials, so local magnates and rapacious clerks are able to exploit them continuously. The local riffraff treat the fishing boats as their own storehouses and use the fishermen's children as their sleeping mats, yet none of the fishermen dare to utter a word about it.

Translated by Lily Hwa

55.

Infant Protection Society

During the Age of Division and the T'ang dynasty, when Buddhism flourished, monasteries undertook many charitable activities and social welfare services. By late traditional China members of the gentry had taken over much of the responsibility for charity and ran such organizations as free schools, orphanages, soup kitchens, and winter shelters for beggars and vagrants. Managing such enterprises was one of the major functions upper-class men fulfilled in their communities.

The following discussion of infanticide and ways to discourage it was written by Yu Chih. He had started an Infant Protection Society in his home village in Wu-hsi county, Kiangsu province, and from 1843 to 1853 it had supported between sixty and one hundred infants every year. His account of this society reveals several aspects of gentry management of charitable activities: it shows the high moral impulses that could lead to philanthropy; it testifies to how much a few members of the gentry knew of the everyday reality of the life of the poor; and it recounts the practical and financial difficulties involved in undertaking charitable projects.

In the cities it is customary to have orphanages where deserted children are taken in. . . . However, the countryside is extensive and travel is difficult, so poor people cannot afford to bring their children into the city. Thus, when poor families have too many children, they are often forced by practical considerations to drown the newborn infants, a practice which has already become so widespread that no one thinks it unusual. (People even give it euphemistic names such as "giving her away to be married," or "transmigrating to the body of someone else." The custom has become so deeply rooted that no one attempts to discourage it.) Not only are female infants drowned, at times even males are; not only do the poor drown their children, even the well-to-do do it. People follow each other's example, and the custom becomes more widespread day by day. (There is a case where one family drowned more than ten girls in a row; there are villages where scores of girls are drowned each year. We who dwell in the country

witness the crime with our own eyes—a scene too brutal to be described.) As soon as the infants are born into this world, they become the victims of murder. They struggle in the water for a long time before they fall silent. On hearing their cries, one is brought to the brink of tears; on talking about it, one's heart is rent with sorrow.

Alas! Who is not a parent? Who is not a child? How can anyone be so cruel? Is it that people are evil by nature? No. It is that the custom has become so prevalent that people can no longer see the cruelty in it. Yet, Heaven encourages life, and man abhors killing. Charitable people who are determined to accumulate good deeds even buy live animals just to release them! Why not save *human* lives! If we who live in the country, who see and hear this crime committed daily, simply look on without trying to save the infants, how can we excuse our own guilt? (This matter may not have come to the attention of the city officials and the country gentry. It is necessary to inquire about the matter from poor women in order to obtain details.) This is why we have to cry aloud for these infants and seek help from the charitable gentlemen of the entire nation.

When we look into the charitable institutions available, we find that, besides orphanages, there are foundling homes and nurseries which take in infants for temporary stays and transport them for the villagers. Yet, in the case of newborn infants, the little bodies might not be able to survive the trip. Therefore, adopting the principle of Su Tung-p'o who saved infants in Huang-o, and P'eng Nan-yün who wrote on saving those who were being drowned, we have formulated a way to offer subsidies of cash and rice to make it possible for parents to raise their children at home instead of sending them to orphanages.

We have formed a society named "The Infant Protection Society." Whenever there is a birth in our area, if the parents are truly too poor to raise the child themselves, our bureau will, according to regulations, provide them with cash and rice for six months so that they can care for the child for that period. Only when it is absolutely impossible for them to raise the infant at home will the society try to transport him or her to an orphanage as a life-saving measure. Our aim is to make the parents keep the infant, at first perhaps for the subsidy, and then out of love—for, as the baby grows, the parents will become more attached to him or her day by day. Our expenses are modest, yet a great many lives can be saved. . . .

The following are the regulations of the Society, which can be adopted by anyone interested.

1. When the Society is first established, a bureau should be set up in a temple or any other public place since there is no time to construct a separate building. All members should share the duties of the bureau. A head should be elected out of those who are of means and of reliable character. Several other trustworthy and capable members should be elected as solicitors and inspectors. It is necessary that all the members work together toward a common goal for only then can the Society achieve long-lasting results.

2. Contributions can be solicited in large lump sums or small donations, in the form of cash or grain—all depending on the local situation of the region. It can be done by calling a meeting within a clan, a village, or even a county; the more funds acquired, the better.

All members have to work together to change this immoral custom and save lives.

3. As the number of people who drown their children is on the increase in rural areas, the Infant Protection Society is established to provide subsidies for the very poorest families only, to discourage them from killing their own children without having to use an orphanage. Therefore, any household that can manage to raise its infants is not eligible for support from the Society.

4. In the area served, whenever an infant is born and the parents are indeed too destitute to keep it, they should report to the bureau of the Society, accompanied by neighbors who are willing to serve as witnesses. The inspector of the bureau will then go personally to the home to examine the situation. If it is truly as reported, the Society will give the parents one peck of white rice and two hundred cash. Afterwards, they can claim the same amount each month, identifying themselves with tickets, for a total of five months. (The exact period can be lengthened or shortened according to individual needs; the amount of subsidy is also flexible.) After five months, if they definitely cannot afford to keep the child, then the Society will provide transportation to an orphanage. (Those who can raise the child, but only with much difficulty, should be persuaded to do so. Even if the Society has to provide rice for two or three more months, whenever a life can be saved, action should be taken.)

5. Records are to be kept in the bureau. After the birth of the child, the parents must report the exact hour, day, and month of birth to the bureau as well as the name of the family, the village, and the county. The inspector then should look over the infant; record finger prints, toe prints, and the direction, location, and shape of the hair swirl on the head. Then the bureau should give out tickets on which is written the exact number of months of subsidy the parents are to receive. Two months later they should bring the child to the bureau for inspection, or the inspector should visit the family. If the infant dies from disease, the subsidy should be terminated on the day the death occurs. Should anyone fail to report the death of such an infant, the witnesses are to be held responsible.

6. In extremely destitute families, if a widow is pregnant and has no sons to continue her dead hus-

band's family line and no other means of suppor
then the subsidy can be increased after a meeting of
the Society members (the period is either three or four
years, the amount flexible). In this way, not only does
the Society take care of orphans, but it actually spon-
sors chastity; this will be of no small aid to virtuous
customs.

7. If a mother in a poor family should die immediately after childbirth and the infant, left without
anyone to nurse it, faces imminent death, then the
bureau, after making sure of the facts, should give an
extra five hundred cash a month to provide for a wet
nurse. This subsidy can be continued for three years.

8. With time, it is to be expected that corruption
will occur. Once a subsidy system is started, there inevitably will be people who are capable of raising
their children and yet pretend to be poor to obtain the
money and rice. Therefore, the investigators must be
careful; only those who are confirmed to be actually
destitute should receive the subsidy. Also, one should
change people's ways of thinking by constantly and
sincerely teaching them about the divine retribution
which awaits those who drown infants.

9. When the Society is established, a geographic
boundary must be set to facilitate inspections. If one
tries to give help to whoever seeks it, then funds will
not be sufficient, and it will be difficult to investigate
cases because of the distances. Therefore, we ten-
tatively set a limit of ten *li*; we are not able to provide
help for those who live outside of the ten-*li* radius.
When an infant is registered at the bureau, if it is
winter, one coat filled with cotton and one wrapping
blanket will be allotted; if it is spring or autumn, one
lined gown.

10. Although the purpose of the Society is to persuade
poverty-striken families to keep their children instead
of drowning them, in some cases the parents may be
ashamed to accept charity or may have their minds
set on drowning the infant because they already have
too many children at home. In others, the parents
may be in such straitened circumstances that keeping
the infant is definitely impossible. In such cases, one
should try hard to persuade them to find ways to solve
their problems, without meddling in their private affairs.

11. Infants who are brought to the bureau should be
provided with wet nurses immediately. If there is a

woman with milk who is willing to be the wet nurse
to pay for her own child, then one should pay her
three years' salary according to regulations. Or, the
first year she may get two pecks of rice a month, and
only one peck each month through the rest of the two-
year period. Since boys are usually adopted, the
bureau should give out birth certificates to prevent
future lawsuits concerning the rights to the child but
should not subsidize them with money or rice.

12. Poxes are the most dangerous diseases of infants,
especially small pox, which is easily spread. Therefore, in the first and second or eighth and ninth
months, one should give inoculations and tell the wet
nurses to watch carefully. The bureau should provide
some funds for medication and supply some medicine
in cases of emergency.

13. Whenever a child is sick, it should be reported to
the manager of the bureau, who will then pay a doctor to see the patient until he or she is fully recovered.
If the mother of a new-born infant is ill or unable to
produce milk, she should also report to the bureau
and receive a subsidy for health care and medication.

14. The regulations of this Society are set for the extremely poor. We are sure that the households which
are capable of raising their own children will not
stoop to such meager assistance, nor would they send
their children to orphanages. And yet, simply out of
impatience with having too many children, or merely
due to the custom of the region, some of these families
may also have drowned their children. After the
establishment of this Society, they will hesitate to do
so. By and by the infants will all be able to escape
cruel early deaths.

15. After the Society's proposal to the county government has been approved, a general notice of prohibition will be drawn up. Should anyone, despite the
Society's efforts, insist on the evil practice of drowning children, he will be convicted and punished if
discovered: No one should be lenient with him. Our
hope is to change the customs in part by pressure from
the outside but more by persuasion from the inside.
This is by no means too harsh.

16. Although the Society is formed to protect infants,
it also helps mothers, for in an extremely poor
household, the livelihood of the family depends on
weaving done by the housewife. A day without work
means a day without food. In such cases, whenever

the wife is in labor or cannot work, the family faces starvation. The woman who is laden with a hundred worries and has nowhere to turn will hardly be capable of returning to work as early as the second or third day after giving birth; if she does it is very possible that she will catch a cold or have other complications which may lead to critical problems. On the other hand, if she can get a small subsidy, she will be able to rest a few days, the infant can be saved, and the mother also can be nourished. This is doing two good deeds at once.

17. Although the Society will provide transportation of unwanted children to orphanages, the cases in which that is necessary should constitute less than twenty to thirty percent. At the time of the birth of the infant, either because of poverty or anger or because the mother has to nurse other people's children, the parents may not wish to keep the infant. But after four or five months the child can already laugh and play, and is very lovable. The parents are then unable to part with him or her. (Those who endeavor to keep their child can again be divided into two groups; the truly hard-pressed ones should qualify for subsidy for several more months.)

The most serious matter in this world is human life, and the greatest of all charitable deeds is the saving of human lives. Of all kinds of life-saving, ours is the most urgent. I humbly hope that the gentlemen who are concerned about the ways of the world will advocate our purpose and spread our practices wherever they go and to whomever they meet. It does not matter whether the scale is large or small; each life we save is worth saving. Every time we establish a bureau, we will save numerous lives, which is no small matter. If these established regulations have faults, then they should be modified according to the specific local situations. It is our greatest hope that our fellow workers will do so.

Once I asked a friend from another part of the country if people there also drowned female infants. He said no, in his region there was no such custom. I expressed great admiration for the goodness of the people in that area. A few months later, I met this friend again, and he spoke to me in great alarm. "Would you believe it!" he exclaimed. "What you told me the other day was true! I'm so glad that you woke me up from my ignorance. Otherwise I would have missed a fine opportunity for doing good."

When I asked him for the details, my friend told me that when he returned home from our meeting, he asked a midwife about the drowning of female infants and found out that the custom was rather prevalent in his hometown. Upon this discovery he called town meetings and admonished the villagers; he also offered to protect infants and worked out village contracts to prohibit such practices. Since then he has been able to save five or six lives.

The above is a good example of the situation: the custom is prevalent in most places, yet people are not aware of it unless they give it special attention. We scholars tend to close our doors and devote ourselves to studying, thinking that by doing so we are concerning ourselves with the people and the universe. Little do we know that right outside our doors there are countless infants crying out to be saved from death! (People who refuse to bother about what happens outside their doors often do so on the grounds that they do not want to interfere with the affairs of others. Yet when it comes to saving lives, one should not insist on such principles. Otherwise the best opportunities to accumulate good deeds will be missed.)

Now, since the custom of drowning female infants is most prevalent in rural areas, charitable people in the cities and towns can do very little where they are. In their case, the best course is to investigate which regions have such wicked customs, then try to save the infants by expounding the principles of divine retribution. They should realize the significance of saving lives and should not be afraid of difficulties. For time does not wait for man; one's hair turns white quickly and one grows old. Once the best chance of doing good passes, it will be too late to repent. Cases of divine retribution for drowning female infants are too numerous to be fully listed. Those who want to help should print illustrated books on this subject to warn the foolish and the ignorant. Also, abortion by taking drugs often causes deaths; pictures against this practice should be printed as appendices to the books. As to children born from illicit relations, they should tell midwives that they will receive 400 to 500 cash as a reward if they bring such illegitimate children to the Protection Societies. In this way they will be able to save quite a few lives in secret.

The lives of men concern Heaven, and Heaven encourages life. Therefore, the saving of human lives is of utmost importance. If a man takes the life of another, not only will he be executed for the crime in this world, he will be punished in the other world as well. Wicked forces result from grievance; together they form the wheel of retributions, and misfortune will certainly befall the guilty. On the other hand, if a man saves a life or a score of lives, even hundreds of lives, imagine the bountiful reward he will receive! Whether it is a grown man's or a mere infant's, a life is a life; therefore, one should not let this chance to accumulate good slip by.

The custom of drowning female infants has become for many a mere habit. Although there are laws prohibiting it and books advising against it, they cannot reach the common people who are ignorant of reason and unable to read. However severe and earnest these laws and books may be, they cannot penetrate into every household and get to the people on the streets. In such cases, the only thing one can do is to compose catchy slogans and folk songs with themes of retribution and propagate them in villages and towns. When ignorant men and women hear these, they will understand them and be inspired and warned. Only then can this age-old, widespread custom be changed. If the blind minstrels that rove the countryside can be taught such songs, then they can make a living with them and at the same time can awaken the world. This is doing two good deeds at once and is the very best way to accumulate merit.

Translated by Clara Yu

56.

Mid-Century Rebels

Over the centuries China witnessed thousands of violent uprisings. Yet no period suffered so many as the mid-nineteenth century, from 1850 to 1873, when the vast T'ai-p'ing Rebellion brought in its wake the Nien Rebellion in the North, Moslem rebellions in the Southwest and Northwest, a Miao rebellion in the Southwest, secret society rebellions along the coast, and many more.

Traditional Confucian historians interpreted rebellion in terms of the dynastic cycle. When a dynasty first came to power, according to this theory, it was fresh and vital, but as time went on, moral decay would begin to choke it. Venal officials would exploit the people but at the same time be too weak to govern them effectively, and so uprisings would begin to break out. Modern historians have added an economic component to this analysis. With governmental decline, the economy would suffer, and the people would become progressively poorer. Many peasants would have to sell out to landlords at deflated prices, and at the same time the government would be weakened because of dwindling tax receipts. Attempts by the government to boost revenues by raising taxes would only result in the further impoverishment and disaffection of the people. Society would then become increasingly militarized on the local level; bandits would strike an area, and the local populace would organize a militia in self-defense. People would look at various groups through which they might express their hostility and dissent, such as secret societies, lineages, religious and ethnic organizations, and bandit and militia units.

Rebellions varied considerably in their origins and organization. Some were started by bands of hungry peasants, others by well-organized secret societies that had elaborate ideologies incorporating elements from popular Buddhism and Taoism. The T'ai-p'ing Rebellion even made use of some Christian beliefs. Nevertheless, virtually all rebellions which had any success also invoked the Confucian theory of the mandate of Heaven: the Emperor had ceased to rule with virtue; therefore, he had lost his mandate and his subjects had the right to rebel.

Sources for the goals, organizing principles, and behavior of rebels are scarce. Most peasants did not write. When rebellions failed, the documents they produced were destroyed as dangerous. The officials who suppressed the rebels wrote reports, but most of them lacked firsthand knowledge, objectivity, or sympathy. To overcome some of these shortcomings, the mid-century rebellions are probed here through four sources of differing origin. The first is a group of proclamations of the Small Sword Society, issued when they took over the city of Amoy on the coast of Fukien and preserved by British diplomats stationed there. The Small Sword Society was one of the secret societies that joined in the general initiative of the T'ai-p'ings to take several cities in the early 1850s. These proclamations reveal typical rebel ideology—for instance, evoking the name of the Ming dynasty and the Han people as an anti-Manchu gesture. The second source is the "confessions" a group of rebels made after their capture. These rebels were members of bandit groups loosely related to the T'ai-p'ings. The third source is a request for military aid sent in by members of the gentry of that same area. These two pieces, which were also preserved by British officials, can be used together to analyze the social milieu that gave rise to banditry and rebellion. The fourth source is an account of the background of the Moslem rebellion in Yunnan written by a seventy-one-year-old Moslem in 1931 based on what he had heard as a child decades earlier. In the mid-nineteenth century 20 to 30 percent of the population of Yunnan was Moslem.

224

After this revolt Tu Wen-hsiu, the leader of the Moslems, was able to rule the province for sixteen years (1856–1873).

PROCLAMATIONS OF THE AMOY SMALL SWORD SOCIETY

1

The Grand Marshal Huang of the Ming dynasty and the Han people, in order to safeguard the lives of the commoners and merchants, proclaims martial law:

I have heard that Heaven and Earth change their course of order: after a time of great prosperity, there must follow a period of chaos; and after a period of great turmoil, there must arise a general desire for peace.

The Ch'ing dynasty has been governing China for more than two hundred years. Corruption of officials and oppression of the people clearly indicate that its mandate has come to an end. I now lead the Righteous and Benevolent Army to save the people and to punish those who have been cruel. I have ordered that my soldiers shall pillage neither the merchants nor the common people nor shall they rape women. The arrival of my armies will not cause the slightest disturbance to the people. If any soldier disobeys my orders I shall punish him in accordance with martial law, permitting no favoritism. You, the merchants and the people, should apply yourselves to your tasks and should not be frightened. I am strict in abiding by my words and enforcing my orders. You should obey them unerringly.

10th day of the fourth month of 1853

2

Concerning the safety of the people and normal business:

I, the Grand Marshal, have led my army to recover the southern provinces, to stabilize peace for the four classes of people, and to eliminate bad officials.

Since the Emperor of the Ch'ing government is young and ignorant, power has been concentrated in the hands of wicked advisors, and officials of the prefectures and counties plunder the wealth of the people and use it to ingratiate themselves with their superiors. As a result the people are oppressed by greedy officials.

I, the Grand Marshal,/have led the Righteous and Benevolent Army and have recovered Hai-ch'eng, Chang-chou, Kuan-k'ou, and T'ung-an. My army has advanced with irresistible power. If my subordinates have any unruly soldiers who rape women and create disturbances in the streets, you should report them to my officers immediately. I shall execute them and display their heads in public in accordance with the law.

All the people—merchants and commoners alike—should carry on with their work and trade as usual. Do not be afraid of my soldiers. After issuing an order I enforce it immediately and do not tolerate offenders. My orders must be obeyed.

3

In the name of the Grand Ming dynasty, Marshal Huang of the Han people proclaims:

It is well known that the way to good government is through benevolent policies; yet military strength is essential in governing a state. At this moment I have already conquered Amoy and must now appoint capable persons to govern it. When employing capable individuals in the government, one should pay special attention to their military ability. For this reason those who are able to pacify the world must exert care in choosing men.

Now the people of Amoy come seeking to take the oaths and join our society. There are hundreds of millions of them. If I do not proclaim the rules of recruitment, I am afraid that the wrong persons will be selected, thereby causing an unnecessary waste of time and resources. With the proclamation of this edict, those of you who have obtained the righteous banners from me and who are willing to reconstruct the nation with me should be very careful in the recruitment of more members. Only the young and the strong and those with experience in the martial arts should be selected as our members. We must eliminate the very old, the very young, and the disabled. In other words, we must eliminate all those over sixty years of age and all those under sixteen. Only by following this method can we strengthen our forces. Do not transgress this order.

15th day of the fourth month, 1853

A STATEMENT OF VOLUNTARY SURRENDER BY MEMBERS OF THE KWANGSI ROVING BANDIT GROUP

We men from Kwangtung—Ta Li-yü, Chang Chao, Chang Kuei-ho, Wen Hsi—and we men from Kwangsi—T'ien Fang, Huang Shou, and Liang Fu—make this appeal.

We were born in a time of prosperity and were

good people. We lived in towns and were taught to distinguish right from wrong. But because of continuous flooding in our area, we could not get a grain of rice to eat even if we worked hard in the fields, and we could not engage in business because we lacked the funds. As a result we all joined the bandits.

Not long ago we came to Kwangsi to try to make a living. We met others who had come from our hometowns. We pitied each other because of our sad situation, and together we began to imitate outlaws in order to relieve our hungry stomachs. In other words, no one forced us to join the outlaws. We were driven to join them because we were desperate. Given the chance, we would have returned gladly to our normal way of life.

We thought constantly of our families, but we could not return to them. Indeed, we were drifting on a hungry, painful sea and knew not when we would reach the other side. We hope Your Excellency will forgive our past sins. We hope you will think of the great benevolence of our imperial house and give us a chance to start a new life. Grass and trees are without feeling, yet they still appreciate the dew and rain that falls upon them to nourish them. Men are conscious beings; therefore how could we forget your great benevolence if you should allow us a new life? We are laying out our situation sincerely to you. We hope you can state clearly your intention. If you are willing to forgive us, please issue a statement of amnesty. If we could again become children of Heaven and return to the kingdom of benevolence and longevity, we will serve you as loyally as your dogs and horses. We will obey all your orders, and we will be willing to serve in your military camp. We have presented our situation to you. Knowing that we have bothered Your Honor with our petty matters, trembling we await our punishment. We sincerely present our case to Your Excellency.

We, humble people, Big-Headed Yang, Lo Ta, Hou Chiu, Wang Liu, Lü Hsiung-chieh, report our grievance and appeal to you. . . .

We hate the army runners who recently made heavy demands on us and disturbed our villages. They used the excuse of establishing a local militia to cause trouble for the good and honest people and create opportunities for the wicked ones. The words they used were virtuous-sounding; yet the deeds they actually perpetrated were most wicked. They allied themselves with government officials and formed cliques so that they could oppress our village and make excessive demands whenever they wished. They

falsely reported that certain persons were connected with the bandits. This was due to personal grudges against the accused or to the fact that they wanted to obtain rewards. They burned down our houses and took all we had; they robbed us of our property and threatened our lives. Therefore we banded together to insure our own safety. Those who still remain in the village may run away someday while those who have left can hardly come back. Therefore, for each ordinary person who ran away, there was one more bandit, and the numbers of bandits became greater and greater. Since there are so many of us, we could not survive except by pillage, nor could we save our lives if we did not fight against the imperial troops that were sent out to exterminate us. As a consequence, we have offended the court and hurt the merchants.

We have always wanted to correct our behavior and to purge ourselves of our beastly nature. We would have liked to return to our homes to enjoy long and happy lives, but we have been left rambling around, wandering through unknown places because the officials did not have mercy on us. Usually after interrogating a bandit, they would kill him or at least expel him. Therefore those who sincerely wanted to correct their past sins were actually risking their lives. If we had surrendered to the officials, we also would have had to depend on their mercy. The thought of it tortures us day and night.

Now, fortunately, Your Excellency has arrived in this area with a commission to pacify the people. You have loved the people like your own children; you have disciplined yourself strictly; you have worked diligently for the good of the nation and have relieved the suffering of the masses. We hope that you will understand our situation and judge fairly. We hope you will treat us leniently and extend your benevolence to us. We are willing to sell our weapons and buy cows for farming. We render all our respect and gratitude to you.

We respectfully report our situation to you.

MEMORIAL OF LI YÜ-YING, CHÜ-JEN DEGREE HOLDER, AND T'AN TUAN-YÜAN, SHENG-YÜAN DEGREE HOLDER, FROM WU PREFECTURE, KWANGSI PROVINCE

Our dynasty has followed the teachings of the ancient sages. As a result everyone in Jung county has lived in harmony for a long time. The population was increasing, and the resources were plentiful; even our dogs and chickens never had to fear disturbance. . . . However, in 1846 bandits and rebels began gathering on the east side of Liang-hsü and disturbed our local tranquility. As their power grew, their influence spread. They even captured the city and took the government officials prisoner. There was no order in the city, and the rebels roamed everywhere. Gentry members were killed and captured; women were raped. Corpses were left lying all over the ground; houses were left in ashes; the farmers' fields were thick with weeds. It was sad indeed to see these things happen. . . . They pillaged property even at great distances from their base area and forced the people who were under their control to pay land taxes to them. They connived to force officials to send up false reports saying that loyalist forces had recaptured areas that had fallen to the rebels. The bandits used official seals and issued false edicts to the populace. It was intolerable to have these ruffians dominate the local government!

Last year we were lucky to have the Governor and the Governor-General decide to lead out their armies to destroy the bandits at Hsün-chou. The Governor then promised to transfer the army to Jung county where the local militia was trying to consolidate its positions pending the arrival of the government troops. The militia have been fighting for a long time and have become quite weary. I am afraid that, if the local militia collapses, the bandits will roam all over the county and prove very difficult for the government troops to control.

The local militia is capable of mustering 10,000 troops, all battle-tested veterans who hate the rebels. It is our opinion that, if only we could get a skilled commander, the militia would be quite effective against the rebels. Unfortunately, we have not been able to get an experienced officer to lead them. There have been constant arguments over battle plans, and the militia has never acted in unison. As a result we have often been defeated by the rebels. The Prefect and Governor-General appointed a pair of officers to supervise the local militia. They issued orders, gave out banners and seals, but did not come to take command personally. The local militia, therefore, has not been united and cannot contribute much to alleviating the critical situation.

Now that the Governor of Kwangsi province has dispatched his army to wipe out the bandits in Hsün-chou, we hope that, after finishing with the bandits there, it will come immediately to Jung county to exterminate the rebels and save the people. If Your Ex-cellency sympathizes with all that the people have suffered, please hasten to have the army come here to suppress the rebels. . . . We might suggest that you consolidate the militias of T'eng, P'ing-nan, Pei-liu, Ch'en-ch'i, and Hsin-i counties under your command so that the bandits may not escape our troops by hopping back and forth across county borders. When the government armies arrive in Jung county have them train the local militia so that it can put up a better defense against the bandits. We would suggest also that you proclaim a general amnesty for those who were forced to join the rebels. We have confidence in the strategy of encircling bandit hideouts; we are sure they could not resist your attacks and their days would be numbered. . . .

Huang P'eng-fen and Feng Wei-jeng are two leaders well respected by the local militia. If you were to appoint them commanders, they would get co-operation and would be able to help achieve the goal of ridding our area of rebels. When your armies arrive here we would personally like to join them to take your orders and give you assistance if needed. With your great talent and ability as a high civil and military official, you will certainly save our people from their hardships. . . .

With the greatest of humility we present these opinions to you.

THE CONFLICT OF THE HAN CHINESE AND THE MOSLEMS AT THE COUNTY OF PAO–SHAN, IN THE PREFECTURE OF YUNG–CH'ANG, AND THE REASONS FOR TU WEN–HSIU'S UPRISING

Yung-ch'ang was the name of a prefecture during the Ch'ing dynasty. The largest county inside the prefecture was called Pao-shan. It was divided into five zones—East, West, North, South and Central—referred to as the five towns. The administration of the area outside the five towns was divided into seven guard stations, each with its own name.

In 1840 the Chinese population in the county had entered into an alliance, pledging brotherhood and burning incense. It was called the Incense Alliance Society. The members addressed each other as "brother," following the example of the Society of Brothers and Elders, but remaining independent of it. The objective of the Society was to terrorize people. Delinquent youth and members of evil gentry families imitated them and formed eight Incense Brotherhoods in the towns during the next several years. Each

Incense Brotherhood had a leader, referred to as Boss. Boss Chuang controlled the town; Boss Keng lived outside the South Gate; Boss Meng lived in Chin-chi village; Boss Wan lived on Plank Bridge Road; and Boss Ts'un on Sand Bar Street. All of the Bosses put on conspicuous displays, but Boss Wan of Plank Bridge Road carried it the furthest. Every time he went out, he imitated the style of a Governor-General by hiring a runner to clear his way. He sat on the eight-man sedan chair, which was a copy of the golden chair of Bright Honor Temple, used only during festivals for the gods. The sedan chair was covered with tiger skin and the footrests were golden carved lions; sitting on it, Boss Wan looked like a heavenly deity. There were 500 to 600 armed guards who accompanied him, and four persons swinging censers walked before the sedan chair as if it were a procession for deities. Their arrogance was indescribable. Occasionally when local civil or military leaders met the Boss, they had to yield way to him. The later disturbances in Yunnan in which millions of Han Chinese and Moslems were killed arose from these eight Incense Brotherhoods.

The Han Chinese in Pao-shan county were very superstitious. Every year on the 29th day of the third month, they honored the five deities from the five mountains. Two days before, eight men would carry the sedan chairs to greet the idols of the five deities from the East, South, West, North, and Central Mountains and place them in the Longevity Hall. Monks and Taoist priests were called to recite passages from scriptures, perform the kowtow, and worship devoutly for two days. On the 29th, the people held a great celebration, had prayer meetings, and brought the five gods from the Longevity Hall to the Eastern Temple, south of the city. But the procession had to pass the Clear Truth Mosque located on Common Brilliance Street which housed about 200 Moslem disciples. Every time the procession passed the Mosque, there were several dozen Moslems watching. They looked down on the Chinese and their method of worship. Some of the mischievous students even laughed at and mocked the passing Chinese. They threw sucked cane sugar remains and fruit peels at the people walking in front of the five sedan chairs. This angered the Chinese spectators and the sedan chair carriers. They argued, and fighting ensued. This happened every year and soon deep hatred and resentment grew between the two factions. Although rational people asked the Moslem teachers to restrain and confine the students, some of

the students still scaled the walls and made trouble. . . .

The Han Chinese brought this matter to the officials of the county, who investigated the matter and had one Moslem student named Ma Yu-teh put to death. Nevertheless, the troublemakers continued to act up. They would make the wild claim that by attacking "paganism" they were furthering the true Moslem religion and were thereby blameless of any wrong-doing. They did not seem to realize that in their actions lay the roots for the destruction of their families and race. The real culprits behind all this trouble were the teachers who had led these Moslem students astray. Indeed it was the teachers who inflamed the students with the dubious proposition that by attacking "paganism" they were furthering the true religion and were thereby blameless of any wrong-doing.

Outside of the Dragon Spring Gate was Dragon Spring Temple. Inside the temple was an Incarnation Hall where people believed the deceased would be reborn. In the seventh and tenth months the local people gathered there to perform ceremonies and young widows went to mourn their deceased husbands. The Moslem youths often flirted with these women, and the Han Chinese in turn hurled insults at the Moslems. Finally oral recriminations gave way to brawls and fights.

In 1843 the conflict between the Han Chinese and the Moslems was reaching a crisis. . . . The hatred between the two groups was steadily intensifying, and the Incense Alliance Society finally decided to exterminate the Moslems. In 1845 Shen Ying of Chinchi, the Boss of the Lu-t'ang Ch'ang who had been taught the mystic skill of imperviousness to bullets fired from guns, was chosen by the Incense Brothers to be their leader and charged with exterminating the Moslems. He managed to form an alliance with the gentry of the area. All signed an oath: "The gentry and people of Yang-ch'ang commission Shen Ying to lead the militia to destroy the Moslems in the prefecture. All of the officials, both civilian and military, agree to take responsibility for this action. If, after the Moslems have been exterminated, any superior official takes outrage at the action and decides to punish the participants, all of the local civilian and military officials will take the blame and will not let Shen Ying be punished. Shen Ying is only carrying out orders."

After gaining this pledge from the gentry, Shen Ying secretly selected 3000 strong men from Chin-chi and on the 2nd day of the ninth month hung a rope on the city wall whereby his men could gain admittance to the city after the gates had been closed. Within the city the gentry ordered all of the Han Chinese to burn incense by their doors throughout the night. This was done under the pretext of worshiping the door god. When the attack began any household which was found not to be burning incense at its door was wiped out completely. The militia was concerned only with killing the Moslems and did very little looting. More than 1300 households, or 8000 Moslems who lived in the city and in its southern suburbs, were put to death. A few hundred managed to escape and fled to the forest, where they hid out for three days until the Magistrate called them back and allowed them to reside in the yamen to escape being killed too. Their suffering cannot be described. In 1847 a second massive anti-Moslem campaign was begun. The local Han Chinese killed Moslems wherever they found them—even travelers from elsewhere and candidates on their way to take the examinations. Even more were killed than before. Since this was the year for the triennial civil service examinations, virtually all of the Moslem candidates coming there were killed. Those Moslems who had sought the safety of the government compound fared no better. Han mobs attacked and burned the place. The officials jumped the wall and fled. All of the government buildings were burned to ashes and the Moslems were either cremated alive or put to the sword. The Han mob thereupon blamed the Moslems for starting the fire in order to escape any retributive actions on the part of the authorities. Thus the city Moslems were exterminated.

In the countryside similar slaughter began on Plank Bridge Road, where there were 1200 to 1300 households, of which 300 were Moslem. In the fourth month of 1845 a Moslem youth and a Han youth got into an altercation. The Moslem youth began singing a song: "Bind the rice seedlings with straw, the new replaces the old." The Han youth replied, singing: "The Moslem herds an old pig, which leads its offspring."

The Moslem regarded this as a great insult, and a fight broke out. It was at this time that the Incense Association was strong and looking for any excuse to pick a fight. Here they found one. Before the Moslems realized what was happening, bands of aroused Han Chinese attacked their homes and killed great numbers of them. They were not allowed to live on Plank Bridge Road any longer, so they went to Pao-

shan county to seek help. The officials came back with them to try to smooth things over, but the Han Chinese ignored the officials' orders to let the Moslems return to their homes. Some of the local ruffians even took pieces of tile and mud balls and hurled them at the officials, who retreated in fright.

Since the local government could not protect them, the Moslems decided to seek help from fellow Moslems in Yün-chou. There was a Moslem bully there named Big Elephant who had a gang of over eighty men. He agreed to come to help. When he arrived at Pao-shan county, however, the local Moslems were trying to cooperate with the officials in solving the problem; therefore they sent an emissary to Big Elephant to call off the raid. The Yün-chou Moslems refused, saying they were confident of victory and would return as soon as they had taught the Han Chinese a lesson. They attacked Chin-chi but were beaten back by Shen Ying. As they retreated they burned and pillaged. They even kidnapped government officials and military men. This made a peaceful solution to the problem impossible, and once more, Moslems were slaughtered in the cities and in the countryside.

The Moslems sent a delegation of Ting Ts'an-T'ing, Mu Wen-k'o, Tu Wen-hsiu, Liu I, and others to the capital to petition the Tao-kuang Emperor, who heard their appeal and ordered Lin Tse-hsü, Governer-General of Yunnan and Kweichou to lead out an army to punish the Han offenders.* In 1846 Lin led out his army but found that there was a Moslem uprising at the time. . . . He thereupon wrote to the Emperor: "There are good people among the Han Chinese, and there are bad people among the Moslems." Instead of taking military actions on a large scale, Lin sought to punish individual abuses.

Lin Tse-hsü stationed his army at Yung-p'ing. He ordered the Yung-ch'ang officials to round up the people accused of murdering Moslems and bring them to Yung-p'ing for judgment. Several hundred were apprehended. . . . The local Han populace freed them from their cages, however, on their way to trial. They went to Chin-chi and held parties and performed dramas. Another massacre of Moslems then commenced. Moslems were killed on sight. . . .

When Lin Tse-hsü heard that the Han Chinese

---

* Lin Tse-hsü (1785–1850) was a famous official whose efforts to suppress the opium trade played a part in starting the Opium War.

had freed the prisoners from jail, he issued dozens of proclamations threatening the jailbreakers. These were posted in the streets of Yung-ch'ang and said: "If you do not listen to the orders of the government, I will send an army to punish you. All of you will be exterminated; not even your dogs and chickens will remain alive."After reading the proclamation, Shen Ying held a meeting of his followers to determine how best to deal with the situation. Shen decided that he could not defeat the government army and so made up his mind to rely on the guarantees he had elicited from the local officials. He obeyed Lin's order and submitted to arrest along with several of his loyal followers. . . . Between 500 and 600 people were arrested and sent to Yung-ch'ang for trial. More than 200 people were condemned to death, and 200 to 300 people were sentenced to military exile on the frontier.

Lin Tse-hsü asked Shen Ying, "How could you dare kill so many people?"

Shen presented four of the oaths in which the civil and military leaders had supported him and said, "I was only carrying out the orders of the civil and military officials."

Lin replied, "You are only an ordinary citizen, and yet you presumed to act as executioner for so many Moslems. The civil and military officials have already been dismissed from their offices. Do you really expect your life to be spared?"

Lin then gave the order for Shen to be beheaded. Of the 3000-odd Moslems of Pao-shan, those who had not been killed were ordered to sell their property to the Han Chinese at a minimal price and move to Kuan-nai-shan on the west bank of the Lu River, a miasmic place. Only the very timid Moslems consented to move out there; those with any sort of backbone refused to go. They murmured, "The government will drive us to our deaths if they force us to move to such a noxious place." They therefore dispersed in every direction. It is hard to describe the tragedy of those who were homeless and wandered around from place to place without any shelter. Hunger and cold forced some into banditry. This made the Chinese all the more inclined to kill Moslems. . . .

The Moslems could not tell from moment to moment whether they would be killed by the Han Chinese. They had no place to live. They were threatened and harassed by the Yunnan province officials. Under these circumstances they saw little

alternative to a death struggle with the Han Chinese. . . .

In 1856 Tu Wen-hsiu rose up in rebellion and occupied Ta-li. The Moslems elected him as their Grand Marshal. . . . Gradually he gained control of I-hsi prefecture. Tu maintained, "The conflict between the Han Chinese and the Moslems began over trifles. It has developed into a tragedy of mutual bloodletting because of poor management by the civil and military officials at Yung-ch'ang county and of Yunnan province. As a result, the mutual killing spread throughout Yunnan. The fault lies not with the people but with the officials." Tu thus proclaimed that he would launch a revolution. He wanted to bring Moslems and Han Chinese together to fight against the Manchus and reestablish a native Chinese empire.

A proclamation said: "I hate the evil officials who decided to support the Han Chinese in exterminating the Moslems. As a result, the people cannot survive because they are killing each other. I will uphold righteousness and unify the Han Chinese and Moslems. I will hold high the flag of righteousness, expel the Manchu barbarians, reestablish the Chinese empire, eradicate corruption, and save the people from lives of hardship.". . .

After this declaration of revolution, Tu treated the Han Chinese well. They could live in safety and engage in their businesses peacefully. Han Chinese scholars and degree holders were appointed to office to assist Tu in civil and military affairs. They changed some of the Ch'ing customs, reintroducing Ming clothing and hair styles. This clearly implied that Tu wanted to revive the ethnic Chinese empire. In I-hsi a group of over 300 Chinese gentry presented him with a wooden tablet. On it were inscribed the words of praise: "The man who will unify the nation." They also sent him some couplets whose words have now been forgotten. That Tu Wen-hsiu did have revolutionary ideals and that he was somewhat successful in unifying the people are indicated by the fact that he was able to resist the Manchus for eighteen years. To his misfortune, he did not appoint his officials properly, and there was great disharmony among his generals. He never captured the capital of Yunnan and his kingdom collapsed after eighteen years.

The Han Chinese had never forgotten the conflicts with the Moslems. They supported Tu's kingdom when it was strong, but they deserted it when it declined. . . . Furthermore, many of Tu's subordinates were rude and even harassed the people, so the Han Chinese came to dislike him and the Moslems. Such words as "rebellion" and "Moslem traitors" appeared in the histories and biographies. None said that Tu launched a revolution. From this one can see that rude and impudent behavior can cost dearly. Indeed, later generations of Moslems must remember this lesson and should not rely on their fierceness and energy alone to get things done. Otherwise, it will be too late to repent mistakes when disaster has been brought down upon the Moslem clans and offspring.

The above description was based on what I heard when I was young from older Han Chinese who lived in Pao-shan and witnessed what had happened. I have recorded it to admonish posterity.

Translated by Jeh-hang Lai

57.

The Conditions and Activities of Workers

With the development of commerce and industry came the appearance not only of prosperous merchants and manufacturers, but also their employees. Little is known of the lives or social conditions of these people, since they ordinarily did not write. There are, however, occasional descriptions of what they were not supposed to do. For instance, independent craftsmen and merchants had long formed guilds, which set standards and prices and provided welfare benefits, but workers were normally discouraged or prohibited from forming such associations. The first selection below is an example of a prohibition against organizing by workers which was carved in stone and preserved in the textile manufacturers' guildhall in Su-chou.

Further evidence of the lives of workers can be found in official reports of cases in which workers were particularly ill treated. The description of the condition of the miners in Hunan given below falls into this category. In this case, after receiving the report, the central government approved the provincial government decision to enact a special law severely punishing owners and foremen who captured, enslaved, or killed workers.

PERMANENT PROHIBITIONS OFFICIALLY ENGRAVED ON STONE

This bulletin is issued jointly by the three county Magistrates (with ten promotions and ten commendations) of the prefecture of Su-chou in Chiang-nan: Magistrate Ch'en of Yüan-ho county, Magistrate Wu of Ch'ang-chou county, and Magistrate Wang of Wu county. The matter concerned is as follows:

In the spring of 1870, Shen Yu-shan, Wang Ch'eng-chung, Sun Hung, Tai Mei-t'ing, Lü Chin-shan, Chu P'ei-ho, and others made a report to the Ch'ang-chou county government. They identified themselves as manufacturers of Sung-chin textiles and said that Ts'ao A-chuan, Ku T'ing, and other textile workers had formed a union and tried to coerce them to donate money on the pretext of making offerings to the patron gods of the trade. Some time later, Shen Yu-shan, et al., charged that Ts'ao A-chuan and his

gang had formed another trade union under a different name to threaten and disturb people in the profession. In both cases the former Magistrate of Ch'ang-chou issued prohibitions against such organizations.

Nevertheless, in the eighth month of this year, Lü Chin-shan, Ning Chin-shan, Shen Yu-shan, and Wang Ch'eng-chung again reported that, although Ts'ao A-chuan had died, a certain Wang P'ei had taken his place and gathered a gang to create disturbances. Threatening to strike, they pasted posters all over town urging negotiation for wages, selected auspicious dates to present offerings to the patron gods, and extorted contributions from people in the business for that purpose. Our former Magistrate, Wan, once more sternly prohibited such actions.

When the current Magistrate came to office, Lü Chin-shan, Jen Chin-shan, Wang Jen-chung, and Shen Yu-shan reported to him that Wang P'ei, Jen

Fu, Chou Hung, Ku T'ing, Wu Szu-shou and others were still blackmailing and disturbing the people. They asked that the culprits be prosecuted and petitioned for a permanent injunction against such activities to be engraved on stone tablets. After the hearing, the Magistrate punished Wang P'ei and obtained his written promise never again to start trade unions, set trade regulations, or collect money on any pretext. The Magistrate also granted the request for a tablet permanently prohibiting such activities.

The petition of Lu Chin-shan, *et al.*, further stated:

> The people in the Sung-chin textile business are scattered in our two neighboring counties, Wu and Yüan-ho, and so are Wang P'ei's followers. Consequently, we consider it necessary for tablets of prohibition to be erected in all three counties. We beg our Magistrate to ask the Magistrates of Yüan-ho and Wu counties to cooperate, so that the troublemakers will never dare to break your rulings, and we of the textile profession need never again trouble you with such complaints.

Besides granting the petition and the request for prohibition tablets, we Magistrates now exonerate all those in the Sung-chin textile profession. You should make note of the fact that the organization of trade unions has long been prohibited. From now on, if Wang P'ei or any of his men dare to violate the law and attempt to form unions or guilds to put pressure on fellow workers, it should be reported to the government so that we can prosecute them. Let it be known that we will not be lenient toward violators of this ruling. Be advised and abide by the law.

Special bulletin issued on the 19th day of the eleventh month of 1878.

Translated by Clara Yu

INVESTIGATION REPORT

The Magistrate's report stated:

The southeast portion of Lei-yang county is rich in coal, which has attracted many entrepreneurs. Hundreds of coal pits of various sizes have been exploited for a long time, so that by now the coal veins lie under water which must be removed before mining can be started. To manage the water pumps, the mine owners hired foremen, known as "Water Men."

To fill this post they usually picked the worst elements of the local population, men who are extremely violent and wicked. These men, allied with local gangsters, have formed a Blue Dragon Society and accumulated huge amounts of money. To trap poor people, they established gambling dens and sold opium; then they lent them money at usurious rates. Moreover, they colluded with wine shops and restaurants to raise their prices. Badly in debt, the poor people had no choice but to sell themselves to the mine. They would also sometimes capture travelers passing through and force them to work in the mine.

The foremen built near the pit dark, damp earthen cubicles which had only a single opening. Surrounded by stockades, both the entrance and exit of these cubicles were controlled by the foremen. These were known as "Sealed Drums." People lured, bought, tricked, or kidnapped were all incarcerated in such "Drums," and were called "Water Toads." Their clothes and shoes were stripped off, and they were forced to work manning the water pumps in alternating shifts day and night without respite. No consideration was given to their hunger and cold. Those who looked tired had their backs whipped, and those who attempted to escape had their feet slashed. Moreover, because it is freezing in the pits and the work is extremely heavy, the weaker miners usually died within a fortnight, and the stronger ones suffered from rotten legs and swollen bellies within a couple of months. Without rest and medication, they perished helplessly. What was most pitiful was that those "Water Toads" who survived were still kept in the "Drums" during the spring suspension in order to be used as water pumpers again the next season. They were called "Pension Rice."

This situation was kept hidden from the outside world. The dozens or hundreds of "Water Toads" who died at each mine every year were buried in the caves nearby. Not even their relatives were informed of their deaths. The local officials have strictly and repeatedly prohibited such practices. However, these mine owners and the "Water Men" used artful excuses to get around the law. Now we have summoned the mine owners for inquiries and have informed them of the permanent prohibition against "Water Men," "Water Toads," "Sealed Drums," and "Pension Rice," and we have received their guarantees which have been filed as documents. In addition, we are investigating secretly and carefully. If there are any more cases like these, they shall be severely prosecuted. And if there are any allied gangsters, runners, or any officials who conceal the crimes, they shall be severely punished too. We have prepared a draft regulation concerning the situation and are now presenting it to you. Please examine it and draw up a memorial.

Translated by Jane Chen

58.

Marriage Contracts

A majority of marriages undoubtedly fitted the standard model: the wife and husband came from families of nearly equal status; their families exchanged gifts of relatively similar value; the wife moved in with the husband's family; any children she bore belonged to the husband's family and took their name. Nevertheless, exceptions could and did occur, most commonly among the poor. A family with no sons could bring a son-in-law into its house either to be the heir or at least to father an heir for the family in the next generation. When a family could not afford to raise a daughter, it could give her out as a "child-bride" to be raised in the house of her future husband, whose family stood to gain because it did not have to provide any wedding presents. Families could also sell their daughters as concubines, thereby losing any ordinary kinship rights over them. Many other variations were also possible.

Since all marriages, and especially nonstandard ones, were in part financial transactions, agreements were regularly drawn up to prevent later disputes. Below are given three late-nineteenth-century marriage contracts written for commoners in Taiwan, then a part of Fukien province.

1

This "getting a husband to support a husband" contract is drawn up for and signed by Wang Yün-fa.

Years ago, I married Li San's daughter, Li Hsiu-liang, who is now twenty years old. We have lived together for four years. Hsiu-liang is very filial to my parents and she takes care of the household without creating trouble or stirring up quarrels. It makes one very content to have such a good wife.

Unfortunately, some time ago I contracted a disease and have become paralyzed. We are poor and have no source of income to meet our expenses. Although at the present time we are not starving, we have considered the fact that the most unfilial thing one can do is not to have heirs. When my wife's youth expires, it will be impossible to have a son. After long discussions, we have decided that there is no other alternative: if we insist that Hsiu-liang be faithful to me, the whole family will be without support. The only solution is to "get a husband to support a husband." We have, therefore, consulted a matchmaker, and it has been arranged for Hsiu-liang to be married to Wu Chiu-sheng's first-born son, Wu Chin-wen, who will come to live with us. We have, on this day, agreed that there will be no betrothal presents, but that Wu Chin-wen should provide the family with twenty dollars a month to help with expenses. Regardless of how many sons and grandsons Wu and Hsiu-liang may have, they will be heirs to the Wang family as well as to the Wu family.

This document is written evidence of the irrevocable agreement reached by both parties.

Signed, Wang Yün-fa, in the third month of 1869
Preparer of document: Cheng Ju-shui
Matchmaker: Mrs. Ch'en (nee Hsü)
Witnesses: Wang Chin-fa and Wang T'ien-fu

2

This marriage contract is jointly signed by Wu Kao and Liu Tsao.

Wu Kao and his wife (whose maiden name is Ch'en) have a daughter by the name of Wu Mein-niang. She is twenty-two years old. (The exact time of her birth was not recorded, and therefore her combination of the stems and the branches is not known.)* Since their daughter did not marry when she first reached adulthood, Wu Kao and his wife have now decided to find her a husband who would become a member of the Wu family, and thereby continue the family line. They are very happy to have been advised that Liu Tsao's twenty-one-year-old nephew, Ch'en Hsiang-kuan, is an honest man and a good match for their daughter. The three parties have agreed that there will be no betrothal presents. An auspicious day will be selected for Ch'en Hsiang-kuan to come to the Wu family to be married. Later, when they have sons, Ch'en must select one—it does not matter which—as the heir of the Wu family. If they should have only one son, then he should be made heir to both the Wu and the Ch'en families. An agreement has been reached by all parties in person that Ch'en Hsiang-kuan should stay at Wu Kao's house for eight years. At the end of this period, if Ch'en and his wife would like to move out and start their own household, Wu Kao should provide them with twenty silver dollars as capital for a business. However, Ch'en Hsiang-kuan from then on will take on the responsibility for continuing the worship of the guardian spirits and ancestral tablets of the Wu family. If, before the end of the agreed term, Ch'en should desire to move out, he should help support Wu Kao and his wife by giving them thirty silver dollars; he would also, as heir to the Wu family, be responsible for the worship of the guardian spirits and ancestral tablets. In any case, should Ch'en Hsiang-kuan ever become distinguished for any reason, his sons—the heirs to the Wu family as well as those of the Ch'ens—should share the titles and the benefits. On the other hand, Ch'en Hsiang-kuan has no claim whatsoever to the meager estate of the Wu family.

This document is drawn up in two copies, each to be held by one of the two contracting parties, as evidence of the union of the two families through the happy marriage.

Signed, Wu Kao and Liu Tsao, in the first month of 1881
Preparer of document: Chang Yün-hsi
Matchmakers: Liu Hai
Chang Ch'an
Witness: (wife of Wu Kao) Ch'en

3

This document is drawn up for and signed by Lin Yu-chang.

My wife (whose maiden name is Ch'en) and I have a first-born daughter by the name of Wang-lien, who is now fifteen years old. Although she is of age, we have not yet promised her to anyone. Pressed by extreme poverty, we now wish to give her away to become a concubine.

We have entrusted the matter to a matchmaker, and it has been arranged that she should become the concubine of Wu Min-kuan. The two parties and the matchmaker have discussed the matter and agreed on the price of 200 silver dollars. The money has been received in full by me, Lin Yu-chang, and the matchmaker. Now Wu Min-kuan is free to select an auspicious day for the marriage. I hereby swear that this girl is the first-born daughter of me and my wife; that she has not been engaged to anyone else; and that she is not a kidnapped child or of suspicious origin. If any question concerning the girl's birth should arise, I am solely responsible, and the buyer will not be involved. I sincerely hope my daughter will give birth to many sons for the Wu family. Once she is sold, all her ties with me are cut.

This written evidence of the sale is to be kept by the buyer for later purposes.

It is clearly recorded here that, on this day, Lin Yu-chang and the matchmaker have personally received in full 200 silver dollars.

Signed, the father of the girl, Lin Yu-chang
in the twelfth month of 1886
Preparer of document: Ts'ai Wen-ping
Matchmaker: K'ang A-hsiu
Witness: (the girl's mother) Ch'en

Translated by Clara Yu

---

* Hours, days, and years were all specified by combinations of the ten "stems" and twelve "branches." The particular combination at the moment of one's birth was believed to have an effect on one's fortune, and so in arranging marriages a fortuneteller would compare the combinations for the prospective mates.

59.

Genealogy Rules

To facilitate ancestor worship and a general reverence for forebears, from at least the Han dynasty men kept records of their ancestors' names, dates, and accomplishments. In the later dynasties more detailed genealogies came to be needed by lineages that owned property or had other privileges to confer on their members; such lineages had to have accurate lists of their current membership and the kinship relationships among them. Thus the flourishing of large lineages in the Ming and Ch'ing dynasties led to the compilations of huge genealogies listing thousands of past and present lineage members.

Below are the rules established by the Liu lineage of Wan-t'ung in Anhui for the compilation of their genealogy. This list was included in the preface to the genealogy they published in 1870. Principles of family and lineage composition are carefully set down in these rules, which also explain which activities and accomplishments most enhance family honor and therefore deserve recognition in the genealogy.

PRINCIPLES OF THE GENEALOGY

1. Our genealogy combines the methods of Ou-yang Hsiu and Su Shih,* and uses charts together with biographical accounts. Its chief aim is to provide concise and clear facts about our family lineage. Lengthy details of specific cases will be given in other records.

2. The illustration of the family tree begins with our first ancestor; the first section lists the five generations from him to his great-great-grandson, the next section lists the next five generations, and then the next five generations, and so on. Thus, starting from the outer branches, one can trace the ultimate origin of one's heritage; starting at the beginning, one can survey the development of the branches.

3. In each section of five generations, the branches and households are listed in order, beginning with the

eldest son. First are listed the descendants of the oldest son, then those of the second son—that is, the second branch—and so on. In this way, the record has a clear outline and will not become confusing because of too many details given at once. This method is followed through the branches and subbranches.

4. Compiling a genealogy is different from writing history. History is written to distinguish good governments from bad ones, and to set down rules and models for later generations; therefore, it should include both good deeds and bad ones. In compiling a genealogy, the purpose is to clarify the ancestry and development of a lineage and to deepen its virtuous and righteous tradition; therefore only good deeds are recorded.

5. Our genealogy, following the example of historical writings and our family regulations handed down from the Han and T'ang dynasties, records each family member's name, polite name, order of birth,

* Two Northern Sung statesmen and writers credited with creating the standard model for genealogies used during the later dynasties.

studio name, birth date, age attained, and the location and direction of his tomb. Those who are buried in one grave are recorded as "buried together."

6. If a living lineage member's name is offensive because it contains the same word as an elder member's name, he should change it. If he is dead, then when his name is recorded in the genealogy, another word with a similar pronounciation is substituted.*

7. If a member of the lineage passed a civil service examination, or was a student of the county, province, or capital colleges, or was a local elder, these facts are recorded under his name in the lineage chart. If he became an official, his title is recorded so as to make known his achievements.

8. In order to extend our respect to the families to which we are related, a wife whose father was an official is designated as "daughter of official so-and-so." If her father did not hold an office, yet was virtuous and lived to an old age, she is described as "daughter of retired scholar so-and-so." In all other cases, I simply record, "daughter of so-and-so."

9. A daughter whose name is listed in her father's biography is designated as "married (or betrothed) to so-and-so," to make clear her own family. If her husband or her sons achieve distinction of which our family can be proud, their titles of office are recorded.

10. An adopted heir who is the son of a member of our own lineage is listed under his natural father, with a note saying that he has been adopted by so-and-so. Under his adoptive father's name, it is recorded that a second, third, or fourth son of so-and-so has been adopted into this household, and that the first son of this adopted heir cannot be given in adoption to any other household. Following the established rules, those lineage members whose order of births have become confused are not listed in this genealogy. Those who become adopted heirs of families of a different surname from ours have the fact noted under their names in order to make it possible for them to resume their original name and return to our lineage.

11. The genealogy is designed to pass on the true lines of descent as well as to eliminate its false seeds.

* Avoidance of the personal names of immediate forebears was an old custom dating back to antiquity.

All persons of a different last name from ours, including stepsons who follow their mothers into our family, are not allowed to be heirs because they are not of the same flesh and blood. Thus there are specific prohibitions against such successions. If these are not strictly observed, the purity in our family heritage will be in jeopardy and the true purpose of compiling this genealogy will be defeated. That is the reason for the following rules. Anyone who adopts a son of a different surname from ours and thereby tinges the purity of our lineage will be dealt sixty blows of the staff. Anyone who allows his son to be adopted by a family of a different surname receives the same punishment. So does anyone who, in adopting an heir from our own family, causes confusion in the order of births. Such an adopted son should then be returned to his natural father, and another heir should be chosen in his place.

12. A wife who, after her husband's death, marries again, or a wife who has been divorced by her husband, is not mentioned in her husband's biography, even though she has borne him children. This is because the relationship between the husband and the wife was terminated. Under the sons' names, however, it is mentioned that their mother was so-and-so who remarried or was divorced, since a son cannot cut his tie with his mother. Should the wife, after having remarried or having been divorced, return to the care of her sons, the record still remains the same, because the relationship cannot be restored.

13. A legal wife who died early without bearing children is recorded in the genealogy, but concubines without children are not mentioned. This is to retain the distinction between their ranks and their degrees of respectability.

14. The concubines are not in reality all the same. Those who are married with proper ceremonies are recorded as being "married," whereas those who are not are designated as being "taken in."

15. A young son of the legal wife precedes an older son of a concubine when they are listed in the biography of their father. This is to uphold the legitimate succession. In the lineage chart, however, all sons are ordered according to their age.

16. Biographies and eulogies are designed to relate facts and to praise virtue and distinction. Regardless of whether he had held an office or not, as long as a

man possessed such virtues as loyalty, filial piety, integrity, or righteousness, and could be a model for his descendants, a biographical sketch is written in praise of him. Whether a woman was a legal wife or a mere concubine, her virtues of chastity, filial piety, and other womanly good deeds are included in the biography of her husband. A daughter's good deeds are also included in the biography of her father. All in all, the biographies should be truthful but inspiring. Those who did not live to fifty years of age are not entitled to a eulogy, only a biography.

17. The names of the male members of the family who indulged in sorcery, Buddhism, Taoism, debauchery, larceny, who misappropriated or sold parts of the family cemetery, or who married indiscriminately are taken off the family genealogy.

18. All the decrees of commendation and bestowment of titles from the Emperors to members of our lineage are respectfully copied and recorded in this genealogy. This is not only to show respect for the Emperors, but also to inspire later generations.

19. All the writings by friends and relatives about late members of our family such as prefaces, inscriptions, anecdotes, biographies, elegies, poems or essays, including those recorded before and those written by renowned writers, are reproduced as models for our lineage.

20. Those writings, notes, poems, and essays written by our ancestors that have withstood the test of time are reproduced in memory of their literary achievements.

21. As the graves contain the body and the physical essence of our ancestors, they should be guarded by our descendants through all ages. In this genealogy, no drawings are made of these gravesites, but in the individual biographies, records of the location and direction of each tomb are kept, so that our descendants will be able to consult them and locate the tombs.

22. The decorum of language in this genealogy is as follows: those who were in office and virtuous, "passed away"; ordinary people "are no longer"; those whose date and place of death are unknown are marked "record lost"; those who had no children are described as "line stopped" instead of "terminated" to show compassion; those who had daughters only are

said to have "no heir," because, although the line has stopped, the family's essence remains.* Male members who died within three months of their births are not included in the category of "early death"; those who died before their eighth year are included in the category, but there is no mourning for them; therefore, these are not recorded in the genealogy. Those who died between eight and eleven years of age are designated by "lower early death," between twelve and fifteen, "middle early death," between sixteen and nineteen, "upper early death." All these three types are recorded in their fathers' biographies. Those who died after their twentieth birthday are all entitled to their own biographical sketches, for they are considered adults. If these members had no sons, they are only listed in the charts, and after five generations, the record stops, because there is no one to continue their lines. Female members who died before they were betrothed are not mentioned in this genealogy, for they did not become wives. For the same reason, women who were betrothed to members of our lineage yet died before the marriage ceremony could take place are not listed in our family genealogy.

23. When lineage descendants move to another part of the country and settle down there, in their biographies such information is given in detail, so that they can be traced over many generations.

24. The ancestral temple is where the spirits of our ancestors stay; it is also where ancestral rites are performed by our descendants. It is important, therefore, to record the buildings, including the shrine in front, the rooms in the rear and the surrounding buildings, as well as the land, which is measured on all four sides and recorded in detail.

25. No one should take a family with the same surname as ours for a branch of our family, regardless of its wealth or power. This is essential in preserving the purity of our lineage.

26. A list of the eldest sons in the primary line of the lineage and a list of our family regulations are appended in this genealogy.

Translated by Clara Yu

---

* Euphemisms for death were also used by historians, who had special terms for Emperors, Princes, officials, and so on.

60.

Families and Lineages of Yen-yüan County

While gross population statistics for large geographical areas survive from as early as the Han, detailed breakdowns of the population, showing the division into villages, lineages, and so on, are very rare. One exception is a list of the population of Yen-yüan county (in the province of Chekiang) derived from a survey made in 1901 and published in the local gazetteer.

Yen-yüan was a relatively hilly area with over 25,000 mou of cultivated land. It had 169 independent and 22 subordinate villages and a population of over 40,000 people in 9,000 households (of which 148 were gentry households, the rest being farmers, artisans, merchants, temporary residents, or entertainers). The proportion of men to women in this county was high, 22,470 men to 17,957 women, probably reflecting a high rate of female infanticide in the preceding several decades. The villages varied greatly in the presence of large lineages. Of villages with more than ten households, thirty-nine were single-lineage villages. Many other villages had two, three, or four large lineages. In quite a few cases a lineage was settled in several areas with members living in a number of different villages. The three sections of this list translated below were chosen to reveal this variability in village lineage composition.

Sha-t'i (south-east): The name of the place is recorded in the local gazetteers of the K'ang-hsi [1662–1722] and Ch'ien-lung [1736–1795] periods. It is contiguous with the villages Shang-shan, Hu-hsiang, and Ch'uan-lei of Ch'in-hsiao. Its inhabitants include the following:

The Fan lineage. Its first ancestor, Fan Liang-chung, was an Imperial Inspector of the Northern Sung dynasty, and moved from Weng-chou to Sha-t'i (according to the *Pen-t'ang chi*). The lineage has lived here for twenty-eight generations. There are 3 scholar's households, with 1 student who succeeded in a civil examination, and 3 young students. In addition, there are 299 households of the Fan clan, with 571 male members and 459 female members.

The Shans moved here from T'ing-hsia. Altogether there are 7 households, with 13 males and 16 females.

The Chous moved here from Shun-t'ien prefecture. One household, 3 males and 1 female.

The Ch'ens moved here from San-shih, 2 households, 6 males and 6 females.

The Chaos moved here from San-shih, and belong to the Szu-mei branch of the Chao clan. Two households, 4 males and 4 females.

One pleasure house, whose head is named Ch'ou, with 5 members.

Hsiao-ch'ien-ao: 5 to 10 *li* from the village of Kung-t'ang. From here a mountain stream meanders through Kan-hsi, Hu-chien, and Shan-lei. On the east side Hsiao-ch'ien-ao touches the village of Lien-shan, on the north side it is contiguous with Ch'in-hsiao. Its inhabitants include:

The Fengs, 6 households, with 12 males and 13 female members.
The Chiangs, 5 households, with 14 male and 12 female members.
The Ts'aos, 2 households, 5 males and 1 female.
The Juans, 1 household, 1 male, 3 females.
The Chengs, 1 household, 1 male and 1 female.
The Wus, 1 household, 5 males and 3 females.
The K'angs, 1 household, 3 males and 3 females.
The Sungs, 2 households, 7 males and 5 females.
The Yüs, 1 household, 3 males and 2 females.
The Fans, 2 households, 6 males and 3 females.
The Chus, 3 households, 13 males and 11 females.
The Tings, 1 household, 1 male and 1 female.
The T'angs, 5 households, 16 males and 13 females.
The Chiangs, 2 households. One is a scholar's household, with one young student, the other has 5 male members and 3 female members.
The Changs, 4 households, 8 males and 5 females.

🔲🔲🔲

Shih-men (south-west): Shih-men is situated at the foot of the Ta-lei Mountain, its inhabitants include:

The Mao lineage, which moved here from the village of Shih-men in Chiang-shan county of Ch'u in the last years of the T'ang dynasty, following Jen Ch'ing-yüan. Hence the name of this village. Among the Maos, there are 8 scholar's households, with 7 state-supported students who succeeded in a civil examination and 6 young students. The rest of the 350 households have 818 male members and 790 female members.
The K'angs, who moved here from K'ang-ling. One household, with 4 male members and 3 female members.
Six pleasure houses with 19 members.

Chin-chu-t'ien: 4 *li* from Shih-men. Its inhabitants are all Maos. There is 1 scholar's household with 1 student who has passed a civil examination. The rest of the 56 households have 136 male members and 112 female members.
Shui-t'ang-wan: 5 *li* from Shih-men. All its in-

habitants are Maos. One scholar's household with 1 student who has passed a civil examination. The rest of the 21 households have 69 male members and 50 female members.
Pien-tan-ling: 4 *li* from Shih-men. All inhabitants are Maos; 18 households with 40 males and 35 females.
Chu-p'ing: 4 *li* from Shih-men. All inhabitants are Maos; 16 households, with 45 males and 26 females.
Sun-chia-shan: 5 *li* from Shih-men. There are 16 households of Maos, including 50 males and 37 females. The Yüans have 3 households, with 8 male and 6 female members. The Yüan family moved here from Yüan-chia-ao.
T'ien-wan: 2 *li* from Shih-men. All are Maos; 13 households with 25 males and 24 females.
Kao-k'eng: 4 *li* from Shih-men. All are Maos; 7 households with 13 males and 12 females.
Shen-lo-k'eng: 5 *li* from Shih-men. All are Maos; 6 households with 13 males and 11 females.
Shih-ling: 5 *li* from Shih-men. All are Maos; 29 households with 46 males and 35 females.
Ta-k'eng: 6 *li* from Shih-men. All are Maos; 18 households with 63 males and 28 females.

All members of the Mao lineage in this section are of its Shih-men branch.

Yen-t'ou (south-east): The name Yen-t'ou did not exist in ancient times. It only became known since early Ming dynasty. First, some members of the Mao lineage moved from Shih-men to Yang-shu, then in 1370 they moved to this location. Now Yen-t'ou has 21 scholar's households, including 2 scholars recommended by the local government, 9 state-supported students, 3 licentiates of the provincial examination, 2 students of rites, and 16 young students. The rest of the 506 households have 1331 male members and 981 female members. In addition, there are 4 pleasure houses with 18 members.
Mao-k'eng (west): 3 *li* from Yen-t'ou. All inhabitants are Maos; 11 households with 31 male members and 32 female members.
Hsü-chia-ch'i (west): 4 *li* from Yen-t'ou. All are Maos. There is 1 scholar's household with one young student; the rest of the 16 households have 50 male members and 46 female members.
Tung-k'eng (north-west): 8 *li* from Yen-t'ou. All are Maos; 18 households with 68 males and 55 females.
Pai-ni-k'eng (west): 10 *li* from Yen-t'ou. All are Maos; 4 households with 10 males and 9 females.

Mao-p'ing (west): 12 *li* from Yen-t'ou. All are Maos; 9 households with 22 males and 18 females.

Hsia-feng-lei (west): 13 *li* from Yen-t'ou. All are Maos; 10 households with 22 males and 15 females.

Tung-chia-p'ing (north): 5 *li* from Yen-t'ou. All are Maos; 16 households with 56 males and 45 females.

T'a-li-k'eng (north): 8 *li* from Yen-t'ou. All are Maos; 10 households with 22 males and 23 females.

Chieh-ling (north-east): so named because the southern part of the mountain ridge (ling) borders (chieh) the Lien-shan district. All inhabitants are Maos; 56 households with 161 males and 112 females.

Han-feng-ling (north): the real border, 5 *li* from the Chieh-ling village. All are Maos; 3 households with 7 males and 5 females.

Pai-shih (north): 10 *li* from Yen-t'ou. All are Maos; 6 households with 22 males and 12 females.

Ta-ao (west): 7 *li* from Yen-t'ou. All are Maos; 23 households with 50 males and 25 females.

Ta-ch'iu-t'ien (east): 13 *li* from Yen-t'ou. All in-habitants are Maos; 8 households with 17 males and 9 females.

Ta-shui-k'eng (north-east): 15 *li* from Yen-t'ou. All are Maos; 43 households with 164 males and 112 females.

T'ieh-shan (north-east): 14 *li* from Yen-t'ou. All are Maos; 12 households with 36 males and 20 females.

Yu-mao-ao (east): 5 *li* from Yen-t'ou. All are Maos; 16 households with 53 males and 36 females.

T'ao-wan (east): 7 *li* from Yen-t'ou. All are Maos; 3 households with 10 males and 6 females.

T'ien-chi-shan (east): 12 *li* from Yen-t'ou. All are Maos; 17 households with 49 males and 27 females.

Ma-luan-fan (north): 16 *li* from Yen-t'ou. All are Maos; 10 households with 25 males and 12 females.

All the members of the Mao lineage in this section are of its Yen-t'ou branch.

Translated by Clara Yu

Part Seven

THE EARLY TWENTIETH CENTURY

Efforts to reform the Ch'ing government and make it strong enough to withstand the foreign threat had begun by the 1860s. Yet hopes for reform faded with China's defeat by the Japanese in 1895 and her humiliation by joint Western and Japanese forces in the wake of the Boxer Rebellion of 1900. Untraditional forms of protest, agitation, and military action were begun by small groups of revolutionaries, the most famous of which was associated with Sun Yat-sen (Sun Chung-shan, 1866–1925). Finally in 1911 a military uprising succeeded, and the last Manchu Emperor agreed to abdicate in early 1912. The decades from then until the founding of the People's Republic of China in 1949 are referred to as the Republican period because monarchy was now repudiated and the Western theory of constitutional republican government was honored, if seldom actually practiced.

Social and political disorder marked most of this period. For a few years the new government unsuccessfully attempted to consolidate its power. Then, from 1916 to 1927 China was politically fragmented with warlords and cliques of warlords ruling their own provinces or regions. In 1926–27 Chiang Kai-shek (1888–1975), the leader of the Nationalist Party, launched a "Northern Expedition," defeating some warlords and making alliances with others. He then established a Nationalist government, which lasted until 1949 (and subsequently on the island of Taiwan). The years from 1927 to 1949, however, were almost as turbulent as those before. Not only were a number of warlords still largely independent, but the Communist Party had control of parts of the country, and after 1931 the Japanese steadily encroached on Chinese territory. From 1937 to 1945 China and Japan were engaged in full-scale war.

The early twentieth century was nevertheless a time

of intense intellectual excitement and rapid social and economic change. The old order based on Confucian ideas was torn apart. The classically educated gentry lost their social position with the abolition of the civil service examinations and the collapse of the monarchy. Modern universities, started in the last years of the Ch'ing, began to produce a new type of intellectual who was deeply concerned with China's fate and attracted to Western ideas ranging from science and democracy to communism and anarchism. Many young people went abroad to study in Japan, Europe, or America. On May 4, 1919, college students and their supporters protested Japan's imperialist advances and their own government's weakness, arousing in the process the patriotic and reformist spirit of a generation of young people. These "May Fourth" intellectuals called for reforms in the family system, the government, and the distribution of economic and political power. Scholars now began to doubt the validity of established views of Chinese history and began studying subjects such as class struggles, power politics, and folklore. Writers imitated Western forms of poetry and fiction and started writing in the vernacular rather than the classical language that had formerly been the mark of the educated man. Widely circulated periodicals brought this new language and these new ideas to literate people throughout the country.

During the early twentieth century, Western-style, capitalist enterprises began to make headway within the Chinese economy. The disruption of the European economy caused by World War I proved especially advantageous to China. A few cities, especially Shanghai, Canton, Tientsin, and Hankow, developed into industrial centers where thousands of people were employed in factories. One of the highest priorities of the Nationalist government was to strengthen the economy, and it undertook measures to modernize the banking, currency, and taxation systems, as well as to improve transportation and communication facilities. Another result of industrialization, however, was union organization and strikes. The greatest of these strikes took place in Shanghai in 1925. Banks and schools closed, 150,000 people stayed away from work, and foreign goods were boycotted in protest against the killing and injuring of strikers by the foreign-controlled International Settlement police.

The development of a small, Westernized, urban elite and urban proletariat in some ways left China more fragmented than ever before, since the vast majority of the peasants remained tied to the countryside and traditional ways of earning a living. Illiterate peasants were little affected by new Western ideas communicated through classroom lectures, magazines, and translated books. Moreover, during the Republican period the standard of living in the countryside stagnated or declined because of the disruption and exploitation by warlords, international economic problems, and continued population growth. By 1930 the population of China had probably reached more than 500 million. The pressure on available land was intensified by the collapse of some local industries, such as silk-raising and cotton-weaving, due to foreign competition. The government and private philanthropic organizations made attempts to raise the level of rural education, create facilities for credit, encourage modern enterprises, form peasant associations, and so on, but gains were usually limited to small areas and short periods. Thus, the Nationalist government remained closely tied to the urban and Westernized sections of the population. At the same time the Communist Party, after 1935 under the leadership of Mao Tse-tung (1893–1976) and settled in Yenan in Northwest China, was concentrating on land reform and winning the support of the rural population.

In Part Seven, selections have been chosen for two reasons: some depict aspects of the major social transformations of this brief period; others provide new kinds of evidence on traditional aspects of Chinese culture and social organization. The early twentieth century saw many new types and forms of written communication. Newspapers and magazines published articles aimed at a broader audience than most previous writing. Western influence in literature led to greater psychological realism in fiction and attempts to portray emotions not previously probed in depth. At the same time there was an upsurge of interest in the lives of the less privileged. Men began to describe the plight of factory hands, slave girls, and tenant farmers with more sympathy than before. A semi-scholarly interest in folklore studies developed, leading to the recording of the habits and beliefs of elements of the population that educated men had hardly noticed before. Because of the abundance of these kinds of sources, many topics for which only indirect inferences could be made for earlier eras can now be examined in some depth and complexity.

Nevertheless, the writing of the Republican period must also be used with care. The authors of descriptions were more influenced by modern, Western ideas than those they were describing, creating a cultural gap between them and their subjects not totally unlike that between Westerners and Chinese (though naturally not as great). Moreover, the passions for reform and desire for change which motivated so much of the writing of the period gives even many descriptive pieces strongly polemical tones. Thus, many of these selections should be read on two levels: as depictions of the social conditions and way of life of those who still did not write much, and also as personal accounts expressing the concerns and values of the new intellectuals.

61.

The Movement Against Footbinding

Footbinding is believed to have originated during the Sung dynasty among the upper class. At the age of seven or eight a girl would have her feet tightly wrapped and slowly bent until the arch was broken, her toes turned under, and her feet only about half the normal size. A few scholars in the eighteenth century attacked this crippling practice, but it was not until 1895 that the first anti-footbinding society was established in Shanghai, concurrently with the establishment of a girl's school. Soon thereafter, branches of this society were formed in other major cities in the South. Activists in the society argued that the practice of footbinding was barbaric, devastating not only to the human body but also to the human mind. Even more alarming to them was the ultimate effect on the strength of the nation, since the pain a girl had to live with when her feet were bound was a tremendous obstacle to any attempt to educate her. To these early reformers, footbinding thus stood in the way of modernization.

This merging of nationalism and women's liberation is illustrated in the career of the early activist Ch'iu Chin (1875–1907). Ch'iu Chin came from a modest gentry family in the treaty port of Amoy. Given a good education along with her brothers and sisters, she did not marry until comparatively late at the age of twenty-one. In 1900 her husband acquired a post in Peking and she was introduced to the social world of the modern reformers. When Peking was occupied by Western troops after the Boxer Uprising in 1900, she became an ardent nationalist. In 1903 she left her husband to go to Japan to study. There much of her time was devoted to radical politics; she even dressed in men's clothing, carried a short sword, and learned to make bombs. In 1906 she returned to Shanghai and for a while taught in a nearby girls' school. The next year she was executed for her role in an abortive nationalist uprising.

Below are three sources showing distinct strands of the movement against footbinding, all dating from the initial decade of the twentieth century. The first is the rules formulated by one of many reform societies formed by local gentry and townsmen. The second is a letter written by an adolescent girl from a middle-class family to her sister. It was later published in a reform-oriented women's magazine. The third is an article written by the activist Ch'iu Chin for a similar magazine. Although these sources testify to the enthusiasm educated segments of the society had for ending footbinding and changing the position of women in the early years of the century, it should be pointed out that these ideas were to take decades to penetrate more deeply into Chinese society.

ANTI-FOOTBINDING SOCIETY OF HUNAN: RULES AND REGULATIONS ON MARRIAGE

1. The purpose of organizing this society is to provide opportunities for members to arrange marriages for their children so that girls who do not bind their feet will not become social outcasts. For this reason, society members must register the names and ages of all their children, and this information will be made available to all members in their selection of mates for their children.

2. Every member is entitled to make selections among the registered children. However, marriages

with nonmembers' families are allowed if the young ladies do not have bound feet.

3. In selecting mates for their children, members must observe strict compatibility of age and generation. Furthermore, no match can be made unless both families agree to it. No member is allowed to coerce, intimidate, or use any other forms of undesirable persuasion in arranging a marriage.

4. Since society members have come from all parts of Hunan province, marriages can be arranged between families situated very far apart. The society encourages men of vision and determination to willingly send their daughters to distant places to be married.

5. A matchmaker may be engaged to arrange the marriage contract. Local customs and rituals may be followed regarding the exchange of gifts. The society suggests that frugality and simplicity be observed by all members, regardless of how wealthy they are. Furthermore the bride's family is not allowed to demand wedding gifts from the groom.

6. Similarly, in preparing the bride's dowry, the society recommends frugality and simplicity. The groom's family should still observe all the courtesies and should not vent their dissatisfaction with the dowry by ill-treatment of the bride.

7. The marriage ceremony should be discarded because ancient rituals are no longer suitable for today. However, members are allowed to follow the commonly accepted rituals and ceremonies of the Ch'ing dynasty because sometimes, for the sake of expediency, we have to do what others do. However, the society recommends that members be guided by frugality and simplicity.

8. The clothing worn by members' daughters should conform with the accepted style. However, their footwear should conform to the style of their brothers. There should be no exceptions, because other styles of footwear may be shocking and offensive to other society members, thus injuring the girl's chances for marriage.

9. If people want to have worthy daughters, then they must promote women's education. If men want their wives to be worthy, then they must donate money to establish local women's schools. The size of the school is determined by the amount of the contribution. By helping other people's daughters learn, one

also helps one's own wife because only after women's education has been popularized can the foundations of a marriage be solid.

10. The above rules have been written one by one in a very simple and lucid style so they can be easily understood by everyone. If anyone feels he cannot follow any of them, he should not join the society. Furthermore, we urge all applicants to study these rules carefully to avoid future regrets.

A LETTER FROM CH'EN SHU-HSIEN TO CH'EN PAN-HSIEN

When I received your letter of the 13th, I wanted to write back to you immediately. However, something important came up on the following day, and since then I haven't had a free moment. I feel very guilty and ashamed for putting off writing back to you, but I am sure you won't be angry at me; perhaps when I tell you the reason for this delay, you will even be happy for me.

Well, it all started when I heard Shang Yu's speech denouncing footbinding. Afterwards, Eighth Sister and I decided to unbind ours. We told Father and he said that we could do it if we wanted to, but as he saw it, large feet will not be accepted by society as a whole, even though Shang Yu supports it. Furthermore, he said that large feet really aren't very attractive anyway. At the time I thought that, bound feet or no bound feet, I would have to stay in the house all the time anyway since there was no place to go. (I was in An-ch'ing at the time and all the women there had bound feet; besides, An-ch'ing did not have a woman's publication office nor did it have women's schools or organizations to promote women's education and freedom.) So, when I heard Father say that large feet are not very attractive, Eighth Sister and I decided to put it off for a while. Later (back home) I read an article in a women's newsletter published by Miss Chi-fen in which she urged all women to stop binding their feet. At the same time I also heard a speech delivered by Miss Chang Ching-hsien telling us that footbinding is contrary to the principles of Heaven and man and harmful to our country and our people. One by one she eloquently attacked the evils of footbinding. It was such a good speech that since that day I have not bound my feet very tightly. One reason is that the pain is so hard to live with; another is that, although I wasn't able to unbind them then, I hoped to be able to do so someday.

One day Sister Ch'a told me that she was going to attend a meeting at the Literary Society School with Wu Ya-nan and Wu Jo-nan and asked me to join them. At first I was reluctant because the girls at the Literary Society School are all well educated and very articulate on the subject of patriotism while I am not. Furthermore, my Mandarin is not fluent so I was afraid that I wouldn't understand anything that was said and I did not want to be embarrassed. Then it occurred to me that nowadays most educated people are passionately patriotic. If they saw that I was not a well-informed person, wouldn't they treat me sympathetically and instruct me? I decided to muster up some courage and go; if I could learn something new or gain a new insight into things, it would be very good for me indeed.

Thus, on Thursday I went with Sister Ch'a and met Jo-nan and Ya-nan and talked with them for a couple of hours. I was very impressed by them. They were most vocal and articulate against footbinding and I felt as if I had listened to a well-prepared lecture. I believe that Sister Ch'a has already written you all about that night so I need not elaborate upon it. When I went home that night I thought to myself that all the women there are so ambitious, planning to promote women's education and publish newspapers and magazines; some even said that after two more years of study, they are going to An-ch'ing to liberate all the women in our province. This experience left me both elated and ashamed. Chinese women have never considered themselves responsible citizens, and this has made China weak. I felt happy because today women like Miss K'ang, Miss Shih, Miss Ch'a Fan, Miss Ch'ing Ch'i, Miss Chu Chun, Miss Ch'ing-yun, Miss Chin-ch'ing, and Jo-nan, Ya-nan, and you have all vowed to rescue the 200 million Chinese women. We now have our own newspaper, and women's schools are being established one after another. I believe if we all work hard together, we will get our rights and enjoy freedom and equality. However, I was also ashamed of myself because all these years I have failed to acquire any knowledge and I am powerless to educate and influence illiterate and other unfortunate women. I have decided to unbind my own feet because I would be ashamed to go to meet anyone with these ugly bound feet. I discussed this matter with Eighth Sister, and we decided to unbind our feet now and in the fall to enroll in the Literary Society School.

This is what I have decided to do and I don't know whether Heaven will allow me to do it, but I intend to give it my best. Remember you told me once, "If there is a will, there is a way." I will try not to let you down.

You wrote that there are many things you wanted to tell me but you were afraid I'd take offense. You were wrong. If not, then you don't know what is in my heart. As stupid as I am, I still should know what's right and what's good for me, shouldn't I? You told me what has been happening and that everyone should pursue an education. These things are good for me; how can I but like hearing them? You are in school with a very busy schedule but you still took the time to write me. I am very grateful. You said in your letter that if you acted against the teachers' wishes, you would get punished. When I read that I was very angry. But I guess if we are to pursue knowledge, we must swallow our pride and anger, and when we graduate, they can no longer humiliate us. After you get this letter, if you don't have any time, don't worry about writing back to me. You can wait until you find time—I don't mind, really. Although I want you to write me often, I know you are in school every day and you must also write to other people. I would feel uncomfortable and guilty if you were to neglect your school work just to write to me. I still have many things to tell you, but I'll stop here and continue another time, for it's been too long since I got your last letter and you might be worried about me if you don't hear from me soon.

Your sister, Shu-hsien
5th day, fourth month, 1903

AN ADDRESS TO TWO HUNDRED MILLION FELLOW COUNTRYWOMEN

by Ch'iu Chin

Alas! The greatest injustice in this world must be the injustice suffered by our female population of two hundred million. If a girl is lucky enough to have a good father, then her childhood is at least tolerable. But if by chance her father is an ill-tempered and unreasonable man, he may curse her birth: "What rotten luck: another useless thing." Some men go as far as killing baby girls while most hold the opinion that "girls are eventually someone else's property" and treat them with coldness and disdain. In a few years, without thinking about whether it is right or wrong, he forcibly binds his daughter's soft, white feet with white cloth so that even in her sleep she cannot find comfort and relief until the flesh becomes rotten and the bones broken. What is all this misery for? Is it just so that on the girl's wedding day friends and neighbors will compliment him, saying, "Your daughter's feet are really small"? Is that what the pain is for?

But that is not the worst of it. When the time for marriage comes, a girl's future life is placed in the hands of a couple of shameless matchmakers and a family seeking rich and powerful in-laws. A match can be made without anyone ever inquiring whether the prospective bridegroom is honest, kind, or educated. On the day of the marriage the girl is forced into a red and green bridal sedan chair, and all this time she is not allowed to breathe one word about her future. After her marriage, if the man doesn't do her any harm, she is told that she should thank Heaven for her good fortune. But if the man is bad or he ill-treats her, she is told that her marriage is retribution for some sin committed in her previous existence. If she complains at all or tries to reason with her husband, he may get angry and beat her. When other people find out they will criticize, saying, "That woman is bad; she doesn't know how to behave like a wife." What can she do? When a man dies, his wife must mourn him for three years and never remarry. But if the woman dies, her husband only needs to tie his queue with blue thread. Some men consider this to be ugly and don't even do it. In some cases, three days after his wife's death, a man will go out for some "entertainment." Sometimes, before seven weeks have passed, a new bride has already arrived at the door. When Heaven created people it never intended such injustice because if the world is without women, how can men be born? Why is there no justice for women? We constantly hear men say, "The human mind is just and we must treat people with fairness and equality." Then why do they greet women like black slaves from Africa? How did inequality and injustice reach this state?

Dear sisters, you must know that you'll get nothing if you rely upon others. You must go out and get things for yourselves. In ancient times when decadent scholars came out with such nonsense as "men are exalted, women are lowly," "a virtuous woman is one without talent," and "the husband guides the wife," ambitious and spirited women should have organized and opposed them. When the second Ch'en ruler popularized footbinding, women should have challenged him if they had any sense of humiliation at all. . . . Men feared that if women were educated they would become superior to men, so they did not allow us to be educated. Couldn't the women have challenged the men and refused to submit? It seems clear now that it was we women who abandoned our responsibilities to ourselves and felt content to let men do everything for us. As long as we could live in comfort and leisure, we let men make all the decisions for us. When men said we were useless, we became useless; when they said we were incapable, we stopped questioning them even when our entire female sex had reached slave status. At the same time we were insecure in our good fortune and our physical comfort, so we did everything to please men. When we heard that men liked small feet, we immediately bound them just to please them, just to keep our free meal tickets. As for their forbidding us to read and write, well, that was only too good to be true. We readily agreed. Think about it, sisters, can anyone enjoy such comfort and leisure without forfeiting dearly for it? It was only natural that men, with their knowledge, wisdom, and hard work, received the right to freedom while we became their slaves. And as slaves, how can we escape repression? Whom can we blame but ourselves since we have brought this on ourselves? I feel very sad talking about this, yet I feel that there is no need for me to elaborate since all of us are in the same situation.

I hope that we all shall put aside the past and work hard for the future. Let us all put aside our former selves and be resurrected as complete human beings. Those of you who are old, do not call yourselves old and useless. If your husbands want to open schools, don't stop them; if your good sons want to study abroad, don't hold them back. Those among us who are middle-aged, don't hold back your husbands lest they lose their ambition and spirit and fail in their work. After your sons are born, send them to schools. You must do the same for your daughters and, whatever you do, don't bind their feet. As for you young girls among us, go to school if you can. If not, read and study at home. Those of you who are rich, persuade your husbands to open schools, build factories, and contribute to charitable organizations. Those of you who are poor, work hard and help your husbands. Don't be lazy, don't eat idle rice. These are what I hope for you. You must know that when a country is near destruction, women cannot rely on the men any more because they aren't even able to protect themselves. If we don't take heart now and shape up, it will be too late when China is destroyed.

Sisters, we must follow through on these ideas!

Translated by Nancy Gibbs

62.

The New Prefect

By the first decade of the twentieth century even people who did not advocate specific reforms or changes generally believed that their society and government were corrupt and decadent. Novels of social and political criticism, satire, and exposure were written in considerable numbers and enjoyed a wide popularity.

The following vignette about a venal and ludicrous Prefect is from the novel Exposure of the World of Officials, *written by Li Pao-chia (1867–1906) during the last decade of the Ch'ing dynasty. Ch'ü Nai-an, the new Prefect, had begun his career as a menial runner, but because of his wife's friendship with the ninth concubine of the Governor, he was able to gain the high and powerful post of Prefect.*

Ch'ü Nai-an's predecessor, Wang Po-ch'en, was a Prefect in his probation period who had hardly been at his post for a year. It so happened that this was the time for tax collection, and the in-rush of silver made him all the more enthusiastic. He figured that he could make a killing in one season; then, even if he had to leave office at the end of the year, he would have made enough money to rest for a few years as a candidate for office waiting for another chance. However, as the proverb goes, "Too much happiness brings sorrow." Barely had ten days passed since the tax-collection season began when he received a telegram from his hometown. His father had died.

When an official lost a parent, he had to report to his superior immediately and retire from office in observance of a three-year mourning period. With that, all Wang Po-ch'en's projected gains from tax-collecting would vanish into thin air. So, when he read the telegram, he quickly assessed the situation, then tucked it away hurriedly, and told the attendants not to say a word about it. Little did he know that a telegram dispatched to the Prefect from another government office was no small news, and people were very curious about its content. Although

Wang Po-ch'en tried to cover it up, it soon aroused suspicion, and rumors began to circulate.

Wang Po-ch'en now knew it was impossible to keep the news from everybody so he sent for his secretary in charge of bookkeeping, another in charge of tax revenue, and a few of his favorite assistants. When everybody had arrived, he asked them to step into a suite in the back of the office, then closed the door behind them and asked the two secretaries to be seated. Suddenly he dropped down on his knees before them. Although these people by now had learned the news, they all pretended to be shocked. "What is the matter?" they cried. "Please stand up. We cannot possibly allow you to honor us in this way!" Saying so, the two of them also went down to their knees.

But Wang Po-ch'en would not get up; he prostrated himself on the floor and cried, "I have received a telegram from my hometown. My father passed away two days ago."

The secretaries sighed in faked sorrow. "What?" they asked. "Was he ill? Why didn't we hear anything about it?"

"Well, he is dead. We cannot call the dead back to

life," Wang Po-ch'en said. "I now beg you to help those of us who are still alive. In my family there are scores of people waiting to be fed. As soon as my father's death is reported, I will have to observe three years of mourning. How can I make it without any income? I must entrust everything to you two."

Then, pointing at the assistants, he continued, "These men have all followed me for a long time, and they all wish to see me stay on in this post as long as possible. If you two can put a lid on the news for twenty to thirty days, I'll try to postpone my report of my father's death until I can get a few dollars together for traveling expenses. This will be a great favor to me; even my father will be grateful to you if he learns of it in his grave."

The proposition so stunned the two secretaries that for a long time they could not reply. The bookkeeper was the first to come to his senses. He thought, "The earlier he retires, the less money we earn. If he wants to conceal the death of his father, it really has nothing to do with us. Why don't we let him do it? In this way, while doing him a favor, we can get some profit too."

He then conveyed his thoughts to the tax-revenue secretary, and the two of them consented to Wang's proposition. As to the assistants, they naturally would not have liked to see their master leave early, so everyone agreed not to break the news. Wang Po-ch'en now crawled down again on the floor and performed a kowtow to the two secretaries. When he accompanied the people out, he made it a point to talk and laugh as naturally as possible as if nothing had happened.

On that same day, the two secretaries discussed the matter. "We have barely started collecting grain taxes. How can we get them all in within twenty days? We have to figure out a way to induce the peasants to pay their taxes as soon as possible." Finally, the two came up with a plan for lowering the tax rate. This is how it would work: For a tael of silver, if the original tax was set at four strings of cash, they would cut it down to 3.8 or 3.6 strings, but the reduction would only apply if the tax was paid up within a limited period of time. When the peasants saw there was profit in it, they would rush to pay their tax. In this way, not only could the tax revenue be gathered quickly, but the Prefect could gain more popularity.

When the two secretaries had the plan worked out, they presented it to Wang Po-ch'en, and the Prefect immediately sent out bulletins to all the towns and villages. As expected, the peasants all rushed in to take advantage of the reduction. Within two weeks sixty to seventy percent of the revenue had been collected and the private gains of Wang Po-ch'en grew massive.

The two secretaries again held a discussion. "We have already gathered more than half of the revenue," they said. "It is time to ask our master to report the death of his father. A few days will pass before the next Prefect can be appointed; by then we will probably have eighty to ninety percent of the tax collected. There should be a little left for the next Prefect so that he won't talk. If we take everything, there may be trouble."

But when they gave their advice to Wang Po-ch'en, he was too greedy to quit. The two then decided, "We've done quite a job for our master. If he conceals the news any longer, we are not to be held responsible for the outcome."

When these words reached Wang Po-ch'en, he was outraged. "It was *my* father who died," he cried out in anger. "I'll take all the responsibility for concealing it. What does it have to do with them?" Not until these angry words escaped him did he realize what he had said. "Oh!" thought he, "now I have said it myself. If the news leaks out, I'll be in deep trouble. Well, I guess I'll have to settle for less now."

He then formally announced the sad news, together with an uninvited explanation: "Such an important matter has to be based on letters. A mere telegram is not reliable enough. It is just like the appointments of government officials which have to be confirmed with formal documents and cannot go into effect with an order by telegram. Therefore, although I received a telegram days ago, the delay of my report is really not against regulations."

Once the news spread throughout the prefecture, guests poured in to console the Prefect on his terrible loss. Wang Po-ch'en, pretending he had just confirmed the news, dutifully performed a crying scene, but without tears. Afterwards he reported the matter to his superior, returned his official seal, and set up a memorial tablet in his office. When the mourning notices were dispatched, all the officials and local gentry came to pay their condolences. Soon afterwards, the new Prefect, Ch'ü Nai-an arrived.

Before reporting to his new post, Ch'ü had figured that it was just about time for tax-collecting, so he could hardly wait to take over the office. But when the Prefectural seal was turned over, he found that ninety percent of the revenue had already been collected by his predecessor. He was so furious that he could hardly utter a word. Upon inquiry, he found that the former Prefect had encouraged the peasants to pay their taxes early by cutting 400 coins of cash from the tax per tael of silver. An old proverb goes, "A good deed never gets beyond the doer's gate; a bad deed travels a thousand *li* away." The rumor that Wang Po-ch'en had delayed reporting his father's death for more than a fortnight was by now on everyone's lips, and some officious person passed it on to Ch'ü Nai-an in order to win his favor. After that Ch'ü hated Wang Po-ch'en even more bitterly. . . .

When Ch'ü Nai-an held hearings in the prefectural court, he vented his venom against his predecessor by deliberately contradicting the former Prefect's verdicts. No matter who was right or who was wrong, the party who won in the court of Wang Po-ch'en would automatically lose in that of Ch'ü Nai-an and vice versa. Whatever plea had been rejected by the former Prefect would without question be granted by the present one.

One day, Ch'ü was presiding over a hearing concerning a dispute between a man named Chang and another named Sun. Chang had owed money to Sun for over twenty years, and had not paid it back, so Sun took him to court. The case was presented to the former Prefect's court, and Wang Po-ch'en ruled that Chang should return part of the sum to Sun immediately, the rest to be paid up later. At this point, the office changed hands. When Chang brought in the money, Ch'ü Nai-an, not Wang Po-ch'en, was in the Prefect's seat. Just to overturn Wang's decision, Ch'ü ruled that Sun must present his witness to the loan in order to get the money.

"My lord," Sun pleaded, "the transaction was made over twenty years ago. The witness has died. Anyhow, there is the written receipt, and Chang also acknowledges the loan. Aren't these enough?"

"Fart!" snarled the Prefect. "Chang decided to pay you the money, I didn't. No witness, huh? Do you think I can let the matter go so easily? The money will be kept in court until you produce the witness. Case dismissed!" And the two confounded people were driven out of the courtroom.

In another case, a certain man named T'ien promised his daughter to the son of another man, whose name was Fu. Then, T'ien went back on his word, slandered Fu's son, and betrothed his daughter to the son of another man, Huang. Fu sued T'ien during Wang Po-ch'en's term, and it was ruled that Huang should return the engagement gifts. T'ien was

reprimanded for his behavior, and the daughter was still to be married to the son of Fu. After Ch'ü Nai-an took office, Huang again came to appeal to the court, whereupon Ch'ü Nai-an ruled that T'ien should marry his daughter to Huang's son.

Fu went down on his knees and pleaded with the Prefect, but gained nothing but a scolding: "Your son is a good-for-nothing. That's why no one wants him as a son-in-law. If your son can improve himself, then he will get a wife someday. You should go home and educate your own son. What are you doing here creating a disturbance in court? This is ridiculous! If you don't stop this nonsense, I will have to order you beaten." Fu was then thrown out of the courtroom.

A couple of days later, Ch'ü Nai-an again held court. In the first case, a certain Hu Lao-liu had reaped some rice from the fields of another man, Hsü Ta-hai. Ch'ü Nai-an briefly looked over Hsü's written complaint, asked him a few questions, and sent him out of the courtroom. Then he called for the defendant.

When Hu Lao-liu came in, Ch'ü Nai-an pounded his gavel and exclaimed, "You son-of-a-bitch, why did you reap the rice that someone else planted?" Then he ordered the court attendants to beat Hu three hundred times with a staff.

"That's not the whole story, my lord," Hu Lao-liu wailed, pleading to be heard.

But the Prefect said, "Later, later. After the beating." The attendants now dragged Hu down to the floor, gave him the beating, then set him up on his knees again.

"What else do you have to say?" asked the Prefect. "Make it brief."

"My land is adjacent to the land of Hsü Ta-hai," Hu said. "He encroached on my land and planted on it. I tried to reason with him, but he wouldn't listen. That was why I went and reaped the rice. It was on *my* land!"

"So that's what happened. All right," said the Prefect, "bring the plaintiff in again." When Hsü Ta-hai was brought in, Ch'ü scolded him: "First you wronged this man, then you dared to bring him to court. You also deserve to be beaten three hundred times."

"But I didn't do anything wrong," Hsü argued.

"Nobody in this world ever admits that he is wrong. Shut up!" Then the Prefect turned toward the attendants and ordered, "Come, come, give it to him!" Before Hsü Ta-hai could say another word, he was thrown on the floor and beaten. After the punishment, Ch'ü Nai-an told the two to sign the papers and concluded that the case was solved.

In the next case, Lu Lao-szu complained about Ch'ien Hsiao-lü, claiming that the latter had insulted him after heavy drinking. So the Prefect ruled that the defendant be beaten one hundred times. After the beating, the defendant said, "My lord, I never drink. I get a headache at the mere sight of alcohol. How could I have gotten drunk and insulted him? He's a liar."

Ch'ü Nai-an then had the plaintiff brought in, reprimanded him for libel, and ordered him beaten a hundred times also. The case was then closed.

The third case was a family dispute between a wife and a concubine. The wife's name was Kou and the concubine's Lü. The husband was called Chu Lo-t'o. The truth was, the concubine was mean and ferocious and scratched the wife's face. Since the husband could do nothing to stop her attacks, the wife had decided to seek justice in court.

Ch'ü Nai-an glanced over the written complaint and called in the wife. Hardly had she explained the situation when the Prefect became outraged. "All the wives in the world are wicked," he declared. "If you had set a good example for the concubine, would she have dared to fight with you? This is your own fault. You think I have the time to bother about such trivial matters? Your complaint is dismissed!"

Then he summoned the husband and demanded, "Why did you bother to get a concubine when your wife is so mean?" He went on to lecture him: "If you had to have a concubine, you should have kept her in a separate house. Now that you allowed them to live under one roof, you have to learn to control the situation. But no, you had to come to court with your family problems. What do you think I am? Do you think that I, the Prefect, besides waiting on my superior officials and collecting taxes for the Emperor, have time to keep an eye on your household affairs? Even if I had three heads and six arms to do my work, I would not be able to bother about these things! You just go home and keep them in separate places. I can guarantee it will work out all right."

"But they did live apart," said the husband. "Then my wife found out about the concubine and made a scene."

"Then it is actually your wife's fault," concluded the Prefect, and only after much begging did the wife escape a beating. The case was also pronounced solved.

The next case involved two country bumpkins, one called Yang Kou-tzu, the other, Hsü Hua-tzu. The two men had argued over a chicken, each claiming that it belonged to him. When the dispute could not be solved by reason, it ended up in a fight. Yang, the stronger of the two, injured Hsü by kicking him on the right leg, and that was how the two of them ended up in the courthouse.

Ch'ü Nai-an first ordered an examination of the victim's leg, and then he said to Hsü, "He kicked you on your right leg, didn't he? Well, I will also beat him on his right leg, then." And he ordered the court attendants to do just that.

The number of strokes went over one hundred and Yang's right leg became all black and blue. When it approximated the color of Hsü's bruises, Ch'ü Nai-an ordered the beating to be stopped. All this time he kept praising himself: "Is there any other Prefect who is as fair as I am?"

Still, the ownership of the chicken had not been decided, and the two could not be reconciled. Ch'ü then said, "This chicken is the source of your fight; it is no good. Let me help you solve the problem." Thus speaking, he suddenly put on a stern face and declared, "Neither of you shall get the chicken. It is to be confiscated." Turning toward the attendants, he further ordered, "Take it to the kitchen. And bring these two out to sign the papers. Case closed!" And out went the two, limping, their eyes still fixed on the chicken that was being taken to the Prefect's kitchen.

So the hearings went on. In one single day, Ch'ü Nai-an took care of some twenty to thirty cases, more or less in the same manner as described above.

The next day, as he was just about to begin another session of hearings, a court clerk came in with a thick stack of petitions and reported to him, "My lord, these are petitions to withdraw complaints. These people all have heard how very discerning you are, and they no longer wish to pursue their lawsuits. Would you please look through them to see if these petitions are to be accepted?"

"Of course, all of them are to be granted," replied Ch'ü Nai-an. Then he thought, very much pleased with himself, "I've been quite annoyed by the quarrelsome nature of the people in Hsing-kuo Prefecture. And now, look, I've held court only a few times, and they're already calming down a great deal. It just goes to prove that when good government is combined with proper punishment, no people are too unruly to be controlled. The Emperor is promoting a clean-up campaign in the justice system; if I can stay at my post for a few more months, I will certainly have a very efficient government with little administrative work."

Little did he know that during those few days he had already provoked loud complaints among the people in Hsing-kuo, who now cried in chorus:

"Prefect Wang has retired, and now we have gotten this incompetent fool. How can we ever survive his term in office?"

Translated by Clara Yu

63.

Rural Education

By the nineteenth century, village schools of the type portrayed in selection 53, "The Village Headman and the New Teacher," were commonplace throughout China. Those who could possibly afford to do so sent boys to school for three or four years, generally from about age seven to age eleven, when the boys were not yet old enough to do much productive work. Within three or four years, a student could learn arithmetic and enough characters to read contracts, shop signs, and stories written in the vernacular language. And there was the added attraction that a child who showed extraordinary talent might somehow rise through the civil service examination system. After the abolition of the examinations in 1905, the curricula of many schools was modernized to include training in science, mathematics, and foreign languages. A major motivation for the change was that those who mastered modern subjects came to have the best prospects; they might gain government scholarships for study abroad, especially in Japan, or at least find jobs in the emerging modern sectors of the coastal cities.

Below is an account written for a teacher's magazine by Yu Tzu-i about his experiences introducing modern subjects in a small rural school in the vicinity of Shanghai in 1907–8. Yu was looking back on his experience after twenty years and does not hide his nostalgia for the place and time. Still, from his description something of what it must have been like to be a student or a teacher in such a school can be discerned. One can also see some of the cultural differences that had come to separate those with modern educations from those without.

The events described here took place in a coastal area east of Shanghai at the end of the Kuang-hsü period [1875–1909]. In the fall, I was notified by the Ministry of Education to take a post in a private rural elementary school, one which still exists. . . . The principal was an old gentleman from the area who had once been the teacher of one of my colleagues at the ministry. Besides him, there was a teacher who had graduated from the ministry's normal school and had come to the school ahead of me. Thus, one was my senior and the other was my student; I filled in the position between them to form a complete teacher-student relationship. . . .

The school building was to the left of a temple. As a matter of fact, it had been converted from half of the temple. . . . More than thirty students were in the grade school, each of the four grades having only one class, while only six or seven students were in the extension school. The normal school graduate took charge of most of the grade-school courses, and I taught one or two subjects, too. For the extension school, the principal and I took care of most of the teaching duties. The old gentleman taught courses like Chinese, history, and geography, while I taught natural science, mathematics, English, and so on. Other courses like drawing, crafts, music, and gymnastics were partly taken care of by the normal school graduate, and partly combined with the grade-school classes.

Why did the students in a rural extension school have to learn English? At the time, I wondered about that, too. The reason was the environment. There was a need for it, since the place was no more than thirty or forty *li* away from Shanghai. Many successful figures from this area had struck it rich in Shanghai. In fact, the founder of the school had been a local poor boy before he went to Shanghai and made his fortune by working there. His first fortune came from undertaking a task for a foreigner. Therefore, local people with a little ambition, both parents and children, all wanted to go to Shanghai to pursue their careers. And they always had to know at least a few sentences of some foreign language in order to have a better chance, regardless of whether they aimed at business or industry.

At the very first English class, I asked the students about their ambitions. Almost all of them answered with some goal in Shanghai. One of the students had an interesting answer: "I will first attend the extension school. But, as soon as there's a chance, I'll leave for Shanghai. One of my relatives works as chief cook there. He is now trying to get me a job as a waiter in a big foreign restaurant. To do this, won't I have to know some foreign language?" His father owned the South-North Grocery Store in the town. The little master of a store wanted to go to Shanghai to be a waiter in a foreign restaurant—isn't the temptation of a lucky strike amazingly great? His father often came to the school to chat, and his notions were similar to his son's.

The people there respected me very much because I was sent by the ministry, wore western-style suits, and could teach their children the language which might someday lead them to acquire a great fortune. Probably they took me as a prototype of the foreign God of Wealth. Who knows! But, in fact, the English I taught was bookish. . . .

Surprisingly, in the first-grade class there were two girls, even though during the Ch'ing dynasty coeducation was prohibited. These two girls were comparatively older and one of them was already engaged to a student in the extension school. (In the countryside, children could be engaged as early as three or five years of age, so being engaged at the age of fourteen or fifteen was not at all unusual.) With some flexibility the old principal admitted the female students, disregarding the regulations. Although he was old, he always encouraged girls to go to school, and, fortunately, there was no one who knew the educational regulations. As long as the head of the school was respected in the community, he could do whatever he pleased. As Heaven was high and the Emperor was far away, he did not have to worry

about any interference, so long as he was trusted locally. The regulations set by the Emperor were not as important as the trust of the local people.

Even for the curricula of the school, we never followed the imperial regulations. The subject most emphasized in the Ch'ing dynasty was the classics. The old principal himself was expert in them, but he knew that such recondite philosophy was really beyond the children. Therefore, all he offered for the first grade was a course in morality. Even in the extension school, we simply applied the most plausible and practical ideas of the classics to courses like Chinese or history. The local people never criticized the school curricula or activities because they trusted the old principal.

In rural areas up to that time, farmers had never dreamed of extracurricular activities or games after class. The sound of reading was expected from a school, but noise and shouting were taken as signs of naughtiness on the part of the children. How could they be so impolite to the teacher! Should anyone hear gleeful sounds, he would assume the teacher was absent. How could a teacher indulge the students that way!

To eliminate such an ingrained prejudice was not at all an easy job. Therefore, we started with some trial games. At first, we did nothing more than bounce a small rubber ball, and we did that only after class had been dismissed. Subsequently, the students became more and more interested in this. The old principal was no less spirited, and one day he brought a rubber ball filled with rushes. We then organized soccer teams and set up a goal made with bamboo poles on the vacant lot west of the school building. Thereafter, we played soccer before and after class every day.

Parents of some of the students came to the school frequently, and the old principal always explained honestly the importance of exercise: "By nature children want to play around. If we prohibit them from playing in public, they will play secretly anyway, which might be dangerous. In addition to the regular courses, they should be allowed to play. When playing a game, they should follow the rules. Besides, there is always a teacher supervising as an umpire. . . ." These were the best reasons for our extracurricular activities. We preached in this way, and the local farmers believed what we said. . . .

The founder of the school had established a rule limiting each meal to one dish of meat or fish and one kind of vegetable. He wanted frugality to be the fundamental principle of this school, fearing that the rural children would become modern good-for-nothings after they entered a modern school. . . . Together with the boarders, we sat around one table when we ate and usually had three huge dishes of food. The one in the middle had plenty of meat or fish, while the two on each side were full of the same kinds of vegetables. Vegetables in the countryside were, of course, the cheapest and freshest food. . . . I had lived at many schools in Shanghai, Wu-hsi, Nanking, Hang-chou, and Wu-hu. To summarize my experiences, the food of those schools was always so terrible that I would not eat it until I had to. Sometimes I had unpleasant feelings when the matter of dining was even mentioned. But the experience of eating at this rural elementary school was so good that I still feel like talking about it now. . . .

I taught the natural sciences, which at that time was called "physics." In the extension school, this course could be handled as in regular senior grade schools, all the methods being found in school manuals. However, there was no such course as general science or local geography and history for grade schools, so I had to invent one. First, I divided the grade school into two groups, the advanced class being the third- and fourth-grade students and the elementary class being the first- and second-graders. I taught different topics in the same course at the same time. The materials were the common phenomena observed in that area. I did not confine myself to natural sciences, but also covered the basic notions of geography and history.

The school had very few specimens or pieces of laboratory equipment. At first, I had planned to make a large-scale purchase upon arrival at the school. However, this was not only impossible but actually unnecessary. When I set out from the ministry, I had already given thought to the situation. To supplement my own reference pictures, I asked the department of natural science at the ministry for a biconvex mirror, a set of dissecting instruments, and a few wide- and narrow-necked bottles. These constituted all the apparatus I had for the teaching of natural science. According to present prices, they probably cost me less than five dollars. After arriving at the school, I made a net for catching insects and small water creatures out of three feet of wire, one thin short bamboo stick, and one yard of white cloth.

The subjects of our study were the phenomena observed in the vicinity. How do the white lentils climb up the bamboo fences beside the river bridge?

Why is the pumpkin as big as the stone plinth while its flower is as small as a cup? Why does the pumpkin not sweeten until it is dried in the sunshine? These were questions arising from agriculture. There were not very many students in the extension school, which was very convenient for both in-door study and out-door observation. Our footprints could be found in the cotton field everyday. The flowers withered, the fruit grew, the fruit split, and the cotton floss appeared. Various results of observations were reported daily. The students brought some real things to school, together with many questions. The floss came out of the cotton fruit. What is the basic function of the floss for the cotton plant itself? How do human beings make use of the floss? These were typical questions.

What are the names of the water plants, the flowers, and the weeds growing beside the embankment and around the fields? How do they grow up by themselves while the pumpkins and the cotton trees need to be planted? What is the use of the wild flowers and weeds? What harm do they do? These were also the topics of our study. The countryfolk rarely paid attention to the relations between agricultural products and weeds. By investigating them, we found that they were very significant. Thus, research on root preservation and weeding methods became our major topic for quite some time. . . .

What are the dragonflies doing on the water surface? Why did the grasshoppers in the paddy field change from green to brown when the plants dried out? How do they breathe without noses? These are sample questions of our insect study. Inspired, the students caught some insects every day and brought them to the class with all kinds of questions. What are their names? How do they live? What are their advantages and disadvantages? (Advantages and disadvantages were judged by the insects' food and way of life.) The children were mostly motivated by curiosity; real issues of human interest were not their major concern. However, life and the history of life apparently were somewhat romantic. And, to approach the true issues of human interest through the romantic questions about life was much more appropriate for the youngsters. I tried this approach, and it proved to be much more interesting than dealing directly with the issues of interest to the adult world. . . .

In the little river behind the school building there were many aquatic animals. We caught some and kept them in a wide-mouthed bottle which I had brought from the ministry. This actually became a temporary aquarium. How do the fish swim. How do they manage to dive and surface? Since human beings drown if they fall into the water, how is it that fish stay alive in the water but die without it? The school was not far from the coast, and there was a coastal town which was a major market. Our study of the life of fish reminded us of the fish market on the sea. The students thus reported many phenomena which they had been observing since they were young, many of which were totally new to me. Not only did I teach them, they also taught me a lot. . . . What they reported were the local experiences and legends, and what I taught was the scientific knowledge stated in the books. Combining these two resources, we found some conclusions which we thought were more convincing. . . .

The students told me many legends about ghosts, spirits, and immortals. Although I took them to be fiction, the students deeply believed them to be true. The elimination of superstitions was not at all an easy task to begin. I might passively argue against superstitious legends, but how could a single mouth fight against the beliefs of thousands of people? A much better way was to actively encourage the students to study science. The scientific attitude would make them suspicious of everything and motivate them to seek a thorough solution to every problem, so that they would no longer stick stubbornly to superstitions. For this reason, I did not point out that their fairy tales were nonsense. Instead, I raised some questions to arouse their suspicion about the existence of the ghosts and immortals which they believed in. Moreover, I described the phenomena of gravity, combustion, and so on. I did not get into the issue of whether there are ghosts and gods or not, leaving it to their own future judgment. If I had had a long period of time to work at this, I probably would have been able to uproot the superstitions totally.

In the quiet countryside, we met only a few acquaintances every day. Thus, it was an unusual event when, one day, a tall, thin man with a beard came to visit our school. Not used to seeing visitors from other places, the rural children gathered around him so tightly he could hardly move. After greeting the guest, the principal realized that he was an education inspector sent by the provincial government. A diligent and enthusiastic inspector, he visited a rural school as secluded as ours in spite of how difficult it

was to get to. At that moment, I was about to teach general science to the grade school class, so he entered the classroom with me. Standing in the corner, he listened through the entire class. . . .

The provincial education inspector invited the teachers and principals in the vicinity of the provincial capital to attend a meeting at which he evaluated every school in detail. Having a high opinion of our school, he especially extolled me for the general science class I had taught that day, saying that it had been one of the most successful classes in the whole county. He criticized an old teacher for misinterpreting one word in class. However, that old teacher, who was also present, looked the word up in the *K'ang Hsi Dictionary* right there and proved himself to have been correct. Our principal said that although the old teacher might have no idea at all about modern knowledge and new teaching techniques, he was definitely learned in the classics and could not have made a mistake in interpreting words. The provincial education inspector indeed had undervalued him. Because of that event, the meeting ended in disharmony.

One night, a special messenger came from the ministry. Not knowing what had happened, we were taken by surprise. The Shanghai daily newspaper, which was available in the countryside, had recently reported that the Empress Dowager and the Emperor were both seriously ill. But, since the newspaper was always at least one day getting to us, we had not heard of their deaths yet. Being near Shanghai, the ministry had telephones and was always well-informed. Hence, they already knew of the deaths one after the other. Informed of the proper rites for schools, they sent a special messenger to deliver a mimeographed notice to us, telling us to suspend classes, hang a piece of white cloth, bow three times every day to the north, and weep in mourning.

Early the next morning, the food manager brought the white cloth and hung it on the front gate of the school. We announced the suspension of classes after the students had come. We then removed all the desks and chairs in the grade school classroom to make a temporary hall for the ceremony. In order for so many students to perform the kowtowing ceremony, we needed several dozen kneeling cushions. The clever old principal went to the temple and borrowed all the rush kneeling mats used for religious rites. The mats on which old ladies sat to chant the name of Buddha suddenly became our devices for mourning the death of the Empress

Dowager and the Emperor. These kneeling mats were usually used only once a year. That year, however, they were in the spotlight for the second time shortly after they had been used—they certainly were lucky! Perfunctorily we performed the ceremony three times every day: the principal led and the students followed. At first when the students were asked to weep in mourning, they would suddenly burst into naive laughter. If that had happened at a government institution, it would have been regarded as extremely rude. However, in the far-off countryside, no one cared.

With the New Year's vacation approaching, it became time for final exams. I discussed with the old principal and the other teacher the idea of purchasing some rewards for the diligent students in order to encourage studying. We agreed, and during our spare time we went downtown to buy some colorful paper, pens, ink, and such at the stationery store. We tried to make the prizes as accessible as possible: any student who had tried hard in one or two subjects would get at least some reward. On the last day of class, we gave the prizes, which made everyone beam with smiles. In addition, I told the students in the extension school to write to me on the stationery during the vacation. They kept their promises, for I did indeed receive their letters after I returned home.

Translated by Jane Chen

64.

The Shanghai Builders' Guild

Western influence on Chinese life was felt most strongly in the port cities with large foreign settlements. Shanghai, a relatively minor city until it was opened to foreign trade in 1846, became the most Westernized of all, a center for Western manufacturing and commerce and the home of thousands of Westerners who lived according to their own customs and laws in the French Concession and the International Settlement. In the "treaty ports," Chinese merchants and manufacturers were both challenged and confused by their encounter with Westerners. Western capitalist ideology favored businessmen; it honored the pursuit of profit and considered financial success a sign of talent and virtue. Yet Chinese entrepreneurs found it difficult to embrace this new ideology wholeheartedly, since competition with Western firms often proved disastrous to their own businesses. Many conservatives opposed all foreign methods and continued to maintain traditional ways.

The following account of the founding of the Shanghai Builders' Guild shows what one of its leading members thought about these problems in 1911. The author wished to stimulate the pride and self-confidence of the guild members by congratulating them on their success in mastering the Western challenge, but he was by no means entirely traditional in his outlook. His account was carved on a stone tablet and kept in the guild hall.

Shanghai is China's largest commercial port. It has a population of 800,000 and a market area extending as far as thirty *li*. The buildings are as densely packed as the teeth of a comb, one built next to another. The taller ones shoot straight up in the sky, almost touching the clouds. Their magnificent design and elegant decoration, their sturdy structure and delicate craftsmanship, all speak of the highest achievements of China's most perfected industry: the building industry.

Almost all the people engaged in our profession come from Ning-po, Shao-hsing, or Shanghai itself. There is one significant exception, and that is Mr. Yang Chin-ch'un, who came from Szechwan and yet proved to be the most reputable builder in our country. I made Mr. Yang's acquaintance in 1897. At that time he had just organized the Guild as a means of benefiting everyone in our profession. But the

organization, undermined by those who were jealous of him, soon collapsed.

Ten years later, Mr. Yang again called our fellow craftsmen to action. After appealing to the government, we finally succeeded in electing twelve new board members to replace the old ones. Each of the twelve was assigned specific duties, and another person was elected to coordinate their activities. The Guild then collected funds for the construction of a Guild Hall. The Guild has provided medical assistance and funeral arrangements for its members, has formulated regulations for our profession, and has acted as mediator in quarrels and lawsuits. People in our profession have willingly accepted its authority. Mr. Yang planned to set up an elementary school and four night schools for the apprentices, but unfortunately he passed away without seeing those projects materialize. His undertakings, however, were brought to completion by Mr. Ku Lan-chou, Mr. Chiang Yü-sheng, and others. Three years have now passed since the second founding of our Guild. . . . [It] has now expanded into a large-scale organization, and I have been asked to write an essay about it.

I have a number of comments to make. In China, scholars are respected but artisans are looked down upon. People think highly of the Way and despise skills. Lofty scholars and officials like to indulge in empty words, while shunning any practical work. If anyone dares to mention an innovation in manufacturing, he will immediately be denounced for "pursuing the insignificant" or for "practicing worthless crafts." As a result, we who engage in practical work also tend to feel inferior and do not dare to defy the scholars and officials. Thus, our knowledge gradually narrows, our skills deteriorate, and our tools fall out of date. Foreigners then exploit this opportunity to export their goods to our country. Since they are able to appeal to our customs and our tastes, they drain our wealth. As we use their merchandise, we grow to like it; yet when we wish to imitate their manufacturing methods, we cannot obtain the secrets unless we learn from the foreigners themselves. Consequently, our governments have foreign clerks; our factories have foreign craftsmen; our schools have foreign teachers. The European fad comes sweeping through our country like a flood, and there is no stopping it.

The construction business is the only one that has not yielded, because from mere sketches we can build tall buildings and pavilions, porches and columns. With our measuring yards we can calculate the quantity of building materials needed, be they of metal, wood, mortar, or stone. Furthermore, we understand the likes and habits of the foreigners without having to learn from them; we can draw revenue from them without allowing them to set themselves up in our profession, preventing them from robbing us of our profit. Thus it can be said that in China with its 400 million people, there is only one profession independent of foreign influence, the construction industry.

A person must first be able to stand on his own feet before he can have independence, and only when he has independence is he able to grow strong. Likewise, only when every citizen is strong can the whole nation, the whole race gain strength. On the other hand, one person alone is powerless; we must unite in tens, hundreds, thousands, and tens of thousands in order to gain strength. To have a strong nation it is necessary to combine the strength of thousands and tens of thousands of people as if they were one. In other words, independence is a basic ingredient for strength, and unity is the highest achievement of that strength. Our Builders' Guild, for instance, is a vital, united organization. Its charitable operations are but a minor function; they are not its spirit or essence. What is its spirit? It lies in resistance to foreign encroachment and the care of our fellow members. What is the essence? It lies in the oneness of our members' minds and in the improvement of our knowledge and skills. We do not have to appear intimate with each other; we do not have to count the number of our meetings. Our spiritual ties will be so strong that we will be inseparable; our fraternal love will be so intense that it will not dissipate even if we are confronted with frustration and suffering. Our ties are as strong as metal or stone, as tight as glue. We are attracted to each other like magnets or amber. When we make mistakes, we admonish each other; when we do good deeds, we encourage each other; when corrupt practices are uncovered, we eliminate them together; when there are profits, we share them together. We will be friends and teachers to each other, promoting progress in our profession, so that eventually we will be able to compete in the world market. Then and only then will we have achieved our goal of independence. I despair because China has not become stronger, yet I rejoice that our construction profession is independent. I would like therefore to promote the spirit of our Guild as an example for all the 800,000 citizens of Shanghai.

Our Guild Office is situated at No. 32, Attainment Embankment, 5th Block, 25th Ward inside the north gate of Shanghai (the new "Bliss Street"). The members who have made donations include Yang Chin-ch'un [and thirty-four others], who are all from Shanghai. Altogether we have obtained 2,746 dollars and 27,813 taels of silver from these donors. The purchase of the land, the construction of the building, and the organization's expenses all depended on these donations. Our Shao-hsing members Wei Ch'ing-t'ao, Feng Chia-hsiang, Yü Chi-ch'en, and Shen Jui-ch'un also contributed one thousand taels, which was used to supplement the construction costs of the Guild Office. The Ning-po builders have their own guild.

Written in the seventh month of 1911.

Translated by Clara Yu

65.

On Freeing Slave Girls

The efforts to raise the status of women by ending footbinding and forced marriages attained wide support from the new intellectuals of the "May Fourth" generation. Efforts to "liberate" women now were extended further to include ending concubinage and the common practice of bonding young girls as household slaves. The following article on slave girls was published in a 1920 issue of the popular Woman's Magazine. *It was written by a man but was aimed at the growing audience of literate women. Its author is typical of intellectuals of the period in his humanitarian goals and somewhat naive and idealistic view of the possibilities for improving people and institutions.*

Why am I writing this essay? Because I believe that the Chinese institution of slave girls is bad. First of all, slave girls are not treated like people, but tortured as if they were animals; in fact, some are treated even worse than animals. These slave girls have no one to tell their troubles to and no place to seek help. Looking at this from a humanitarian point of view, this institution is indeed wrong. Secondly, since their masters do not treat them as human beings, the slave girls themselves never learn to behave as such. They set out to take advantage of their masters in everything they do. When they go shopping, they often lose money; when they are told to work, they are lazy and cut corners, not caring if their laziness causes inconveniences for other people; and when they cook, they purposely waste fuel, rice, oil, and salt. In the end it is the masters who lose out. For these two reasons we can agree that the institution of slave girls must be abolished.

Nowadays people who are imbued with new ideas understand these arguments, so I need say no more. But their proposals tend to be too lofty, too general in scope, too detached from reality. Although their ideas make sense, they are difficult to carry out. The ideas I

have put down in this essay, however, are not merely empty talk, for they could easily be put into practice!

Why do I say that many people's ideas are too lofty and general? Nowadays people with new ideas are all talking about women's liberation, the liberation of all women. Isn't that too broad? There are already many independent women in our society who have no need to be liberated. Weaker, uneducated, and dependent women do need help and support in order to become self-reliant, but the help they need is not liberation. Women who do need liberation fall into the following three categories: (1) prostitutes, (2) concubines, and (3) slave girls. These women are virtually bound hand-and-foot by others. They have had their rights to freedom taken away from them, and their lives are often hard and bitter. In the name of humanity, how can we not first liberate these women whose lives are a living hell? Furthermore, if they are not liberated, not only will they themselves suffer, but many others will indirectly be made to suffer too. If we want to change our society, we must first liberate these women.

Since these three categories of people are different, our methods of liberating them should also be different. For example, it would be more difficult to liberate prostitutes and concubines, so in this essay I shall limit my discussions to how to liberate slave girls. I am not saying that prostitutes and concubines should not be liberated, nor even that their liberation can be delayed. But this essay is written for women with new ideas who I am hoping will carry out this liberation movement without help from men. In reality, it is easier for women to liberate slave girls then prostitutes and concubines, so we might as well begin with the simplest. . . .

Why should women liberate slave girls without help from men? Since both educated women and slave girls are females, women might be more sympathetic. Moreover, slave girls usually work for women, so the power to free them is in the hands of women, not men. Therefore, I suggest that this job should be done by women themselves. As I see it, the job can be divided into two stages: discontinuing buying slave girls, and freeing the ones already owned.

There are two ways to free slave girls. Concerning the slaves you own yourself, since you have the power to free them, do so immediately. For example, if I own a slave girl and I want to free her, I can go ahead and do so. Concerning the slaves you do not own, you must persuade others to liberate them. For example, if my mother, sister, or neighbors own any and I want them free, I must persuade the owner to free them. If they do not heed me, I must try again; if they still do not listen, I should try a third time, a fourth time. . . . Eventually I will reach my objective. These two ways are the only ways to liberate slave girls, and they can be carried out by everyone.

But what is to be done after they are given their freedom? This is indeed a great problem. In my opinion, the best course is to take them into your family as your daughters. You should send the younger girls to school to be educated, and in their after-school hours they should be taught to work around the house. They should be encouraged to do any work which they are fitted to do, which would benefit the whole family, and which would not injure their health. As for the older girls, you could arrange marriages for them, of if you keep them at home, you should teach them housework as well as the ways of the world. When they marry, you must be cautious and think of their happiness instead of the amount of money you will get. If you treat them like this, they will then treat you like real mothers and not want to be dishonest or take advantage of you. You should instruct the girls who have already acquired bad habits

of cheating and not expect them to change their ways too readily. Sometimes punishment may be necessary as long as you are guided by your conscience. (In dealing with your own children, a certain amount of punishment is inevitable, but punishing them does not change the affection you feel for them.) In sum, we must treat liberated slave girls as our own daughters.

Some people have pointed out that servant girls once had parents who, because they needed money, sold them into slavery. No matter how sympathetic we feel toward them, it would be much better to return them to their natural parents without demanding that the money be returned. This idea sounds good but poses serious difficulties. First, more often than not, the parents of these slave girls have moved away and cannot be located. Second, if the parents have sold them once, can you feel assured that they would not sell them again? That would be no liberation at all. Therefore this method should only be used with extreme caution.

I have been discussing how to free servant girls and care for them after they gain their freedom. There is one more thing I must mention. I find that no matter what a thing is, if only one person does it, the majority consider it strange and opposition to it is enormous. But if the same thing is done by many people, others consider it perhaps worth doing and opposition is slight. Therefore I suggest that if women are to liberate slave girls, it would be best to organize a society. If all unite and work together then this would be a simple thing to do. The society might adopt these rules:

1. The society shall be called the Society to Free Slave Girls.
2. Members of the society must all be female.
3. The duty of each member is to free slave girls she owns and to persuade others to free ones she does not own.
4. The society has no other business.

From these rules we see how easy it would be. Organizing this society could be done with a minimum of red tape since members need only quietly assume their responsibilities. Furthermore, this type of liberation frees one girl at a time; therefore it is easier to carry out than mass liberation. Since the girls would continue to reside in their former masters' houses as members of the households, it would be quite easy to carry out.

Some people might say, "This is all very well and good, but what about the slave owners who are not so enlightened? Might they not refuse to free their slaves at your suggestion and maltreat them as usual anyway?"

I would answer, "I have no doubt cases like that will occur. But if four or five people out of every ten free their slaves after listening to me, I will consider my efforts to be half successful." Those who agree to this liberation with their mouths and not their hearts must be persuaded again and again; and if we can convert one or two of them, our success will increase by yet another ten to twenty percent. As for those people who cannot be persuaded, they will soon lose the respect of their peers. Everyone wants face, and I am sure they will change their minds under the pressure of public opinion. Furthermore, the society should investigate the treatment and living conditions of freed slaves and attempt to raise the girls' level of consciousness about themselves and about the world around them. If these three steps are carried out simultaneously, how can the movement not succeed?

I am writing this essay in the hopes that others might carry out my ideas. Originally I intended to launch this movement myself, but then I realized that this society to free slave girls should be organized by women themselves. Since I myself do not own any slave girls, I have none to free. My duty is to write this article and hope that modern educated women will carry this matter to its conclusion.

Translated by Nancy Gibbs

66.

My Old Home

A major achievement of the intellectuals of the Republican period was the creation of a new literary genre, the modern short story. Western literature and literary theories were the stimulus for this activity, but very quickly Chinese writers turned from derivative imitations of Western stories to ones firmly rooted in Chinese experience. Part Seven includes stories by three writers, Lu Hsün, Mao Tun (selection 74), and Shen Ts'ung-wen (selection 75). These stories were chosen not only because they reveal the interests of intellectuals in personal psychology and social relations, but also because they portray the ways of thinking and modes of behavior of nonintellectuals with much more sensitivity and attention to intimate details than any other kind of source.

"My Old Home" was written in 1921 by Lu Hsün (1881–1936), the first important fiction writer of the twentieth century and widely considered the best writer of his generation. Sent to Japan on a government scholarship, Lu Hsün studied medicine and read Western literature and philosophy. Returning to China in 1909, he taught and began his career as a writer. In 1920 he was offered a position in Peking University and visited his old home to arrange for moving his mother there. This story concerns that trip and deals with one of the major problems of the new intellectuals: the difficulty they faced in overcoming ingrained class barriers so that they could communicate effectively with ordinary people neither educated nor modern.

Braving the bitter cold, I traveled more than seven hundred miles back to the old home I had left over twenty years before.

It was late winter. As we drew near my former home the day became overcast and a cold wind blew into the cabin of our boat, while all one could see through the chinks in our bamboo awning were a few desolate villages, void of any sign of life, scattered far and near under the somber yellow sky. I could not help feeling depressed.

Ah! Surely this was not the old home I had remembered for the past twenty years?

The old home I remembered was not in the least like this. My old home was much better. But if you asked me to recall its peculiar charm or describe its beauties, I had no clear impression, no words to describe it. And now it seemed this was all there was to it. Then I rationalized the matter to myself, saying: Home was always like this, and although it has not improved, still it is not so depressing as I imagine; it is only my mood that has changed, because I am coming back to the country this time with no illusions.

This time I had come with the sole object of saying goodbye. The old house our clan had lived in for so many years had already been sold to another family, and was to change hands before the end of the year. I had to hurry there before New Year's Day to say goodbye forever to the familiar old house, and to move my family to another place where I was working, far from my old home town.

At dawn on the second day I reached the gateway of my home. Broken stems of withered grass on the roof, trembling in the wind, made very clear the reason why this old house could not avoid changing hands. Several branches of our clan had probably already moved away, so it was unusually quiet. By the time I reached the house my mother was already at the door to welcome me, and my eight-year-old nephew, Hung-erh, rushed out after her.

Though mother was delighted, she was also trying to hide a certain feeling of sadness. She told me to sit down and rest and have some tea, letting the removal wait for the time being. Hung-erh, who had never seen me before, stood watching me at a distance.

But finally we had to talk about the removal. I said that rooms had already been rented elsewhere, and I had bought a little furniture; in addition it would be necessary to sell all the furniture in the house in order to buy more things. Mother agreed, saying that the luggage was nearly all packed, and about half the furniture that could not easily be moved had already been sold. Only it was difficult to get people to pay up.

"You must rest for a day or two, and call on our relatives, and then we can go," said mother.

"Yes."

"Then there is Jun-tu. Each time he comes here he always asks after you, and wants very much to see you again. I told him the probable date of your return home, and he may be coming any time."

At this point a strange picture suddenly flashed into my mind: a golden moon suspended in a deep blue sky and beneath it the seashore, planted as far as the eye could see with jade-green watermelons, while in their midst a boy of eleven or twelve, wearing a silver necklet and grasping a steel pitchfork in his hand, was thrusting with all his might at a *zha* which dodged the blow and escaped between his legs.

This boy was Jun-tu. When I first met him he was just over ten—that was thirty years ago, and at that time my father was still alive and the family well off, so I was really a spoilt child. That year it was our family's turn to take charge of a big ancestral sacrifice, which came round only once in thirty years, and hence was an important one. In the first month the ancestral images were presented and offerings made, and since the sacrificial vessels were very fine and there was such a crowd of worshippers, it was necessary to guard against theft. Our family had only one part-time labourer. (In our district we divide labourers into three classes: those who work all the year for one family are called full-timers; those who are hired by the day are called dailies; and those who farm their own land and only work for one family at

New Year, during festivals or when rents are being collected are called part-timers.) And since there was so much to be done, he told my father that he would send for his son Jun-tu to look after the sacrificial vessels.

When my father gave his consent I was overjoyed, because I had long since heard of Jun-tu and knew that he was about my own age, born in the intercalary month, and when his horoscope was told it was found that of the five elements that of earth was lacking, so his father called him Jun-tu (Intercalary Earth). He could set traps and catch small birds.

I looked forward every day to New Year, for New Year would bring Jun-tu. At last, when the end of the year came, one day mother told me that Jun-tu had come, and I flew to see him. He was standing in the kitchen. He had a round, crimson face and wore a small felt cap on his head and a gleaming silver necklet round his neck, showing that his father doted on him and, fearing he might die, had made a pledge with the gods and buddhas, using the necklet as a talisman. He was very shy, and I was the only person he was not afraid of. When there was no one else there, he would talk with me, so in a few hours we were fast friends.

I don't know what we talked of then, but I remember that Jun-tu was in high spirits, saying that since he had come to town he had seen many new things.

The next day I wanted him to catch birds.

"Can't be done," he said. "It's only possible after a heavy snowfall. On our sands, after it snows, I sweep clear a patch of ground, prop up a big threshing basket with a short stick, and scatter husks of grain beneath. When the birds come there to eat, I tug a string tied to the stick, and the birds are caught in the basket. There are all kinds: wild pheasants, woodcocks, wood-pigeons, 'blue-backs.' . . ."

Accordingly I looked forward very eagerly to snow.

"Just now it is too cold," said Jun-tu another time, "but you must come to our place in summer. In the daytime we'll go to the seashore to look for shells, there are green ones and red ones, besides 'scare-devil' shells and 'buddha's hands.' In the evening when dad and I go to see to the watermelons, you shall come too."

"Is it to look out for thieves?"

"No. If passers-by are thirsty and pick a watermelon, folk down our way don't consider it as stealing. What we have to look out for are badgers, hedgehogs, and *zha.* When under the moonlight you hear the crunching sound made by the *zha* when it bites the melons, then you take your pitchfork and creep stealthily over. . . ."

I had no idea then what this thing called *zha* was—and I am not much clearer now for that matter—but somehow I felt it was something like a small dog, and very fierce.

"Don't they bite people?"

"You have a pitchfork. You go across, and when you see it you strike. It's a very cunning creature and will rush toward you and get away between your legs. Its fur is as slippery as oil. . . ."

I had never known that all these strange things existed: at the seashore there were shells all colours of the rainbow; watermelons were exposed to such danger, yet all I had known of them before was that they were sold in the greengrocer's.

"On our shore, when the tide comes in, there are lots of jumping fish, each with two legs like a frog. . . ."

Jun-tu's mind was a treasure-house of such strange lore, all of it outside the ken of my former friends. They were ignorant of all these things and, while Jun-tu lived by the sea, they like me could see only the four corners of the sky above the high courtyard wall.

Unfortunately, a month after New Year Jun-tu had to go home. I burst into tears and he took refuge in the kitchen, crying and refusing to come out, until finally his father carried him off. Later he sent me by his father a packet of shells and a few very beautiful feathers, and I sent him presents once or twice, but we never saw each other again.

Now that my mother mentioned him, this childhood memory sprang into life like a flash of lightning, and I seemed to see my beautiful old home. So I answered:

"Fine! And he—how is he?"

"He? . . . He's not at all well off either," said mother. And then, looking out of the door: "Here come those people again. They say they want to buy our furniture; but actually they just want to see what they can pick up. I must go and watch them."

Mother stood up and went out. The voices of several women could be heard outside. I called Hungerh to me and started talking to him, asking him whether he could write, and whether he would be glad to leave.

"Shall we be going by train?"

"Yes, we shall go by train."

"And boat?"

"We shall take a boat first."

"Oh! Like this! With such a long moustache!" A strange shrill voice suddenly rang out.

I looked up with a start, and saw a woman of about fifty with prominent cheekbones and thin lips. With her hands on her hips, not wearing a skirt but with her trousered legs apart, she stood in front of me just like the compass in a box of geometrical instruments.

I was flabbergasted.

"Don't you know me? Why, I have held you in my arms!"

I felt even more flabbergasted. Fortunately my mother came in just then and said:

"He has been away so long, you must excuse him for forgetting. You should remember," she said to me, "this is Mrs. Yang from across the road. . . . She has a beancurd shop."

Then, to be sure, I remembered. When I was a child there was a Mrs. Yang who used to sit nearly all day long in the beancurd shop across the road, and everybody used to call her Beancurd Beauty. She used to powder herself, and her cheekbones were not so prominent then nor her lips so thin; moreover she remained seated all the time, so that I had never noticed this resemblance to a compass. In those days people said that, thanks to her, that beancurd shop did very good business. But, probably on account of my age, she had made no impression on me, so that later I forgot her entirely. However, the Compass was extremely indignant and looked at me most contemptuously, just as one might look at a Frenchman who had never heard of Napoleon or an American who had never heard of Washington, and smiling sarcastically she said:

"You had forgotten? Naturally I am beneath your notice. . . ."

"Certainly not . . . I . . ." I answered nervously, getting to my feet.

"Then you listen to me, Master Hsün. You have grown rich, and they are too heavy to move, so you can't possibly want these old pieces of furniture any more. You had better let me take them away. Poor people like us can do with them."

"I haven't grown rich. I must sell these in order to buy. . . ."

"Oh, come now, you have been made the intendant of a circuit, how can you still say you're not rich? You have three concubines now, and whenever you go out it is in a big sedan-chair with eight bearers. Do you still say you're not rich? Hah! You can't hide anything from me."

Knowing there was nothing I could say, I remained silent.

"Come now, really, the more money people have the more miserly they get, and the more miserly they are the more money they get . . ." remarked the Compass, turning indignantly away and walking slowly off, casually picking up a pair of mother's gloves and stuffing them into her pocket as she went out.

After this a number of relatives in the neighbourhood came to call. In the intervals between entertaining them I did some packing, and so three or four days passed.

One very cold afternoon, I sat drinking tea after lunch when I was aware of someone coming in, and turned my head to see who it was. At the first glance I gave an involuntary start, hastily stood up and went over to welcome him.

The newcomer was Jun-tu. But although I knew at a glance that this was Jun-tu, it was not the Jun-tu I remembered. He had grown to twice his former size. His round face, once crimson, had become sallow and acquired deep lines and wrinkles; his eyes too had become like his father's, the rims swollen and red, a feature common to most peasants who work by the sea and are exposed all day to the wind from the ocean. He wore a shabby felt cap and just one very thin padded jacket, with the result that he was shivering from head to foot. He carried a paper package and a long pipe, nor was his hand the plump red hand I remembered, but coarse and clumsy and chapped, like the bark of a pine tree.

Delighted as I was, I did not know how to express myself, and could only say:

"Oh! Jun-tu—so it's you? . . ."

After this there were so many things I wanted to talk about, they should have poured out like a string of beads: woodcocks, jumping fish, shells, zha. . . . But I was tongue-tied, unable to put all I was thinking into words.

He stood there, mixed joy and sadness showing on his face. His lips moved, but not a sound did he utter. Finally, assuming a respectful attitude, he said clearly:

"Master! . . ."

I felt a shiver run through me; for I knew then what a lamentably thick wall had grown up between us. Yet I could not say anything.

He turned his head to call:

"Shui-sheng, bow to the master." Then he pulled forward a boy who had been hiding behind his back, and this was just the Jun-tu of twenty years before,

only a little paler and thinner, and he had no silver necklet.

"This is my fifth," he said. "He's not used to company, so he's shy and awkward."

Mother came downstairs with Hung-erh, probably after hearing our voices.

"I got your letter some time ago, madam," said Jun-tu. "I was really so pleased to know the master was coming back. . . ."

"Now, why are you so polite? Weren't you playmates together in the past?" said mother gaily. "You had better still call him Brother Hsün as before."

"Oh, you are really too . . . What bad manners that would be. I was a child then and didn't understand." As he was speaking Jun-tu motioned Shui-sheng to come and bow, but the child was shy, and stood stock-still behind his father.

"So he is Shui-sheng? Your fifth?" asked mother. "We are all strangers, you can't blame him for feeling shy. Hung-erh had better take him out to play."

When Hung-erh heard this he went over to Shui-sheng, and Shui-sheng went out with him, entirely at his ease. Mother asked Jun-tu to sit down, and after a little hesitation he did so; then leaning his long pipe against the table he handed over the paper package, saying:

"In winter there is nothing worth bringing; but these few beans we dried ourselves, if you will excuse the liberty, sir."

When I asked him how things were with him, he just shook his head.

"In a very bad way. Even my sixth can do a little work, but still we haven't enough to eat . . . and then there is no security . . . all sorts of people want money, there is no fixed rule . . . and the harvests are bad. You grow things, and when you take them to sell you always have to pay several taxes and lose money, while if you don't try to sell, the things may go bad. . . ."

He kept shaking his head; yet, although his face was lined with wrinkles, not one of them moved, just as if he were a stone statue. No doubt he felt intensely bitter, but could not express himself. After a pause he took up his pipe and began to smoke in silence.

From her chat with him, mother learned that he was busy at home and had to go back the next day; and since he had had no lunch, she told him to go to the kitchen and fry some rice for himself.

After he had gone out, mother and I both shook our heads over his hard life: many children, famines, taxes, soldiers, bandits, officials and landed gentry, all had squeezed him as dry as a mummy. Mother said that we should offer him all the things we were not going to take away, letting him choose for himself.

That afternoon, he picked out a number of things; two long tables, four chairs, an incense burner and candlesticks, and one balance. He also asked for all the ashes from the stove (in our part we cook over straw, and the ashes can be used to fertilize sandy soil), saying that when we left he would come to take them away by boat.

That night we talked again, but not of anything serious; and the next morning he went away with Shui-sheng.

After another nine days it was time for us to leave. Jun-tu came in the morning. Shui-sheng did not come with him—he had just brought a little girl of five to watch the boat. We were very busy all day, and had no time to talk. We also had quite a number of visitors, some to see us off, some to fetch things, and some to do both. It was nearly evening when we left by boat, and by that time everything in the house, however old or shabby, large or small, fine or coarse, had been cleared away.

As we set off, in the dusk, the green mountains on either side of the river became deep blue, receding toward the stern of the boat.

Hung-erh and I, leaning against the cabin window, were looking out together at the indistinct scene outside, when suddenly he asked:

"Uncle, when shall we go back?"

"Go back? Do you mean that before you've left you want to go back?"

"Well, Shui-sheng has invited me to his home. . . ." He opened wide his black eyes in anxious thought.

Mother and I both felt rather sad, and so Jun-tu's name came up again. Mother said that ever since our family started packing up, Mrs. Yang from the bean-curd shop had come over every day, and the day before in the ash-heap she had unearthed a dozen bowls and plates, which after some discussion she insisted must have been buried there by Jun-tu, so that when he came to remove the ashes he could take them home at the same time. After making this discovery Mrs. Yang was very pleased with herself, and flew off taking the dog-teaser with her. (The dog-teaser is used by poultry keepers in our parts. It is a wooden cage inside which food is put, so that hens can stretch their necks in to eat but dogs can only look on furi-ously.) And it was a marvel, considering the size of her feet, how fast she could run.

I was leaving the old house farther and farther behind while the hills and rivers of my old home were also receding gradually ever farther in the distance. But I felt no regret. I only felt that all around me was an invisible high wall, cutting me off from my fellows, and this depressed me thoroughly. The vision of that small hero with the silver necklet among the watermelons had formerly been as clear as day, but now it suddenly blurred, adding to my depression.

Mother and Hung-erh fell asleep.

I lay down, listening to the water rippling beneath the boat, and knew that I was going my way. I thought: although there is such a barrier between Jun-tu and myself, the children still have much in common, for wasn't Hung-erh thinking of Shui-sheng just now? I hope they will not be like us, that they will not allow a barrier to grow between them. But again I would not like them, because they want to be akin, all to have a treadmill existence like mine, nor to suffer like Jun-tu until they become stupefied, nor yet, like others, to devote all their energies to dissipation. They should have a new life, a life we have never experienced.

The access of hope made me suddenly afraid. When Jun-tu asked for the incense burner and candlesticks I had laughed up my sleeve at him, to think that he still worshipped idols and could not put them out of his mind. Yet what I now called hope was no more than an idol I had created myself. The only difference was that what he desired was close at hand, while what I desired was less easily realized.

As I dozed, a stretch of jade-green seashore spread itself before my eyes, and above a round golden moon hung in a deep blue sky. I thought: hope cannot be said to exist, nor can it be said not to exist. It is just like roads across the earth. For actually the earth had no roads to begin with, but when many men pass one way, a road is made.

Translated by Yang Hsien-yi and Gladys Yang

67.

The Hai-Feng Peasant Association

Among the many foreign ideas and ideologies to attract the attention of intellectuals in the first two decades of the century was socialism. Particularly after the success of the Bolshevik revolution in Russia in 1917, Marxism gained more and more adherents, and in 1921 the Chinese Communist Party was founded. During the 1920s the main base of support for the new Communist Party was in the cities, among urban intellectuals and unionized factory workers. However, some progress was also made in organizing peasants.

Below is an account by P'eng P'ai (1896–1929) of his pioneering attempts to found peasant unions in 1921–1923. P'eng became interested in agrarian socialism while a student in Japan from 1918 to 1921. On his return he joined the Communist Party and began to put his ideas into practice. The account below covers the period of his initial success. He later had to flee Hai-feng when the local military authorities decided to suppress the unions.

THE BEGINNING OF A PEASANT MOVEMENT

In May, 1921, I was the Head of the Education Bureau of Hai-feng county. Still dreaming of realizing social revolution through education, I called for all the students in the county, most of whom were children of the wealthy, to celebrate the "May First" Labor Day at the county seat. That was an event unprecedented in the history of Hai-feng. Not one single worker or peasant participated in the celebration. The pupils of the First Elementary School paraded the streets, holding red banners with "Join the Reds" written on them. It was truly childish. The gentry class of Hai-feng thought that we were now going to practice property-sharing and wife-sharing, and they started numerous rumors, attacking us before [the Governor] Ch'en Chiung-ming. As a result, I was discharged from my duties, and, one after another, all the progressive teachers and school principals I had appointed also lost their positions.

At that time we were fighting a confusing battle

with Ch'en Chiung-ming's hometown paper, the *Lu An Daily*. Along with comrade Li Ch'un-t'ao and others I published a few issues of *Red Heart Weekly* as the mouthpiece of the workers and peasants. In fact, not a single worker on the streets or peasant on the farm was behind our journal or even had a hint of what we were doing. One day when I returned home, my little sister tried to prevent me from entering the house. She said, "I don't know why, but Mother is crying and says she is going to kill you." First I thought she was joking, but when I went into the family hall, I saw that indeed my mother was weeping.

It turned out my seventh younger brother had gotten hold of a "Letter to Peasants" which we published in the *Red Heart Weekly* and read the essay aloud. When my mother happened to hear it, tears flowed down her cheeks. Finally she burst out into loud wails, crying, "Our ancestors must have failed to accumulate virtue, for here we have a prodigal son. Your grandfather worked hard for what we have to-

269

day. If you carry on like this, our family will certainly be ruined!" I tried my best to console her, and she finally calmed down.

At that time it occurred to me that if the peasants could read this essay, they would be very happy, perhaps as happy as my wailing mother was upset. Besides, I was confident that peasants could be organized. Consequently, I abandoned the senseless war of words with the *Lu An Daily* and took up practical action in the farm villages. At the time, all my local friends were against it. They said, "Peasants are extremely disorderly. You won't be able to organize them. Plus, they are ignorant and resistant to campaigns of any kind. You'll just be wasting your energy."

My family could be considered a large landowner. Every year we would collect about 1000 piculs of grain and had over 1500 peasants under our control. Since my family had less than thirty members altogether, each member had fifty peasants as slaves. Consequently, when they heard that I wanted to start a peasant movement, my relatives all hated me with a passion (except for my third elder brother and fifth younger brother). My oldest brother would have liked to kill me, as would all the others in our lineage and village. The only thing I could do was ignore them.

On a certain day in May, I started my own campaign for the peasant movement. The first place I went to was a village in Red Mountain. I was dressed in a white Western-style student suit and wore a white hat. A peasant about thirty years of age was mixing manure in front of the village. When he saw me coming, he said, "Sir, how are you? Are you here to collect taxes? We are not putting on a play here."

"No, I'm not here to collect taxes for plays," I replied. "I'm here to be your friend. I know you have hardships, and I would like to talk with you."

To which the peasant said, "Yup, hardships are our destiny. So long now. We don't have the leisure to talk with you. Excuse me." And he hurried away.

After a little while, another peasant came along. He was a little over twenty and seemed more sensible. He asked me, "Sir, to which battalion do you belong? What is your rank? What is your business here?"

I replied, "I am not an official nor a military officer. I was a student, and I've come here to make friends with you."

He laughed and said, "We are useless people, unworthy of aristocrats like you. You must be kidding! Good-bye." Without a moment's hesitation, he turned and walked away. I was going to say something, but he had already gone too far to hear me. I became very distressed, especially when I recalled my friends' warning that my efforts would be a waste of energy.

When I was entering a second village, the dogs bared their teeth at me and barked fiercely. I took this demonstration of power for a sign of welcome and went straight into the village. But then I saw that all doors were locked. The villagers had all gone into town or into the fields. By the time I hurried to a third village, it was already twilight, and I was afraid that the villagers might suspect me of foul play, so I didn't go in. Instead, I headed for home.

Arriving home, I found that not one soul in my own family would talk to me. I had become an enemy. They had already eaten, and the only thing left was some rice gruel. I had a bit of the gruel and went to my room. I opened my diary and tried to record my achievements for that day, but all I could write was a big zero.

I spent all night trying to figure out methods that would work. At dawn I crawled out of my bed, had a bite of breakfast, and went back to the villages. On my way, I saw many peasants coming into the city, carrying bundles of potatoes or urine barrels on a pole over their shoulders. Whenever I met them on a narrow road, I would respectfully step aside to let them pass. Now, city folks usually would not make way for country folks. Instead, peasants who carried loads had to make way for the empty-handed city people. Thus I figured that at least some of the peasants would notice my respect towards them.

I found myself back at the village I had visited the day before. This time I encountered a peasant of forty, who asked me, "Sir, are you here to collect land rent?"

"No, no, I am here to help you collect your due. Someone owes you money, and you've forgotten it. I'm here to remind you."

"What!" the man exclaimed. "I'll be lucky not to owe others money. Who'd owe anything to me?"

"Don't you know?" I told him. "The landlords owe you a lot. Year in and year out, they sit at home and do nothing, and you work in the fields until you drop dead. In the end they are the ones who get the yields as rent. The piece of land worth at most 100 dollars has been tilled by you for a hundred, a thousand years—and how much grain have you submitted to the landlords? We think it's really unfair. That's why I'm here to talk with you, to find out a way to get even with the landlords."

The man smiled and said, "That'll be great indeed! But we will be locked up and beaten up if we only owe them a pint or a tenth of a pint. Such is fate—those who collect rent always collect rent, and those who till the fields always till the fields. Goodday, sir. I've got to go to town."

"Big brother, what is your name?" I asked.

"My name is—uh, I live in this village. Come again when you have time."

I realized that he was unwilling to tell me his name, and decided not to press him.

There were women working in the village, but most men were out in the fields. Since it was not proper for me to talk to women, I lingered for a long while, but finally moved on to another village.

Although I went through several villages that day, the result was the same as the day before: zero. The only difference was that in my diary I wrote down a few more sentences.

That evening, two things suddenly occurred to me. First, my language was too formal and refined; much of it was lost on the peasants. I would have to translate the jargon into everyday language. Second, my appearance, physique, and clothing were all different from the peasants'. They had long been oppressed and cheated by those who looked different, and naturally suspected that I was an enemy. Also, my appearance indicated my class, and thereby alienated the peasants. I decided, therefore, to wear simpler things. I also came up with a new plan. The next day, instead of going to the villages, I would go to the crossroads where I would meet more peasants.

The next day, I went to a main road in front of Lung-shan Temple. This road was the principal artery for traffic between the Red Mountain, Pei-hu, Ch'ih-an and Ho-k'ou regions. Every day, countless peasants passed by and rested in front of the Temple. I took this opportunity to talk to them, explaining the reasons for their hardships and the remedies, pointing out to them the evidence of landlords' oppression and discussing the necessity for the peasants to unite. At first I was talking to only a few people, but as the listeners increased, I began giving speeches. The peasants were, however, only half credulous. On that day, four or five peasants actually talked to me, and a dozen or more listened. It was a great achievement.

THE UNITED STRUGGLE OF SIX PEOPLE

After that day, I spent two weeks at intersections, talking to the peasants who passed by or giving speeches. Those who talked to me increased to a dozen or so, and my audience now consisted of thirty or forty, a major step forward. One day, as I walked

into town, I noticed something rather peculiar about how people in the stores looked at me. Then, many relatives started to come to see me, bringing food with them, and asking about my "illness." I was really puzzled. Later, a servant told me, "You'd better just stay home and rest from now on." I asked him why, and he replied, "The people out there all say you've gone mad. You ought to rest and take care of yourself." I almost died of laughter. I later discovered that it was a rumor started by the gentry, but many peasants in the villages also believed that I was insane. They seemed to be afraid of me and tried to avoid me. Nevertheless, I continued my campaign in front of Lung-shan Temple.

One day I gave a speech, saying that if the peasants could unite, they would be able to reduce their rent, and the landlords would be powerless. The various oppressive measures such as the three lease rules, presents to landlords, home delivery of rent, rent increases, and suspension of leases could all be eliminated. At this moment a peasant about forty years old shouted in a loud voice, "You're just shooting off your mouth! All this talk of reducing rent! As long as your family's Ming-ho estate keeps harassing us for rent, I won't believe a word of it."

Before I could make a reply, a young peasant beside me stood up and retorted. "You're wrong," he said. "The land you till belongs to Ming-ho. If Mingho reduces its rent, only you benefit. What about me? I don't till Ming-ho's land. The problem is not how to plead for the lowering of rents, but whether we can unite as a group. This is like a chess game; victory belongs to those who have the best strategies. If we do not have any strategy, we will eventually lose, and it will be no use begging from others. We are not talking about your personal problems, but the problems of the majority."

I was very happy to hear this and said to myself, "Here is a comrade!" After asking his name, I invited Mr. Chang Ma-an to come to my place to talk that night. I expressed my joy when he arrived, and he said to me, "Often, after listening to your speech, we argue with the villagers who are still 'asleep.' They are always afraid that you are telling lies. But a few of us really believe you."

"Who are they?" I asked.

He named Lin P'ei, Lin Huan, Li Lao-ssu, and Li Ssu-hsien. "They are all good friends of mine," he added.

"Do you think we should ask them to join our discussion? Would you go get them while I prepare some tea?"

He agreed, and in a little while the tea was ready and Chang came back with his friends, all young peasants under thirty who spoke and acted enthusiastically. After I learned their names, I started to talk about the peasant movement with them. I raised a difficult problem, "Every day I go to the villages to propagate my ideas, but the peasants pay no attention to me and refuse to talk. Do you have a solution?"

Lin P'ei said, "The reasons are, first, the peasants are too busy. Second, what you say is too profound; sometimes even I can't understand you. Third, you lack people you know to lead the way. The best time for us to go is around seven or eight at night, when there is a lot of free time in the villages. Then you need to make things easier to understand. And we can also lead the way for you."

When I heard what he said, I realized how smart he was. He also warned me in a very serious manner that I should never show any contempt for the gods when I talk to the peasants. This was a comment that gave me even more respect for him.

"Let's start a Peasants' Union now," suggested Li Lao-ssu. "If more people join us, that's great; but even if no one joins, we'll keep it going. How does that sound?"

"Great idea," I said. "Tomorrow I'll go with two of you to the villages, and at night we'll make a public speech." They all thought that was a good plan, and it was decided that Chang Ma-an and Lin P'ei should go with me the next morning.

We continued our discussion for a long time. After the meeting, I wrote "Victory is in sight."

The next morning, after breakfast, my peasant friends Chang and Lin came to get me, and we went to the villages around Red Mountain. Because of their introduction, the villagers felt close to me and talked to me sincerely. I asked them to come to the lecture that night, and they responded enthusiastically. When evening came, they had tables, chairs, and lights all prepared for me. I had an audience of sixty to seventy. Children were in front, men behind them, and women in the rear. I talked about the causes of the hardships peasants endured, the facts of landlords' exploitation, and the ways to peasants' liberation. I used the question-and-answer format, and the peasants approved of what I said. I also came to know that they could understand me. I concluded my speech by saying that the next time I would play a phonograph and give a magic show. I promised to let them know in advance.

The next day we went to other villages, and the results were equally encouraging. On the third day I announced that I would give a magic show and a lecture. When the time came, more than 200 peasants turned up. They applauded my show and listened to my lecture. For the next week or two I used this method, which proved very successful. But I began to notice that Lin P'ei and Chang Ma-an appeared pensive, distressed, and listless. I thought that the landlords must have started rumors that made them worry, so I asked them what was wrong. At first they wouldn't say anything, but when I pressed, one of them said, "Our parents and brothers are very upset because we spend our time with you instead of working in the fields. My parents scolded me, saying 'You hang around with P'eng P'ai. P'eng P'ai won't starve to death, but you sure will!' This morning when I was leaving the house, my father came very close to hitting me. And it's not just my parents; my wife and my brothers are equally upset. That's why I'm dejected."

After deliberating for a long time, the three of us came up with a plan. I went and borrowed three silver dollars from a friend, and gave them to Lin P'ei. When Lin returned home that day, he took the coins out of his pocket, counted them, and dropped them on the floor, making noises. Sure enough, his mother asked him where he had gotten the money. He answered, "Who'd go out there without pay? Do you think I only run around for fun? I'm doing this for money." When his mother heard this, her anger turned into joy. His brothers also stopped their criticism. His wife, of course, was only too delighted to see that her husband had money. After this act, Lin P'ei turned the money over to Chang Ma-an, who also did the same thing in front of his mother, with equal triumph. The money was then returned to my friend. This ruse bought us about a week's time, during which Lin and Chang could work hard. They progressed rapidly and were actually able to give speeches afterwards.

However, nothing was more difficult than asking the peasants to join the Union. They would always say, "I'm all for it. When everyone else has joined, I will certainly do so." We explained to them that if everyone were to think that way, the Peasants' Union would not be a reality in even a thousand years. We told them that joining the Union is like crossing a river. On this shore is hardship, on the other side happiness; each and every one of us is afraid of drowning, and no one dares to be the first to cross the river, but by joining the Union we can cross the river together, hand-in-hand. We described the Peasants' Union as an organization of mutual assistance in which all members are as close as brothers. Some of the peasants were persuaded by our argument and agreed to join in, but when I wrote down their names in a register, others became apprehensive and hurried away. I had to stop using the register. Still we could only enlist a couple of people in a week, and after over a month's effort, we only had around thirty members.

At about this time, an accident happened in the Yün-lu village of Red Mountain. The daughter-in-law of a member of our Union, who was only six years old, fell into an outhouse and drowned. Thirty or forty people from her family came to Yün-lu. They charged our member with murder and were determined to avenge the girl's death. The thirty members of our Union held a meeting to decide on counter-measures, and we agreed to go to Yün-lu to reason with the avengers. When we arrived, we asked them on what grounds they made their accusations and recorded all their names in a notebook. We bluffed them, saying, "You're all tricked." Not knowing what we had up our sleeves, they all became apprehensive because their names had been put down on paper. Then a district chief named Cho Meng-mei came to mediate, suggesting that our friend be punished. He was driven away by the members of the Union, and only barely escaped a beating. The avengers were now even more intimidated. They pleaded with us: "At least let us examine the body."

We said to them, "Go ahead, if you dare to. If you're not afraid of being put in jail, you can go right ahead and open up the coffin!" The women were all frightened when they heard the word "jail," and they pulled at the shirts of their men, wanting to go home.

Upon this we pressed even harder for them to leave. They asked us, "We came here on account of our relative. What does it have to do with you?"

"Don't you know we have formed a Peasants' Union?" we replied. "The Union is a union for the poor. Its members are all closely united, closer than real brothers. What concerns one concerns all. Today, this friend of ours is in trouble, and we have come to help him, risking our own lives. Since you are also peasants, someday you will certainly join the Union, and once you do so, we'll help you just as we've helped him. Now, why don't you go home."

Crestfallen, they left, and there was not the least bit of damage done to us. News got around, and many peasants learned that the brothers of the Union were loyal to each other and were able to help each other. We also used this incident for the purpose of propaganda: "We have no power if we are not united. We will be taken advantage of if we have no power. To have power, join the Peasants' Union immediately." And membership gradually increased.

Not long afterwards, we found that some peasants would try to get others' land to till, and landlords would increase rent and change tenants. So the Union drew up some regulations to prevent such incidents. Briefly, these regulations were:

1. Unless permission is given by the member and by the Union, no one may encroach on a member's rented land.
2. Unless the member relinquishes his lease and the Union gives its permission, no one may rent the land already rented to a member of the Union. Violators are subject to severe punishment.
3. In case a landlord takes back his land from a member by means of increasing the rent, and as a result a member's livelihood is in danger, he may ask for help from the Union, which will either persuade nearby members to allow him to till part of their land, or will introduce him to another trade.

After the regulations were publicized, there was no longer any competition for land among our members, and the landlords also were afraid to raise the rent of members of the Union. At times, non-members would fight for the land already rented by our members, but under the advice of the Union's representatives, they would usually quickly return the land to the members. Once, a landlord became annoyed and refused to lease his land to the original tenant (i.e., a member of our Union). We then announced a boycott, and the landlord, fearing that his land would lie fallow, was forced to lease the land back to the member. This was another victory for us.

When the peasants rowed their boats into the cities to collect nightsoil, etc., local ruffians would force them to pay a fee of two cents to anchor their boats on the pier. If a peasant failed to comply, his rudder would be removed, and to claim his rudder, he had to pay several dollars. The peasants were all annoyed by this, and our Union declared that this would have to stop. Our strategy was as follows. Whenever these ruffians passed by the villages or brought their boats by, we would charge tolls. If they refused to pay us, we would also refuse to pay the "pier fee." In this way, the pier fee was abolished without much ado.

We also discovered that peasants easily got involved in quarrels, and as a result allowed themselves to be used by the gentry class. They would file lawsuits in the courts and end up breaking up their families and losing everything they ever owned. For this reason, we sent out notices to the members of the Union, telling them that any quarrels or disagreements among members should first be reported to the Union. If any member should fail to report a case to the Union, but instead went straight to the gentry or the courts, he would be expelled from the Union even if he was in the right, and the Union would use all its power to support his opponent. When a member of our Union had a confrontation with a non-member, he also had to report to the Union. In negotiating with a landlord, if a member did not report to the Union, the Union would not be responsible for his failure.

From then on, the locus of political power moved from the hands of the gentry and the rich to the Peasants' Union. The police and judicial branches of the local government witnessed a decrease in "business," which made the policemen and judges resent the Union. As the Union was able to solve many problems for the peasants and won many victories for them, its membership increased daily.

FROM THE RED MOUNTAIN UNION TO THE HAI–FENG CENTRAL UNION

By now it was September, 1922. We had about 500 members, most of whom were from the twenty-eight villages of Red Mountain. So we set a day in September to hold the Founding Assembly of the Peasants' Union of Red Mountain. Besides the members, the principal of the high school, Li Yüeh-t'ing, and the principal of the elementary school, Yang Szu-cheng, attended the assembly and gave speeches. Huang Feng-lin was elected as the head of the Red Mountain Union. The meeting ended with a tea party, and the members all went home happy. This founding assembly influenced the people of the various villages, and applicants grew in number. On the average we were getting ten new members every day.

The procedure for joining the Union was as follows. The applicant had to appear in person at the Union Headquarters and pay a membership fee of twenty cents. (Originally we had intended to have them pay a registration fee plus yearly or monthly membership dues, but we were afraid that this might

be too complicated for them, so, for clarity and propaganda purposes, we decided to charge twenty cents per year. But we planned to change it when the peasants became more experienced as members of the Union.) Then they would receive a briefing and a membership card (the words were printed on a blank calling card) like this:

PEASANTS' UNION MEMBERSHIP CARD
Date   Address   Name
No work, No food. Cooperate! Unite!

At this time the Union issued manifestoes and publicized its benefits. In addition, we continued our campaign efforts day and night. In October, we had an average of twenty new members every day. Following the example of Red Mountain, numerous other areas all established their own regional unions. The county seat was now surrounded on all sides by union organizations, and the time had come for us to prepare for a Hai-feng Central Union.

A "Funeral Expenses Co-op" was formed by the Union. Any member of the Union could join the co-op, and we reached a total of around 150 members. The rule was that for any member who died or who lost a parent, every other member would donate two cents for funeral expenses. The first day this method was announced, a member's father died. The members each put out two cents, which came to more than thirty dollars, and they also went to attend the funeral. The member concerned was delighted. On the fifth day, another member's father died. As the members of the "Funeral Expenses Co-op" could no longer afford the two cents, the Union had to advance the money, which was to be paid back by the co-op later on. On the seventh day, a member died, and the Union had to advance another thirty dollars. The members of the co-op panicked: five or six people had died within the first ten days; what were they to do if the trend should continue? An assembly was held, and it was decided that the co-op would be temporarily discontinued, and that it would be resumed when the funds of the Union became more sufficient.

A medical dispensary was also established. It was located on the main street of Hai-feng. The doctor in charge was an enthusiast of the Peasants' Movement and a trained Western-style physician. Any member of the Peasants' Union who needed medicine could present his membership card and get a 50 percent discount. Non-members could also get medicine, but at the full price. All members were entitled to the free clinic operated by the doctor, whose wife also delivered babies for no charge. Any medicine used in connection with natal care was also half-priced, and usually came to twenty or thirty cents only. This brought many peasants to the dispensary for medicine and for deliveries. We also caught some non-members posing as members, using borrowed membership cards. We had to add several regulations on the membership card, restricting its use to members themselves. We also made up a rule that a member must pay two cents for the replacement of a lost membership card.

On the first day of January, 1923, the Hai-feng Central Union was established. The total membership had reached 20,000. And the population within the Union's jurisdiction was 100,000, a quarter of the population of the entire county. On that day, more than sixty village representatives of the Union came for the assembly, the procedure of which was:

1. The chairman announced the purpose of the assembly.
2. The representatives made their reports.
3. The chairman reported on the preparation for the Central Union.
4. Speeches.
5. Elections.
6. Discussion of regulations.
7. Proposals.
8. Banquet.

P'eng P'ai was elected as the President of the Union, Yang Ch'i-shan the vice-president, Lao Ching-ch'ing the treasurer, Lin P'ei the manager, Chang Ma-an the investigator . . . (the rest has escaped my mind). . . .

One problem that we discussed during the Assembly was that membership dues might have to be increased to support the Central Union. We investigated other possibilities and came up with the following idea. Peasants sold their goods in the sweet-potato markets, the sugar markets, the green

vegetable markets, the bean markets, the rice markets, the firewood markets, the pig markets, and the hay markets, all of which were controlled by the gentry, the local landowners, and the temple priests. We figured that the sweet-potato markets alone must produce at least 500 dollars in income. If we took account of all the markets, then there would be 3000 dollars to 4000 dollars. Could we take over the rights to these markets? If we took over the markets, we would inevitably come into conflict with the gentry. So, the first thing to do was to negotiate with them. If they were stubborn, our plan was to move the sweet-potato market, and within three days, all other markets would follow suit and move to other places. The Union then took action. We first made a model steelyard, and sent a member to the sweet-potato market to supervise the sales. The gentry protested heatedly. The Union then put out notices for all the peasants of the county, ordering them to move their sweet-potatoes to stands next to their neighborhood Union offices and prohibiting them from selling sweet-potatoes in the old market. As a result, we won the battle and took control over the sweet-potato market. The income from the market was allocated to support the dispensary. . . .

Concerning the work of the Department of Education, the peasants were afraid of the "New Education" program. Whenever the subject was mentioned, fear would show up on their faces. . . . The Union, however, created a new slogan, "Peasant Education," which meant the founding of peasant schools. Our "Peasant Education" program was different from the "New Education" program. It aimed at teaching peasants to keep accounts so landlords could not cheat them, to write letters, to use the abacus, to write the names of various feeds and agricultural tools, and to operate the Union. That was all. The peasants were all for the program. Besides, the Union hired teachers for them at a low cost, provided school facilities, and did not charge the students. No wonder the peasants were happy.

Where did the funds for the schools come from? Each village where a Peasant School was formed set apart a piece of land of suitable size, and this was the "school's field," rented by the school from a landlord. The seeds and manure were paid for by the Union; the tilling tools, animals, and human labor were provided by the students' families, who would divide among themselves the duties of tilling and sowing. When the time came for weeding, the teacher of the school would lead the students to the "school's field," and divide them and the field into four parts. Each group of students would be responsible for a part of the field. A contest would be started, and, in no time, the fields would be pruned, while the students had learned something about farming. When the grain was ripe, the students' relatives again went out to the fields to reap the harvest. The rent was paid to the landlord, and the rest of the harvest became the teacher's salary. Within a month after this system was started, a dozen such Peasant Schools were founded, including night schools, all of which were under the leadership and supervision of the Union's Department of Education. From then on, over 500 village children, hitherto completely deprived of an opportunity for education, attended school. . . .

At this time the Hai-feng Central Union reached its peak of activities. The county Magistrate of the time, Weng Kuai-ch'ing, who was Ch'en Chiung-ming's most trusted man, disapproved of the Union, but he dared not ban it, and we were allowed more freedom to develop our programs. Also, the Union had by now acquired considerable power. The slogans we used for the peasants were:

1. Reduce rent.
2. Abolish the "three lease rules."
3. Abolish presents to landlords (chickens, ducks, rice, or money).
4. Don't give bribes to the police.

The slogans we used for outsiders were:

1. Improve agriculture.
2. Increase peasants' knowledge.
3. Perform charitable deeds.

Our plan was not to reduce rent until after five years of preparation.

Soon it was the Chinese New Year of 1923. Dragon dancers and music troupes from all the villages came to celebrate, and the Union organized a New Year's Festival for all peasants in Hai-feng. On the 16th of the first month, the Festival was held at the grass-carpeted field in front of the Tung-lin Ancestral Temple at Ch'iao-tung. More than 6000 members and 3000 non-members participated, and the banners of each village's bands, dragon dancers, and music troupes danced in the air. The sequence of the Festival was (1) Music, (2) The chairman announced the purpose of the Festival, (3) Speeches, (4) Songs and music, (5) Dragon dances, (6) Three cheers for the peasants, (7) Firecrackers. The speakers included P'eng P'ai, Huang Feng-lin, and Yang Ch'i-shan, who pointed out that before the proletarian revolution was realized, there could be no joyous New Year, for New Year's Day was a time for the exploiters to oppress us and to demand us to pay our debts. We were now united in our hardships, not in joy. However, this was an opportunity in which we might demonstrate our strength to our enemies, and awaken the spirit of revolution in ourselves. We were prepared for a battle with our enemies. This was the reason why, on the one hand, we felt weighed down by our emotions, but on the other hand elated.

On that day, we issued 2000 new membership cards, and received over 400 dollars in dues. It was the highest point in the history of the Union. After that, around 100 new members would join each day, and we could hardly keep up with the work. Every day about 300 peasant friends would come to the Union for information, for conversation, and to sign up as members. We were extremely busy.

But we also caught the attention of the landlords, who said, "We didn't think they would succeed. We thought all that talk was nonsense. But now, it actually has happened!" . . .

Translated by Clara Yu

68.

The Dog-Meat General

The abolition of the monarchy and the literary civil service examination system did not put an end to abuses of power or incompetence on the part of officials. To the contrary, disorder provided leeway for the rise of warlords, many of whom were not only incompetent and corrupt, but also brutal and destructive.

Below is an account of Chang Tsung-ch'ang (1881–1932), a poor boy who, in less than thirty years, rose from juvenile delinquent to general to governor of a province. When the Nationalist Party succeeded in its Northern Expedition against the warlords in 1928, Chang retreated to Manchuria, then to Japan. On a visit back to his native area in 1932 he was assassinated by the son of one of his earlier victims. The article below was written after his death, based on the responses a magazine received when it solicited accounts of his cruelties and oppression from its readers.

Chang Tsung-ch'ang, nicknamed "Dog-meat General" and "Lanky General," was from I county in Shantung. His father was a trumpet-player (hired for funeral processions, etc.) and barber, and his mother was a shamaness. At the age of twelve or thirteen, Chang started helping his father by playing the cymbals. When he was fifteen or sixteen he went with his mother to Yin-k'ou, and worked as a servant in a gambling house, mixing with pickpockets and thieves. The gentry of the town, annoyed, drove him away. He then fled to Kuan-tung [in Manchuria] to join the "bearded bandits." His mother stayed on at Yin-k'ou, and lived with the proprietor of a bathhouse, then with a cobbler, then with a cloth vendor. The cloth vendor, in a fit of jealousy, killed the cobbler, and was sent to jail. Because of this, Chang's mother was sent into exile. Lacking any means of transportation, she gave herself to a rickshaw puller so that he would take her back to I county. In this way she returned to the trumpet-player. But the trumpet-player was too poor to support her, so he sold her to a grain wholesaler named Chia for some millet.

We all know that Chang Tsung-ch'ang had two fathers, and this is the explanation.

When the revolution started in 1911, Chang led about 100 "bearded bandits" from Kuan-tung to Yen-t'ai [in Shantung] to join Commander Hu Ying's army. When Hu resisted the revolutionary forces, Chang went to Shanghai to join the regiment commander of the revolutionary army. At that time, there was a truce between the North and the South, and the regiment commander resigned, but not before he had made Chang, who was not only strong but also brave, the leader of his men. Chang and his army were then reorganized by Commander Ch'eng Te-ch'uan of Kiangsu. Now called "Kuang-fu" troops, they were sent to Feng-p'ei and Hsiao-i to put down bandits, and were under the Division Commander Leng Yü-ch'iu. When the Second Revolution started and Leng was defeated, Chang took over Leng's soldiers and gained even more military power. However, because Chang was connected with Leng, his troops were soon dissolved by Feng Kuo-chang, the honorary title "model supervisory regiment" given him was but an empty name. From then on, Chang made a profession of murdering his revolutionary comrades. The assassination of Shanghai's Commander, Ch'en Ch'i-mei, was Chang's doing. Because of this, Chang was taken into the confidence of Feng Kuo-chang. When Feng was the national Vice President, he appointed Chang as the Chief of his personal guards. . . .

Chang was very brave in battle, but he had no mind for strategy. His soldiers were mostly bandits, and therefore very valiant warriors, which by and large accounted for his success in military ventures. But he also had an advisor who assisted him in military maneuvers, the fortune-teller T'ung Hua-ku. During the Feng-tien-Chihli warfare, Chang was stationed to the east of the Hsi-feng Pass. One day, Chang came across T'ung and went up to him for advice. T'ung told him that his physiognomy revealed that he would achieve great distinction. He also predicted that the next day, when the Chihli troops passed by train, the train would derail, and if Chang would take this opportunity, he could attack them and win a big victory. The next day, Chang stationed his troops to wait for the Chihli troops. Just as T'ung had predicted, the train derailed, and Chang routed the enemies. At the time of the battle T'ung paced back and forth on top of a hill, his hair untied, his mouth uttering words of magic. After the battle, Chang asked T'ung to step down from the hill, and with utmost deference appointed him as his military advisor. From then on, Chang followed T'ung's words to the letter where military action was concerned.

It turned out that the fortune-teller was rather shrewd. The night that he met Chang, he hired a few peasants to remove the screws connecting the rails over a bridge, thereby causing the derailment. Because he knew Chang could easily be fooled, he used a fairytale as a steppingstone to a career. At any rate, on account of Chang's military distinctions, he was finally appointed as Governor of Shantung. . . .

Not long after Chang became Governor, two phrases were heard all over the cities: "Cut apart to catch light," and "listen to the telephone." The former referred to the human heads which were treated like watermelons, cut in halves to bask in the sun; the latter referred to the same, except the heads were hung from telephone poles, and from afar they seemed to be listening on the telephone. At the same time, at the train stations along the Chiao-chi and Ching-p'u lines, people started to hear the strange expression "My head is my passport; my ass is my

ticket." This was because people were being regularly kicked, beaten up, abused in vile language, and spat in the face by the soldiers. To the sights of the city of Chi-nan there were also added White Russian soldiers, who were drunkards, ruffians, and rapists. Living in Shantung at this time, one could really feel the truth in the saying "A man's life is less valuable than that of a chicken."

Soon after Chang Tsung-ch'ang came to his post, he unveiled his ugly nature and started his vile deeds. Under his "steel sword" policy, the once-flourishing academies disappeared, the better students fled, and the provincial assembly was silenced. On the other hand, clever people moved with the current and began buttering Chang up. Upholding the philosophy that "In an age of chaos, don't miss the chance to loot during the fire," they went after offices. From circuit Intendants and county Magistrates to bureau Chiefs, all positions were refilled with much pomp. Whenever these henchmen went to a local district, their first priority was to extort and exploit, so that they could repay past favors and secure future ones, whereas the people were becoming skinnier daily. Too true was the proverb "In the official's house, wine and meat are allowed to rot, but on the roads are the bones of those who starved to death."

Chang Tsung-ch'ang came to Shantung in June of 1925, and he fled on the 30th of April, 1928. In these three years he took a total of 350,000 dollars of the people's blood money.

Chang Tsung-ch'ang was a warmonger, by nature fond of disorder. After his arrival in Shantung, there was not even one day of peace. In the Lu-su war, Chang fought with Sun Ch'uan-fang back and forth between Pang-fu, Hsü-chou, Han-chuang, and Lin-ch'eng. In the Lu-yü war, he battled Chin Yün-o and Li Chi at Mount T'ai. In the battle at Pa-li-wa, he almost lost all his arms and men. In the battle at Nan-k'ou, he fought side by side with the Feng-t'ien and Chihli troops against the Nationalist army, forcing them into Kansu and Shensi. During the Nationalists' Northern Expedition, Chang fought like a wounded beast along the Chin-p'u railroad.

After each battle, the field was strewn with bodies. The loss of the soldiers required replacement, which in turn required military funds, which resulted in higher taxes. When funds were raised, more soldiers were drafted, and another war was in the making. This cycle was repeated again and again. This was the way Chang Tsung-ch'ang ruled the province of Shantung from 1925 to 1928. The white banners of recruitment flew all over the province, and young people were driven straight into their graves. In such a situation, how could the people of Shantung escape hardship and poverty?

Taxation

During the less than four years that Chang Tsung-ch'ang ruled, there was not one day that he failed to take money from the people. Besides the regular taxes, there were special taxes and blatant extortions. Whenever he needed a sum of money, he would issue an order to several counties for them to come up with the cash. And when he spent the money, well, that was the end of that. Thus, the people of Shantung were really in deep water, and they suffered more than the rest of the nation.

The regular land taxes were eight to twenty dollars for each tael of land value. After the Northern Expedition, the Provincial Bureau of Finance released a statistics report showing that "From the day Chang Tsung-ch'ang came to Shantung till the day he left, the recorded land taxes, tributes, and special taxes that he collected amount to a sum which, if figured by regular rates of taxation, would exceed all taxes to be paid until 1939."

Below are the various types of taxes he collected:

1. One-time special land tax for military reconstruction
2. One-time special tribute rice for reconstruction
3. One-time special land tax for suppressing the Reds
4. Tribute rice for suppressing the Reds
5. Special land tax for military purposes
6. Supplementary land tax for military purposes
7. Supplementary tribute rice for military purposes
8. Supplementary tax for the Li-tung Pass
9. Special tax for relief funds
10. Special supplementary tax for river conservancy works
11. Supplementary tax for highway works
12. Tax for barracks works
13. Military loans
14. Government bonds for reconstruction
15. Special tax on tobacco and liquor
16. Government sales special tax
17. Registration fees for establishments
18. Stamp tax for registrations
19. Registration fees for real estate
20. Tax for license to distribute paper currency
21. Stamp tax on paper currency
22. Long distance telephone fees
23. Tax on tobacco seeds
24. Fines on tobacco saplings
25. Business license fees
26. Donations for army shoes
27. Pension certificates for the families of soldiers in the First Army Corps who were killed in the Chia-tzu war
28. Pension certificates for the families of the soldiers in the Chih-lu Army Corps who were killed in the war against the Reds
29. Fees for license to examine tobacco
30. Stamp tax for license to sell tobacco
31. Donations for the construction of a living shrine for Chang Tsung-ch'ang
32. Donations for a bronze statue of Chang Tsung-ch'ang
33. Advance for firewood and straw
34. Donations for the entertainment of the officers and soldiers
35. Restaurant taxes
36. Tax on dogs
37. Tax on dwellings
38. Tax on wealthy families
39. Poll-tax
40. Exclusive sales of opium by government operated stores
41. Tax on opium-pipe lighters
42. Tax on light vehicles
43. Tax on rickshaws
44. Stamp taxes
45. Tax on livestock
46. Local tax on already-taxed foreign goods
47. Tax on vegetables
48. Exclusive sales of nightsoil by government operated "golden-juice" stores
49. Tax on prostitution houses
50. Tax on theatrical performances
51. Tax on chickens . . .

Flooding the Market with Paper Money

Chang Tsung-ch'ang issued the following paper currencies:

1. Banknotes of the Provincial Bank of Shantung
2. Military stamps
3. Co-op certificates

Altogether several tens of millions of dollars were

issued, all without any reserve to back them up. When he was losing his battles on the frontiers, these forms of currency came to be regularly discounted and financial chaos resulted. Chang's soldiers continued to use his paper money for purchases, however, without accepting a discount on the face value. If anyone objected they would use their fists, legs, and foul tongues against their opponents. For this reason, arguments and fights were frequent, and the merchants suffered. There is a story that a store refused to accept military stamps. Chang gave orders to arrest the owner, who was beaten up and then shot.

Extortion for Military Expenses

In order to raise funds to pay his soldiers and buy arms, Chang Tsung-ch'ang frequently "borrowed" from various banks and commercial unions. Though these were loans in name, they were extortions in fact. The Kung-li Banking House, which had operated in Shantung for over a decade, went out of business because of such extortions, and its manager went into exile. . . .

Building a Living Shrine and Casting a Bronze Statue

To manifest his own "merits and distinctions," Chang planned to build a living shrine and a bronze statue for himself along the Ta-ming Lake of Chi-nan. The expenses were extorted from the people. He shipped a full trainload of granite from Mount T'ai for the construction. But because of the rapid advance of the troops of the Northern Expedition, there was not enough time for the actual work to begin. However, the "donations" for these purposes had been collected in full. . . .

Youth Squads

Chang Tsung-ch'ang especially recruited an army of teenagers for his son, calling them "young students of war." Their arms were specially designed small foreign-made rifles, and they were given good uniforms, food, and pay. Chang appointed his son the leader, and put several thousand such youths under his control. The youth squads were stationed at the southern barracks of the Chinan area. When they were in training, they would sing the children's song, "There is a fat little baby in our family." Consequently, they came to be known as the "Baby Squads.". . .

Not Paying the Troops

Chang kept all the money that he extorted from the people for his personal use, seldom paying his soldiers. Consequently, his men lost their confidence in him, and he lost many battles. In order to improve the morale, he raised some money to pay the men, but it turned out to be too little. When each soldier only got fifty cents, they said to each other, "Let's fight another fifty cents' worth of war for Chang Tsung-ch'ang."

Salvos Against Heaven

In the summer of 1927, there was a severe drought in Shantung. Not a drop of rain fell, and the crops were all dying. Chang Tsung-ch'ang ordered a general fast and personally went to the "Dragon King Temple" to pray for rain. But the Dragon King was apparently not impressed, and the drought continued. In a rage, Chang slapped the Dragon King's face many times. He then went to the Chang-chuang Arsenal and fired cannon balls into the sky for hours, so as to vent his anger at Heaven. Nevertheless, it still did not rain. . . .

State Sales of Opium

Chang Tsung-ch'ang decreed that opium could only be sold by the state, but an opportunist opened up a store in a newly built shopping center, calling it "Opium Quitting Center." But in fact it was an opium store, and every month this person presented a gift of "State sales tax on opium" to Chang.

Educational Background

Once Chang Tsung-ch'ang held a meeting of high-ranking military officers in the governor's office, and these officers introduced themselves, one saying, "I graduated from X university," another saying, "I am attending Y university." Hard-pressed, Chang Tsung-ch'ang said, "I, Chang Tsung-ch'ang, am a graduate of the College of the Green Forest."*

Drafting Soldiers

Chang literally dragged young people from the streets to become his soldiers so that he could send them to the frontiers, using their flesh against the cannon balls of the enemy. Many students were dragged away,

* The Green Forest was a term for the hideout of bandits.

and only after negotiations, were released. In order to prevent such incidents, the schools issued each student a cloth tag with his name and the school's seal printed on it. In this way the students were distinguished from the common people.

Clearing the Streets

Whenever Chang came out of his office, he would clear the streets, and all traffic was stopped. The main street in front of the governor's office was sprinkled with clean water. In front of his motorcade, he had the showy white Russian cavalry squad. Soldiers were stationed all along the streets, their rifles loaded with real bullets, their backs to the street. All precautions were taken against possible assassins. . . .

Translated by Clara Yu

69.

The General Strike

Unionization of China's urban workers began with the May Fourth Movement in 1919 and made considerable progress in the early 1920s, aided by organizers from the young Communist Party. It led to fifty major strikes in 1921 and ninety-one in 1922. The first serious violence against strikers took place on February 7, 1923, when the soldiers of the warlord Wu P'ei-fu attacked striking railway workers and killed sixty-five. During the following two years, anti-union repression became widespread. The incident that created the greatest uproar occurred on May 30, 1925, when the English police in the International Settlement in Shanghai shot at a group of demonstrators, killing ten. A general strike was then organized, which involved 150,000 workers, merchants, and students and lasted three months. For over a year sympathizers throughout China contributed money, boycotted foreign goods, and staged strikes. In the meantime, the Communist Party had formed an alliance with the Nationalist Party to overthrow the warlords and establish a national government. Members of the Communist Party joined the Nationalist Party and tried to continue their labor union work within the framework of the alliance. For example, during the Northern Expedition, Communists aided the advance of Chiang Kai-shek's army by organizing peasants and workers along the way. The alliance between the two parties was, however, fragile, since the Nationalists drew their strength from the bourgeoisie and landlords, whom the Communists opposed.

Below is an account of a strike held in Shanghai during the Northern Expedition, organized by the Communist-led General Labor Union. The account appeared in a Communist Party newspaper, Guide Weekly, *shortly after the strike. It reveals both the goals and avowed principles of the labor union movement as well as the fragility of the alliance of the Nationalists and Communists. Less than three months after it was written, Chiang Kai-shek ordered an attack on the unions and a purge of Communists from the Nationalist Party. For months thereafter, Communists were hunted down and killed. Not until 1936 would there again be any semblance of cooperation between the Nationalists and the Communists.*

A RECORD OF THE SHANGHAI
GENERAL STRIKE

By Shih Ying
Recorded 6 A.M., February 27, 1927

On February 19th the working class of Shanghai started a historic struggle which has unleashed the anger of the urban masses and launched the common people's fight for political power. A new page has been turned in the revolutionary history of China; a

heroic record has been added to the history of the working class of the world.

The February 7th Movement of 1923 and the May 30th Movement of 1925 had different characteristics, a result of their historical and social causes. The heroic February 7th Incident demonstrated that the first struggles of the Chinese working class were struggles for political freedom under the rule of feudal warlords. The fierce May 30th Movement showed, in addition, that during a time of increasing nationalism, the working class was determined to revolt against imperialism. These two movements led to the Northern Expedition to eliminate the warlords. The unity formed by the Chinese working class was itself a political unity, and the principle that motivated the actions of the workers was "political power to the masses for the revolution."

Once the Northern Expedition had begun, the spirit of revolution shook every city and village. Since Shanghai is the most important city in our country, the workers there are the leaders of the entire working class, endowed with a natural responsibility in this historic, revolutionary struggle. Thus, it was among the working masses of Shanghai that the general strike broke out on February 19th. But this was no mere strike; it was a revolution. The initial stage lasted only five days; yet, since the workers went back to work, revolutionary activities have continued to increase. The following is a record of what happened in the initial stage of the revolution.

Prelude to the Strike

On the eve of the February 19th strike, the victorious Northern Expedition forces had claimed control of the nearby province of Chekiang. Although the actual military victory was some distance away, it struck fear in the warlords controlling Shanghai. The uncertainty of their rule provided an opportunity for the masses to take revolutionary action, thus igniting the strike. This strike was a political, not an economic one; its purpose was to overthrow the rule of warlords Sun Ch'uan-fang and Li Pao-chang, establish the political power of Shanghai's revolutionary masses (including the workers), support the Northern Expedition, and expedite the victory of the national revolutionary war. For these reasons, the workers of Shanghai rose to lead all oppressed people in their revolutionary struggle, and the general strike began. Immediately before the February 19th strike, the central organization of the workers of Shanghai, the General Labor Union, held an assembly and issued the following order:

Order for a General Strike

To all worker-friends of Shanghai:
The power of the people's revolution is increasing daily! The Northern Expedition is victorious, and Sun Ch'uan-fang's resistance has collapsed. The masses must now rise and overthrow the forces of the warlords. The General Labor Union therefore declares a general strike for the entire city of Shanghai. Its purpose is to eliminate the remaining power of the warlords and demonstrate the strength of the revolutionary masses. As soon as you receive this order, go on strike. After the strike begins, obey the orders of the General Labor Union in an organized and orderly manner. Remember, do not go back to work until you are advised to do so.

Strike in support of the Northern Expedition!
Strike to overthrow Sun Ch'uan-fang!
Long live the people's political power!
Long live the workers' freedom!
Long live the workers' unity!

Issued by the General Labor Union
of Shanghai on February 19th

When the strike began, the General Labor Union issued a manifesto and seventeen economic and political demands:

Manifesto of the General Strike

Our people's revolutionary movement has intensified since the May 30th Movement. The warlord Sun Ch'uan-fang who controlled the Southeast has been defeated by the bravery of our revolutionary masses.

Shanghai belongs to the citizens of Shanghai, who have for decades been oppressed by the warlords. The imperialist powers have used Shanghai as their base to encroach on China, and now they are continuing to menace our nationalist movement by military means. We citizens want to overthrow the dark rule of the warlords and to resist the advance of the imperialists. Ever since the May 30th Movement, workers of Shanghai have been bravely struggling for our people's freedom and liberation. At this moment, the forces of Sun Ch'uan-fang have been routed, but the imperialists are still threatening us with guns and cannons. If we do not destroy these dark, reactionary powers, our people will never see the dawn of freedom.

In order to destroy these dark, reactionary powers, the people must rise up and protest by going on strike in industry, in business, and in schools. Once the working class has begun its protest, the revolutionary masses must also take action to speed the elimination of the warlords and to assist in the victory of the Northern Expedition forces. For these reasons, this General Union now calls for all workers of Shanghai to begin demonstrating the power of the masses by organized, orderly means. We hereby declare a general strike, effective today. The following are the minimum political and economic demands we make for the workers of Shanghai:

1. Continued resistance against imperialism.
2. Elimination of the warlords' underhanded power politics.
3. Liquidation of all reactionary forces.
4. Establishment of a government that truly protects the welfare of the people.
5. Rights to hold meetings, to form associations and to strike, as well as freedom of speech and freedom of the press.
6. Recognition of the labor union's rights to represent the workers.
7. Higher wages and a minimum wage for workers.
8. An end to inflation and protection of the livelihood of the workers.
9. An eight-hour work day.
10. Sundays and festivals are to be paid holidays, with double pay for work on those days.
11. Hiring of the unemployed. No closing of factories on the pretext of strikes.
12. An end to employers' physically or verbally abusing workers, or reducing their wages at will.
13. An end to employers' firing workers without the consent of the labor union.
14. Compensation for work-related injuries and deaths.
15. Health care plans for the workers, and half-pay when sick.
16. Equal wages for male and female workers. Improvements in the treatment of working women and children. Six weeks of maternity leave with full pay. No heavy physical labor for children.
17. Better working conditions in the factories. More doors, windows, skylights, and lavatories.

The above are the goals of the present action taken by the workers of Shanghai. We want to struggle side by side with the people of all classes in our society to destroy the remaining power of the warlords, and we hope the new government will accept these demands made by our workers.

Issued by the General Labor Union
of Shanghai on February 19th

The Massive Strike

The strike began at 6 A.M., February 19th. . . . Tallied according to different professions, the striking workers included the entire textile industry; the entire city communications service; salespersons belonging to the Commerce Union, and those who worked in such stores as Foremost, Peace, New, and Beautiful;

gold- and silversmiths; makers of tea cases; tailors of Western-style clothing; makers of canvas, incense, tea, carpets, and pig-bristle products; workers at a dozen metal and machine works; crews of the Ancient line's Kwangsi, Shansi, Kuang Shun-t'ien, Kansu, and Ningpo ships; the Sun Bright line's Mt. Lu, Fortune, and Shang-yang; the Peaceful line's Prosperity; and Mt. Chou line's Mt. Chou; also all the workers of the Commercial, Colorful, Lovely, Chinese Merchant, Black, and Stone Presses. The total number of striking workers exceeded 150,000.

On the second day of the strike (February 20th), the number of strikers rose sharply to a total of over 275,000. Most of the increase came from those professions that had been restrained by the capitalists on the first day or had not received the order to strike. Included were 60,000 workers from the silk factories of North Sluice; 40,000 workers in the construction business; 100,000 workers from businesses such as imports, soy sauce, rice, second-hand clothes, herb medicine, and fabrics. Five hundred workers in public transportation also joined in. The number of striking textile factories in the Sandy Crossing area increased to twenty-five, which added another 15,000 workers to the strike. The dock workers of Whangpoo and Sixteen Shops also numbered 10,000. . . . All in all, in these four days, more than 360,000 workers joined in the strike, making it the biggest not only in the history of Shanghai, but in the entire nation. It demonstrated the heightening of political consciousness and the rapidly developing organization of the Shanghai working class. . . .

White Terror

On the first day of the strike, Li Pao-chang, Defense Commander of Shanghai and a henchman of Sun Ch'uan-fang, struggled to retain power by lashing out at the masses. He immediately contacted the Labor Departments of the Concessions and instituted a reign of white terror.

Within six hours of the strike, bustling, prosperous Shanghai became lifeless. All the trolleys stopped running; no ships entered or departed; the doors of post offices were bolted; department stores were closed; all factories were shut down, their sirens echoing one another but unable to call in a single worker. All these developments made the police and military patrols on the streets tremble; the ruling class, terrified and enraged, began to strike back with massacres.

Those slaughtered—our front-line soldiers—were

workers handing out strike literature on the streets. The martyrs of the first day were two workers, Ts'ai Chien-hsün and Shih A-jung, from the metal and machine works of South City. They were arrested for distributing strike literature and were immediately beheaded. On the second day of the strike, a worker selling trolley tickets was shot at the West Gate for giving out leaflets about the strike. Two of the students who made public speeches at Ts'ao Family Crossing were arrested and beheaded immediately. At the old West Gate, citizens who were reading strike literature were killed by the Big Sword Brigade. One head was hung from a telephone pole, and two bodies were left lying on the streets. Two workers, one from Lucky Life Iron Factory and the other from Heroic Tobacco Factory, walked past a group of policemen and annoyed them by their presence. They were arrested and shot. A worker from an import store, Wang Tung-wen, was also killed. In North Sluice, two students were arrested and killed. In the same area, the workers' clubhouse of the Commercial Press situated at Pao-shan Road was raided; fourteen workers were arrested, and two were shot. Others who were arrested during the day included twelve workers of the Iron Factory at the International Settlement, five workers from the Rainbow Coal Company, nine workers from East Landing, five female workers from the Wu-sung Textile Company, seventeen from Ying-hsiang Harbor, six from Willow Landing, seven from South City, and more than fifty students who were staying in the dormitories at Shanghai University. In addition, many people disappeared without a trace, perhaps having been murdered or arrested. The total number of casualties must have been over one hundred.

The white terror was a further incentive to the revolutionary workers, students, and citizens of Shanghai: It led to the struggle of the masses to seize weapons by force on the 21st and 22nd.

On the first day of the strike, Li Pao-chang publicly gave the order to "kill on sight." In the Chinese territory as well as in the Concessions, police and military brigades patrolled the streets, stopping and searching people. Security was especially tight in the Chinese territory. One could see soldiers everywhere, wearing swords on their backs and holding placards of warning. With such patrols on the streets, fear gripped the city. All businesses closed in South City, North Sluice, and part of the French Concession. Li Pao-chang's soldiers began looting and provoking citizens at will, arresting and killing those who dared

to show their indignation. In South City and East Landing, the inhabitants did not even dare to look at the soldiers when they passed by them. In East Landing, a peddler who cried out "Mai Ping" ("selling cakes") was accused of saying "Ta pai ping" ("beat the routed soldiers"). He was arrested, beaten up, and stabbed repeatedly with bayonets but passers-by did not even dare to turn and look.

At seven o'clock in the evening, all traffic in the Chinese territory stopped. Also, from that time on, foreign troops were allowed to set up defenses outside of the Concessions, and Chinese soldiers were permitted to enter the Concessions to arrest members of labor unions, the Communist Party, and the left wing of the Nationalist Party. The foreign imperialists and the reactionary forces of the warlords were now fully cooperating in carrying out the white terror.

The Warlords' Massacre Policy and the Right Wing of the Nationalist Party

Who were the ringleaders of the massacre? Who were the masterminds behind the white terror? The answer is the Western Hills Conference group—the right-wing faction of the Nationalist Party.

The headquarters of these rightists was situated at 44 Dragon Road in the French Concession. The recently established mad-dog *Chiang-nan Evening News* was the mouthpiece of their organization. The leaders of this right-wing group were none other than those denounced by Sun Yat-sen and expelled from the Nationalist Party: Chang Chi, Chou Lu, Hsieh Ch'ih, and so on. Right after the general strike began, Chü Cheng and company advised Li Pao-chang (who held 2000 dollars' worth of stock in the *Chiang-nan Evening News*) that "the only thing for you to do now is to resist the Party's forces in the front and kill workers in the rear." Thus the savage warlord Li Pao-chang was assured of protection by the Nationalist Party and provided with a policy of terror against the strikers.

We are not libeling the rightists of the Nationalist Party when we say that they are responsible for the massacre. It is a fact supported by the words of the *Chiang-nan Evening News*. Before the strike began, the paper had already predicted that the masses would be sacrificed. After the massacre had been carried out, the paper made a great deal of noise, accusing the Communists of sacrificing the masses. When the massacre aroused the anger of the citizens of Shanghai, the paper reported it, and at the same time advised Li Pao-chang to change his "kill on sight" policy. Undoubtedly, the right-wing Nationalists are the instigators of the massacre; they are the reactionaries, the counterrevolutionaries, and therefore enemies of the people.

The Struggle for Arms

The killings under the white terror naturally provoked the red terror of the revolution. An eye for an eye, a terror for a terror: this is the condition in which revolutions begin, and this was the condition for the Shanghai masses—workers and ordinary citizens alike—on February 21st, the third day of the strike.

When the time for a revolution is ripe, a general strike will directly lead to mass riots; when premature, the masses will continue their struggle for arms. When the weapons are in the hands of the warlords, white terror results; when the masses get hold of the weapons, armed revolutionary struggle explodes. This is a lesson in Marxism-Leninism, a lesson to be learned by the working class of Shanghai.

Having no weapons, the Shanghai workers had to snatch them out of their enemies' hands. The white terror that followed the strike made the working masses determined to struggle for arms. Beginning on the evening of the 21st, workers of the various regions began fighting the police and soldiers. On the 22nd, sailors who opposed the warlords' massacre policy and sympathized with the workers' movement opened unauthorized artillery fire on the Kao-ch'ang-miao Arsenal. That evening, heated battles broke out in South City and North Sluice, in which workers and citizens attempted to seize weapons. They were not completely successful because not everyone joined in and because the enemy still struggled to retain power. However, the cannonade made the enemy officers and soldiers run for shelter in the Concessions. On the 22nd, during their attacks on the defense lines and sentries of the police and military forces, workers of various regions succeeded in acquiring quite a few weapons; they also shot and killed a police captain while returning fire. Such was the first heroic effort to wrest weapons from armed enemies with our bare hands. These actions continued into the evening of the 23rd in the North Sluice and South City regions. The workers raided several police stations and were engaged in battles for hours. The stalemate came to an end when the masses retreated safely, the police not daring to chase after them. All these events show

that armed revolutionary struggle has begun in Shanghai. . . .

Fighting for Political Power

What was the purpose of the Shanghai workers' general strike and armed struggle? The rightists, who do not understand the situation of the revolution and are afraid of the power of the working class, suspect that the workers of Shanghai want to form a labor government. This is incorrect. The present aim of the Shanghai workers is to form not a labor government, but a citizens' government, a democratic government under the Republic. However, the fight of the workers *is* a fight for political power.

In this revolution of an oppressed people in a semicolonial state, in this revolution of Shanghai's citizens against the rule of imperialists and warlords, the struggle of the workers bred the struggle of the citizens; the revolt of the workers led to the revolt of the citizens; the political power of the workers ensured the political power of the citizens. Therefore, the slogan of the Shanghai workers was "to establish a representative government." Again, the purpose of the Shanghai workers' general strike and armed struggle was to take over political power and to lead all oppressed Shanghai citizens to form a democratic government belonging to them.

On the fourth day of the strike, when armed struggle broke out and the navymen suddenly opened artillery fire on Kao-ch'ang-miao, the unity of the armed forces and the workers in revolution was demonstrated, and the necessity and possibility for soldiers and workers to seize political power was proved. Incidentally, on that same day, representatives of all classes of Shanghai society (merchants, workers, students) and of both revolutionary political parties (the Nationalist Party and the Communist Party) formed a "Provisional Revolutionary Committee of the Citizens of Shanghai," which further proved the necessity and possibility of the citizens' establishing their political power. On the evening of the 22nd, this Provisional Revolutionary Committee issued an order, still in effect, for the mobilization of all navy and army troops to disarm the warlords. This Revolutionary Committee is an advisory board for the revolution as well as an intermediary step toward a representative government. This Revolutionary Committee is the child of the general united strike and the revolutionary actions of the masses, yet its historical and revolutionary significance is timeless.

The Revolutionary Justice of the Masses

In terms of history, the most significant events of the five-day general strike are the armed struggle and the beginning of the struggle for political power. Another action of the masses is worth noting, however, and that is their revolutionary justice.

On the 22nd, nearly 10,000 workers from Willow Landing gathered for a demonstration. A henchman by the nickname of "Little Trickster" had been discovered spying on the workers. As he had conspired with detectives and policemen and was responsible for the arrests of the workers' leaders, the people seized him and brought him before the dais to be judged by the masses. When the majority of the workers cried out "kill him," the chairman put the issue to a vote. A unanimous verdict was reached, and "Little Trickster" was executed on the spot.

This was a revolutionary judgment passed by the masses—terror answered with terror, counterrevolution met with revolution. By the verdict of the masses, a henchman of the industrial thieves was punished by death. Such is the law of the revolution. Certainly, the reactionaries and the counterrevolutionaries are opposed to such a verdict and call it a vicious act of the masses. But this was an eminently fair action; the enemy killed dozens of our people, we now only justly punished one. When power is in the hands of the revolutionary masses, the architect of this massacre, Li Pao-chang, should also receive the same punishment.

Returning to Work in Order to Enlarge the Struggle

Up to this point, the mass action of the general strike had developed along two correct lines; first, taking over arms for the struggle, and second, fighting for the political power of the citizens. However, because the military power of the revolution still lagged far behind, the time was not yet ripe for the revolution and the masses suffered losses. While the organized political power was still intact, on the fifth day of the strike, the Shanghai General Labor Union called for all workers to return to work at 1 P.M. the next day (February 24th) in order to prepare for an even greater struggle.

On the morning of the 24th, the order to return to work was issued:

To all our worker-friends of Shanghai:
When this Union ordered the general strike, 400,000 organized workers responded. Within a few hours, our coordinated actions shook the warlords' power, and the bustling city of Shanghai turned into a battlefield of revolution. This was the first time since the May 30th Movement that all Shanghai workers have been engaged in such a great and honorable struggle. During the five-day strike, our citizens rose in revolt, and the revolutionary navymen attacked our enemies—a great symbol of the alliance of workers and soldiers. Our strength is now known to our enemies. The Union, seeing that the struggle will be a long one, has decided not to fight alone, for fear of bearing excessive losses. For this reason, we command all our worker-friends to return to work as of 1 P.M., the 24th of this month. We must prepare for a greater struggle to come.

Long live the great strike of the workers of Shanghai!

Fight for more power!

Long live the Shanghai General Labor Union!

Issued by the Shanghai General Labor
Union, February 24th

Declaration of the End of the Strike

To all the citizens of Shanghai:
We, the working class, went on a general strike to protest tyrannical government and to show our support for the Northern Expedition. Our strike lasted five days, during which workers and citizens made great sacrifices. Now we are forced by various factors to declare a temporary end to the strike. Although the strike is halted for the moment, our struggle against the tyrannical rule of the warlords, our fight for our political power and for improvement in workers' lives will continue. During the strike, the citizens of Shanghai showed their sincere sympathy, for which we are grateful. Although we have taken the advice of businesses to return to work, we hope the revolutionary citizens of Shanghai will continue to join our fight against the dark powers, until we have completely overthrown tyranny.

Our call for returning to work is not a retreat, but a preparation for a greater struggle.

Issued by the Shanghai General
Labor Union, February 24th

The Process of Continuing the Struggle

Once the order to return to work was issued, some workers went back even before noon. From noon until the next morning, more than 300,000 workers returned to their jobs. But the five-day strike had not been brought to a conclusion by any means.

All the workers and oppressed citizens of Shanghai are in the midst of a continuing struggle to gain victory. The general strike was by no means a failure. It produced results. The experience we gained and the lessons we learned during those five days—especially the solutions we found through struggle—exceeded the sum total of all lessons learned since the May 30th Movement. This is a critical moment in the history of the working class of Shanghai; it now has duties to fulfill.

The following slogans are the emerging political aims of the workers of Shanghai. They also outline the actions of the masses:

1. Down with Li Pao-chang!
2. Drive out the Chi-Lu army!
3. Support the Northern Expedition!
4. Uphold the Republic!
5. Start mass uprisings; seize weapons!
6. Kill the reactionaries!
7. Avenge the dead!
8. Establish a representative government!
9. Get rid of foreign armies and reclaim the Concessions!

Translated by Clara Yu

70.

Funeral Processions

Funerals were important occasions in religious and social life from earliest times. Funeral processions served as great parades that entertained onlookers while symbolically reinforcing social distinctions and kinship connections. Special garments worn by the mourners revealed how closely they were related to the deceased. Also part of the processions were emblems of the rank and accomplishment of the family.

Below is an account of two funeral processions written in 1924 by Ku Chieh-kang (b. 1895), a prominent historian and intellectual. Unlike earlier ritual texts which merely state the rules or expectations for funerals, Ku's account gives a full description of two processions as they were actually organized. Ku's theme is the changes in funeral practices caused by the overthrow of the old gentry class with its codes of ritual and the consequent increasing importance of money in establishing social status. It should be pointed out, however, that such critiques were not new to the twentieth century. As early as the Han, writers lamented how funerals had become occasions for the display of wealth, and that those who could not afford lavish preparations felt their social status to be jeopardized.

The city of Su-chou has always been known for impressive and elaborate ceremonies, but nowadays this display of wealth and luxury has taken on a different character. In the past, the right to conduct lavish ceremonies was strictly reserved for the gentry and official classes, whereas now it has been taken over by the wealthy merchant class. Any novelty will soon become the fashion after the social elite has adopted it. Previously, elaborate ceremonies sometimes made life difficult for exalted households, but now that the class system has been overthrown, the painful task of keeping up with one's neighbors falls on everybody.

There are numerous occasions for lavish and elaborate ceremonies, the most important of which are weddings and funerals because they represent the greatest events in a person's life. A marriage celebration may be embellished to impress people, but its lavishness can never compare with a funeral. Marriages are affairs arranged by the older generation for the younger. If they are conducted with frugality,

people may laugh, but they will not scold or criticize. Besides, parents often have more than one child and cannot afford to put on an elaborate show for each one. If they did not give their younger children the same lavish weddings, they would appear to be partial. Funeral ceremonies, on the other hand, are quite different because these are affairs conducted by the younger generation for their elders. If the arrangements are too simple, older relatives will make critical remarks, and sons will be accused of unfilial behavior and face the disapproval of society. Moreover, when there are many sons in a family, the responsibility and cost for one funeral can be shared by all the brothers. As more people naturally means more resources, they can be more free with their money.

The burial aspect of a funeral is not given much attention because cemeteries are located outside of the city where few on-lookers are present. The most elaborate part of a funeral is the procession because it passes through city streets and avenues where spectators gather. For this reason, preparation for the funeral procession is the single greatest task for the bereaved family; it is also an important occasion for those who are eager to watch a good show. Before the procession takes place, news of it has already spread to every corner of the city: "On such and such a day, a procession from the House of _____ will pass through such and such streets." People with nothing to do wait along those city streets.

When a procession is well planned and lives up to the expectations of the crowd, there are words of praise from the spectators, such as, "This family certainly lives up to its reputation!" The sons, wearing mourning clothes and surrounded by mourning curtains, are comforted when they hear such words. However, if the procession is not outstanding or if it compares poorly with another one held that day, people ridicule it, saying things like, "Do they think this is good enough for us to watch?" Then all the preparations and all the money are wasted. Not only are their expenses and efforts in vain, but the family will long after be branded with an unfavorable reputation. When their name is mentioned, people will say, "Oh, how those sons slighted their parents!" or "That family has no face!"

In Peking, a funeral procession of a middle class family includes just the casket. Sons and male relatives walk ahead of it and female relatives and friends walk behind. This, after all, is the idea behind a funeral procession. People who are slightly better off hire young boys dressed in traditional costumes and musicians to lead the procession. It is believed that the dead person still has consciousness and feelings and his soul must be coaxed by the music to follow the procession. This is not an unreasonable explanation for the musicians' presence. But this kind of funeral procession is not seen in Su-chou. People here feel that it would not only cause one to lose face but also invite ridicule and criticism. Having no procession at all would almost be better. Therefore, under the cover of darkness, when everyone is sound asleep, a family hires a few coolies to carry the casket onto a boat and row it via canals to the city gate. At daybreak, when the gate opens, the casket is carried to the burial ground. This practice is called "burying the dead secretly," and is not condemned by the people of Su-chou who sympathize with families in difficulty. But those families who conduct a funeral procession through the streets must meet the current standard of extravagance. The streets of Su-chou are very narrow, so a funeral procession can cause quite a traffic jam; the longer the procession, the worse the traffic problem. But spectators do not mind it at all; they even complain when the traffic congestion is over too soon. It seems that people no longer regard funeral processions as funeral processions, but as parades in religious festivals.

In my childhood I took part in funeral processions of family friends. At that time, the processions were not long and mourning guests riding on horseback were a rare sight. Today, few guests are willing to walk; almost all of them ride horses. Furthermore, the items in a procession change constantly with new things added almost every day. How do we explain this phenomenon? In the past, the items in a procession were determined by a person's rank in office, and he could not make additions wantonly. But now that tradition has been overturned, and the people of Su-chou have been greatly influenced by the Shanghai merchants' "spirit of extravagance." And once things begin to change, they never stop.

About five or six years ago, there were two funeral processions to Su-chou from Shanghai which people have not yet forgotten. One was that of Mr. Sheng Hsüan-huai, the other that of Mr. Hsi O-ming. Mr. Sheng was on the board of directors of Shanghai Coal and Gas Company. He owned a resort in Su-chou (the noted Liu Gardens outside of Yen Gate). After his death, his family was supposed to spend 100,000 dollars to send his casket in a boat procession to his garden here. I was not present in Su-chou at the time so I have no first-hand knowledge of just how exciting that occasion was, but according to many people, it was something never experienced before, a once-in-a-lifetime thrill. Mr. Hsi was a paint manufacturer in Shanghai. After World War I broke out, the supply route for European paint was cut off; the price of paint soared sky-high, and paint manufacturers became enormously wealthy. But Mr. Hsi died before he could enjoy his new-found wealth. His family felt very sorry about it and conducted a particularly lavish funeral for him, hoping his soul would rest in peace. Ever since then, elaborate and lavish processions have become a common practice in our city.

Two years ago, within three months, our family held two funerals. I still have the accounts for both processions. One was for my sister who died in Hangchou. After her casket was settled in the funeral home there, her soul tablet was brought home to Su-chou. The other funeral was for my grandmother. The procession began at our house and ended in a funeral home two *li* away. I must declare right away that our family is not one that flaunts its wealth, but our position required us to meet the current standard of lavishness. Our two processions were rated slightly above average. After the reader has finished these accounts, I hope he does not accuse us of being too extravagant. Perhaps he can imagine the pride and joy of those rich families who can extravagantly flaunt their wealth, and at the same time the pain and anxieties of those families who are in financial difficulties but still must keep up appearances.

I. The procession for "bringing home the soul tablet" (sister)
   1. oblong paper lantern, hanging from a pole
   2. placard demanding silence and reverence (carried over the shoulder)
   3. placard demanding people to clear the way
   4. gongs
   5. regimental insignia of the Manchu dynasty
   6. picture of a dragon on a placard
   7. placard on which is written the official rank of the deceased
   8. melon-shaped paper decorations hanging from a pole
   9. military band (brass instruments and drums)
   10. ten embroidered banners
   11. seven Taoist priests
   12. *papier-mache* float to fetch the soul (all floats carried by men)
   13. pavilion-shaped float made with pine needles
   14. seven Buddhist monks
   15. parasol made with pine needles
   16. small pavilion-shaped float carrying a picture of the deceased
   17. ten silk umbrellas
   18. brass musicians
   19. glass lantern
   20. paper effigies of spirit deities
   21. male relatives and friends
   22. picture of a tiger on a placard
   23. cymbals
   24. large parasol
   25. large fan
   26. kerosene lantern
   27. large parasol for a rider on horseback
   28. Ting stallion of a high-ranking Manchu regiment (decked out with military ornament)
   29. name of the lineage on a placard
   30. small paper lantern
   31. sedan chair carrying the soul tablet

32. accompanying sedan chairs for female mourners and guests

II. Funeral procession (grandmother)
   1. a load of coins to buy passage on the road
   2. horse to clear the way
   3. gentleman's horse
   4. six long horn players
   5. stallions from Ch'ung regiment (decked with military ornaments)
   6. stallions from Piao regiment (decked with military ornaments)
   7. oblong paper lantern with the lady's rank written on it
   8. two pairs of yellow placards
   9. nine pairs of tinfoil placards
   10. six-man military band
   11. umbrella for a rider on horseback
   12. horse of high-ranking Manchu official
   13. yellow parasol
   14. a staff with feathers tied on it (the higher the rank, the more feathers)
   15. dragon staff
   16. palace-style fan
   17. palace-style lantern
   18. six swinging censers
   19. yellow pavilion-shaped float carrying a large board on which is written the lady's rank, conferred by the Emperor

The above completes the first part of the procession. All the items after 5 are used to set off the pavilion float (19). Since the honor was conferred by the Emperor, the float is accompanied by a palace fan, palace lantern, and other paraphernalia associated with him. Items 5, 6, and 9 were associated with the office of the Manchu Military Governor and were originally used in military ceremonies. During the Ch'ing dynasty an official had to hold a rank of three or higher before permission was given by the Military Governor to include these items to glorify the pavilion float (19) in his funeral procession. The office of the Military Governor is now abolished, and it would seem that his power has been taken over by the funeral directors.

   20. effigies of two spirits who clear the way
   21. effigies of the four guardians of the Buddhist temple
   22. pavilion-shaped float carrying a soul banner
   23. oblong paper lantern

24. placard demanding silence and reverence
25. Manchu regimental insignia
26. placard demanding that people clear the way
27. gongs
28. placard on which is written the official rank of the deceased
29. melon-shaped paper ornaments on a pole
30. picture of a dragon on a placard
31. embroidered banner
32. nine musicians
33. pavilion-shaped float carrying incense burner
34. silk ribbons tied to a staff
35. nine Taoist priests
36. pavilion-shaped float carrying offerings of food and drink
37. five pairs of silk-covered placards
38. eight riders on horseback (not in mourning clothes)
39. ten-man orchestra
40. picture of deceased on a large placard (to be placed at grave site)
41. silk parasol
42. nine Ch'an monks
43. open sedan chair
44. four placards with the word "libation" on them
45. five pairs of placards with the word "libation" written on them
46. elegiac couplets from friends (each couplet written on two long strips of white cloth tied to a bamboo pole)
47. drum player
48. pavilion-shaped float carrying elegies
49. ten paper umbrellas with "Amita Buddha" written on them
50. woodwind musicians in ancient costumes
51. picture of the deceased in an open sedan chair
52. male guests
53. picture of a tiger on a placard
54. cymbals
55. the titles of the deceased on a placard
56. eight riders (in mourning clothes)
57. large parasol
58. large fan
59. Western-style lantern (square glass lanterns)
60. umbrella for rider
61. horse of high-ranking Manchu official
62. string musicians
63. young boy
64. young novice carrying the streamers which harbor the soul

65. glass lantern
66. sedan chair for the soul tablet, decorated with baskets of real and artificial flowers

This completes the second part of the procession. The important items are 22, 51, and 66. Effigies of the four guardians (21) were suggested by our family accountant, but my family felt that since it was something new and not widely used, we should eliminate it. Perhaps it has by now become a necessary and popular item. The guests (52) used to walk in the procession, but nowadays they no longer do so. (In recent years, many guests even ride rickshaws.)

67. numerous placards, each exhibiting an official title the deceased once held
68. decorative placard
69. managers of the procession
70. brass players
71. a strip of white cloth stretched between two bamboo poles
72. Western-style lantern (square glass lantern)
73. umbrella for rider
74. paper lantern
75. gong and wooden clappers
76. riderless horse
77. casket on a bier, carried by thirty-two people
78. white sedan chair
79. sedan chair with a white top
80. sedan chair for female relatives and guests

Of the above items, the most important is, of course, the casket (77).

Just take a look! In a funeral procession the important items should be the casket (77), sedan chair for the soul (66), and the pavilion-shaped float with the soul banner (22). In nine out of ten cases, the certificate of rank (19) is a forgery. The picture of the deceased in the sedan chair (51) must be carried back home again after the burial; therefore it does not count. The white cloth (71), white sedan chair (78), guests (52), and guest sedan chairs (80) are also necessary. They add up to seven items only. In actuality, the procession was blown up twelve times its necessary size—eighty items in all! We must attribute this "something growing out of nothing" phenomenon to the innovativeness and creativity of our citizens.

When I have some spare time, I would like very much to look into the origins of each of these items—which were the earliest in existence and which were later additions. Elderly persons have told me that years ago a funeral procession consisted of only the casket, personal honors of the deceased, and six or seven other things such as the gongs, parasols, musicians, large fan, and a brass band. They had a special term for this basic unit, but I have forgotten it. The processions I saw in my childhood consisted of this basic unit and a few additional items: the spirit to clear the way, placard demanding silence and reverence, and Buddhist monks and Taoist priests. The military band and woodwind players were added on just within the last ten years or so. Drummers were included even later. The soft and sweet sound of the woodwinds and the clamorous sounds of drums are ridiculously incompatible. The feathered staff and the dragon staff were originally used in temple ceremonies. They were carried in parades during religious holidays, festivals, and fairs, but now they are used as the vanguard for the pavilion-shaped float carrying the rank of the deceased (19). It seems things have gotten more and more out of hand. People have included stilts, floats, treasure chests, and the four professions (fisherman, woodcutter, farmer, scholar) to their processions today.

My family did not wish to flaunt its wealth and only wanted to "do the right thing"; therefore we did not include anything new. But the items we did include make me sad. I have always wanted to read the descriptions of imperial funerals written in our dynastic histories and compare them with the ones of today to find out whether the Emperors of old were as extravagant in death as the commoners of today. I have not done this, but I dare to predict that the extravagance of people today far surpasses that of the Emperors. They were checked by rules of ceremony, and our extravagance has been analyzed and determined by thousands of spectators.

How much did a funeral procession cost? Unfortunately I do not have an exact figure. But our family accountant made an estimate of my grandmother's funeral procession, and I have kept his figures, which are as follows:

1.	labor fee for craftsmen to make placards, floats, etc.	60.00
2.	material cost for placards, floats, silk, cloth, etc.	60.00
3.	payment for sedan chair carriers and their meals	2.00
4.	musicians playing long horns	8.00
5.	Ch'ung stallions	9.60
6.	Piao stallions	6.40
7.	Taoist priests	3.00
8.	Ch'an monks	3.50
9.	Buddhist monks	3.00
10.	orchestra	9.00
11.	drummers	7.00
12.	woodwind players	6.00
13.	string players	3.00
14.	military band	5.00
15.	manager of the funeral	35.00
16.	manager of the procession	15.00
17.	manager for pavilions and lanterns	15.00
18.	grooms	5.00
19.	forty-eight horses	48.00
20.	assistants	3.00
21.	[deleted in the original]	4.50
22.	twenty-six hired hands to carry placards, etc.	30.00
23.	rented sedan chairs	15.00
24.	temporary altar on the road	3.00
25.	cost of white cloth	3.00

The estimated cost was 370 dollars. If we include the other expenses of the funeral, the total cost was between four and five hundred dollars. Our house was located less than two *li* from the funeral home, yet we spent between four and five hundred dollars just to send the casket there. This indeed is too wasteful. But when you think about it, you really cannot say that it was too extravagant. The two processions of the Sheng and Hsi families started from Shanghai and covered a distance that could be traveled in one and a half hours by train; yet they used more than 100,000 dollars. My family's total expense was only one-third of one percent of that. In comparison, our frugality could be considered exemplary.

At this point, my curiosity is once again aroused. I believe that families like the Shengs and Hsis should make their funeral expenses accessible to the public. That would be interesting indeed! I for one would not even know how to begin planning a procession that would cost even one one-hundredth of what theirs did. Extravagance like theirs can make a person boil with rage or sigh with envy. The people who watched your funerals years ago are now dead. Your wealth probably is exhausted. Why don't you make your accounts public so students of local customs can have more research materials?

Translated by Nancy Gibbs

71.

My Wife and Children

The relations between husbands and wives and between parents and children have, of course, always been impor-tant in people's lives, but before the twentieth century they were considered too private a matter for public revela-tion. Twentieth-century writers, however, have been willing to explore these areas in fiction and essays.

The following essays about his family were written by Chu Tzu-ch'ing (1898–1948) on three separate occasions between 1928 and 1934. Chu came from a gentry family and attended Peking University, graduating in 1920. Thereafter he taught literature at several middle schools and universities. He also wrote poetry, criticism, essays, and sketches, which brought him considerable fame as a writer.

CHOOSING MY SPOUSE

Because I was my family's eldest grandson and eldest son, talk about getting me a wife started even before I was eleven years old. At that time the topic made no sense to me at all, and I did not understand why it had been brought up so early.

My great-grandmother's family was from a village in a small county of northern Kiangsu where members of our family had lived for generations. I may have been there too, but in my stupid way, I do not have the least recollection of it. My grandmother, smoking her opium pipe on the couch, would often tell stories of the place, mentioning this or that farmer's name. At first, it was rather misty, just like the white smoke curling up from her pipe. But in time, almost unconsciously, I became familiar with the scene, and it held my interest, second only to the place where we lived. The place she spoke of was called Flower Garden Village. Therefore, when I heard that a girl from there had been selected to be my future bride, I found it perfectly reasonable and did not object at all. Every year someone would come from the fields there, dressed in a short blue cotton jacket (instead of a long gown), an old-fashioned

long-stemmed pipe between his teeth, and bring us a good supply of barley flour, dried sweet potatoes, and such. There would occasionally be mention of the girl—that she was about four years older then me, fairly tall, with bound feet—but at that time I was more excited about the barley flour and the dried potatoes.

I remember, it must have been in my twelfth year, when a message came reporting that the girl had died of tuberculosis. No one in our family showed much sadness; perhaps they had seen her only when she was small and, with the passage of time, hardly remembered what she was like. My father was then in government service in some other province, so my mother, getting very impatient about my marriage, asked the tailor to be matchmaker. He came often to our house to make clothes for all of us and also went to a lot of other people's houses where he could observe all the ladies and girls, so he was a good choice. The tailor came back with the news that he had found a rich family with two daughters, one by a secondary wife; he had spoken for the older girl born by the main wife. He said her family wanted to have a look at the prospective bridegroom, so my mother agreed and fixed a date.

The tailor brought us to a teahouse. I remember it was winter. On that special day, Mother made me put on my brownish-red brocade long gown, a black brocade formal jacket, and a black satin skull cap with a red knot on top, and she repeatedly admonished me to mind my manners. At the teahouse we met the man who was to look me over. He was square-faced with large ears, about the age I am now, wearing a cotton gown and jacket as if he were in mourning for someone, but he was quite amiable. He never stopped looking me up and down and asking me questions such as what books I had read. Afterwards the tailor told us that the man had been careful in his inspection; he had noted that the middle line of my upper lip is long, a sure sign of long life. He had also watched me walk to make certain there was nothing wrong with my legs. On the whole he had approved of me, so now it was up to us to look them over. Mother dispatched a trusted old manservant who came back to report that the older of the two sisters was bigger than me, really filling her chair when she sat down. The younger sister, however, was slender. Mother said fat women cannot bear children, like so-and-so among our relatives, so she asked the tailor to go back and speak for the younger daughter. The family was miffed at this and refused, and so the matter fell through.

At a mahjong party, Mother met a lady with a daughter who, she hinted, was a very smart girl. Mother became interested. When she got home she mentioned that the girl was about my age, still a child actually, romping about. After a few days she asked someone to find out how the other side would feel about an engagement. The girl's father was an official of even lower rank than my father. That was one year before the Revolution, when things like that still mattered, so they were quite pleased to connect their family to ours. Things were about ninety-nine percent fixed when a hitch occurred. Mother somehow found out that a widowed maidservant, employed by our great aunt, knew all about that family. The maid was asked to visit to be interrogated. At first she did not want to come out with the truth, but she finally did: the girl in question was originally adopted, but they loved her as much as if she had been born into the family. Mother lost all interest. Two years later we heard that the girl had fallen sick with tuberculosis and had acquired the opium habit. Mother said, "It's lucky we had not definitely settled the betrothal." To the extent that I understood things, I fully agreed.

In the year of the Revolution, Father contracted typhoid and several doctors were called in. Among them was one Dr. Wu, who eventually became my father-in-law. One day the servant who was usually sent for the doctor came with the news that one of the doctors had a daughter. Since Father was sick, Mother's concern for my affairs was greater than ever. Once she had heard the news, she followed up on it. The servant had only made a casual remark and could not give any details; so next time the doctor came, Mother had someone ask his sedan chair bearers if he had a daughter, which they confirmed. Mother then consulted Father, and they entrusted an uncle to get the doctor's reaction to their proposal. That day I was at Father's bedside and overheard their conversation. Uncle first found out for certain that the girl had no one else yet, then he said, "How about someone from this family of old X here?" The doctor expressed approval, and talk stopped there. Next, the bride had to be inspected. Mother again sent her trusted maidservant, and this time the report was not bad, except for one thing: she had somewhat big feet. As the matter had already been as good as settled by then, Mother merely told the sedan chair bearers to tell the girl's parents they should bind her feet a little.

After the bride had been brought and the wedding performed, she told me that she had hidden from the inspection and that the girl that had been looked over had been someone else. As to the message that the sedan chair bearers had brought back, it had caused quite a commotion. Father-in-law scolded Mother-in-law: "I told you long ago to bind her feet, but you didn't believe me. Now, see how people talk about it!" Mother-in-law retorted, "I definitely will not bind her feet! Let's see what they're going to do about it!" But they managed to find a compromise until the bride was brought over and wed.

CHILDREN

I am now already the father of five. Thinking of the metaphor that Yeh Sheng-t'ao* likes to quote about the snail that carries a house on its back makes me feel uncomfortable. Recently one of my relatives teased me, saying, "You are getting 'skinned'!" That disturbed me even more. Ten years ago when I had just married, I read Hu Shih's *Sundry Notes*† where he

---

* B. 1894, a leading writer and editor.
† Hu Shih (1891–1962), leading philosopher and writer.

says that many famous men never got married. He also quotes Bacon to the effect that whoever has taken a wife has his life "set." That startled me as if awakening me from a dream, but my family had married me off and I had had nothing to say about it. What could I do? Once I had a wife, along came five children, a heavy burden for my two shoulders; I really wonder how I can go on. Not only is my life "set" but I also worry about how the children will grow up.

Being an egotist through and through, I am not much as a husband, even less as a father. Of course, "Esteem children and grandchildren" and "Youth is the basic unit" are philosophical and ethical principles which I recognize. Once you have become a father, I know, you cannot just shut your eyes and ignore the rights of the children. Unfortunately, many of my ideas remain mere theory; in actual fact, I cope with the situation in the old-fashioned traditional way, savage in style, just like any ordinary father. Only now when I am almost middle-aged do I realize a little of my own brutality, and when I think of the corporal punishment and scolding the children have had to endure, I am at a loss to find excuses. Like touching an old scar, it still hurts to think of it. Once, reading a translation of Arishima Takeo's "With the Young,"* I was moved to tears by his noble and deeply sincere attitude. Last year my father enquired about A-chiu, who was then still with me at White Horse Lake, saying in his letter, "Since I never neglected you, I wish you would also not neglect him." I thought this remark very touching. Why am I not capable of my father's loving kindness? I will never forget how he looked after me. Human nature may really be polarized; I am certainly inconsistent, swinging back and forth like a pendulum.

You have probably read Lu Hsün's "The Happy Family." Mine is indeed such a happy group. At our daily lunches and dinners, two tidal waves seem to be descending on us. First, the children keep running to and fro between the dining room and the kitchen to check on things, urging Mother or me to give out the order to serve food. The hurried patter of many little feet, accompanied by much hilarity and shouting, lasts until that order is given. Then the running and shouting resume as the order is transmitted by many mouths until it reaches the maid in the kitchen. Then back again they rush for the fight for stools: one shouts "I want to sit here"; the other complains

"Brother won't let me sit"; brother retorts "Sister hit me"; whereupon I have to assume the role of peacemaker. At times, though, they become so adamant that I cannot stand it. I start shouting and, if that does not settle it, I may lose my temper, and down comes my heavy hand on someone. Then finally, after a few tears, all will find their seats and order will be restored. Next the arguments will break out about large bowls versus small bowls, red chopsticks versus black ones, rice or gruel, tea or soup, fish or meat, bean curd or carrots, with mutual accusations of dipping too often into the meat and vegetable dishes. Mother, as usual, tries to calm everyone down, but with little obvious effect. Then my rather irascible nature will not be able to stand it any longer and, of course, I will apply the old-fashioned method, thereby managing to subdue them instantly. More tears, but finally everyone will be busy with bowls and chopsticks, some wiping tears from reddened eyes. When the meal is over and they leave their seats, off they go helter-skelter, leaving behind a mess of food droppings, rice, sauce, bones, crumbs and a jumble of chopsticks and spoons in the pattern of a colorful map.

Apart from eating, the children's main pursuit is play. The big ones come up with big ideas and the small ones with small ideas, and no one will go along with the others' wishes. Then the quarrels start again, and either the big ones bully the small ones, or the small ones manage to browbeat the big ones; anyhow, the victimized party will personally bring his or her complaint to Mother or me. Most likely I will again apply the old-fashioned method of settling the argument, but sometimes I just pay no attention. The most annoying are the fights for toys. Even if both have similar toys, one insists on the other's, and no one will give up anything he has. In a situation like this, inevitably tears will have to flow from someone's eyes. Not all of this happens every day, but a good measure of it does. If I want to read a book or write something at home, I can guarantee that my attention will be diverted several times every hour, or I will be forced to get up once or twice. On rainy days or Sundays, when most of the children are home, it has happened that I could not read even one line or write one word. I often tell my wife, "All day our home is like a battlefield with large armies in motion." This goes on not only during the daytime, but even at night when there is the commotion of babies being fed or the sick being tended to.

I was only nineteen the year I married. I was

* D. 1923, Japanese author and social idealist.

twenty-one when we had A-chiu, twenty-three when we had A-ts'ai. At that time I was like a wild horse that could not stand saddle, reins, and bridle. I knew I should not run away from it and yet, unconsciously, I tried to. Thinking back to those days, I see that I really gave the two children a hard time; my acts of violence were unpardonable. When A-chiu was only two and a half years old, we lived on the school ground at Hang-chou. Seemingly for no reason, this child was crying all the time and was also very wary of strangers. When he was not near Mother, or when he saw a stranger, he would start bawling his head off. Since many people lived around us, I could not let him disturb the whole neighborhood, but we also could not avoid having many visitors. I was most annoyed by his behavior. Once I purposely got Mother out of the room, closed the door, put the boy on the floor and gave him a good spanking. Even now, when we talk about it, Mother finds it unpardonable. She says my hands are too harsh. After all, the child was only two and a half. In recent years I have often felt sad at the thought of that incident. Once it also happened with A-ts'ai in T'ai-chou. She was even smaller, just past a year, hardly able to walk, possibly because she was very much attached to her mother. I put her in a corner and let her cry and yell for three or four minutes. It made her sick for a few days, and Mother said it was really a heartless thing to do. But my sufferings were genuine too.

Once I wrote Yeh Sheng-t'ao that my plight due to the children sometimes got to be unbearable and gave rise to thoughts of suicide. Although in saying this I was merely venting my anger, I really have been in this mood sometimes. Later, with more children, and having to bear my suffering for some time, I found the sharp edges of my youth had become blunted and added age had increased my rational judgment. I became more tolerant, recognizing that in the past I really had been "anything but a perfect father," as I wrote to another friend. However, I still believe that my children in their early years were much more of an annoyance than other people's. I think it may have been mainly due to our ineptness at bringing them up. Yet if we invariably scolded them and had them take all the blame for what should have been our responsibility, it was certainly a shameful cruelty on our part.

Yet I must admit there was also happiness in the true sense. As anyone will tell you, the little ones are always adorable, those captivating little mites and little darlings. A-mao is now five months old. When you touch her chin or make faces, she will open her toothless mouth and give out a gurgling laugh. Her smile is like a flower unfolding. She does not like to be inside for long and if she is, she cries out loudly. Mother often says, "The little girl wants to take a walk; like a bird, she has to flit away once in a while."

Jun-erh was three just last month; a clumsy one, he cannot yet speak well. He can only say three- or four-word sentences with no regard for grammar and a blurred pronunciation, getting every word out only with great effort. It always makes us laugh. When he wants to say *hao* [good], it comes out like *hsiao* [small]. If you ask him, "Are you well?," he will reply "small" or "not small." We often make him say these words for the fun of it, and it seems he now suspects as much and has recently begun to say a correct *hao*, especially when we purposely want him to say *hsiao*. He has an enamel cup which we bought for about ten cents. The maid had told him, "This is ten cents." All he remembered were two words "ten cents" and he therefore used to call his cup "ten cents," sometimes abbreviated to "cents." When that maid left, the term had to be translated for the new one. If he is embarrassed or sees a stranger, he has a way of staring open-mouthed with a silly smile; we call him a silly boy in our native dialect. He is a little fatty, with short legs, funny to look at when he waddles along, and if he hurries, he is quite a sight. Sometimes he imitates me, clasping his hands behind him and walking with a swinging gait. He will then laugh at himself and also make us laugh.

His big sister A-ts'ai is over seven years old and goes to elementary school. At the table she prattles along breathlessly with stories of her schoolmates or their parents, whether anybody wants to listen or not. She always ends with a "Dad, do you know them?" or "Dad, did you know that?" Since Mother does not allow her to talk while eating, she always addresses herself to me. She is always full of questions. After the movies, she asks whether the people on the screen are real, and if so, why they don't talk. The same with photographs. Somebody must have told her that soldiers beat up people, which prompted her to ask, "Are soldiers human beings? Why do they beat people?" Recently, probably because her teacher made certain remarks, she came home and asked, "Whose side is Chang Tso-lin on?* Are Chiang Kai-shek's soldiers helping us?" Endless questions of this type are

* Chang Tso-lin (1873–1928) was the warlord in Manchuria.

used to pester me every day, and often they back me into a corner for want of an answer. When she plays with Jun-erh, they make an incongruous pair, one big and one small, and there is constant quarreling and crying. But sometimes they seem to get along. For instance, one might hide under the bed and the other try to squeeze in in pursuit. Then out they come, one after the other, from this bed to that. All one hears is their laughter, shouting, and panting, as Mother would say, just like little dogs. Now in Peking there are only these three children with us since, when we came north last year, Grandmother took A-chiu and Chuan-erh back to stay at Yang-chou for the time being.

A-chiu loves books; he likes to read *Water Margin, The Journey to the West, Heroes of the Sword, Little Friend,* and so on. He reads whenever he has a spare moment, sitting or lying down. The only book he dislikes is *The Dream of the Red Chamber,* which, he says, has no flavor, and indeed a ten-year-old can hardly be expected to appreciate its flavor.

Last year we had to leave behind two of the children. Since A-chiu was a bigger boy and since Chuan-erh had always been with Grandmother, we left them behind in Shanghai. I remember very clearly the morning of our parting. I brought A-chiu from the hotel at Two Stream Bridge to where Mother and Chuan-erh were staying with some friends. Mother had told me to buy something to eat for them, so at Ssu-ma Street I went into a restaurant. A-chiu wanted some smoked fish, which I bought for him along with some cookies for Chuan-erh. Then we went by streetcar to Hai-ning Street. When we got off, I noticed an expression of apprehension and discomfort on his face. I had to hurry back to the hotel to prepare things for the journey and could say only one or two words to the children. Chuan-erh looked at me silently while A-chiu turned to say something to Grandmother. I looked back once, then left, feeling myself the target of their recriminatory glances. Mother later told me that A-chiu had said behind my back, "I know Father prefers little sister and won't take me to Peking," but this was really not doing me justice. He also pleaded, "At summer vacation time, you must come and pick me up," which we promised to do.

Now it is already the second summer and the children are still left waiting in far-away Yang-chou. Do they hate us or miss us? Mother has never stopped longing for her two children. Often she has wept secretly, but what could I do? Just thinking of the old

anonymous poem, "It's the lot of the poor to live with constant reunions and separations," saddened me no end. Chuan-erh has become even more of a stranger to me, but last year when leaving White Horse Lake, she spoke up in her crude Hang-chou dialect (at that time she had never been in Yang-chou) and her especially sharp voice: "I want to go to Peking." What did she know of Peking? She was just repeating what she had heard from the big children. But still, remembering how she said it makes me terribly sad. It was not unusual for these two children to be separated from me, and they had also been separated from Mother once, but this time it has been too long. How can their little hearts endure such loneliness?

Most of my friends love children. Shao-ku once wrote to reproach me for some of my attitudes. He said that children's noises are something to be cherished. How could anyone hate them as I had said? He said he really could not understand me. Feng Tzu-k'ai* wrote an article for his *Viewing China,* which is all "amiable talk from a most kindhearted man." Yeh Sheng-t'ao often talked about his worries too, such as what middle school to send the children to after they finished elementary school. He brought this topic up with me two or three times. Those friends made me feel ashamed of my own attitude. Recently, however, I have grown more aware of my responsibilities. I think, first of all, I must get all my children together. Next, I must give them strength. I have personally witnessed the case of a man who, although very fond of his children, grossly neglected them by not providing good educations for them. Not that he was spoiling them in any way; it was merely that he lacked the patience to take good care of them. As a result, they will never amount to much. I think if I go on like I have, my children will be in even greater danger. I must make plans, must let them gradually know what it takes to become a good human being. But do I want them to become like me? Once at White Horse Lake where I was teaching lower middle school, I had asked Hsia Mien-tsun this question, to be considered from the standpoint of the teacher-pupil relationship. He answered unhesitatingly, "Of course!" Recently, I came to talk with Yü P'ing-po† about raising children and he had a clever answer: "In any case, do not make them worse than we are." Yes, indeed, raising them to be not worse than we are, that would do! Likeness to oneself need not be of any concern. Pro-

---

* B. 1898, artist and essayist.
† B. 1899, poet and scholar.

fession, world view, and so on—let them figure that out for themselves. Whatever they decide for themselves, they will value. Merely to guide them and help them develop themselves seems the most enlightened path to follow.

Yü-t'ung once said: "Only if we have our children graduate from universities can we say that we have fulfilled our parental duties." S. K. disagreed: "Consider also in this context your own economic ability and the children's capabilities and goals. If they graduate from middle school and cannot, or will not, go on to higher studies, let them do something else; even becoming workers, for instance, would not be improper at all." Of course, a person's social value and success does not altogether depend on his school education. By insisting that our children be university educated, we only follow our personal prejudices. I cannot decide these issues now, especially since the times are so unstable. How can one possibly foresee the future? It is a good thing the children are still small; we can wait and see what happens. All that we can do at present is to give them basic strength, breadth of mind, and good judgment. Since they are still children, it is of course too early to talk about high and far-off objectives; we should rather start out slowly from what is near at hand and basic. This, quite naturally, will proceed from the way I am. "It is up to each individual to solve for himself the mysteries of life!" Be it glory, misfortune or an undistinguished fate that awaits them, let each exert himself to the utmost of his strength. I only hope that with all these reflections I will from now on do well as a father; that would satisfy me completely. The call of the "madman" to "rescue the children"* is a frightening warning to all of us!

TO MY DEPARTED WIFE

Ch'ien, time flies so fast! Although it seems like an instant, it has already been three years since you passed away. In these three years, I do not know how much has changed in the world, but you would not be interested in that, I know. Your main worry would be the children and then me. The children and I, in equal parts, made up your world when you were alive; now in death, if you have knowledge, it must still be that way. So let me tell you about us. I went home last summer. Mai-erh has grown very strong; he is now a head taller than I am. Jun-erh, Grand-

---

*In Lu Hsün's story "Diary of a Madman."

father says, is the best behaved, but he is not as chubby as he used to be. Ts'ai-erh and Chuan-tzu are both well. Number Five is complimented by everybody on her good looks, but she developed boils on her legs and had to sit all day on her bamboo bed, pitiful to look at. As to Number Six, how shall I tell you? You know, before you died you also talked about him to Grandmother. That child was added for no good purpose. Try as he may, he could not make it, so he gave up last spring. A few months after he was born, your tuberculosis got serious. I urged you not to get so close to the child, to just supervise the maidservant and let her take care of him. But you could not bear to; one moment you would pick him up, the next you would carry him. However, considering how sick you were yourself, worrying about the child was quite something. That summer, when he was sick all the time, you kept busy the whole day—hot water, medicine, keeping him cool, keeping him warm—you had no time even to sleep and never gave a thought to yourself. When he looked slightly better, you were overjoyed and a dry smile came to your waxen face. I could only sigh to myself.

I never would have believed a mother would be able to do what you did. Starting with Mai-erh, you breast-fed all of the first four children. In the beginning you had not heard of feeding them at fixed times; later you found out but still could not adjust. How often the children's crying woke you up at night, especially in the oppressive heat of summer! I doubt if you ever had enough sleep. During the day you still had to cook and look after the children with little time to spare. You were not strong to begin with, and the four children wore you down during those seven or eight years. When the fifth one came, you were really no longer up to it; you did not have enough of your own milk but fed the baby yourself with powdered milk and hired a special maidservant to look after him. Even when the baby slept with the maidservant, you never stopped worrying. If he would cry at night, your ears would prick up and you would rush over if the crying did not stop quickly.

Early in 1927, I came to you in Peking but left Mai-erh and Chuan-tzu at home [in Yang-chou]. For those three years we could not bring them up to Peking, so that was a time of painful anxiety for you. You did not mention it much, but I knew. You later said your sickness was caused by too much worrying. Naturally, there is some truth in that, but the main reason is that you wore yourself out bringing up the children. Of your short married life of twelve years, you spent eleven on the children, never sparing your-self. What strength you had, you gave, right up to the end. You loved all your children equally, whether boys or girls, big or little. The old saying "As you store grain for days of hunger, boys are raised to pro-vide for old age" never entered your head; you just kept loving them with all your heart. Frankly, you did not concern yourself much with matters of educa-tion; as long as the children were well and fed and played happily, that was plenty. No wonder, since you yourself grew up that way. But after all, the children were still small, and eating and playing was all that really mattered. When your illness got seri-ous, the one thing you never could let go of was the children. When you were mere skin and bones, you still did not give up hope for recovery, always saying, "If I die, the children will suffer." When later there was talk of sending you home, the thought of seeing Mai-erh and Chuan-tzu again made you quite willing to go. The thought that you might never come back again did not occur to you. Only when I sent you off did you cry uncontrollably and say, "Will we ever see each other again?" How poignant! I know what was on your mind; you were thinking of bringing all our six children back to me again. Ch'ien, I am quite sure that was what you were thinking.

Apart from the children, you had me on your mind. It is true that your father was still alive, but your mother had died and he had remarried, so you did not feel so close to him anymore. During the first year of our marriage, you still were attached to your old home, but by the second year the children and I held all your attention and you had no time to worry about your father. Do you still remember that first year? I was in Peking and you were left at our home. People wrote me that you did not like to stay there and often returned to your parents' home. I was angry and wrote you immediately scolding you. You asked someone to write in reply that there had been some matters you had to attend to so you had to return. That was your first, and maybe last, time to protest and argue. I did not write you again there-after. During the summer vacations, when I re-turned, I had much on my mind, but on seeing your smiling face, I relaxed. After that, you gradually turned your heart from your father to me. You sold your gold bracelet to help pay my tuition, telling me to repay it later, which I never did.

In my family you had to suffer a lot of annoy-ances, and because of us, your family too gave you some trouble, all of which you endured. It was all because of me, I know. That time when I left my job at a middle-school in my native town in mid-term, people at home made fun of you and also told you to get out. Where could you go? You had to go home to your family who received you icily, and you had to live in that "ice-house" for three months. It was with some difficulty that I was able to move you out of there and then move all of us to another province. That is where we built up our little family.

Although you were not from a wealthy family, you were brought up by doting parents. Now, as housewife, you had to do everything with your own hands. You did not seem a bit perturbed, and even went about it happily. The chore of preparing the food was usually yours alone, but the eating was done by the rest of us; you had at most two or three bites with your chopsticks. You were not a bad cook either; an expert of long standing even once praised your cooking. You also did a good job at keeping our clothes clean; in summer you always personally washed my long silk gown. You were never idle at home. For each of the early childbirths, you always got up after only four or five days; you said lying around at home was against "good order," but ac-tually your getting up was not in "good order." Since we had so many children in the house, how could we keep good order?

When you were in Chekiang, you had to flee twice because of military troubles. I was in Peking all that time, so it was left to you to bring Mother and all the children out, hiding here and dodging there. The last time you even had to walk quite a few *li* across a mountain range. Both times, everything depended on you. In addition to bringing along Mother and the children, you also brought box after box of my books because you knew how fond I was of them. In those twelve short years, you had more worries than some people do their whole lives. Ch'ien, how were you able to endure it? You took on your shoulders some of my worries and responsibilities and they wore you down. I will never be able to pay you back the debt I owe you!

You wasted a lot of energy on my confounded books. The first time when your father's servant brought them along from our hometown to Shang-hai, he made a few uncalled-for remarks which made you so angry that you even cried in front of your father. The second time, you carried the books along when you were fleeing the city; everybody called you stupid, but you had your own way of reasoning: "How can a teacher teach without books? Besides, it's the hobby that he is fondest of." You did not know that it actually would not have been such a great pity to lose them. But how could you have known? I had never discussed these matters with you. Anyhow, I am most grateful for your considerate thoughts.

During those twelve years you suffered great hardship because of me and had but a few happy days. The time that we lived together adds up to less than five years. Regardless of how miserable your life was, whether you were left all by yourself or were with me, you never showed bad temper or became angry with me and never uttered one word of complaint about me or your unhappy lot. Frankly, I am an ill-tempered man who is apt to vent my anger on a third party. If that happened to you, you merely sobbed and shed tears but never answered back or raised your voice. But then, I too had only you alone in whom I trusted. Some things I discussed with you because in the whole world only you really sympathized with me. You not only suffered on my behalf but even took a share of my hardship off my shoulders.

Most of my present vigor and strength was nurtured by you. Over the years I have been sick very seldom, but I am a most impatient invalid. When I am sick, I groan and moan incessantly and make myself a nuisance to those who care for me. You once had the experience for only one or two hours but that was troublesome enough. You were frequently sick but never complained loudly or made a nuisance of yourself, in part not to disturb me, but also because you felt there was nobody else to do your chores. I have a bad temper and do not like to hear of people being sick, it is true. Later, when you ran a fever every day, you pretended it was malaria brought up from the south, always keeping the true state of affairs from me. Even when you were compelled to lie down, you quickly sat up when you heard my footsteps. After a while I got to wondering and had a doctor examine you. What a shock! One of your lungs had already decayed, leaving a big hole. The doctor urged you to move to the Western Hills for recuperation, but you would not leave the children and did not want to spend the money. Even when told to stay in bed at home, you would not neglect your household chores. The more I watched you, the more I became convinced that it would not do, so I sent you home. I knew then that there was little hope, but I did not expect the end would come in less than a month. I had had hopes of seeing you again, but it was not to be. Did you ever think it would end the way it did? Father told me that after returning home

you stayed in a separate little house but worried because there was no guest room, which would make it inconvenient if I came.

The summer before last, I went back and visited your grave. Your resting place is below that of the grandparents, which makes me feel that you are not alone. Only, the plot is somewhat small and the graves seem crowded. It may give the living a feeling of discomfort, but wait, I will find a way to improve the situation. There was a lot of greenery growing on the graves and dew dampened my cotton shoes. You had been buried a little over half a year. Some earth had come off one end of the grave, but otherwise it was not obvious that it was new. This year I went back with [my second wife] Yin. We had intended to visit your grave, but she got sick and we could not go. We wanted to let you know that all five children are well. We will do our utmost to raise them well so they will be worthy of their mother. You, dear Ch'ien, do not worry, and rest in peace.

Translated by Ernst Wolff

72.

Birth Customs

The daily life of peasants, especially in inland areas, was slow to change in the early twentieth century. Most peasants continued to follow traditional religious practices based on long-ingrained beliefs in spirits, ghosts, Yin and Yang, and so on. They also maintained traditional social forms, perhaps especially with regard to family life. This conservatism can be seen in the description given below of the customs surrounding pregnancy and birth followed by peasants in P'u-ning county in Kwangtung province. It was published in 1936 in a magazine devoted to reports of folklore and folk customs. The customs this article described may have been essentially religious in character, but they also served to shape family life and the experience of women.

Pregnancy is a very serious matter so a pregnant woman must respect the following taboos:

1. She should not attend any magic shows because if she were to see through the tricks and cause the magician embarrassment, the resulting trouble would be dangerous and unlucky.
2. She must not go to temples or houses of witchcraft. It is believed that gods and spirits are most high, pure, and powerful beings who protect all people with impartiality and must be respected. A pregnant woman, however, is an offensive sight to them, so it would be most irreverent for her to visit a temple.
3. She must not climb up fruit trees, reach for things in high places, or carry heavy objects. According to common belief, if a thing is handled by a pregnant woman, it becomes unlucky. For example, if she climbs up a fruit tree, it will bear no fruit the coming year. . . .
4. She should not quarrel with anyone.
5. She should not go on long journeys or visit her relatives.

6. She should not go to large gatherings or crowded places.
7. In the few months before and after giving birth, she must wear a rain hat and carry an umbrella when she goes out, rain or shine, night or day.
8. She must not step on goose droppings.
9. She must not eat chicken, goose, or carp.

The mistress of the house should consult a diviner on behalf of the pregnant woman to find out whether the unborn baby is a boy or a girl and to pray for its protection. If the pregnant woman is the mistress of the house, she must ask a neighbor woman to act on her behalf. The gods that peasant women revere most are the Mother of Birth, the Old Man and Old Lady of Pox, the Equal of Heaven, and various local gods of the earth. If the woman wants the baby to be a boy, she should pray to these gods and promise to repay them with gifts after the birth of her child. . . .

A young woman, after her marriage and particularly after conception, should pay visits to older women in the village who have had many sons or who live in comfortable circumstances to ask them for instructions and advice. She should listen to them and follow their instructions carefully so that she too may someday enjoy such good fortune.

When the day of birth approaches, the woman should let other people do all heavy work for her, unless the family is too poor to get outside help. At certain times she is not even allowed to wet her hands with water. A medication made with thirteen types of herbs must be prepared. If the family is well-off, they should pray to the god of medicine and implore him to protect the woman from illness; they should also burn incense and buy ginseng and other nourishment for her. After giving birth, the mother must take a tonic to replenish her blood. This preparation is a traditional one, passed from one generation to the next.

A midwife from the village is engaged to help with the delivery. If the baby is a girl, very little fuss is made; friendly neighbors come and wish the mother a rapid recovery. However, if the baby is a boy, there are elaborate ceremonies. Even the cutting of the umbilical cord must be done by a lucky woman who cuts it with a bamboo writing brush which has been split in half. Since the brush is an instrument of the gentry class, this is a symbolic gesture signifying that the child will learn to read and write and escape the life of a poor, hardworking peasant. Girl babies enjoy no such privileges because they are not valued. Even if one were to become rich and famous someday, the honor could go to another house and no good whatsoever would come to her own family.

After the baby is born, the following important tasks must be performed:

1. *Naming the child.* A male member of the household must dress in his best clothes and ask a member of the gentry or a well-educated man to name the baby. Special care must be taken lest the name contain a character found in the names of the father or an uncle. If the child does not have a sweet disposition, if he or she is often sick, has an unfavorable horoscope, has five elements not compatible with those of the parents, the name given by the gentleman is put aside temporarily and instead a vulgar name, such as "dog," "pig," or "stupid," is given to the child to ward off calamity. In extreme cases, the child must even address his or her own parents as "foster mother" and "foster father."

2. *Offering prayers to the gods.* Requests for prayers must be made to the monks and priests of the temples. The gifts to the gods consist of three incense sticks, a pair of red candles, twenty-four hard gold nuggets, 480 small gold foil nuggets, eight silver chalices, candies and cakes, three bowls of red dumplings, and a dish of meat, all of which express the family's gratitude and appreciation.

3. *Ushering in the God of the Bed.* This god's place is under the child's bed and his duty is to keep the child safe. At this point he must be ushered under the bed. On the 7the day of the seventh month in the child's fifteenth year, he will be ushered out again.

4. *Notifying friends and relatives.* The most important people to notify are the wife's family, close relatives, and good friends. In the villages very often the neighbors are relations anyway, so there is no need to go through this process. The announcement of a birth is usually accompanied by a sweet rice pudding. After being notified, rich families should send presents to the new baby, such as bolts of fabric, toys, gold and silver jewelry, pig's feet, or eggs. Poorer people should send pork and eggs. Gifts from the maternal grandparents are more elaborate, consisting of children's clothes, eggs and pork boiled in wine, pig's feet, fresh eggs, red rice dumplings, and all the things needed by a convalescing woman. . . .

If the baby is a girl, the gifts and ceremonies are much simpler. No announcement is sent and few presents are given to the baby, just noodles and white sugar. The maternal grandparents do not make much of a fuss either. . . .

Three days after the baby is born, he or she is bathed in water scented by twelve different types of flowers and herbs. One week after birth, the baby gets a first hair cut. The head is shaved except for one tuft of hair in front and another in back; afterwards, ointment is rubbed into the scalp. On the same day, the neighborhood children are invited to eat soft-boiled eggs and brown sugar so they will be nice to the new baby as he or she grows up.

A family in better circumstances gives a party when the baby completes one month of life. A cook is hired to prepare an elaborate dinner for friends and neighbors called the "feast after one full month."

Translated by Nancy Gibbs

73.

The Life of Beggars

For centuries beggars and street entertainers were a common feature of large cities. "The Attractions of the Capital" (selection 27) briefly described a number of hustlers and entertainers who sought money on the streets of Hang-chou in the Sung dynasty. Below is a description of the beggars active in Peking in the 1930s from a book on the social life of the area. While the existence of hundreds or even thousands of beggars in a large city like Peking can hardly be taken as a sign of prosperity, in this author's view the beggars themselves were not in desperate straits and their presence enlivened life in the city.

In Peking, begging for a living is an old and time-honored profession. Born into this tradition and never having opportunities for education or employment, old and young beggars alike firmly believe that begging is their only way to make a living. "Aggressiveness in begging and strength in numbers" is the byword of the beggars of China, and Peking is the city where their guild originated and flourished. According to older beggars, a certain Emperor was once reduced to begging before he became successful. Later, as an exalted Emperor, he bestowed his blessings on the beggars and granted them special permission to beg at every door, elect a leader, and establish a guild in every city. While there is no evidence to substantiate their story, the guild regards it as a trustworthy historical record because it increases its own importance. I shall now, after a careful study, present my findings about the way of life and the different styles of the beggars in Peking.

THE LEADER OF THE BEGGARS' GUILD AND HIS POWER

There is a beggars' guild in Peking which has all the beggars in the city under the control of its leader and his few trusted subordinates. This guild is a highly structured organization in which rank and status are closely observed and its influence is extensive. Not only must the local beggars show absolute obedience to the leader's orders, but any beggar coming from outside the city must pay a courtesy call on him in order to get permission to beg in the streets. This registration ceremony is referred to as "paying courtesy to the leader." The leader of the guild is appointed for life and lives in a fairly comfortable style. After he dies his successor is selected by the guild members from among those with the highest standing and prestige in the organization. Then the rest of the beggars are ranked approximately by age, the oldest called "Brother Number One," the next, "Brother Number Two," "Brother Number Three," and so on. Children are called "apprentices." The leader of the guild has the power to command and mediate. For example, if two beggars have been quarreling over territory, the leader mediates and they must accept his decision. When the townspeople hold weddings or birthday celebrations, the leader pays them a visit asking for donations on behalf of all the beggars. When a beggar becomes sick or dies, the leader must buy medicine and have him cared for or collect money for his burial and report his death to the authorities.

DONATIONS RECEIVED
DURING CELEBRATIONS

Soliciting for donations on festive occasions has become customary for the beggars. When a household celebrates a wedding or a birthday, the leader of the beggars' guild comes and extends his congratulations, whereupon the family manager usually gives him money, ranging from forty cents to one dollar. A family holding a birthday celebration generally gives more money than one celebrating a marriage because filial sons holding a birthday celebration for their parents do not want beggars to loiter about their front door saying unlucky things. After the leader gets the money, he posts a notice on the front door of the house: "This exalted household is having a celebration and our brothers are not to disturb them." Beggars who recognize this slip of paper shun the place the way small devils keep away from [the devil catcher] Master Chiang. If a family refuses to donate, a crowd of beggars soon creates disturbances at their front door and one never knows what embarrassing thing they might do next.

FORMS OF ADDRESS AND
TYPES OF CRYING

When begging on the streets, the beggars must call out to different types of people with different forms of address such as, "big master," "great master," "honorable master," "madame," "your ladyship," "young master," "sir," "young lady," "honorable proprieter," "honorable official." They must appraise a person on the spot, determine his status, and address him with the appropriate title. How to do this is a required skill for all the beggars in Peking, one earnestly passed on from master to apprentice. Two types of beggars must also be trained to cry properly, those who cry and run about the streets, and those who beg while sitting in one fixed place. Women and children must weep with correct pitch and rhythm. One often sees them crouching on the side of the road wailing and chanting with tears in their voices, touching people's hearts with their words; or one sees women wailing while walking down the streets, dragging young children behind them. When they are given money, they stop their pitiful crying and pour out their gratitude. Male beggars must shout wildly or exhibit their deformities and injuries. All these techniques must be studied and mastered. After a day of begging with them, the income gained can be quite impressive.

THE MASTERY OF SKILLS

Some beggars learn a variety of skills when they are young, such as balancing tricks, juggling, sword dancing, and magic. These skills are not taught by the guild leaders but by special masters, even professional entertainers and boxers who are looking for extra income. As long as the beggars pay for their lessons and the lessons do not interfere with begging, they are free to engage teachers for these skills. A skilled beggar makes more money than the wailing, chanting, and singing kind.

Beggars also carry a variety of utensils such as bamboo baskets and glazed bowls for holding money, rice bags and iron pots for holding food, and canes for chasing dogs away and self-defense. Sometimes people give beggars old clothes that are still in fair condition, which they then wear under the tattered jackets which show their destitution. For the skilled beggar, other items are necessary, such as musical instruments, gongs, drums, wooden clappers, theatrical swords, daggers, lances, and various equipment for animal acts.

HOSTELS FOR BEGGARS

Outside of Peking's Ch'ao-yang Gate, in the region south of T'ien-ch'iao, there are many hostels for beggars. Users are charged one copper cash per night and must leave in the morning. In the winter months, most of these hostels provide heat in a large room called the "fire room." Wood is burned in a hole dug in the middle of the floor which everyone sits around for warmth. The customers are old and experienced beggars who are idle during the cold weather. Among them there is usually someone who teaches "The Falling of Lotus Petals" and other traditional begging songs. Most young beggars use this opportunity to accept a master. Sometimes when the weather is so cold no one goes outside, the hostel's cook will make a large pot of porridge for all to eat. There is a charge for this, but a day's stay is only five copper cash. Male and female beggars all share the same room, and no one dares take off shoes or clothes while sleeping because they will be gone the next morning. According to my research, Peking has nine of these hostels, an institution which does not exist in the warmer and milder south.

TRADITIONAL BEGGING SONGS

The older beggars pass on to their disciples not only skills for survival but also a variety of songs and rhymes. Lucky phrases are skillfully worked into the lyrics of begging songs. The lyrics are memorized but can be easily changed to meet different circumstances. When a beggar encounters someone who refuses to give anything, he can instantly change the lyric to mock the man and make him feel uneasy. I have jotted down some of the most common lyrics:

Well-wishing songs: "Turtle crawls to your door; your wealth will soon soar." "Madame gave me a couple of coins; madame will live a thousand years." "Old master you are most kind; this year you'll get a thousand gold pieces." "Madame took pity upon me; sons and grandsons you'll soon have."

Unpleasant verses: "If you don't give me money, I won't survive this year." "Don't give me money? I don't care! Save your money for your coffin!" "If you won't give, I won't ask. We'll see how you feel when your son dies!"

The well-wishing songs must be sung with a sad but strong voice to evoke people's sympathy and make them give voluntarily. Generally, families holding celebrations do not refuse beggars because no one wants to hear their curses at such a time.

The beggars in Peking all refer to their profession as "living off the streets" for the obvious reason that they spend their entire lives in streets and alleys. Because of the economic decline of villages in the region in recent years, the number of beggars in Peking has increased sharply. Everywhere one hears loud wailing and lamenting and sees strange and unusual tricks and gimmicks. I have listed them as follows:

1. *Sword Slappers.* The beggars hold two long broad swords. Baring their chest, they slap the blades on it, breathe in deeply, then let out a loud grunt. This type is found most frequently during temple festivals and other holidays. A sword slapping beggar first addresses himself to a passer-by, grunts, and then slaps himself with his swords. He continues to do so until his flesh is red and swollen and covered with speckles of blood. He is quite pitiful to look at.

2. *Brick Slappers.* These beggars sit in the middle of the street slapping their bare chests and backs with a brick until their upper torso is covered with blood. This, too, is horrifying to see. These beggars grunt and shout just like the sword slappers. The above two types of beggars are not allowed to walk about but must remain seated in one place.

3. *Walking Brick Slappers.* These beggars walk down the streets while slapping a brick against their breasts, crying, "Master, madame, have mercy on the blind and deformed." Then they let out a pathetic sigh and hit themselves with the brick. As they repeat the crying and chanting, the brick serves as a percussion instrument setting the rhythm for the melodic wailing.

4. *Street Criers.* These beggars, carrying willow staffs and baskets, roam the city streets and lament. They are mostly old and weak and do not hurt themselves, but their income is much less than the types already mentioned. The last two types of beggars are allowed to walk the city streets, but they are never permitted to knock on people's doors.

5. *Head Nailers.* These beggars hold a few long nails between their lips and carry bricks. Each beggar penetrates the skin of his head with a sharp nail so it stands on the top of his head. Without saying a word he begs at doors. If he is given money right away, he leaves immediately; if not, he taps the nail into his head with the brick causing a crackling noise. Usually the nail is stuck into a tumor or a wart; when it is driven in deeper, blood drips down his face, creating a horrible sight. Once he bleeds, he usually will not leave until given a generous sum of money. This type of beggar is supposed to beg on one side of the street only.

6. *Head Cutters.* These beggars carry a sickle and get intoxicated before begging at doors. If not given money, one of these beggars takes the sickle between his thumb and forefinger until just a few millimeters of blade show, then passes the blade over his head until blood oozes out. He then falls to the ground and does not get up until the person gives generously.

7. *Treasure Counters.* These are the most commonly seen beggars in Peking and can be divided into three types.

   a. The first holds two beef shoulder bones from which dangle bells and colored ribbons. He begs and sings while keeping time by clapping the bones together and jingling the bells.

   b. The second carries a big piece of bamboo in his right hand and a small one in his left. Scraping them against each other, he sings and begs.

   c. The third type wears a colorful cap with a pom-pom on top. He holds two blue ceramic bowls in his hands and knocks them against each other to make a tinkling sound as he begs and sings. Some of these beggars wear rouge and powder and look very disgusting. I have recorded some of their songs: "I've begged here and I've begged there. When you eat dinner I'll be right here." "Shopkeeper, you'll soon be rich. When you eat your dinner, you'll see me." "Shopkeeper, don't get mad; the sooner you give, the sooner I'll leave."

8. *Sack Carriers.* These beggars carry cloth sacks on their backs and beg from door to door. They must address people as "uncle" and "aunt" only and not as "master" and "madame"; otherwise it is a violation of rules for which they can be expelled from the guild.

9. *Falling Lotus Petals.* Two beggars, wearing colorful clothes and caps, paint their faces with rouge and powder and carry bamboo staffs with holes drilled into each segment and filled with a few copper cash. While begging, they sing and dance, swinging their arms and legs, spinning around, and jumping up and down as if they were mad. Those who do not have colorful clothes often make do with ordinary rags.

10. *Jade Drummers.* These beggars have long bamboo cylinders covered with tightly stretched skin, which they strike as they sing a slow and melodious song.

11. *Frame Balancers.* These beggars balance a chopstick on the tip of their nose and place a small cup on top of the chopstick. Thus balanced, they beg from door to door.

12. *Eel Threaders.* These beggars carry an iron hook and pass it through a hole previously punctured in their noses. Until paid, they continue to stand at someone's front door, pushing the hook back and forth.

13. *Nodding Phoenixes.* These beggars puncture a hole through the bridge of their noses and push a thick needle through it. Then they balance a small bowl on one end of the needle. Rocking and singing, they go from door to door.

14. *Frozen Meat.* Beggars in the North often use their children to get money. In extremely cold weather, they strip the youngsters and place them near shops and stalls to arouse sympathy from passers-by and

shopkeepers. These children become accustomed to such inhumane treatment; some even develop resistance to very cold weather. These beggars must remain in one fixed place.

15. *Snake Charmers.* As North China is cold and harsh, only small green snakes are kept by snake charmers who carry them in bamboo cages and go from door to door to offer entertainment. These beggars are well versed in the art of handling snakes and also offer their services to capture snakes or sell snake skins and gall bladders for their restorative powers. During religious festivals, they catch water snakes and sell them to devout old ladies who later turn them loose. The next day they recapture them from the water and sell them again, turning an impressive profit.

I shall now list various ways deformed and invalid beggars can beg. They are not allowed to beg from door to door but must remain on the streets. Going down the streets, shouting pitiable cries, they try to arouse sympathy from passers-by to make them give of their own free will.

16. *Sunset Beggars.* Blind beggars aided by walking sticks who call out to passers-by and collect money in a straw hat.

17. *Light Gropers.* Blind beggars who squat on the street and grope their way around slowly while begging.

18. *One-eyed Dragons.* One-eyed beggars who lean on a staff and pretend to be totally blind though actually able to see quite well.

19. *Rollers.* Beggars with totally disabled hands and feet who lie in mud rolling and howling. They are accompanied by other beggars who take care of them and collect the money. This type of beggar has the biggest income.

20. *Wall Starers.* Beggars with disabled legs who pad their knees and hips with cotton and move about the street on their hands and knees.

21. *Wooden Hands.* Beggars with paralyzed legs who hold two wood blocks and move about the street, dragging their bodies behind them.

22. *Moving Carts.* Paralyzed beggars who lie on wooden carts pushed and dragged by two companions. Wailing and crying, they pass through the

streets, and passers-by can throw money into the moving cart.

23. *Rock Carriers.* Male beggars who carry invalid females on their back, moaning and lamenting, through the city streets.

Translated by Nancy Gibbs

74.

Spring Silkworms

By the 1930s the belief of the early activists that social and political reforms could be easily implemented had largely faded; intellectuals were instead blaming China's problems on the economic and social structure, which kept so large a part of the population on the margin of existence, and more and more of them were calling for thorough-going transformations of society. Not only communists and socialists, but also intellectuals influenced by Western liberalism came to believe that China could only be made strong if Chinese society were changed.

To awaken concern for the oppressed, a number of novelists and short story writers turned to the methods of Western social realism to write about the lives and work of peasants and laborers. Mao Tun (pen name of She Te-hung, b. 1896) was perhaps the most successful of such writers. A committed leftist, he was also a serious author who had read the works of such European authors as Dickens, Zola, and Chekhov. In "Spring Silkworms," written in 1932, he explores the world of a family of peasants caught by economic forces they cannot comprehend, much less master.

Old Tung Pao sat on a rock beside the road that skirted the canal, his long-stemmed pipe lying on the ground next to him. Though it was only a few days after "Clear and Bright Festival," the April sun was already very strong. It scorched Old Tung Pao's spine like a basin of fire. Straining down the road, the men towing the fast junk wore only thin tunics, open in front. They were bent far forward, pulling, pulling, pulling, great beads of sweat dripping from their brows.

The sight of others toiling strenuously made Old Tung Pao feel even warmer; he began to itch. He was still wearing the tattered padded jacket in which he had passed the winter. His unlined jacket had not yet been redeemed from the pawn shop. Who would have believed it could get so hot right after "Clear and Bright"?

Even the weather's not what it used to be, Old Tung Pao said to himself, and spat emphatically.

Before him, the water of the canal was green and shiny. Occasional passing boats broke the mirror-smooth surface into ripples and eddies, turning the reflection of the earthen bank and the long line of mulberry trees flanking it into a dancing grey blur. But not for long! Gradually the trees reappeared, twisting and weaving drunkenly. Another few minutes, and they were again standing still, reflected as clearly as before. On the gnarled fists of the mulberry branches, little fingers of tender green buds were already bursting forth. Crowded close together, the trees along the canal seemed to march endlessly into the distance. The unplanted fields as yet were only cracked clods of dry earth; the mulberry trees reigned supreme here this time of the year! Behind Old Tung Pao's back was another great stretch of mulberry trees, squat, silent. The little buds seemed to be growing bigger every second in the hot sunlight.

Not far from where Old Tung Pao was sitting, a

grey two-storey building crouched beside the road. That was the silk filature, where the delicate fibres were removed from the cocoons. Two weeks ago it was occupied by troops; a few short trenches still scarred the fields around it. Everyone had said that the Japanese soldiers were attacking in this direction. The rich people in the market town had all run away. Now the troops were gone and the silk filature stood empty and locked as before. There would be no noise and excitement in it again until cocoon selling time.

Old Tung Pao had heard Young Master Chen— son of the Master Chen who lived in town—say that Shanghai was seething with unrest, that all the silk weaving factories had closed their doors, that the silk filatures here probably wouldn't open either. But he couldn't believe it. He had been through many periods of turmoil and strife in his sixty years, yet he had never seen a time when the shiny green mulberry leaves had been allowed to wither on the branches and become fodder for the sheep. Of course if the silkworm eggs shouldn't ripen, that would be different. Such matters were all in the hands of the Old Lord of the Sky. Who could foretell His will?

"Only just after 'Clear and Bright' and so hot already!" marveled Old Tung Pao, gazing at the small green mulberry leaves. He was happy as well as surprised. He could remember only one year when it was too hot for padded clothes at "Clear and Bright". He was in his twenties then, and the silkworm eggs had hatched "two hundred per cent"! That was the year he got married. His family was flourishing in those days. His father was like an experienced plough ox—there was nothing he didn't understand, nothing he wasn't willing to try. Even his old grandfather— the one who had first started the family on the road to prosperity—seemed to be growing more hearty with age, in spite of the hard time he was said to have had during the years he was a prisoner of the "Long Hairs."*

Old Master Chen was still alive then. His son, the present Master Chen, hadn't begun smoking opium yet, and the "House of Chen" hadn't become the bad lot it was today. Moreover, even though the House of Chen was of the rich gentry and his own family only ordinary tillers of the land, Old Tung Pao had felt that the destinies of the two families were linked together. Years ago, "Long Hairs" campaigning through the countryside had captured Tung Pao's grandfather and Old Master Chen and kept them

working as prisoners for nearly seven years in the same camp. They had escaped together, taking a lot of the "Long Hairs'" gold with them—people still talk about it to this day. What's more, at the same time Old Master Chen's silk trade began to prosper, the cocoon raising of Tung Pao's family grew successful too. Within ten years grandfather had earned enough to buy three acres of rice paddy, two acres of mulberry grove, and build a modest house. Tung Pao's family was the envy of the people of East Village, just as the House of Chen ranked among the first families in the market town.

But afterwards, both families had declined. Today, Old Tung Pao had no land of his own, in fact he was over three hundred silver dollars in debt. The House of Chen was finished too. People said the spirit of the dead "Long Hair" had sued the Chens in the underworld, and because the King of Hell had decreed that the Chens repay the fortune they had amassed on the stolen gold, the family had gone down financially very quickly. Old Tung Pao was rather inclined to believe this. If it hadn't been for the influence of devils, why would a decent fellow like Master Chen have taken to smoking opium?

What Old Tung Pao could never understand was why the fall of the House of Chen should affect his own family? They certainly hadn't kept any of the "Long Hairs'" gold. True, his father had related that when grandfather was escaping from the "Long Hairs'" camp he had run into a young "Long Hair" on patrol and had to kill him. What else could he have done? It was "fate"! Still from Tung Pao's earliest recollections, his family had prayed and offered sacrifices to appease the soul of the departed young "Long Hair" time and time again. That little wronged spirit should have left the nether world and been reborn long ago by now! Although Old Tung Pao couldn't recall what sort of man his grandfather was, he knew his father had been hard-working and honest—he had seen that with his own eyes. Old Tung Pao himself was a respectable person; both Ah Sze, his elder son, and his daughter-in-law were industrious and frugal. Only his younger son, Ah To, was inclined to be a little flighty. But youngsters were all like that. There was nothing really bad about the boy. . . .

Old Tung Pao raised his wrinkled face, scorched by years of hot sun to the colour of dark parchment. He gazed bitterly at the canal before him, at the boats on its waters, at the mulberry trees along its banks. All were approximately the same as they had been

---

* The T'ai-p'ing rebels were called "Long Hairs."

when he was twenty. But the world had changed. His family now often had to make their meals of pumpkin instead of rice. He was over three hundred silver dollars in debt. . . .

Toot! Toot-toot-toot. . . .

Far up the bend in the canal a boat whistle broke the silence. There was a silk filature over there too. He could see vaguely the neat lines of stones embedded as reinforcement in the canal bank. A small oil-burning river boat came puffing up pompously from beyond the silk filature, tugging three larger craft in its wake. Immediately the peaceful water was agitated with waves rolling toward the banks on both sides of the canal. A peasant, poling a tiny boat, hastened to shore and clutched a clump of reeds growing in the shallows. The waves tossed him and his little craft up and down like a see saw. The peaceful green countryside was filled with the chugging of the boat engine and the stink of its exhaust.

Hatred burned in Old Tung Pao's eyes. He watched the river boat approach, he watched it sail past and glared after it until it went tooting around another bend and disappeared from sight. He had always abominated the foreign devils' contraptions. He himself had never met a foreign devil, but his father had given him a description of one Old Master Chen had seen—red eyebrows, green eyes, and a stiff-legged walk! Old Master Chen had hated the foreign devils too. "The foreign devils have swindled our money away," he used to say. Old Tung Pao was only eight or nine the last time he saw Old Master Chen. All he remembered about him now were things he had heard from others. But whenever Old Tung Pao thought of that remark—"The foreign devils have swindled our money away"—he could almost picture Old Master Chen, stroking his beard and wagging his head.

How the foreign devils had accomplished this, Old Tung Pao wasn't too clear. He was sure, however, that Old Master Chen was right. Some things he himself had seen quite plainly. From the time foreign goods—cambric, cloth, oil—appeared in the market town, from the time the foreign river boats increased on the canal, what he produced brought a lower price in the market every day, while what he had to buy became more and more expensive. That was why the property his father left him had shrunk until it finally vanished completely; and now he was in debt. It was not without reason that Old Tung Pao hated the foreign devils!

In the village, his attitude toward foreigners was well-known. Five years before, in 1927, someone had told him: The new Kuomintang government says it wants to "throw out" the foreign devils. Old Tung Pao didn't believe it. He heard those young propaganda speech makers the Kuomintang sent when he went into the market town. Though they cried "Throw out the foreign devils," they were dressed in Western style clothing. His guess was that they were secretly in league with the foreign devils, that they had been purposely sent to delude the countryfolk! Sure enough, the Kuomintang dropped the slogan not long after, and prices and taxes rose steadily. Old Tung Pao was firmly convinced that all this occurred as part of a government conspiracy with the foreign devils.

Last year something had happened that made him almost sick with fury: Only the cocoons spun by the foreign strain silkworms could be sold at a decent price. Buyers paid ten dollars more per load for them than they did for the local variety. Usually on good terms with his daughter-in-law, Old Tung Pao had quarreled with her because of this. She had wanted to raise only foreign silkworms, and Old Tung Pao's younger son Ah To had agreed with her. Though the boy didn't say much, in his heart he certainly had also favoured this course. Events had proved they were right, and they wouldn't let Old Tung Pao forget it. This year, he had to compromise. Of the five trays they would raise, only four would be silkworms of the local variety; one tray would contain foreign silkworms.

"The world's going from bad to worse! In another couple of years they'll even be wanting foreign mulberry trees! It's enough to take all the joy out of life!"

Old Tung Pao picked up his long pipe and rapped it angrily against a clod of dry earth. The sun was directly overhead now, foreshortening his shadow till it looked like a piece of charcoal. Still in his padded jacket, he was bathed in heat. He unfastened the jacket and swung its opened edges back and forth a few times to fan himself. Then he stood up and started for home.

Behind the row of mulberry trees were paddy fields. Most of them were as yet only neatly ploughed furrows of upturned earth clods, dried and cracked by the hot sun. Here and there, the early crops were coming up. In one field, the golden blossoms of rapeseed plants emitted a heady fragrance. And that group of houses way over there, that was the village where three generations of Old Tung Pao's family were living. Above the houses, white smoke from many kitchen stoves was curling lazily upwards into the sky.

After crossing through the mulberry grove, Old Tung Pao walked along the raised path between the paddy fields, then turned and looked again at that row of trees bursting with tender green buds. A twelve-year-old boy came bounding along from the other end of the fields, calling as he ran:

"Grandpa! Ma's waiting for you to come home and eat!"

It was Little Pao, Old Tung Pao's grandson.

"Coming!" the old man responded, still gazing at the mulberries. Only twice in his life had he seen these finger-like buds appear on the branches so soon after "Clear and Bright". His family would probably have a fine crop of silkworms this year. Five trays of eggs would hatch out a huge number of silkworms. If only they didn't have another bad market like last year, perhaps they could pay off part of their debt.

Little Pao stood beside his grandfather. The child too looked at the soft green on the gnarled fist branches. Jumping happily, he clapped his hands and chanted:

Green, tender leaves at Clear and Bright,
The girls who tend silkworms,
Clap hands at the sight!

The old man's wrinkled face broke into a smile. He thought it was a good omen for the little boy to respond like this on seeing the first buds of the year. He rubbed his hand affectionately over the child's shaven pate. In Old Tung Pao's heart, numbed wooden by a lifetime of poverty and hardship, suddenly hope began to stir again.

II

The weather remained warm. The rays of the sun forced open the tender, finger-like, little buds. They had already grown to the size of a small hand. Around Old Tung Pao's village, the mulberry trees seemed to respond especially well. From a distance they gave the appearance of a low grey picket fence on top of which a long swath of green brocade had been spread. Bit by bit, day by day, hope grew in the hearts of the villagers. The unspoken mobilization order for the silkworm campaign reached everywhere and everyone. Silkworm rearing equipment that had

been laid away for a year was again brought out to be scrubbed and mended. Beside the little stream which ran through the village, women and children, with much laughter and calling back and forth, washed the implements.

None of these women or children looked really healthy. Since the coming of spring, they had been eating only half their fill; their clothes were old and torn. As a matter of fact, they weren't much better off than beggars. Yet all were in quite good spirits, sustained by enormous patience and grand illusions. Burdened though they were by daily mounting debts, they had only one thought in their heads—If we get a good crop of silkworms, everything will be all right! . . . They could already visualize how, in a month, the shiny green leaves would be converted into snow-white cocoons, the cocoons exchanged for clinking silver dollars. Although their stomachs were growling with hunger, they couldn't refrain from smiling at this happy prospect.

Old Tung Pao's daughter-in-law was among the women by the stream. With the help of her twelve-year-old son, Little Pao, she had already finished washing the family's large trays of woven bamboo strips. Seated on a stone beside the stream, she wiped her perspiring face with the edge of her tunic. A twenty-year-old girl, working with other women on the opposite side of the stream, hailed her.

"Are you raising foreign silkworms this year too?"

It was Sixth Treasure, sister of young Fu-ching, the neighbour who lived across the stream.

The thick eyebrows of Old Tung Pao's daughter-in-law at once contracted. Her voice sounded as if she had just been waiting for a chance to let off steam.

"Don't ask me; what the old man says, goes!" she shouted. "He's dead set against it, won't let us raise more than one batch of foreign breed! The old fool only has to hear the word 'foreign' to send him up in the air! He'll take dollars made of foreign silver, though; those are the only 'foreign' things he likes!"

The women on the other side of the stream laughed. From the threshing ground behind them a strapping young man approached. He reached the stream and crossed over on the four logs that served as a bridge. Seeing him, his sister-in-law dropped her tirade and called in a high voice:

"Ah To, will you help me carry these trays? They're as heavy as dead dogs when they're wet!"

Without a word, Ah To lifted the six big trays and set them, dripping, on his head. Balancing them in place, he walked off, swinging his hands in a swimming motion. When in a good mood, Ah To refused nobody. If any of the village women asked him to carry something heavy or fish something out of the stream, he was usually quite willing. But today he probably was a little grumpy, and so he walked empty-handed with only six trays on his head. The sight of him, looking as if he were wearing six layers of wide straw hats, his waist twisting at each step in imitation of the ladies of the town, sent the women into peals of laughter. Lotus, wife of Old Tung Pao's nearest neighbour, called with a giggle:

"Hey, Ah To, come back here. Carry a few trays for me too!"

Ah To grinned. "Not unless you call me a sweet name!" He continued walking. An instant later he had reached the porch of his house and set down the trays out of the sun.

"Will 'kid brother' do?" demanded Lotus, laughing boisterously. She had a remarkably clean white complexion, but her face was very flat. When she laughed, all that could be seen was a big open mouth and two tiny slits of eyes. Originally a slave in a house in town, she had been married off to Old Tung Pao's neighbour—a prematurely aged man who walked around with a sour expression and never said a word all day. That was less than six months ago, but her love affairs and escapades already were the talk of the village.

"Shameless hussy!" came a contemptuous female voice from across the stream.

Lotus's piggy eyes immediately widened. "Who said that?" she demanded angrily. "If you've got the brass to call me names, let's see you try it to my face! Come out into the open!"

"Think you can handle me? I'm talking about a shameless, man-crazy baggage! If the shoe fits, wear it!" retorted Sixth Treasure, for it was she who had spoken. She too was famous in the village, but as a mischievous, lively young woman.

The two began splashing water at each other from opposite banks of the stream. Girls who enjoyed a row took sides and joined the battle, while the children whooped with laughter. Old Tung Pao's daughter-in-law was more decorous. She picked up her remaining trays, called to Little Pao and returned home. Ah To watched from the porch, grinning. He knew why Sixth Treasure and Lotus were quarreling. It did his heart good to hear that sharp-tongued Sixth Treasure get told off in public.

Old Tung Pao came out of the house with a wooden tray-stand on his shoulder. Some of the legs of the uprights had been eaten by termites, and he wanted to repair them. At the sight of Ah To standing there laughing at the women, Old Tung Pao's face lengthened. The boy hadn't much sense of propriety, he well knew. What disturbed him particularly was the way Ah To and Lotus were always talking and laughing together. "That bitch is an evil spirit. Fooling with her will bring ruin on our house," he had often warned his younger son.

"Ah To!" he now barked angrily. "Enjoying the scenery? Your brother's in the back mending equipment. Go and give him a hand!" His inflamed eyes bored into Ah To, never leaving the boy until he disappeared into the house.

Only then did Old Tung Pao start work on the tray-stand. After examining it carefully, he slowly began his repairs. Years ago, Old Tung Pao had worked for a time as a carpenter. But he was old now; his fingers had lost their strength. A few minutes' work and he was breathing hard. He raised his head and looked into the house. Five squares of cloth to which sticky silkworm eggs were adhered, hung from a horizontal bamboo pole.

His daughter-in-law, Ah Sze's wife, was at the other end of the porch, pasting paper on big trays of woven bamboo strips. Last year, to economize a bit, they had bought and used old newspaper. Old Tung Pao still maintained that was why the eggs had hatched poorly—it was unlucky to use paper with writing on it for such a prosaic purpose. Writing meant scholarship, and scholarship had to be respected. This year the whole family had skipped a meal and with the money saved, purchased special "tray pasting paper." Ah Sze's wife pasted the tough, gosling-yellow sheets smooth and flat; on every tray she also affixed three little coloured paper pictures, bought at the same time. One was the "Platter of Plenty"; the other two showed a militant figure on horseback, pennant in hand. He, according to local belief, was the "Guardian of Silkworm Hatching."

"I was only able to buy twenty loads of mulberry leaves with that thirty silver dollars I borrowed on your father's guarantee," Old Tung Pao said to his daughter-in-law. He was still panting from his exertions with the tray-stand. "Our rice will be finished by the day after tomorrow. What are we going to do?"

Thanks to her father's influence with his boss and

his willingness to guarantee repayment of the loan, Old Tung Pao was able to borrow the money at a low rate of interest—only twenty-five per cent a month! Both the principal and interest had to be repaid by the end of the silkworm season.

Ah Sze's wife finished pasting a tray and placed it in the sun. "You've spent it all on leaves," she said angrily. "We'll have a lot of leaves left over, just like last year!"

"Full of lucky words, aren't you?" demanded the old man, sarcastically. "I suppose every year'll be like last year? We can't get more than a dozen or so loads of leaves from our own trees. With five sets of grubs to feed, that won't be nearly enough."

"Oh, of course, you're never wrong!" she replied hotly. "All I know is with rice we can eat, without it we'll go hungry!" His stubborn refusal to raise any foreign silkworms last year had left them with only the unsalable local breed. As a result, she was often contrary with him.

The old man's face turned purple with rage. After this, neither would speak to the other.

But hatching time was drawing closer every day. The little village's two dozen families were thrown into a state of great tension, great determination, great struggle. With it all, they were possessed of a great hope, a hope that could almost make them forget their hungry bellies.

Old Tung Pao's family, borrowing a little here, getting a little credit there, somehow managed to get by. Nor did the other families eat any better; there wasn't one with a spare bag of rice! Although they had harvested a good crop the previous year, landlords, creditors, taxes, levies, one after another, had cleaned the peasants out long ago. Now all their hopes were pinned on the spring silkworms. The repayment date of every loan they made was set for the "end of the silkworm season."

With high hopes and considerable fear, like soldiers going into a hand-to-hand battle to the death, they prepared for their spring silkworm campaign!

"Grain Rain" day—bringing gentle drizzles—was not far off. Almost imperceptibly, the silkworm eggs of the two dozen village families began to show faint tinges of green. Women, when they met on the public threshing ground, would speak to one another agitatedly in tones that were anxious yet joyful.

"Over at Sixth Treasure's place, they're almost ready to incubate their eggs!"

"Lotus says her family is going to start incubating tomorrow. So soon!"

"Huang 'the Priest' has made a divination. He predicts that this spring mulberry leaves will go to four dollars a load!"

Old Tung Pao's daughter-in-law examined their five sets of eggs. They looked bad. The tiny seed-like eggs were still pitch black, without even a hint of green. Her husband, Ah Sze, took them into the light to peer at them carefully. Even so, he could find hardly any ripening eggs. She was very worried.

"You incubate them anyhow. Maybe this variety is a little slow," her husband forced himself to say consolingly.

Her lips pressed tight, she made no reply.

Old Tung Pao's wrinkled face sagged with dejection. Though he said nothing, he thought their prospects were dim.

The next day, Ah Sze's wife again examined the eggs. Ha! Quite a few were turning green, and a very shiny green at that! Immediately, she told her husband, told Old Tung Pao, Ah To . . . she even told her son Little Pao. Now the incubating process could begin! She held the five pieces of cloth to which the eggs were adhered against her bare bosom. As if cuddling a nursing infant, she sat absolutely quiet, not daring to stir. At night, she took the five sets to bed with her. Her husband was routed out, and had to share Ah To's bed. The tiny silkworm eggs were very scratchy against her flesh. She felt happy and a little frightened, like the first time she was pregnant and the baby moved inside her. Exactly the same sensation!

Uneasy but eager, the whole family waited for the eggs to hatch. Ah To was the only exception. We're sure to hatch a good crop, he said, but anyone who thinks we're going to get rich in this life, is out of his head. Though the old man swore Ah To's big mouth would ruin their luck, the boy stuck to his guns.

A clean dry shed for the growing grubs was all prepared. The second day of incubation, Old Tung Pao smeared a garlic with earth and placed it at the foot of the wall inside the shed. If, in a few days, the garlic put out many sprouts, it meant the eggs would hatch well. He did this every year, but this year he was more reverential than usual, and his hands trembled. Last year's divination had proved all too accurate. He didn't dare to think about that now.

Every family in the village was busy "incubating." For the time being there were few women's footprints on the threshing ground or the banks of the little stream. An unofficial "martial law" had been imposed. Even peasants normally on very good terms stopped visiting one another. For a guest to come and frighten away the spirits of the ripening eggs—that would be no laughing matter! At most, people exchanged a few words in low tones when they met, then quickly separated. This was the "sacred" season!

Old Tung Pao's family was on pins and needles. In the five sets of eggs a few grubs had begun wriggling. It was exactly one day before Grain Rain. Ah Sze's wife had calculated that most of the eggs wouldn't hatch until after that day. Before or after Grain Rain was all right, but for eggs to hatch on the day itself was considered highly unlucky. Incubation was no longer necessary, and the eggs were carefully placed in the special shed. Old Tung Pao stole a glance at his garlic at the foot of the wall. His heart dropped. There were still only the same two small green shoots the garlic had originally! He didn't dare to look any closer. He prayed silently that by noon the day after tomorrow the garlic would have many, many more shoots.

At last hatching day arrived. Ah Sze's wife set a pot of rice on to boil and nervously watched for the time when the steam from it would rise straight up. Old Tung Pao lit the incense and candles he had bought in anticipation of this event. Devoutly, he placed them before the idol of the Kitchen God. His two sons went into the fields to pick wild flowers. Little Pao chopped a lamp wick into fine pieces and crushed the wild flowers the men brought back. Everything was ready. The sun was entering its zenith; steam from the rice pot puffed straight upwards. Ah Sze's wife immediately leaped to her feet, stuck a "sacred" paper flower and a pair of goose feathers into the knot of hair at the back of her head and went to the shed. Old Tung Pao carried a wooden scale-pole; Ah Sze followed with the chopped lamp wick and the crushed wild flowers. Daughter-in-law uncovered the cloth pieces to which the grubs were adhered, and sprinkled them with the bits of wick and flowers Ah Sze was holding. Then she took the wooden scale-pole from Old Tung Pao and hung the cloth pieces over it. She next removed the pair of goose feathers from her hair. Moving them lightly across the cloth, she brushed the grubs, together with the crushed lamp wick and wild flowers, on to a large tray. One set, two sets . . . the last set contained the foreign breed. The grubs from this cloth were brushed onto a separate tray. Finally, she removed the "sacred" paper flower from her hair and pinned it, with the goose feathers, against the side of the tray.

A solemn ceremony! One that had been handed down through the ages! Like warriors taking an oath before going into battle! Old Tung Pao and family now had ahead of them a month of fierce combat, with no rest day or night, against bad weather, bad luck and anything else that might come along!

The grubs, wriggling in the trays, looked very healthy. They were all the proper black colour. Old Tung Pao and his daughter-in-law were able to relax a little. But when the old man secretly took another look at his garlic, he turned pale! It had grown only four measly shoots! Ah! Would this year be like last year all over again?

III

But the "fateful" garlic proved to be not so psychic after all. The silkworms of Old Tung Pao's family grew and thrived! Though it rained continuously during the grubs' First Sleep and Second Sleep, and the weather was a it colder than at "Clear and Bright," the "little darlings" were extremely robust.

The silkworms of the other families in the village were not doing badly either. A tense kind of joy pervaded the countryside. Even the small stream seemed to be gurgling with bright laughter. Lotus's family was the sole exception. They were only raising one set of grubs, but by the Third Sleep their silkworms weighed less than twenty catties. Just before the Big Sleep, people saw Lotus's husband walk to the stream and dump out his trays. That dour, old-looking man had bad luck written all over him.

Because of this dreadful event, the village women put Lotus's family strictly "off limits." They made wide detours so as not to pass her door. If they saw her or her taciturn husband, no matter how far away, they made haste to go in the opposite direction. They feared that even one look at Lotus or her spouse, the briefest conversation, would contaminate them with the unfortunate couple's bad luck!

Old Tung Pao strictly forbade Ah To to talk to Lotus. "If I catch you gabbing with that baggage again, I'll disown you!" He threatened in a loud, angry voice, standing outside on the porch to make sure Lotus could hear him.

Little Pao was also warned not to play in front of

Lotus's door, and not to speak to anyone in her family. . . .

The old man harped at Ah To morning, noon, and night, but the boy turned a deaf ear to his father's grumbling. In his heart, he laughed at it. Of the whole family, Ah To alone didn't place much stock in taboos and superstitions. He didn't talk with Lotus, however. He was much too busy for that.

By the Big Sleep, their silkworms weighed three hundred catties. Every member of Old Tung Pao's family, including twelve-year-old Little Pao, worked for two days and two nights without sleeping a wink. The silkworms were unusually sturdy. Only twice in his sixty years had Old Tung Pao ever seen the like. Once was the year he married; once when his first son was born.

The first day after the Big Sleep, the "little darlings" ate seven loads of leaves. They were now a bright green, thick and healthy. Old Tung Pao and his family, on the contrary, were much thinner, their eyes bloodshot from lack of sleep.

No one could guess how much the "little darlings" would eat before they spun their cocoons. Old Tung Pao discussed the question of buying more leaves with Ah Sze.

"Master Chen won't lend us any more. Shall we try your father-in-law's boss again?"

"We've still got ten loads coming. That's enough for one more day," replied Ah Sze. He could barely hold himself erect. His eyelids weighed a thousand catties. They kept wanting to close.

"One more day? You're dreaming!" snapped the old man impatiently. "Not counting tomorrow, they still have to eat three more days. We'll need another thirty loads! Thirty loads, I say!"

Loud voices were heard outside on the threshing ground. Ah To had arrived with men delivering five loads of mulberry branches. Everyone went out to strip the leaves. Ah Sze's wife hurried from the shed. Across the stream, Sixth Treasure and her family were raising only a small crop of silkworms; having spare time, she came over to help. Bright stars filled the sky. There was a slight wind. All up and down the village, gay shouts and laughter rang in the night.

"The price of leaves is rising fast!" a coarse voice cried. "This afternoon, they were getting four dollars a load in the market town!"

Old Tung Pao was very upset. At four dollars a load, thirty loads would come to a hundred and twenty dollars. Where could he raise so much money! But then he figured—he was sure to gather over five hundred catties of cocoons. Even at fifty dollars a hundred, they'd sell for two hundred and fifty dollars. Feeling a bit consoled, he heard a small voice from among the leaf-strippers.

"They say the folks east of here aren't doing so well with their silkworms. There won't be any reason for the price of leaves to go much higher."

Old Tung Pao recognized the speaker as Sixth Treasure, and he relaxed still further.

The girl and Ah To were standing beside a large basket, stripping leaves. In the dim starlight, they worked quite close to each other, partly hidden by the pile of mulberry branches before them. Suddenly, Sixth Treasure felt someone pinch her thigh. She knew well enough who it was, and she suppressed a giggle. But when, a moment later, a hand brushed against her breasts, she jumped; a little shriek escaped her.

"Aiya!"

"What's wrong?" demanded Ah Sze's wife, working on the other side of the basket.

Sixth Treasure's face flamed scarlet. She shot a glance at Ah To, then quickly lowered her head and resumed stripping leaves. "Nothing," she replied. "I think a caterpillar bit me!"

Ah To bit his lips to keep from laughing aloud. He had been half starved the past two weeks and had slept little. But in spite of having lost a lot of weight, he was in high spirits. While he never suffered from any of Old Tung Pao's gloom, neither did he believe that one good crop, whether of silkworms or of rice, would enable them to wipe off their debt and own their own land again. He knew they would never "get out from under" merely by relying on hard work, even if they broke their backs trying. Nevertheless, he worked with a will. He enjoyed work, just as he enjoyed fooling around with Sixth Treasure.

The next morning, Old Tung Pao went into town to borrow money for more leaves. Before leaving home, he had talked the matter over with daughter-in-law. They had decided to mortgage their grove of mulberries that produced fifteen loads of leaves a year as security for the loan. The grove was the last piece of property the family owned.

By the time the old man ordered another thirty loads, and the first ten were delivered, the sturdy "little darlings" had gone hungry for half an hour. Putting forth their pointed little mouths, they swayed from side to side, searching for food. Daughter-in-law's heart had ached to see them. When the leaves were finally spread in the trays, the silkworm shed at once resounded with a sibilant crunching, so noisy it drowned out conversation. In a very short while, the trays were again empty of leaves. Another thick layer was piled on. Just keeping the silkworms supplied with leaves, Old Tung Pao and his family were so busy they could barely catch their breath. But this was the final crisis. In two more days the "little darlings" would spin their cocoons. People were putting every bit of their remaining strength into this last desperate struggle.

Though he had gone without sleep for three whole days, Ah To didn't appear particularly tired. He agreed to watch the shed alone that night until dawn to permit the others to get some rest. There was a bright moon and the weather was a trifle cold. Ah To crouched beside a small fire he had built in the shed. At about eleven, he gave the silkworms their second feeding, then returned to squat by the fire. He could hear the loud rustle of the "little darlings" crunching through the leaves. His eyes closed. Suddenly, he heard the door squeak, and his eyelids flew open. He peered into the darkness for a moment, then shut his eyes again. His ears were still hissing with the rustle of the leaves. The next thing he knew, his head had struck against his knees. Waking with a start, he heard the door screen bang and thought he saw a moving shadow. Ah To leaped up and rushed outside. In the moonlight, he saw someone crossing the threshing ground toward the stream. He caught up in a flash, seized and flung the intruder to the ground. Ah To was sure he had nabbed a thief.

"Ah To, kill me if you want to, but don't give me away!"

The voice made Ah To's hair stand on end. He could see in the moonlight that queer flat white face and those round little piggy eyes fixed upon him. But of menace, the piggy eyes had none. Ah To snorted.

"What were you after?"

"A few of your family's 'little darlings'!"

"What did you do with them?"

"Threw them in the stream!"

Ah To's face darkened. He knew that in this way she was trying to put a curse on the lot. "You're pure poison! We never did anything to hurt you."

"Never did anything? Oh, yes you did! Yes, you did! Our silkworm eggs didn't hatch well, but we didn't harm anybody. You were all so smart! You shunned me like a leper. No matter how far away I was, if you saw me, you turned your heads. You acted as if I wasn't even human!"

She got to her feet, the agonized expression on her face terrible to see. Ah To stared at her. "I'm not going to beat you," he said finally. "Go on your way!"

Without giving her another glance, he trotted back to the shed. He was wide awake now. Lotus had only taken a handful and the remaining "little darlings" were all in good condition. It didn't occur to him either to hate or pity Lotus, but the last thing she had said remained in his mind. It seemed to him there was something eternally wrong in the scheme of human relations; but he couldn't put his finger on what it was exactly, nor did he know why it should be. In a little while, he forgot about this too. The lusty silkworms were eating and eating, yet, as if by some magic, never full!

Nothing more happened that night. Just before the sky began to brighten in the east, Old Tung Pao and his daughter-in-law came to relieve Ah To. They took the trays of "little darlings" and looked at them in the light. The silkworms were turning a whiter colour, their bodies gradually becoming shorter and thicker. They were delighted with the excellent way the silkworms were developing.

But when, at sunrise, Ah Sze's wife went to draw water at the stream, she met Sixth Treasure. The girl's expression was serious.

"I saw that slut leaving your place shortly before midnight," she whispered. "Ah To was right behind her. They stood here and talked for a long time! Your family ought to look after things better than that!"

The colour drained from the face of Ah Sze's wife. Without a word, she carried her water bucket back to the house. First she told her husband about it, then she told Old Tung Pao. It was a fine state of affairs when a baggage like that could sneak into people's silkworm sheds! Old Tung Pao stamped with rage. He immediately summoned Ah To. But the boy denied the whole story; he said Sixth Treasure was dreaming. The old man then went to question Sixth Treasure. She insisted she had seen everything with her own eyes. The old man didn't know what to believe. He returned home and looked at the "little darlings." They were as sturdy as ever, not a sickly one in the lot.

But the joy that Old Tung Pao and his family had been feeling was dampened. They knew Sixth Treasure's words couldn't be entirely without foundation. Their only hope was that Ah To and that hussy had played their little games on the porch rather than in the shed!

Old Tung Pao recalled gloomily that the garlic had only put forth three or four shoots. He thought the future looked dark. Hadn't there been times before when the silkworms ate great quantities of leaves and seemed to be growing well, yet dried up and died just when they were ready to spin their cocoons? Yes, often! But Old Tung Pao didn't dare let himself think of such a possibility. To entertain a thought like that, even in the most secret recesses of the mind, would only be inviting bad luck!

IV

The "little darlings" began spinning their cocoons, but Old Tung Pao's family was still in a sweat. Both their money and their energy were completely spent. They still had nothing to show for it; there was no guarantee of their earning any return. Nevertheless, they continued working at top speed. Beneath the racks on which the cocoons were being spun fires had to be kept going to supply warmth. Old Tung Pao and Ah Sze, his elder son, their backs bent, slowly squatted first on this side then on that. Hearing the small rustlings of the spinning silkworms, they wanted to smile, and if the sounds stopped for a moment their hearts stopped too. Yet, worried as they were, they didn't dare to disturb the silkworms by looking inside. When the silkworms squirted fluid in their faces as they peered up from beneath the racks, they were happy in spite of the momentary discomfort. The bigger the shower, the better they liked it.[1]

Ah To had already peeked several times. Little Pao had caught him at it and demanded to know what was going on. Ah To made an ugly face at the child, but did not reply.

After three days of "spinning," the fires were extinguished. Ah Sze's wife could restrain herself no longer. She stole a look, her heart beating fast. Inside, all was white as snow. The brush that had been put in for the silkworms to spin on was completely covered over with cocoons. Ah Sze's wife had never seen so successful a "flowering"!

The whole family was wreathed in smiles. They were on solid ground at last! The "little darlings" had proved they had a conscience; they hadn't consumed those mulberry leaves, at four dollars a load, in vain. The family could reap its reward for a month of hunger and sleepless nights. The Old Lord of the Sky had eyes!

Throughout the village, there were many similar

scenes of rejoicing. The Silkworm Goddess had been beneficent to the tiny village this year. Most of the two dozen families garnered good crops of cocoons from their silk worms. The harvest of Old Tung Pao's family was well above average.

Again women and children crowded the threshing ground and the banks of the little stream. All were much thinner than the previous month, with eyes sunk in their sockets, throats rasping and hoarse. But everyone was excited, happy. As they chattered about the struggle of the past month, visions of piles of bright silver dollars shimmered before their eyes. Cheerful thoughts filled their minds—they would get their summer clothes out of the pawnshop; at Spring Festival perhaps they could eat a fat golden fish. . . .

They talked, too, of the farce enacted by Lotus and Ah To a few nights before. Sixth Treasure announced to everyone she met, "That Lotus has no shame at all. She delivered herself right to his door!" Men who heard her laughed coarsely. Women muttered a prayer and called Lotus bad names. They said Old Tung Pao's family could consider itself lucky that a curse hadn't fallen on them. The gods were merciful!

Family after family was able to report a good harvest of cocoons. People visited one another to view the shining white gossamer. The father of Old Tung Pao's daughter-in-law came from town with his little son. They brought gifts of sweets and fruits and a salted fish. Little Pao was happy as a puppy frolicking in the snow.

The elderly visitor sat with Old Tung Pao beneath a willow beside the stream. He had the reputation in town of a "man who knew how to enjoy life." From hours of listening to the professional storytellers in front of the temple, he had learned by heart many of the classic tales of ancient times. He was a great one for idle chatter, and often would say anything that came into his head. Old Tung Pao therefore didn't take him very seriously when he leaned close and queried softly:

"Are you selling your cocoons, or will you spin the silk yourself at home?"

"Selling them, of course," Old Tung Pao replied casually.

The elderly visitor slapped his thigh and sighed, then rose abruptly and pointed at the silk filature rearing up behind the row of mulberries, now quite bald of leaves.

"Tung Pao," he said, "the cocoons are being gathered, but the doors of the silk filatures are shut as

---

[1] The emission of the fluid means the silkworm is about to spin its cocoon.

tight as ever! They're not buying this year! Ah, all the world is in turmoil! The silk houses are not going to open, I tell you!"

Old Tung Pao couldn't help smiling. He wouldn't believe it. How could he possibly believe it? There were dozens of silk filatures in this part of the country. Surely they couldn't all shut down? What's more, he had heard that they had made a deal with the Japanese; the Chinese soldiers who had been billeted in the silk houses had long since departed.

Changing the subject, the visitor related the latest town gossip, salting it freely with classical aphorisms and quotations from the ancient stories. Finally he got around to the thirty silver dollars borrowed through him as middleman. He said his boss was anxious to be repaid.

Old Tung Pao became uneasy after all. When his visitor had departed, he hurried from the village down the highway to look at the two nearest silk filatures. Their doors were indeed shut; not a soul was in sight. Business was in full swing this time last year, with whole rows of dark gleaming scales in operation.

He felt a little panicky as he returned home. But when he saw those snowy cocoons, thick and hard, pleasure made him smile. What beauties! No one wants them?—Impossible. He still had to hurry and finish gathering the cocoons; he hadn't thanked the gods properly yet. Gradually, he forgot about the silk houses.

But in the village, the atmosphere was changing day by day. People who had just begun to laugh were now all frowns. News was reaching them from town that none of the neighbouring silk filatures was opening its doors. It was the same with the houses along the highway. Last year at this time buyers of cocoons were streaming in and out of the village. This year there wasn't a sign of even half a one. In their place came dunning creditors and government tax collectors who promptly froze up if you asked them to take cocoons in payment.

Swearing, curses, disappointed sighs! With such a fine crop of cocoons the villagers had never dreamed that their lot would be even worse than usual! It was as if hailstones dropped out of a clear sky. People like Old Tung Pao, whose crop was especially good, took it hardest of all.

"What is the world coming to!" He beat his breast and stamped his feet in helpless frustration.

But the villagers had to think of something. The cocoons would spoil if kept too long. They either had

to sell them or remove the silk themselves. Several families had already brought out and repaired silk reels they hadn't used for years. They would first remove the silk from the cocoons and then see about the next step. Old Tung Pao wanted to do the same.

"We won't sell our cocoons; we'll spin the silk ourselves!" said the old man. "Nobody ever heard of selling cocoons until the foreign devils' companies started the thing!"

Ah Sze's wife was the first to object. "We've got over five hundred catties of cocoons here," she retorted. "Where are you going to get enough reels?"

She was right. Five hundred catties was no small amount. They'd never get finished spinning the silk themselves. Hire outside help? That meant spending money. Ah Sze agreed with his wife. Ah To blamed his father for planning incorrectly.

"If you listened to me, we'd have raised only one tray of foreign breed and no locals. Then the fifteen loads of leaves from our own mulberry trees would have been enough, and we wouldn't have had to borrow!"

Old Tung Pao was so angry he couldn't speak.

At last a ray of hope appeared. Huang the Priest had heard somewhere that a silk house below the city of Wusih was doing business as usual. Actually an ordinary peasant, Huang was nicknamed "The Priest" because of the learned airs he affected and his interests in Taoist "magic." Old Tung Pao always got along with him fine. After learning the details from him, Old Tung Pao conferred with his elder son Ah Sze about going to Wusih.

"It's about 270 *li* by water, six days for the round trip," ranted the old man. "Son of a bitch! It's a goddam expedition! But what else can we do? We can't eat the cocoons, and our creditors are pressing hard!"

Ah Sze agreed. They borrowed a small boat and bought a few yards of matting to cover the cargo. It was decided that Ah To should go along. Taking advantage of the good weather, the cocoon selling "expeditionary force" set out.

Five days later, the men returned—but not with an empty hold. They still had one basket of cocoons. The silk filature, which they reached after a 270-*li* journey by water, offered extremely harsh terms— Only thirty-five dollars a load for foreign breed, twenty for local; thin cocoons not wanted at any price. Although their cocoons were all first class, the people at the silk house picked and chose only enough to fill one basket; the rest were rejected. Old Tung Pao and his sons received a hundred and ten dollars for the sale, ten of which had to be spent as travel expenses. The hundred dollars remaining was not even enough to pay back what they had borrowed for that last thirty loads of mulberry leaves! On the return trip, Old Tung Pao became ill with rage. His sons carried him into the house.

Ah Sze's wife had no choice but to take the ninety odd catties they had brought back and reel the silk from the cocoons herself. She borrowed a few reels from Sixth Treasure's family and worked for six days. All their rice was gone now. Ah Sze took the silk into town, but no one would buy it. Even the pawnshop didn't want it. Only after much pleading was he able to persuade the pawnbroker to take it in exchange for a load of rice they had pawned before "Clear and Bright".

That's the way it happened. Because they raised a crop of spring silkworms, the people in Old Tung Pao's village got deeper into debt. Old Tung Pao's family raised five trays and gathered a splendid harvest of cocoons. Yet they ended up owing another thirty silver dollars and losing their mortgaged mulberry trees—to say nothing of suffering a month of hunger and sleepless nights in vain!

Translated by Sidney Shapiro

75.

The Orange Grower and the Old Sailor

A perspective on rural life in the 1930s quite different from that of "Spring Silkworms" is provided by the following vignette. Its author, Shen Ts'ung-wen (b. 1902), is the modern writer who most loved and appreciated the countryside, especially his native region of west Hunan. Shen had grown up in a small town but later saw much of the hardness and cruelty of modern life. He was sent to a military school at age thirteen and from fifteen to seventeen served in a regional army, witnessing about 700 decapitations. Subsequently he held a series of minor posts and traveled widely, living in both Peking and Shanghai for periods of time. From 1924 on he published regularly, mostly short stories.

"The Orange Grower and the Old Sailor" is from Long River, *a semi-fictional account of people and places along the Yangtze in the area where Shen grew up. It was written in the early 1940s, during the war with Japan, when Shen was away from his native region, teaching college in Kun-ming. The story itself is set some years earlier, during the mid-1930s. Its major theme is the resilience of the villagers despite a succession of petty wars and misguided government policies.*

The Ch'en River is a tributary of the Yüan, which it flows into just north of Ch'en-chi, the county seat. Lü Family Landing is about 140 *li* from Ch'en-chi and used to serve as a wayferer's station midway up the Ch'en River. It was much like any other small port; products of eastern Kweichou such as tung oil, timber, tobacco, leather, white wax, mercury, and indigo for dying cloth, as well as hemp, bamboo, and other agricultural products from the banks of the Ch'en were shipped downstream, while bolts of patterned cloth, kerosene, matches, sea food, white sugar, cigarettes, and canned goods were shipped upstream.

Most of the cargo boats had to stop at Lü Family Landing for customs inspection since the provincial revenue officials were stationed there; hence the town had become quite prosperous. There were several large oil presses, each producing over 10,000 barrels of tung oil per year, to be sold to distributors in Han-

k'ou and Ch'ang-te. There were at least ten magnificent ancestral temples full of red lacquered tablets inside. Each year during the spring and autumn festivals theatrical stages were set up across from these halls for opera performances. In addition, the town had many temples honoring the Fire God, the General-Who-Stilled-the-Waves, the God of Wealth, and in particular, the Heavenly Empress, whose temple was the one most frequented by traveling merchants. All these edifices symbolized the hopes and beliefs of the people of the area. There were also some ten small inns which, together with a government-licensed "Rehabilitation Center for Opium Addicts," served passing travelers and petty merchants.

Since Lü Family Landing was a port, there was the usual number of idlers who sponged off others, supernumerary government officials, widows who supported themselves by making small loans, prostitutes with big breasts and buttocks, fortunetellers, and chessplayers. . . . In other words, there was a certain liveliness about the place owing to too much idle money, too many idle people, and a lot of spare time. Since the town had both money and goods, some 180 soldiers from various units were stationed there, nominally charged with maintaining the peace, but in reality serving as nothing more than parasites.

The 3rd, 8th, 13th, and 18th of each month were market days, when peasants who lived within twenty *li* of Lü Family Landing would come to trade what they had for what they lacked. They would bring pigs, sheep, cows, dogs and other domestic animals, as well as stone mortars and wooden pestles. The traveling merchants from Kiangsi and Pao-ch'ing, who brought rock sugar, salt, bolts of cloth, paper, pipe tobacco, firecrackers, and other goods, would also set up booths in the marketplace. On market days, people would come from all over, some on foot, some by small wooden boat, and some by bamboo raft. Since cotton cloth, solid-colored or patterned, was something everyone needed, trading in this item was especially brisk. And since draft oxen, pigs, and sheep were closely connected with the lives of peasants, these noisy, ill-tempered animals were always present on market days. Trading was done amidst shouts, curses, promises, and oaths sworn to many gods. After a successful transaction, all parties would go to the refreshment booth for a drink and a good time so that market days were noisy, lively occasions.

Itinerant silversmiths and women who sold needles and thread were in high demand. The highly skilled silversmiths demonstrated their techniques of enameling and goldplating in their booths; blowing flames with a fine tube, they made inlaid jewelry while a hundred curious country women crowded around to admire their work. Finally, there were fortunetellers and "doctors" who pulled teeth and sold Red Cross Brand plasters and magic cure-all tonics.

During spring and summer, the mill owner would bring a black mule and the oil press owner a yellow bull to one corner of the market. There they would set up a tent, enclose it on all sides with canvas, and provide stud services. When naughty children sneaked a glimpse at this peep-show, the village elders would suddenly emerge from inside and chase them away shouting. The whole affair was handled, in fact, more seriously than a Christian marriage ceremony. As for the sailors on the Ch'en River, they were only too happy to stop at Lü Family Landing, scrambling on shore to look for prostitutes and play a few harmless games which would cool their pent-up fire without violating their taboos.

Although Lü Family Landing was only a small port, it had everything. Here Three Castles Cigarettes and canned lichees and loganberries could be bought as presents. But in the villages on the other side of the river, things were quite different. There the rural way of life was faithfully followed and preserved, people's natures and local customs not in the least influenced by the port town. For example, when a traveler passed through the orange groves during harvest season, he was not charged for oranges he ate to quench his thirst. However, in Lü Family Landing the old ladies at the ford in the river charged money for even the sourest tangerines, even though their purpose was more to pass the time than to make money.

Turnip Creek was a relatively well-to-do village near Lü Family Landing. Through the middle of this village ran a small creek which had its source in a grotto some three *li* away. The creek bed was narrow but the water ran clear and swift eastward to join the Ch'en. The villagers used this to their best advantage, building one dam after another to fill ponds for fish, to irrigate the fields, and to power the rice mills. Upstream there were seventeen dams and twelve mills which, taken together, had a significant effect on the local economy. The underwater sandbars were rich with fine gold flakes so the creek was also called the "Golden Sand Creek." During mating season in the spring, willow fish and bream would swim up the creek at night so the pools at the back of the dams were filled with delicious fish. The soil was rich with loam and sand, and the place was famous for producing big juicy turnips. Therefore, quite appropriately, it was named Turnip Creek.

For their livelihood, the people of Turnip Creek grew turnips and other vegetables. However, the area was most famous for its oranges, and nearly every family owned a medium-sized grove. Even those who did not own any farmland had a few orange trees planted around their houses and next to sewer pits.

Among the rich families who owned large orange groves, the most prominent was the family of T'eng Ch'ang-shun. Like many people in the area, T'eng Ch'ang-shun had been quite poor in his youth and had worked as a hired hand on one of the river boats. Later he bought a small single-masted craft and rowed it from one wharf to another along the Yüan River, loading it with cargo to sell. Downstream, he carried mountain goods and vegetables; upstream, he transported miscellaneous consumer goods. Since he had agile feet and a pair of hands willing to work and was honest and reliable, within five years he began to prosper. He bought a large boat and expanded his business, changing his status from laborer to helmsman, and finally to wealthy shipowner.

When it was time for him to marry and raise a family, he chose a girl from Kao Village whose family owned a sugar mill. She brought with her a part of her family's wealth as well as her own intelligence and resourcefulness. Both husband and wife were healthy and hard-working; their hands were never idle and their savings rapidly increased. Then Ch'ang-shun remembered the proverb "Like a tree spreading its roots, so must a man settle down." He felt more like a branch drifting on the waters than a tree spreading roots and was not happy with the way he lived. Therefore, after discussing their situation, the couple finally consulted a fortuneteller. As a result, they decided to settle down in Turnip Creek, where they bought a vegetable garden and a house. While Ch'ang-shun still sailed his boat up and down the Yüan River, his wife remained at home with their children, taking care of the fields and gardens and raising pigs and chickens. When Ch'ang-shun's ship sailed upstream transporting goods to the Hung River, he would anchor his boat at Ch'en-chi and hurry home to see his wife and children, sometimes bringing along a sailor or two. During the orange harvesting season, he would refuse all other customers. Loading the boat with his oranges and taking his wife and children along, he would sail down to Ch'ang-te to show his family a little of the world downstream. There he could easily sell his oranges for a good price since they were neatly packaged and sweet and he had many steady customers. A month later, the boat would be loaded with goods from the various stores along the Ch'en River to be transported back to Lü Family Landing. With their own savings the family would also buy miscellaneous items which they could sell in their village for a profit. Thus loaded, they would return to Lü Family Landing to celebrate the New Year.

During the twenty years of the Republic, it was hard to determine just how many dozen civil wars, large and small, the people of the Yüan River Basin experienced. These wars completely ruined many boat owners who had their sailors drafted and their boats confiscated, requisitioned, or heavily taxed. Many of the oil firms were taxed or held for ransom by either bandits or the army and had to declare bankruptcy. The world was changing and the Yüan River Basin was no exception. As the proverb says, "In ten years many make a fortune and many lose one."

Our T'eng Ch'ang-shun, partly from luck, but mostly because of his resourcefulness, managed to maintain his business throughout these various changes. He increased not only his wealth but also the number of his children, till he had two sons and three daughters. His sons, once grown and married, became his business associates, each sailing a boat with three cabins and four sculls along the Yüan River while Ch'ang-shun himself stayed at home taking charge of the fields. His oldest daughter was also married and the two younger ones were engaged and lived at home. He had three grandsons, the oldest of whom was already six, old enough to dry straw and chase ducks down to the river. Ch'ang-shun was fifty-six years old and had been working for nearly forty years. He often complained that he was getting old, that his bones were rattling and he needed a rest. But during harvest, when the rice had to be husked and milled and when other family members and the hired hands were busy, he would not hesitate to hoist two large baskets of grain on a pole across his shoulders and run toward the mill at the mouth of the creek. Scurrying down the road, he would never let any younger person get ahead of him.

Since he had a family and a prospering business in Turnip Creek, Ch'ang-shun was considered a prominent member of the village. Because of his family business, his age, and his upright and honorable character, he was respected and trusted by his fellow villagers. Consequently, whenever the village had to deal with some public matter, he would assume the position of leadership. If, for instance, an army unit were passing through and a reception were to be held in the town hall at Lü Family Landing, T'eng would be elected to represent Turnip Creek. In addition, he could write a few characters, was well versed in geomancy, physiognomy, and herbal medicine, and kept himself informed about current events. . . . All this served to increase his importance at Turnip Creek.

His two sons had accompanied him on the boat ever since they were young; consequently they were thoroughly familiar with all the hazardous sandbars and rocks along the course of the Yüan River (and, naturally, even more so with the Ch'en River). Like their father, they were popular and gained the trust of many firms. By the time they were able to sail by themselves, the "two young T'eng Masters" were just as highly regarded as their father.

Owing to their mother's care and supervision, the T'eng girls were healthy, industrious, and skillful workers. Since they worked outside under the sun every day, their skin was tanned to a reddish-brown color. In a happy family of old and young, of parents, brothers, and sisters, the girls grew up to be lively and honest. They were sincere and kind toward others and loved to laugh out loud. Regardless of the task, they treated it like a game and completed it in an atmosphere of friendly competition. The three girls, like flowers nurtured by sunlight, rain, and dew, budded and bloomed. Four years earlier, when the oldest daughter was seventeen, she was married to a man from the T'ien family of T'ung-mu-p'ing who was in the cinnabar trade. The second daughter, now sixteen, was betrothed to a family who owned an oil store in Kao Village, but since the young man was away from home, the marriage had been postponed. The third daughter was only fifteen and had just become engaged in the tenth month of the previous year. After the young fellow had graduated from the county elementary school, he had gone on to the Provincial Normal School and had three years before he would graduate. So this marriage would also be delayed.

Of the three daughters, the oldest was the most capable at running a household, the second was the most reliable and honest, but the third was the prettiest. She was petite, with long legs, a small mouth, and white teeth. The bridge of her nose was very straight and, although her eyebrows arched elegantly, there was a certain wildness in her eyes. Her face, hands, and feet were well sun-tanned, and she carried herself with the charm and style well suited to her healthy dark beauty. Since she was the youngest in the family she was named Sis. The rest of the family all spoiled her a little but, since she was clever and courteous, she did not try to outshine anyone else. Her innocence and gentle nature won her the affection of those around her and she was very much loved and admired.

The family did not believe seriously in any one religion, but it faithfully observed the birthdays of Kuan Yin, the God of Wealth, the King of Medicine, and all other gods of popular Buddhism and Chinese mythology. On such days, they would burn incense, eat vegetarian meals, and contribute money to those in charge of the observances. In addition, the family faithfully devoted themselves to all the festivals and taboos existing in their agrarian society. If they were to take a trip during the first month, they would first consult the almanac for an auspicious day. In the fourth month, they would visit the graves of their ancestors and offer them sacrifices. On the 5th day of the fifth month, they would make the eight-jeweled plaster against the five poisons and give it away as presents. After they had drunk the wine that restores vitality, the whole family would change into their new clothes, go into Lü Family Landing to watch the dragon boat races and cheer for the boat from their own village. In the sixth month, they would feast on carp, eggplant, and the newly harvested rice. During the harvest month, they would brew a large cask of rice wine to refresh the hired hands who had worked for them all year long. On the 15th of the seventh month, the Festival of the Dead, they would burn paper money for their deceased ancestors. The girls would be kept especially busy on this occasion. In good spirits they would fold foil into the shapes of small gold and silver ingots and carry them to the riverbank to be burnt at twilight. Then they would set lotus-shaped lanterns afloat in the water to illuminate the path for the disembodied souls to reach the Western Paradise. In the eighth month, during the Moon Festival, they would send someone to the market to buy mooncakes and other necessities and the whole family would climb a hill, have a picnic, and enjoy the dry, crisp air of autumn. At the winter solstice, they would spread lime at their front door in order to "exterminate" the hundred pests. On the 8th of the twelfth month, they would cook the eight-jeweled pudding. In short, they carefully followed local customs and observed the almanac instructions to the letter, gaining a sense of joyous release and solemn reverence from these occasions.

A family like this one, in want of neither food nor clothing, would be considered quite fortunate under normal circumstances, but this was not the case. Their little village, like so many other places in this world, seemed, against all logic or reason, to have something wrong with it. There are people on this earth who work with either their hands or their heads, cooperating with nature to increase the earth's production of food and wealth. But at the same time there are others who, through age-old customs, hold special privileges and give very little to the world. In Lü Family Landing these latter people used all sorts of methods and excuses to extract from those who were bound hand-and-foot to the land whatever little income they had earned. Besides the regular land and grain taxes, a surtax on land and grain taxes, and additional security taxes, there were the irregular but unavoidable exactions such as the militia defense loans, the militia maintenance costs, and the ammunition cost for bandit extermination and village "purification." As for the wealthy, they were easy targets for kidnapping, blackmail, and robbery. Consequently, although a person spent one dollar on the gods, he had to shell out at least twenty times that amount for men. And those with large incomes had more expenditures.

The world was changing, and in times of change as in times of revolution, villagers lose their savings. T'eng Ch'ang-shun was well-acquainted with this principle; and in spite of all his money, his world still had not changed for the better. He simply explained this as "bad luck." Whenever country people could not solve a problem, they almost always attributed their troubles to "bad luck." By so doing, they could increase their power of endurance, adapt themselves to unfair treatment and unfortunate incidents, and still maintain a dim ray of hope for the future. Ch'ang-shun understood very well that it was only their "bad luck" that the world was not at peace; therefore, he and his family passed their days in the usual way. Fortunately, his family was big, the soil was productive, his boats had had no accidents, and in the countryside he was still regarded as a rich man. Despite the various changes in the world, the family still fulfilled all its religious and social obligations such as holidays, sacrifices, funerals, and marriages. Whether it was honoring the gods at year's end or arranging marriages for his children, his family always did everything properly.

There was another man who understood that the world was changing and who used "bad luck" to explain the misfortunes he suffered amidst the changes he quietly endured. He was an old sailor whose life was like a story, simple but unusual. His fate was just the opposite of that of T'eng Ch'ang-shun, who had decided to put out his roots on land. When the old sailor was young, he too had lived his life on the waters. After he was married and had children, his property consisted of two boats; sailing one himself and hiring someone else to operate the other, he transported goods up and down the Yüan River. Just as his business was on the rise and as his oldest son was reaching twelve, old enough to become his assistant, an evil star suddenly descended on his door and held his family, old and young, in its invisible clutches. His wife and two sons contracted dysentery from eating a

watermelon and died within a few days of each other. Just to keep the story going, it seemed, the evil star spared the old sailor and let him go on living alone. Seeing that the evil star had descended upon him, the old sailor could do nothing but sell one of his boats to purchase three coffins to bury his wife and sons. He continued to survive as best he could, blaming everything on his "bad luck", and sailed his boat up and down the Yüan River.

At first he thought that, since he was just a little over forty, perhaps he could rely on his energy and make a new life for himself if his luck would change. But misfortune never comes just once. Less than three months after the death of his loved ones, he loaded his boat with tung oil and tobacco and headed for Ch'ang-te. In the middle of the Yüan River the boat hit a large rock and split in two. He watched as his cargo fell into the water and was carried away by the currents. Angry and frightened, he clutched an oar and floated for nearly three *li* before reaching shore. Only after he had climbed onto the bank did he realize that not only was the cargo lost, but a merchant who had been supervising the shipment had been drowned and two of his eight sailors were missing.

After this incident he was left with nothing. The owner of the oil firm who had hired him did not cause trouble since he believed that shipping was very dangerous to begin with, its safety solely in the hands of Heaven, and that the old sailor had lost his boat because of his "bad luck." He was even willing to lend the old sailor three hundred strings of cash to buy a smaller, older boat in order to slowly recoup his losses. But the old sailor, having suffered two successive blows, lost all his self-confidence; he was convinced that all was lost and trying anymore would be useless. Like other disappointed people, he wanted only to run—as far away as possible. After a while, he disappeared from the Yüan River region and no one seemed to know where he had gone. As winter turned into spring and the four seasons rotated in succession, the people of Lü Family Landing forgot all about him.

Some fifteen years later, the old sailor suddenly reappeared on the streets of Lü Family Landing. When he first turned up, he was recognized only by those over forty. In one glance they could tell that his fifteen years in the outside world had not gone well. His hair had turned completely white and one of his arms apparently had been injured rather badly for he could hardly move it. He looked weary, his clothes were old and faded, and the small bundle on his back could not have weighed very much. He had, in fact, returned to get a loan of five hundred strings of cash from old friends and neighbors in order to buy a boat and start his business again, although he would be competing with much younger men.

It was customary for the local people to help others willingly in such a circumstance. As the contributions were being collected, the matter came to the attention of T'eng Ch'ang-shun. He, too, had begun his life as a boatman and depended on the waters for his livelihood. Now that he saw this distant cousin of his looking so worn and weary and in need of a rest, he made a suggestion to him. "Old friend, it seems to me that you're tired of being a water duck. You're not young anymore yet you don't seem to care where you put your old bones. That's not good. You should have a rest. Why don't you come and live with us for a while? There's always enough plain tea and rice for one more. The world is changing everyday and you and I are becoming useless. Why don't we let your young nephews run the shipping business? You and I can relax and enjoy our rice and vegetables. You have only to come and live with us—and I want you to—and we will treat you like one of the family."

The old sailor closed his little eyes into a narrow slit and fixed his gaze on Ch'ang-shun. Shaking his injured arm, he heaved a sigh and started to smile. Then nodding his head and thinking to himself, he agreed to Ch'ang-shun's kind proposal. That same day, he slung his tiny bundle onto his back and returned with Ch'ang-shun to the orange grove in Turnip Creek.

He was considered a guest but, being a country person, he could never keep his hands idle, so he helped out whenever he could. Moreover since he had seen a lot of the world, could hold his liquor, and was very friendly, everyone in the house was very good to him and loved him like a real uncle.

He lived there for nearly two years, but even though he was completely accepted by the family, he never felt at ease about leading such a parasitic life. Although he was old in years, his heart was still young and he began thinking of ways to gain his independence. But as Ch'ang-shun had pointed out, the transport business was really for the young and strong; a man nearly sixty could have no part in it. There were, however, many members of the T'eng lineage in the area. Some owned boats, some oil stores, and some orange groves. When profits were good, they would contribute some of their take to build temples to honor their ancestors, to do a good

deed for their sons and grandsons, and to give public recognition to the diligence and frugality of the lineage members. Besides these private ancestral temples, there was a public one that had been built on a grand scale through the contribution of the lineage branches. Surrounding it was a large piece of land, owned jointly by the lineage, whose income was put toward annual sacrifices and support of a free school. The private ancestral temples were usually built and maintained by individual families and used as family shrines. As it happened, a widow of the T'eng lineage whose husband had prospered from an oil business bought the entire plot of land on top of Maple Tree Mound, and built an ancestral temple there. She needed an older man to work as caretaker but had been unable to find one, so Ch'ang-shun put in a few good words for the old sailor, and he got the job.

Maple Tree Mound was close to the highway and overlooked the banks of the river where many travelers and boats would pass. Many passers-by as well as boatmen would come to the mound to rest, smoke, and lift the heavy loads from their shoulders. In front of the ancestral temple were several dozen large maple trees, under which rows of stone benches stood. There the old sailor set up a small stall and sold refreshments. In the eyes of the passers-by he looked very dignified acting as the owner of the mound; therefore his life was more pleasant and comfortable than it had been as a guest under someone else's roof. In his leisure time, he would cross the river to Ch'ang-shun's house to visit. He could sit awhile, repeat some local gossip, go to see the newly born calves in their pen, or go down to the kitchen and help himself to a sweet potato, a corn pone, or a bowl of thick rice gruel. Sometimes, carrying a small bamboo basket, he would go to market and walk around looking at the cow pens, rice stalls, and farm implement displays. On the way back he would stop at the meat counter, sit down on a low wooden bench next to the booth, and listen to the merchants discussing market conditions or the boatmen chatting about the news downstream—the prices of things or the ups and downs of boat families in the Ch'en River Valley. If he met a government runner, he would find out all about the latest dispatch from the county seat and the whereabouts of the militia. When evening came, his thoughts would turn to home and on the way back he would buy a few necessities, some salt, a plug of tobacco, or half a gourd of wine. Sometimes he would feel compelled to sample the wine, so often he would arrive home with only half of what he had purchased.

Because of "bad luck," which had tricked him in his prime, the old sailor was unable to recover from the blow and was left alone in his old age. Compared with the other people of Lü Family Landing, he seemed to be a little peculiar; he had, after all, lived through so much. Despite his old age and feebleness, he had the curiosity and the inquisitiveness of a child. This combination of eccentricity and inquisitiveness made the local people consider him a rather strange person. In fact, when he had first returned, some people thought that, during those fifteen years he had spent in the outside world, he must have gained at least some wisdom, if not wealth. Therefore he was regarded with some interest. But these villagers were practical; after a couple of years, when they neither saw gold nor heard words of wisdom, they soon lost their interest in him and turned their attention elsewhere. The only people who really understood and loved him were Ch'ang-shun and his family.

Although advanced in years, the old sailor was still young at heart. He could not change himself but he believed that the world would undergo many changes. Whether they would be good or bad, life would never remain the same. This belief had been proven true four years previously when both the Communist and the Nationalist troops passed through the area in succession. He firmly believed that many more events would take place in the future and tomorrow would never be the same as today. When he had heard that the "New Life"* was coming, he was quite excited. He was the first person in the area who actually had any fantasies about this movement. In fact, even though everything else in the world was different, the old sailor's life had long ago been determined, and this little spot on earth would undergo even more changes than he ever dreamt of.

After the old sailor had crossed on the ferry with Ch'ang-shun's two younger daughters, they followed a small path by the river leading toward Turnip Creek. Still uneasy about the New Life Movement, he asked, "Sis, when you and your sister went to market today, were there a lot of people?"

Amused by his question, Sis answered him with one of her own. "Why wouldn't there be a lot of people at market, Uncle?"

"I meant, were there many soldiers there?"

The second daughter answered, "I heard that there was gambling at the market; they set up twenty

---

* A movement to improve moral and social behavior begun by Chiang Kai-shek in 1935.

tables and charged two dollars a table. I also heard that the Commander had his Mauser on as he drank with the Captain at the noodle shop. The Captain's face flushed ever so red and he kept on calling the Commander his brother. No one knew what they said to each other though."

The old sailor muttered to himself, "Gambling! In times like these I guess some people still prefer money to their skins!"

Her curiosity aroused, Sis asked, "What do you mean preferring money to their skins? It's not as if bandits are. . ."

The old sailor wrinkled his brow and tried to visualize the scene between the Commander and the Captain toasting and playing finger games with each other. The expression on his face reminded Sis of how her third brother and some of the townspeople had looked as they were criticizing the river police some time ago. The story was so bizarre and a telling of it would mean using words that were too coarse for her, so she merely laughed.

The old sailor muttered, "Sis, you're laughing; you're laughing because you think I'm old and my head is all muddled, aren't you?"

She replied, "I was laughing at my third brother who was so dumb that he almost got himself into big trouble."

"What happened?"

"Oh, it's an old story. It happened last year. I'm sure you've heard it already."

When the old sailor remembered the story, he broke out laughing in spite of himself. Then he became serious again. . . . He said, "Pretty soon, pretty soon these shameless scoundrels will have gotten enough money out of us and leave. But others will come."

Sis still did not understand him and asked, "Who will be coming here? Tell me, you're driving me crazy with the suspense."

The old sailor put on a condescending air and answered her as if she were a small child, "You wouldn't understand anyway, Sis. However, think of me as a prophet like Wang Pan-hsien. When I say something is coming, it will come. Remember last year when the Red Army came, followed by the Government Army and all of you escaped to the hills for nearly two months? Well, I predict that soon you'll have to run again! If you don't, they'll threaten to kill your father if he doesn't pay up. . . . No matter who you are, when they stretch out their hands and say, 'Hand it over,' you'll have to oblige. They won't be satisfied with just one or two thousand, not them. They may even take your gold rings and silver necklaces from your trousseau. Sis, are you willing to part with them? . . . They should die of the plague, that's what they deserve!"

The second daughter, who was a little older and a little more serious-minded, noticed that underneath his jesting tone the old sailor was dead serious, so she asked him in a hushed voice, "Uncle, are you saying the southern and northern armies are fighting each other again and are going to march through here?"

"It's not the war or the army," the old sailor said. "What's coming is much worse than the army!"

"What is it? What will it do when it comes? The militia here have guns. Won't they fight back?"

"Ha, the militia! What good are they? They'll all run away and, if they don't hurry fast enough, they'll be captured one by one to settle a twenty-year-old score!"

Sis was annoyed. "Uncle, listening to you is like listening to someone chewing on a clam. I feel I've been shut inside a drum and my ears are buzzing from listening to the rat-ta-tat and tum-te-tum-tum."

As they were crossing the stone bridge over Turnip Creek, Sis saw her father talking to a revenue officer in their garden. Ch'ang-shun had a branch of a bamboo tree in one hand and swung it back and forth; he appeared very relaxed and happy. The revenue officer had come down to buy some oranges as a present for his friends in T'ao-yüan county, so two workers had climbed up the trees with bamboo baskets. Sis hurried to her father's side.

"Daddy, Uncle has some important news for you."

Ch'ang-shun had not seen the old sailor for nearly two weeks, so he first asked him why he had not come over, then about the urgent news. Eying the tax man, the old sailor remembered the high-handed manner of the letter-writing officer at the government office and decided he did not want to share his news with any revenue officer. He thought that if he could keep this news from the government people, they might eventually be caught unprepared, a fitting punishment. Therefore he refused to say anthing in the officer's presence and mumbling something he walked away toward a large orange tree. Ch'ang-shun understood the old sailor and knew that his important news would be nothing more than idle gossip of the county or trivial stories about the police along the river.

"Excuse me a moment, Mr. Secretary," Ch'ang-shun said. "Sis, why don't you take Uncle to the bam-

boo garden and show him the large cellar we have dug?" Turning his head, Ch'ang-shun caught a glimpse of all the purchases in his second daughter's shopping basket. "What! More things? Are you planning to open a store here? What about the large fishhook I asked you to buy? You forgot all about it, didn't you? What am I going to do with you? You never buy anything we need, and what you do buy we can easily do without. I can see that you'll never make a good wife!"

Scolding his daughter in front of his guest, Ch'ang-shun was like a man who patted his child's head and expressed his love through reproaches, his voice full of warm affection. The girl smiled as she listened to him. But when the fishhook was mentioned, she realized that she had indeed forgotten all about it. "I told Sis to take care of that," she answered. "It was she who forgot all about it."

Sis laughed too, but she refused to acknowledge the fault. "Daddy, I never forget anything you ask me to do. But every time second sister asks me to do something, she confuses me so. Today she was talking the whole time we were at the market and dragged me to the stock pavilion to look at some calves. So I remembered only the calves and forgot all about the fishhook. The T'ien family from T'ai-ping Creek brought two small brindled calves. Somebody offered twenty-six dollars, but Mr. T'ien wouldn't let them go for under thirty. If only I had had thirty dollars, I would have bought them. They were such a cute pair."

Ch'ang-shun replied, "Sis, you really do talk nonsense sometimes. What would you do with two calves?"

She replied, "Do? They're so cute and when they're grown they can plow the fields."

"And what are you going to do when you grow up, Sis?" Her father's intention was to tease her. According to the old saying, "A young man should marry and a young girl, wed," so Sis should marry when she grows up. Realizing that the meaning behind the joke was not to her advantage, Sis did not argue, but picked a stalk of dog-tail, put it in her mouth, and ran toward the bamboo grove. Her sister called out and ran after her, giggling. The old sailor, however, stayed behind to watch the orange pickers and did not go to see the new cellar.

The revenue officer's eyes followed the departing girls. "Mr. T'eng, you are really lucky to have such a nice family. The orange harvest this year was excellent, wasn't it. You must have made 2000 dollars already. It must be true that to own land is to have wealth."

"Mr. Secretary, you have no idea of our difficulties," answered Ch'ang-shun. "What are these watery fruits worth? How can one make a fortune from them? Besides, the world is not at peace, so it's not easy to make a living nowadays. Mr. Secretary, you don't know the poverty of us country folks. If we had any extra cash, do you think the authorities would let us bury it in our cellars?"

The revenue officer laughed and said jokingly, "Mr. T'eng, how you carry on. Are you afraid I'm going to borrow money from you? Is that why you keep talking about poverty, poverty, and more poverty? Everyone knows that you're the richest man in Turnip Creek. As for silver, I'll bet there are thousands and thousands of ingots piled in your cellar."

"My dear sir, I would be only too happy to have silver in my cellar. But alas, all I have is sweet potatoes. Mr. Secretary, it's people like you who are well off. You needn't worry about anything. If the sky falls, there are tall people to prop it up for you; if the ground sinks, there are people to fill it in for you. You eat and drink and live comfortably and get rich effortlessly by sitting back and collecting small amounts at a time."

"As the saying goes, 'The grass is always greener.' How would you know our difficulties? We follow the bureau chief from one place to another and try to muddle through somehow. Last month he didn't come to the office at all because he was convalescing at the home of widow Wang in T'ung-wan Creek. God only knows what illness he had! Downstream the rumor is that the main office is about to replace its chief. When they do, they'll replace everyone high and low. So we'll have to pack our suitcases and wait to be kicked out."

The old sailor, hearing them speaking of possible changes in the government staff, assumed that perhaps it had some relationship with the New Life. He interrupted them to ask, "Master Secretary, has the county government been busy lately?"

"I'd say that they're busy over nothing."

"Master Secretary, my guess is that something important is. . . I am sure it's true. . . . I heard people say that it's definitely. . ." The old sailor stammered, not knowing how to continue. He had not planned on saying anything at all, but he could not keep it in any longer.

Ch'ang-shun thought that his news had only to do with the transfer or removal of the local militia, so he asked, "Have there been any changes in the militia?"

"No, I heard people say that the New Life is coming soon."

He wanted to emphasize the words "New Life," to get Ch'ang-shun's attention. But for some reason when the words left his lips, they were muffled and hushed. His audience did not hear him so the old sailor had to repeat himself, "The New Life is coming. It's true."

Both the revenue officer and the owner of the orange grove were quite startled and exclaimed almost simultaneously, "Did you say the New Life is coming?"

Actually, the reason for their astonishment was the fact that the term New Life had made the old sailor so nervous. Both men were truly puzzled. However, the old sailor was quite satisfied with their reaction. He answered them in absolute seriousness as if he were swearing an oath: "Yes, yes. It's coming. That's what they all say. When I was on Maple Tree Mound I saw with my own eyes a spy disguised as a monkey trainer. He asked me how far it was to our district and hurried off after I told him. He had shifty eyes like a spy but tried to act like a gentleman. I bet you anything that it was all an act."

The two men could not suppress their laughter. The New Life Movement was after all not a man or a party. If it came, it came; a spy was not necessary. Besides, what was there to fear? It was not something to worry about. Fairly well-informed about the news from downstream, both men knew what the New Life Movement was and therefore were not a bit frightened by it. They listened to the old sailor and could not help thinking that his nervousness was a bit funny. The revenue officer related to them some of the recent news concerning the New Life Movement that he had read about in a Shanghai newspaper. However, it became apparent that he did not understand the meaning behind the movement either, so he stopped talking.

Ten days earlier, Ch'ang-shun had heard from a few boatmen a little about the New Life Movement. For example, one should walk on the left side of the street, button all the buttons on one's shirt, not go about barefoot or shirtless, learn to act speedily and keep clean. . . . As the old sailor listened to Ch'ang-shun, he no longer regarded it as a dangerous and fearful thing; instead, he thought it annoying and ridiculous. Just imagine what would happen if the New Life Movement came to the countryside! If one had to walk on the left side, how could people gather during market days? If one could not go about shirtless, how could one pull a boat into the water? If people acted speedily, then the ferries would overturn when they rushed on board. Furthermore, wouldn't people shove and push and start fights? If a person had to be clean all the time, how could he ferment bean curd and bean sauce and how could he spread manure on his vegetable patch? Wouldn't being completely buttoned lead to heat rash on hot days? In brief, the conditions of the movement were unthinkable and unworkable. Villagers in general thought that it was only for city dwellers. Those boatmen who had been to Ch'ang-te actually saw soldiers and students standing by the government buildings on the main streets interfering with pedestrians. When a citizen had not fastened all his buttons as ordered, he was struck a few times as an example for others. The boatmen also noticed that as soon as people walked out of the city gates and reached the river, they urinated and nobody cared! Therefore, most people, even those who were punished, still did not have the slightest idea of what the movement was all about.

When Ch'ang-shun heard the old sailor telling him that the New Life Movement was coming to the countryside, he asked him his sources. Naturally, he was not able to furnish any but only insisted, "It's true, it's really true." At this point they all broke out laughing for they realized that, if the New Life Movement could not be enforced outside the city gates of Ch'ang-te, it certainly could not be handled in and around Lü Family Landing. Moreover, if even village heads could be paddled if they walked on the wrong side of the street, how many flat boards must the place have for the rest of its citizens?

Just then the two workmen who had gone up in the orange trees climbed down with their filled baskets. The revenue officer took out a dollar and asked Ch'ang-shun to accept it as a token of his appreciation. But Ch'ang-shun, shaking his hands, refused: "Mr. Secretary, you are one of us. What is this money for? If you want oranges, just come and take a load away. Oranges are grown for people to enjoy. We're not strangers, so do not treat me like one."

The revenue officer protested, "This will not do at all. If I took thirty or fifty just for myself, that would be one thing. But I'm sending them as presents. You know the old saying, 'It's not proper to present Buddha with borrowed flowers.' "

"It's all the same! It doesn't matter. If you want to send some to your friends or relatives, by all means come again and get several loads. The more one picks these things, the more they grow."

The revenue officer insisted on paying for them but the orange grove owner adamantly refused. "Mr. Secretary, you really make a stranger of me. It looks to me as if I'm not worthy to be your friend."

"Mr. T'eng, you don't understand. I have the same temperament as you people up-river. I'm straightforward and don't use fancy words. Please take the money this time so I can come again later."

The old sailor saw that they were both being too stubborn to get anywhere so he interrupted, "Master T'eng, see how frank the secretary is? Why don't you just accept his money?"

But Ch'ang-shun still felt uneasy, so he ordered a hired hand to climb up an old tree and pick fifty of the largest oranges for the secretary, who was anxious to return to town. After thanking Ch'ang-shun profusely, he hurried off, followed by the workers carrying large baskets of oranges.

The old sailor observed, "He's a kindly man who doesn't smoke or drink. I heard that his ancestors were once governors of Kweichou."

Sis, having changed into a simple blue cotton dress, ran up to them from the house dragging a large white dog on a leash. Seeing her father still talking to the old sailor, she said to him, "Daddy, Uncle said the New Life is coming. Do we have to hide under Chi-liang Bridge again?"

Ch'ang-shun replied very casually, "If it comes, let it, Sis. We won't hide from it."

"Aren't you afraid of trouble?"

Ch'ang-shun could not help himself from laughing. "Sis, if you're afraid then run off and hide with Uncle. I won't hide, nor will the rest of the family. We're not afraid of trouble. Besides, there won't be any."

Sis's eyes were clouded with confusion. "What's all this about?" She wanted the old sailor to explain, but he was a bit embarrassed and he kept blinking his eyes. His voice was strained and anxiety-ridden.

"I'll bet you, I'll bet you this little finger that they'll come. Sis, your father understands Yin-Yang. In June this year we had a flood and didn't the gold carp from the dam swim down the large river into Lake Tung-t'ing? That wasn't a good omen. We will have no peace this year, even if we offer sacrifices to the dead ten times, even if twenty-four catties of sandalwood incense are burned, and even if we give enough nuts and fruits to Taoist priests to make their stomachs bloat with gas."

Ch'ang-shun laughed and said, "Let's not worry about it. If it comes, let it. We'll go in and drink some wine and have venison and mushrooms in hot pepper sauce."

The old sailor, realizing that he was beaten, still persisted, "Master T'eng, I'll bet you these four fingers that there will be trouble. If I'm wrong, I'll bite them off."

Yao-yao had great faith in her father. When she saw that he was quite calm and unaffected, she turned to tease the old sailor. "Uncle, did you dig up a pot of gold last night? Are you crazy with worry that someone might steal it from you? You know, once a skunk has been caught in a bamboo trap, it's even scared of bamboo splinters. The New Life is not going to snatch away your gold."

The old sailor pointed his injured, lifeless arm in the direction of gold maple trees, blazing in the sun, and replied jokingly, "Look, Sis, there's my treasure. People say that underneath the maples there is a mandrake root. In a thousand years, it will grow hands and feet and even a pigtail. During the nights of the full moon, it will come out and run around. If you dig it up and cook it with a white-feathered, black-boned chicken and eat it, you'll live forever. When I dig it

up and cook a chicken with it, I'll only invite you to eat it with me. Then the two of us will fly up to the sky and become immortals. I have many friends in the Palace of Long-Life so we won't be lonely there. But since I'm hungry now, I'll just have to settle for some of your venison."

One of the workers nearby happened to believe in these myths. He asked quite sincerely, "How is that you don't invite me to share that dinner with you? When you all become immortals and live in a large garden, you'll still need someone to plant peaches for you."

"You're right. Of course I'll invite you. Just wait."

"I'll just eat the toe of the mandrake, that's all I want."

"Or better still, one of your own toes would do nicely too."

The old sailor had mentioned that Ch'ang-shun understood Yin-Yang, and indeed, he was well acquainted with the geomancy of the area. Ch'ang-shun was not particularly concerned about the gold carps swimming into Lake Tung-t'ing, but he knew intuitively that this area was a bit out of the ordinary. Trees stood in harmony with the grace and majesty of the landscape. This area could indeed produce a great man! But the time was not right for his appearance. Who would it be? It left him vexed and puzzled.

Translated by Nancy Gibbs

Part Eight

THE PEOPLE'S REPUBLIC

The war with Japan, lasting from 1937 to 1945, produced massive social disorder. Much of East and South China was occupied and everywhere the economy was severely strained. With the defeat of the Japanese by allied forces, civil war between the Nationalist government and the Communist Red Army resumed. Although starting with only a fourth as many soldiers, in less than two years of actual fighting the Communist forces were victorious. On October 1, 1949, the establishment of the People's Republic of China was proclaimed. The three decades which followed were a time of vigorous reform and reorganization, which left few areas of Chinese life untouched. The central institution for both formulating and implementing these changes was the Communist Party.

During the initial decade of Communist leadership, some of the social groups that had earlier impeded the introduction of structural reforms in Chinese social life were decisively struck down. The rural landowning elite was eliminated through a land reform program that redistributed agricultural holdings among all peasants. Then the possible emergence of a new landlord class was prevented by the collectivization of agriculture, accomplished by the end of 1956. At the same time, the urban-based capitalists who had gained influence in the Republican period were undermined by the socialization of industry. These changes were intended to enhance rapid economic growth by placing considerable economic resources under the direction of a newly reconstituted Chinese bureaucracy. Accompanying these domestic changes was a strict limit on foreign intervention within China, first by a Chinese alliance with the Soviet Union against the former imperialist powers, and then by the rejection of Soviet influence by the end of the 1950s.

Although the goals of the Communist Party were clearly revolutionary, they also encompassed the traditional longing of Chinese leaders for national wealth and strength. A strong commitment to the raising of liv-

ing standards was at odds with the poverty of China's economic base, and with the associated need to accumulate capital for investment in future industrial growth. Nevertheless, significant improvements in the living conditions of the bulk of the population were made possible by a more equitable distribution of the limited resources available. And measures such as improvement in the transportation of grain and increased political control of markets eliminated the ancient scourge of famine. Social services, including basic health care and primary education, were extended to the vast peasantry, still 80 percent of the population. But within this context of improved material security, China's leaders encouraged austerity and hard work so as to maximize the economic surplus to reinvest for long-term growth.

One of the most striking changes brought about by the new government was the extent of participation in public life by ordinary citizens, traditionally regarded by their rulers as politically passive. The conscious mobilization of China's masses was pursued in part to assure popular support for the social reforms being introduced but also to maximize labor power. In the absence of large-scale capital, China's leaders relied extensively on the physical labor and emotional energy of the populace.

All these social and economic changes introduced new experiences into the lives of ordinary citizens. Rapid industrialization demanded new skills and created new occupations, especially in urban China, but increasingly in the rural areas as well. In the countryside, new collective institutions drastically limited the social significance of kinship relationships. Graduates of urban high schools were sent by the million to live in the countryside, in the hopes of weakening traditional disdain for manual labor and creating an obstacle to the growth of a class of persons who work only with their minds. Nevertheless a new elite can be discerned in the party cadres who occupied the positions of authority in the government, factories, schools, and communes.

Many previous cleavages and sources of diversity were overcome in the 1950s and 1960s. Occupational and geographical mobility were extensive, and the movement of persons among places and jobs broadened the store of cultural experience shared among the Chinese people. Use of a standard dialect based on North Chinese pronunciation was successfully promoted. And because class distinctions were sharply diminished and education more widely spread, the former division between upper-class and popular cultures significantly narrowed.

The many changes introduced by the Communist Party can easily be discerned, but it is more difficult to judge their impact on the outlook, values, and assumptions of the people who have witnessed them. How suc-

cessfully has the Communist Party promoted new moral principles and work habits? Such questions are especially difficult to answer because of the establishment of a much more closely regulated press after 1949. The most accessible sources are newspaper and magazine articles and other books and pamphlets issued quite consciously to influence ways of thinking. Thus we have voluminous sources for what people have been taught, which must in time strongly influence their thought patterns. These do not provide entirely idealized views, since instruction and exhortations often give examples of common types of mistaken ways of thinking, and criticism of those recently removed from power has repeatedly been encouraged. Still our evidence often seems to fall too neatly into black and white categories. It is possible that people now think in these ways, but we must keep in mind the chance that this dichotomy is a product of the limitations of our sources. We do not have the personal letters, stories circulated solely for their popular appeal, and descriptions of activities recorded merely as aids to memory which in earlier periods could keep us from confusing what people wanted others to think and the actual principles and models people followed in their daily lives.

76.

Land Reform

From the early 1930s until 1952, land redistribution was the major policy pursued by the Communist Party when it gained control of rural areas. Each village would be visited by a group of party cadres who would organize committees of poor peasants and supervise the classification of the inhabitants into five categories: landlords (those who lived off the rents of their lands); rich peasants (those who rented out some land but worked the rest themselves); middle peasants (those who worked their own land without the help of tenants or hired hands); poor peasants (tenants and owners of small plots who also rented or worked for wages); and hired hands (those with no land who worked for wages). In periods when more radical courses were taken, not only landlords but also rich peasants and even some middle peasants would have their land confiscated and redistributed. They would also be publicly criticized and punished for their past offenses; some were even executed. During the war with Japan and after 1948, more moderate measures were generally followed both in expropriation of land and humiliation of landowners.

This revolution in landholding marked one of the greatest turning points in Chinese history. The landowning elite was eliminated, the source of its income and influence abolished. Much of the power landowners had previously wielded in local affairs was taken over by peasant leaders and representatives of the Communist Party.

Changing the attitudes of deference and submission which had previously characterized most poor peasants required considerable organizational talent and skill on the part of Communist cadres. Below is a fictional and probably idealized description of how a group of peasants learned "to stand up" and assert their rights against a landlord. It is part of the novel, Sun Shines over the Sangkan River, *written in 1948 by Ting Ling (pen name of Chiang Ping-chih, b. 1907), a writer well known since the 1920s. In 1932 Ting Ling became a member of the Communist Party, and in 1936, after several years in a Nationalist prison, she joined the Communist base in Yenan. She participated in land reform in several villages in North China during one of its more radical phases in 1946–47, an experience that provided her with the basis for this novel. As an example of "socialist literature," this story was meant to be edifying and help shape a new way of thinking, but it also conveys a sense of some of the social realities of the period.*

After breakfast when Kuo got to Old Han's house, he found only three of Landlord Chiang's nine tenants in the courtyard. At the meeting the day before, when Comrade Wen had explained many principles to them which they appeared to understand, they had agreed to go as a group today to ask for the title deeds. So when six of them failed to show up, the other three decided to separate and look for them.

As he searched, Kuo thought excitedly about the possibilities of the situation. He had been cultivating ten *mou* of arid land belonging to Chiang, and reluctantly paying four piculs of rice as rent. Every year he argued with Chiang in vain over those four piculs, burning with frustration because the land was so poor that it yielded only four to five piculs altogether. Unless he did odd jobs on the side, he could barely eke out enough from one year to the next even to pay for drinking water. He had thought several times of giving up the land, but it would not be easy to find any elsewhere. Now he thought that if only he could be given this parcel of land through the land reform act, he would have a solid base for the future. Not only would the land provide him with enough to eat but, since he was young and strong, if he tightened his belt, he might earn enough from it to buy one or two more *mou*. With that much property he would never have to worry again. He wanted that land and was determined to get it, whatever the difficulties. So he strode off enthusiastically to look for the others, eager to get his hands on a title deed, that mysterious object which could so vitally affect his entire life.

One by one, all the tenants showed up, including a youth of seventeen named Wang and three timid old men who seemed glad that the young men were there to lend them moral support, but who nevertheless remained comparatively quiet. After the exhortations of the previous day's meeting, they were now willing to go and ask for the deeds. But, as they told Comrade Wen, Landlord Chiang, having been a ward chief, was a good talker and experienced in dealing with others; so he probably would not give the deeds up willingly.

Comrade Chang agreed that Chiang was a slippery customer, noting that he had told the fortune-teller White Snake to spread rumors that the Emperor born of the real dragon was in Peking, and also that he had sent his wife ever day to work on Vice-Head Chao's feelings. These few tenants would probably be no match for him. To test their mettle, Comrade Wen asked, "Are you still afraid?"

They all chorused in reply, "With you comrades beside us, we're not afraid!"

Then Cheng, the Chairman of the Peasants' Association, told the following story of Tenant Hou. The year before, when Landlord Hou's land was divided up, Tenant Hou had also been forced by the cadres to go and settle up with the landlord. The landlord, who was lying in bed when he arrived, had shouted, "Who's that in the yard there?"

"It's only me, Uncle," Tenant Hou had replied.

"Oh, you. What do you want?"

"Nothing," said Tenant Hou. "I just came to see you, Uncle," whereupon he picked up a broom and started sweeping the path.

"Oh!" said the landlord. "You really are a good sort after all. I thought you had come to settle accounts like the rest of them. Well, if you want to settle up, you'll have to go to the King of Hell and let him decide whose property this is to be! By the way,

Nephew, you can forget about that ten thousand dollars you owe me. After all, we're from the same family. After all these years we can count on each other's friendship."

"Oh, that's not necessary, that's not necessary. . . ." Tenant Hou had protested.

When Tenant Hou came out and the people asked him if he had settled accounts, he said, "Yes, it's all settled. I still owe him ten thousand dollars!" Later, the Peasants' Association had given him one and a half *mou* of land, but he returned it secretly.

"You people won't follow the example of Tenant Hou, will you?" challenged Cheng. "He's the kind of man who would rather die than stand up for what he believes in."

They smiled and replied, "We aren't such weaklings as to want to make a laughing-stock of ourselves!"

Yet, even though the tenants had been reminded of their past misfortunes and had given their word, Comrade Wen was far from reassured. Then, on an inspiration, he glowered like a landlord and demanded gruffly, "What are you doing here?"

Kuo caught on at once and answered, "We've come to settle accounts with you."

"Settle accounts, eh? Very well!" Comrade Wen continued. "You've been farming ten *mou* of arid land belonging to me. Did I force you to work it, or did you ask to? At the time you started, the terms were spelled out quite clearly in black and white: the rent would be four piculs a year. Have you always paid up? And now you want to settle accounts, eh? Fine! First, pay me what you owe me; then we'll settle up! If you don't want to farm the land anymore, that's all right with me. I can find plenty of others who do. Now, let me ask you: whose land is it, yours or mine?"

"Can the land grow crops for you by itself?" countered Wang.

Kuo chimed in, "Let me tell *you*, Chiang! Everybody knows that when you were ward chief, you used Japanese backers to buy up all our rationed cloth. And that time I repaired your house for you, you agreed to pay me one pint of rice a day. But I worked one month and three days, and you gave me only ten pints of rice. Think about it! Am I telling the truth or not?"

"Of course, it's true," replied Comrade Wen, still playing the part of the landlord. "But wasn't that rationed cloth used for an awning when we had a play? I didn't take it! When you worked on my house, wasn't the food you ate for one month and three days to be counted? I didn't underpay you! Another thing: the year before last, before the Japanese left, you accused me and I paid you then all there was to pay. Is there no end to your extortions? I worked for the Eighth Route Army too."*

This made them all furious and they started shouting, "Fine! You say we extort. But if we hadn't sweated, you couldn't have had such an easy time of it! How much land did you have before, and how much do you have now? Would you have been able to grow so fat without our blood and sweat? If you don't produce those title deeds today, we'll beat you to death. . . !"

As they shouted, they saw Comrade Wen and the others laughing, and they soon began to chuckle too. One of them remarked, "Chairman Wen, you really make a good landlord!" And another said, "Just like Chiang, he's a tough customer to deal with!"

Then Comrade Wen asked what they would do if Chiang's wife followed the example of Landlord Li's wife and came out crying and snivelling.

"We wouldn't pay any attention to the whore!" they shouted.

Kuo said, "The first year that bitch was here, she asked me one day to help them turn their millstone. Of course, I didn't dare refuse. Then, after the wheat was ground, I had to do the millet. It took me until evening to finish. Then I cleaned up the stone for them, stabled the mule, and fed it hay. Only as I was about to leave did she say, 'Have a bowl of gruel before you go.' But just then Landlord Chiang returned, and as soon as he came in he shouted, 'What do you mean by coming here while I'm away? Carrying on with my wife! Damn it! I'll have you sent to the ward office and sentenced to hard labor!' And that woman just sat inside not saying a word! No matter what I said, Chiang wouldn't believe me. I finally had to go to Hsia-hua-yüan twice to fetch coal for him before he would let me off. If it hadn't been for that bitch, I wouldn't have gotten into that mess. I want to settle accounts with her, too, and if she cries, I'll hit her! I certainly won't act like my old man!"

Comrade Wen asked them some more questions to which they gave satisfactory replies. He wanted to give them more encouragement, but they could contain themselves no longer, and someone cried, "We've got it all straight now. Let's go!"

* The Eighth Route Army was the army of the Communist Party active in North China during the war against Japan.

"We're bound to come out of this the winners," said Wang confidently. "Don't worry!"

Comrade Wen saw them to the street and watched them set out with curious villagers following behind. Cheng also tagged along to see how they would make out.

The nine of them swept like a gust of wind up to Landlord Chiang's door. Kuo was the first one through the big gate with the others close behind. There was no one in the courtyard. From the north room came the sound of furniture being moved. Kuo dashed up the steps and burst in. Chiang was standing in the middle of the room. From the way the poor tenants had come rushing in, he guessed they were after the title deeds, but he was not afraid of them. Calmly he said, "Did the Peasants' Association tell you to come? Well, ask for anything you want! I understand the situation because, remember, I've been with the Eighth Route Army too. Only be sure to get everything straight yourselves; don't let other people cheat you! Young Wang, are you here too?"

The others were speechless. Only Kuo spoke up loudly, "We understand the whole situation too, Chiang! We've come to settle accounts for all these years!"

"Settle what accounts?" Chiang began indignantly. But noting the expressions on their faces and hearing steps in the courtyard, he immediately changed his tone. "You and I both know there's going to be land reform in the village. That's good! I have a fair amount of land, more than I can cultivate myself, and I told the cadres long ago that I had decided to make a gift of it. Let everyone have land to farm and food to eat! That's only fair!"

Hearing that Chiang was going to make a present of the land, Wang lost his head and demanded testily, "What about the title deeds?"

In response, Chiang opened a drawer and took out a package, saying, "I got this ready a long time ago. I was just thinking of sending it to the Peasants' Association, but now you've come along at just the right time. There are twelve sheets here for 53.3 *mou* of land—all pretty good land, too. I'm young and can take hard work, so it doesn't hurt me to give away so much. Wang, your five *mou* are included. Take that to the Peasants' Association. If you think it's still too little, tell them Chiang says he can give some more. After all, I'm the village head. I ought to set an example for others!"

"Chiang! What are you up to . . . ?" Before Kuo could finish, Wang snatched the package and ran out, and the others, seeing him running away with the title deeds, took off after him. The crowd outside could not imagine what had happened. As they caught sight of Wang and the others rushing through the gate, Cheng hurried over and asked, "What are you doing? What's the idea?"

Wang held his hand up, unable to contain his excitement, restless as a cock after a fight, unable to speak. Another tenant next to him shouted, "We've got them! We've got the title deeds! As soon as we went in, he handed them over!" There was nervousness rather than delight in his voice. By then Comrades Wen and Yang and the others had arrived. Thinking that the tenants had been frightened and had turned back, they asked at once how things had gone. Young Wang was clutching the package firmly in childlike excitement.

"Didn't you say anything?" asked Comrade Wen. "Did you just take his title deeds and leave without saying anything?"

They looked at him quizzically, wondering what was wrong. Comrade Wen explained, "We want to settle accounts with him; we don't want him to give land away. That land is ours! What right does he have to say he'll give it away? We don't want *his* land. What we want is our *own land*. It doesn't do any good for you to run off with the title deeds without settling accounts. He'll just say we're unreasonable then, won't he?"

When the inexperienced tenants heard this, they realized, "You're right! We went to ask for what he owes us! How did he manage to shut us up so quickly? It was all the fault of that good-for-nothing boy, Wang. As soon as he ran out, everyone followed. Let's go back! Come on!"

"What about Kuo? Has he gone home?" They suddenly realized he was still alone in Landlord Chiang's house. Nobody had seen him come out. "Come on!" With renewed courage, the group reversed direction and hurried back.

When Wang and the others had rushed out, leaving him behind, Kuo had become anxious and called after them, "We haven't settled our scores yet. What are you running off for?" But no one had heard him. Just as he was nearing his wits' end, Chiang's wife darted in from the inner room, looked him up and down once disdainfully, then said to Chiang in her syrupy voice, "Really, what a gang of thieves! Did they take all the title deeds away?"

Kuo whirled around and glared at her, saying, "Who are you calling names? Who's a thief?"

The woman's long, dishevelled hair framed a small, pale face. The bridge of her nose was pinched a purple red. Her upper lip was very short, revealing a row of irregular teeth which were all the more noticeable because two of them had gold crowns. Still ignoring Kuo, she walked around him as if he were so much dirt and scolded Chiang, "You idiot! You let them take all the land that you had paid for. You hadn't stolen it, had you? Couldn't you reason with them? Communizing, communizing! Well, all your property has been communized now. I suppose if they tell you to share your women, you'll do that too! Let's see how you like being a cuckold tomorrow!"

"Dammit!" yelled Chiang. "Shut your stinking mouth!" He knew it was no use giving her a wink. Turning impatiently to Kuo, he yelled, "What are you still hanging around here for? I gave away your ten *mou* of land too. Why don't you go home?"

"We haven't settled scores yet," said Kuo quietly. He knew the tenants had said that they had come to settle accounts but, now that he was left all alone, he felt tongue-tied. How he detested that woman! But hit her? He could not raise his hand. Leave? He did not want to show weakness. He was not afraid of Landlord Chiang, but he felt awkward. Just then, he caught sight of Wang and the others coming back. Feeling as happy as a released prisoner, he could not help shouting, "Wang!"

Wang marched straight into the room, brushing past Kuo, threw the title deeds onto a table, and bellowed, "Who wants you to give away your land? It's our land that we want, now!" Then he winked at Kuo, looking very confident.

Immediately, Kuo knew what to do. Drawing himself up to his full height, he said, "Okay, Chiang, we won't count earlier scores. Just since the Japanese came. You say how much that land of yours has yielded, and we won't bother with the rent reductions we were supposed to get. Let's just say I should take half the yield. In that case, you made me pay every year about a picul and a half more than I should have. Then there was the grain tax I paid for you for nine years at compound interest! How much do you think *you* ought to repay *me*? And then, there's the wages you owe me. You kept making me do this, that, and the other for you. That's got to be counted too."

A shout came from behind him: "Hey, Chiang! I didn't farm your land for five or six years for nothing either!"

By this time many other villagers, hearing the tenants were settling scores with Landlord Chiang over his rent, had come to watch the excitement. Seeing Chiang caught off guard inside, they joined the attack through the window, shouting, "The bastard! When he was ward chief he made us pay taxes and do his bidding as army porters, sending our men to Tang-shan and Hung-shan, and some of them never came back. We want his life in exchange!"

When the tenants saw the crowd outside, they grew bolder. The three old ones had not meant to say anything originally, but now they joined in the shouting too. One of them cursed: "You rogue, Chiang! Do you remember New Year's Eve the year before last when you brought guards to my house and took away all my pots and pans, just because I was three pecks of rent behind? On what charge was my property confiscated? On New Year's Day we didn't even have a mouthful of gruel to eat at home. Old and young alike were crying. You heartless brute!"

Outside the shouting grew even more menacing: "Beat the dog to death! Shoot him!"

Seeing that things were going badly, his wife hid herself inside, afraid of being beaten. Chiang was in a rage but dared not act tough anymore, thinking, "Damn! Now I'm in for it. Discretion is the better part of valor." He was afraid to think, "All right, let them shoot!" But his mind was in turmoil. He thought of Landlord Chen Wu who had been beaten by the peasants. Making up his mind, he ran inside, brought out another red package, bowed to the ground before them all and, with a glum look, entreated them, "Good masters, I've let all my neighbors down. Please be generous. I really owe too much to each of you. I can't possibly repay. The only thing to do is take the land as payment. These are my title deeds. They're all here, a hundred and twenty-seven *mou*. If you'll all be generous, I'll be a good citizen from now on. . . ."

Now that he was humbled and all the title deeds had been produced, the crowd began to subside, for they had not planned any further settlement. Reluctantly, they took the title deeds, saying: "All right, we'll work it out and see. If there's too much, we'll give some back; but if there's not enough, you'll have to think of a way to make it up. Let's go!" Those inside and those in the yard all started leaving together. The trampling of feet could be heard, interspersed with some curses which, however, were filled with satisfaction. Chiang went into the courtyard to look dejectedly after their retreating figures. He gazed at the gray sky and sighed involuntarily. Inside, his wife burst into bitter wailing.

The disposition of Landlord Chiang's land was entrusted to the nine tenants who had taken his title deeds to the Peasants' Association. This was something they had never hoped for even in their wildest dreams. The nine of them crowded into Kuo's house, and the Peasants' Association sent Han to help them write an account. They did not know how to begin, feeling merely that they had to find an outlet for their pent-up emotions. Their lives during the last three days had changed too drastically, especially in the case of the three old men, one of whom said, "Ah, the day before yesterday when the Peasants' Association asked me to describe all the hardships I've had in my life, I thought, in all these scores of years, has one single good thing ever happened to me? Happiness no sooner reaches me than it turns to sorrow. That year when my wife had given birth and people came to congratulate me on being a father, I thought, 'Eh, why make all this fuss? She's lying in bed waiting for me to go and borrow some millet to make gruel.' All day I tried in vain to borrow some, so the next day I took some bedding to pawn for three pints of rice. . . . Another year I owed Landlord Chiang one picul and eight pecks for rent and he was pressing me for it. We didn't even have husks at home, but I was afraid of him—if he grew angry, he could send you off as a porter for the army. There was nothing I could do, so I sold my eldest girl. Ah, why worry about her? At least she found a way to live. I didn't cry; in fact, I felt pleased for her sake—anyhow, I had nothing to say about it. I had already stopped being human; I couldn't feel like a man. So I didn't say a word. When the Association told me to go for the title deeds, I was afraid. I'm old. Why make enemies for the young folks? But I didn't dare say I wouldn't go, so I followed along with the rest. My, who could have believed that the world really has changed! Just think, Chiang's twenty-odd acres of land are in our hands now! Who could have imagined it? I know I ought to be pleased but, strangely enough, I actually feel sad, remembering all my past troubles."

Another said, "I always used to think that I was indebted to Landlord Chiang, that I must have owed him something in an earlier life as well as in this one, making it impossible to ever pay him all back. But yesterday when everybody reckoned things up like that, why, I've cultivated his land for him for six years, paying eight piculs rent a year, while he didn't lift a finger except to use his abacus! Six eights are forty-eight piculs, plus compound interest. With that, I could have bought fifty *mou*, not fifteen! We were poor, too poor ever to rise to our feet. Our children and grandchildren had to work like animals just because the landlords lived on our rent. The more we provided them with, the tighter they held on to us. But we're not beasts after all, we're men! Why should we live like horses in harness, working without stopping until our hair is white! Now at last we see things clearly. Ah, our sons and grandsons won't be ground down like our generation!"

"We've got Chiang's land in our hands," said the third old man. "But he's still the village head. There are still people who're afraid of him, who have to obey him. This time we've got to take the job away from him! Another thing: he's not the only rich person who's exploited us. It's no good unless we overthrow them all. So, I say this is only the beginning."

"Chiang usually gives himself airs," said another. "Look how he tried to browbeat us when we went in, and then how he suddenly went soft, like wax by the fire, cringing and scraping. I think it was just because there were so many of us. There's strength in numbers, and he knows we've got powerful support with the Eighth Route Army and the communists backing us up!" . . .

On returning to the Peasants' Association the previous day, Comrades Wen, Yang, and Chang had talked things over with the others and decided to divide up Landlord Chiang's land first. Since, at the moment, it was not possible to hold a mass meeting to elect a committee for dividing up the land, it was decided that the tenants should make a preliminary division, to be discussed by the masses later, in order to heighten the villagers' enthusiasm and increase their confidence. Accordingly, these nine men were chosen as a temporary land division committee.

When this news spread, many villagers grew excited. Group after group went to the cooperative to lodge complaints with the Peasants' Association against Chiang, demanding to go and settle scores with him too. They asked for his property to be confiscated, saying he had no right to go on living in such a good house. It was a house he had built when he was ward chief, built with the people's sweat and blood! And why should he be allowed to store so much grain? He had a double wall full of grain. Everybody knew there was a narrow lane at the back of his house where he stored it. Why should he be allowed to keep so many clothes in his wardrobe, now that so many people had nothing to wear? They raised pandemonium, and some pushed their way into Landlord Chiang's house while he was busy pulling all the strings he could, calling on the cadres, hoping they would leave him a little more land. When

the villagers saw he was out and about, they were afraid the cadres would be deceived and listen to him. Then even more of them went to find Comrades Yang and Wen and ask to have all Chiang's property moved out. Wen, who was afraid of going too far and was unthinkingly clinging to a few "policies," felt that such an act would be beyond the scope of land reform. He wanted to have nothing to do with it and even urged the villagers to hold off. But the people refused to leave, some wanting to move the things out themselves. When the militia arrived, they sneered at them, "What are you doing here? Have you come to keep an eye on us?"

Comrade Yang had a long talk with Comrade Wen and finally won his consent to have all of Chiang's movable property temporarily confiscated by the Peasants' Association. Wen realized that as matters stood, some action must be taken, so he turned the matter over to the Association.

Cheng headed the unit that pasted up notices telling of the property being sealed and giving orders to seal up all chests, containers, and unoccupied rooms, leaving only one bedroom and kitchen for Chiang to use for the time being. But crowds of people, still doubtful, followed to watch and said, "We won't touch a thing, only watch. It's all right now that the Association is taking charge. As long as you are not keeping these things for Chiang we approve."

Standing to one side, they made suggestions and supervised the work, until finally even the containers of oil and salt for daily use were all sealed up. Chiang had returned by then and, bowing repeatedly to them all, begged them not to seal up so much. His wife, her eyes red from weeping, sat sullenly on the millstone in the courtyard. Seeing her, someone suggested that the millstone be sealed up, but another answered, "They can't move it very far, so there's no need to seal it up!"

77.

Hu Feng's Letters

The revolutionary alliance that overthrew the Nationalist government united people of diverse backgrounds and values, including both peasants and urban intelligentsia. As long as they faced a common enemy during the civil war, different groups cooperated, but latent tensions surfaced after peace was restored. Hu Feng (pen name of Chang Ku-fei, b. 1903), a leading editor and literary critic, reveals the buildup of those tensions in letters he wrote during the period 1944–1955.

The deliberate politicization of art and literature was a key component of the Communist Party's program. Mao Tse-tung's 1942 "Talk at the Yenan Forum on Art and Literature" established a militant tone for the Party's aesthetic policies: artists were to integrate themselves with ordinary people, and their work was required to serve the needs of the revolution. Liberal notions of art for art's sake had no place in Mao's scheme. Hu Feng's earliest letters reveal misgivings about this doctrine. Although he had been a member of the League of Leftist Writers since the early 1930s, compared to Mao, Hu was a liberal. Where Chinese Marxism was materialistic and collectivist, Hu was an idealist and an individualist. These intellectual differences were exacerbated by personal conflicts with the Party's chief literary bureaucrat, Chou Yang.

Hu's letters reveal a search for the best tactics for advancing liberal views within a society where few of those in power were liberals. No successful method was found. After participating in public criticism of the important **Literary Gazette** *in 1954, Hu was himself criticized, with Mao Tse-tung taking a personal hand in preparing a series of* **People's Daily** *articles that published Hu's letters and denounced him for his bourgeois values and counter-revolutionary activity. Hu Feng's public career ended with his arrest in 1955.*

Chungking, 11/1/1944

To Shu Wu:

Yesterday I finished a quick reading of the book *Philosophy of Mankind* and felt as if I had fought my way through a great battle and been rewarded with some new ideas. . . .

The book seems to say much too little about individualism, which is merely touched on in conjunction with collectivism. This shows caution, yet dwelling on that topic would have been the only way in which to make the volume truly worthwhile. How criticism and censure have made their effects felt! . . .

There should be a chapter on the exalted position of the mind too. This would bring out the independence and power of ideas and show the spirit of sacrifice. It should be the climax of the entire volume, serving as a death blow to the materialistic ideas of these rascals.

Chungking, 7/29/1945

To Shu Wu:

The only thing that matters now is that our magazine has been completely encircled. . . . I have suffered quite a lot because of this magazine. I have thought the matter over a thousand times already. Fighting individual battles will not solve anything; eventually we shall be overwhelmed. I really do not know what to do. There seems to be only one way out: if we make concessions, then the periodical may be saved. On the other hand, if we must make concessions, then why publish it at all?

Peking, 5/30/1949

To Lu Ling:

The world of literature and art is enshrouded by an atmosphere of great melancholy. Many seem to be in shackles, although everybody hopes for the best. Many are like the unhappy little daughters-in-law in our old Chinese family system, who are always fearful of a beating that may come at any moment but who must go on living. . . .

Peking, 1/12/1950

To Lu Ling:

Victory will be ours, although the road may not be an easy one, and more intensive and vigorous efforts must yet be made. It is not too pessimistic to estimate that it will take five years.

As for our little magazine, let us continue to improve it. We must not see it as a major battleground in any sense; but we must remember that if we so much as cough, someone will take note of it and criticize us.

Peking, 3/15/1950

To Shu Wu:

In Shanghai the field of literature is dominated by several big names, so we can hardly publish any books or periodicals there. Also, in Peking the field is much too crowded. Both in Wu-han and Hunan, where the pattern set in Hong Kong is being followed, there seems to be a great deal of confusion. The Northeast, however, is free from such pressure, or at least if pressure is there, it must be extremely weak. Besides, Tientsin is nearby, where the literary movement is prospering. With Lu Li and his associates taking charge of literary matters there, prospects for the future are indeed bright.

Shanghai, 8/13/1950

To Chang Chung-hsiao:

The circumstances are now such that many among the reading public, cut off from each other, have become blinded. First of all, with "public opinion" standardized, the average reader finds it difficult to discern what is right. Second, the great majority of readers live in organized groups in a suffocating atmosphere of pressure. Third, in matters of literature and art, the easiest way out is allegiance to "mechanism."

Yet in spite of these conditions, the seeds of opposition are found everywhere; people are clamoring for something better. This makes it difficult for the "leaders" to exert pressure, although they feel pressure itself is absolutely necessary.

What will the final outcome be? I wonder if some signs will be visible in half a year's time. It is important that the reading public speak up, as well as those under pressure or oppression. Slowly we shall see whether a chink can be found. As it is, all the magazines are under close supervision. If this barrier cannot be torn down, we shall all die of suffocation.

Shanghai, 8/24/1950

To Keng Yung:

It is a good idea to send your letter back to them every time it is returned; this will create a problem for them. But did you change your last name last time? It would, of course, be best if you had used another name, although if you did not the last time, you should not do so now. Furthermore, in the composition of the letter you must be analytical and lucid, bearing in mind that, besides factionalism, they are also hampered by incompetence. The most important thing is that your letter possess the power to convince the readers, although in all probability, it will not be published by the journal.

Shanghai, 6/26/1952

To Lu Ling:

First, in dealing with Kun I [apparently a code name for Chou Yang], no matter whether he uses hard or soft tactics, our attitude toward him should be good-natured, and we should try to soften his blows. We must have respect for hard facts. We cannot risk taking the offensive haphazardly, nor should we retreat too readily. This is important. We must let him realize that, while he can use us, he cannot bully us.

Second, there are three ways open to us: (1) to hold on to that periodical and concentrate our attack on it; (2) to make known our criticisms at once; or (3) to record our views but put them aside for the moment and wait for developments. Let us wait for actual developments before deciding on anything. At one of the small group meetings you might explore how to deal with that periodical. At any rate, we should certainly be getting preparations under way.

Shanghai, 5/30/1952

To Lü Yüan:

In the reform campaign, the important thing is to speak in praise of the leadership and undertake a self-review. Except for those within the same discussion group, it would not be wise in the discussions to touch on anybody not immediately concerned. Before Liberation, each person fended for himself; since Liberation, each is supposed to work under the leader of his or her own group. There cannot be too close a relationship between any two people. . . .

If an individual must give his views at all, he should give only his impressions. . . . If we are asked what influences have affected us, we might mention the good influences, such as our desire to go among the masses to reform ourselves. In fact, have we not already asked for such an opportunity? As for the bad influences which have affected others, that is their business. . . .

Shanghai, 3/17/1952

To Lu Ling:

Tien has been told by the director that the time is ripe to discuss my case. Please verify this when Po-shan comes around. If true, then there will be some fun. I rather suspect that the honorable Ch'iao's "indisposition" is an excuse to take time off to study my case. At the moment I am undecided whether or not to ask for a hearing to present my views in person.

Shanghai, 6/13/1952

To Lu Ling:

Since the Ministry is sending people to direct guidance work, it is best to finish our preparations. As I see it, the conclusions reached at the small discussion meeting will not be accepted, so the Ministry will do everything again. However, you must give your views concerning that shameless person; without question, you must expose his real self. As for the article mentioned, it is not to be taken as final but is intended for further discussions. You can attest that you heard it this way, and besides, that nobody agreed with him completely.

Please tell how he schemed to become a professor and how everybody was dissatisfied with him, . . . how after Liberation we advised him to stay in Nan-ning, and how all the time he wanted to come out so he could climb up the ladder. Mention that, when he arrived in Peking, he always spoke sarcastically and everybody disliked him. . . .

Concerning the matter of forming a small clique, say that you know nothing about it. Also mention that many of the articles contributed to our magazine by individuals had to be rejected. Also point out that we never held meetings to discuss the articles intended for submission. . . .

Peking, 11/7/1954

To Fang Jan and Chi Fang:

The developments here deserve watching. Today the Second Augmented Meeting of the Federation of Literary and Art Circles was held. Speaking to the assembly, I pointed out that the problems of the *Gazette* are not unique, rather that they manifest the inclinations of those in leadership positions. I cited cases to prove that from its very first and second volumes it had already shown the follow-

ing trends: In outlook, it capitulated to the capitalist class and at the same time discriminated against young and revolutionary writers who did not side with it. In the field of ideology, it developed sociological concepts of the common and vulgar sort and bowed to formalism in the matter of style. I further pointed out that in the past few years it had gone steadily downhill. By saying this, I meant to divert the meeting from the case concerning the periodical to a review of the situation as a whole.

I have not finished my speech yet. At the next meeting, Hsü will speak and will make his denunciation.

I had at first hoped that you people would take part in the review. But now I would like you at least to speed up the writing of your article. Be sure to paint a clear picture of persecution based on factionalism, at the same time pointedly bringing out the capitalist character of their ideology.

SPEECH TO THE FEDERATION OF LITERARY AND ART CIRCLES, PEKING, 11/11/1954

Armed with sociological ideas of the common and vulgar sort, the commentators and critics became arrogant. They would not look upon writers as their comrades-in-arms or as comrade-workers. They would appear at times as political tutors, at times as tactical lecturers, and, worst of all, at times as petty judges about to render their verdicts. In short, one was forced to write according to their prescribed formulas and their rules. Their attitude toward creative productions was one of extreme rigidity and cruelty. They paid no attention to the conditions of the individual writers or to the requirements of creative production, nor did they care about the real contents of their own productions or look into the matter of objectivity. Developed to the extreme, all of this subjected the writer to a formula to demarcate class status. It rendered writers practically helpless and made it imperative that even the slightest details in their works conform to the directions and distorted interpretations of the commentators and critics. . . .

The *Literary Gazette* has been published for five years. Why is it that only now questions are being raised about it?. . . It did not passively suppress free discussion. On the contrary, it resorted to active means, such as criticizing others to avoid being criticized or having to make a self-criticism.

During the past five years various literary reform

campaigns have been undertaken: the "Three-Anti," the "Five-Anti," and many other campaigns of ideological reform within the Party. Yet all along, the *Gazette* has been remolding the general populace without reforming itself, behaving as if it had no mistakes or defects of any kind at all.

Secondly, shouldn't the *Literary Gazette* be closely attuned to the general public? Obviously it should. Yet from the very beginning, it had adopted an attitude of despising and keeping away those readers who did not side with its views, and particularly those opposed to them. It organized a correspondent's network composed of readers who favor its views and circulated among this restricted group a publication known as the "Internal Circular for Correspondents." This circular is a means by which the *Gazette* issues orders and directives to its correspondents to organize and guide attacks against other people. . . . The correspondents are encouraged to write letters, to convene group discussion meetings, to prepare articles, and generally to create the impression of a popular front. If they do all of these things obediently, they are rewarded. If they bring up mildly opposing views, they are criticized for being questionable in ideology. If their offenses prove to be serious, they are no longer allowed to serve as correspondents and are banished from that privileged group.

And what exactly is the result? A sense of blind obedience is fostered among the general populace with consequent adverse effects. . . . Some of the correspondents form a small privileged group while the *Literary Gazette* itself operates in the position of the big boss, having under its control those correspondents purporting to give it popular support.

Peking, 12/13/1954

To Fang Jan:

I presume you have seen all of the articles and literature published. The waste involved in this matter must have been enormous. . . . Blinded by illusions which were too optimistic, we have tended toward adventurism without making a concrete analysis of actual conditions. For this I must bear the main responsibility.

Peking, 1/26/1955

To Chi Chih-fang and Jen Min:

It has been a long time since I wrote you last. I hope you are both well. There are now new developments in the situation. Please take the things that have come to pass and those that will shortly transpire in a cool-headed manner and with silent reserve. Do not act hastily or take part in discussions since this will only make things worse. I hope you will also stop our sympathizers from doing anything. Do not write any letters or articles expressing your views. This is no time for discussions. We are under criticism and censure.

You are in the teaching profession, so it is best that you do not get involved. If it is absolutely necessary, just give a few of your criticisms of me. . . .

Peking, 2/8/1955

To Chang Chung-hsiao:

Do not feel sad and by all means stay calm. There are many things we must put up with. We must find renewal through forbearance, for the sake of our enterprise and more important things to come. Hence, at the coming meetings do not be hesitant. Speak out in criticism of Hu Feng and others. As for Hu, he is quite willing to write articles criticizing himself if those above wish it. It does not matter, for the masses will be able to determine how much he is in the wrong and how much he is in the right.

MY SELF–CRITICISM
(*PEOPLE'S DAILY*, 5/24/1955)

In the course of the current campaign criticizing capitalist ideology, I have begun to realize my serious errors. Their fundamental cause has been my thinking that the revolution of the bourgeoisie and its stand were synonymous with those of the working class. I glossed over the differences in principle between them. These errors have been exemplified in ideology by my confining myself to the narrow viewpoint of realism instead of adhering to political principles; by my distorting and disregarding the viewpoints of the working class; by my contradicting Marxist principles with respect to certain fundamental issues; and by my disobeying the line advocated by Chairman Mao in the fields of art and literature. They are exemplified in my way of doing things; in my attitude of refusing for a long time to undergo thought reform; in my advocating individual heroism of the sort which results in praising oneself all the time; in my giving vent to narrow factional sentiments; in my utter lack of the spirit of self-criticism; and in my tendency to deviate from the masses and collectivization. Because of my attitude of considering myself to be right all the time, I persisted in my errors and disregarded the criticisms of my comrades as well as their wishes and expectations. As a result, not only did I avoid correcting my errors but I continued in them and allowed them to grow.

78.

The State Budget and the Standard of Living

Despite the peasant origins of most of the cadres and Red Army soldiers who won the civil war, the leaders of the Communist Party began their task of rebuilding the country on the standard Marxist premise that socialism presupposes industrialization. Thus, in the early 1950s much effort was devoted to Soviet-style economic planning, which would concentrate available resources for the development of heavy industry. To do this required the promotion of many technical experts to positions of authority and the establishment of a much larger and more complex bureaucracy than was needed during the Yenan period. The daily lives of citizens were inevitably altered as the government sought to transform them into a well-disciplined work force. Even peasants were affected when in 1955 their cooperatives were organized into larger-scale collectives to improve productivity and make collection of grain tax easier.

There are few sources that reveal directly how Chinese responded to these major transformations of their lives. The article below, from a July, 1956, Tientsin newspaper, presents what the government wanted people to think and by implication some of the complaints people made.

State expenditure on economic and cultural construction has been considerably increased this year while that on national defense has been decreased. Spending for agriculture and light industry is way up, while the increase for social, cultural, and educational services is 26.39% higher than 1955. Spending on scientific work has more than doubled to meet the demand for mastery of science. Budgetary expenditure for minority areas is up 32.56% over 1955, an above-average increase. These statistics indicate that the government attaches importance to improving the people's living standard through developing production and industrializing the country. Concern over the people's living standard is, it might be said, one of the striking features of the 1956 budget.

The number of new workers employed by various sectors of the national economy will reach 840,000 in 1956. The average raise for office employees and workers will be 14.5%. There will be greater in-

creases for production department and key construction department workers, higher scientific and technical personnel, higher technical workers, rural primary school teachers, personnel of supply and marketing cooperatives, and personnel of rural people's councils whose wages were low in the past. Additional income made by all office employees and workers due to these increases in wages will reach 1.25 billion dollars.

Wages are an important issue in the relations between the working class and the state. In our country the working people are the masters of the state and carry on production for society as well as for themselves. It is precisely because of this that their labor activity can be brought into full play while they get reasonable pay according to the principle of "to each according to his work" and improve their life by continual elevation of their productivity. Workers' wages have recently increased every year. By the end of

1955, workers' wages were up 80% over 1950. The workers are also getting greater and greater social welfare benefits. Sick and disabled workers can get proper care and aged workers can get appropriate treatment after they retire; more nurseries, hospitals, and spare-time cultural and technical schools have been started. The state appropriates about one billion dollars as a labor insurance fund, a figure equivalent to 14% of wages. This is apart from the large sums of money spent by the state on housing projects for the workers. Thus, the life of our working masses is not merely constant but is improving by degrees.

However, in the past our policy on wages was not without defects. In the three years from 1950 to 1952 when the national economy was rehabilitated, workers' wages were increased comparatively fast in order to make up for the low wage rate and the irrational wage system of the Nationalist regime. By 1952, industrial labor productivity was up by 33.3% over 1950 while workers' wages averaged an increase of 57.7%. In the three years from 1953 to 1955 when the period of planned construction was ushered in, the increase in wages was slowed down and lagged behind the development of production and elevation of productivity. This was a defect even though allowance should be made for the fact that beginning in 1953 the state launched into construction which required the concentration of financial resources and in 1953 and 1954 agriculture was hit by major calamities. Yet in 1955, even though productivity was raised further, a good harvest was gathered, and peasants' income increased, wages for workers still were not adjusted. The old system of reward was done away with but a new system of reward was not instituted quickly enough. The supply of subsidiary foods was not adequately ensured; house building fell behind schedule; some enterprises did not show adequate concern for the lives of their workers. All such defects could not but slow improvement in workers' lives and hinder development of their productive capabilities. These defects will in the main be corrected along with this year's reform of the wage system. A new system of reward is being worked out; supply of subsidiary foods is being improved; measures are being taken with regard to workers' living quarters and industrial safety. In 1956 the central government ministries and their subordinate offices will build houses with a total floor space of 13 million square meters for workers and office employees and will gradually build the necessary subsidiary structures such as living quarters.

Gradual improvement of the peasants' living standard is a constant concern to the state. Its policies are to: (1) help the peasants increase production and income; (2) place no heavy burdens on them; (3) require no excessive quantities of unified purchase of grain; (4) gradually reduce the price differential between manufactured goods and farm produce to keep them at a reasonable ratio.

This is the first year for agricultural collectives, and peasants' production morale is high. The state plan envisages a further 9.3% increase this year in collective and sideline production. State financial aid and loans to the peasants this year are greater than they were in any year in the past and will reach 2.2 trillion dollars, more than double last year's. State investments in agriculture, forestry, and water conservancy projects are 48.3% higher than in 1955. The state has also stepped up supply of the means of agricultural production. Barring extraordinary natural calamities, overfulfillment of the 1956 agricultural production target is certain.

The main burden on the peasants is the agricultural tax. In past years, we collected agricultural tax according to the following principles: "collect a percentage of the standard yield as tax; reduce and exempt tax according to regulations; do not increase tax on increased yield." From 1950 to 1952, the period of economic recovery, the amount of tax paid by the peasants increased year by year. At that time, the People's Republic of China had been only recently founded and was confronted with the danger of American imperialist aggression. During the "resist-U.S., aid-Korea, protect home, and defend country" movement, the peasant masses declared their holdings and yield truthfully, paid the agricultural tax enthusiastically, and made immense contributions to the state. In 1953, during the period of national economic construction, the government adopted a policy of stabilizing the peasants' burden by keeping the total amount of agricultural tax at the 1952 level of 38.8 trillion catties for three years. Actually, only 35.1 trillion catties were collected in 1953 and 38 trillion catties in 1954 and 1955. The proportion of tax to output has dropped since 1951; it averaged 14% during the period of economic rehabilitation and 12% during the period of planned construction. With production stepped up, the surplus grain in the hands of the peasants after delivering the agricultural tax increased each year. Average surplus grain per capita of farming population amounted to 432 catties in 1950, 521 catties in 1952, and 566 catties in 1955. . . . Because agricultural production has increased to a considerable extent in 1956, the proportion of tax to output will not exceed 12% and will be smaller than the 1952 figure of 13.2%. Surplus grain in the hands of peasants after delivering agricultural tax will reach 611 catties on the average, or 45 catties more than in 1955. Thanks to the state policy of stimulating production and rationalizing the tax, the peasants are enabled to keep the greater part of their increased income. This is a great stimulus to their productive activity.

With regard to grain, the government enforced in the autumn of 1953 a policy of unified purchase and unified sale in order to meet the growing needs of the people and ensure stable market prices. In 1955 the government enforced the "unified production, purchase, and sale of grain" policy, which improved the methods and cut the quantity of unified purchases. In this way, the surplus grain left at the free disposal of the peasants will increase along with the development of production.

Concerning the ratios between the prices of manufactured goods and farm produce, the state adopted appropriate measures, thanks to which the prices of farm produce were raised, those of manufactured goods were relatively reduced, and the differential between them was gradually narrowed. Figures from ten county seats disclose that in 1955 the price differential between manufactured goods and farm produce was narrowed by 18% over 1950. With the same quantity of farm produce the peasants could get more manufactured goods in return.

It will be seen that all these policies are ones essential to improving the peasants' living standard and strengthening the worker-peasant alliance. While our work still has its defects, generally speaking we are dealing correctly with the relations between the state and the peasantry, between town and country, and between industry and agriculture. . . .

The above illustrates the interest of the government in raising the material and cultural level of the people. In our country the people are masters of the state. They regard the interests of the state as the highest and most fundamental interests of individuals. They understand that their interests can be fundamentally ensured only when production is developed, the country is made rich and mighty, and socialist construction is successful. On the other hand, our state is a democratic one and the interests of the people are its fundamental interests. The sole aim of economic and cultural construction is to raise the material and cultural level of the people. Moreover, only when the people lead a better life and take more interest in the results of their labor so as to raise their productivity can the state gain further progress. In a word, the interests of the state are closely connected with those of individuals and it would be wrong to neglect either. That being so, we should keep an appropriate part of the national income for social accumulations and set aside another for consumption by individuals.

79.

A New Young Man Arrives at the Organization Department

The growth of bureaucracy, with its nonegalitarian spirit and reliance on experts, was not without its critics; indeed, Mao himself was a leading one. From the time of victory in 1949 Mao worried that the revolutionary fervor of Party members would wane, that they would lose touch with the people and become authoritarian bureaucrats. Efforts to reform the Party from within proved difficult, and in 1956–57, Mao launched a campaign to expose the Party to the criticism of intellectuals under the slogan "Let a Hundred Flowers Bloom." Although most intellectuals were cautious at first, once criticism started to pour out it soon became a torrent. At this point Mao and other Party leaders abruptly changed the policy of toleration and launched an attack on the critics for harboring rightist ideology.

The following story by Wang Meng, published in People's Literature *in 1956, was a product of the "Hundred Flowers" period. It was widely read and became a subject of controversy. Wang's mockery of this one sleepy and inefficient Party office earned the praise of many who were troubled by the growth of bureaucratic red tape, but it also elicited considerable hostility from officials unaccustomed to this manner of criticism. During the public discussion of his story, Wang Meng was criticized for sentimentality and despondency, traits said to be characteristic of bourgeois intellectuals with few ties to the masses. Wang's literary career did not continue, although Mao Tse-tung later ruefully remarked that the Party had dealt too harshly with his point of view.*

The main characters in the story are:

> Lin Chen—new Party member and young man in the Organization Department of the District Party Committee
>
> Chao Hui-wen (female)—a secretary of the Organization Department
>
> Liu Shih-wu—Vice Director of the Organization Department
>
> Chou Jun-hsiang—Secretary of the District Party Committee
>
> Li Tsung-ch'in—Assistant Secretary of the District Party Committee
>
> Han Ch'ang-hsin—chief of the Factory Party Organizational Development Section
>
> Wang Ch'ing-ch'uan—Director and Party Branch Secretary of the Gunny Sack Factory
>
> Wei Ho-ming—Organization Committee Member of the Factory

I

It was March; a fine spray of something between rain and snow was in the air. A pedicab stopped in front of the District Committee door and a young man jumped down. The driver glanced at the large plaque hanging on the door and politely told his passenger, "If you're coming here I won't take any money."

From the messenger room, a demobilized soldier named Old Lü came limping out and, after inquiring about the young man's reason for coming, hastened to help him move his slightly damp bags from the pedicab and then went off to call the Organization Department's secretary, Chao Hui-wen. When she came, she clasped both of Lin Chen's hands and said, "We've been waiting for you a long time."

Lin Chen had known Chao Hui-wen from the time they were both in the primary school teachers' Party branch. Her two large eyes shined out from her pale but beautiful face with warmth and affection. Under them, though, weary shadows had appeared. She took Lin up to the men's dormitory, put down his bags, opened them up, aired out the damp blanket, and made up the bed, pausing frequently to flip her hair back, just like all other capable and attractive women cadres.

"We've been waiting for you a long time!" she repeated. "Six months ago when we wanted to have you transferred here, the Cultural Section of the District People's Council absolutely refused to let you go. Afterwards the District Party Committee's Secretary went directly to the District Chief for a man, and only after going through another fight with the Personnel Office of the Education Bureau were we finally able to get you transferred."

"I just heard the day before yesterday that I was to be transferred to the District Party Committee," Lin Chen said. "What does it do?"

"Everything."

"And the Organization Department?"

"It does organizational work."

"Are you busy?"

"Sometimes yes, sometimes no."

Chao, giving her full attention to making up the bed, shook her head disapprovingly like a big sister and said, "Young man, you've just no understanding of cleanliness! Just look at that pillowcase! It's already turned from white to black. And the top of the blanket is steeped in the oil from your neck. And look at the creases in the sheet . . . it's worn as thin as gauze. . . ."

Lin felt that as soon as he had entered the door of the District Party Committee—just when his new life was starting—he had encountered a close friend. With holiday-like exuberance, he ran down to the office of the Department's Vice Director, Liu Shih-wu, to report. As Lin Chen knocked at the door, his heart pounding, Liu was sitting with his head raised, a cigarette dangling from his lips, thinking about the Organization Department's work plan.

The Vice Director enthusiastically and cordially greeted Lin and took him over to a sofa while he himself sat on the edge of his desk. Moving around the papers piled up on the glass-topped desk, he asked casually, "How are things?" His left eye narrowed a little while his right hand flicked off the cigarette ash.

"The Branch Secretary informed me I should come the day after tomorrow but, as I had nothing to do at the school, I came today. I'm a bit afraid I won't be up to the work of the Organization Department. I'm a new Party member and I was a primary school teacher before. My past work and the work in the Organization Department are a little different. . . ."

Lin Chen uttered these long-since-prepared words very unnaturally, like a primary school student first meeting his teacher. The room was very warm. In the middle of March winter was just on the way out, and with the fire in the room, the frost on the windows melted in dirty streaks. Beads of perspiration broke out on his forehead and he groped in vain for his pocket handkerchief.

Liu Shih-wu mechanically nodded his head and carelessly extracted a manila folder from the middle of the great pile of papers. Opening it, he took out Lin Chen's Party membership registration form and with a keen eye quickly glanced over it. Tiny wrinkles appeared on his broad forehead, and he shut his eyes for a moment. Then, supporting himself on the back of the chair, he stood up and the padded jacket hanging loosely over his shoulders slipped down. With a familiar, completely lethargic voice he said, "Good, right, very good. The Organization Department is really short of cadres. You've come at the right time. No, our work isn't difficult. If you study it, you'll be able to do it; that's the way it is. Besides, your work at the lower level . . . rather successful, wasn't it?"

Lin sensed a note of irony in Liu's voice and agitatedly shook his head. "No, my work wasn't good. . . ."

A faint smile appeared on Liu Shih-wu's not-too-clean face, his eyes flashed intelligently, and he continued, "Of course, it is possible that you may have difficulties, it's possible. This is important work we do. One comrade in the Party Center has said organizational work is the housekeeping of the Party. If the house is not well cared for, the Party will have no strength." He continued without waiting for a question, "How do we care for the house? By developing the Party and strengthening its organization, augmenting its fighting power, building Party life on the basis of centralized leadership, criticism and self-criticism, and close ties with the masses. If we do this well, then the Party's organization will be strong, lively, and vigorous, and will be able to unite and lead the masses in carrying out ever task of socialist construction and transformation. . . ."

He constantly cleared his throat, but when he came to certain often-used phrases, he rattled them off as one word. For instance, he said, "Build Party life on . . ." but when you listened, it sounded like "Build Party life ratitiratitirat." He blandly handled all those concepts that Lin Chen thought terribly profound with the skill of someone manipulating an abacus. Lin Chen listened intently but still was unable to grasp the meaning of all Liu said.

Finally Liu Shih-wu assigned Lin his work. But as Lin was about to leave, Liu halted him with a question asked in a completely nonchalant manner, "Do you have a girlfriend, little Lin?"

"No. . . ." Lin Chen blushed instantly.

"A big boy like you still blushes?" Liu Shih-wu laughed out loud. "You're only twenty-two; there's no hurry." Then he added, "What's that book in your pocket?"

Lin Chen took out the book and read off its name: *The Tractor Station Manager and the Chief Agronomist.*

Liu took the novel and, opening it in the middle, read a few lines. "Is this what they recommend to you youngsters to read?" Lin nodded.

"Lend it to me and let me look it over."

"Do you have time to read novels?" Lin asked in amazement, looking at the pile of papers on the Vice Director's desk top.

Liu hefted the book once or twice, testing its weight, and squinted slightly. "What? I'll go through a thin book like this in half an evening. I read the four volumes of *Silent Flows the Don* in a week."

When Lin Chen went toward the general offices of the Organization Department, the sky had already cleared and shiny rims had appeared around the few remaining wisps of clouds. The big courtyard of the District Committee was bathed in sunlight. Everybody was busy: a comrade dressed in uniform clutching a briefcase under his arm hurried across the yard. Old Lü of the messenger's office was carrying two large iron teapots to the conference room. You could hear a woman comrade saying stubbornly into a telephone receiver: "That won't do! At the latest tomorrow morning! No. . . ." You could also hear a now fast, now slow tapping—an unfamiliar hand using a typewriter. "She's like me," he thought, "a new arrival," guessing on some unknown evidence that the typist was a girl. He stood around a bit in the hall, looked at the dazzling courtyard of the District Committee, and was happy at this beginning of his new life.

II

Including Lin Chen, there were twenty-four cadres in the Organization Department. Of these, three were temporarily off on assignment to the Office for Eliminating Counterrevolutionaries, one was studying half-time for his college entrance examinations, and one had taken maternity leave. Of the remainder, four persons did cadre work, and fifteen were separately assigned to different bureaus, factories, and schools in connection with Party building work. Lin Chen was assigned to a factory liaison organ to do Party recruitment work.

Li Tsung-ch'in was not only the Director of the Organization Department but the Assistant Secretary of the District Party Committee as well. However, he did not often ask about the affairs of the Organization Department so that in reality the work was in the hands of the Department Vice Director, Liu Shih-wu. Another Vice Director was in charge of cadre work. The person who actually directed Lin Chen's work was the chief of the Factory Party Organizational Development Section, Han Ch'ang-hsin.

Han Ch'ang-hsin's manner was completely different from Liu Shih-wu's. He was twenty-seven and wore a blue serge naval uniform which was so clean that even if it had been beaten hard, not a fleck of dust would have fallen from it. He was a big man with a strong face, which was, however, pockmarked from acne. Patting Lin on the shoulder, Han explained in a loud voice, which he continually broke with even louder laughter, what Lin's work was to be. Lin thought, "He's more like a leading cadre than the leading cadres themselves." This impression was strengthened by a conversation he heard between Han and a Branch Organization Committee member. "Why did you only talk for half an hour? I told you over the phone to discuss the 'recruitment plan' for at least two hours!" To which the Organizational Committee member mumbled about the month's production tasks being heavy. Han Ch'ang-shin interrupted him and said pompously, "So just because production tasks are heavy, recruitment work cannot be conscientiously looked into? That's opposing regular work to special work and a manifestation of 'the Party not looking after the Party' attitude."

Lin Chen was unable to figure out what "opposing regular work to special work" and "the Party not looking after the Party" meant. He was familiar with another set of phrases: "The five links in the classroom" and "Intuitive teaching methods." But he very much respected Han Ch'ang-hsin's vitality and energy in going swiftly to the heart of the question and issuing instructions.

He turned his head and saw Chao Hui-wen leaning on a table stenciling some materials. She looked doubtfully at Han Chang-hsin, frowned, and then, straightening the imitation amber comb in her hair, looked out the window with a slightly worried expression.

That evening, some of the cadres went out to take part in group organizational activities. Others rested, but Chao Hui-wen continued stenciling "Experience in cultivating and uplifting cadres in Taxation Branch Offices." Tired after a whole day's work, her wrist ached, and she constantly had to put down the stylus in the midst of writing to shake her wrist and blow on it. Lin Chen offered to help, but she refused, saying, "If you do the copying, I'll still be worried about it." So Lin Chen helped her to neatly pile up the already stenciled pages and gave her moral support by standing at her side. While she copied, she frequently lifted her head to look at Lin who finally asked, "Why do you keep looking at me?" Chao bit her stylus and mischievously smiled.

III

In the fall of 1953 Lin Chen, newly graduated from Normal School, had been a candidate member of the Party and was sent to the District Central Primary School as a teacher. Even though he was a teacher, he still preserved the habits of his high school life: every morning he lifted barbells; every evening he wrote in his diary; and before every important holiday—May 1, July 1 . . . he went around everywhere asking people their views of him. Once someone predicted that within three months he would become just like the older adults who did not lead such regulated lives. But not long afterwards, several teachers somewhat enviously said: "This boy doesn't have any cares or worries, no family ties, nothing but work. . . ."

He did not fail to live up to expectations. In the winter of 1954, because of his teaching accomplishments, he was given a prize by the Ministry of Education. Perhaps people believed that this young teacher could thus steadily, contentedly, and happily pass through his whole youth. But no. Lin Chen with all his childlike purity also had his problems. After a year, he punished himself with even more worries. Was it because of the stimulus of the high tide of socialism, or the call of the All China Youth Socialist Activists Conference, or because he was getting older?

He was already twenty-two and remembered when he was in Junior High School he had written a composition with the title "When I am X years old." He had written "When I am twenty-two I want to . . ." Now that he *was* twenty-two his life history seemed to be a blank page—no accomplishments, no creations, no adventures, not even love . . . he had never even written a letter to a girl. He worked hard but comparing the little he had accomplished with the youth activists, he was not happy with the way his life was speeding by. He settled on a plan to study and do everything; he wanted to stride the world with seven league boots!

Now that he had received his instructions to transfer to another job, his composition could read, "When I am twenty-two years old I will become a Party worker," and perhaps his real life was about to begin. He restrained his interest in primary education work and children and nurtured his hopes for his new position. After he had a conversation with his Party Branch Secretary about the transfer, he stayed up the whole night thinking.

It was thus that Lin Chen, *The Tractor Station Manager and the Chief Agronomist* in his pocket, excitedly mounted the stone stairs of the District Party Committee filled with sacred visions of the life of a Party worker (based upon the portrayals of omnipotent Party secretaries of the movies). But when he met those busy and confident leading comrades, heard those sharp quarrels and exalted analyses, he blinked his light brown eyes and was a little afraid. . . .

The fourth day that Lin Chen was at the District Headquarters, he went to the Tung-hua Gunny Sack Factory to look into the conditions of Party recruitment work during the first quarter of the year. Before going, he looked over the relevant documents and read a small volume entitled "How to Carry out an Investigation Study." He repeatedly asked Han Ch'ang-hsin for advice and carefully and elaborately wrote out an outline for himself. Then he mounted the bicycle supplied to him and rapidly rode out toward the Gunny Sack Factory.

The guard at the factory entrance, as soon as he heard Lin was a Party Committee cadre, did not even ask him to sign his name but trustingly invited him to go on in. He walked through a large empty yard, past a huge open storage bin filled with hemp and a building which rumbled with the sound of machinery. Then, rather nervously, he knocked at the door of Wang Ch'ing-ch'uan, the Factory Director and concurrent Party Branch Secretary. Receiving a reply of "Come in," he entered slowly, fearing that if he moved quickly he would display his lack of experience. He saw a fat-faced, thick-necked, short man playing chess with a slick-haired humpback. The short comrade lifted his head, playing with a chess piece, and after asking Lin whom he wanted to see, impatiently waved his hand and said, "Go over to the Branch Party Office in the adjoining building and ask for Wei Ho-ming; he's the Organization Committee member." Then he lowered his head once more and continued with the chess game.

Lin Chen found the ruddy-faced Wei Ho-ming and began questioning from his outline: "In the first quarter of the year how many persons did you recruit?"

"One and a half." Wei replied harshly and abruptly.

"What's this 'half'?"

"One person was passed, but the District Committee has already delayed two months in approving him."

Lin Chen took out a notebook and noted this down. Then he continued, "How was the recruitment work carried out? What experiences did you have?"

"The procedure was the same as before—as laid down in the Party Constitution."

Lin Chen looked at the person sitting opposite him. Why were his remarks as dry as week-old bread? Wei leaned his cheek on his hand and looked away as if he were thinking of something else.

Lin asked, "What were the results of your recruitment work?"

Wei replied, "I just told you," in a manner which showed he hoped to end the discussion quickly.

Lin Chen did not know what to ask next. He had spent a whole afternoon preparing an outline and now after talking for five minutes he had used it all up. He was quite embarrassed.

At this moment the door was pushed open by a forceful hand. The short comrade came in and snapped at Wei, "Do you know what was in that letter that just came?"

Wei dully nodded his head.

The short comrade paced back and forth and then, standing with legs apart in the middle of the floor, said, "You've got to think of a way out! The question of quality was raised last year. How is it you have to wait until the contractor writes a letter to the Ministry of Textiles? It is shameful if in the high tide of socialism our production cannot gradually be raised!"

Wei Ho-ming coldly looked at the short man's face and said, "Who are you talking about?"

"I am talking about all of you!" The short man waved his hand, including Lin Chen in his gesture.

Wei Ho-ming was trying to keep his anger under control and looked quite frightening. His face turned even redder and standing up he asked, "And you? You don't have any responsibility?"

"Naturally I am responsible." The short comrade calmed down. "I am responsible to the higher levels. No matter how they deal with me, I've got to take it. You are responsible to me. After all, who made you production chief? Be careful. . . ." Finishing, he looked threateningly at Wei Ho-ming and then left.

Wei sat down, opened up all the buttons on his cotton jacket and took a deep breath. When Lin Chen asked who that man was, Wei sarcastically replied, "You don't know him? He's the factory director, Wang Ch'ing-ch'uan."

Then Wei told Lin in detail all about Wang Ch'ing-ch'uan. Originally, Wang worked in some central ministry but as punishment for some involvement with a woman, he was assigned to this factory as Deputy Factory Manager in 1951. In 1953 the Factory Manager was assigned elsewhere and Wang was promoted to that position. He never did anything but run around in circles, hide in his office, sign papers, and play chess. Every month at the Union meeting, the Party Branch meeting, and the Youth League meeting he would make a speech criticizing the workers for not carrying out mass competition well, for their indifference to quality, for their economistic ideology. . . . Wei had not finished when Wang Ch'ing-ch'uan pushed open the door again. Looking at the watch on his left wrist he orderd: "Inform all responsible persons in the Party, League, Union, and Administrative Departments that there will be a meeting at 12:10 in the Factory Manager's office." Then, slamming the door, he left.

Wei Ho-ming mumbled, "You see what sort of a person he is?"

Lin said, "Don't keep these complaints to yourself. Criticize him, tell the higher levels about all this. They cannot possibly condone this sort of Factory Manager."

Wei smiled and asked Lin, "Old Lin, you're new here, aren't you?"

"Old Lin" reddened.

Wei explained, "Criticism doesn't work. He generally does not join in such meetings; so where are you going to criticize him? If by chance he does join in and you express your views, he says, 'It's fine to put forth opinions, but you've got to have a firm grip on essentials and consider the time and place. Now we should not take up precious time put aside for discussing national tasks by giving vent to personal opinions.' Fine. So instead of taking up 'valuable time,' I went around to see him myself, and we have argued ourselves into this present situation."

"And how about informing the higher levels?"

"In 1954 I wrote letters to the Ministry of Textile Industry and the District Party Headquarters. A man named Chang from the Ministry and Old Han from your office came around once to investigate. The conclusion of the investigation was that 'Bureaucratism is comparatively serious but most important is the manner of carrying out work; the tasks have been basically completed. It's only a question of shortcomings in the manner of completing them.' Afterwards Wang was criticized once, and they got hold of me to encourage the spirit of criticism from bottom to top, and that was the end of it. Wang was better for about a month. Then, he got nephritis. After he was cured he said he had become sick because of his hard work, and he became as he is now."

"Tell the upper levels again."

"Hmph. I don't know how many times I've talked with Han Ch'ang-hsin, but Old Han doesn't take any notice. On the contrary he lectures me on respect for

authority and strengthening unity. Maybe I shouldn't think this, but I'm afraid we may have to wait until Wang embezzles funds or rapes a woman before the upper levels take any notice."

When Lin left the factory and mounted his bike again, the wheels turned round much more slowly than they had on his way to the factory. He frowned deeply. The first step in his work was filled with difficulties, but he also felt a kind of challenge—this was the time to show one's fighting spirit! He thought and thought, until his bike strayed into the express lane and he was stopped and scolded by a policeman.

IV

After finishing lunch, Lin Chen could not wait to go off to Han Ch'ang-hsin to report on the situation. Han was wearily leaning on the sofa, his big form looking heavy and clumsy. He took a box of matches out of his pocket and, choosing one stick, began picking his teeth.

While Lin poured forth a disconnected account of what he had seen and heard at the Gunny Sack Factory, Han tapped his toe on the floor and kept saying, "Yes, I know." Afterwards, he patted Lin on the shoulder and cheerily said, "If you didn't understand conditions the first time out, it's not important. The next time will be better."

"But I understand the situation regarding Wang Ch'ing-ch'uan," said Lin, opening his notebook.

Han closed the notebook and told him, "Right, I've known about this situation for a long time. The year before last the District Committee told me to settle it, so I severely criticized him, pointing out his shortcomings. We talked for at least three or four hours. . . ."

"But there weren't any results. Wei Ho-ming said he was only better for one month."

"Even one month is something. Moreover, it certainly was not for only one month. Wei's ideology is questionable if as soon as he meets anyone he starts to tell all about his superior's faults. . . ."

"Well, was what he said true or not?"

"It's hard to say. Naturally this ought to be solved. I've talked it over with the District Committee Assistant Secretary, Comrade Li Tsung-ch'in."

"And what did the Assistant Secretary think?"

"He agreed with me that the problem of Wang Ch'ing-ch'uan ought to be solved and can be solved. . . . Only, you shouldn't go diving into it just like that."

"Do you mean *me*?"

"Yes. This is the first time you've gone to a factory, and you don't understand the entire situation. Your job isn't to solve the problem of Wang Ch'ing-ch'uan; in fact, to speak frankly, a more experienced cadre is needed for his problem. Besides, it isn't that we haven't considered the affair. . . . If you go jumping into this business, you won't get out for three months. Are you completely familiar with the first quarter's summary on party building? The upper levels are anxious to receive our report!"

Lin Chen was silent. Han patted him on the shoulder again. "Don't be upset. There are 3,000 Party members in our district and a hundred-and-some-odd branches. Do you think you can know all of their problems as soon as you arrive?" He yawned, the pockmarks on his tired face standing out redly. "Ahhhh—I'd better take my afternoon nap."

"Then how should I go about investigating Party recruitment work again?" Lin asked hopelessly.

Then Han Ch'ang-hsin again rose to pat his shoulder, but Lin involuntarily moved away. Han self-confidently said, "Tomorrow we will go together; I'll help you investigate. How about that?" Then he took Lin off with him to the dormitory.

The next day, Lin Chen was very interested to see how Han Ch'ang-hsin would go about investigating conditions. Three years earlier when he was in the Peking Normal School, he had gone off to observe teaching in practice. The teacher stood in front and lectured while Lin and the students listened. This time, Lin adopted the same attitude; opening his notebook, he prepared to note down carefully Han's modus operandi.

Han asked Wei Ho-ming, "How many Party members did you recruit?"

"One and a half."

"Not 'one and a half,' but two. I'm inquiring about your recruitment work, not about whether the District Committee has approved them or not." Having corrected him, Han continued, "How did these two men complete their production quota?"

"Very well. One exceeded his by seven percent and the other by four percent. The factory wall newspaper shows . . ."

When he started to talk about production conditions, Wei seemed to take on a little more life, but

Han interrupted him, "What shortcomings do they have?"

Wei Ho-ming thought for some time and then vaguely mentioned some defects. Han made him give some examples. After this Han again asked him about the Party activists' completion of their quarter's production tasks, seeking figures and concrete examples. But when the manner in which advanced workers overcame difficulties and developed innovations came up, he showed no interest.

After they returned, Han quickly scribbled off a hand-written draft "Summary of Conditions Regarding Recruitment Work at the Gunny Sack Factory" whose details were as follows: ". . . During this quarter (January-March 1956) the Gunny Sack Factory Branch Office basically carried through a positive and careful plan of recruiting new Party members. In Party building work it achieved definite results. Newly approved Party members Chu and Fan received the glorious encouragement of becoming Communist Party members, strengthened their outlook as owners of their own tools, and in the first quarter exceeded their heavy production quotas by seven percent and four percent respectively. The great mass of positive workers within the Party Factory Branch were influenced by the good example set by Chu and Fan, and were stimulated by their decision to achieve acceptance into the Party. They developed their positive attitude and creativity and magnificently completed or exceeded their production quotas for the quarter. . . ." (Below was a series of figures and concrete examples.) "This proves: 1. Party building work not only does not interfere with production work, but in fact greatly stimulates it. Any work method which uses as a pretext the urgency of production work to disregard Party building is mistaken. 2. . . . But at the same time it must be pointed out that Party building work in the Gunny Sack Factory still has certain shortcomings . . . such as . . ."

Lin Chen held the sheet of fine paper on which the "Summary of Conditions" was written and read it over and over. There was an instant when he doubted whether he had been to the Gunny Sack Factory or whether the last time he had gone to the factory with Han he had fallen asleep. Why was it there were so many things he absolutely could not recall? He suspiciously asked Han, "What is the basis for all this?"

"Wei Ho-ming's report that day."

"The production results were due to their Party building work?" Lin began to stammer.

Han shook out the crease in his trousers and said, "Naturally."

"No, Wei didn't say that last time. They were able to raise production, but perhaps it was due to expanding competition, perhaps because the Youth League established a supervision post, but not necessarily because of the achievements of Party building work. . . ."

"Naturally, I don't deny that. Various factors all worked together. You cannot split them apart metaphysically in an analysis and say this is a result of X and that is a result of Y."

"Then if we were writing a summary of rat catching work during the first quarter could we also use these figures and examples?"

Han smiled broadly at Lin's inexperience and said, "You have to be somewhat flexible. . . ."

"How do you know their production tasks were heavy?"

"Do you think there could be any factory now with light tasks?"

Lin was dumfounded.

V

Work in a District Committee is tense and serious; in the Secretary's office meetings go on till the small hours of the morning day after day. From the phoneticization of Chinese to the prevention of meningitis, from labor insurance to lectures in political economy, nothing escapes discussion by the District Committee. Once Lin Chen went to the mailroom to pick up a newspaper and saw an enormously thick document with the title written on the first page "A Report by the Party Organization of the District People's Council on Adjusting the Methods of Distributing, Managing, and Administrating Joint Public-Private Enterprises and on Carrying Through the Report of the Municipal Committee on the Wage Question in Joint Public-Private Enterprises." With a feeling of reverence he gazed at the document—as thick as a book—and its long title. Sometimes too, he also felt that the attitudes of cadres in the District Committee were flippant and casual. They chatted nonchalantly in the office, read newspapers, and joked about the subjects Lin Chen thought most serious. For example,

when the Youth League supervision post started its work, and Han Ch'ang-hsin half-sarcastically said, "Our young friends are all in a sweat."

The one session of the Work Meeting of the Organization Department that Lin sat in on was also very interesting. They were discussing a temporary task assigned by the Municipal Committee, everyone smoking, joking, interrupting; they met for two hours, dragging the meeting on with no results whatsoever. Then Liu Shih-wu, who had been sitting musing for some time, put forward a proposal and immediately an animated discussion started with many people putting forward brilliant suggestions that filled Lin with amazement and respect. He felt that the last thirty minutes of discussion were ten times more effective than the first two hours of the meeting.

Sometimes at night there was light in every room of the District Committee: in the first conference room the fat businessmen from industry and commerce exchanged views with the head of the United Front Department; in the second conference room, a number of teachers of study groups argued heatedly about the relationships between "price" and "value"; several young men excitedly waited for their interviews prior to being admitted to the Party; a certain strict Party Secretary from the Municipal Committee unexpectedly appeared in the Secretary's office asking the Deputy Secretary to report on the circumstances of carrying through the wage reform. . . . At this point the sound of voices became chaotic; shadows rushed back and forth; the telephone rang intermittently. It seemed to Lin Chen as though he were listening to the very pulse beat of the District Committee and that the old, nondescript courtyard of the District Committee had become glorious and imposing.

In the midst of all his impressions, the most striking and fresh was of Liu Shih-wu. Liu had an enormous amount of work to do: frequently several telephone calls would come all at the same time urging him to go and hold meetings. Yet, after only a short time he had finished *The Tractor Station Manager and Chief Agronomist* and passed it on to Han Ch'ang-hsin. Moreover, he had already committed to memory the draft Chinese phonetic alphabet published the month before and had started to make notes at meetings using the phonetic alphabet. Some documents passed to him he would merely skim the title and conclusion, sign his name, and send them on. With others only a few pages long, he might linger for a whole afternoon, minutely making all kinds of notations on them. Sometimes Liu would be listening with half an ear as Han made a report and at the same time apparently reading over some entirely different matter. He would listen and listen and then suddenly point out, "You didn't say that the last time you made a report!" Han would smile artificially while Liu's eyes flashed; but Liu would not dig any deeper into the question and would go back to looking over the other matter before him while Han Ch'ang-hsin regained his composure and loudly and animatedly continued with his report.

Lin Chen also had his doubts about the relation between Chao Hui-wen and Han Ch'ang-hsin. Han's attitude toward everyone was one of back-slapping, casualness, intimacy—everyone was "Old Wang," "Old Li." It was only toward Chao that he preserved a polite, formal attitude. He would say, "Comrade Chao, where is Party Bulletin number 104?" Chao also treated him very circumspectly.

Strangely enough, Lin was unable to decide definitely whether his new environment was good or bad. Just as in elementary school, he got up every morning to work out with the barbells and he still gave people an impression of "purity," even of naiveté. But he was turning things over in his own mind much, much more now than in elementary school. He had to judge everything and everybody.

It was April; the east wind was gently blowing, the no-longer-beloved stoves stuck away in dark corners of storerooms, with only the black soot on the ceilings of every room to provide a lasting trace of their existence. In previous years at this time Lin Chen had gone tramping through the Sleeping Buddha Temple or the scenic spots of the Western Hills with a band of bouncing children to search out signs of spring on early blossoming peach and pear trees and in black turgid brooks. . . . But there was no echo of the new season in the life of the District Committee which continued to move to the same tense rhythm and complicated tempo. And so, when one morning Lin plucked a ripe, tender bud from the weeping willow tree in the courtyard, he felt a twinge of sadness because spring had come so quickly and he had done nothing of significance to welcome in that beautiful season. . . .

One night at nine o'clock, Lin entered the door of Liu Shih-wu's office. Chao Hui-wen was already

there, wearing a dark brown sweater. Against the glare of the light her face seemed even more ashen. When she heard someone enter the room she quickly turned her head, but Lin caught a glimpse of the faint traces of tears on her cheekbones. He turned around to leave, but Liu, smoking a cigarette, gestured to stop him, saying, "Sit down here, we have just about finished talking."

Lin sat down in a corner and glanced through a newspaper by the light of the lamp some distance away. Liu, inscribing circles in the air with the stub of his cigarette said with sincerity, "Believe me, I am right. All young people are the same, filled with admiration for each other in the beginning and then gradually discovering defects until they feel everything is common and ordinary. Don't make unrealistic demands. How can you say you cannot go on living together? There's no cruelty, no desertion, no question of politics or morals. It has only been four years. Your ideas come straight out of Soviet films. In reality, life is just the way it is."

Chao Hui-wen did not say anything but flipped her hair back and, as she was about to leave, smiled sadly at Lin Chen.

Liu Shih-wu walked over to Lin and asked, "What's new?" He threw away his cigarette butt and drawing out a new one, lit it, and puffed on it greedily several times. Slowly exhaling white smoke, he explained to Lin, "Chao Hui-wen and her husband have broken up again. . . ." He opened the window. A puff of wind blew several sheets of paper off the desk. They could hear laughing voices and bicycle bells in the front courtyard as a group was just leaving a meeting. Liu threw away his half-smoked cigarette and stretched. Leaning on the window, he said in a low voice, "It's really spring!"

"I want to talk about some matters regarding my work since I have come to the District Committee. I have some problems I don't know how to solve." As he said this to Lin he picked up the papers which had fallen to the floor.

"Right, fine," said Liu Shih-wu, still leaning on the window sill.

Lin started with his visit to the Gunny Sack Factory. ". . . I went into the Factory Manager's office and saw Comrade Wang Ch'ing-ch'uan. . . ."

"Was he playing chess or poker?" Lui asked, smiling.

"How did you know?" Lin was amazed.

"We can always predict what he will do at a particular time," Liu Shih-wu said slowly. "He is obsessed by chess. One time half way through a meeting here he went out to the bathroom. When he didn't come back I went out to find him. . . . He had seen Old Lü and the son of the District Committee Secretary playing chess and stayed around to watch and comment on the side."

Lin paid no attention to his companion's digressions but resolutely continued describing the situation as he saw it. Liu shut the window, drew up a chair, and sat down. He rested both hands on his knees and, with a slight shake of his head, said, "Wei Ho-ming is hot-headed. He no sooner arrived than he began to bicker with Wang Ch'ing-ch'uan. . . . You know, Wang is not an ordinary person, not so simple as you may think. After the victory over Japan, he was sent into the Nationalist army and became a Deputy Brigade Commander—a first rate intelligence agent. In 1947 communications between us were cut and only reestablished after Liberation. He was sent to undermine the enemy but he himself was infected by some of the habits of the Nationalist officers which he can't seem to shake off. In reality though he's a brave old comrade."

"So that's how . . ."

"Yes." Liu Shih-wu nodded his head seriously and continued, "Naturally, this does not exonerate him. The Party sent him to defeat the enemy, not to model himself on them, and so his mistake is unforgivable."

"How can we solve this mess? Wei Ho-ming says this problem has already dragged on for so long. He's written letters everywhere. . . ."

"Yes." Liu stopped to cough for a moment and then, gesturing, said, "Right now there are so many problems in low level cells. How can you expect to solve them one by one using handicraft methods? That's to labor like an elephant and bring forth a mouse. Besides, the upper echelons are always breathing down your neck with more assignments. Just fulfilling them is a heavy job. The art of being a leader is to be able to combine general and specific problems, along with the tasks laid down by your superiors and those problems existing in the lower levels. Again, it's a fact that Wang doesn't work hard, but it hasn't deteriorated to the point of a slow-down; his work style is somewhat crude, but no violation of law or discipline is involved; obviously this isn't a problem of punishment by the Organization Bureau but of ordinary education. Looked at from every angle, the time is not yet ripe to solve this problem."

Lin was silent, unable to decide which was right: Nastya's dictum of "absolute intolerance of evil" or Liu Shih-wu's "theory of ripe conditions." Whenever he thought of a factory manager like Wang he found it unbearable, and yet he was unable to refute Liu Shih-wu's "art of leadership." Liu added, "Actually, it's not just one cadre who has this kind of defect. . . ." This made Lin open his eyes even wider and feel that there was nothing in common between this and the contents of the Party lessons he had heard in primary school.

Next, Lin recounted how Han went about "investigating" and writing up a short report. He said he felt that to adjust a report in that manner was not very honest. Liu laughed aloud. "Old Han . . . that one . . . really brilliant. . . ." After he finished laughing, he took a deep breath and told Lin, "Right, I'll pass on your opinion to him." Seeing that Lin hesitated, Liu asked, "Still something bothering you?"

Then Lin Chen bravely came out with it: "I don't know why, but, since I've come to the District Committee, I've discovered many failings; the Party leadership organs that I had imagined were not like this. . . ."

Liu put down his tea cup. "Naturally, what you imagine is always good; but reality is just what it is. The key is not whether or not there are weak points but what is vital. In the District Committee's work, including the Organization Department's work, which matters—our accomplishments or our shortcomings? Obviously the accomplishments; the shortcomings are only shortcomings in the course of progress. Our great work is accomplished by exactly those imperfect organizations and Party members."

After having left the office, Lin had a strange feeling. A talk with Liu was like a catharsis, but his own fixed judgments and clear views had turned foggy and indistinct. He felt even more unsure of himself.

VI

Not long afterwards, Lin Chen was the target of severe criticism in a Party small group meeting. The situation developed as follows. During one of Lin's visits to the Gunny Sack Factory, Wei Ho-ming told him that because the quality standard set for the quarter had not been met, Wang Ch'ing-ch'uan had fiercely lectured the workers. The workers had their own views on this, and Wei planned to call a discussion group together, collect these views, and pass them on to the higher authorities. Lin approved of this method and thought that in this way the "ripening of conditions" could be hastened. Three days later Wang came into the District Committee in a blind rage, looking for the Assistant Secretary, Li Tsung-ch'in. He complained that Wei Ho-ming—with the support of Lin Chen—had formed a faction to carry out anti-leadership activities and moreover, that the workers in the discussion group Wei directed were all suspect because of their backgrounds. . . . And at the very end, he requested that his own resignation be accepted. Li Tsung-ch'in criticized a few of Wang's shortcomings and agreed to prevent Wei from convening his discussion group again. "As for Lin Chen," he said to Wang, "we will give him some much deserved instruction."

In the criticism meeting, Han Ch'ang-hsin analyzed: "Comrade Lin Chen did not discuss the issue with the leadership but on his own responsibility agreed to Wei Ho-ming's calling of a discussion group. This, to begin with, is a kind of unorganized, undisciplined behavior. . . ."

Lin Chen refused to concede and said, "Not requesting permission from the leadership was an error. But I do not understand why we not only fail to investigate spontaneously the views of the masses but on the contrary prevent the lower levels from putting forth their views!"

"Who says we won't investigate?" Han Ch'ang-hsin raised one leg. "We are completely in control of the situation at the Gunny Sack Factory. . . ."

"In control but making no effort to solve the problem; that's what's so painful! The Party Constitution says that Party members must struggle against anything that works against the interests of the Party. . . ." Lin Chen's face paled.

Experienced Liu Shih-wu began to make his statement. He always made a point of entering at a discussion's most crucial point.

"Comrade Lin Chen's enthusiasm is very praiseworthy, but for him to lecture the Organization Department cadres on the Party Constitution after having been here only a month is a little presumptuous. Lin believes that, by supporting criticism from the bottom up, he is doing a very fine thing, and his motive is no doubt very noble. But criticism from the bottom up must be initiated by the leadership. For example, let's ask Comrade Lin to think about the following: First, isn't it true that Wei Ho-ming has a personal grudge against Wang Ch'ing-ch'uan? It would be very difficult to say otherwise. Then, for Wei Ho-ming so eagerly to call a discussion group together may have had a personal objective, couldn't it? I think that's not entirely impossible. Second, were there people in the discussion group whose backgrounds are in doubt and who may have ulterior motives? We've also got to consider that point. Third, can the convening of that kind of a meeting give the masses the impression that Wang Ch'ing-ch'uan is on the verge of being punished and thereby lead to confusion all around? And so on. As to Lin Chen's ideological condition, I want to put forward very frankly a guess: a young man easily idealizes life; he believes life should be a certain way and then demands that it be that way. Those who do Party work must consider the objective facts and whether life can be that way. Young people also easily overestimate themselves and aspire to too much. As soon as they go to a new work post they want to struggle against every shortcoming and be a 'Nastya' type of hero. This is a valuable and lofty idea but it is also a kind of vanity. . . ."

Lin Chen wavered for a moment as if he had received a blow. He bit down tightly on his lower lip to hold in his anger and pain. Screwing up his courage, he asked again: "But what about Wang Ch'ing-ch'uan? . . ."

Liu Shih-wu jerked his head up and interrupted, "Tomorrow I will have a talk with him. You are not the only one with principles."

VII

Saturday night was Han Ch'ang-hsin's wedding night. When Lin Chen entered the hall he could not stand the thick, choking, smoky air, the litter of candy wraps on the ground, the constant roar of loud laughter in the air; and, without waiting for the ceremony to begin, he beat a retreat.

The Organization Department office was dark. He turned on a light and saw an envelope on his desk from his fellow workers at the primary school containing a letter signed by the small hands of the children. "Teacher Lin, are you well? We really, really miss you. The girl students all cried. Then afterwards they stopped crying. Afterwards we did arithmetic. The problems were very, very hard, and we worked for a long time at it. Finally we were abel to do it. . . ."

Looking at the letter, Lin Chen could not help smiling to himself. He picked up a pen and corrected "abel" to "able" and planned to write back to tell them to be careful the next time to avoid such mistakes. It was as if he could see Li Lin-lin with her beribboned pig-tails, Liu Hsiao-mao who loved to paint with water colors, and Meng Fei who always bit his pencils. . . . When he abruptly raised his head from the letter, he saw the telephone, the blotter, and the glass table top. The children's world he was so familiar with was far away. Now he found himself in an unfamiliar environment. He thought of the criticism he received at the Party small group meeting two days earlier. Could it be that he was really wrong? Was he really clumsy, childish, and youthfully overzealous? Perhaps he really ought to reevaluate himself, do all his regular duties well, and after a few years when he had "matured," again try to enter into other things.

The explosive sound of applause and laughter came from the wedding hall.

A soft hand fell on his shoulder and Lin turned his head with a start. The lamplight hurt his eyes. Chao Hui-wen stood silently at his side; women comrades all had the knack of walking up on you quietly.

She asked, "Why aren't you at the festivities?"

"I am too lazy to go. You?"

"I ought to go home," Chao said. "Come along, and we'll chat a while there. It's better than sitting here brooding by yourself."

"I don't have anything to brood about," Lin protested, but he accepted her kind invitation.

Chao Hui-wen lived in a small courtyard not far from the District Committee. Her son was sleeping in a small, light blue bed happily sucking his forefinger. Chao kissed him and drew Lin into her room.

"Doesn't his father come home?" Lin carefully asked.

Chao Hui-wen shook her head. Her room looked as if it had been furnished very hastily. The walls appeared too austerely white because they were entirely bare of any decoration. A washbasin was stuck by itself over in one corner; an empty flower vase on the window sill stupidly opened its mouth; only the radio on the small bed table seemed likely to be able to disturb the silence of the room.

Lin Chen sat down in a wicker chair, while Chao Hui-wen remained standing against the wall. Lin, pointing at the flower vase, said, "You ought to put some flowers in it," and motioning toward the wall remarked, "Why don't you buy a few pictures to hang on the walls?"

"Ordinarily I am not in, and so I haven't paid any attention to those things." Then, pointing at the radio, she asked, "Should we turn it on? Every Saturday evening there's good music."

The radio lit up and a soft, dreamlike melody floated in from far away, slowly changing and becoming more stirring. The poetic theme being played on the violin clutched at Lin Chen's heart. He leaned his cheek on his hand and scarcely breathed. His youth, his quests, his failures all seemed to find expression in this music.

Chao Hui-wen leaned against the wall with her hands behind her back, inattentive to the fact that the whitewash was coming off on her clothes. She waited until the end of the movement and then, in a voice like the music itself, said: "This is Tchaikovsky's 'Capriccio Italien,' it makes you think of the South, of the sea. When I was in the Cultural Workers' Troop, I often listened to it and gradually came to feel this music was not being performed by someone else but sprang straight out from inside me. . . ."

"You were in the Cultural Workers' Troop?"

"After I was at the Military Affairs Cadres' School I was assigned to it. In Korea I used my clumsy voice to sing for the troops. I am a husky-voiced singer."

Lin reappraised Chao Hui-wen as if he were seeing her for the first time.

"Don't I look like a singer?" At that moment the station shifted to "The Opera Stage," and she turned the radio off.

"If you were in the Cultural Workers' Troop, why do you sing so little?" Lin asked.

She did not reply but went over to the bedside and sat down. Then she said, "Let's talk a bit, Little Lin. Tell me, what's your impression of our District Party Committee?"

"I don't know, I mean, it is still not clear."

"You are not quite happy with Han Ch'ang-hsin and Liu Shih-wu, are you?"

"Perhaps."

"In the beginning I was that way too. Coming here from the army and comparing its strictness and precision with this, I could not get used to a lot of things. I offered them many suggestions and once had a bitter quarrel with Han Ch'ang-hsin, but they smiled at my childishness, smiled at my constant suggestions even though I was not doing my own work well; and, gradually, I discovered my strength was not up to struggling against the shortcomings of the District Committee. . . ."

"Why not?" Lin Chen jumped up as if stung and frowned.

"That was my fault," Chao admitted. She took a pillow and placed it on top of her lap. "At that time I felt my own level was too low and that I was far from perfect. For me to try to correct those comrades whose levels were so much higher than my own was really impractical. Moreover, Liu, Han, and some other comrades do certain work extremely well. When you scatter their defects in among our accomplishments, it's like scattering dust in the air: You can smell it but can't grab hold of it."

"Exactly!" Lin struck his left palm with his right fist.

Chao Hui-wen was also a bit agitated. She threw off the pillow, and speaking still slower, said, "The work I do is general office routine; leadership cadres don't often ask about it. In addition I have a number of personal responsibilities so I keep quiet. I go to work and copy and write, and leave work to wash the baby's diapers and buy milk powder. I feel that I'm growing old very fast. The enthusiasm and imagination I had in my days at the Military Cadres' School has flown away, goodness knows where."

She was silent, squeezing her beautiful white fingers one by one. Then she continued, "Two months ago, Peking entered the high tide of socialism. Workers, shopkeepers, even capitalists letting off strings of firecrackers and beating drums came to the District Committee to tell of their joy. Many sent applications to enter the Party directly to the Organization Department. The main street was changed overnight. The whole District Committee was ablaze with lights every evening, and during meals the cadres of the Financial and Propaganda Departments chattered incessantly about various features in the high tide of socialism. But our Organization Department? Very little change! We made some telephone calls asking for development figures; we added a few examples on last year's pattern and wrote up a general summary. Most recently, everyone had to conduct an investigation into conservative ideology. The Organization Department also investigated—by lackadaisically calling three meetings, writing up a report, and that was it! Oh, I'm all mixed up. In the high tide of socialism, every sound of a string of firecrackers going off stung me; when I stenciled the notification of admission of new Party members my hand shook with excitement. But is there any chance to improve our work in this office?"

She took a deep breath, paced back and forth, and then continued. "When I spoke about my own way of thinking at a Party small group meeting, Han Ch'ang-hsin said smugly, 'You can't deny that our ratio of completed recruitment figures is the highest of any District, can you? You can't deny that the Municipal Committee has asked us to write up our experiences, can you?' Then he started his analysis, saying that the reason my feelings were not optimistic enough was that I was dissatisfied with general office work. . . ."

"In the beginning, Han makes a terrific impression on everyone, but when you actually come into contact with him . . ." Lin again recounted the story about making the report on the Gunny Sack Factory.

Chao nodded in agreement. "Although I haven't put forward any views for the last year or two, there hasn't been a minute when I haven't been looking at things. Everything in life looks differently on the inside and the outside. To do something so it glitters on the outside isn't difficult. For example, when Han takes charge he gives instructions in a loud, clear voice; in reports he knows how to dredge up vivid examples; in analyzing problems he knows how to string together generalizations; and so he seems a vigorous and capable cadre and floats complacently along on top of the world."

"But Liu Shih-wu?" Lin Chen asked. "He certainly isn't shallow like Han Ch'ang-hsin, but his individual opinions and analyses seem cynical. I simply cannot understand why he tolerates a factory manager like Wang Ch'ing-ch'uan. And when you want to express an opinion, his criticism makes you go round and round until it seems that his is the only road to follow. . . ."

"Liu Shih-wu has one pet phrase: 'That's the way it is.' He's seen through everything and believes everything is just the way it is. Using his own way of speaking, he knows what is 'right' and what is 'wrong' and that 'right' will inevitably be victorious over 'wrong,' but not in the twinkling of an eye. He knows everything, has seen everything—the experience a person gets from doing Party work is really not inconsequential—and so he can no longer be bothered; he no longer loves and also no longer hates. When he smiles at imperfections, it's nothing but a smile; when he expresses his appreciation for achievements, it's nothing but appreciation. He is satisfied that he has the ability to deal with everything and that there is no further need to study zealously anything except factual matter like the phonetic alphabet. When he feels that conditions are ripe and that it's necessary to do something, he grasps the thing in his hand, teaches this, arranges that, as if he were everyone's superior.

Taking his experience and intelligence into account, he naturally can do some things easily and so he's all the more self-confident." Chao poured out mercilessly the words that had gone around in her head during so many sleepless nights. . . .

"Our District Committee Assistant Secretary and Department Chief, doesn't he pay any attention?"

Chao became even more excited and said, "Li Tsung-ch'in's health isn't good. He wants to do theoretical work and dislikes the District Committee work which is too concrete for him. He is only nominally the head of the Organization Department and has passed everything on to Liu Shih-wu. That's a rather ordinary 'extraordinary' phenomenon; there's a whole group of old Party members whose health is bad, or whose cultural level is low, or who, because they are some big wheel's spouse, hold the titular rank of Factory Manager, School Principal, or Secretary but whose Assistant Factory Manager, Executive Officer, secretary, or whatever does the actual work."

"What about our Secretary, Chou Jun-hsiang?"

"Chou has too much work to do. He's busy with the suppression of counterrevolutionaries, the transformation of private industry . . . all 'shock missions.' Our Organization Department's work, generally speaking, never has any urgent, immediate tasks, and so he doesn't pay much attention to it."

"So . . . what then?" Lin only now began to understand the complexity of things, as if every shortcoming were connected, from top to bottom, with a whole series of reasons.

"Yes." Chao sat in deep thought, drumming with her fingers on her leg as if on a piano, and then, smiling into the distance, said, "Thank you. . . ."

"Thank me?" Lin Chen thought he had not heard correctly.

"Yes, for when I see you it's as if I were young again myself. You often fix your eyes on some faraway place and you're always imagining things, like a fantasy-loving child. You're also extremely easily excited, and you blush at practically anything. But you're also not afraid of anything and protest against all that's bad. I have a kind of woman's intuition that a big upheaval is on the way."

Lin Chen blushed again. He certainly had not expected this frank an appraisal and felt ashamed at his helplessness. He mumbled, "Well, I only hope it is a real affair and not a tempest in a teapot." Then he asked, "You've thought so much, analyzed this so clearly; why do you keep it all bottled up inside you?"

"I don't feel I can do anything about it," Chao said, placing her hand on her chest. "I look and think, think and look; sometimes I think so hard I can't sleep. I ask myself, 'Your work is in general office routine; can you understand all these things?'"

"How can you think that? I think that what you've been saying is completely correct! You ought to speak to the District Committee Secretary about what you've just said, or write a letter to the *People's Daily*. . . .

"Goodness, listen to you." Chao smiled and flashed her glistening teeth.

"Why say 'listen to you'?" Lin got up unhappily and scratched his scalp hard. "I've also thought about it many times. I think a person can correct himself in the course of fighting rather than wait until he's first correct before entering into a fight!"

Chao suddenly pushed open the door and went out leaving Lin alone in the vacant room. He smelled the aroma of soup, and she came back quickly carrying a long-handled pot, skipping like a little girl. She uncovered the lid and said dramatically, "Come, we're going to eat water chestnuts, done-to-a-turn water chestnuts. I haven't been able to find anything else good to eat."

"From the time I was small I've loved cooked water chestnuts," bubbled Lin Chen. He took the pot, chose a large one and bit into it without peeling it. Then wrinkling up his eyebrows, he spat it out. "This is a bad one, sour and rotten." When Chao laughed, Lin angrily threw the squashed up sour water chestnut on the floor.

By the time he was getting ready to go, it was late at night and the clear sky was filled with apprehensive little stars. An old man hoarsely singing "Fried dumplings boiling in the pot!" pushed his cart past. Lin stood outside the door while Chao faced him in the doorway, her eyes flashing brilliantly in the dark. She said, "The next time you come, there will be pictures on the walls."

Lin Chen smiled appreciatively. "And I hope that you will take up singing again!" He pressed her hand once, then breathed in deeply the fresh fragrance of the spring night and felt a warm spring gush up in his heart.

VIII

Han Ch'ang-hsin had been recently promoted to the position of Vice Director of the Organization Department. This, along with his recent marriage seemed to make a new man of him. Shaving became a daily habit, and, after he went to see a Clothing Exhibition, he bought himself a new suit of clothes. But he cut down on his personal investigations of ongoing work and confined himself to signing documents, listening to briefings, and conducting interviews. Liu Shih-wu was as busy as ever. . . .

One evening after dinner, Han Ch'ang-hsin returned *The Tractor Station Manager and the Chief Agronomist* to Lin Chen. Tapping the cover of the book with his finger and nodding his head, Han said: "It's very interesting, but a little fantastic. It must be quite a lot of fun being an author, describing everything in such extravagant ways. If in the future I ever get rheumatism or am punished for any mistakes, I think I'll write a novel."

Lin took the book and tucked it away in the bottom of his drawer. Liu Shih-wu, sitting in another corner of the room on a sofa, was wrapped up in studying the end game of a chess match, but when he heard Han Ch'ang-hsin's remarks he said scathingly, "It is not entirely beyond the realm of possibility that Old Han will get rheumatism or be punished for his mistakes. As for a novel, I think we can rest at ease that we won't see his masterpiece on this planet." He said these words without the slightest bit of humor so that Han hastily turned his head away and pretended not to have heard them.

Then Liu called Lin Chen over, told him to sit down alongside him, and asked, "Have you read any new novels recently? If they were good ones I'd like to borrow them."

Lin said he had not. Liu Shih-wu shifted his body so that he was lying sideways on the sofa, put his hands behind his head, half-closed his eyes, and drawled, "Recently I read a translation of the second part of *Virgin Soil Upturned* [by Mikhail Sholokhov] in *Literary Translations*. Damn well written, extremely vivid. . . ."

Lin Chen asked skeptically, "Do you often read novels?"

"I'm glad to say I like to read as much as you—novels, poetry, even fairy tales. Before Liberation my favorites were Turgenev's novels. By the time I was in the fifth grade of primary school, I had already read *A Nest of Gentle Folk*. I cried over the old German, Lundman, and loved Elena. Although Yenshelov does not write too well . . . his books do have a tone of freshness and emotionalism." He suddenly stood up and walked closer to Lin, leaned over on the back of the sofa and continued, "I still love to

read, and when I do, I am completely entranced. Then when I've finished I feel nothing. You know." He sat down next to Lin and half-closed his eyes. "When I read a good novel I dream of a pure, beautiful, transparent life. I wish I could become a sailor, or a white-coated researcher studying red blood cells, or a gardener. . . ." He smiled as Lin had never seen him smile before—not with his head but with his heart. "But as things are I have to take charge of the Organization Department." He spread his fingers.

"Why do you think there's such a difference between actual Party work and that in fiction? Is Party work not pure, beautiful, transparent?" Lin Chen asked in a friendly and concerned manner.

Liu Shih-wu shook his head several times, coughed, stood up again, and leaned a little further away. Sarcastically he said, "A Party worker really should not read novels. For example," he gestured in the air, "take Party recruitment: a novelist could write 'many new fighters entered into the front ranks of the proletariat in our great work, hurray!' But our Organization Department is plagued by worries; an organizational member of a certain branch is found to have neglected to perform his duty in a satisfactory manner and cannot even give a clear presentation of the historical background of a new recruit; over 100 applications are awaiting approval, but the Organization Department simply has no time to proceed with the processing of the cases; although approval of new recruits must be decided by members of the standing committee at a meeting, when they are told that a meeting will be held for this purpose, they ask for leave; the Public Security chief often falls asleep at meetings held to approve new members. . . ."

"You're wrong!" Lin Chen said loudly, finding this as hard to take as if being insulted himself. "It's very strange. . . ." He could not go on.

Liu Shih-wu laughed lightly and called Han Ch'ang-hsin. "Come on, look at this end game in the paper. Would it be better to move the rook or the knight first?"

IX

Wei Ho-ming told Lin Chen he wanted to return to the workshop as a worker. "I can't do this job of being the organizational member of the factory Party branch and the production chief."

Lin still tried to persuade him to write a report for the Party newspaper on the opinions he had collected. Moreover he chided him, "You're running away. Don't you have confidence in the Party and the State?"

After this, Wei Ho-ming and several of the workers with the strongest views wrote a long letter and secretively mailed it off to the paper. Even Wei had some misgivings: "Suppose this is again a 'factionalist' act? We will only be punished!" Feeling more than somewhat guilty, he shoved the letter into the mailbox.

In the middle of May, the *Peking Daily* published the letter from the masses exposing the bureaucratic work style of Wang Ch'ing-ch'uan under a sharp, clear headline. This letter over the signature "A group of workers at the Gunny Sack Factory" angrily demanded that those in authority settle this question. The editor of the *Peking Daily* pointed out in a note: "Authorities concerned should immediately check into the matter thoroughly. . . ."

Chao Hui-wen was the first one in the Organization Department to discover the item and called Lin Chen over to look at the paper. Lin was so excited his hand shook, and he looked for a long time before he could even compose a sentence. He thought, "Good, the matter is finally out in the open! Now the time is ripe."

He handed the paper over to Liu Shih-wu, who read it over carefully and then, shaking the pages, said, "Good! The surgery has begun!"

Party Secretary Chou Jun-hsiang walked into the office at just that moment. "Do you have all the information on the Wang Ch'ing-ch'uan case?" he asked.

Liu answered calmly, "There's no question but that certain unhealthy conditions have been existing in the Gunny Sack Factory's Party Branch. We've checked into this matter in the past, and I had a talk with Wang Ch'ing-ch'uan just recently. At the same time, young Comrade Lin has also made an investigation of it." He turned to Lin, "Comrade Lin, tell us your findings about this case."

Someone knocked at the door. Wei Ho-ming rushed in, his face not ruddy but pale, and said that Wang Ch'ing-ch'uan had become very angry after reading the *Peking Daily* and was trying to identify the writers of the letter.

With the publication of the case in the Party newspaper and the personal demand for a full report by the District Committee Secretary, Liu Shih-wu became a different person—a person of quick decision and drastic action. This thorough change in character caught Lin Chen by surprise. Once Liu

made a decision, he could work exceptionally well. He turned over all the rest of his work to other people and for several days went to the Gunny Sack Factory every day with Lin. He went into the workshop and thoroughly investigated everything about Wang Ch'ing-ch'uan and sought out the opinions of the workers. He next consulted all departments concerned in the case, and in a little over a week's time, the whole case of Wang Ch'ing-ch'uan had been cleared up: he was dismissed from his administrative position and from the Party.

The meeting in which Wang Ch'ing-ch'uan's case was discussed lasted until midnight. When it ended it was raining—sometimes hard, sometimes lightly, but continuously. The rain was cold on the face. Liu Shih-wu and Lin Chen went off to have some dumplings at a nearby restaurant which was a newly opened Joint State-Private Enterprise and both clean and comfortable. Because of the bad weather there were few customers and Liu and Lin were able to avoid the hot stove where the dumplings were boiling away in a pot, and sat down at a table in a corner.

They ordered meat dumplings and Liu asked for wine. He took a drink and then, counting on his fingers, said in an emotional voice, "This is the sixth time I've taken part in disciplinary action against responsible cadres who have committed mistakes. The first few times my heart was very heavy." Because he had spoken intensely at the meeting, his voice was rather hoarse. "Party workers are like doctors; their responsibility is to cure the diseases of others while remaining unaffected themselves." He tapped the table lightly with a finger. Lin Chen nodded in agreement.

"What day is today?" Liu Shih-wu asked suddenly.

"May 20th."

"May 20th, that's right. Nine years ago today I was shot in the leg by the 208th Division of the Youth Army."

"Hit in the leg?" Lin did not know much about Liu's background.

Liu Shih-wu did not say anything for a few minutes. He listened to the sound of the rain, which just then was coming down in sheets, and sniffed the damp air. A sopping wet boy dashed into the shop to avoid the rain, his hair dripping water. "Give me a dish of pork leg," Liu told the waiter. Turning to Lin, he continued. "In 1947 I was the chairman of the Self-Government Association at Peking University. When we joined the demonstration parade on

May 20th that year, the dogs of the 208th Division shot me in the leg." He rolled up his trouser leg and showed Lin an arc-shaped scar, then standing up, he said, "Isn't my left leg shorter than my right?"

Lin Chen looked at Liu for the first time with admiration and respect. Liu took a few drinks from his glass, his face turning slightly red, and sat down. He passed a few pieces of meat over to Lin Chen and then, leaning his head to one side, said, "At that time . . . how young and zealous I was! How I wish . . ."

"Aren't you young and zealous anymore?" Lin Chen probed.

"Of course I am." Liu Shih-wu toyed with his empty glass. "But I am so busy! So busy that everything has become common and wearisome. Since Liberation I haven't slept for eight full hours on one single night. I have to deal with this man and that, but I have no time to deal with myself." He leaned his cheek on his hand and looked at Lin Chen with an air of complete sincerity. "Yes, a Bolshevik must be rich in experience but pure in mind. . . . Another glass of wine!" Liu lifted up his glass and motioned to the waiter.

By this time Lin had already begun to be moved by Liu's deep and sincere confessions. Liu continued gloomily, "There's a saying that a common disease among cooks is that they have no appetite; they have to cook all day and are surrounded by nothing but dishes and meals. We Party workers have created a new life, but this new life is incapable of arousing us."

Lin Chen started to move his lips but Liu Shih-wu waved his hand to indicate he did not want to argue. He sat quietly, leaning on his chin and staring off at nothing. "The rain is easing off. It's very good for this year's wheat crop." Liu sighed heavily after a long pause. Suddenly he said, "You are a good cadre, better than Han Ch'ang-hsin."

Lin Chen in his confusion pretended to be busy with his food.

Liu Shih-wu stared at him for a while and, smiling good-naturedly, asked, "How has Chao Hui-wen been getting on lately?"

"Her state of mind seems fine," Lin said casually. He picked up a piece of meat with his chopsticks and saw Liu eying him with that familiar, flashing glance.

Pulling his chair closer to Lin Chen, Liu said

slowly, "Forgive me if I am too direct but I feel it is my duty to tell you . . . "

"What?" Lin held his chopsticks motionless in the air.

"As I see it, Chao Hui-wen's feelings toward you are not . . . "

Lin Chen laid down his chopsticks with a trembling hand.

By the time they walked out of the dumpling shop the rain had stopped. Stars reappeared from behind the clouds and the wind was even colder. The rain water ran in rills down the gullies on both sides of the street. Lin Chen ran back to the dormitory in a daze, feeling as if it had been he rather than Liu who had been drinking the wine. Everyone in the dormitory was fast asleep and the silence was broken only by the rising and falling sounds of snores. Lin Chen sat on the edge of his bed, felt the wet cuff of his pants, and became inexplicably sad. The beautiful, pale face of Chao Hui-wen floated before his eyes. He was only a callow, inexperienced, uninformed young man. Sad, sad . . . He went over to the window and laid his face against the wet, icy glass.

The members of the Standing Committee of the District Party Committee met to discuss the Gunny Sack Factory problem with Lin Chen participating as an observer. He sat in a corner, nervous, excited, his palms wet with cold sweat. In his pocket he had an outline of his planned several-thousand-word-long statement. He was prepared to move from the Gunny Sack Factory into problems in the Organization Department's work. He felt that the exposure and solution of the Factory problem had created an excellent opportunity to ask the leadership to evaluate the work of the Department. The time had come!

Liu Shih-wu was just in the process of a step-by-step, detailed report on the case. Secretary Chou Jun-hsiang sat in deep thought using his left fist to support his strong, broad soldier-like face. He held down a piece of paper with his right wrist and from time to time made a few notes. Li Tsung-ch'in was scribbling characters in the air with his forefinger. Han Ch'ang-hsin was also there and seemed to be concentrating on tying and untying his shoelaces. Several times Lin Chen wanted to speak but his heart throbbed so he could not catch his breath. He wondered whether making such a bold statement the first time he appeared at a Standing Committee meeting would be overly presumptuous. "Don't be afraid, don't be afraid," he encouraged himself. He thought of the time he had plunged into the water at school in Ch'ing-tao when he was eight. Then, too, his heart had pounded and he had angrily told himself, "Don't be afraid, don't be afraid!"

Liu Shih-wu's report was finally approved by the Standing Committee and a discussion of the next item on the agenda was about to be started when Lin Chen raised his hand.

"If you have anything to say, don't raise your hand, just go straight ahead and say it," Secretary Chou Jun-hsiang said, smiling.

Lin Chen stood up, causing his chair to squeak, took out his notebook, and looked at his outline. He did not dare to look at his audience. He said, "Wang Ch'ing-ch'uan as an individual has been dealt with. But how shall we guarantee that a second and third 'Wang Ch'ing-ch'uan' will not appear? We ought to take this opportunity to review the shortcomings of the District Committee's Organization Department. First, we have only grasped Party recruitment but have not given the attention necessary to consolidating the unity of the members at the lower levels in order to prevent internal conflict and aimless drifting. Second, we know there are problems that we've been putting off, trying to find solutions. Wang Ch'ing-ch'uan came to the factory a full five years ago. The problem existed from the very beginning and became more and more serious. . . . Specifically, I think both Comrades Han Ch'ang-hsin and Liu Shih-wu are responsible."

There was a momentary stir among those present. Some coughed, some put out their cigarettes, some opened their notebooks, others moved their chairs.

Han Ch'ang-hsin shrugged his shoulders, ran his tongue once around the rim of his teeth, and said scornfully, "We often hear these 'second-guessers': 'Why didn't we take care of it sooner?' Naturally the earlier the better. When the case of Kao Kang and Jao Shu-shih was made public, people asked, 'Why didn't we discover it earlier?' With Beria it was the same, 'Why didn't we discover it earlier?' Neither the Organization Department nor Comrade Lin Chen are in a position to guarantee that there will be no second or third 'Wang Ch'ing-ch'uan.'"

Lin raised his head and glared angrily at Han Ch'ang-hsin. Han only smiled coldly. Lin held his anger in check and said, "Old Han knows that a person is expected to have shortcomings but he does not

know that to progress by overcoming these shortcomings is even more proper. Old Han and Director Liu both recognize the first and so they adopt a tolerant and even indifferent attitude toward all kinds of important defects." Finishing, he used his hand to wipe the sweat off his forehead. He himself did not know how he had dared to speak so sharply, but, anyway, it had been said and he felt as if a heavy load had been lifted from him.

Li Tsung-ch'in stopped painting characters in the air with his forefinger. Chou Jun-hsiang looked at Lin Chen and then shifted his eyes over to the audience. The wooden chair on which he was sitting squeaked under his heavy body as he turned to Liu Shih-wu and asked, "Do you have any comment?"

Nodding his head, Liu Shih-wu said, "Comrade Lin Chen's views are correct. His spirit is an inspiration to us."

He walked leisurely over to the side of the table, poured a cup of tea, and rubbing the teacup meditatively, he said, "But coming to the Gunny Sack Factory case, it is a little more difficult to say. We admit we have not done enough to consolidate Party work. We have too few cadres. We are not even able to do the work of Party recruitment satisfactorily. But the disposition of the case of Wang Ch'ing-ch'uan was both timely and effective. The atmosphere at the meeting when the dismissal of Wang Ch'ing-ch'uan was announced was unprecedentedly exuberant. Some backward workers were made more aware of the Party's impartiality and unselfishness. One old worker broke into tears while he was speaking on the rostrum. Everyone spoke of their thanks to the Party and to the District Committee!"

Lin Chen said quietly, "Yes, it is just because of this that I feel that our indifference, procrastination, and irresponsibility in our work is a crime against the masses." He raised his voice higher. "The Party is the heart of the people and the working class. We do not permit dust in the heart; we cannot permit defects in the Party organs!"

Resting his clasped hands on his knees, Li Tsung-ch'in said deliberately, as if he were speaking and thinking how to construct his sentences at the same tim " "I believe there are two main bones of contention between Lin Chen on the one hand and Han Ch'ang-hsin and Liu Shih-wu on the other; one is the question of balancing principle and practicality, . . . the other . . ."

Lin Chen interrupted with surprising audacity and said, "I hope you will not only make a cold, general analysis . . ." He was afraid if he said any more he would burst into tears.

"Why?" Chou Jun-hsiang asked, then continued sternly, "A cold, general analysis is a lot better than impulsive and high-sounding words. Comrade, you get excited too easily. The organization work of the Party cannot be properly done by reciting lyrics." Turning to the audience, he said, "Let's go on to the next item on the agenda!"

After the meeting ended, Lin Chen was so furious he was unable to eat dinner. The Secretary's attitude was far from what he had expected, leaving him disheartened and discouraged. When Han Ch'ang-hsin and Liu Shih-wu asked Lin to take a walk with them, as if they had paid no attention to his dissatisfaction with them, he realized all the more clearly how inadequate his strength was to stand up to them. He smiled to himself bitterly and thought, "So you thought you would accomplish something great merely by speaking to the Standing Committee!" He opened his drawer and took out the Russian novel which Han Ch'ang-hsin had sneered at, opened up the first page and read printed there: "Live like Nastya!" He muttered to himself, "It's not easy!"

XI

After office hours the next day, Chao Hui-wen called out to him, "Come and have supper with me. I'll make dumplings for you." He wanted to decline but she had already gone.

Lin worried over the invitation for some time and ended up eating in the mess hall first and then going to her home. The meat dumplings were just ready when he arrived. For the first time Chao wore a dress, a dark red one with an apron tied around her waist. Her hands were covered with white flour and like a diligent housewife she told Lin, "I've put fresh beans in the dumplings. . . ."

Nervously, Lin Chen said, "I've already eaten."

Chao Hui-wen did not believe him and ran off to get him chopsticks. Lin repeated again that he had really eaten and she discontentedly ate by herself. Lin sat down to one side and looked here and there, rubbed his hands, shifted his seat. That same warm and painful feeling welled up inside him again. His heart ached as if something had been lost from it. He simply did not have the courage to look at her beautiful face, shining pinkly with the reflection of her dress.

"Little Lin, what's wrong?" Chao stopped eating.

"N-nothing."

"Tell me." She looked at him fixedly.

"I presented all my opinions at the Standing Committee meeting yesterday and the District Committee's Secretary didn't even notice them."

Chao chewed on a chopstick and thought a bit, finally saying firmly, "It cannot be so. Perhaps Comrade Chou Jun-hsiang just doesn't give his views lightly."

"Perhaps," Lin said, wanting to believe it but not quite able to. He lowered his head, not daring to meet Chao Hui-wen's concerned glance directly.

Chao ate a few more dumplings and then asked, "Anything else?"

Lin's heart beat wildly. He raised his head and saw her sympathetic and encouraging eyes. He said softly, "Comrade Chao Hui-wen . . ."

She put down her chopsticks and leaned against the back of the chair, a little surprised.

"I want to know if you're happy," he said in the firm, strong voice of a grown man. "I saw your tears that time in Liu Shih-wu's office. Then it was spring . . . and afterwards I forgot about it. I get by myself somehow and I do not know how to care about others. But are you happy?"

She looked at him rather doubtfully and then shook her head. "Sometimes I also forget. . . ." Then nodding her head she said, "Yes, I will. I will be happy. But why do you ask?" She smiled quietly.

Lin Chen told her about what Liu Shih-wu had said. "Please forgive me for telling you all this nonsense of Liu Shih-wu's. I really like to talk and listen to symphonies with you. You're wonderful, that goes without saying. . . . Maybe there are things here which are not nice, not proper. . . . I may have overlooked things. I am afraid that I have disturbed you," he apologetically concluded.

Chao Hui-wen smiled gently, frowned, then raised her thin arm and rubbed her forehead. She shook her head, as if shaking off some unpleasant thought, and turned around. She walked over to the wall and, halting in front of a new oil painting hanging there, looked at it silently. The subject was spring and showed the early spring sun shining brightly on a mother and her children in a Moscow street.

A moment later, she turned and quickly sat down

on the edge of her bed. With one hand holding the bedrail, she said very quietly, "What is this you're saying? Really! I couldn't do such thoughtless, inconsiderate things. I have a husband and a son. I haven't spoken to you of my husband yet, have I? We were married in 1952, when I was only nineteen, really too young to be married. He was demobilized from the army and became a Section Chief in a Central Ministry. Gradually he became infected by a kind of wild ambition. He fought over position, quarreled over salary, and was unable to get on with his fellow workers. We were only together from Saturday night to Monday morning. His theory is that either love is exalted or it's nothing. We quarreled . . . but I'm still waiting. He is off on a job in Shanghai now, but as soon as he comes back we will have a long talk. So what have you been talking about?

"Little Lin, you are my best friend, and I respect you very much. But you're still a child—perhaps it's not right to call you that. I'm sorry. We have both hoped for the same genuine sort of life; we both hope the Organization Department will become a true Party work organ. I feel as if you were my younger brother. You want to rouse me from my lethargy, don't you? Well, life ought to have the warmth of mutual help and friendship. I've always had an aversion for coldness. That's all there is. Is there any more? Can there be any more?"

Lin distractedly said, "I should not have been influenced by what Liu Shih-wu said."

"No." Chao Hui-wen shook her head. "Liu Shih-wu is a clever man. His warning was perhaps not entirely uncalled for, afterwards. . . ." She heaved a deep sigh and said, "That is that."

She collected the chopsticks and bowls and went out. Bewildered, Lin stood up and paced back and forth. He thought and thought . . . as if there were something else he had wanted to say, and then, it was gone. What did he want to say? Nothing had happened. Somethimes the current of some feeling flowed into one's life and both aroused and troubled one; then the current flowed out again leaving not a trace behind. But was there really no trace? There was left a pure and beautiful memory, faint but unforgettable.

Chao Hui-wen entered the room again bringing along her two-year-old son and carrying a briefcase. The boy had already met Lin Chen several times and affectionately greeted him as "wuncle"—he could not say "uncle" correctly. Lin Chen lifted him up in his strong arms, and the gray room was immediately filled with the sound of a child's laughter.

Chao opened the briefcase and took out a sheaf of papers. As she leafed through them, she said, "This evening I want to let you read a few things. I've already written a draft on some of the problems in the work of the Organization Department that I've seen in my three years here and some of my own opinions. This . . ." She embarrassedly touched a piece of drawing paper. "Probably this is funny. I've set up a competitive system for myself, measuring myself today against myself yesterday. I've made out a chart. If I make mistakes in my work—copy a name incorrectly in a notice of admission to the Party or make a mistake in adding the figures on new Party members—then I draw in a black cross on the chart. If I haven't made any mistakes, then I draw a red flag. If for a whole month there's nothing but red flags, then I buy a pretty scarf or something else as a reward for myself. Does this seem like a nursery game? Do you think it is funny?"

Lin listened carefully and then said gravely, "Not at all, I respect your . . ."

By the time Lin Chen got up to leave it was already very late. He stood outside the gate. Facing him at the gate, Chao spoke to him, her eyes shining in the dark. "It's a beautiful night, isn't it? Do you smell the fragrance of the pogoda tree? Those ordinary little white flowers are more delicate than peonies and stronger than plum blossoms. Do you smell them? Well, goodnight. Until early tomorrow morning when we meet again, when we both throw ourselves into our great but annoying work again. Afterwards, in the evening, look for me and we will listen to the beautiful 'Capriccio Italien.' Then I'll boil you some water chestnuts, and we will throw the peels on the floor until it's completely covered. . . ."

For a long time Lin stood leaning against the big pillar in the Organization Department courtyard, just staring, looking up at the night sky. The south wind of early summer brushed his face. When he had arrived it was the end of winter. Now it was early summer. He had passed his first spring in the District Committee.

Until now he had never thought he had any special feeling for Chao Hui-wen. She was only a friend, a big sister. But when he thought of her friendship, a warm and yet sad and guilty feeling welled up inside him. He really had not thought out why he had this feeling. But because of it and Liu Shih-wu's hints, he felt still more uneasy, that something unfortunate might happen. That was why he had made that frank confession to Chao Hui-wen. But when Chao also made the same kind of confession, when she said she still considered him an intimate friend, when she spoke of the need for warmth between people, when she described her plan for striving for self-improvement, her every movement and gesture, her animation made her seem dearer and a gush of real love, beyond anything he had dreamed of, welled up from deep within his heart! No! She had a husband. She could not love him, he must not love her. People were so complicated! All things were not, in Liu Shih-wu's phrase, "Just that way." No, they were certainly not "just that way." And just because things were not "just that way" each person had to deal seriously and conscientiously with everything and everyone in a straightforward manner. And because of this, if you saw something unreasonable, something which could not be tolerated, then it should not be tolerated and you should fight against it once, twice, three times, as long as was necessary to change it. Despair and gloom were of no use . . . and as for love, under the circumstances one must grit one's teeth and bury it deep in one's heart!

"I must become more active, more enthusiastic, but above all stronger. . . ." Saying these words to himself in a low voice, Lin Chen took a deep breath of the cool night air.

On the other side of a window he saw the green desk lamp and large profile of the late-working District Party Secretary. He firmly, impatiently knocked on the door of the Party leader's office.

80.

Developing Agricultural Production

Soon after the redistribution of land was accomplished during Land Reform, the socialization of agricultural production took place with the formation of collectives in 1956 and then their amalgamation into communes in 1958. Communes are large units encompassing from five to over fifty thousand people. As administrative units they combine agricultural, educational, commercial, and welfare functions. Communes are in turn divided into production brigades and work teams, which often correspond to old villages or neighborhoods. With the establishment of communes private ownership rights to land, tools, and draft animals were largely abolished. Except for the produce from small private plots, the income of a team is distributed to residents according to how many work points they earn based on the number of hours they work at tasks graded according to difficulty. The creation of communes coincided with Mao's ambitious effort to speed up industrialization through a "Great Leap Forward." Although most of the industrial projects soon had to be abandoned, communes survived.

Reorganizing the social and productive life of China's millions of peasants has been an enormous task, and it is not surprising that the government has had to shift priorities periodically and make persistent efforts to motivate both the administrators and the peasants to adopt the spirit necessary for the new system. Enthusiasm for collective enterprises flagged during the "three lean years" of 1961–1963, but was promoted again in the following years. Below is an article from a December, 1965, **People's Daily** *which describes some of the strategies followed by the cadres in one brigade in south China.*

POLITICS MUST BE RELIED UPON IN THE LAST ANALYSIS

by Huang Yu-ch'ing
Secretary, Party Branch, Yüan-feng
Production Brigade,
Huan-ch'eng Commune, Chung-shan County

The task of guiding and stimulating agricultural production cannot be accomplished through administrative orders, nor through material incentives. The correct way is to place politics in command and begin by making a good job of ideological and political work. A review of what has happened with our brigade over the last several years will prove that the development of production depends in the last analysis on politics.

In the period from 1960 through the first half of 1961, our brigade cadres did not step up ideological and political work and did nothing to heighten the masses' class consciousness and enthusiasm for production. Instead, they kept commune members in line through various kinds of systems such as deducting work points or launching criticisms at meetings. As a result, many commune members did not know for whom they labored and displayed no initiative toward collective production. When the cadres were with them, they grudgingly forced themselves to work; when the cadres left, they relaxed. Consequently, their efficiency was very low and the quality of their work poor.

In the second half of 1961 the brigade cadres tried to promote production by means of material incentives. For instance, in order to quicken the speed of transplanting, anyone transplanting an extra O.1 *mou* of land was given a reward of a duck's egg or twenty cents in cash. On the surface, it looked as though many commune members had become very energetic and the transplanting quotas were exceeded every day. Actually, the quality of work was very poor. Production was not properly carried out, and due to expenditures for rewards in cash and in kind, in the end less income was distributed to the commune members. Thus, it will not do to rely on systems alone, and material incentives do not work.

Beginning in 1963, the brigade cadres found themselves helpless. Following a policy of laissez-faire, they relaxed their leadership. The results in terms of production became even worse.

Then in 1965, after the socialist education movement began, our leadership nucleus was strengthened and ideological and political work stepped up. The Party branch of the brigade carefully armed all Party members and cadres with the thought of Mao Tsetung and organized youths and commune members to study the works of Chairman Mao, telling them the histories of individual villages and families as a part of their class education. After such study, many people raised their ideological consciousness and became more enthusiastic about production. Many commune members demanded that collective production be made successful, and set the pace by working energetically.

When the early crop was grown this year, as a prominent place was given to politics, the enthusiasm of the commune members was maximized. We achieved a harvest bigger than any ever seen before in history, with the average per *mou* output 549 catties. Every household paid its debts and still had a higher income than before. There was something set aside, too, for stepping up capital construction on the farms.

The experience and lessons I have gained over the past several years have made me realize that in promoting production it is imperative to place politics in command and to start by properly carrying out political work among all the people. Commandism*, coercion, and sole dependence on material incentives do not contribute to successful production.

---

* "Commandism" refers to the behavior of cadres who give orders without paying attention to the thoughts of the masses.

81.

The Correct Handling of Love, Marriage, and Family Problems

Like the ancient Legalists, the leaders of the Communist Party have seen the patriarchal family as an obstacle in the way of rational and efficient operation of the government and economy. Moreover, they inherited the sentiments of the late-nineteenth and early-twentieth-century reformers who saw the old family system as oppressive to youth and women. While changing family behavior has not been one of the highest priorities of Party leadership, they have given it attention periodically. Youth have been encouraged to place duty to the state before duty to their family. Women have been mobilized to work outside the home in the fields and factories. In 1950 a Marriage Reform Law was enacted, which prohibited involuntary marriages and established the right of divorce and the right of women to own property. The government also encouraged dating rather than marriages arranged by parents and tried to break down the customary sexual segregation of the countryside. It condemned early marriage on the grounds that it deflected the energies of youth from productive work and led to too high a birth rate.

While promoting change, the Party leadership also recognized dangers in undermining parental authority and weakening the sense of filial duty, since Chinese society remained too poor to afford separate housing for each young couple or a national system of pensions or health insurance. Sons were still expected to support their elderly parents, and one son generally lived with them. Thus, the government had to try to promote family institutions strong enough to provide basic welfare purposes but not so strong as to jeopardize the authority of new political units. Some of the difficulties this balance entails can be seen in the three selections below, drawn from a handbook published in 1964 for the use of rural cadres.

WHAT SHOULD ONE PAY ATTENTION TO WHEN HE FALLS IN LOVE?

We have already said that young men and women must have a correct point of view toward love when they fall in love. Here we shall talk a little about a few concrete problems to which one should attend when falling in love.

First, with regard to the problem of dating between young men and women, may young men and women date each other in public? Of course they may. So-called friends ought to be comrades in our socialist society. Sentiment between friends is lofty, and the relationship between one and the other is equal and cooperative, full of solidarity and love. Common ideals, common interests, common lives of labor and war have bound us together tightly and have created a brand-new comradely relationship between us. This sort of comradely relationship encourages us to progress, and it advances our solidarity. It is beneficial to socialist construction and at the same time makes our lives happier and more blissful. Under such circumstances, why shouldn't young men and women court each other publicly?

But in real life there are some people who always look askance at any relationship between a man and a woman. As soon as they see a man and a woman together, they are scandalized without looking into the true circumstances. They say this and that and make all kinds of criticisms to make people feel ashamed. There are also some people whose heads are full of ridiculous formulas. As soon as a young man and woman start to see each other often, they brand them for having an "improper style" and claim that "the relationship between the sexes is impure." Because of this, some young men and women become anxious. If they love someone, they don't dare declare their love. When they start courting, they hide here and there, not daring to see people, as if they had done something disgraceful. This is a problem worthy of our attention.

How should young men and women treat others' criticisms when they fall in love?

1. We must clear away the remnants of feudal ideology in our minds and treat the relationship between the sexes correctly. When we see a man and a woman talking together, we should not be greatly surprised. We should, moreover, not gossip or interfere with them. When a man and woman meet, they should be open-minded and not be suspicious of each other. If you love another person, you must give it serious consideration. After due consideration, if you want to propose, then propose. You need not suppress it in your heart and create suffering. If you and the other person build up a proper relationship and fall in love, even if you do encounter ridicule or interference from others, you need not feel troubled by it and may disregard it. You may also explain it to them and, if necessary, make observations on the situation to the party or the League in order to request support.

2. When they fall in love, young men and women must be particularly careful to balance well the relationship between love and work. They should not forget everything else when they fall in love, but should change love into a kind of motive power to encourage themselves to work, learn, and progress better.

3. In falling in love, one should never have improper sexual relationships as a result of temporary emotional impulses. This is immoral.

In sum, as long as we treat these problems seriously, others will not "gossip." Even if some people talk nonsense, we can still stand up to it. Facts always will prove that their opinions are wrong and our actions are honest.

Second, on the problem of "unrequited love."

"Unrequited love" means that the love relationship is broken.

We know that in love itself there exist two possibilities. One possibility is that it continues to develop and leads to marriage. The other possibility is that it breaks up midway, and the love relationship terminates. The process of falling in love is a process of mutual understanding and increasing friendship. After a considerable period of mutal understanding, if one side feels forced and proposes to break off the love relationship, this is normal and means that the love between the two has not matured. A proverb says, "The melon that is gathered by force is not sweet." Love is something that cannot be forced. If love is immature and thus the love relationship is broken off, it is not necessary to create trouble for oneself. But there are some young men and women who cannot treat this problem correctly. According to them, it seems that as soon as you fall in love you must get married. Otherwise you feel cheated. Because it is "unrequited love," it creates "the greatest suffering." One cannot eat or sleep; one feels dispirited at work and even loses interest in living. This is wrong in the extreme. One should have a correct attitude in dealing with "unrequited love." First, one should understand clearly his goals in life. If one has a lofty goal in life, then one's work, learning, and progress will not be affected by setbacks in love. Second, one should be philosophical. Since the other no longer loves you, you should not put something into it that is not there.

Third, on the problem of "fickleness in love."

"Fickleness in love" is a bourgeois conception of love. Its characteristic is: "Love the new and detest the old. The other hill seems higher than this one."[1] It manifests itself in changeability and untrustworthiness. One loves X today and Y tomorrow. It is a very flippant attitude. This is completely different from normal love. When a young couple feels lovingly toward each other and builds up a love relationship, they should respect each other and make their love develop and strengthen without cease. If in the process of falling in love one party feels that the love is strained and that the love relationship cannot indeed be maintained, then, based on a serious and cautious

[1] "The grass is always greener on the other side."

attitude and after conscious consideration, it is also quite normal that the love relationship be broken off. This is beneficial to oneself, to the other person, to one's future life, and to society. But "fickleness in love" is different. Its purpose is hedonistic enjoyment. When you enjoy each other, you are "in love." When you have had enough, then "take off." When you have the money, it is "love"; when the money is all used up, "take off." Responsible to no one, enjoyment is supreme and the individual comes first. These are deceitful acts of love and ought to be vigorously opposed.

Fourth, on the problem of matchmaking by family and relatives.

Some young people are introduced to their partners by family and relatives. Is this way of doing things good?

This should be analyzed concretely, for one cannot say whether it is good or bad in general. Generally speaking, it is best for young men and women to find their beloveds by themselves and to build up a love relationship through common labor and common struggle. Some people, due to limitations of various sorts, cannot help but ask others to introduce them to a partner. It is all right to do so. But if there is no mutal understanding or love toward the partner one is introduced to, then there should be a process of mutual understanding and building up of love. This process is absolutely essential. Some young people rely on the one-sided opinion of a matchmaker; they meet a few times and agree to get married right away. This way of doing things is too rash. We should say that one ought to have more contact with the person he is introduced to so as to learn to understand one another, but not rely on "love at first sight." If you hand over your "heart" after only one meeting, then it is not serious enough. "Love at first sight" often means you only see the superficial phenomena of the other's looks, clothes, manners etc., but cannot see the other's "real heart." Some young people often give away their hearts before they see the other's. How can this be reliable? Therefore, when you ask others to introduce a partner, if you yourself are not yet familiar with the other person, then, in addition to listening to the opinions of the person who makes the introduction, you should also listen to the opinions of people familiar with that person. More important, there must be a process of mutual understanding. This, too, is the process of falling in love.

We may see from the above problems that in the question of love and marriage there exists a struggle between new and old thinking. In order to deal correctly with the problems of love and marriage, we must oppose the remnants of feudal ideology and the ideology of the bourgeoisie. We must draw a clear boundary line with these two kinds of ideology and carry out a vigorous struggle. These, then, are the problems young men and women must pay attention to in the process of falling in love.

WHAT AGE IS BEST FOR MARRIAGE?

There is a proverb in our country: "When a man grows up, he should marry; when a woman grows up, she should wed." But how old is considered "grown up"? What age is suitable for marriage? In actual life, everyone has his own view.

In raising this problem, there will perhaps be someone who will say, "There is no necessity for asking. The Marriage Law stipulates that when a man is 20 and a woman is 18, they may marry. As long as they have reached these ages, it is appropriate to marry."

True, Article 4 of the Marriage Law states: "Only when a man is 20 years of age and a woman 18 may they marry." These are the legal ages for marriage. If a person has not reached the legal age, but gets married anyway, he commits an act contrary to the national law. Why does the Marriage Law have this kind of stipulation?

The regulations concerning the age of marriage in our Marriage Law stem from the degree of consciousness of the vast masses. The legal reason is opposition to the old society's system of early marriage. For several thousand years, the custom of early marriage had been widespread in China. Moreover, the reactionary ruling class of former generations made early marriage the law. Not until after Liberation and the establishment of the People's Government was opposition to the evil custom of early marriage raised and the regulation promulgated in the Marriage Law. But sweeping away evil customs that have been transmitted for several thousand years is not something we can accomplish in one morning. Therefore, when we regulated the age of marriage, we took the masses' level of consciousness into consideration. The age of marriage, as stipulated in the Marriage Law, is the minimum age of marriage. One must at least reach this age before he can marry. Therefore, the legal age of marriage of "20 for men and 18 for women" is not the most appropriate age for marriage. The most appropriate age for marriage is determined on the premise of obedience to the legal marriage age and according to such conditions as the physical development and the work, labor, study, and financial situation of both man and woman.

Then what age, after all, is more suitable for marriage? Generally speaking, marriage is more appropriate for men between 25 and 30, and for women between 23 and 28, for only at this age has a person's physical development completely matured, a certain degree of knowledge and skill been grasped, and economic life is self-reliant and the capability for an independent life is achieved. Although this age is several years more than the minimum age of marriage stipulated in the Marriage Law, there are many advantages to marriage at this time. The advantages are as follows:

First, it is advantageous for young people's political and ideological progress. The period of youth is a period when they study, progress, and accept the truth most quickly. It is the time for a man to secure political direction and a time when he initially establishes his philosophy of life. To marry at a later date will enable youth to have more energy for studying the works of Marxism-Leninism and of Chairman Mao, for attending to national events and collective tasks, and for having more energy for participation in class struggle, production struggle, and scientific experimentation. He can strengthen the exercise of and raise unceasingly the level of his ideological consciousness and political theory. If one marries too early, he will always be bothered by household affairs, and his political and ideological progress will be affected. After a long time, it may cause political backwardness.

Second, one can concentrate one's energies in study and work, build a good foundation, and make more contributions to socialist construction. We know that a person from the age of 20 to 30 has the most energy; the power of retention and understanding is likewise strongest. He is especially sensitive to new things and can accept new things and new knowledge comparatively faster. It is the golden time for study and for work. During this time, if one concentrates his energies on strengthening his political training and diligently learning skills well, he can then build a good foundation and contribute more of his power to the socialist construction of the fatherland. But if one gets married too early and has children, then the many household affairs will dissipate his energy and affect his study and his work.

It will be very difficult to make such a contribution to the state, nor will it be advantageous to one's individual progress.

Third, one can better manage the family's economic life and the relationship between husband and wife. During the period of youth, some young people are still studying and they are still not independent economically, and others are just beginning to participate in productive labor and work; their income still does not amount to much. To get married a few years later, when one has stronger political training and better work skills, when the financial income is greater and one can correctly handle problems, means that one is capable of handling the relationship between husband and wife well. When the family is harmonious, it is of benefit to production and to work. If one gets married too early, one will encounter much difficulty in arranging one's own life. Because one lacks the ability to lead an independent life, it may even lead to discord in the family.

Fourth, it is also beneficial to the physical development of both men and women, as well as to the education of the children. The period of youth is precisely a time for physical growth. A proverb says, "At twenty-two and three one leaps a little (i.e., grows in height); at twenty-four and five, one blows a little (i.e., grows in strength)." This has a bit of truth. The physiological characteristics of humankind, generally speaking, are that women from 12 to 14 and men from 14 to 16 begin to enter a period of puberty. Overall, development does not approach maturity until around 20, and only at about 25 does the body completely grow to maturity. To marry at a later age is beneficial to health, and to marry too early is harmful to health. At the same time, to marry too early often creates excessive births. It is harmful to health, to child rearing, and to the entire society as well.

To sum up, marriage should not be entered into too early. We youth, in considering the age of marriage, should consider several aspects of the issues mentioned above.

There are some young people who know that there are many advantages to late marriage, but have deep worries. For instance, some people worry that a late marriage will make delivery difficult and will affect reproduction. There are also some who worry that if they marry late, they won't find good prospects, etc., etc. These worries are all superfluous. In fact, late marriage will not have any effect on reproduction, nor will it make deliveries difficult. Many bedside experiences by medical experts have proven that the period between 20 and 40 is the time when man's reproductive faculty is most energetic. As far as chances for pregnancy and ease of delivery are concerned, there is no great difference (within this age span). The worry and fear that late marriage will lead to difficult delivery or to a slimmer chance of pregnancy is baseless. When we say this, there will perhaps be someone who will cite such-and-such an example of so-and-so who married after 30 and then had complications in delivery. But is this created by late marriage? No, it is not. There are many reasons for complications in delivery and for sterility. There are people who also suffer from complications in delivery and from sterility even though they were married at around the age of 20. Thus we cannot say that late marriage will necessarily lead to complications in delivery and to sterility. We must believe in science, but not in hearsay that has no scientific basis.

Some people are afraid that they cannot find a good prospect. This is an influence of the ideology of early marriage. Whether a young person—be it man or woman—can find an ideal partner or not does not depend on a few years' difference in age. The most important thing is one's political views, attitude toward labor, style of life, and quality of thought. If one's political views, attitudes toward labor, style of life, and quality of thinking are good, even if one is a little old, he can still find a good mate. Furthermore, if both young men and women start courtship and marriage a few years later, a new social trend will be formed. Then the concern and fear that when one is older he will not be able to find a good partner will also cease to exist.

We talked about the worries some people have about late marriages. Here we shall talk about the mistaken ideas of some people regarding late marriages.

Some people fear that if one gets married late, he wastes his youth. They say such things as, "A girl of 17 or 18 is a flower. If a man reaches 30 and a woman 24 or 25, they will waste their youth." They also say, "The golden age of a man's life is around 20. One should use this wonderful time to set up a small happy family as soon as possible." These sayings are either influenced by the early marriage ideology of feudal society or more or less reflect the philosophy of love of the bourgeoisie. This is very wrong. As was discussed earlier, we, the young people of new China, should have lofty purposes in life and farsighted ideals and ambitions. We should offer our precious youth to the great cause of socialist construction. We should relegate problems of love and marriage to second place. Only this kind of life is significant. Only in this way are we forever young and progressive from day to day.

Some people think that by getting married early one can benefit from children, but that if one marries late one cannot enjoy the benefits of children. They say, "By planting rice early, one harvests early. By getting a wife early, one enjoys happiness early." This is also the influence of thinking inherited from the old society. Now we are in a socialist society. If one uses that kind of old perspective in building the new society, it will no longer apply. For a young person of new China to continue to accept the influence of old thinking is truly disgraceful. From this we can see that to advocate marriage at an appropriate age is an urgent demand for young people. It is also a great event signifying the struggle between the new ideology and the remnants of feudal ideology and the ideology of the burgeoisie. It is a great event in the transformation of customs. Young friends, you should thoroughly break down the evil custom of early marriage and be the first to establish a new trend.

HOW SHOULD ONE TREAT ONE'S PARENTS?

Young men and women after marriage should respect and support the parents of both partners, and make their lives in their declining years happy and comfortable.

Respecting one's parents is a virtue of the laboring masses of our country. Under the cruel exploitative system of the old society, thousands upon thousands of good laborers were made homeless and destitute and unable to serve their parents. Only under the leadership of the Communist Party and Chairman Mao, when the three mountains of imperialism, feudalism, and bureaucratic capitalism were overturned and the socialist system established, was the wish of the people realized, namely, that "at old age there be refuge, in middle age there be employment, and in youth there be guidance, and that the widows and widowers, orphans, the childless, and the disabled all obtain support" [from *The Book of Rites*]. Young men living in this era of Mao Tse-tung should passionately love this age. In treating their parents, they should also create a new trend of respect for parents.

Some young people would like to evade this problem. As soon as someone mentions respect for one's parents, they feel that this is "stale feudalism" and they say such things as: "We are the youth of the new age. Why should we hang on to this feudal tail?" They regard respect for one's parents as a residue of feudalism, and this is a miscomprehension. We advocate that to respect one's parents and to make them feel the warmth and comfort of family life is a duty that all children should perform. It is also the new morality of the new society. This is completely different from the "filial piety" of which the feudal landlord class spoke.

Parents spend a great deal of time and energy in raising children. Generally speaking, as long as they are diligent laboring people, have made contributions to their children and to society, parents should be respected. One should especially respect those old people who have lost the ability to work. But there are some young people who look down on their parents and are displeased because they have "old-fashioned minds" and are "talkative." They cannot get along with their parents because of this, and they feel "hampered" by old people all day long: "not free," "not at ease." For the sake of convenience and to save trouble, they clamor about splitting up the family and leading their own lives. This kind of looking down on old people and not caring for them is obviously wrong.

Parents who lived in the old society for a long time were obviously influenced in their thinking by the old society. It is not surprising that they still have "old-fashioned minds." When parents are getting on in age, it is also inevitable that they will become repetitive in speech. At the same time, one should also make clear what the meaning of having "old-fashioned brains" really is. For instance, some parents advocate diligence and economy and oppose spendthriftiness. If one considers this "old-fashioned minds," it is wrong. "Talkativeness" also depends on what it is they are "talkative" about. If one has shortcomings and the parents continuously remind and teach one because of their love for their children, then this kind of "talkativeness" has its advantages. Even if it is supposed that parents do indeed have some conservative superstitions and "old-fashioned minds," one should still not treat them with a tough attitude, but should patiently tell them about new things and new rationales, and help them accept new things and new truths. Sometimes, if parents are "talkative" about trifling matters, when children

hear it, they don't have to argue. If what the old people say is correct, then they ought to obey; if what they say is incorrect, then they should explain it patiently. What is so difficult about that? Even if old people have some shortcomings, children should not use them as an excuse for not respecting their own parents. Even more, they should not attempt not to take care of the old, or clamor about splitting up the family, or desire quietness and comfort by themselves. For those who are married, if conditions allow them to live together with their parents, and the elders can always guide them, this should be considered a good thing. Why should one be afraid of being "controlled by old people" and become so "easily peeved"?

To support one's parents is an obligation that children should also feel. If some young people forget their parents after marriage, begrudging the fact that parents are old and bereft of ability, regarding support of their parents as an "extra burden," fearing that parents will take advantage of them and that they will themselves suffer losses, they will push out their parents and not take care of them. This kind of thinking and conduct is immoral and shameful.

Between parents and children there is no such thing as who suffers losses and who does not. To rear children is a duty parents should fulfill, and to support parents is also an obligation the children should fulfill. If one says that when children have the ability to work and when parents cannot work because of old age, children will regard supporting their own parents as suffering a loss, then what can one call this situation when in the beginning parents suffered hunger and cold in order to bring up their children, and when they become old their children refuse to support them? Some young people use "distribution in accord with one's labor" as an excuse to push out their own parents and not pay any attention to them; this is an illegal act. The Marriage Law of the People's Republic of China clearly stipulates that ". . . children have an obligation to support and aid their parents. Neither party should mistreat and desert the other." As young people of the new China, everyone should be a model of obedience to the national law. When we say "distribution in accord with labor" and "those who do not labor cannot eat," we refer to those people who can work but do not, and to those lazy people who like to enjoy themselves. This does not include those old people who have lost the ability to work. With respect to those old people who have lost the ability to work, even the state and society take care of them all the time. How can their own children evade the responsibility? If some people want to desert their parents, then they ought to think about it very carefully; when you yourself were young, did you also receive "distribution according to labor" when you ate or clothed yourself? And when you yourself become old and your children do not take care of you, how will you feel then?

To treat elders badly or to desert one's parents is not permitted by the law of the state. It is also a manifestation of the ideology of the bourgeoisie. We know that all exploiting classes are selfish and do not recognize any familial relationships. For the sake of personal enjoyment of life they could disregard all morality, even to the point of murdering one's parents for money. Now, if there are young people who do not support the old because they themselves want to live happily, such thought and conduct are unmentionable in public. It is apt to leave a bad taste among the masses.

Young men and women, after marriage, should respect and support their parents. They should also deal correctly with the problem of the influence of parents' thinking.

In our socialist society, the growth of young people depends chiefly on the Party's education. But parents' thinking also exerts an important influence on the younger generation. There are young people who still do not understand this clearly, especially young people who were born into families belonging to the exploiting class. Because they have, in varying degrees, been subject to the influence of the ideology of the exploiting class, some of them cannot draw a clear boundary line between themselves and their families. They think, "It has been so long since Liberation. My parents are not different from other commune members. Aren't they all eating rice in accord with work points?" Obviously, the perception of such young people is very blurred. They only see superficial phenomena, but do not understand that at present there still exist classes and class struggle in our country. They do not understand the complexity of class struggle. For instance, the overturned landlord class, which on the surface is very honest and obedient to the leadership and participates in labor, bears deep in their bones a bitter hatred for the laboring people. To transform these people into new men is not easy. If they only see some superficial phenomena, thinking that they have become "straight" by

participating in labor and relaxing their class vigilance, then we cannot supervise and transform them well, and sometimes this will even cause one to lose his own revolutionary standpoint. Therefore, young people who come from exploiting class families ought to rebel against the class into which they were born and walk the path of socialism. In treating one's parents, one should pay attention to drawing ideological boundaries clearly. One ought to use one's correct thought to influence them, but one should never let the exploiting class ideology of parents influence one's own thinking.

Some people may not be fully convinced by our arguments. They may say, "Class struggle is a social phenomenon. Why do we have to drag it into the relationship between parents and children? All parents under heaven love their children. How can they want to harm them? What you say may be too exaggerated."

No, it is not exaggerated at all. Indeed, parents in general all love their children, but love itself has its class nature. Different classes have different kinds of love for children. For example, some parents encourage their children to participate in productive labor, to constantly undergo training in the most difficult posts. This is true love. But for the exploiting class, this kind of love is regarded as harmful. They treat their children as their personal property and want them to obey their own wishes in doing things. They do not allow their children to receive revolutionary tempering. They tell their children to seek fame and profit, to indulge in enjoyments. If children do not obey them, they are considered "disobedient" and "without ambition." This kind of love, according to the proletariat, is poison to children. Therefore, whether parents' love for children is true love or not has to be determined through class analysis, but it cannot be generalized. Some young people say, "Dear Father and Dear Mother are not as dear as the Communist Party." This is really correct. To determine whether or not parents' love is true or false, we must see if their opinions accord with the Party's demands upon us. If they are in accord, then it is love. If not, then it is not love. It can even be harmful. On this problem, the most important thing is to rely on and listen to the Party. If one insists on this principle, one's head is clear; one knows right from wrong, and one will be able to deal well with the problems of the family.

82.

The Spring Festival

Ceremonies and festivals have always played an important role in shaping people's outlooks. Consequently, it is not surprising that the new government has introduced new holidays (especially October 1, the anniversary of the founding of the People's Republic in 1949) and has also made efforts to change religious beliefs and practices and even to alter secular elements of popular festivals.

Certainly the most important Chinese holdiay prior to 1949 was the lunar New Year. As seen in the following January, 1965, newspaper article, this celebration, now called the Spring Festival, did not lose all its former meaning or popularity. Nevertheless, the government was attempting to rid it of extravagance and of its more overtly religious elements. The past practice of lavish New Year's consumption fit in poorly with the government's admonitions to save and invest for China's future economic well-being. Later, during the Cultural Revolution, "feudal" Spring Festival activities were more harshly criticized.

HOW ONE CAN OBSERVE THE REVOLUTIONIZED SPRING FESTIVAL HAPPILY BY FREEING ONESELF FROM THE BONDAGE OF THE OLD IDEAS AND OUT-OF-DATE CUSTOMS

The Spring Festival is coming. It is an ancient festive occasion dating back to antiquity; therefore, a large number of old feudal and capitalist customs have been handed down with it. The people of Shanghai who are just now making big strides forward on the broad road of socialism are demanding to pass the socialist Spring Festival in a revolutionary spirit by promoting proletarian ideas, annihilating bourgeois beliefs, and reforming old customs. All of us did so at the Spring Festival last year, and we are making further preparations to do the same this year. However, some people who have been more rigidly bound by the old customs have some scruples and doubts about the problem of passing the Spring Festival with a revolutionary spirit, and so they

hesitate. Here are instances which we have encountered in our contact with the residents in some parts of Shanghai. In presenting these reports, we ask all of you to act as "staff officers" and discuss these questions in order to help these people find solutions to their worries and doubts and gain a correct view so that all of us may stride forward together. . . .

During the period of the Spring Festival, the first and most important of the superstitious activities is worshipping gods and ghosts and burning incense and joss paper. Such activities have decreased in number year by year through our efforts to publicize the problem and educate the people about it. For instance, on the day of the Spring Festival last year, the number of people going to the Old Temple of the City God to burn the first incense in the early morning decreased by seventy-three percent in comparison with the year before last. In Ching-an Ward, among the four resident groups of the Kang-chia-chiao Neighborhood Committee, sixty households worshipped gods and ghosts during the Spring Festival the year before last; only thirty of them did so last year. This year most of them have pledged not to conduct any more such superstitious activities. However, the problem remains that it is only "most of them" and not all of them. A few of these people still feel uneasy about giving up such worship. An old lady who has always worshipped gods and burned incense is told by others not to do so again and retorts, "Why shouldn't I? If I offend the gods, won't I invite unexpected misfortunes?" A retired old worker is also making preparations to offer a meal of sacrifice to his deceased wife, saying, "She suffered a miserable life in the old society; I will offer a good meal to her so that she may share with us the happiness of the new society."

All the instances cited above are cases of people who have always believed in the presence of ghosts and gods. There are also people who followed the masses last year in doing away with superstitious activities at the Spring Festival, but now are beginning to think again about the gods and ghosts. On Wan-chun Street off Wan-hang-tu Road lives an old lady by the name of Chu who in past years would invariably go to the temple to burn incense every festival. Last year, she was educated during the Spring Festival season and pledged never to engage in superstitious activities again. On the eve of the last New Year, she accompanied her old husband to visit the "Great World" amusement park for pleasure. However, it so happened that as they were returning home from the park she stumbled and fell. Later, her daughter had a prolonged illness. Therefore, the old lady began to worry and told people that the Buddha was angry because she had not offered sacrifices to the gods and the Buddha. Now she is thinking about going to the temple to burn incense again.

Naturally, there are only a small number of people like this old lady Chu who will go back to their old practice of engaging in superstitious activities. Most people are raising their consciousness step by step and doing away with the incense and joss paper. But, why should they do away with them? And, how can they do away with them? There are different views on this problem. The following situation occurred in the residential sections of Yang-pu and Cha-pei Wards on the festival evening of the Winter Solstice. Some families offered meals for sacrifice and burned joss money to their ghosts while murmuring: "Ghosts of our ancestors, please come and eat your fill! From now on, we will not offer meals for sacrifice or burn joss money to you anymore. We will

not burn incense or repeat the name of Buddha. It's not that we don't want to do so, but that at present all the people are eliminating superstition. Buddha and all our ancestors, please forgive us and don't be angry with us. We have also heard that one of the families prayed while performing the ceremony of "sending off the God of the Kitchen to Heaven": "You, Sir, God of our Kitchen, you have worked hard during the year. You are also getting old and should have retired by now. Furthermore, all the people are eliminating superstition, so we don't dare receive you back again. . . ." According to our information, this year during the Spring Festival, there are still some people who are going to hold "farewell dinners" for the "gods and ghosts." They are doing everything possible to get permission to prepare a final sacrificial meal to say "good-bye" to them.

In handling the above-mentioned cases, we have seen people using persuasion and scientific propaganda. However, some people are still coexisting peacefully with superstitious thinking though they do not believe in gods and ghosts themselves. In Ching-an Ward, members of the family of an actor burn incense all day long and repeat the name of Buddha without interruption. People always see the smoke coming out from his house and hear a voice chanting "Nan-wu-ah-mi-tu-fu . . ." inside. An old lady in his family is engaging in superstitious activity. The cadres of his neighborhood committee have criticized him, saying that he was propagandizing on the stage to reform old customs and eliminate superstition but allowed his family to set up a shrine of the Goddess of Mercy at home. They wanted him to change old customs and habits at home as well. The actor replied, "I don't believe in such things myself. My old mother wants to do them, and I can't do anything about it." As a matter of fact, he was afraid of stirring up "family troubles."

During the period of the Spring Festival, feudal superstition is expressed mainly by worshipping gods and offering sacrifices to ghosts. In addition, it is manifested in various fields of daily life. For instance, when people make rounds of New Year visits, they always use euphemistic expressions. They drink tea of "treasure," and eat "sweet in heart" candies and "up step by step" or "being promoted continuously" sugarcanes. On New Year's Eve, people are not supposed to wash their clothes; and on the first day of the first moon, they should not sweep the floor or use cutlery, and small children should not cry, etc. Though most of these old customs have been changed or eliminated, there are still people who cannot give them up. They are doing their best to keep a stock of sugarcanes, olives, oranges and other things to be able to go "up step by step" and find the "treasure." When others try to dissuade them, they argue, "These are small matters. Why do you bother me about so many things?"

In addition to superstitious activities, people also pay New Year visits and express good will during the Spring Festival. Can good will have a class basis? How should one handle the good will? These are problems which deserve our discussion.

Good will is mainly expressed by paying visits to relatives and friends, so the first problem to be taken into consideration is the kind of relatives and friends we should pay visits to during the festival. Many people take the opportunity to visit their class brothers and comfort those among their relatives and friends who are dependents of martyrs and soldiers, sick and old people, and those with various difficulties. This is very commendable. However, some people are confused in their thinking about the line demarcating classes; they are ready to express their good will to class antagonists and exploiters, paying them New Year visits and offering them greetings.

When we visit our relatives and friends, can we express our real good will by carrying something with us? We have seen that many people are ready to carry the new socialist style with them on such visits. However, there are also a good number of people who are getting ready to take presents to make a show of their bourgeois extravagance. Some of them say, "This year the market has almost everything for sale. If we don't give gifts, people will call us stingy." Others say, "If we visit our relatives and carry nothing with us, the elders will think we do not know the customary rules. For instance, my sister took several pieces of fruit along when she paid a visit to a certain relative. If when I visit this relative, I take nothing, I will feel ashamed of myself and the neighbors will gossip about me. That will be most embarrassing." Furthermore, some people are standing at the crossroad. They think that it is not only vulgar but also extravagant to give away too many presents, but they also think that they cannot but "follow the custom." They are waiting for the new style of the society to push them ahead with a gust of favorable wind.

Besides paying visits to relatives and friends and giving away presents during the New Year Festival, people also want to hold "family gatherings." Here is

one such incident. Recently a woman called at a certain government department to make a request to get her son back home from Sinkiang where he was working in support of construction so that they could have a New Year "family gathering." The comrade in charge told her that insisting on holding a New Year's Eve dinner with the whole family gathered together was a reflection of her narrow-minded views about the family and an example of an old custom. Today, all of us should advocate the great gathering together of the people of the whole nation and advocate that good children should cherish the hope of going to distant places. Those two had been separated for only about one year, so it was not necessary for the son to rush back home for a family gathering from a place thousands of *li* away. Instead, the woman should be encouraging her son to study energetically and train himself in the skills needed for the construction of the fatherland. This woman felt rather "sorry" for herself and thought that she was passing the festival this year well in all respects except for missing her son. Comrade readers, please help her comprehend: what is her "feeling" for her son? Is she right or not?

Furthermore, some parents are making all sorts of preparations to amuse their children with food and drinks, new clothes and games. Some of them have made several suits of new clothes; others have saved twenty or thirty dollars for year-end "lucky money" for their children. It used to be claimed that without doing these things, parents could not express their "love for their children" or enable their children to enjoy the holiday. Some parents said, "When we were young, we were so poor that we could not even have a good meal. Now, our life has improved; we should let our small children eat their fill and dress themselves nicely." As in the above case, what is this "feeling" for their children? Do we want such "feeling"?

Another problem concerns diligence and praticing economy. On festivals and New Year's days, especially on such popular traditional festivals as the Spring Festival, it is permissible and also normal for us to improve our standards of living in suitable degrees and serve better dishes than on ordinary days, so long as we do not indulge in lavish feasts. However, from some instances which we have learned about, it may be seen that extravagance is reemerging. Under the Shih-ying Neighborhood Committee, a small property owner recently bought nearly 200 dollars worth of pork. In the Chin-lin East Road section of Huang-pu Ward, someone has bought the pork of two and a half pigs. Under the Kang-chia-chiao Neighborhood Committee, a worker, his wife, and three children have withdrawn all their money from four recently matured monthly savings accounts. The worker intends to spend all his savings plus his wife's annual bonus from her factory job during the Spring Festival. On Nan-yang Road, a worker heard some time ago that the price of pork had dropped, so he borrowed twenty-four dollars from the mutual aid funds with the intention of buying pork to celebrate the Spring Festival. In some parts of Shanghai, the residents are busily getting ready to make huge purchases of "New Year goods." Some households on the Wei-hai-wei Road are making preparations to hold New Year's Eve dinner parties. They say, "This year, the situation is very good; the market is full of supplies. Our relatives will come together, and we all must enjoy a very good dinner." When other people advised them to spend less money, they replied, "It's money we saved. We will buy things to feed ourselves and make us grow and will waste nothing. Mind your own business." Under such influence, some people who have less money begin to imitate; though at first they wanted to be thrifty, when they see what others are doing they feel pressed by the "situation." In Ju-ho Lane along Peking East Road, a woman complained: "I saw other people making preparations to spend several hundred dollars for the festival. What am I going to do for myself?"

Apart from all the problems mentioned above, there are many other aspects of the Spring Festival which concern the movement to reform old customs and habits. For instance, with respect to amusements and social gatherings, some people think about playing mahjong in their homes or dormitories. They give as their "reason" that this is good "fun" and is no concern of others. They say, "It's New Year time, and we play only for small stakes. . . ."

Mentioned above are some thoughts and problems of the residents in Shanghai with respect to the movement to observe the revolutionized Spring Festival in a proper manner. We should point out that they are, on the one hand, not the most important thoughts and problems of the masses of people at the present time, and, on the other hand, not a full reflection of all the concrete thoughts and problems among the local residents. Our purpose in making these reports is to invite all of you to discuss this matter and to give you something to aim at so that we may further publicize the significance of revolutionizing the Spring Festival. Dear readers, having read the above reports, please express your opinions on these problems from the materialist-scientific viewpoint, from the proletarian class viewpoint, and from the socialist-communist viewpoint.

83.

Lei Feng, Chairman Mao's Good Fighter

In traditional China, tales of individuals who exemplified extremely virtuous or self-sacrificing behavior formed a regular part of moral education. Young people were instructed in the tales of filial sons and steadfast women; adults enjoyed stories and plays in which characters were either paragons of virtue or of evil. In contemporary China this method of moral instruction has continued, albeit with significant changes in the characteristics of the people to be admired.

Of the many men and women held up for emulation in the last three decades, the one who has become best known undoubtedly is Lei Feng (1939–1962). After his death in a trucking accident, there were repeated campaigns to "learn from Lei Feng." He was born into a poor peasant family in Hunan, and his childhood was a series of tragedies. When he was five, his father died, having been pressed into service as a coolie by the Japanese army. The next year his elder brother, a child laborer in a factory, died of tuberculosis. Then his younger brother perished from typhoid fever and malnutrition. His mother took a job as a servant, but hanged herself after being raped by her employer, leaving Lei Feng an orphan at the age of eight. The bitterness of Lei Feng's past intensified his enthusiasm for the social reforms introduced in the People's Republic. As a worker and soldier he was exemplary in his adherence to revolutionary attitudes and spartan living, qualities China's leaders have encouraged for their value in combating selfishness and promoting industrialization.

The following anecdotes about Lei Feng's sincerity, devotion, and good deeds come from a biography published in 1968.

When Lei Feng finished his studies in the senior primary school in 1956, a nation-wide movement of agricultural collectivization was surging forward like a spring tide, and the industrialization of the country was being pushed forward on a large scale. Life with all its richness was beckoning to every young person, and many took up jobs in industry and agriculture after they left school. Like a fledgling bird Lei Feng was anxious to try his wings, so he took a job as a messenger in the local authority offices, dispatching letters and notices and helping to compile statistics, charts, and forms. Whenever there was some work which he thought he could do, he would always

volunteer to do it, so everyone was pleased with his work and attitude.

Later, at the age of seventeen, Lei Feng was transferred to work in the Party committee office of Wang-cheng county, where he began a new life. During the day he worked hard and in the evening he attended a spare-time middle school run by the county government. "The Party has rescued me from the depths of misery and enabled me to lead such a comfortable life," he often thought to himself. "How shall I repay its kindness?" He provided the answer by the excellent way he worked—taking good care of public property and making himself a driving force in the office for the sale of government bonds. It was not surprising that his comrades later cited him as a model worker.

Lei Feng worked under Chang, Secretary of the County Party Committee, a friendly and kind man to whom he became very attached. He dispatched letters and documents for Chang and made sure to be by his side whenever needed in the countryside or at a meeting. When Chang worked late into the night, Lei Feng would see he had everything he needed, such as hot water and tea. Although the Secretary was very busy, he always tried to find time to tell Lei Feng revolutionary stories about the armed uprising against the counterrevolution of Chiang Kai-shek launched by the Chinese Communist Party in Nanch'ang, Kiangsi on August 1, 1927, about the struggle waged by Chairman Mao in establishing the revolutionary base in the Ching-kang Mountains, as well as episodes of the Red Army's Long March and the War of Resistance against Japan. In a story about the Autumn Harvest Uprising led by Chairman Mao in Hunan, he described how a Party member was arrested during a fight, how he was tortured cruelly by the enemy but refused to yield, preferring death to submission. When Lei Feng heard this he exclaimed, "That's the kind of man I want to be!"

"Very good," said Secretary Chang, "then work well, study hard, and try to become a member of the Youth League and Communist Party. Remember, always try to make greater contributions to the cause of revolution."

Lei Feng remembered every one of Secretary Chang's words. He made a special point of trying to learn from his comrades in the County Party Committee. Once when he accompanied Chang to a meeting, he saw a screw lying on the road. Thinking it a useless thing, he kicked it away. When Chang turned round and saw what he had done, without saying a word he bent down, picked it up and put it in his pocket. Lei Feng was surprised. "What does a Party Secretary want with a screw?" he wondered. Several days later Lei Feng was about to send a letter to an agricultural machinery plant when Chang handed him the screw and told him to send it to the workers there. "Ours is a poor country," he said. "We have to work hard to build it up. A screw is a small thing but a machine can't work if it is missing one. Remember, drops of water go to make a stream and grains of rice fill a bin." Lei Feng stared at the Secretary with wide-open eyes. From that time on he

never squandered a single cent and deposited all his savings in the bank.

Secretary Chang helped Lei Feng not only with his day-to-day problems but also with his political studies and ideological remolding, enabling him to raise his class consciousness steadily. They became very close, and Lei Feng always felt happy and content in working with Chang, no matter how difficult or exhausting a job he was given. In fact, he seemed to develop inexhaustible energy and could stay up night after night without feeling tired.

The warmth of brotherhood, the deep class love of his comrades, often made Lei Feng compare his present life with the bitterness of his past. Whenever he thought of his mother, he felt a stab of pain and hot tears would roll down his cheeks. Once Secretary Chang saw Lei Feng sitting alone crying. "What's the matter?" he asked. Then taking out a handkerchief and handing it to him he said, "Don't cry. Take this and wipe your eyes."

"All right," Lei Feng sobbed.

Chang paused. Then he took Lei Feng's hand and stroked his head, saying, "It's good to think a lot about the past. You mustn't forget it. A revolutionary should draw strength from his past sufferings and let them spur him on to do better work for the revolution." With tearful eyes Lei Feng gazed at the Secretary, stirred by every one of his words.

Pointing to the scar on the back of Lei Feng's hand, Chang continued, "The sufferings you've gone through are the sufferings of the proletariat and the sufferings of the Chinese people. Your present happy life has been given by the Party and Chairman Mao and is the product of the blood shed by countless revolutionary martyrs. You're still a young man. You must study harder and harder, because in the future you'll be asked to do many, many things for the revolution. . . ."

From then on Lei Feng made even bigger strides in his work and studies, and when he became a member of the Communist Youth League on February 8, 1957, he felt greatly honored. . . .

December 3, 1959, after the yearly conscription began, the secretary of the general Party branch made a recruitment speech. Afterwards Lei Feng went back to his room, excited and a little nervous. As the hours ticked into the night sleep still eluded him. Thoughts of the early days after Liberation when he had tried to get into the People's Liberation Army flooded back into his mind. At that time he was only a little boy and the army had refused to take him, but now that he was an adult they would have no grounds to turn him down, especially as he wanted so much to help actively defend the motherland. Then he thought of the newly set-up plant which would soon begin production and be of so much use to the nation. Should he desert it now? Finally he came to a decision. "I used to be a poor orphan, but now I'm a master of my country. If I don't join up, who will?"

It was snowing. Registration was to start at eight the next morning, but Lei Feng was so agitated that he felt he could not possibly wait. He had learned that the man in charge of registration, Secretary Li of the general Youth League branch, was on duty in the office attached to the workshop; so he got up at three in the morning, scrambled into his clothes and hurried off to the office, determined to be the first one to register. When Li opened the door he said with an understanding smile, "Why aren't you in bed at this time of the night?"

"Secretary Li, I want to register for enlistment," Lei Feng replied.

"You . . . well, you'd better put more clothes on first. If you catch cold you'll be unable to carry a rifle." Li then disappeared into the office, picked up a padded coat from his bed and put it around him. Then he asked him to sit on his bed and tell him why he wanted to enlist. If Lei Feng had been prepared for the question he would have been able to rattle off a number of sound reasons, but Li's sudden and completely unexpected query caught him so much unawares that he just did not seem to know how to answer it. "I was a poor boy in the old society," he fumbled, "and I have suffered a lot. After Liberation I began to enjoy a really happy life, but it didn't come easily. Anyone who leads a happy life after suffering for so long would want to defend it. That's only natural."

Li thought about his request for a few moments and said, "You're right—very right—to want to defend the motherland. But, you know, you're not all that tall, and not very strong either. I'm not really sure whether you'll be able to pass the physical examination."

Sensing that Li was unofficially supporting his request, Lei Feng pressed him still further. "Secretary Li, can I say I've got your approval?" Li smiled as Lei Feng continued, "If I get the plant's approval I won't be afraid of any examination. In any case, a small man makes a nimble fighter, you know." As Lei Feng wrote "I want to join the army" in the register, he could not help thinking of the bitterness of his past. . . .

After the physical tests had been given at the plant, four workers were notified that they had passed—but Lei Feng was not among them. He did not know he had been turned down by the doctors until a few days later when the leading cadres at the plant gave a special send-off meal for the four who had passed the tests. When he realized his position, he was stunned. Bitterly disappointed, he made straight for Li and furiously demanded, "Why is my name not on the list? Tell me, why?"

Li pointed to a chair and asked Lei Feng to sit down. "You know, lots of people have registered, and it's impossible to accept every one of them. Because of your physical handicaps we could not approve your enlistment. But don't be upset. If you stay at the plant you can make equally important contributions to the country's socialist construction. . . ."

Interrupting him, an impatient Lei Feng implored, "I want to enlist, and I have the right to enlist. Please contact the people in charge of conscription again and speak on my behalf."

Li was embarrassed. He knew that it was not only Lei Feng's duty but also his right to enlist. However, as the list of conscripts had already been decided on, it was too late to make any alterations. Then what could he do? Pondering the matter, he promised that he would contact the drafting center in Liao-yang to see if anything could be done. Lei Feng felt relieved.

Later that day Li asked Lei Feng to have a meal with him and the four men just before they were due to go to Liao-yang for a final general examination. When Lei Feng saw how pleased and excited the four men were, he became depressed. He just sat and picked at the food without any appetite. After the meal he returned to his room and sat on the bed where an irritating thought crossed his mind. What would he do if the drafting center refused to accept him? Would it not be better if he went there himself and made a personal request to enlist? The next day he told his superiors he wanted leave to go to the center.

When he arrived at the drafting center in Liao-yang he was received by the Deputy Political Commissar, named Yu. After he had explained why he wanted to enlist, he said, "Imperialism still exists in the world and class enemies within our country are always trying to stage a comeback. Whenever I think of this I feel I must take up arms and defend the motherland."

Yu was pleased with this energetic, outspoken young man. But running his eye over Lei Feng he knew he was probably not up to the required standard. After a pause he said, "You'd better have a check-up first." Yu's words filled Lei Feng with a tremendous relief, dispelling his dejected mood. His face brightened up instantly. He was so happy, in fact, he did not know what to say, and his eyes sparkled with joy.

Lei Feng returned to the plant and took additional leave to go to the medical center, where he saw youngsters from various places, all of whom had come for a physical examination. He noticed that they were all much taller and bigger, and he began to feel rather nervous, afraid that he might fail the examination. Still he refused to let himself get downhearted even though he was as much as a head shorter than the others. When his height was being measured he secretly stood on tiptoe, but the doctor spotted him and said, "No point trying to fool me, comrade!" Then he patted Lei Feng on the shoulder and told him to stand properly. Seconds later he had taken his measurement and was calling out, "Height: 1.54 meters."

Lei Feng looked up at the doctor, a worried gleam in his eyes. "I know I'm small but I'm a bulldozer driver, you know," he told him. "Just look at my muscles—I'm really strong." The doctor smiled and said nothing, continuing the examination.

When it was Lei Feng's turn to stand on the scale he pressed down with all his strength but they only registered forty-seven kilograms. The doctor shook his head and murmured, "Ah, less than fifty kilograms.!"

"But I came without my breakfast," Lei Feng explained. "If I'd had a heavy meal, I'm sure I'd have reached the mark."

"Can a meal increase your weight by three kilograms?" asked the doctor, trying to suppress a smile. Finally he said, "Your height may pass the lowest requirement but your weight cannot."

Lei Feng was dumbfounded. Then as the doctor was writing down his weight on the form, he implored him, "Doctor, please make it fifty. I pledge to make up for it afterwards. If enlisted, I'll do my best to improve my physique through physical exercises." He hoped against hope that the doctor would comply

with his request, but in reality he knew that it could not be.

His troubles did not end there, for the next examination by the surgeon revealed that Lei Feng's breathing was affected by a deformed bone in his nose. Lei Feng grew more dispirited. After he had taken off his clothes for a body checkup, the surgeon noticed a scar on his back and asked how he got it. Lei Feng became misty-eyed as he explained. "Doctor," he said, "this scar stands witness to all the wrongs I suffered in the old society. It's because I want to make sure the people will not suffer this kind of wrong again that I decided to join the army."

The surgeon sympathized with him and realized how badly he wanted to join the army, but he could do nothing to help him for he was obviously below the army's standard. Yet he felt he could not simply turn him down outright, so he suggested, "Perhaps the best thing is for you to explain everything to the leaders of the drafting center; maybe they could make an exception in your case."

Taking his advice, Lei Feng hurried off to the drafting center. Making his case to an officer in charge of conscription, he begged, "Please, let me join the army."

"We know all about your case," replied the officer rather stiffly, "but we can only enlist recruits if they're fit. Since you're not qualified, there's no point in going on about enlisting. People should work for the construction or defense of the motherland according to their respective ability."

"Do you mean I can't join up?" Lei Feng cried. "Oh, comrade, please help me. Special consideration should be given to special cases. Although I'm not up to the mark, I'm sure I'll make a good soldier." The officer now found himself moved by Lei Feng's obviously sincere plea. No, he could not just send him away without any hope at all. "I'll tell you what," he said in an encouraging tone, "why don't you go back and wait for our notification?"

Hearing this, Lei Feng immediately thought that he had been approved. Approved! He wanted to skip with joy. "All right," he beamed. "I'll go back to the plant and wait. But you must notify me as soon as possible." The officer smiled.

Back in the plant Lei Feng found that time dragged by. After two days without news he could wait no longer. Determined to enlist he asked those in charge for some more leave and began to pack. Some clothes for which he had no immediate use he gave to

Uncle Lu. He packed three volumes of Chairman Mao's works, several notebooks containing his diary, and a few everyday things. Carrying his suitcase, he went to the drafting center again. As soon as he saw the officer in charge of conscription he said, "I've come to report for duty."

The nonplussed officer looked him in the eye. "We've studied your case and still can't solve it," he told him. "What have you brought your luggage for? What will you do if you can't enlist?"

"Why, I thought everything had been settled," Lei Feng said rather uneasily. "You know I'm really in earnest about joining the army!"

"Comrade, we know that," the officer said. "But your physical condition isn't up to standard and we can't send a young man like you to the officer who signs on recruits."

"Please tell me who he is."

"Battalion Commander Ching."

"I'll go and see him then."

Lei Feng rushed straight to Commander Ching's office and explained why he had come. Then quite spontaneously he found himself pouring out all the wrongs he had suffered in the old society and weeping as he did so. The Commander was so moved by his story that tears trickled down his face. Yu, the Deputy Political Commissar of the drafting center, had already spoken to the Commander about Lei Feng and suggested special consideration be given to his request. Now as he heard the young man's story he agreed that something should be done for him. He told Lei Feng to wait for a moment in his office and went off to discuss the case with Yu. Soon the matter was settled—Lei Feng would be accepted as a recruit. . . .

In 1958 Lei Feng had begun to study Chairman Mao's writings regularly. He had made it a rule to study one hour every morning and in the evenings up to ten or eleven o'clock. Every spare moment at work in the coal yard of the An-shan Iron and Steel Company he would study Mao's *Selected Works*. After joining the army he had managed to complete volume three while boiling water for the amateur cultural troupe. Then the army leadership called on the men to "study Chairman Mao's works, follow his teachings, act in accordance with his instructions, and be his good soldiers." Lei Feng took this call to heart and wrote it down on the front covers of his copies of Chairman Mao's works. But where the authorities had asked the men to "study Chairman Mao's works," he added "every day" so that he would study them more diligently. Lei Feng's job as a driver often took him to various places, but wherever he went he always carried a satchel containing different essays by Chairman Mao, which he read at every opportunity. Soon his comrades described his satchel as a "mobile library."

About this time one of his comrades grumbled, "There's so much work to do we haven't got enough time for our personal affairs or even rest." Lei Feng did not agree, and to encourage himself to work and study even harder he wrote this passage in his diary, which he remembered from a book he had once read:

How do you put a screw into a piece of wood which is perfectly smooth and has no holes? You use force and screw it in. Then just as a screw has to be forced and screwed in, so when you study you should bore firmly into the subject.

It was with this spirit that Lei Feng was able to complete Chairman Mao's *Selected Works*, from volume one to four. Among the many essays he read over and over were: "In Memory of Norman Bethune," "Serve the People," "Carry the Revolution Through to the End," "On Practice," and "On Contradiction." Some of the volumes were so worn that the edges of the pages were tattered and frayed, but he still kept reading them over and over again, and every time he read them he got something new out of them. As he read the essays he marked them in all kinds of ways, with lines and dots, with blue ink, and with red and blue pencil. He also made brief notes interpreting various passages. Once he came to this passage in the essay "Rectify the Party's Style of Work": "Every Party member, every branch of work, every statement, and every action must proceed from the interests of the whole Party; it is absolutely prohibited to violate this principle." He underlined this passage heavily with a red pencil and wrote in the margin: "Take this to heart!"

Lei Feng found an inexhaustible source of strength and wisdom in Chairman Mao's works, and he gradually came to understand the meaning of life, of revolution, and of the laws of social development. He learned how to treat one's enemy and one's comrades, and what attitude one should take toward work. He felt he could see things more and more clearly, that his vision of life was broadening, and that a big new world was opening up before him. Following the teachings of Chairman Mao, Lei Feng gradually became a dedicated proletarian fighter. This is what he wrote in his diary:

> After having studied volumes one, two, three, and four of the *Selected Works*, I feel most deeply that I know how to be a man and the purpose of my life. . . . I think one should live to make others live better.

Lei Feng studied Chairman Mao's works in three ways. He applied what he studied as he went along; he studied and applied creatively; and he used Chairman Mao's teachings to remold his ideology and guide his actions. Whenever he came across a difficult problem in his life, he would immediately turn to Chairman Mao's works to draw strength from them.

One day Lei Feng drove up to the barracks with a truckful of grain and the comrades came out to help him unload it. Among them was Old Wang who belonged to Lei Feng's squad and was known for his great strength. He could carry a sack of grain weighing more than two hundred catties and run fairly fast with it. As Lei Feng was small and unable to carry such a heavy load, he and another comrade stayed on the truck and passed the sacks down onto the shoulders of the rest of the men. When Old Wang's turn came, he leaned against the truck and teasingly said to Lei Feng, "If you're a better man than I am, why don't you come down and carry a sack?"

Lei Feng did not reply. Then Old Wang added, "Ah, I knew all along that you didn't have the guts to compete with me. Of course not—you're so small!"

"Stop trying to needle me," Lei Feng replied calmly. "We need people to carry the sacks and we also need people to hand them down from the truck. Let's see if you can carry as much as I can move. How about that?" Lei Feng had not meant to challenge him, but his pride had been hurt by Old Wang's cutting remarks about his size.

That night he reread the essay "In Memory of Norman Bethune" by Chairman Mao until he came to this passage:

> We must all learn the spirit of absolute selflessness from him. With this spirit everyone can be very useful to the people. A man's ability may be great or small, but if he has this spirit, he is already noble-minded and pure, a man of moral integrity and above vulgar interests, a man who is of value to the people.

When he read the passage, everything seemed to fit into place and he began to see things in a new light. No longer did he have a feeling of wounded pride or a brooding sense of grievance. "Although I'm small, I'll do my best," he pledged, "to emulate Comrade Bethune's spirit of utter devotion to others without any thought of self."

A few days later the men decided to collect fodder in the mountains. Their plan was to set out after breakfast and return in the early evening, taking their lunch with them. After breakfast the thought suddenly crossed Old Wang's mind that it would be a nuisance taking lunch with him, so he ate his quickly before they set off. As soon as they were in the mountains the men set to work quickly and diligently, collecting grass and hay. At noon they sat on the mountain slope in two's and three's and began to eat their lunch. Lei Feng opened his lunch box and was about to eat when he saw Old Wang sitting by himself without any lunch. "He must have forgotten it or lost it on the way," Lei Feng thought to himself. Offering his own lunch he said, "Come on, take this." Old Wang looked at the lunch box, then at Lei Feng, shook his head, and refused to accept it. "Take it," Lei Feng said as he forced the lunch box into Old Wang's hand. "You'll be able to work better on it."

"If I take it, what are you going to do?" said Old Wang, handing it back.

"My stomach is a bit upset and I don't feel like eating," Lei Feng replied. Then he walked away pressing his hand against his stomach as if it hurt.

Holding the lunch box in his hand, Old Wang stared into space as Lei Feng slowly went away. Then he thought to himself, "Imagine, I actually said he's a small fellow and can't do anything big. I'm a big fellow all right, but I've never given my lunch away to anyone.". . .

Because Lei Feng earnestly studied Chairman Mao's writings, worked hard, remained loyal to the Party and the revolutionary cause, and because he made strict demands on himself, he was given the honor of membership in the Chinese Communist Party on November 8, 1960. It was the greatest day in the twenty-two years of his life. With gratitude he wrote this in his diary:

> November 8, 1960, I will never forget this day. This is the day when I had the honor of being made a member of the great Chinese Communist Party, thus realizing my highest ideal.
> Oh, how thrilled my heart is! It is beating

wildly with joy. How great the Party is! How great Chairman Mao is! Oh, Chairman Mao, it is you who have given me a new lease on life! When I was struggling in the fiery pit of hell and waiting for the dawn it was you who saved me, gave me food and clothing, and sent me to school! I finished my studies in the senior primary school, put on the red scarf, and then was given the honor of being admitted to the Communist Youth League. I took part in the nation's industrial construction and later became a soldier in the armed forces of the motherland. It was under your constant care and guidance that I, a former poor orphan, became a Party member, a man with some knowledge and political consciousness.

Now that I have joined the Party, I have become stronger and my vision has broadened. I am a Party member and a servant of the people. For the freedom, emancipation, and happiness of mankind and the cause of the Party and people, I am willing to climb the highest mountain and cross the widest river, to go through fire and water. Even at the risk of death I will remain forever loyal to the Party. . . .

In Lei Feng's company there was a man named Hsiao Chiao who had enlisted at the same time as he. Hsiao never complained about his work or drill, and his behavior was exemplary in every way. His only flaw was that he lagged behind in his studies, being particularly backward in arithmetic, which often gave him a headache. Gradually, however, he became resigned to the situation, a fact which soon began to worry Lei Feng. Once when Lei Feng was helping him with his arithmetic, Hsiao said, "I've had little education. I can't get the hang of all these things—addition, subtraction, multiplication, and division."

Trying to boost his confidence, Lei Feng told him, "Nothing is too difficult if you have the will to do it. Where there's a will, there's a way. To a revolutionary no difficulty is too great to overcome." Later he got hold of a copy of an old newspaper which carried a story describing Chairman Mao's concern for the education of soldiers. Showing it to Hsiao he said, "Look, here's a story written just for you!"

"Just for me?" Hsiao Chiao was puzzled.

"Listen to how really concerned Chairman Mao is about our studies!" Lei Feng said as he began to read the story, explaining it bit by bit in the hope that this would encourage his comrade. Hsiao Chiao listened attentively, nodding his head from time to time. When Lei Feng had finished it, Hsiao decided on the

spot to buy some pencils and exercise books as soon as possible.

"You don't have to bother with those things," said Lei Feng, handing him a fountain pen and an exercise book which he had anticipated he would need.

Hsiao Chiao was moved by Lei Feng's generosity but hesitated to accept the gifts. "If you give those things to me," he told Lei Feng, "what are you going to use?"

"Take them, I've got more," smiled Lei Feng. "If you want to be a part of the modernized Liberation Army, you must get an education."

Grateful to Lei Feng for his help and encouraged by the interest he had shown in him, Hsiao Chiao began to study arithmetic with much more concentration and initiative. And whenever he came up against something he could not grasp, he would go to Lei Feng and ask him to explain it. Checking up on his progress, Lei Feng asked him a few days later to solve a number of arithmetical problems. Running his eye over them Hsiao Chiao was sure they were easy. Then he took out his pen and got to work on them. A few minutes later he had answered all the questions correctly. Lei Feng's eyes lit up. "You've made marvellous progress," he said with a broad smile.

"But without your help I wouldn't have gotten anywhere," Hsiao Chiao acknowledged. . . .

Not so long afterwards Lei Feng had to change trains at Shen-yang, this time en route for Fu-shun. It was just after five in the morning. With his knapsack on his back he passed the ticket barrier and walked onto the platform. As he was going through the underground passage he saw a white-haired woman carrying a big bundle on her back; she was walking with difficulty, using a stick. Lei Feng hurried up to her and asked, "Auntie, where are you going?"

"I've come from the other side of the Great Wall and am going to Fu-shun to visit my son," the old woman gasped.

Seeing that she was going his way Lei Feng quickly took her bundle and carried it for her. Supporting her with his hand, he said, "I'll accompany you to Fu-shun." Grateful for his help, the old woman kept addressing him as "my boy."

When they got on the train Lei Feng saw that all the seats were taken, and while he was wondering what to do, a student stood up and gave his seat to the old woman. Lei Feng stood beside her. After the train had started he took out two pieces of bread which he had bought at the station and gave one of them to the old woman. "Take it yourself, my boy, I'm not hungry," she said.

"Please take it, Auntie, and let's have a snack," Lei Feng said as he pressed the bread into the old woman's hand. She took it, so moved that her hands trembled and she did not know what to do or say. Then she squeezed up to the next passenger and made some space for Lei Feng. "Sit down here, my boy," she said beckoning to the seat.

The words "my boy" made Lei Feng feel that his mother was talking to him. He sat beside the old woman and began to chat with her. "My son is a worker," she said. "He left home several years ago but I've never visited him and don't know where he lives." She took out a letter and showed it to Lei Feng.

Lei Feng could not recognize the address, but seeing that the old woman anxiously wanted his help he said, "Don't worry, Auntie, I'll help you to find your son."

The train had reached the outskirts of Fu-shun. Huge buildings and tall chimneys began to rise up as the train sped by. The old woman obviously had never seen such big buildings before and she kept on looking out of the carriage window with surprise on her face. "Auntie, this is our coal capital," Lei Feng explained. "The coal produced here is known for its quantity and quality. When you see your son, let him take you around and show you all the sights."

"Oh, I must see the sights," said the old woman. "I never knew I'd see such a big place in my lifetime!"

When the train arrived at the station Lei Feng put his bundle in a check room and helped the old woman to the street, carrying her bundle for her. Supporting her with his hand, he led her through the town inquiring after her son. After almost two hours of inquiries they finally found him. The first thing the old woman said to her son was, "If it weren't for the kindness of this boy, Heaven knows when I'd have found you!" When it was time for Lei Feng to say goodbye to the pair they held his hands tightly, reluctant to see him go. Finally, they all walked along together for some distance before parting.

It may be asked why Lei Feng was so interested in helping others. The reason may be seen in this passage of his diary:

> Man's life is finite but the cause of serving the people is infinite. It is my wish to devote my finite life to the infinite cause of serving the people.

84.

Housing in Shanghai

Before 1949 most urban residents lived in rented quarters owned by relatively wealthy landlords. Thereafter, the government gradually took over more and more of the apartment houses in the big cities, starting with those owned by the largest landlords. In Shanghai, by 1966 the government had charge of 80 percent of all dwelling units. Management of publicly owned housing, therefore, had come to require a large bureaucracy in charge of apartment assignment and building maintenance. The following article suggests some of the bureaucratic problems entailed in such a task. It was published in a Shanghai newspaper in November, 1965.

BOTH MAKE CONCESSION FOR MUTUAL ADVANTAGE

The Northern Shansi Road Housing Administration Office in Cha-pei Ward received a letter from resident Wu Ta-te of T'ien-t'ung Road. Both he and his wife were working. Wu said that besides his main home he had a room of eighteen square meters on the second floor of a house on Chou-chia-tsui Road in Hang-chiu Ward. In it he had to accommodate his elderly parents and two children. Every morning, his mother took the children by bus to his home on T'ien-t'ung Road, then sent them to school while she stayed to do household chores; in the evening, she took the children back to Chou-chia-tsui Road. Wu found it inconvenient to have two homes and wanted to have the whole family living together. The comrades of the housing and administration office introduced him to several families to arrange an exchange of houses, but nothing was accomplished because no one liked his.

At that time, a Chang family, consisting of husband and wife and five children, lived in a room of only eleven square meters at Lane 346 on Ch'i-p'u Road. They found their room too small and made a request to the Northern Shansi Road Housing Administration Office for improvement in their living conditions. The housing administration personnel noted that as Chang was working at a factory in Hang-chiu Ward, if Wu Ta-te's room on the Chou-chia-tsui Road were given to him, he could save time and money in going to work and at the same time improve his living conditions. This was an unusual opportunity and both parties were taken to see the houses.

When Chang saw the room on the second floor and noted that it faced south, was dry and spacious, had both water and power supplied, was in a quiet neighborhood and close to his factory, and had reasonable rent, he was well pleased. Yet, when he thought that his own room was small and in a noisy front partition, he was worried that the other party might not want the exchange. Wu Ta-te's mother also went from the back door of her son's residence to see Chang's room about ten houses away and was satisfied with its location. Making a tour inside, she saw the room was a front partition on the ground floor that saved the trouble of climbing upstairs. Its shortcoming was that it was rather noisy and had seven square meters less space. As she looked around, she thought to herself, "The house is close to my son's and on the ground floor, too. It saves me the trouble of traveling back and forth daily and makes it easy for all members of our family to look after one another. Better take it though it is small and somewhat noisy." She immediately expressed her willingness to accept the exchange.

A month or so had elapsed but Chang still had failed to turn up to arrange with Grandma Wu for the exchange, even though she had asked for it several times. The truth was that Chang's wife had lived on Ch'i-p'u Road for many years. Although she thought her room too small and wanted to exchange it for a larger one, she was reluctant to leave the locality if she did not have to. She also did not like the new place because she was not used to living on the upper floor and thought the staircase too narrow. Therefore the matter was left unsettled. When Chang's factory authorities learned this, they studied the matter with Chang and his wife and advised them not to miss this excellent chance to exchange a small home for a larger one, which would solve the problem of over-crowding, provide a quiet place to sleep, and be close to the factory. They also pointed out that the willingness of the other party to make the exchange revealed their sincere attitude and correct thinking, so Chang should also assume a correct attitude and be willing to give something for what he was gaining. To ask for a spacious, good, convenient, quiet, and totally ideal apartment was an unrealistic goal. Taking all of this into consideration, Chang and his wife saw that their notions had been unrealistic and decided to make the exchange.

Now the two households have what they wanted after exchanging houses with each other.

85.

Red Guards

The most turbulent period in the People's Republic's first three decades was the Cultural Revolution, 1966–1969. Begun by Mao Tse-tung as a campaign to prevent bureaucratization, produce a new socialist spirit and culture, and give young people born under the new regime the experience of a revolution, it soon grew to much larger proportions than any other previous campaign. The formation of the Red Guards played a key role in the course of the Cultural Revolution. Maoist leaders strongly encouraged the organization of middle school, high school, and college youth into Red Guard units, both to educate them in revolution and to provide the Maoists with important allies in their combat with less radical leaders. In June, 1966, almost all schools and universities were closed as students devoted full time to Red Guard activities. That fall eight massive Red Guard rallies were held in Peking, attracting, it is said, more than eight million youths.

The four selections below each take up a distinct strand in the Red Guard experience. "Long Live the Revolutionary Rebel Spirit of the Proletariat!" is a passionate manifesto demanding that young people learn revolution by practice. "Red Guards in Nan-ning and Liu-chou Take to the Streets to Clean Up the Four Olds" is a newspaper article describing the enthusiasm Red Guards displayed for purging China of objects and habits that they judged to reflect feudal or bourgeois influences. "March Forward Valiantly Along the Road Pointed Out by Chairman Mao" is a report issued by eleven middle school Red Guard units. It recounts the experiences of one band of young people who marched to Peking in emulation of the Red Army's legendary march from southeast to northwest China in 1934–35. Such activities were later encouraged by the government, eager to keep Red Guard traffic from completely overwhelming China's limited rail system. Massive nationwide travel by youth was unprecedented in Chinese society and contributed to the development of national, rather than local identity among the younger generation. All three of these pieces date from the summer and fall of 1966. "Factual Account of the September 11 Bloodshed" is from a Red Guard newspaper published during the following year, in September, 1967. It may well be exaggerated, but does reveal the role of violence as Red Guard groups were increasingly plagued by factionalism later in the Cultural Revolution. To overcome this violence, toward the end of the Cultural Revolution Red Guard organizations were placed under the supervision of worker and soldier "Mao Tse-tung Thought Propaganda Teams."

Besides providing evidence of the nature of a major political movement, descriptions of Red Guard activities also provide rare insight into some of the dynamics of social organization in the 1960s. By looking at how young people acted when given considerable leeway to organize their own groups and set their own goals, we can infer some of their values and attitudes and how they were shaped by the institutions and groups to which they belonged.

LONG LIVE THE REVOLUTIONARY REBEL SPIRIT OF THE PROLETARIAT!

Revolution is rebellion, and rebellion is the soul of Mao Tse-tung's thought. Daring to think, to speak, to act, to break through, and to make revolution—in a word, daring to rebel—is the most fundamental and most precious quality of proletarian revolutionaries; it is fundamental to the Party spirit of the Party of the proletariat! Not to rebel is revisionism, pure and simple! Revisionism has been in control of our school for seventeen years. If today we do not rise up in rebellion, when will we?

Now some of the people who were boldly opposing our rebellion have suddenly turned shy and coy, and have taken to incessant murmuring and nagging that we are too one-sided, too arrogant, too crude and that we are going too far. All this is utter nonsense! If you are against us, please say so. Why be shy about it? Since we are bent on rebelling, the matter is no longer in your hands! Indeed we shall make the air thick with the pungent smell of gunpowder. All this talk about being "humane" and "all-sided"—let's have an end to it!

You say we are too one-sided? What kind of all-sideness is it that suits you? It looks to us like a "two combining into one" all-sideness, or eclecticism. You say we are too arrogant? "Arrogant" is just what we want to be. Chairman Mao says, "And those in high positions we counted as no more than the dust." We are bent on striking down not only the reactionaries in our school, but the reactionaries all over the world. Revolutionaries take it as their task to transform the world. How can we not be "arrogant"?

You say we are too crude? Crude is just what we want to be. How can we be soft and clinging towards revisionism or go in for great moderation? To be moderate toward the enemy is to be cruel to the revolution! You say we are going too far? Frankly, your "don't go too far" is reformism, it is "peaceful transition." And this is what your daydreams are about! Well, we are going to strike you down to the earth and keep you down!

There are some others who are scared to death of revolution, scared to death of rebellion. You sticklers for convention, you toadies are all curled up inside your revisionist shells. At the first whiff of rebellion, you become scared and nervous. A revolutionary is a "monkey king"* whose golden rod is might, whose supernatural powers are far-reaching and whose magic is omnipotent precisely because he has the great and invincible thought of Mao Tse-tung. We are wielding our "golden rods," "displaying our supernatural powers" and using our "magic" in order to turn the old world upside down, smash it to pieces, create chaos, and make a tremendous mess—and the bigger the better! We must do this to the present revisionist middle school attached to Tsinghua University. Create a big rebellion, rebel to the end! We are bent on creating a tremendous proletarian uproar, and on carving out a new proletarian world!

Long live the revolutionary rebel spirit of the proletariat!

RED GUARDS IN NAN-NING AND LIU-CHOU TAKE TO THE STREETS TO CLEAN UP THE "FOUR OLDS"

According to a *Kwangsi Daily* report, on August 23, Red Guards and revolutionary teachers and students in the city of Nan-ning, inspired by the revolutionary spirit of revolt shown by the Red Guards in the capital, and filled with great revolutionary pride, took to the streets to post revolutionary leaflets and big-character posters and carry out oral propaganda. Using the thought of Mao Tse-tung as a weapon, they violently attacked all old ideas, old culture, old customs and old habits. They demanded that Nan-ning be built into a great school of Mao Tse-tung's thought.

A group of Red Guards in the Second Middle School in Nan-ning climbed up to a traffic policeman's stand and, through the medium of loudspeakers, read aloud to the people their Manifesto of Revolt: "Today, the clarion call for the Great Proletarian Cultural Revolution has been sounded, and the battle between the proletariat and the bourgeoisie has begun. We must promote the fearless spirit of the proletariat—the spirit of staining our bayonets with blood—and the revolt against feudalism, capitalism, and all demons and monsters. Backed by Chairman Mao and the Party Central Committee, this revolt is

---

* The Monkey King is a famous character from the Ming novel *Journey to the West*.

sure to succeed. Let the thought of Mao Tse-tung shine upon every corner. . . ."

Revolutionary "young generals" of the Kwangsi College of Arts formed four propaganda teams for the purpose of replacing bourgeois ideology with proletarian ideology and getting rid of the old to make way for the new. In no time they composed a revolutionary song entitled "Raise the Iron Broom of the Revolution," and sang it in the streets and shops. With revolutionary pride, they sang: "Sweep and break. Raise the iron broom of the revolution to sweep away the vestiges of feudalism, uproot the bourgeois ideology, hold aloft the red banner of the thought of Mao Tse-tung, establish proletarian and destroy bourgeois ideology, destroy a lot and build a lot, and construct a new socialist country." The masses around them sang with them.

Red Guards of the Kwangsi Nationality College in a remote suburban area arrived in the morning at the Station for the Reception of the Masses operated according to the revolutionary rules. These Red Guards proposed to change the names of streets, places, and stores—such as People's Livelihood Road, People's Rights Road, Emperor Ridge, and White Dragon Bridge—into new names with revolutionary content. They proposed getting rid of all poisonous things in barber shops, tailor shops, and book-lending shops immediately. In shops that the Red Guards of the Nan-ning Ninth Middle School and revolutionary teachers and students visited, they were received warmly by the workers and employees, who were determined to respond to their revolutionary proposals.

The workers of the Handicraft Product Center of Nan-ning said, "We have long wanted to discard artistic products decorated with emperors, kings, generals, prime ministers, scholars, and beauties. Now that you have come to support us, we'll take immediate action." They immediately tucked away the carved standing screens and hanging screens and hung more portraits of Chairman Mao in the shop.

The workers of the New South Barber Shop at the suggestion of the Red Guards took down the pictures showing decadent bourgeois hair styles such as the "wave-type" and "big western style" and indicated that they would in future refuse to do such bizarre hair styles for their clients.

Fourteen Chinese and Western medicine shops under the Medical Company of Nan-ning held workers' forums one after the other and, after discus-

sion, that same night adopted new signboards expressing revolutionary ideas.

The revolutionary masses of the city's cultural palace and museum listened to the broadcasts at eight o'clock in the morning and by nine had posted a big-character poster at Prince Liu Park. They thought that the term "Prince Liu" reflected feudal bureaucratic ideas and was incompatible with the spirit of the times. They thought the name should be changed into "People's Park," so immediately wrote "People's" on a piece of paper and pasted it on top. This suggestion was warmly supported by the revolutionary masses passing by.

MARCH FORWARD VALIANTLY ALONG THE ROAD POINTED OUT BY CHAIRMAN MAO

Our long march team was made up of eight boys and three girls averaging eighteen years of age. We started out from Peng-pu on September 11, and crossed Anhui, Kiangsu, Shantung, and Hopei provinces. After forty-four days of walking we had covered a thousand kilometers and arrived in Peking to be alongside our beloved leader Chairman Mao.

Chairman Mao has said, "Our policy must be made known not only to the leaders and to the cadres but also to the broad masses." Vice Chairman Lin Piao has said, "The whole country should become a great school of Mao Tse-tung's thought." As Red Guards of Mao Tse-tung's thought, it was our glorious duty to disseminate his ideas. We decided to organize our long march team to spread propaganda and to do our bit in the great cause of turning the whole country into a great school of Mao Tse-tung's thought.

At the same time, we knew we had never been tested in revolutionary struggles, even though we all come from railway workers' families and have been brought up under the red flag. In the Great Proletarian Cultural Revolution we learned that young people cannot become worthy successors to the proletarian revolutionary cause if they have not tempered themselves in the storm of class struggle, integrated themselves with the workers and peasants, and remolded their world outlook. The long march, we decided, was a good way of tempering and remolding ourselves.

These were the considerations that became decisive in our determination to undertake a long march. Before we left, we spent several days studying "The Orientation of the Youth Movement," "Serve the People," "In Memory of Norman Bethune," "The Foolish Old Man Who Removed the Mountains," and some other writings by Chairman Mao. We armed ourselves with Mao Tse-tung's thought; his teachings unified our ideas and increased our confidence and courage.

When the day for our departure arrived, we were all very excited. We made a pledge addressed to Chairman Mao: "Our most beloved leader Chairman Mao! The brilliance of your ideas is the light that guides us in heart and mind. We are resolved to fulfill your words, 'Be resolute, fear no sacrifice, and surmount every difficulty to win victory.' We shall not falter in getting to Peking." . . .

To make a start is always difficult. The first day we walked twenty-seven kilometers. Many of our schoolmates suffered swollen feet and had to clench their teeth with each step they took. Even when we stopped and rested, our backs and feet really ached. A few of us debated about going back home; whether to go forward or retreat became a question of revolutionary determination. It was a crucial moment. To solve the problem, we studied a passage in Chairman Mao Tse-tung's works in which he says, "How should we judge whether a youth is a revolutionary? . . . There can only be one criterion, namely, whether or not he is willing to integrate himself with the broad masses of workers and peasants and does so in practice."

We took this as a mirror in which to examine our own ideas and decided that the purpose of our long march was to integrate ourselves with the masses, to learn from the workers, peasants, and soldiers, and to train ourselves as proletarian revolutionary successors who can truly stand all tests. "How shall we wage revolution if we can't even pass this first test?" we asked ourselves. "No! We must keep on. To go forward means victory!" In this way we applied Mao Tse-tung's ideas and prevailed over the vacillating muck in our minds. We all became more confident than ever.

We all carried knapsacks as well as gongs, drums, and study material. On the average we each carried a load of about fifteen kilograms. But we plucked up our courage and kept going, though the weather was very hot. At the time our clothes, and even our knapsacks, were soaked through with our perspiration.

We sang. At any difficult moment we all sang the

wonderful lines from Chairman Mao's poem: "The Red Army fears not the trials of a distant march; to them a thousand mountains, ten thousand rivers are nothing"; and we also sang: "We count the myriad leagues we have come already; if we reach not the Great Wall, we are not true men!"

Each of us had a quotation from Chairman Mao Tse-tung written on a placard fixed to his knapsack. The one behind read it aloud in turn, and all of us took it up in chorus. It raised our spirits and helped to shore up our determination. For Chairman Mao's words brought to mind what the old Red Army did on its 12,500-kilometer Long March. It gave us fresh energy and the will to persist. Each step we took, we told ourselves, brought us a step closer to our great leader, Chairman Mao.

Our journey from Hsü-chou to Han-ch'uan presented us with another difficult test. That day we arrived at a small place where we had planned to eat, only to find the public mess hall closed. We could have asked the peasants to cook a meal especially for us but decided not to, since we knew that they were busy with farm work. We put on our regular propaganda performance and walked on, very thirsty and hungry. The weather was broiling. We felt almost completely exhausted. But we read aloud Chairman Mao's statement: "Give full play to our style of fighting—courage in battle, no fear of sacrifice, no fear of fatigue, and continuous fighting." We recalled that the Chinese people were hungry every day before Liberation. When the old Red Army on the 12,500-kilometer Long March crossed snow-capped mountains and marshlands, they were reduced to boiling their leather belts and digging up roots for food. They often went hungry. What did it matter if we missed our meals for one day? It was an opportunity to show our determination. Our revolutionary predecessors endured hunger for the sake of those to come. If we now tempered ourselves we could make a better contribution to the Chinese and the world revolution, so that the great masses in the world would not go hungry. This was the gist of our talk and our thoughts, and so we no longer felt hungry. In fact, we marched on with greater vigor, and, as we walked, we beat our gongs and drums and sang revolutionary songs. That day we kept our average of four propaganda performances.

On the way we met a number of leading members of various institutions. With the best of intentions, they advised us to go to Peking by train. We must have looked tired to them. Some of them even offered us train tickets, but, in every case, we refused. We felt that come what may, we would not give up our objective half-way. We persisted northward on foot to gain and exchange revolutionary experiences.

We Red Guards are reserves of the Chinese People's Liberation Army. We knew we had to follow its example, the finest example of adherence to Chairman Mao's teachings. The army feared no trials, strictly applied the Party's policies, and maintained high discipline. We consciously tried to emulate it during our long march by applying the three main rules of discipline and the eight points for attention which Chairman Mao himself formulated for the Chinese People's Liberation Army long ago.

None of us ever bought any sweets on the way or had any food other than our regular meals. We never wasted a grain of food and took great care of public property. We washed our own clothes, did our own mending, and cut one another's hair instead of going to a barber. In short, we were very thrifty in our way of living. We made a particular effort to temper ourselves by plain living, especially in the matter of food. The more we did so, we felt, the better we could remold our ideology. Guided by Mao-Tse-tung's thought, we overcame one difficulty after another and successfully stood the test we had set ourselves— the first real test in our lives.

Chairman Mao said, "The Long March is a manifesto, a propaganda force, and a seeding-machine." On our long march, too, a fundamental task was to spread Mao Tse-tung's ideas. And we persisted though we were often very tired. Altogether we gave some 120 performances in over 100 villages and small railway stops. We estimate our total audience at more than 10,000 people. We also distributed 400 pamphlets containing the decisions of the Party Central Committee, speeches by Party leaders, and editorials of the *People's Daily* and 10,000 leaflets and posters with Mao Tse-tung's ideas.

Our first performances were, indeed, a test for us! Only three of us had any experience. We were afraid people would laugh at us, but we remembered Chairman Mao Tse-tung's words: "It is often not a matter of first learning and then doing, but of doing and then learning, for doing is itself learning." We decided we must "learn to swim by swimming," as the Chairman taught. There was plenty of enthusiasm once we arrived at our decision. We composed our items at odd rest moments and rehearsed them on the way, gradually mastering the art of putting on a

show including choral singing, solo singing, ballad recital, dialogue, and singing combined with acting.

One evening we arrived at a village where the people asked us to put on a performance. It was just one kilometer from the railway station where we were to have a meal and rest. We had been walking most of the day and were very tired, and what is more, we had missed our lunch and were very hungry. What were we to do? We held a discussion and decided to give the performance. What were hunger and fatigue to us compared with the joy of meeting the people's wishes and disseminating Mao Tse-tung's thought!

We put down our knapsacks and performed whenever there was an audience. One day, we put on a show for three housewives. Our persistence in spreading Mao Tse-tung's thought insured us of a hearty welcome everywhere from the revolutionary masses. One old worker said to us very sincerely after watching us perform: "You are really good Red Guards of Chairman Mao! We of the older generation feel more assured with such good successors growing up." . . .

One young worker at a Teng-hsien railway station presented us with his most prized possession—a small plaster cast of Chairman Mao—together with a letter in which he wrote: "Though we are at different revolutionary posts, we are one and the same in our determination to give our very lives in defense of Chairman Mao and to carry the great proletarian cultural revolution through to the end. We shall safeguard our impregnable proletarian state whatever the cost. In presenting you with this likeness of our great leader Chairman Mao, I am sure it will give you infinite strength on your journey." These deeply felt words greatly moved us, and thereafter wherever we stayed, we placed the statue in the most conspicuous place. Indeed, it always gave us fresh strength. . . .

At Feng-t'ai station near Peking, we went to see the nationally famous engine, the "Mao Tse-tung Special," and had a talk with members of the crew. It was a great experience, for they are fine students of Chairman Mao's works. What they told us opened our minds and made us all the more determined to study Chairman Mao's books and work for the revolution, and especially to study the three much-read articles and use them in remolding our ideology. We decided we would devote the whole of our lives to becoming truly reliable successors to the proletarian revolutionary cause.

All along the way the workers and peasants

showed great concern for our well-being. Very often a railway worker's wife would insist on doing our washing and mending. Keeping close to the railway line all along our route, we had many indications of the deep class comradeship of the workers. It brought to mind the popular verse: "Great as is Heaven and Earth, they are not as great as the good brought by the Party. Dear to us as our parents are, they are not as dear as Chairman Mao. Fine and good as many things are, none is as fine as socialism. Deep as the deepest ocean is, it is not as deep as class comradeship." Our hearts were linked by this class comradeship with the hearts of these people whom we had not met before.

Our forty-four-day trek gave us the chance to learn how excellent traveling on foot is as a means to gain and exchange revolutionary experience. For it tempers your proletarian ideology, steels your willpower, and helps you to revolutionize your thinking. We learned a great many things we could not get from books and also gained personal experience of many things we had read about. In particular, we have deepened our understanding of the brilliant thought of Chairman Mao.

Of course, we have taken only the very first step in the 10,000-*li* long march that lies before us, the first step along the glorious road which Chairman Mao has shown us. We need to improve our creative study and application of Chairman Mao's works and to continue to temper and remold ourselves in the furnace of the great Cultural Revolution. We must revolutionize ourselves and become young militants who are really reliable successors to the cause of the proletarian revolution, for that is what Chairman Mao expects of us.

FACTUAL ACCOUNT OF THE SEPTEMBER 11 BLOODSHED

The appalling September 11 bloodshed which shook the municipality took place after the signing of the September 1 Agreement and the announcement of the September 5 Order approved by Chairman Mao. This was not a mere accident; it was a bloody slaughter of the revolutionary rebels and revolutionary masses, instigated by the handful of bad leaders of the conservative organizations manipulated by the capitalist-roader authorities in the Party. Its aims were to provoke large-scale violent struggle, to sabotage the implementation of the September 5 Order, to apply pressure on the Party Central Com-

mittee and the Canton Military District Command, to interfere with the ongoing movement of supporting the army and cherishing the people, and to alter the direction of the struggle to criticize T'ao Chu.* It was a deathbed struggle waged by the bourgeois reactionaries. After this incident, the conservatives— manipulated by the capitalist-roaders in the Party— cranked up the propaganda machines. They screamed "stop thief" while they themselves were the thieves. They confused right and wrong, wantonly started rumors, and vilified and attacked the revolutionary rebels in an attempt to cause trouble for other people and acquit themselves of their crimes of murder. How malicious their intentions were!

To rectify any misconceptions, we give below a comprehensive though brief account of the on-the-spot investigations of the incident made by the Red Flag Commune of Chien-kuo Restaurant under the Food and Drinks Section of the "Workers' Revolutionary Alliance" and by the Elementary Education Red Headquarters.

On September 11, the "Spring Thunder," "District Headquarters," "Doctrine Guards," and other conservative forces in Canton gathered their men in Fo-shan, Shao-kuan, Chung-hua, and other suburban areas to attend the so-called inauguration of the "Revolutionary Committee of Workers in the Canton Area" held at Yüeh-hsiu-shan Stadium. A little past nine o'clock in the morning, seventy-two trucks loaded with peasants from Chung-hua arrived in Canton via Chung-shan No. 5 Road. Because there were crowds of people at the junction with Peking Road, the trucks had to move slowly. As the thirty-second truck approached the intersection, the masses discovered some weapons in it and immediately mounted the truck to investigate. There they found a pistol, a hand grenade, and a dagger. The onlooking revolutionary masses felt deep indignation at this open violation of the agreement to keep arms under bond and unanimously roared their condemnation, some of them indignantly tearing from the truck the flag of the Alliance of Poor and Lower-Middle Peasants in Areas Around Chung-hua. Seeing that their secret had been uncovered, one of the men in the truck, in order to escape being caught, pulled out a pistol and was about to shoot. Fortunately, the masses were highly vigilant and immediately ran forward to snatch it. Later when the men of the Red Garrison Headquarters and the Workers' Pickets ar-

* Mayor of Canton.

rived, the masses handed the man over to them, together with the arms found in the truck.

The masses did not reproach the members of the suburban peasant's alliance, but instead had friendly chats with them and carried out ideological work among them, giving them water to drink and cigarettes to smoke. The peasants came to realize that they had been deceived and that they should not have come into the city. A leader of these peasants said, "We don't know what we came here for. The higher authorities told us that we didn't have to work today and had to come here for a meeting. Each of us was given two dollars and fifteen wage points." The peasant brothers in those trucks which did not drive away were later persuaded by the army comrades to take a rest in the assembly hall of the Kwangtung Provincial People's Council. The broad revolutionary masses expressed warm welcome to them for their awakening and their revolutionary refusal to take part in the violent struggle provoked by the Workers' Committee under the District Headquarters.

At about eleven o'clock in the morning, two trucks loaded with bricks and members of the Doctrine Guards and "Hung Pan Tsung" of the No. 46 Middle School sped along Chung-shan No. 5 Road toward the Financial Department Building. The masses on the road laughed at them, and some people threw banana peels and handbills at them, whereupon the Doctrine Guards stopped their truck and one of them threw a piece of a brick at the crowd, wounding someone. Another Doctrine Guard got down from the truck and struck out at the onlooking masses with his leather belt. The masses were indignant at this and loudly condemned the Doctrine Guards "for attempting to kill," then they quickly surrounded the trucks. Seeing this, the Doctrine Guards at once started their trucks and pressed hard on the accelerators. As the trucks pulled away from the pursuing masses, the Doctrine Guards pulled out their pistols and shot at them. They fired a few shots and wounded four men, one in the head, one in the chest, one in the hand, and one in the foot. After that, the Doctrine Guards sped towards Yüeh-hsiu-shan.

At noon, despite the ironclad facts that the arms of the Chung-hua suburb Poor and Lower-Middle Peasants' Alliance had been discovered and that the Doctrine Guards had shot and wounded the masses, the presidium of the "Revolutionary Committee of Workers in the Canton Area" wantonly started a rumor at the meeting that the "Red Flag Faction"

had amassed their men at Chung-shan No. 5 Road (actually the masses at the road junction were unorganized and many of them were children) to sabotage their demonstration. . . . They stirred up public opinion in favor of a violent struggle and read a so-called statement of protest.

At 1:15 P.M., the Revolutionary Committee of Workers in the Canton area started its parade. The parade contingents wanted to pass Chi-hsiang Road and go westward along Chung-shan No. 5 Road, but the road was crowded, particularly at the intersection. A handful of heartless and rabid leaders of the District Headquarters ran two of their trucks into the crowds at speeds of over forty kilometers per hour. The first truck crashed into a pillar supporting the balcony of the Urban Services Bureau building. The second bumped into a trolley bus which was stopping at Chung-shan No. 5 Road. One person (a child) was killed on the spot, and two others were injured. The masses raged with indignation over these atrocities, and picking up pieces of bricks on the roadside, launched a brave counterattack. The bad leaders used machine guns, pistols, hand grenades, and other murderous weapons to start their premeditated massacre. From the time the Doctrine Guards fired their guns to the time the Central Investigation Corps and the army unit arrived at the scene, the District Headquarters and the Doctrine Guards fired more than 200 bullets and threw four hand grenades. According to incomplete statistics, thirteen persons among the revolutionary masses were killed (nine of them died on the spot and the other four died in the hospital) and one hundred fifty-five were wounded, seventeen of them seriously. Of the wounded, seventy-three were sent to Chung-shan Hospital, forty-three to Provincial People's Hospital, thirty-six to Municipal No. 1 Hospital, eleven to Municipal Workers' Hospital, and five to Yüeh-hsiu Area Hospital. (Those sent to military hospitals are not included in the above figures.) Apart from this, countless people were injured by bricks thrown by the District Headquarters and the Doctrine Guards. In Chienkuo Restaurant alone, forty-five persons who were less seriously injured came in to have their wounds dressed. Moreover, the District Headquarters and the Doctrine Guards beat and kidnapped seven persons from among the revolutionary masses and took them away in four trucks, the license numbers of which were: 3-318, 15-1458, 15-10029, and 15-14944.

These facts have been written in blood. They cannot be reversed no matter what rumor the Spring Thunder, District Headquarters, Doctrine Guards, and other conservative organizations may start. There must be a reckoning of their crimes in sabotaging the September 5 Order and the September 1 Agreement.

86.

My Accusations

The rapid pace of change in the People's Republic has been sustained by the Communist Party's commitment to reshape Chinese society. Many new attitudes have been produced indirectly through such structural changes as industrialization, collectivization, and expanded educational opportunity. Yet the Party has also at times attempted to directly modify people's thoughts and behavior by subjecting them to intense social pressure. The most dramatic method used is "struggle sessions," which have accompanied many reform campaigns and political movements.

The following account was made by Li Ken-lien, widow of a language teacher who committed suicide under political pressure early in the Cultural Revolution. In it she describes her experience as an object of political struggle. Her accusation is itself a speech given in a struggle session against her former adversaries. An important theme in her criticism is the abuse of power by highhanded bureaucrats. Even in the Cultural Revolution, the greatest of anti-bureaucratic campaigns, there was a proliferation of new committees and organizations established to coordinate the movement. Some of these proved as remote and self-serving as the old organizations they were designed to change. Li's particular charges may have been exaggerated for political effect, but the overall tenor of her critique of bureaucracy certainly expressed feelings held by many Chinese.

Comrades and comrades-in-arms among the revolutionary rebels:

I am grateful to the Party, Chairman Mao, and other revolutionary comrades for allowing me—the family dependent of a victim—to make accusations here against Party committee members Lai Chu-yen and Ma Ch'ing-jui and Work Group leader Li X of the Engineering Bureau. These men persecuted Ch'en Liang to death by implementing the instruction of Liang Hsiang, member of the sinister Municipal Committee and follower of the bourgeois reactionary line of Liu Shao-ch'i, Teng Hsiao-p'ing, and T'ao Chu.

My husband, Ch'en Liang, was a language teacher of the middle school section of the Sparetime Engineering College of the Engineering Bureau. As soon as the movement began, he was named by the Party Committee and Work Group of the Bureau as

"little Teng T'o."* The Party Committee and Work Group of the Bureau hoodwinked the masses into using big-character posters to entrap him. Ma Ch'ing-jui and Li X ignored a number of his pleas, and on July 6 through 9 last year, they organized the whole Bureau to hold four days of large and small struggle meetings. At the July 9 struggle meeting, Ma Ch'ing-jui hurriedly announced in public that Ch'en Liang was one of the three kinds of "anti" elements [i.e., one who opposed the Communist Party, socialism, or the people]. On the evening of July 11, when I returned to my unit to study, Ch'en Liang took his two sons out. That evening, he first killed them, then himself. . . .

Ch'en Liang's family background and personal history were honorable. An urban pauper by birth,

* A writer who had written a piece interpreted as ridiculing Mao.

he was himself a revolutionary serviceman. In the old society, his father died when he was one year old, and he lost his mother at three. He was brought up by his elder sister who worked for others to earn wages for his upkeep. After drifting around for a time, he was sent to an orphanage. At the age of seven, in order to make a living, he was forced to work for a priest of an imperialist Church, but because he resisted oppression, he was driven out by the priest on three occasions. He had nowhere to go and could only beg for his living in the streets.

Ch'en Liang owed his emancipation to the liberation of old China by Chairman Mao and the Communist Party. In June 1949, he joined the great Chinese People's Liberation Army. Because he was less than sixteen years old at that time, he could only join the "little devil" unit. When he had been tempered in the crucible of the People's Liberation Army, he went to study in an accelerated middle school and acquired the cultural standard of a senior middle-school graduate. He served as a people's teacher until 1954, when he became a language teacher.

From what I know of Ch'en Liang's way of life over the past eight years, he had never acted against the Party or socialism, nor had he any enmity against the people. He had not committed any mistakes in past political movements. He was not a landlord, rich-peasant, counterrevolutionary, bad or rightist element, and had not joined any reactionary organization. . . .

After Ch'en Liang committed suicide, the Party Committee and Work Group of the Engineering Bureau worked in collusion with the Party General Branch and the work team of the bookstore to persecute me also. Lai Chu-yen, Ma Ch'ing-jui, and Li X attempted to cover up the damning evidence of their persecution of him. They said Ch'en Liang committed suicide for fear of punishment and that the Engineering Bureau concurred because the finding had been reached by the Public Security Bureau on the spot.

Comrades, why is it that, up to today, the family dependents of the deceased have not been clearly told what offense he had committed and what made him commit suicide? Stranger still, at first they dared not admit that they had struggled against him. When I pressed the question further, they answered: "It is definite that Ch'en Liang was never struggled against. The teachers of the college only wrote a few big-character posters against him. Although not many such posters were written, he became so panicky that he committed suicide for fear of punishment."

After Ch'en Liang was forced into committing suicide, Li X announced to the masses of the college that he was a "murderer" and that he "committed suicide for fear of punishment." Patting his own chest, he also said, "I shoulder the principal responsibility for the death of Ch'en Liang," adding, "Every movement claims the lives of a few persons. There is nothing unusual in this." He wanted to seal the lips of the masses.

Apart from this, whenever I questioned these men, they either gave me an ambiguous reply or intimidated me. Li X told me that, if I forced them to disclose Ch'en's offense, it would prove I had no faith in the Party and my outlook would become questionable. What nonsense! This handful of persons actually dared to regard themselves as the personification of the Party!

Let me tell you, Lai Chu-yen, Ma Ch'ing-jui, Li X, and others: Today we are backed by Chairman Mao, and we dare to unhorse you handful of capitalist roaders in authority who obstinately cling to the bourgeois reactionary line. If you refuse to admit your guilt before Chairman Mao and the revolutionary masses you will come to no good end.

Apart from making every effort to cover up the damning evidence of their persecution of my husband, Lai, Ma, and Li also sent men to the bookstore where I work to discuss with people of the Party general branch and the work team how to deal with me. The work team sent someone to discuss ideology with me day and night and wanted me to "draw a dividing line" between me and Ch'en Liang. They said, "Ch'en Liang cheated you by not leaving you a single word before he died. It can be seen that this man had no affection for you." They also said, "You must not be emotional about Ch'en or allow his past affection for you to obscure your understanding of his reactionary nature." Seeing that these words could neither shake my understanding of Ch'en Liang, the man with whom I had lived for eight years, nor bring me to hate his "reactionary nature," they went further to provoke my grief and pain over the loss of my children. They told me over and over, "Whether Ch'en Liang was one of the three "anti" elements or not, his murdering your children was serious enough to make him an active counterrevolutionary which he further proved by committing suicide to resist the movement. . . ."

Later, I moved in with a girl friend. (Before Ch'en Liang killed himself, he had written a letter to this friend asking her to look after me.) The Cultural Revolution Office of the bookstore also directed the leader of the Cultural Revolution Group of my unit to go to my friend's home and require her to give an account of what I had said and done. The leader of the Cultural Revolution Group also intimidated that girl friend, saying, "Li Ken-lien is of questionable family background, and her problems will be dealt with at a later stage." Then the leader hinted that she should ask me to move elsewhere. My friend was reluctant to do this out of the fear that I might be pushed too far and commit suicide. That leader of the Cultural Revolution Group actually said, "After her removal from your place, the bookstore will carry out some ideological work on her, and should she still choose to follow her husband and commit suicide, let her do so!" . . .

My undesirable family origin is something I did not choose. However, since taking up work in the bookstore at the age of sixteen, I have made no mistakes for more than ten years, and I long ago deserted my family. I joined the Communist Youth League in 1956 and served as a group leader on the Branch Committee and in other capacities. Last year, I resigned from the Youth League due to age. What problems do I have that must be dealt with later? This accusation simply reflects the rivalry between T'an Li-fu's "reactionary pedigree theory" and the "class origin theory" of the Party; between the theory of not taking account of class origin versus emphasis on political performance. . . .

After I lost my happy family and beloved children, I was filled with grief and pain; my mind was unstable. One day in the middle of August, I stayed home from work because I was sick. The leader of the Cultural Revolution Group came to my home to "visit me." In her conversation with my mother, she said that before his death Ch'en Liang had not only left a letter for me but had also left letters to the Party Committee and the hotel manager to explain why he had to take the road that he did. After I learned of this, I still did not dare ask the Engineering Bureau and the bookstore organization for my letter. . . .

At that time, the revolutionary young fighters who came from Peking to establish revolutionary ties [i.e. Red Guards] also encouraged me to go to the Engineering Bureau to claim the letter and clear up the problem. I then had faith in the Cultural Revolution Group and relied on them, thinking that they would stand for justice and give me support. Actually, they toed the line of those in authority and the work team, and all of them worked in collusion to persecute me.

Therefore, on December 2, I sent a letter to the Engineering Bureau through the Chairman of the Cultural Revolution Group asking him to turn over the letter written by Ch'en Liang to his family and to inform me of Ch'en Liang's offense. Because I received no reply after several days, I went in person on December 5 to the Engineering Bureau to see the person in charge of the Cultural Revolution Group. Its chairman received me but pretended ignorance of the case and directed me to see Li X, leader of the work team. In my presence Li X gave the following answers to my questions: (1) The letter left by Ch'en Liang for his family dependents and all his materials were handed over to the College. (2) The Engineering Bureau made public all the materials used in the struggle against Ch'en Liang and the letter left by him for his family. (3) When the bourgeois reactionary line was first criticized and repudiated, the masses were allowed to discuss things again according to the spirit of the "Sixteen-Point Decision." Since the masses did not raise any questions, Ch'en Liang was not guilty of following the bourgeois reactionary line. (4) Granted that Ch'en Liang was not one of the three "anti" elements, yet judged by his subsequent acts, he was an active counterrevolutionary.

Two days after Li X refused to hand over the letter to me, Wu XX, leader of the Cultural Revolution Group of the bookstore came to tell me, "The letter left by Ch'en Liang says nothing in particular; it only asks you to heed what the Party and Chairman Mao say and work hard." I asked him why, if this were really so, I had not been informed of the letter at the time, and why they had first denied that there was such a letter? The leader of the Cultural Revolution Group replied, "You were not informed of the letter left for fear that it might grieve you." . . .

On May 20, the representative of the fighting detachment of the bookstore came with me to demand that Secretary Lai Chu-yen of the Party Committee of the Engineering Bureau hand over the letter left by Ch'en Liang. In reply, Lai said that because he was not clear about the details of the case, he must discuss the matter with Ma Ch'ing-jui and Li X before he could give us an answer. We called on Lai again on May 23, and he claimed that since the letter left by Ch'en Liang was a document found on the spot and was connected with the case, according to the provisions of judicial procedure, it should not be handed over to his family dependents. We asked him to tell us which policy of the Central Committee stipulated that a letter left by a dead person should not be handed over to his family dependents. Because Lai was unable to answer, he had to send for the Chief of the Security Section to confront us. As a result, Chief Hsü XX of the Security Section made known that he had consulted with the second Division of the Public Security Bureau and was of the opinion that the letter left should be handed back to the family dependents. Thereupon, Lai Chu-yen could only define his attitude and agreed to return the letter left to the family. However, he said that he did not know who had kept this letter and would have to find out. We were told to return on May 24 for it.

However, Lai Chu-yen made himself unavailable to us on May 24 and 25. On the morning of May 26, the representative of the rebels of the bookstore and I found Lai Chu-yen at the Red Flag Headquarters of the College. The Bureau later sent representatives to join us, but Lai again claimed that the letter in question was kept in Li X's office. We waited for one hour, but when Li X turned up, he said that the letter

was not in his office but in the Cultural Revolution Office. Lai then got hold of the man from the former Cultural Revolution Group, but the latter lied, saying that the letter in question had disappeared when the materials were handed over in February. . . .

I have devoted nearly a year's effort to getting back the letter Ch'en Liang left me. They had all along told me that the letter in question was a "document found on the spot" and was "top secret material" which could not be shown to anybody, but I was never told that it had been lost. . . .

I have made up my mind and will fight resolutely to the end to clear up the case of Ch'en Liang. I once again lodge the strongest protest. Liang Hsiang, Lai Chu-yen, and Ma Ch'ing-jui must carry out the directive of the Military Commission of the Central Committee, and Comrade Ch'en Liang must be openly rehabilitated. Finally, I appeal to the revolutionary rebel organizations: I hope you will support me in the name of justice, defend Chairman Mao's revolutionary line, and expose the bourgeois reactionary line of the sinister Municipal Committee and the Engineering Bureau which has diverted the target of the struggle and persecuted the revolutionary masses.

87.

The Nature of Diseases

Most fields of traditional art and scholarship have been held suspect by the Communist Party leadership because in the past they were practiced and developed by members of the literati class. An exception, however, has been made for Chinese science; the achievements of early doctors, botanists, geologists, engineers, and so on have been widely praised. In the case of medicine, although many of the methods and drugs of Western medicine have been adopted, old theories based on Yin and Yang are also studied by medical personnel. In addition, worldwide publicity has been given to areas in which traditional Chinese techniques excel, such as the use of acupuncture for anesthesia.

Below are excerpts from a comprehensive manual of Chinese medicine issued by the New Medical College of Kiangsu in 1972. In this manual all diseases are analyzed according to the theory of Yin and Yang and ch'i (life force, breath). This selection can be usefully compared to the one from the Yellow Emperor's Classic of Medicine *included earlier under the Han dynasty (selection 11, "The Interaction of Yin and Yang").*

HIGH BLOOD PRESSURE

High blood pressure is caused by over-stimulation in the upper nerve centers and is characterized by a rising of the blood pressure in the arteries. Based on its symptoms, it belongs to the realm of such diseases as "headache," "dizziness" and "Yang liver" and is directly connected with "palpitations" and "paralysis" in Chinese medicine.

Cause and Theory

The underlying cause of this disease is the over-abundance of Yang or the over-depletion of Yin. The factors leading to the occurrence of the disease are extended periods of tension and strong emotional stimuli such as worry and anger, for these can lead to the imbalance of Yin and Yang of the liver and the kidneys; either the liver's Yang dominates, or the kidneys' Yin weakens. This is reflected in the symptoms showing repletion in the external and exhaustion in the internal. The excess of the Yang in the body,

when accompanied by emotional stimuli, strengthens the *ch'i* in the heart and the liver, which in turn causes the over-exuberance of the Yang. As a result, fire and wind are disturbed and the symptoms of "wind Yang attacking upward" appear. If the fire turns saliva into phlegm, then symptoms of "phlegm fire burning inward" will appear. When the over-exuberance of Yang continues for a long time, the Yin fluid will be depleted. Old patients and ones with weak livers and weak kidneys will easily have the rising of exhausted Yang or even exhaustion of both Yin and Yang. Usually, in the early stage, the symptoms are those of excessive Yang, and in the late stage exhaustion of both Yin and Yang or predominant exhaustion of Yang.

If the disease is allowed to last for a long time, or if there is a sudden development for the worse so that the wind Yang carries phlegm through the meridians and even attacks the brain, then dangerous consequences such as paralysis and unconsciousness may result. It is also possible to have the complication of heart failure resulting from the total exhaustion of the heart and kidneys, which causes the circulation of *ch'i* and blood to fail.

Diagnosis and Cure

To cure this disease, it is necessary to differentiate between the symptoms of repletion and depletion. The former usually results from wind Yang and phlegm fire, and should be cured by calming the liver, eliminating the wind, clearing out the fire, and dissolving the phlegm. The latter should be further differentiated into Yin and Yang symptoms. One should nourish the liver and the kidneys when their Yin is depleted. If the case is complicated by the exhaustion of the Yin of the heart, then one should nurture the heart. If the exhaustion of Yin is extended to Yang, Yang should also be remedied. It often happens that the symptoms of repletion and depletion occur at the same time, so one has to take both into consideration when treating the patient. For example, in a case of depleted Yin and repleted Yang, the symptoms are headache, dizziness, blurred vision, flushing easily when engaged in physical activity or when excited emotionally, thirst, loss of weight, backache, weak legs, involuntary ejaculation, reddened tongue, and thin and rapid pulse.

ARTHRITIS

This disease is characterized by sore joints, local swelling, or deformation; it includes rheumatic arthritis, pseudo-rheumatic arthritis, bone arthritis and the like. In Chinese medicine it belongs to such categories as paralysis, aching rheumatism and acute joint rheumatism.

Cause and Theory

When the *ch'i* in the body is low, and the resistance is weak, then the evil elements of wind, cold, and dampness will invade the body. They pass through the meridians, block the joints, and affect the circulation of *ch'i* and blood; the blockage results in pain and paralysis. Therefore, the ancients say, "When the three *ch'is* of wind, cold, and dampness come together, they combine and cause paralysis."

Because of the different proportions of the three evils in the combination, the symptoms vary. Arthritis caused mainly by wind is called "moving paralysis"; that caused mainly by cold is called "aching paralysis"; and that caused mainly by dampness is "stationary paralysis." If the body is affected

by the evil rheumatic heat, or if the body itself has a Yang excess when attacked by rheumatic elements from outside, or if the three evils of wind, cold, and dampness, having stayed too long in the body, have blocked the meridians and joints, then heat paralysis may arise.

If the disease is prolonged, or if the person has a weak liver and weak kidneys, conditions which cause insufficient *ch'i* and blood, then the evil *ch'i* will stay in the meridians. As a result, the saliva will thicken into phlegm, and the poorly circulating blood will form into clots, which in turn may cause the swelling, deformation, inflexibility, or locking of the joints. In the end the joints may lose their use.

Now, if the rheumatic heat goes from the external to the internal, it may harm the *ch'i* and the Yin. If the paralysis happens intermittently, the evil *ch'i* may block the meridians and cause difficulty in the circulation of *ch'i* and blood. In both cases, the heart may be robbed of its nourishment and palpitations will result.

Diagnosis and Cure

The diagnosis of this disease should be based on correct determination of the dominant evil element, whether it is wind, cold, dampness or heat. Then one can cure the patient by dispelling the wind, dispersing the cold, removing the dampness, or quenching the heat. In cases where phlegm and blood clots co-exist and the joints are deformed, one should strive to dissolve the phlegm and capture the wind, to reduce the clotting and restore blood circulation. At the same time one should clear the meridians to reduce the aching, thus achieving the principle of "if free-flowing, then no pains."

If the disease has been prolonged to such an extent as to affect the *ch'i* and blood in the viscera and harm the liver and the kidneys, then one should repair the *ch'i* and blood and nourish the liver and the kidneys.

DIABETES

China became acquainted with diabetes earlier than any other country in the world. It was treated in the *Yellow Emperor's Classic of Internal Medicine,* and there are detailed records of continuous discussions about its symptoms and complications in later periods. According to its symptoms, diabetes belongs to the category of draining diseases in Chinese medicine.

Cause and Theory

This disease is closely connected with weakness of the kidneys and insufficiency of Yin. The immediate causes for its occurrence include intemperance in eating and drinking and excessive intake of fried, greasy food; blockage in the middle heater; malfunction of the spleen and the stomach; heat and unrest, injuring the Yin fluid; failure to nourish the lungs and kidneys. There are two major courses of development of this disease, the exhaustion of Yin and heat-unrest, and one can arise from the other. When heat burns the lungs, there is excessive intake of fluid; when heat fills the spleen and the stomach, there is excessive eating of food; when there is depleted fire in the kidneys, urine becomes voluminous.

If the disease is allowed to become prolonged, the exhaustion of Yin often leads to the exhaustion of Yang and of *ch'i*. In late stages there may even appear symptoms of injured Yang in the kidneys. In other cases even the early stages show signs of weakened *ch'i*.

A patient who remains uncured for a long time may develop complications such as tuberculosis, ulcers, and blindness as a result of extreme Yin exhaustion and heat-unrest. When the Yin fluid is reduced excessively and the Yang becomes unrestrained, there may appear symptoms of ketone acidosis, irritability, thirst, sunken eyes, reddened lips, dried tongue, headach, and hyperventilation. In the end the patient may, because of total exhaustion of both Yin and Yang, lapse into a coma, his limbs turning cold and his blood pressure dropping.

Diagnosis and Cure

The major symptoms of diabetes are excessive drinking, eating, and urination, and loss of weight and strength. Depending on the symptoms, one can categorize them into upper, middle, and lower drainages. Thirst and the intake of water belong to the upper drainage, that of the lungs; hunger and the intake of food belong to the middle drainage, that of the stomach; and the need to urinate belongs to the lower drainage, that of the kidneys. However, in actual cases often all three are present. As all three drainages result from Yin depletion and heat-unrest, the method of cure is cultivating the Yin fluid, quenching the heat, and tempering the unrest. For prolonged cases in which the injury of Yin extends to Yang, one should mend the Yang of the kidneys by warm medications.

Translated by Clara Yu

88.

Modern Models for Family Life and Marriage

Despite the Marriage Reform Act of 1950 and decades of exhortation, patterns of authority in family life did not readily change, nor were all old customs abandoned. For instance, marriages continued to involve expensive gifts (especially from the groom's to the bride's family) and residence in the groom's parents' home. During the Cultural Revolution and the decade which followed, such "feudal" or "Confucian" practices were repeatedly condemned.

Below are two newspaper articles providing exemplary models of how young people could lead the way to institute change. The first is from an October 1968, People's Daily *and the second from a February, 1975, issue of a Canton newspaper.*

NEW SOCIALIST ATMOSPHERE IN THE FAMILY

Vice Chairman Lin Piao teaches us: "China is a great socialist state of the dictatorship of the proletariat with a population of 700 million. It needs unified thinking, revolutionary thinking, correct thinking. That is Mao Tse-tung's thought. Only with this thinking can we maintain vigorous revolutionary enthusiasm and a firm and correct political orientation."

Just as the state needs unified thinking to be a revolutionized state, so a family needs unified thinking to be a revolutionized family. My father is a representative of the Poor and Lower-Middle Peasant Association of the commune. He is a rebel who dares to rebel against others, but not against the old patriarchy as represented in himself. He would not listen to the opinion of others, but wanted everyone to listen to him. In fighting against my father's old ideas and habits, I myself was guilty of preserving some self-interest. I feared that fighting patriarchy would cause hostility between my father and me and consequent gossip.

Last March I attended a conference of activists in

the study of Chairman Mao's works in rural areas, which was convened by the Liaoning provincial military area command. At the conference, I was truly inspired by the story of how a new daughter-in-law had dared to rebel against the old ideas of her husband's father. I thought, "Since I am afraid to rebel against the old ideas of my father, I'm protecting the 'four olds' [old ideas, old culture, old customs, and old habits]. But how am I to rebel?" Then I thought of Chairman Mao's teaching: "If our task is to cross a river, we cannot cross it without a bridge or a boat. Unless the bridge or boat problem is solved, it is idle to speak of crossing the river." I decided to use the daughter-in-law's story as a "boat" to accomplish the task of "crossing the river." Returning to the production brigade, I transmitted the spirit of the conference to all the commune members and retold the story of the new daughter-in-law. My father was present at the meeting and afterwards I asked him, "What did you learn from this?"

He answered, "The new daughter-in-law rebelled against the old father. Good." This meant that my father was on the "boat." So striking the iron while it was hot, I asked him to organize a family study class

407

that evening. He was a bit strained and nervous and tried to shift his ground, saying, "You'd better do the job, I . . ."

Returning to the issue, I said, "You still can't drop your airs. Is it that you're afraid you'll lose your authority? You are the head of our group; you must kindle the fire yourself." As he had no real reason for putting it off, my father agreed.

After a meeting that evening I rushed back home, eager to learn how my father had "fought self." Standing outside the house by the window, I heard him say, "That new daughter-in-law is a real revolutionary. She dares to rebel against the old father-in-law. That's real democracy! But I hear that some in my family are still scared of me. What is there to fear? If you have opinions, bring them out! From this day onwards I'll put off my patriarchal airs and break the old custom of one man being the master of a family. I'll hand over power."

I laughed as I entered the room and said, "What father says is good. In the new society we have to establish a new family atmosphere based on Mao Tse-tung's thought. You, father, are the head of our study group. You are not to hand over power but to hold firmly to the power of Mao Tse-tung's thought. From now on, in word and deed, we will obey anyone whose words coincide with Mao Tse-tung's thought."

My brother added, "As to the older ones, we must take care of their livelihood as well as their political thinking. We must care for each other, love and help each other politically, and set up a new revolutionary relationship in our family."

My father happily declared, "I will hold fast to the power of Mao Tse-tung's thought. Now let anyone who has opinions express them boldly. If I'm wrong, I will immediately correct myself."

My mother, who often disputed with my father over household jobs and invariably failed to persuade him to do as she wished, was the first to speak up. She said, "Don't you remember that at the Moon Festival last year you wanted to have something to drink? I bought half a bottle, but you thought it was too little, so you threw your chopsticks away and upset the dinner. Actually, there was enough in half a bottle for several drinks, but you were afraid that people would laugh at you for being stingy and buying only half a bottle. That was nothing other than bourgeois thinking. To tell you the truth, you actually owe the half bottle of wine to the leadership of Chairman Mao! In

the old society sometimes you didn't have even porridge, let alone a drink. I see you've forgotten your past."

My mother's words touched my father on a tender spot, and his face flushed. But he soon calmed down and cited a quotation from Chairman Mao: "If we have shortcomings, we are not afraid to have them pointed out and criticized, because we serve the people. Anyone, no matter who, may point out our shortcomings." He then asked modestly for other opinions.

My brother's wife, who had never dared to say "no" to my father, then plucked up courage and said in a timid voice, "Chairman Mao teaches us to divide one into two when looking at a problem, but father sometimes sees a person in one stance only. No one is perfect. If he's one of us, we must help him enthusiastically and not regard him as a die-hard who will not change." Though she did not mention any names, we all knew she meant those class brothers in our village who were comparatively backward in thinking.

Then my third sister, who was rather excited, spoke, "Last year when the Hsin-sheng Passenger Car Plant moved away, some bricks were left behind. When father saw other people picking them up, he ordered us to get some. We said they were the property of the state and argued against it, but father wouldn't listen to us. He said, 'What's that! The property of the state! They were discarded there. If other people can pick them up, why can't we?' Father, you had better reconsider what this kind of thinking and acting leads to!"

At this family study class, everyone spoke his mind. My father listened deferentially and accepted nearly all our opinions. From that time our family changed, and a new revolutionary atmosphere was established in our home. For instance, during the busy spring sowing season this year, my father wanted to enlarge the windows of our house and put in glass panes, which would have meant four to five days' work. In the past we had to listen to him because he had patriarchal "authority." But this time my brother said, "Chairman Mao calls us to 'grasp revolution and promote production,' yet we are to busy ourselves in household jobs. This is going against collective production." My father immediately canceled his plan and led the whole family to take part in the farming activities of the production team.

DARE TO DO AWAY
WITH OLD CUSTOMS

It was a day in the middle of October last year. The masses of people in Szu-hsin Brigade (Ni-wan Commune, Tou-men county) joyously ran about passing the words: "Uncle Chin-hsi is taking a son-in-law today."

Let's hear the story about Uncle Chin-hsi taking a son-in-law.

Old poor peasant Huang Chin-hsi's daughter Ping-tsai fell in love with Ho Hua-shen of Wei-kuo Brigade, Pai-chiao Commune, and they planned to get married. This event made Chin-hsi rejoice on the one hand and grieve on the other. He was happy because thanks to the good leadership of Chairman Mao and the Communist Party, his whole family was free and his children had all grown up; he grieved because he had no son and his four daughters one after the other had all gotten married and left the family. He thought to himself, "How wonderful it would be if my son-in-law could come to live with me and take care of me when I get old." His daughter understood how he felt and suggested that Ho come to settle in her family. He consented.

When news of this spread, a small number of people still influenced by feudal ideas began to criticize. Some said, "A fine young man like him can find a wife without difficulty. Why should he have to join the family of his wife? What a shame!" When Ho's father heard these erroneous views, he also thought that as it had been a practice for women to marry into their husband's family since ancient times, his son would be looked down upon and meet "bad luck" if he did as planned.

Ho studied conscientiously the relevant writings of Chairman Mao and the ten new things of Hsiao-chin-chuang, and came to realize that "times have changed, and men and women are equal." If women could go settle in their husbands' families, then men could also go settle in their wives' families. Revolutionary young people must take the lead to break with traditional concepts like "men are superior and women inferior." Therefore, he patiently tried to enlighten his father, saying, "As long as we act in accordance with Chairman Mao's instructions, the cadres and masses will give us support." He also said, "If it's 'unlucky' for a man to join his wife's family, what kind of 'luck' did you have when you followed the old practice and took a wife into your family before liberation?" This refreshed his father's memory of the miserable past. Ho's grandparents had both died of poverty and illness under the merciless oppression of the landlords. His father worked for the landlords from early childhood, and was beaten and scolded all the time. By the time he took a wife, he had neither house nor land to his name and borrowed some money to buy a ruined boat for a house. The family led a desperate existence. After Liberation, under the leadership of Chairman Mao and the Communist Party, they became masters of their own and led an ever happier life. After recalling this bit of family history, Ho Hua-shen's father repudiated the doctrines of Confucius and Mencius, like "three cardinal guidances and five constant virtues" and "men are superior and women inferior," and raised his consciousness. In the end, he even supported his son's decision to settle in his bride's house.

Ho and Ping-tsai then went ahead with their wedding preparations. They both agreed to have their wedding the new way, not accepting betrothal money or presents or giving a feast. Huang Chin-hsi felt it was a bit niggardly not to spend a little money treating his relatives to a few drinks on this happy occasion of taking a son-in-law. Therefore, he intended to invite a few relatives and friends for a small wedding party. When Ping-tsai learned what her father felt, she said to him, "You said that when you got married, you didn't give any betrothal money or presents and didn't give a wedding feast. Why didn't you feel niggardly then?"

"That was before Liberation," he answered. "Then I was so poor that there wasn't a single grain of rice in my pot. How could I afford to buy presents and give a wedding feast? It's different today; we're now well-off. A wedding is a great event which justifies spending a little money."

In order to help her father raise his level of understanding, Ping-tsai patiently explained, "Even though we're better off today doesn't mean we can spend money at will. Indulging in extravagance and waste is an old habit of the exploiting classes, while industry and thrift are the good virtues of us poor and lower-middle peasants. We must do away with the existing habits and customs and old conventions of the exploiting classes, and erect the new style of the proletariat. If there are to be standards for weddings, then make them the standards of the proletariat."

Her father agreed with this and raised his consciousness. He even gave his consent to their preparing the wedding in an economical way. On the day of the wedding, they insistently refused gifts, did not give a feast, and did not follow any of the feudal superstitious customs. After the wedding, they immediately plunged into the battle of grasping revolution and promoting production.

89.

Population Control and the Four Modernizations

After the death of Mao Tse-tung in 1976, the leaders responsible for many of the most radical policies of the past decade were ousted from power. The new leaders, Hua Kuo-feng and Teng Hsiao-p'ing, turned much of their interest to economic development. In 1977–1980 the catchwords were the "Four Modernizations," that is, modernization of agriculture, industry, science, and the military. Competitive entrance examinations were reintroduced for universities, ending the practice of favoring peasants and workers over intellectuals. The problems China faced for rapid expansion and improvement of industry came to be more openly discussed, and advice and techniques from foreign countries actively sought. For the first time in decades, hundreds of Chinese were sent abroad to complete their education.

The article below, from an October, 1979, Canton newspaper, is typical of this new trend in its realism about China's problems. It was written by Li Mei-lin, Deputy Director of the Kwangtung Provincial Family Planning Office.

Controlling population growth must be viewed from an explicit fundamental standpoint; that is, it must be considered in terms of its strategic significance for accelerating the realization of the socialist Four Modernizations. If our family planning is done well, we can speed up the progress of the Four Modernizations; if it is not, it will hold back the Four Modernizations. Using facts as the sole criterion of truth, we should take stock of our experience, positive and negative, in the population problem over the last thirty years and lower the natural population growth to a more reasonable level.

China has the largest population of any country in the world. China's population growth is distinguished by a large base, a high birth rate, and a rapid growth rate. At the time of Liberation in 1949, China's population was over 540 million. Now it has risen to over 900 million. Of this number, about 600 million were born after Liberation. The population had a net

increase of over 400 million in thirty years, nearly doubling. In 1949, the population of Kwangtung was 30.1 million, but by 1978 it had reached 55.92 million. Of that number, 36 million were born after Liberation. That is a net increase of 25.8 million, or 85.7 percent of the population in the early years of Liberation. This is very fast for population growth.

In dealing with population growth we are facing a new problem, the population growth peak. The peak of the birth rate is determined by how many people enter their childbearing years. Because in the 1950s we did not pay attention to family planning, population growth rose sharply, and those who were born in that period are now entering their childbearing years. If we take Kwangtung as an example, because of the 36 million people born after Liberation, every year from 1980 on, the number of persons reaching marriageable age will gradually increase from 500,000 couples to 600,000–800,000 couples. If every couple has two children, by the year 2000 that generation born after Liberation alone will have given birth to nearly 36 million more people. According to statistics provided by the agencies concerned, after the population of those born after Liberation throughout the entire country reaches the childbearing years, even strictly adhering to the plan that each couple have only two children, the country's population will climb to 1.2 billion by the end of the century. This kind of population growth cannot be ignored.

Our population is large in terms of our cultivated land, creating a major contradiction. If we do not control population on a planned basis, this contradiction will become increasingly acute, and the matter of food will inevitably become critical. At present in China there is an average of 1.5 *mou* of land per person. Moreover, agricultural production is backward, food grain output per unit area is low, and, in terms of the average volume of food grain produced per person, China has one of the lowest standards in the world. We already face the serious contradictions of large population, limited land, and food grain production that cannot catch up to population growth. For this reason, we must resolve to adopt effective measures to control population at an appropriate level. Otherwise, the development of the Four Modernizations will be hindered. . . .

To realize the Four Modernizations, it is necessary to have a large amount of capital accumulation and a fairly high rate of accumulation; yet, on the other hand, it is also necessary gradually to improve the people's standard of living. How can we give consideration to both of these needs? The first way is to expand production and practice strict economy. Apart from this, under the existing state of affairs in which our country's population base is large and increasing rapidly while production is insufficiently developed, lowering the rate of population growth can be an important measure in managing the relationship between accumulation and consumption. . . .

Recently, some departments concerned estimated that the expenditures for one child from conception and birth to the age of sixteen is 6,900 dollars in a major city, 4,800 dollars in a provincial city, and 1,600 dollars in the rural areas. Kwangtung began to give attention to family planning in 1965. In 1965 the birth rate in Kwangtung was 36.28 per thousand, but in 1978 it was 20.11 per thousand. That is a reduction of 16.17 per thousand over twelve years. Altogether over 6.9 million fewer people were born. This re-

duced the national and family expenditures by over 350 billion dollars; saved nearly 4.3 billion catties of food grain; reduced the number of children starting school annually by 580,000; and reduced the burden on medical care, housing, employment, and nonstaple foods. It can be seen that doing a good job on family planning can lighten the burden on the nation, increase accumulation, and accelerate the Four Modernizations.

The relationship between consumption and population reproduction is even closer. It is an objective economic law that population production must be in line with the production of material goods. This is especially the case when the means of livelihood which can be supplied by social production are insufficient. If population growth cannot be controlled it will affect the standard of living and will influence the entire nation's scientific and cultural level.

The people's standard of living is a matter of food, clothing, and shelter. As I said earlier, our nation's average grain output per person is one of the lowest in the world. Since Liberation, the total output of food grains in the entire country more than doubled, from 210 billion catties in 1949 to 565 billion catties in 1977. In twenty-eight years our food grain increased at an average rate of 3.3 percent, surpassing the rate of population growth of 1.9 percent. However, if we base our calculations on the twenty-year period from 1957 to 1977, the average annual increase in food grains was 2 percent and the average annual population growth was also about 2 percent, so that the two canceled each other out. If we take into consideration the increase in grains used for industry and the like, our actual average grain ration is not much better than it was in 1957.

Housing is an important element in the people's standard of living and it is also very closely related to population growth. From 1956 to 1977 the nation invested over 30 billion dollars in urban housing. Recently housing construction reached 500 million square meters. According to statistics, from late 1977 the average area of urban housing per person was 3.6 square meters, a decrease of .9 square meters from the 4.5 figure for the early Liberation period. The housing situation in Kwangtung is even more critical. According to statistics for ten large- and medium-sized cities in Kwangtung, 115,000 households were without housing or lived in housing with less than 2 square meters per person. Thus, it is obvious that even though every year the nation spends money to resolve the problem of housing the people, the housing shortage has not been alleviated. An important reason is the rapid growth of the population.

Planned control of population growth would also help in raising the scientific and cultural level of the nation. In old China, the educational level was very low. Although we made great progress after Liberation, the gap between us and economically developed countries is still wide. The ordinary worker in Japan has finished upper middle school, but in China there are 100 million young people who are illiterate or semi-illiterate, and 5 million of them are in Kwangtung. In 1977, of every 10,000 people, in America 456.4 were in college, in Japan 156.8 were in college, in Yugoslavia 156.8 were in college, in France 141.4 were in college, in Germany 117.1 were in college, in England 112 were in college, but in China only 6.1 were in college. To achieve the Four Modernizations we need not only workers in quantity but, more important, workers of quality, that is, ones who have a degree of culture and the ability to be expert at one thing and good at many others. But to train a person to be this kind of worker requires a capital investment of over 10,000 dollars. If we can control the natural population growth to under 10 per thousand by 1985, we can reduce the number of persons in school throughout the country by 50 million. . . .

To control the rate of population growth effectively, we must conscientiously take stock of our positive and negative experience on the population question over the last thirty years and improve research on population theory. Why has the rate of China's population growth been so rapid since Liberation? One important reason is that we adopted mistaken theory, superficially proclaiming the viewpoint that "more people is a good thing," as if the more people the better, even to the point of claiming it as an important principle of historical materialism. We adopted a policy of "look but don't see" toward population problems actually in existence, even to the point of creating an anarchistic attitude toward population growth, which has had disastrous effects. In the early 1950s, many scholars who studied the population question put forth good ideas about planned growth for China's population. Mr. Ma Yin-ch'u once in December 1956 and again in May 1957 published essays proposing that planned control of China's population be undertaken. Particularly commendable is that he saw the dual importance of the population question. He said, "A large population is, of course, an extremely great asset, but an extremely great liability as well," and he pointed out that "Too

many peope will retard technological development and scientific progress." Looked at today, these viewpoints still have great practical significance. If at that time we had adopted this correct idea and the Party and nation had as serious a regard toward the population as they have today, probably China's population would not have increased as fast as it has in the last twenty years, and the problem would not have reached its present proportions. But Mr. Ma Yinch'u's foresight and wisdom brought on criticisms; it was "Malthusianism," "denied the superiority of the socialist system," and "lacked sympathy for the 600 million people"; he was tarred with one political brush after another. Many other scholars who studied the population question were not condemned as reactionary population theorists or Malthusians, but they were called rightists and suffered the same fate as Mr. Ma Yin-ch'u. Thus, theoretical workers did not dare to study demographic theory, and practical workers could not formulate with assurance effective policy measures to control population.

In the 1950s, Kwangtung was quite active in research on population theory, and many comrades proposed some very good ideas. In the early 1970s, some theoretical workers in Shan-t'ou set forth the view that the production of people and the material means of production go hand in hand. To promote research on population theory, in the winter of 1975 two population theory study courses were offered at the provincial party school. In December 1977, the State Council Family Planning Leadership Team Office held a "National Conference on Population Theory Study Class Work" in Shan-t'ou. The response was very enthusiastic about the research on population theory which we had begun. Now, under the new conditions, we want to liberate thinking, take stock of experience, make a clear distinction between what is Malthusianism and what is Marxist population theory, eliminate the bad influence of the metaphysical view that having a lot of people is always a good thing, breach the forbidden zone of socialist population questions, carry out thoroughly the policy of encouraging diverse ideas, advocate seeking truth from facts, raise population theory research to a new level, promote planned population growth, and contribute to the acceleration of the Four Modernizations.

Translated by William L. MacDonald

Glossary

Amita Buddhism. The school of Buddhism that stressed salvation in the Pure Land, a paradise ruled over by the Amita Buddha. While on earth the Amita Buddha had promised entry into his paradise to those who sincerely called on his name.

Analects (Lun yü). The record of the sayings of Confucius, one of the thirteen classics.

Board of Civil Office. The central government organ concerned with personnel issues such as the assignment of men to office.

Book of Changes (I-ching). One of the Five Classics, dating from the Chou dynasty. A divination manual.

Book of Documents (Shu-ching). A collection of purported speeches, pronouncements, and court debates dating from the Chou dynasty. One of the Five Classics. See "The Metal Bound Box," selection one.

Book of Poetry (Shih-ching). One of the Five Classics, dating from the Chou dynasty. See "Songs and Poems," selection three.

Boxer Rebellion (1900). Anti-foreign uprising in northeast China in 1900. The Boxers were a xenophobic, mystic society, which sought to drive the foreigners from China and to restore the glory of the Ch'ing dynasty. In the summer of 1900 they besieged the foreign legations' compound in Peking, but the siege was broken by an international relief force and the rebellion suppressed.

Buddha. Means "the Enlightened." Buddhahood may be claimed by anyone who has achieved enlightenment. "The Buddha" usually refers to the Prince Siddhartha of the Guatama clan (ca. 563–483 B.C.) from the ancient state of Magadha along the modern-day border of Nepal and India. According to tradition, the Guatama Buddha tried then rejected first a life of luxury and then a life of poverty. In the year 528 B.C. he is said to have achieved Enlightenment and began teaching a philosophy of the Middle Way.

cash. A small copper coin.

Ch'eng Brothers. Ch'eng Hao (1032–1085) and Ch'eng I (1033–1107). Early Neo-Confucian philosophers who helped develop the metaphysical concepts of *li* ("principle") and *ch'i* ("material force").

ch'i. Vital energy, material force, ether, breath. A term used both in philosophy and in scientific thinking.

Chieh (traditional r. 1818–1766 B.C.). Last ruler of the legendary Hsia dynasty whose evil ways were said to have caused the downfall of that dynasty.

Ch'ien-lung Emperor (r. 1736–1795). Fourth Ch'ing Emperor who presided over the dynasty at the height of its power. While an able administrator and skillful leader in war, he is also known as a connoisseur of literature, painting, porcelain, and other arts.

chin-shih. "Presented Scholar." Beginning as one of a number of examination degrees offered during the Sui and T'ang dynasties, from the Sung onwards it was the highest and most prestigeous degree. During the Ming and Ch'ing dynasties candidates who had passed the *chü-jen* or provincial level examination could take the examination for the *chin-shih,* offered every third year in the capital. Those who became *chin-shih* could normally expect to receive an official appointment, although delays sometimes amounted to years.

Chu Hsi (1130–1200). One of the greatest of the Neo-Confucian philosophers. Considered the first great synthesizer of the *li hsüeh* (School of Principle). Also known for his great commentaries on the Confucian classics. His configuration of Neo-Confucianism became the official orthodoxy during the Ming (1368–1644) and Ch'ing (1644–1911) periods.

chü-jen. "Recommended Man." A provincial-level degree-holder eligible to hold office and take the capital examinations.

Chuang Tzu (369–286 B.C.). Traditionaly considered to be the second of the great classical Taoist philosophers after Lao Tzu. His writings, consisting of philosophical essays and humorous though pointed anecdotes, have been preserved in a book called the *Chuang Tzu.*

Confucius (K'ung-fu Tzu) (551–479 B.C.). Classical philosopher, one of the most influential thinkers in Chinese history. He was born in the state of Lu (in modern Shantung) and assumed the life of the itinerant scholar-official trying to influence the policies of the great lords of the various classical states. While he never met with great success in the political sphere, he propagated a philosophy of life that was to be highly influential throughout subsequent Chinese history.

Duke of Chou. Early statesman and philosopher, served as regent for his royal nephew from 1115 to 1108 B.C. Admired by Confucius, the Duke of Chou is credited with consolidating the power of the newly founded dynasty.

examination system. The system of recruiting men for office through written and oral examinations of candidates. Most highly developed in the Sung and subsequent dynasties.

Five Classics. The *Book of Poetry*, the *Book of Documents*, the *Book of Changes*, the *Spring and Autumn Annals*, and the *Record of Rites*. All were revered by the Confucians as preserving the most ancient truths.

the five elements or forces. A component of Chinese cosmological thinking developed during the late classical period. The five elements are wood, fire, earth, metal, and water. They are in constant interaction, overtaking and suppressing each other in a fixed progression. Illness, the change of seasons, the change of weather, and even the change of dynasties were explained in terms of these elements.

geomancy. The "science" of locating favorable sites for houses, graves, and so on, according to the vital forces and "veins" of the earth.

Governor. Head of a province. See REFERENCE MATTER.

hexagrams. Graphs of six lines, some broken, some unbroken. Each of the 64 possible hexagrams had a name and the *Book of Changes* offered interpretations of its meaning.

Hsiung-nu. A nomadic people of the steppes north of China who frequently invaded during the Han dynasty. The Hsiung-nu are often identified with the Huns who invaded the Roman Empire in the fifth century A.D.

International Settlement. Area of Shanghai in which foreigners enjoyed many privileges of self-government and immunity from Chinese law (extra-territoriality). The Shanghai International Settlement became extremely important both as a point of foreign influence and trade in China and as a refuge for Chinese seeking to avoid their own country's law.

K'ang-hsi Emperor (1662–1722). The second and probably the greatest of the Ch'ing Emperors. The K'ang-hsi Emperor was successful in breaking the Manchu court factions and concentrating power in the Emperor's hands. He strove to reconcile the Manchu conquerors and their Chinese subjects. The final military conquest of all China by the Manchus was achieved under him.

kowtow (k'ou-t'ou). "To knock the head," a ceremony of one or more kneelings or bowings with the head striking the floor. The kowtow was performed as a sign of respect for one's superiors, especially for the Emperor and for the elders and ancestors of one's family.

Kuan Yin. A Bodhisattva (Buddha-to-be) noted for compassion. Usually conceived of as a female.

kung-sheng. "Senior Student." A middle-level degree holder, sometimes eligible to hold office.

Lao Tzu (traditional dates 604–531 B.C.). According to tradition, the author of the *Way and Its Power* and founder of Taoism as a school of philosophy.

Legalism. Classical philosophical school and important strand in Chinese intellectual history. The Legalists held that the law should be supreme in the land and universal in its application. The Confucian reliance on government of good men was shunned by them on the grounds that men were basically evil. Rather than relying on education and the good will of men in governing the state, the Legalists looked to bureaucratic regulations and rewards and punishments. Legalism became the official ideology of the Ch'in dynasty (221–206 B.C.).

li. A unit of length equal to about ⅓ of a mile.

Long March. Heroic march of the Communist Party and Red Army from their besieged headquarters in Kiangsi province to a new base in Yenan, taking over two years and covering 6,000 miles.

Magistrate. Head of a county. See REFERENCE MATTER.

Manchus. A tribe of the Jurched group, settled in what is present-day Manchuria. By the mid-sixteenth century, they had largely given up their old nomadic ways, and in 1644 invaded China and established the Ch'ing dynasty, which lasted to 1911.

May Fourth Movement. Large-scale protest movement of students and intellectuals, begun in Peking on May 4, 1919, over the agreements at Versailles giving the old German concessions in Shantung province not to China but to Japan. In a broader sense the May Fourth Movement came to represent a general movement among educated Chinese to chart new courses for China's development, especially in the intellectual and cultural sphere.

Mencius (Meng Tzu 372–289 B.C.). Classical philosopher and successor to Confucius. Like Confucius, his attempts to influence the rulers of his time were largely unsuccessful, but his speeches (preserved in the *Mencius*) charted new directions in Confucianism. Especially noted for his theory that rulers rule by the Mandate of Heaven, which can be withdrawn if they mistreat their subjects.

Mongols. Generic term for a number of Central Asian tribes that were united by Chinggis Khan in 1206. Through a series of rapid military conquests, they established a great Eurasian empire. China was subjugated by the Mongols in stages, completed by Khubilai Khan in 1279. After the collapse of their dynasty in China (the yüan), the Mongols proved a military threat to China for several centuries but were never able to reassert their supremacy.

popular Taoism. The term used for the folk religion of the Chinese. It incorporated ancient beliefs in a wide variety of ghosts, spirits, and demons with belief in immortals and the divinity of Taoist sages. After Buddhism was introduced to China, Popular Taoism also developed an elaborate system of clergy and temples. See also TAOISM.

Prefect. Head of a prefecture. See REFERENCE MATTER.

Pure Land. The paradise of the Amita Buddhists.

rules of decorum, ritual, ceremony (*li*). The basic rules of conduct governing traditional Chinese life, prescriptions for socially acceptable behavior. These rules govern interpersonal relations as well as the ceremonies for worship, ancestor veneration, and official activities.

runner. An underling of a Magistrate or Prefect who carried messages, arrested criminals, collected taxes, and performed other assorted duties.

sheng-yüan. Government student. A lower-level degree holder eligible to take the provincial level examinations.

Shun (legendary reign ca. 2255–2206 B.C.). One of the legendary sage emperors of the golden age of antiquity. He was held up as an example of a self-made man of humble origin who achieved greatness as a wise ruler.

Six Boards. The Boards of Civil Office, Revenue, Rites, War, Punishments, and Public Works. Major units of the central government from the T'ang through the Ch'ing dynasties.

T'ai-p'ing Rebellion (1850–1864). Huge upheaval in south and cental China during the mid-nineteenth century. Led by the mentally unbalanced Hung Hsiu-ch'üan, its ideology incorporated elements of Christianity, utopian Confucianism, and mystical Taoism.

Taoism. A classical school of philosophy formulated by Lao Tzu (tr. 604–521 B.C.) and Chuang Tzu (369–286 B.C.). Main strand of thought is the search for harmony with the Tao ("Way"), which is total, natural, spontaneous, nameless, and eternal. Everything that exists or happens does so because of the Tao. Taoists are less rigid than Confucians, seeing the relativity of values and the smallness of human endeavors within the working of the universe. Distinguish from POPULAR TAOISM.

Tatars. See MONGOLS.

Thirteen Classics. Besides the Five Classics, the Thirteen Classics also included the *Ceremonies and Rituals*, the *Rituals of the Chou Dynasty*, the *Ku-liang*, *Kung-yang*, and *Tso* commentaries to the *Spring and Autumn Annals*, the *Analects*, the *Mencius*, the *Erh-ya*, and the *Classic of Filial Piety*. This list of the classics gained favor in the Sung dyansty.

Tso Chronicle. One of the thirteen classics. A historical account presented as a commentary to the *Spring and Autumn Annals.*

The Way (Tao). See TAOISM.

yamen. The headquarters of a local official. The yamen was a walled area that contained buildings for the conduct of official business and also served as the residence for the official and his immediate family and staff.

Yellow Emperor. One of the ancient mythical culture heroes. Associated with Taoism and medicine.

Yenan. A city in Shensi province which became Mao's headquarters shortly after the completion of the Long March and remained so during World War II.

Yin and Yang. Components of Chinese cosmological thinking. Yin is the female, or passive principle, Yang the male, or assertive one. These are complementary principles. Although in nature one rises as the other wanes, no creature, force, or object is purely composed of one in the absence of the other.

Suggestions for Further Reading

Books in English about China and Chinese civilization now number in the thousands, with especially good coverage of the modern period. There is both an extensive monographic literature and many fine books aimed at a general audience. The following suggestions are limited to widely available books, especially paperbacks, and to the topics covered in this sourcebook.

HISTORICAL OVERVIEWS

Fairbank, John K. *The United States and China*. 4th rev. ed. Cambridge, Mass.: Harvard University Press, 1979.

Fairbank, John K., and Reischauer, Edwin O. *China: Tradition and Transformation*. Boston: Houghton Mifflin, 1978.

Hucker, Charles O. *China's Imperial Past: An Introduction to Chinese History and Culture*. Stanford: Stanford University Press, 1975.

Meisner, Maurice. *Mao's China: A History of the People's Republic*. New York: Free Press, 1977.

Meskill, John, ed. *An Introduction to Chinese Civilization*. New York: Columbia University Press, 1973.

Sheridan, James E. *China in Disintegration: The Republican Era in Chinese History, 1912–1949*. New York: Free Press, 1975.

Wakeman, Frederic, Jr. *The Fall of Imperial China*. New York: Free Press, 1975.

RELIGION AND COSMOLOGY

Ch'en, Kenneth K. S. *Buddhism in China: A Historical Survey*. Princeton: Princeton University Press, 1964.

Kaltenmark, Max. *Lao Tzu and Taoism*. Stanford: Stanford University Press, 1969.

Mote, Frederick W. *Intellectual Foundations of China*. New York: Alfred A. Knopf, 1971.

Overmeyer, Daniel L. *Folk Buddhist Religion: Dissenting Sects in Late Traditional China*. Cambridge, Mass.: Harvard University Press, 1976.

Thompson, Laurence G. *Chinese Religion: An Introduction*. 2d ed. Encino, Cal.: Dickenson Publishing Co., 1975.

Welch, Holmes. *The Parting of the Way: Lao Tzu and the Taoist Movement*. Boston: Beacon Press, 1957.

———. *The Practice of Chinese Buddhism, 1900–1950*. Cambridge, Mass.: Harvard University Press, 1967.

Wolf, Arthur P., ed. *Religion and Ritual in Chinese Society*. Stanford: Stanford University Press, 1974.

Yang, C. K. *Religion in Chinese Society: A Study of Contemporary Social Functions of Religion and Some of Their Historical Factors*. Berkeley: University of California Press, 1970.

FAMILY, KINSHIP, AND WOMEN

Ahern, Emily M. *The Cult of the Dead in a Chinese Village*. Stanford: Stanford University Press, 1973.

Baker, Hugh D. R. *Chinese Family and Kinship.* New York: Columbia University Press, 1979.

Cohen, Myron L. *House United, House Divided: The Chinese Family in Taiwan.* New York: Columbia University Press, 1976.

Davin, Delia. *Woman-Work: Women and the Party in Revolutionary China.* Oxford: Oxford University Press, 1976.

Freedman, Maurice. *Lineage Organization in Southeastern China.* London: Atheone Press, 1958.

———, ed. *Family and Kinship in Chinese Society.* Stanford: Stanford University Press, 1970.

Hsu, Francis L. K. *Under the Ancestor's Shadow: Kinship, Personality and Social Mobility in China.* 2d ed. Stanford: Stanford University Press, 1971.

Levy, Marion J., Jr. *The Family Revolution in Modern China.* New York: Atheneum, 1968 (originally published 1949).

Parish, William, and Whyte, Martin. *Village and Family in Contemporary China.* Chicago: University of Chicago Press, 1978.

Pruit, Ida, from the story told her by Ning Lao T'ai-t'ai. *A Daughter of Han: The Autobiography of a Chinese Working Woman.* Stanford: Stanford University Press, 1967 (originally published 1945).

Sidel, Ruth. *Women and Child Care in China.* Baltimore: Penguin Books, 1973.

Wolf, Margery. *Women and the Family in Rural Taiwan.* Stanford: Stanford University Press, 1972.

Wolf, Margery, and Witke, Roxane. *Women in Chinese Society.* Stanford: Standford University Press, 1975.

Yang, C. K. *The Chinese Family in the Communist Revolution.* Cambridge, Mass.: M.I.T. Press, 1959.

Young, Marilyn B., ed. *Women in China: Studies in Social Change and Feminism.* Ann Arbor: Center for Chinese Studies, 1973.

SOCIAL AND ECONOMIC ORGANIZATION

Buck, John L. *Land Utilization in China.* Shanghai: Commercial Press, 1937.

Chen, Jack. *A Year in Upper Felicity: Life in a Chinese Village During the Cultural Revolution.* New York: Macmillan, 1973.

Eckstein, Alexander. *China's Economic Revolution.* Cambridge: Cambridge University Press, 1977.

Elvin, Mark. *The Pattern of the Chinese Past.* Stanford: Stanford University Press, 1973.

Elvin, Mark, and Skinner, G. William, eds. *The Chinese City Between Two Worlds.* Stanford: Stanford University Press, 1974.

Fei, Hsiao-tung, and Chang, Chih-i. *Earthbound China: A Study of Rural Economy in Yunnan.* Chicago: University of Chicago Press, 1945.

Gamble, Sidney D. *Ting Hsien: A North China Rural Community.* Stanford: Stanford University Press, 1968 (originally published 1954).

Greenblatt, Sidney L., ed. *The People of Taihang: An Anthology of Family Histories.* White Plains, N.Y.: M. E. Sharpe, 1976.

Jing Su and Luo Lun. *Landlord and Labor in Late Imperial China: Case Studies from Shandong.* Translated and with an introduction by Endymion Wilkinson. Cambridge, Mass.: Harvard University Council on East Asian Studies, 1978.

Meskill, Johanna Menzel. *A Chinese Pioneer Family: The Lins of Wu-feng, Taiwan, 1729–1895.* Princeton: Princeton University Press, 1978.

Myers, Ramon H. *The Chinese Peasant Economy: Agricultural Development in Hopei and Shantung, 1890–1949.* Cambridge, Mass.: Harvard University Press, 1970.

Myrdal, Jan. *Report from a Chinese Village.* New York: New American Library, 1965.

Oksenberg, Michael, ed. *China's Developmental Experience.* New York: Praeger, 1973.

Perkins, Dwight H. *Agricultural Development in China, 1368–1968.* Chicago: Aldine, 1969.

———, ed. *China's Modern Economy in Historical Perspective.* Stanford: Stanford University Press, 1975.

Rawski, Evelyn Sakakida. *Education and Popular Literacy in Ch'ing China.* Ann Arbor: University of Michigan Press, 1978.

Skinner, G. William, ed. *The City in Late Traditional China.* Stanford: Stanford University Press, 1977.

Smith, Arthur H. *Village Life in China.* Boston: Little, Brown, 1970 (originally published 1899).

Spence, Jonathan D. *The Death of Woman Wang.* Baltimore: Penguin, 1978.

Whyte, Martin King. *Small Groups and Political Rituals in China.* Berkeley: University of California Press, 1974.

Willmott, W. E., ed. *Economic Organization in Chinese Society.* Stanford University Press, 1972.

Yang, C. K. *A Chinese Village in Early Communist*

Transition. Cambridge, Mass.: M.I.T. Press, 1959.

Yang, Martin C. *A Chinese Village: Taitou, Shantung Province.* New York: Columbia University Press, 1945.

THE UPPER CLASS
AND INTELLECTUALS

Beattie, Hilary J. *Land and Lineage in China: A Study of T'ung-Ch'eng County, Anhwei, in the Ming and Ch'ing Dynasties.* Cambridge: Cambridge University Press, 1979.

Chang, Chung-li. *The Chinese Gentry: Studies on Their Role in Nineteenth-Century Chinese Society.* Seattle: University of Washington Press, 1955.

Chow, Tse-tsung. *The May Fourth Movement: Intellectual Revolution in Modern China.* Stanford: Stanford University Press, 1967 (originally published 1960).

Eberhard, Wolfram. *Social Mobility in Traditional China.* Leiden: E. J. Brill, 1962.

Ebrey, Patricia Buckley. *The Aristocratic Families of Early Imperial China: A Case Study of the Po-ling Ts'ui Family.* Cambridge: Cambridge University Press, 1978.

Fei, Hsiao-t'ung. *China's Gentry: Essays in Rural-Urban Relations.* Chicago: University of Chicago Press, 1953.

Goldman, Merle. *Literary Dissent in Communist China.* Cambridge, Mass.: Harvard University Press, 1967.

Grieder, Jerome B. *Hu Shih and the Chinese Renaissance: Liberalism in the Chinese Revolution, 1917–1937.* Cambridge, Mass.: Harvard University Press, 1970.

Ho, Ping-ti. *The Ladder of Success in Imperial China: Aspects of Social Mobility, 1368–1911.* New York: John Wiley, 1964 (originally published 1962).

Hung, William. *Tu Fu: China's Greatest Poet.* Cambridge, Mass.: Harvard University Press, 1952.

Lang, Olga. *Pa Chin and His Writings: Chinese Youth Between the Two Revolutions.* Cambridge, Mass.: Harvard University Press, 1967.

Levenson, Joseph R. *Liang Ch'i-ch'ao and the Mind of Modern China.* Berkeley: University of California Press, 1967 (originally published 1953).

Meisner, Maurice. *Li Ta-chao and the Origins of Chinese Marxism.* Cambridge, Mass.: Harvard University Press, 1967.

Schneider, Laurence A. *Ku Chieh-kang and China's New History: Nationalism and the Quest for Alternative Traditions.* Berkeley: University of California Press, 1971.

Schwartz, Benjamin. *In Search of Wealth and Power: Yen Fu and the West.* Cambridge, Mass.: Harvard University Press, 1964.

Waley, Arthur. *The Life and Times of Po Chü-i, 772–846 A.D.* London: George Allen & Unwin, 1949.

———. *Yuan Mei, Eighteenth Century Chinese Poet.* New York: Grove Press, 1956.

Wang, Y. C. *Chinese Intellectuals and the West, 1872–1949.* Chapel Hill: University of North Carolina Press, 1966.

Wechsler, Howard J. *Mirror to the Son of Heaven: Wei Cheng and the Court of T'ang T'ai-tsung.* New Haven: Yale University Press, 1974.

Wright, Arthur F., ed. *The Confucian Persuasion.* Stanford: Stanford University Press, 1960.

LAW AND LOCAL GOVERNMENT

Bennett, Gordon. *Yundong: Mass Campaigns in Chinese Communist Leadership.* Berkeley: Center for Chinese Studies, 1976.

Bernstein, Thomas P. *Up to the Mountains and Down to the Villages: The Transfer of Youth from Urban to Rural China.* New Haven: Yale University Press, 1977.

Bodde, Derk, and Morris, Clarence. *Law in Imperial China, Exemplified by 190 Ch'ing Dynasty Cases, with Historical, Social, and Juridical Commentaries.* Cambridge, Mass.: Harvard University Press, 1967.

Buxbaum, David C., ed. *Chinese Family Law and Social Change in Historical and Comparative Perspective.* Seattle: University of Washington Press, 1978.

Ch'u, T'ung-tsu. *Law and Society in Traditional China.* Paris: Mouton, 1961.

———. *Local Government in China Under the Ch'ing.* Stanford: Stanford University Press, 1962.

Cohen, Jerome Alan. *The Criminal Process in the People's Republic of China, 1949–1963: An Introduction.* Cambridge, Mass.: Harvard University Press, 1968.

Hsiao, Kung-chuan. *Rural China: Imperial Control in the Nineteenth Century.* Seattle: University of Washington Press, 1960.

Hulsewe, A. F. P. *Remnants of Han Law*, vol. 1. Leiden: E. J. Brill, 1955.

Johnson, Wallace. *The T'ang Code: General Principles*. Princeton: Princeton University Press, 1979.

van der Sprenkel, S. *Legal Institutions in Manchu China*. London: Athlone Press, 1962.

Vogel Ezra. *Canton Under Communism: Programs in a Provincial Capital, 1949-1968*. Cambridge, Mass.: Harvard University Press, 1969 (paperback: Harper Torchbooks).

Wakeman, Frederic, Jr., and Grant, Carolyn, eds. *Conflict and Control in Late Imperial China*. Berkeley: University of California Press, 1975.

Watt, John R. *The District Magistrate in Late Imperial China*. New York: Columbia University Press, 1972.

REBELLIONS, POPULAR MOVEMENTS, AND MODERN REVOLUTIONS

Belden, Jack. *China Shakes the World*. New York: Monthly Review Press, 1970 (originally published 1949).

Bennett, Gordon A., and Montaperto, Ronald N. *Red Guard*. New York: Viking Press, 1972.

Chesneaux, Jean, ed. *Popular Movements and Secret Societies in China, 1840-1950*. Stanford: Stanford University Press, 1972.

Eastman, Lloyd E. *The Abortive Revolution: China Under Nationalist Rule, 1927-1937*. Cambridge, Mass.: Harvard University Press, 1974.

Esherick, Joseph W. *Reform and Revolution in China: The 1911 Revolution in Hunan and Hubei*. Berkeley: University of California Press, 1976.

Feuerwerker, Albert. *Rebellion in Nineteenth-Century China*. Ann Arbor: Center for Chinese Studies, 1975.

Hofheinz, Roy, Jr. *The Broken Wave: The Chinese Communist Peasant Movement, 1922-1928*. Cambridge, Mass.: Harvard University Press, 1977.

Isaacs, Harold. *The Tragedy of the Chinese Revolution*. Stanford: Stanford University Press, 1961 (originally published 1938).

Jen, Yu-wen. *The Taiping Revolutionary Movement*. New Haven: Yale University Press, 1973.

Johnson, Chalmers A. *Peasant Nationalism and Communist Power: The Emergence of Revolutionary China, 1937-1945*. Stanford: Stanford University Press, 1962.

Karnow, Stanley. *Mao and China: From Revolution to Revolution*. New York: Viking Press, 1972.

Kuhn, Philip A. *Rebellion and Its Enemies in Late Imperial China: Militarization and Social Structure, 1796-1864*. Cambridge, Mass.: Harvard University Press, 1970.

Milton, David, and Milton, Nancy Dall. *The Wind Will Not Subside: Years in Revolutionary China, 1964-1969*. New York: Pantheon Books, 1976.

Naquin, Susan. *Millenarian Rebellion in China: The Eight Trigrams Uprising of 1813*. New Haven: Yale University Press, 1976.

Schiffrin, Harold Z. *Sun Yat-sen and the Origins of the Chinese Revolution*. Berkeley: University of California Press, 1970.

Schram, Stuart. *Mao Tse-tung*. Baltimore: Penguin, 1966.

Selden, Mark. *The Yenan Way in Revolutionary China*. Cambridge, Mass.: Harvard University Press, 1971.

Snow, Edgar. *Red Star Over China*. New York: Modern Library, 1938.

Wakeman, Frederic, Jr. *Strangers at the Gate: Social Disorder in South China, 1839-1861*. Berkeley: University of California Press, 1966.

Wright, Mary Clabaugh, ed. *China in Revolution: The First Phase, 1900-1913*. New Haven: Yale University Press, 1968.

TRANSLATIONS

Fiction

Buck, Pearl S., trans. *All Men Are Brothers*. New York: John Day, 1933.

Birch, Cyril, trans. *Stories from a Ming Collection: Translations of Chinese Short Stories Published in the Seventeenth Century*. New York: Grove Press, 1958.

Cao Xueqin. *The Story of the Stone*. Translated by David Hawks. Baltimore: Penguin, 1973.

Chang, H. C. *Chinese Literature: Popular Fiction and Drama*. Edinburgh University Press, 1973.

Chin P'ing Mei, the Adventurous History of Hsi Men and His Six Wives. New York: Capricorn, 1960 (originally published 1940).

Hsia, C. T., ed., with the assistance of Joseph S. M. Lau. *Twentieth-Century Chinese Stories*. New York: Columbia University Press, 1971.

Isaacs, Harold R., ed. *Straw Sandals: Chinese Short Stories, 1918-1933*. Cambridge, Mass.: M.I.T. Press, 1974.

Lao She. *Rickshaw, the Novel Lo-to Hsiang Tzu*.

Translated by Jean M. James. Honolulu: University of Hawaii Press, 1979.

Liu T'ieh-yün. *The Travels of Lao Ts'an*. Translated and annotated by Harold Shadick. Ithaca: Cornell University Press, 1952.

Lu Hsun. *Selected Stories of Lu Hsun*. Peking: Foreign Languages Press, 1960.

Mao Tun. *Spring Silkworms and Other Stories*. Translated by Sidney Shapiro. Peking: Foreign Languages Press, 1956.

———. *Midnight*. Translated by Hsu Meng-hsiung. Peking: Foreign Languages Press, 1957.

Pa Chin. *Family*. New York: Doubleday, 1972.

Ting Ling. *The Sun Shines over the Sangkan River*. Translated by Yang Hsien-yi and Gladys Yang. Peking: Foreign Languages Press, 1954.

Waley, Arthur. *Ballads and Stories from Tun-huang*. New York: Macmillan, 1960.

Wu Ch'eng-en. *The Journey to the West*. Translated and edited by Anthony C. Yu. Chicago: University of Chicago Press, 1977–

Wu Ching-tzu. *The Scholars*. Translated by Yang Hsien-yi and Gladys Yang. Peking: Foreign Languages Press, 1957.

Wu Wo-yao. *Vignettes from the Late Ch'ing: Bizarre Happenings Eyewitnessed over Two Decades*. Translated and with an introduction by Shih Shun Liu. New York: St. John's University Press, 1975.

Nonfiction

Analects of Confucius, The. Translated and annotated by Arthur Waley. New York: Vintage Books (originally published 1938).

Brandt, Conrad; Schwartz, Benjamin; and Fairbank, John K., eds. *A Documentary History of Chinese Communism*. Cambridge: Mass.: Harvard University Press, 1952.

Chan, Wing-tsit, trans. *A Source Book in Chinese Philosophy*. Princeton: Princeton University Press, 1963.

Complete Works of Chuang Tzu, The. Translated by Burton Watson. New York: Columbia University Press, 1968.

de Bary, William Theodore; Chan, Wing-tsit; and Watson, Burton, comps. *Sources of Chinese Tradition*. New York: Columbia University Press, 1960.

Gittings, John. *A Chinese View of China*. New York: Pantheon, 1973.

Mao Tse-tung. *Selected Works of Mao Tse-tung*. 5 vols. Peking: Foreign Languages Press, 1965.

Mencius. Translated by D. C. Lau. Baltimore: Penguin, 1970.

Pan Ku. *Courtier and Commoner in Ancient China: Selections from the History of the Former Han*. Translated by Burton Watson. New York: Columbia University Press, 1974.

Ssu-ma Ch'ien. *Records of the Historian: Chapters from the Shih chi of Ssu-ma Ch'ien*. Translated by Burton Watson. New York: Columbia University Press, 1961.

Sung Ying-hsing. *T'ien-kung K'ai-wu: Chinese Technology in the Seventeenth Century*. Translated by E-tu Zen Sun and Shiou-chuan Sun. University Park, Pa.: Pennsylvania State University Press, 1966.

Yellow Emperor's Classic of Internal Medicine, The. Translated by Ilza Veith. Berkeley: University of California Press, 1966 (originally published 1949).

Original Sources

1. *Shang shu* (Ssu-pu pei-yao ed.) chüan 7/7b-10a. This book is also available in complete translation. See James Legge, trans., *The Chinese Classics* (Oxford, 1893–95), III, or Bernard Karlgren, trans., "The Book of Documents," *Bulletin of the Museum of Far Eastern Antiquities* 22 (1950): 1–81.

2. *Chou I* (Shih-san ching chu-shu ed.), 111a-28a. This book is also available in complete translation. See Richard Wilhelm, trans., *The I Ching or Book of Changes* (New York, 1950).

3. Reprinted from Arthur Waley, trans., *The Book of Songs* (original ed. Boston, 1937), pp. 31, 121, 128–29, 164–67, by permission of Grove Press, Inc., and George Allen & Unwin Ltd.

4. *Ch'un-ch'iu ching chuan chi-chieh* (Ssu-pu pei-yao ed.) 11/8b-12a. The *Tso Chronicle* is translated in the notes of Legge's translation of the *Spring and Autumn Annals* in *The Chinese Classics*, V.

5. *Lun Yü*, 15:31, 1:14, 2:13, 12:4, 16:18, 16:7, 4:16, 15:17, 5:15, 16:10, 13:25, 13:23, 14:24, 15:20, 15:18, 15:19, 15:22, 13:26. 19:9, 1:8, 19:21, 17:24, 14:28, 2:12, 17:6, 12:2, 12:3, 1:3, 13:27, 6:21, 3:3, 4:1, 15:34, 4:5, 15:8, 15:35, 7:29, 15:9, 4:3, 4:7, 14:5, 14:7, 2:7, 1:11, 19:18, 2:5, 4:19, 4:21, 4:18, 13:18. One complete translation of this book is Arthur Waley, trans., *The Analects of Confucius* (New York, 1938).

6. Reprinted from Burton Watson, trans., *The Complete Works of Chuang Tzu* (New York: Columbia University Press, 1968), pp. 187–88, 188–89,

191–92, 227–28, 339–43, by permission of the publisher.

7. Huan K'uan, *Yen-t'ieh lun chiao chu* (Taipei: Shih-chieh shu-chü ed., 1970), 1, pp. 1–11. See also the complete translation by Esson M. Gale, *Discourses on Salt and Iron*, Leiden, 1931 and *Journal of the North China Branch of the Royal Asiatic Society* 65 (1934): 73–110.

8. *I-li Cheng-chu* (Taipei, 1972 reprint) chüan 3. See also the complete translation by John Steele, *The I-li* (London, 1917).

9. Wang Fu, *Ch'ien-fu lun* (Ts'ung-shu chi-ch'eng ed.) 8, pp. 195–208.

10. Liu Hsiang, *Lieh-nü chuan* (Taipei, 1971 reprint of Ming illustrated edition), 3/33b-35a; Fan Yeh, *Hou-Han shu* (Chung-hua shu-chü ed.), 28B, pp. 1003–4 commentary. The *Lieh-nü chuan* has been translated by Albert R. O'Hara, *The Position of Woman in Early China, According to the Lieh Nü Chuan, "The Biographies of Chinese Women,"* (Taipei, 1971).

11. *Huang-ti nei-ching su-wen*, 5, in *Tao tsang* (Taipei: I-wen yin shu reprint.) This book has been translated by Ilza Veith, *The Yellow Emperor's Classic of Internal Medicine* (Baltimore, 1949).

12. Yen K'o-chün, ed. *Ch'üan Hou-Han wen*, in *Ch'üan Shang-ku Ch'in-Han San-kuo Liu-ch'ao wen* (Shanghai, 1948 reprint), 75/3a-b; 98/2a-b; 102/4b-5b.

13. *Hou-Han shu* 71, pp. 2299–2300; Ch'en Shou, *San-kuo chih* (Chung-hua shu-chü ed.) 8, p. 264 commentary; Ch'ang Chü, *Hua-yang kuo-chih* (Ts'ung-shu chi-ch'eng ed.), 2, pp. 16–17.

14. Ko Hung, *Pao-p'u Tzu* (Ssu-pu pei-yao ed.), 50/2a–8a. Another translation of this piece is found in James Ware, *Alchemy, Medicine, and Religion in China of A.D. 320* (Cambridge, 1966), pp. 6–21.

15. Stein 4528, 4366, 1910, 3935, 1177. Texts reproduced in Lionel Giles, "Dated Chinese Manuscripts in the Stein Collection," *Bulletin of the School of Oriental and African Languages* 7 (1935): 820, 826, 830; 9 (1937): 8, 1044.

16. Pelliot 3821. Text reproduced in Jao Tsung-yi and Paul Demieville, *Airs de Touen-houng* (Paris, 1971), plates 68–69.

17. Wang Ting-pao, *T'ang Chih-yen* (Taipei, Shih-chieh shu-chü ed.), 3, pp. 29–30, 40; 4, p. 47; 8, p. 87, 89; p. 94, 95; 11, p. 125.

18. Ikeda On, *Chūgoku kodai sekichō kenkyū* (Tokyo, 1979), pp. 195–196, 198.

19. Niida Noboru, *Tōsō hōritsu bunsho no kenkyū* (Tokyo, 1937), plate 4; Tun-huang wen-wu yen-chiu-so tz'u-liao shih, "Ts'ung i chien nu-pei mai-mai wen-shu k'an T'ang-tai ti chieh-chi yen-p'o," *Wen wu*, 1972:12, 68–71; Niida Noboru, *Chūgoku hōseishi kenkyū: dorei, nōdohō Kazoku, sonraku hō* (Tokyo, 1962), pp. 30–31 and plate 1.

20. Stein 4374, 6537, Text in Niida, *Chūgoku hōseishi kenkyū: dorei, nōdohō kazoku, sonrakuhō*, pp. 570–576.

21. *T'ai-shang kan-ying pien chien chu* (Kyoto, 1970 ed.). This book has been translated several times, including James Webster, The *Kan Ying Pien, Book of Rewards and Punishments* (Shanghai, 1918).

22. "Chung-yang li-chiao shih-wu lun," in *Tao tsang* (Taipei, I-wen yin-shu reprint).

23. Ssu-ma Kuang, *Ssu-ma shih shu-i* (Ts'ung-shu chi-ch'eng ed.), 10, pp. 113–120.

24. Reprinted from H. C. Chang, trans., *Chinese Literature: Popular Fiction and Drama* (Edinburgh: Edinburgh University Press, 1973), pp. 32–55, by permission of Edinburgh University Press and Columbia University Press.

25. Yüan Ts'ai, *Yüan shih shih-fan* (Ts'ung-shu chi-ch'eng ed.), 1, pp. 17–21, 3, pp. 55–56.

26. Fan Chung-yen, *Fan Wen-cheng kung chi* (Ssu-pu ts'ung-k'an ed.), Addendum, 1b–3b. These rules plus all of the amendments have been translated by Denis Twitchett in his "Documents of Clan Administration, I," *Asia Major* 8 (1960): 1–35.

27. "Tu-cheng chi-sheng," in *Tung-ching meng-hua lu, wai ssu chung* (Peking, 1962), pp. 91–101.

28. Chen Te-hsiu, *Chen Hsi-shan chi* (Ts'ung-shu chi-ch'eng ed.) 7, pp. 114–115.

29. Ch'en P'u, *Nung shu* (Ts'ung-shu chi-ch'eng ed.), pp. 1–10.

30. Ch'eng Tuan-li, *Tu-shu fen-nien jih-ch'eng* (T'ang-kuei ts'ao-t'ang ts'ung-shu, 1864), preface, 1a–12b.

31. Kuo Pi, *Yün-shan jih-chi*, in Chu Wen and Juan Wu-ming, ed. *Sung-Yüan ti jih-chi hsüan* (Hongkong, 1957), pp. 112–115.

32. Ming T'ai-tsu, *Ta kao*, 1:43 (pp. 45–46), 2:74 (pp. 217–220).

33. *Ta Ming lü* (Japanese, 1722 ed.), 18/2b–11b.

34. K'uang Fan, *Pien-min t'u-tsuan* (Chung-kuo ku-tai p'an-shu ts'ung-k'an ed., Taipei, 1959), 10/1a–b, 3a–4b.

35. Yang Ssu-ch'ang, "Wu-ling ching-tu lüeh," (Shuo-fu hsü ed.), 1a–13b. This essay is also translated in full by Chao Wei-pang, "The Dragon Boat Race in Wu-ling, Hunan," *Folklore Studies* 2 (1943): 1–18.

36. Quoted in Niida, *Chūgoku hōseishi kenkyū: dorei, nōdohō, kazoku, sonrakuhō*, pp. 763, 773, 781–782.

37. Quoted in *ibid.*, pp. 806–811.

38. Hsü I-kuei, *Shih-feng kao*, in *Wu-lin wang-che i-chu* (1894 ed.), 2/3a–4a.

39. Fu I-ling, "Ming-tai Hui-chou chuang-p'u wen-yüeh chi-ts'un," *Wen wu*, 1960:2 11–13; Chi Liu-ch'i, *Ming-chi nan-lüeh* (T'ai-wan wen-hsien ts'ung-k'an ed.), 9, p. 266.

40. *Shui hu chuan* (Taipei, 1972 ed.), chüan 1–2, pp. 18–30. This novel has been translated in full by Pearl S. Buck, *All Men Are Brothers* (New York, 1933).

41. Chang Han, *Sung-ch'uang meng yü* (1896 ed.), 4/16b-24a; Wang Tao-k'un, *T'ai-han fu-mo* (1633 ed.), 13/21a-23b, 30a-33a.

42. Quoted in Taga Akigoro, *Sōfuku no kenkyū* (Tokyo, 1960), pp. 604–608.

43. *Chin P'ing Mei tz'u-hua* (Tokyo, 1963 reprint of Ming, Wan-li ed.), chüan 2 (round 11), pp. 229–241. This novel has been translated in full by Clement Egerton, *The Golden Lotus*, I–IV (London, 1939).

44. Li Chih, *Fan shu hsü fan shu* (Peking, 1975 ed.), FS 1, pp. 29–31, 2, pp. 45–46, 52–53, HFS 4, pp. 140–141, 101–102.

45. P'u Sung-ling, *Liao-chai chih-i* (Peking, 1962 ed.), 1, pp. 35–37, 86, 72–74; Yüan Mei, *Tzu pu yü* (Pi-chi hsiao-shuo ta-kuan hsü-pien ed.), 4/1a-b, 6/1a, 7/10a, 4/5a-6a, 6/4b, 1/6a-b. Most of the *Liao-chai chih-i* has been translated by Herbert A. Giles, *Strange Stories from a Chinese Studio* (London, 1916).

46. Retranslated from the texts collected by W. Scarborough, *A Collection of Chinese Proverbs* (Changsha, 1926), and Cifford H. Plopper, *Chinese Religion Seen Through the Proverb* (Shanghai, 1926).

47. *Huang li* (Huai-ching-t'ang ed., 1894), "Cheng yüeh hsiao."

48. Yeh Meng-chu, *Yüeh shih pien*, 6/1a-5a, 12a-19a, in *Shang-hai chang-ku ts'ung-shu* (Shanghai, 1936).

49. Chang Ying, *Heng ch'an so-yen* (Ts'ung-shu chi-ch'eng ed.), pp. 1–9. This essay is translated in full in Hilary J. Beattie, *Land and Lineage in China* (Cambridge, 1979), pp. 140–151.

50. Lan Ting-yüan, *Lu-chou kung-an* (1881 ed.), 2/11a-14a, 1/14a-16b.

51. Wang Yu-p'u, *Sheng-yü kuang-hsün yen*, 9, in *Wang Chieh-shan hsien-sheng ch'üan-chi.*

52. Chūgoku nōson kankō chōsa kankōkai, *Chūgoku nōson kankō chōsa* (Tokyo, 1958), VI, 268; Imahori Seiji, "Shindai ni okeru sonraku kyōdotai, *"Rekishi kyōiku.* 13:9 (1965), 38–51 (document, p. 50).

53. Reprinted from Wu Ching-tzu, *The Scholars*, trans. by Yang Hsien-yi and Gladys Yang (Peking, 1957).

54. *Kao-yang hsien-chih* (1826 ed.), 21/36a-b.

55. Wu Yün, *Te-i lu* (Taipei, 1969 reprint of 1869 ed.), 2/1a-6a.

56. Sasaki Masaya, *Shinmatsu no himitsu kessha, shiryō hen* (Tokyo, 1967), pp. 246–248, 1–2, 17–19; Pai Shou-i, ed. *Hui-min ch'i-i* (Shanghai, 1953), I, 3–10.

57. Chiang-su-sheng Po-wu-kuan, *Chiang-su-sheng Ming-Ch'ing i-lai pei-k'o tz'u-liao hsüan-chi* (Peking, 1959), pp. 14–15; *Yang-wu yün-tung* (Shanghai, 1957), pp. 404–406.

58. Rinji Taiwan kyūhan chōsakai, *Taiwan shihō, furoku sandōsho* (1910 ed.), IIB, pp. 129–130, 87, 182.

59. Quoted in Makino Tatsumi, *Kinsei Chūgoku sōzoku kenkyū* (Tokyo, 1949), pp. 71–73.

60. Quoted in *ibid.*, pp. 305, 315–518.

61. Li Yu-ning and Chang Yü-fa, *Chin-tai Chung-kuo nü-ch'üan yün-tung shih-liao, 1842–1911* (Taipei, 1975), pp. 577–580, 423–424.

62. Li Pao-chia, *Kuan-ch'ang hsien-hsing-chi* (Hong-kong, 1958 ed.), 40, pp. 370–374.

63. Yü Tzu-i, "Erh-shih nien ch'ien hsiang-ts'un hsüeh-hsiao sheng-huo-li ti wo," *Chiao-yü tsa-chih* 19 (Dec. 20, 1927): 30533–30545.

64. *Chiang-su-sheng Ming-Ch'ing i-lai pei-k'o tz'u-liao hsüan-chi*, pp. 504–506.

65. Hu Huai-ts'an, "Shih-fang pei-nü i," *Fu-nü tsa-chih* 6 (January 1920): 1–4.

66. Reprinted from *Selected Stories of Lu Hsun*, trans. by Yang Hsien-i and Gladys Yang (Peking, 1960).

67. *Ti-i tz'u kuo-nei ko-ming chan-cheng shih-ch'i ti nung-min yün-tung* (Chung-kuo hsien-tai-shih tz'u-liao ts'ung-k'an, Peking, 1953), pp. 51–70. P'eng P'ai's report has been translated in full by Donald Holoch, *Seeds of Peasant Revolution: Report on the Haifeng Peasant Movement* (Cornell University China-Japan Program, 1973).

68. Kung Yao, et al., "Ho-kuo yang-min t'an-wu ts'an-pao chih Chang Tsung-ch'ang," *I-ching* 6 (May 20, 1936): 316–320.

69. *Ti-i tz'u kuo-nei ko-ming chan-cheng shih-ch'i ti kung-jen yün-tung* (Chung-kuo hsien-tai-shih tz'u-liao ts'ung-k'an, Peking, 1954), pp. 450–466.

70. Ku Chieh-kang, "Liang-ko ch'u-pin ti tao-tzu-chang," reprinted in Ku Chieh-kang and Liu Wan-chang, *Su-Yüeh ti hun-sang* (Chung-shan ta-hsüeh min-su ts'ung-shu, 1928–29), pp. 30–43.

71. Chu Tzu-ch'ing, *Chu Tzu-ch'ing wen-chi* (Peking, 1959), pp. 301–303, 197–204, 275–279.

72. Ku Ying-ming, "P'u-ning ying-hai t'an-sheng ti kuan-su," *Min-su* 1 (1936): 121–125.

73. Liu Hsü, "Pei-p'ing ti ch'i-kai sheng-huo," reprinted in Li Chia-jui, ed. *Pei-p'ing feng-su lei-ch'eng* (Shanghai, 1939), pp. 405–408.

74. Reprinted from Mao Tun, *Spring Silkworms and Other Stories*, trans. Sidney Shapiro (Peking, 1956).

75. Shen Ts'ung-wen, *Ch'ang-ho* (Hongkong, 1960 ed.), pp. 38–64.

76. Adapted from Ting Ling, *The Sun Shines over the Sangkan River*, trans. by Yang Hsien-yi and Gladys Yang (Peking, 1954), pp. 203–217.

77. *Jen-min jih-pao*, May 13, 1955; May 24, 1955; June 10, 1955.

78. *Ta Kung-pao*, July 5, 1956. Trans. adapted from *Survey of China Mainland Press* (hereafter *SCMP*) 1331 (July 18, 1956): 9–11.

79. Wang Meng, "Tsu-chih-pu hsin-lai ti ch'ing-nien jen," *Jen-min wen-hsüeh*, Sept. 1956. Trans. adapted from *Current Background* 459 (June 28, 1957): 1–32.

80. *Jen-min jih-pao*, Dec. 14, 1965. Trans. adapted from *SCMP* 3609 (Jan. 4, 1966).

81. Reprinted from "The Correct Handling of Love, Marriage, and Family Problems," *Chinese Sociology and Anthropology*, 1, no. 3 (Spring 1969): 17–21, 27–32, 42–47. Copyright © 1969 by International Arts & Sciences Press, Inc. Reprinted by permission of M. E. Sharpe, Inc.

82. *Hsin-min wan-pao*, Jan. 14, 1965. Trans. adapted from *Union Research Service* 38 (Feb. 5, 1965): 162–168.

83. Trans. adapted from Chen Kuang-sheng, *Lei Feng, Chairman Mao's Good Fighter* (Peking, 1968), pp. 14–18, 40–46, 60–64, 71, 75–76, 91–93.

84. *Hsin-min wan-pao* (Nov. 2, 1965). Trans. adapted from *Union Research Service* 43 (Apr. 12, 1966): 57–59.

85. New China News Agency release, Nov. 11, 1966 quoting *Hung-ch'i*. Adapted from *SCMP* 3822 (Nov. 17, 1966): 27–28; *Yang-ch'eng wan-pao*, Aug. 25, 1966. Trans. adapted from *SCMP* 3774 (Sept. 6, 1966): 19–20; New China News Agency release, Nov. 19, 1966, adapted from *SCMP* 3827 (Nov. 25, 1966): 19–23; *Tung-fang hung*, Sept. 21, 1967, trans. adapted from *SCMP* 4087 (Dec. 27, 1967): 1–3.

86. *Ch'en Liang An-chien chuan-k'an* (Canton, Jan. 9, 1968). Trans. adapted from *Current Background* 860 (Aug. 12, 1968): 9–0.

87. Chiang-su hsin-i-hsüeh-yüan, *Chung i-hsüeh* (Chiang-su, 1972), pp. 386–387, 415–416, 438–439.

88. *Jen-min jih-pao*, quoted in New China News Agency release, Oct. 24, 1968. Trans. adapted from *SCMP* 4289 (Oct. 31, 1968): 16–18; *Nan-fang jih-pao*, Feb. 8, 1975. Trans. adapted from *Union Research Service* 79 (May 13, 1975): 148–151.

89. *Nan-fang jih-pao* (Canton), October 8, 1979, p. 3.

Index

For broad topical coverage see the Suggested Topical Arrangement (pp. xv–xvi). For definitions of commonly used terms see the Glossary (pp. 414–17). For historical background and dates of events see the Part introductions, and the Chronology of Chinese History (pp. xxi–xxvii).